Jane Alpers

Plate One. *Joined caqueteuse armchair. English; Salisbury. Walnut, dated 1622. The back panel bears the arms of the City of New Sarum (Salisbury), and the chair was presented to the City Corporation in 1622 by Maurice Greene, Mayor. See Chapter Four, Figures 4:59 and 4:61.*

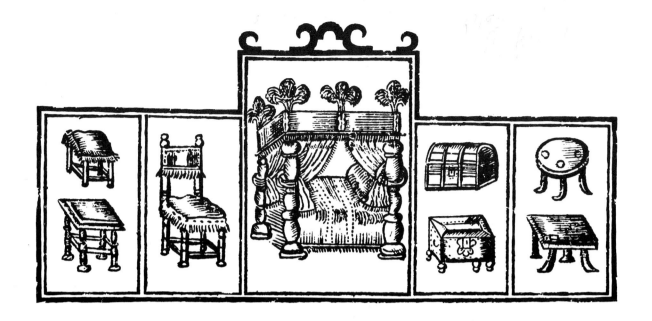

OAK FURNITURE
The British Tradition

A History of Early Furniture
in the British Isles and New England

Victor Chinnery

Antique Collectors' Club Ltd.

British Library CIP Data
Chinnery, Victor
  Oak furniture.
  1. Furniture 2. Oak
  I. Title II. Antique Collectors' Club Ltd.
  749.2   NK2230

Published for the Antique Collectors' Club
by the Antique Collectors' Club Ltd.

Printed in England by
Baron Publishing, Woodbridge, Suffolk

Folding oak bookrest made from a single plank, the only addition being that of the back strut. Early seventeenth century. From an article by Thomas Crispin in Volume 14 No. 6 of *Antique Collecting*.

For my dear wife Janet

"... It hath been ... mine endeavour ... to give unto every limb and part not only his due proportion but also his due place, and not to set the head where the foot should be, or the foot where the head ... "
Henry Denne, *Grace, Mercy and Peace,* 1645.

Contents

List of Colour Plates

Preface

The purpose of this study is to offer a brief illustrated summary of present knowledge concerning the early furniture of England, Wales, Scotland, Ireland and New England; a political entity once known as Greater Britain. The English, as the colonising agents, passed on most of their furniture-making practices into these areas, and so we are chiefly concerned with the influence of English traditions at home and abroad. It is easier to set a geographical focus on our subject than a time-limit. We are concerned with a native tradition of furniture making which used oak as its favourite timber. This means that we must start in the misty areas of the Middle Ages, but where shall we finish? Oak and the other native timbers fell from favour in fashionable circles after the Restoration of the Stuarts in 1660, but in middle class and provincial circles these woods remained in popular use until well after 1800, even though decorative styles were gradually modified. So we are involved with an organic tradition of techniques and materials, both in its heyday and in decline. The pieces shown in these pages are the products of a vigorous and inventive people, adapting their forms to suit changing tastes and circumstances.

But the reader must not think that he can glean any more than the basic principles from a book of this kind. I cannot overstress the value of his getting out to see and handle a variety of furniture for himself, good and bad, grand and humble. The illustrations are presented as a series of comparative examples, and are no substitute for visiting museums, private collections and antique shops, where the budding connoisseur must roll up his sleeves and get to grips with the real thing. Turn it over, pull out the drawers, feel the wear and enjoy the colour in daylight. Learn the feel and the smell of the genuine article, and how to spot replaced parts and outright fakes.

Whilst we are on that tack, I must point out that this book has not been written in order to report on the condition of any of the pieces shown (with rare exceptions), nor to guarantee the authenticity of any item illustrated in its pages. That would be the motive of a *prima donna* dealer, trying to justify the sales he has made in past years. If authenticity and originality are at issue, then each piece must be judged on its own merits. Rather, each photograph has been chosen for its relevance to pertinent aspects of furniture design and construction in our chosen period. Naturally, I have taken the greatest care that only *genuine* examples have been included, and I am confident that each is impeccable as a representative of its type.

Repairs and replacements are always to be regretted, but it is for the individual collector to decide how pure he wants his pieces to be. Any item which has escaped damage and repair should be the more highly-valued for such good fortune, but let us bear in mind the thought that most furniture has undergone some measure of decay or damage in a long working life. Less forgivable are some of the thoughtless 'restorations' and 'improvements' wrought in the nineteenth century or more recently. In other cases, even the repairs themselves are of considerable antiquity, as with the much-restored late medieval cupboard in Louth Church, Lincolnshire, known as Sudbury's Hutch. The churchwardens' accounts for 1666 record payments to "Goody Blackey for a piece of wood. 4s.", and to "Shorte for works about Sudbury Huch. 14s.5d.". Many such remnants would have disappeared but for timely repairs of this sort, and that would have been our loss.

We must be wary of looking through the distorting glass of time. Old furniture does not look the same now as when it was new, and it is a great pity that seventeenth century England did not breed the same tradition for painted views of interiors that existed in Holland. How much more we could have learnt about the use of fabrics and carpets, the colours of walls and woodwork, and the disposition of furniture. The few chance survivals that are still with us fill only a small part of the image conjured up by those magic lists in contemporary wills and inventories, and we must look to these and other evidence for traces of certain transitory classes of furniture which have now vanished, such as basketwork and those tasty upholstery fabrics. Indeed, the evidence for a whole class of people is very sparse in our period, for the furniture and houses of the labouring classes have disappeared almost without trace from the seventeenth century, and almost no real cottage furniture has survived from before c.1750. To gauge their character we must make assumptions based on later examples of traditional type.

Unfortunately, the history and typology of furniture are not simple issues. The ground is littered and pitted with complicated problems such as the state of the furniture-making trades, social conventions, personal idiosyncracy, contradictory nomenclature and modern misconceptions. But if the reader feels totally confused, then I can only urge him to go to the best museum he can find, sit quietly in front of a sympathetic piece of furniture, and ask himself some basic questions. When was it made? What function did it serve? Which class of craftsman was it made by? Which materials did he choose? Does it conform to a conventional decorative type? What has happened to it in the succeeding generations? The answers will provide the first steps towards understanding.

The most difficult problem which faced me when I first approached this study was the thorny labyrinth of which classification I should use. If I must impose some sense of order in Bedlam, then a logical category must be devised. But how should it be determined? Many writers have set out in the past to simplify the story of furniture so that the rest of us might understand it, but they have often left us with a lunatic set of chronologies. What, for example, is the point of trying to classify furniture types by the arbitrary fortunes of Kings and Queens? The comings and goings of Royal Houses do not shift the orbit of the earth, nor the ways of the people. Even the Restoration of Charles II in 1660, often regarded as the most important point of departure in the history of English furniture, pales to some insignificance in the glare of the Great Fire of London of 1666, and the subsequent opportunity to rebuild the greatest city on earth. Yet in provincial England, the furniture of the countryman slowly evolved through all this as if nothing had happened.

The division of furniture timbers into four distinctive periods holds water for only a very limited area of fashionable types (though I am equally guilty of relying heavily on the term 'oak furniture' as a convenient and descriptive shorthand definition). Perhaps I can justify it by reminding myself that the middle classes consistently preferred oak as a cheap and durable material, conducive to their appreciation of thrifty and sensible living. Neither would I dream of limiting the 'Age of Oak' to the period ending with 1660.

The least troublesome approach to a classification would be simply to lump together firstly all the chairs, then all the tables, then all the chests, etc., etc. This has frequently been done, but in the end we are little the wiser. One chair is not necessarily related to another simply by virtue of the fact that they are both *chairs*. The first chair owes far greater kinship to a chest or a bedstead from the same workshop, than it does to another chair made one hundred miles away and in the aesthetic of another social class.

Such kinship groups must be a significant factor in any objective study of early furniture typology. Very few pieces are *unique* to any great extent. Almost every aspect of construction and decoration may be closely compared with similar examples. The ties between members of a group may often be very close. At the closest, they may derive from the same hand or workshop, and they will reflect a subtle sense of unity. More loosely, they may derive from the same district, and the regional style and preferences may be writ large in their form and decoration. Other factors, such as a distinctive decorative motif or a constructional feature, may reach across geographical or class barriers and express a craftsmanlike element of creative pleasure and fitness of purpose. We are only at the threshold of workshop and regional studies, and a rich field of deductions waits to be explored.

In the event, I decided that three basic characteristics are important to all classes of furniture — construction, function and decoration. They cannot *exist* separately, yet they must be *analysed* separately. After an introductory chapter, I have dealt with constructional methods and materials in Chapter Two; the functional types and their nomenclature in Chapter Three; and the aesthetic aspects of social and regional styles in Chapter Four. I apologise if the reader finds this approach unnecessarily cumbersome, but I would not like to offer a more facile interpretation for fear of falling between two stools (to coin a phrase). I do believe that the old glib chronologies based on dynastic successions or a taste for the 'picturesque' are poor meat for a modern generation of collectors and curators, to whom real beauty lies in the discernible truth.

Finally, I should like to put in one small plea to encourage others to follow some objective course of local studies if their time and inclinations will allow. The present generation is offered the last chance to study regional styles at a local level. A good deal of clarification has been achieved in recent years, but there is still much to be done in a field which is not over-endowed with research funds or curatorial interest. Indeed, the time is ripe for the establishment of a studies' centre which can co-ordinate the necessary research and recording activities into all aspects of early and vernacular furnishings.

As an author and furniture historian, I find myself deeply indebted to all those who have ever written on the subject of our great heritage of early furnishings, especially the late R.W. Symonds; to all who have contributed towards the chance preservation of those pieces which are still here for our enjoyment; and to the many people whose kindness and enthusiasm have helped to form my present conception of the subject, whether in conversation or correspondence. But special thanks are due to the following for their particular help and hospitality: Louis and Sarah Stanton; Alun Davies; John Fardon; Tom Burn; William Wells; Brian and Hazel Fox; John and Angela Halsey; Claude Bornoff; David Anderson; and to Robert

Kime, whose initial confidence and encouragement helped me launch into this bottomless pool.

For helpful correspondence, stimulating conversation and invaluable photographic facilities, thanks are due variously to Michael Gray, Ralph Cox, Christopher Gilbert, Mary Bellis, Gene and Sally Foster, Clive Sherwood, Shirley Brown, Lesley Brown, Patrick Sandberg, Ronald Lee, Colin Stock, Dr. Levi Fox, Robert Logan, Betty Smith, Dr. A.W.J. Houghton, Bill Stokes, Roy Barling, Arwyn Lloyd-Hughes, Michel le Coz, John White, John Hardy, Robert Reedman, Olive Smith, Patricia E. Kane and Joyce Caldwell; as well as many individual private owners who wish my gratitude for their help to remain anonymous.

For help and encouragement with my work on the furniture of Salisbury, I wish to thank Monty Trethowan, Harold Cory, Carl Strachan, Peter Newell, Nancy Steele, the Wiltshire Record Office and Penny Carew-Hunt, who transcribed Humphrey Beckham's will and inventory for me. For his help in particular matters, my brother Doug must be mentioned, and all those members of my family who put up with my work. So many people have been of detailed help, yet their names are missing from this list, for which I apologise.

My deep gratitude is due to my publishers, John and Diana Steel, for their equally great reserves of patience and enthusiasm.

My first thanks, which are now recorded last, are due to my dear wife Jan. She has encouraged, cajoled and inspired me at every turn. Without her forbearance and fortitude this work would have been impossible. She has endured midnight conversations and has gone without many of the modern comforts which should rightly have been hers, in order that I might involve myself more fully in this work. Few men are granted the privilege of thanking their wives publicly and in print. This I am pleased to do...

Victor Chinnery
Marlborough
Wiltshire
September 1979

Chapter One

Time and Place

The Historical Context

THE BACKGROUND OF THE PERIOD

THE SOCIAL AND economic history of the early modern period (broadly, from the close of the Middle Ages to the beginning of the eighteenth century, say 1500-1720) has been admirably chronicled by a host of recent authorities, so there is no need to reiterate it here. Over the period of two hundred years or so the political and fashionable face of society changed and developed very profoundly, but for the labouring and artisan classes there was a continuity of inexorable physical and economic factors which limited their ability to improve their own lives. These factors bore directly on the everyday lives of furniture-making craftsmen and the society of men in which they found themselves, and served to shape the mould from which emerges English oak furniture and its family of derivatives. It is necessary for the modern observer constantly to remind himself that the world was then a very different place from ours of today. At every turn the priorities and conditions of life were cast in a more basic and immediate form, in which survival figured high on the list. In a pre-industrial society, most men lived in a close relationship with the natural world and a strong bond still existed between cultural life and the environment, even in the growing towns.

Post-medieval England was throughout a world of great contrasts: of splendour and squalor; of pageantry and corruption; of public bravado and private misery; of political and religious eccentricities; of simple pleasures and the threat of sudden death. Throughout the sixteenth and seventeenth centuries the spectre of the plague hung like an invisible cloud over the head of every man, woman and child in Europe. The contradictory philosophies of the age were characterised by crude superstitions on the one hand and objective scientific thought on the other. It may help us to understand the

Sweet William.

Making hay while the sun shines.

17

domestic and artistic products of Tudor and Stuart England if we first look at the shape of society, and some of the forces at work within it.

The Economic Landscape

At the beginning of the seventeenth century, England was still far short of the rolling sea of tidy fields we know as the agricultural landscape of today. Houses were mainly grouped together, for protection and gregariousness, into small clustered towns and villages, with few of the scattered farmsteads which became an established feature only after the widespread enclosures of the old shared common field. These small centres achieved a degree of self-sufficiency in the production of their own food, with a further dependence on a system of local market towns for a variety of supply and trade. These islands of cultivation still alternated with vast tracts of the pristine forests of deciduous oaks which were the natural vegetation of these islands, and with the wastelands of open heath, scrub and undrained fenland. Even so, some of the lowland areas, especially in the Midlands, had already been converted into great vistas of open field long before the end of the Middle Ages, though the area of land under cultivation had actually declined during the fourteenth century. The extraordinary ravages of the Black Death, which claimed a third or more of the population in 1348 and the subsequent visitations, left villages deserted and their fields reverting to waste or to sheep-grazing.

In the fifteenth and sixteenth centuries agriculture expanded once more and the land surfeit of the previous generation gave way to a land hunger. Sheep pasture represented for the landowner a highly efficient and profitable method of land utilisation. Aided by the superfluity of cleared land and the shortage of labour following the Black Death, sheep farming expanded rapidly and by the middle of the fifteenth century sheep outnumbered the human population by about three to one, and Englishmen had begun to complain that "sheep do eat up men". But the causes and characteristics of this phenomenon are of less significance here than its results.

Firstly, an expanding involvement in sheep farming led to the adoption of enclosures as a method of containing sheep pasture, a method which began to erode the time-honoured rights of the peasantry to tillage and rough grazing. This was only the beginning of a process of enclosures which was to proceed in fits and starts for over four hundred years, but a significant proportion of common land was quickly removed from common usage. Many country people were deprived of their traditional means of livelihood through subsistence husbandry, which led to the abandonment of villages and great hardship to many innocent people. Bands of dispossessed peasants roamed the country as vagabonds, causing problems to townsmen and travellers alike.

As a second effect, the sheep were encouraging greater inroads into the existing stocks of woodland, by their insistent demands for ever more provision of pasture. The great primeval forests were still well represented in the sixteenth century — Epping, Sherwood, the Weald, Arden, Wychwood and Dean still stood along with a score of less romantic names; but the profligate rate at which this most important of the nation's natural resources was being depleted was beginning to place the free supply of timber in jeopardy, especially in districts with a natural dearth of woodland. Timber was the one raw material indispensable to the national economy. It was used, and abused, for a variety of primary applications — as fuel for the home and for industry, as the material for houses, furniture,

Plate Two. *Joined upholstered armchair. English; Warwickshire. Oak, with woollen turkeywork covers, c.1625. Large, comfortable armchairs of this sort were probably not uncommon in middle-class homes throughout the middle part of the seventeenth century, but few examples have survived to reinforce any impression of warmth and comfort in the furnishings of this period. Where fixed upholstery was not used, then wooden armchairs were normally softened with loose cushions.*

19

A country idyll.

implements, bridges, wagons and ships — the shelter, tools and rolling-stock of an insistently consumptive economy. We can imagine the delight with which the virgin forests of the New World were viewed by the earliest explorers and settlers, for whom cedar and walnut figured high in the list of exploitable imports.

The third great result of the expansion of sheep farming, and one which went far beyond mere agriculture in the implications for the economic life of the country, was the proliferation of the wool trade itself. Whereas in the early Middle Ages, England had been the primary producer and exporter of wool for the European market, in the fifteenth century a major cloth industry developed. England became an exporter, not of the raw wool which fed the looms of Italy and Flanders, but of woollen cloth. The demand was chiefly for unfinished broadcloth which would be dressed, dyed and finished in the customer workshops; but it nevertheless provided work at home for a huge new class of rural spinners and weavers, and a rising class of entrepreneurial country clothiers who assembled the finished product for supply via the Antwerp trade. These men not only put gowns on the backs of bourgeois Germans and Hungarians, they also spent their profits freely at home on building and furnishing their houses, and thereby encouraged a new and status-conscious middle class of English traders and professional men. The Merchants of the Staple, the old state-sponsored monopoly which controlled the export of wool, were superseded by the Merchant Venturers of the City of London — merchants who specialised in a broader species of overseas trade. They channelled the cloth trade through London, consolidated the financial supremacy of the capital, and in many ways founded the spirit of exploration that took the English into Ireland, the New World and around the Cape of Good Hope to India and the Far East. Wool was one of the chief sources of English wealth, and the money gained by it established England as a financial power on a world scale and developed many other aspects of English trade and exploration in the sixteenth and seventeenth centuries.

This period witnessed a steady growth in population, especially in the towns, and correspondingly dramatic improvements in agricultural methods in order to feed them. The introduction of revolutionary new crops

Tavern life in the 1660s.

like clover, turnips and potatoes, the spread of enclosures, and the development of new techniques in livestock and field management combined to change the face of the countryside after 1650. Even so, the open road between the havens of settled farmland held real terrors for the traveller, as much by reason of threats from the elements as fears of being accosted by footpads or vagabonds, or of getting lost on the abysmal tracks and byways.

Just as with agriculture, a huge development of industries evolved in the countryside after 1500. Some of these industries were closely based on the processing of agricultural and forest products such as spinning and weaving, knitting, leather working, charcoal burning or barrel making; but others were more concerned with industrial processes such as mining (clay, coal, tin, copper, iron, lead), and the consequent manufacture of finished goods in the form of cast brass and iron wares, edge tools, glass and pottery. These manufacturing industries were regionalised to an extent which is still evident today, and in each area the first spoil heaps, mill ponds and specialised buildings began to put their indelible stamp on the landscape. In many cases, process industries like these had first moved out of the towns in order to escape the restrictive rule of the craft guilds, to be nearer their sources of materials and power, and to find a pool of cheap labour on a part-time basis. Many peasants and small farmers came to divide their time between their agricultural trade on the one hand — dairying, tillage or stock-rearing — and seasonal or spare-time work for sale to itinerant merchants on the other — weaving cloth, knitting stockings, making nails or cutting barrel staves. These peasant workers gained the advantages of a well-spread family economy, earning cash from their activities and providing food from their subsistence farming and the keeping of a pig or two. Such advantages were cruelly denied to a later generation of industrial workers who were herded into the satanic mills and tenements provided by the capitalist masters of the eighteenth century.

The Growth of the Towns

Most organised settlements in Tudor England took the form of small, self-contained villages. The estates of the nobility and the greater gentry also represented quite large individual communities, centred around the great households of family and servants, with their attendant lodgings, cottages and farms; but fewer than ten percent of Englishmen lived in towns of any size in the sixteenth century. This proportion increased steadily over the next two hundred years, but even so, very few towns grew to any considerable size until the floodgates of the Industrial Revolution began to open up after 1750. London was far and away the largest conurbation, with a population which rose from about 50,000 in 1530 to over 200,000 in 1600; then rising to three times that by 1700, despite the setbacks of the Great Plague of 1665 and the losses of property in the Great Fire of the following year (the City was completely rebuilt by 1686).

The next largest cities of Norwich, Bristol and York could boast only a fraction of London's population and wealth (for the relative sizes of the major provincial towns in 1662 see the map and table in Figure 4:56). Estimates of population figures for the period are notoriously unreliable, since the censuses were more concerned with collecting household taxes than counting heads, but it is clear that the average provincial town would today be considered little more than a village. Many of these small towns acted as market centres for the surrounding countryside, where produce and livestock could be bought and sold, local specialities such as cheeses and knitted stockings be assembled for collecting by dealers, news and gossip exchanged, and where country people might acquire those manufactured utensils and commodities which they could not make for themselves. By this process the small towns were an integral part of country life, and the year was punctuated by a series of regular chartered fairs which amplified the agricultural and recreational functions of the weekly market.

Town life depends for its success not simply on a large and active population, but on a high degree and quality of civic organisation. The trade and institutions which guarantee prosperity must be properly (if not democratically) ordered for the common good. The regulation of municipal and commercial life stems from the early merchant guilds, and the most successful corporate towns were those which could attract the interest and participation of rich traders through the provision of efficient services and geographical advantages. The city and borough corporations grew powerful and independent as the growing towns attracted a taxable population,

Puffing Billy.

investments from the gentry and nobility, an influx of skilled craftsmen and small industrial masters, and the benefits of national and international contacts. London possessed all these advantages, the presence of the Court, and much more besides; and the highly-organised corporate life which evolved there became the model for the larger provincial cities, most of which also contained a cathedral, since spiritual and temporal power often worked hand-in-hand.

The English guild system had its roots in the Saxon *frith gild* and the Norman *ceapmanne gilde* and the Hansa. Guilds were essentially fellowships or fraternities organised by members with a common interest, for the furtherance of that interest, and financed by levies and contributions from the membership. In addition to a membership fee, fines could be extracted for special privileges or infringements. In the Middle Ages there was usually some formal religious bond, but the real reasons for the existence of guilds were manifold. Some existed merely to guarantee the welfare of members in time of need, in much the same way as modern contributory pension schemes, or the friendly societies of the nineteenth century; but the most powerful guilds in the early Middle Ages were the merchant guilds, which acquired a high degree of administrative authority in the boroughs, and which developed the systems of local government which gave rise to the city corporations. Democracy came later to these *gilda mercatoria,* which were organised by the whole merchant body of each town in order to protect their own interests and to exclude the intervention of rivals and 'strangers', a protectionism which was enforced with the utmost severity in an age of severity.

Trades Organisation

The merchant guilds also included at first the small manufacturing craftsmen who made and sold their own wares, but as the numbers of independent craftsmen grew in the towns, so they saw their circumstances as different from the merchants and dealers whose business lay solely in the buying and selling of commodities. Accordingly, the craftsmen formed themselves into craft guilds, whereby one of the rules of membership was that any applicant must first prove his abilities in that 'misterie' or trade. In the fifteenth century a conflict arose between the *industrial* interests of the small manufacturing masters and the *commercial* interests of the merchants. In time, the merchant guilds capitulated to the strength of the craft guilds, which held increasing influence over the manual side of their activities. Merchants now tended to join those craft guilds which were involved in the manufacture of the particular goods which formed their usual stock-in-trade. In so doing, the merchants regained some of their former advantages since they now found they had considerable control over the conditions of manufacture and supply, as well as a vested interest in the welfare of the trade. For their part, the artisan craftsmen now had a far greater say in policy decisions, and were able to bring their sound mechanical knowledge into play.

In London, the large population of craftsmen enabled each trade to form a viable guild of its own, but in the provincial cities most guilds embraced several trades with only broadly similar interests, if any. One of the most striking aspects of the social topography of medieval cities is the way in which each trade, with its shops and guild hall, tended to congregate together in the same street or parish. Thus most ancient cities have their Ironmonger Row, Butcher Row (or Shambles) or Fish Street. This accumulation brought in many communal advantages such as a bulk supply of raw materials and the shared use of tools, labour and expensive facilities.

The Rat-catcher.

The guild court tempered any disharmony between competitive individuals, and any member who refused to submit to arbitration could be expelled from the freedom of the guild and would lose his livelihood in that town. As with any closely-governed human relationship, the guild system provided both comfort and frustration.

The nominal religious bond which characterised the medieval guilds proved to be their undoing. With the abolition of their private chapels and chantries under Henry VIII and Edward VI, the craft guilds became disorganised and their charters revoked. But their *raison d'être* was as sound as ever and they reformed themselves on a broader secular basis, with new charters from Elizabeth I or James I, as the new trade companies, secure and confident in their well-tried methods and structure. The new companies formalised the relationship between the dependent classes of craftsmen and the capitalist merchants who orgnised much of the wider distribution and marketing of their products (though, as we shall see, the furniture-making trades generally worked for a more tangible local clientele, and were hardly in need of a distributive service).

The establishment of the craft guilds had been one of the earliest chapters in the continuing history of labour organisation in Britain. The control systems which they evolved were seen to work very well in the conditions of the day, though they were quickly superseded as society itself evolved, and even the new trade companies had lost much of their real power by 1700. The overwhelming principle which guided their actions was that of protecting the circumstances in which the trade could flourish, thereby to guarantee the welfare and prosperity of their members, whilst also guaranteeing a high quality of service and supply to the customer. The trade companies inherited the systems which the craft guilds had pioneered, and put them into practice in the seventeenth century. The companies were run by elected committees of overseers, who were faced with the task of trying to reconcile a number of potentially conflicting interests. They were armed with considerable powers, and we may examine the ways in which these were used to regulate the conduct of trade and competition:

Standards of Workmanship

The craft guilds had always recognised their supervisory responsibility for the promotion of integrity, and their operations were marked from the earliest times by an insistence on the highest standards of craftsmanship and materials. The customer was entitled to a lawful value in return for his money, and the company reserved the right to inspect the produce of their members and to determine standards of quality. Each company appointed some experienced 'viewers and searchers', who would visit the shops of members to inspect their raw materials, finished articles and methods of production. If these did not match up to the required minimum standards, the member could be reported to the court and his faulty goods confiscated. The 'power of search' was in continual use, with searchers licensed by the corporation. This sort of transgression usually merited a fine, but habitual offenders might be expelled from the company.

Matters rarely came to a head in this way because of the stringent safeguards over admission to the company in the first place. The hierarchy set up by a guild organisation was in the form of a rigid social system which the individual entered from the bottom as an apprentice. The conditions of apprenticeship were formally codified by the Great Statute of Artificers in 1563, when it was decreed that in all trades the term of service was to be seven years, and all training was to be completed by the age of twenty-four. Most boys (and sometimes girls) followed their fathers into the same trade, partly because familiarity would breed aptitude (the workshop was usually the family home, and a boy might gain a wide experience of his father's work during childhood), and partly because, as an established freeman, the father would be in a good position to find the most able master and then promote his son's career through the exercise of influence. Under the terms of indenture, the father of the apprentice would pay a fee to the shop master for the acceptance of his son; and in his turn the master undertook to feed, clothe and house his charge, to extend his general education as far as possible, and specifically to train him in the 'misterie' of his craft by setting him to work in his workshop, to learn by example. The apprentice was normally kept well under the eye of the master and his wife, as he lived with the family virtually as an adopted son. Abuses of the system were many and are well-chronicled, but in a rough-and-ready age it served remarkably well to produce an honest and experienced artisan class.

After serving his time, the apprentice was examined as to his capabilities in his craft, and the successful applicant admitted to the freedom of the company. This allowed him to offer his services for employment as a qualified journeyman (paid at daily rates — Fr. *journée*), or to set up his own shop as his own master. The rigid social order which resulted from this system — master, journeyman, apprentice — did much to guarantee the stability of town life in the sixteenth and seventeenth centuries, whilst the rigid control of standards fostered confidence on the part of the consumer.

Protection of Trade Interests

One of the motives behind the early trade guilds was the one which continued to give the biggest problems — that of preserving the rights and prerogatives of craftsmen to practise their trades without the unfair trespass of unqualified or cut-price competitors. In particular companies sought the exclusive rights of their members to use certain processes, without duplication by any other trades. This led to some fierce squabbles within the furniture-making fraternity, especially between joiners and carpenters, over *who* was allowed to do *what*. Companies were very jealous over their rights, and were always ready to defend them by recourse to law or even stronger methods. Riots and street fights were by no means uncommon, and running battles would sometimes be fought between gangs of apprentices, no doubt covertly egged on by the more staid elders of the respective companies. Legal rulings led to a system of demarcations which defined the practices and prerogatives of the different trades, though it often proved difficult to enforce them.

Apart from the legitimate members of other trades, the companies were always troubled by the threat from 'strangers and foreigners' who might set up competition in the town. This term might actually mean foreign craftsmen such as Dutchmen or Flemings, or simply unlicensed artisans from another town, who were either forcibly excluded or allowed to remain on payment of a hefty fine. These circumstances were often catered for in the company ordinances, e.g. in the Charter of the Joyners Carvers and Turners of the City of Chester, 1576:

> "If itt fortune any foriner or stranger to come into this Citty and theire minde to sett upp or occupie the said occupation of Joyner Carver or Turner or buy his freedom of ye said Citty and pay not to ye said occupation ye sum of XLs he shall forfeite ye one halfe of all his worke..."

The furniture trades in London and Norwich felt especially threatened by a large Flemish population, but English complaints were no doubt exaggerated. One of the worst excesses was on 'Evil May Day', 1517, when London apprentices rose against the influx of alien craftsmen and rioted, but the London Joiners' Company seemed to be able to keep the 'strangers' at arm's length in Southwark, at least until after the Great Fire of 1666 and the consequent rebuilding. In provincial cities, the policy of excluding joiners from outside must have been a major factor contributing towards the retention of local styles of decoration, emphasising the retarded and parochial nature of regional furniture after 1650.

Regulation of Trading Conditions

The financial side of market conditions was closely controlled by the overseers. They kept a careful eye on the state of supply and demand, in hopes of maintaining a regular flow of goods and customers. The prices of standard articles were sometimes enforced by them; but more specifically the wages paid to their members were rigidly laid down, to eliminate any unfair competition from an unscrupulous master who might undercut prices by paying his employees a lower wage. In the fourteenth century the 'Statutes of Labourers' attempted to control wages, and to some extent prices, and they marked one of the first attempts by Parliament to substitute national control for local custom, to serve the interests of a money-based economy. Under Elizabeth I the local magistrates were empowered to fix local wages, on proper consultation with the trade companies, and these were rigidly enforced. The average amounts were fourteen pence per day for the chief workmen, twelve pence for the journeymen, and ten pence for labourers and those apprentices who had served four years.

The limitation of wages caused great hardship in times of rampant inflation, such as that suffered under Elizabeth I. The rise in the cost of living hit the skilled artisan very hard, particularly during the occasional years of famine. The trade companies attempted to alleviate some of these problems by attending to the welfare of their members. They would often guarantee to buy produce from members who fell on hard times (albeit at a rather low fixed rate), and maintained a charitable fund to which indigent members could apply for relief. The fund was raised by a levy on the more successful brethren in an attempt to iron out the irregularities of trade and circumstances. The principle was well-expressed at the time: "...whosoever had parte of the gaine in profitable times, must now, in the decay of trade...beare parte of the publicke losses..."

It must be emphasised that this intensive management of trade practices and conditions was purely an urban phenomenon. The guilds and trade companies were controlled by the borough and city corporations, and as such their jurisdiction ended at their boundaries. Rural craftsmen were not obliged to join the nearest guild, nor to follow its rules. The restrictions imposed by guild legislation were admittedly sometimes very irksome, but they did have the effect of maintaining high standards of craftsmanship and materials, so that the products of their members were in very great demand. This was particularly true of London, and it is a fact that young men flocked from the provinces in order to enjoy the privilege of an apprenticeship in the capital.

Class and Society

The nominal equality which we enjoy today under English law is a relatively novel and hard-won principle, both in concept and in practice.

A merry vagabond.

The emancipated citizen of modern Britain must find it difficult to appreciate the conditions which operated in Tudor and Stuart England, where a man's position in the social framework was perhaps the most significant single factor operating in his life, and where very real distinctions controlled the differing circumstances of rich and poor. Wealth is the most pertinent divide between the various classes; and it was wealth, and more particularly the ownership of land and property, which brought legal and social advantage to the ruling classes. At the end of the Middle Ages, English society was still a rigid and highly formalised structure, with the peasant classes held firmly to the land by a system of religious and economic taboos. The great powers were the Crown and the Church, presiding over an economy based almost entirely on agriculture and its products. Administrative power was largely centralised on London even then, but in the shires it was the manorial system which provided the mechanism by which society operated. Men were divided by it into two great classes; the 'upper' or land-owning class, and the 'lower' class of the tenantry and their labourers. The gentry held their manors from the aristocracy or their king, and derived an income from supervising the lives of their tenants, who cultivated the land with the sweat of their brows (or hired the sweat of their neighbours' brows).

But even from the earliest times, this picture was modified by a distinct and growing middle class of traders, suppliers and professional men, who earned their incomes largely from the exchange of goods and services, and the manipulation of money. The Dissolution of the Monasteries freed huge quantities of land and wealth which had been locked in the ownership of the Church, and which passed then into general circulation. The capitalist middle classes developed an axiom which was quite alien to the spiritual principles which had governed much of medieval public life; namely that it was perfectly proper for a man or a nation to devote their efforts towards the acquisition and enjoyment of wealth, and to raise the standard of comfort in this life, even at some little risk to the next. Tudor society offered the man of talent an opportunity to acquire both wealth and position; and the middle classes cultivated a puritan ethic to help them achieve these, by laying emphasis on sober and business-like virtues such as diligence and frugality, thrift and application.

Having acquired some wealth by successful ventures in farming, trading, manufacturing or litigation, the middle classes spent their surplus in predictable ways. The display of wealth was as important as the enjoyment of it, and so they built strong and comfortable houses, and furnished them with sturdy and reliable goods: oak furniture, needlework cushions and carpets, woollen wall-hangings, brass, pewter and silver tableware, and soft feather beds.

Memento mori.

But it is impossible to summarise the state of a nation within the compass of a few sentences, so what better than to work from the general to the particular, and look at one man's personal view of the social structure in which he found himself? The Rev. William Harrison set out to describe Elizabethan England from the inside. His 'Description of England' was published in 1577, and again in 1587 as part of Holinshed's Chronicle. His monumental and fascinating work covers many aspects of his time, and three short extracts are given here in edited form (Appendix I), covering the class system, houses and furnishings, and timbers.

By that time the Tudors had successfully defused much of the power of the medieval barons, and turned them from dangerous war lords into a dependent land-owning aristocracy, subservient to the Crown and bent chiefly on consolidating and administering their holdings. They were no longer quite the rapacious bandits which their ancestors had been, and England had entered into a somewhat quieter phase than that experienced under the medieval kings. Harrison gives a picture of the aristocracy as the highest level of a wider class of gentry, which embraced the knights and other land owners into a great administrative ruling class. But gentlemen were not only born, they could also be made, and the gentry were under a constant pressure from beneath as rich merchants and farmers bought their way in. It became a national obsession for anyone who would be 'reputed for a gentleman' to buy himself a coat-of-arms and a respectable pedigree (both necessary badges of gentility).

The term 'middle classes' is not one used by Harrison, but instead he defined the urban and rural middle estates separately as burgesses and yeomen. It terms of status, these were virtually the same thing, though they could extend from relatively poor shopkeepers and farmers on the one hand, to rich merchants and landowners on the other. Indeed, some of them were better off than the minor gentry, into whose ranks they penetrated by marriage and purchases of manors, land and arms. The townsmen amongst them were mainly traders, manufacturers and professional men (lawyers, clergy, etc.), who not only ran the economic life of the boroughs and city corporations, but also made up the local ruling class through their involvement in the administration of the cities. Such men also ran the guilds, and by thus controlling the means of production, the guilds and trade companies proved a powerful weapon in the hands of the middle classes.

The yeomanry have been defined in several ways, but perhaps the most meaningful is that they made up the more prosperous range of the farming community, on a level with the workshop masters and better tradesmen in the towns. The poorer farmers were the husbandmen, and in general we may accept one hundred acres as the dividing line. Those who farmed more were regarded as yeomen. As A.L. Rowse remarked, "one observes that yeomen had stone slabs over their graves, where the gentry raised marble tombs".

In the sixteenth and seventeenth centuries, the gentry and the middle classes took full advantage of the opportunities they found to improve their lot; and the period is marked by a new fluidity in the social classes, where the fortunes of the individual and his family were free to find their own level. They provided much of the capital, the initiative and the energy for English expansions at home and overseas. The author makes no apology that this study is primarily concerned with *middle class* culture in this period, for most of the surviving furniture which is encountered today derives from just that group; and just as men of different classes may be distinguished and identified by the superficial traits of their dress, speech and manner, so we can broadly gauge the social origins of furniture by its materials, construction and stylistic 'manner'.

The great mass of the lower classes were formed by the artisans, the poor farmers, and their day-wage labourers who were "to be ruled and not rule other". Despite the lustre and brilliance which public and literary life had begun to assume under Elizabeth and her ministers, the lot of the skilled labourer was aggravated by legal and social hardships which progressively

Low tavern life.

deprived the working man of his pride and privileges. Wages were limited by statute, despite rampant inflation and a steadily rising cost of living, and enclosures on the land caused hardship to the peasant farmer. Public health improved throughout the seventeenth century, largely through improvements in public and personal cleanliness and the adoption of a more varied diet; but the steady devaluation of real wages and the inability to improve his own station in life combined to reduce many a working man to a dangerous state of dissatisfaction, contributing to the popular support for the English Civil War.

The Colonial Motive

In addition to economic inequality, the England of the early seventeenth century was also a hotbed of religious and political bigotry. The Laudian regime ruthlessly persecuted puritan and egalitarian elements (Dissenters, Quakers, Levellers, etc.), just as the Catholics and Protestants had persecuted each other in their turn. Men looked round for a haven in which each might practise his own vision of life, unmolested by the stern and disapproving hand of others.

Quakers emigrating to New England.

It was into this climate of despondency that burst the glowing promise of emigration to the New World. Aristocratic and merchant capital was sunk into various projects in the Americas, India and the Far East, and their profits were often enormous. But it is New England which must interest us here, for it was in many ways unique amongst the British colonies of the seventeenth century. There, the new population of settlers consisted almost entirely of ordinary British men, women and children, struggling to build a new society for themselves. In most of the other American colonies (certainly in Virginia, Jamaica and the West Indies) the Englishmen were chiefly upper class adventurers and their mercenaries, merchants, planters and other entrepreneurs, who exploited a labour force drawn from native or imported populations of slaves and near slaves, and carried their wealth back to England in the form of raw materials and commodities.

The settlers of New England quickly developed a working relationship with the local tribes, and learnt from them some of the techniques for survival in the harsh north-eastern winter. The settlers were chiefly drawn from the yeomanry and peasantry, farmers and craftsmen whose special skills suited them for the task in hand. Their motives were partly economic and ambitious, and partly religious and idealistic; and their prize lay in the freedom they gained from the iron grip of the English landowner and the Legislature, or in the freedom to worship as they chose. By emigrating, they were in no sense running away from the realities of life at home. Instead, and they mostly realised this, they were facing an even harsher reality, but one which carried with it the twin prospects of freedom and self-determination. The landless classes saw a chance to acquire and develop their own soil, and an opportunity to found self-governing communities which could be made in the image of their religious and political dreams. The popularity of emigration to New England, and the entrenchment of trade prerogatives through the protectionism of the trade companies, may both be seen as facets of the struggle by the artisan classes to improve their controls in life and to fight off the increasing stranglehold in which they found themselves in the early seventeenth century.

THE BACKGROUND OF THE HOUSE

In the development of the North European house, the provision of shelter was always most closely associated with the need for warmth. A permanent fire was required both for comfort and for cooking, and so the emotional and practical focus of the traditional home was to be found around the hearth or fireplace. The chief room of the house was known to the Norsemen as the 'fire house', but in England this was later contracted to 'houseplace', or 'hall'. Even in very grand houses in the Middle Ages, the hall was the centre of life in the home, though rich families later chose to adopt more private quarters for their own use in the form of a solar or parlour, away from the communal life of the hall. As the rich developed more and more complex series of private apartments in the seventeenth century, so the poor tended to retain the earlier system, and the chief living-room retained its title of 'hall', though some householders could afford the extra luxury of a small parlour. In farmhouses, the hall still retained its early function as a communal eating room for the family and staff of labourers, and often the food was cooked over the main hearth. Separate kitchens were a medieval innovation, but few small houses had the room for such a luxury. The emotional importance of the fireplace was retained in the English domestic scene right up until the present day, but has largely been replaced by the adoption of dispersed central-heating systems. But 'hearth and home' is still a powerful sentiment, and many still prefer an open fire of logs or coal.

> 1632... the Hall or Fier-house of the newe mansion house of the said John Parker...

The provision of a hearth is the most important factor in the consideration of early house plans, since the location of the fire directly affects the circulation of the house and its manner of furnishing. Furniture and architecture both serve the needs of the occupants, and the efficiency and comfort of a house are the outcome of generations of development (the concept of the house as a "machine for living in" was *not* invented in the twentieth century, though earlier generations might have phrased it differently).

Figure 1:1. *Central hearth with reredos (reconstruction) at Hendre'rywydd Uchaf Farm, Llangynhafal, Denbighshire. This open hearth is built on the site of the original hearth in this late fifteenth century timber-framed farmhouse. The iron trammel hangs from a roof beam to support the bronze cauldron over a peat fire. The floor of beaten earth would still be found in many poor rural homes in the seventeenth century.*

Harrison observed the more general adoption of chimneys during the course of the sixteenth century (Appendix I), but he remembered in his youth the more common appearance of the central hearth, with its *reredos,* or back-plate (Figure 1:1). In winter the family would sit and talk or work around this little life-giving arena. Their backs would freeze while their fronts roasted, and the smoke from the peat or log fire would find its way out as best it could through windows or roof vents. The discomforts of a smoky atmosphere and a sooty roof can well be imagined, and it seems that the provision of a canopy over important persons (and sometimes over the whole dais) had a very practical purpose in halls with an open hearth. Accumulations of soot must occasionally have worked loose, with disconcerting effect on those below.

The development of stone or brick wall-chimneys and timber-framed hood chimneys (see Figure 3:5) proceeded throughout the Middle Ages, but by 1500 they were still to be found only in rich houses and monasteries. In the sixteenth century, and especially in the great surge of vernacular building which marked the reign of Elizabeth I, chimneys became the rule rather than the exception. This followed closely on the wider adoption of coal for domestic fires, with its acrid smoke and tarry deposits. Many inventories record the use of iron grates or furnaces in which to burn the 'sea-cole' in conjunction with a chimney, and there is some evidence that portable charcoal grates were used indoors.

> 1540. . . a court chimney made gratewise upon wheels. . .
> 1558. . . cole baskettes, for seacole. . .
> 1590. . . In my owne chamber. . . one iron chimney. . .
>   In the lowe hall. . . one iron chimney. . .
> 1603. . . a cradell of iron to burn sea-cole. . .
> 1680. . . one small furnace with ye irons. . .

The space around the hearth was preserved in traditional homes by reserving a wide chimney opening, supported by a huge fire-beam or 'bressumer' (Figure 1:2). This open hearth or 'inglenook' became the focus

Figure 1:2. *Down-hearth fireplace, with oak bressumer. Cilewent Farm, Dyffryn Claerwen, Radnorshire. The house was in existence in 1579, but this fireplace probably dates from the alterations of 1734.*

of houshold life in the same way as the old central hearth had been, and many were ample enough to accommodate the seated family with all their iron and brass pots, pans, trivets, spits and all the other paraphernalia of down-hearth cookery.

Interior Decoration

As if to signal its importance in the life of the home, the fireplace was enriched to serve as the decorative focus of the room; and the hall fireplace was usually the most elaborate of all (Figure 1:3). In well-to-do homes, the chimney opening was provided with a carved fire surround, and surmounted with a stone, plaster or wooden overmantel, often charged with the arms of the family and its associates. Elaborate wooden overmantels were made and carved by the joiner to match the scheme of wall-panelling and doorcases which completed the room. In a house of quality, all the architectural woodwork of the house was similarly decorated in a style which embraced staircases, room panelling and the movable furniture (Figure 1.4). It is important to remember that newly finished oak furniture and woodwork is a pale biscuit colour, and not the richly patinated warm black-reds which we see today; and so a visit to a room such as this does not give a true impression of its appearance in the seventeenth century.

Figure 1:3. *Joined mantelpiece at the Old House, Hereford. Oak, c.1621. This mantelpiece is in an upstairs parlour, over the room in Figure 1:4. The overmantel is heavily carved, with terminal figures and shields (which must originally have been painted with coats-of-arms).*

Figure 1:4. *Dining hall at the Old House, Hereford. The staircase, panelling and furniture are of various dates in the seventeenth century.*

It is these twin qualities of colour and freshness which are unavoidably missing from any modern reconstruction of a period interior. Whilst we tend to admire the softening and darkening effect of age, we should try to bear in mind the appearance of fabrics, paints and polished wood when they are new, and when they formed the all-important physical background to movable furnishings.

Fabrics of all sorts were an important ingredient in middle and upper class houses of the seventeenth century. Needlework was one of the chief accomplishments of the respectable housewife, and the house was adorned with her handiwork and that of her daughters. Decorative fabrics from the professional hand were also much in demand, and inventories are full of references to hangings, cushions, table carpets, foot carpets, screens, and upholstery materials. Side tables and court cup-boards were usually covered

Figure 1:5. *Woollen tapestry wall-hanging, sixteenth century. This large fragment was part of a larger piece, which in turn must have been part of a set from a room at Winchester College, Hampshire. Whilst a great many pictorial and armorial tapestries are known from this date, this kind of all-over repeat pattern is comparatively rare. The quality of this French or Flemish piece is very good, with a fine and tight weave. The background pattern is 'paned' with alternating widths of red and green.*

with a cloth or 'carpet', but even the latter might be of quite thin material, though turkeywork was very popular too.

> 1588...a livery cubbord with a carpett of Turkey worke. Vs.
>
> 1594...My greatest Turkey carpet lying on the table in the hall...
>
> 1595...One cubborde and a cubborde clothe of Turkie worke...
>
> 1614...A cupboard of walnuttre with a Turkie carpett, the ground redd...
>
> 1624...a livery cupboard and turkey carpet on itt...
>
> 1626...4 Turket carpetts for side cubberds and table...

One rather curious habit (so far unexplained) was the occasional practice of keeping one or two cushions on top of a cupboard or side table:

> 1552...a litle quioshen table...a ioyned quoishen cupbourde...
>
> 1651...1 long Court Cupboard Cushion...
>
> 1672...1 livory board & Darnix cloth & 2 cusheans upon it...

This habit is also found in New England inventories:

> 1659...A livery cuberd wth a cloth and cushion, £1.6.8...
>
> 1 corute cobbord: chusion: cubbord cloth, £1.5s...
>
> 1661...By two small cushins to set on a cubbards head, £2...
>
> 1673...One cowt cubbard a cushen & cloth, £2.10s...

To the modern observer, the wooden-seated chairs and settles of the period represent very cold comfort indeed, but in fact most rooms were supplied with a number of turkeywork, needlework or even plain cloth cushions.

If the room was not panelled ("seeled with oke", as Harrison put it), then it might be hung with fabrics to keep out the winter draughts. The most desirable and effective draught-excluders were the thick woollen tapestries which were imported from Flanders, or later made in this country. Tapestry

Figure 1:6a. *Joined upholstered stool. English. Oak, c.1640. The top is covered with a re-used fragment of tapestry wall-hanging.*

Figure 1:6. *Woollen tapestry wall-hanging, sixteenth century. Another (smaller) fragment of tapestry with a repeat-pattern in two shades of green. The quality here is coarse, and such hangings must once have been common in middle-class houses. This piece has only survived because it was re-used at some time for the seat of an upholstered stool (Figure 1:6a).*

Figure 1:7. *Mural painting. A run of strapwork, from a house at Stamford, Lincolnshire.*

hangings were known by the generic name of 'arras', after the Flemish town which was famous for their manufacture; and other, lighter, materials were also in common use. Sometimes they were of a single colour or a simple pattern with two or three colours, such as the fragments in Figures 1:5 and 6; or the more expensive versions would be lavishly decorated with classical or biblical subjects, landscapes, allegories, birds and beasts, verdures, millefleurs, armorials and many more besides:

> 1552... th'angings of arras of the story of David 4 pair...
> th'angings of tapisterie of the story of Josphe 3 pecis lyned...
> 1601... fowre peeces of tapistrie hanginges with personages...
> six peeces of hanginges imbrodered uppon white damask murry velvet...
> fyve peeces of hanginges called the planetes...
> six peeces of hanginges of red Mockadowe...
> seaven peeces of hanginges of Cloth of gold and silver...
> six peeces of tapistrie hanginges of the story of Ulisses...
> six peeces of tapistrie hanginges of personages and My Ladies Armes in them...
> 1672... The chamber hung about with blue linsey woolsey streaked with white...

We can only begin to imagine the rich and colourful character of rooms hung in this way, but more important in the middle class home was a much cheaper form of painted cloth hangings. These are extremely common in inventories, though very few examples survive today. They were generally made in direct imitation of tapestry, with a similar range of subjects, and were sometimes known as 'counterfeit arras'. These painted or stained cloths were found even in quite poor homes, and may take the form both of room and bed hangings:

> 1536... stained clothes of the lif of St. George...
> Dyninge Parlor...stayned werke conteyning III peeces...
> 1576... the paynted cloths in the hall being the halling...
> 1578... stayned clothes of storyes hanging about the great chamber...
> 1584... the stained clothes that hang behind mine cupboard, and a little story of Tobias that hangeth over it...
> 1585... one peece of stayned cloth of forrest worke hanging about the parlour...
> 1588... To John Steven for three score ells of canvas which doth hang the said chamber, 37s.2d...
> To the goodman Laye the painter for painting the cloths. 51s.8d..
> 1589... a painted clothe of Robin Hoode that hangeth in the hall...
> 1608... also peyneted clothes about the chamber...
> 1672... an olde cheast with soreworne paynted clothes yn ytt...

Decorated wallpapers were also in use throughout the sixteenth and seventeenth centuries, though it is very difficult to gauge just how common they were. They are rarely mentioned in inventories, since they were not

Figure 1:8. *Painted ceiling, at Crathes Castle near Aberdeen (seen from below). c.1602. This is one of a series of finely-preserved polychrome ceilings at Crathes, here depicting the Muses. The paint is applied directly to the surface of the wooden beams and the underside of the floorboards of the upper room.*

Figure 1:9. *Painted ceiling, from a house at Wickham, Hampshire (seen from above). Early seventeenth century. This is a much simpler version than the example from Crathes Castle. It is in a small middle-class house on the village square, and is a rare survival of a once common type. The paint is hidden from below by a later plaster ceiling, and was discovered recently during repairs to the house.*

movable goods; and being of an ephemeral nature very few traces of them remain. Sometimes scraps may be found under later papers or panelling, but most survivors are known because of their use as box and drawer linings (Figures 3:394 and 395). Some were originally pasted straight onto the plastered wall, but many were pasted onto canvas stretched over a light wooden framework and hung on the wall with battens. The earliest paper known in England is the fragment of c.1509 from Christ's College Cambridge. Like all the later papers, it was printed from a woodcut block. The papers found as linings are mostly in black, but other colours include dark blue, red and red-brown. In the later seventeenth century 'flock' papers were introduced from the Netherlands, in which the design was printed first with glue. The paper was then dusted over with flock, the powdered and coloured ends of wool, which stuck to the glue and produced a pattern. Printed papers might also include two or more colours, and further details were sometimes added by stencil.

The subject matter of early paper hangings is highly varied. Some of the most popular were copies of fabric designs, especially silk damasks, and Pepys mentioned the "counterfeit damask" paper used to hang the walls of his wife's closet. Pictorial subjects were very common, as well as floral patterns based on contemporary needleworks. The papers were printed by hand from woodblocks about twelve inches or fourteen inches square, and those intended for wall hangings were made in lengths of twelve feet or so, to be stored and sold in rolls.

If the walls of a room were neither hung with fabrics nor panelled with wainscot, then a simple and colourful alternative was to paint the plaster ground with mural paintings. These were also common in small houses of the sixteenth and seventeenth centuries, but like other schemes of decoration, few examples have survived to give an accurate impression of the newly-finished room. In poorer homes, the notion of 'decorating' a room with an integrated scheme was obviously non-existent; but even poor householders would often whitewash their walls inside and out. This was largely an hygienic measure designed to kill insects and other pests, and even up to the present century the annual limewashing of the house and outhouses was cheerfully known in working-class circles as 'bug-blinding'.

The fresh white of limewash could be varied by the addition of different colouring agents, and until recent years the regional variations in the colourwash used on plastered cottages were very obvious (red-brown in Devon, pink in Suffolk, yellow ochre in the Cotswolds, etc.). To some extent this practice has been revived with the use of commercial colours, but the gaudy Mediterranean palette of ready-mixed modern paints can never replace the subtle blends of local earth-colours mixed with whitewash. Other shades were obtained from vegetable dyes, such as the deep drab blue used in Derbyshire, called 'archil' and derived from the liverwort which grows in the Peak District. Chemical agents were also used, such as red lead to make a brownish-red, or copperas for a light pastel green. The author found a pristine coat of drab red-brown on the plastered wall of a sixteenth century house in Salisbury, which was exposed when some early seventeenth century panelling was removed by workmen.

For those interested in complete authenticity, limewash and other examples of colourwash were always painted over the beams and plaster, and the beams were not left exposed as in modern practice. Even more decorative painting was often continued across structural beams, and many beams retain evidence of painted mouldings and other detail. The painted wooden beams and ceiling in Figure 1:9 are a lucky survival. Here the paint was protected by a later plaster ceiling. The underside of the floor boards was painted with simple red and black flowers and foliage, which gave a bright and vigorous ceiling to the room below. Thousands of similar examples must have disappeared without trace, and no doubt a few are still hidden from view. Simple trail patterns were sometimes painted on cottage walls, and a traditional pattern called the 'witch-worm' was noted in Derbyshire and Yorkshire by Sidney Oldall Addy in the 1890s. No doubt such elementary devices have a long unrecorded history. This one consists of a linear trail with alternating dots, and was painted in a single colour over a different coloured ground (Diagram 1:1).

Diagram 1:1. *The traditional 'witch-worm' pattern noted by Sidney Oldall Addy in his 'Evolution of the English House', 1933.*

In middle- and upper-class dwellings the use of mural paintings was an infinitely more sophisticated process, and continued practices found in Roman villas and medieval churches alike. A preference for religious subjects was a hangover from the Middle Ages, which soon gave way to a wide variety of secular scenes, landscapes and abstract patterns. Many of the scenes are taken from contemporary woodcuts and book illustrations, if not from the painter's own imagination, and scenes from the classics and everyday life alternated with moral tales and cautionary texts. Geometric and floral patterns grew in popularity during the sixteenth century, and *trompe l'oeil* imitations of panelling sometimes substituted for the real thing. Sometimes, even the folds and hooks of tapestry hangings were copied onto the flat plaster, though painted cloths must have been a more effective imitation. Mural paintings were largely superseded by the popularity of cheap wallpapers in the seventeenth century, and most of the fragments known today were found under old wallpaper (often protected by the battened canvas frames) or later panelling.

The Use of Furniture in Interiors

Despite our fairly extensive knowledge of furniture types and related social conventions, we still have only a sketchy view of the predictable ways in which furniture was used in the early house. This is an important and very relevant matter, for the design of individual pieces is often directly related to the exact use for which they were intended, and the exact location for which they were made. A prime example is in the usual form of the long dining table (see Chapter Three). Such a large piece of furniture was a cumbersome object in a small house, and so the layout of the hall was designed expressly to accommodate the large table and the necessary seating.

In Diagram 1:2, five successive standard layouts are shown, all taken from surviving houses. They demonstrate the continuation of the medieval convention of using fixed wall-benches to provide some of the seating, and movable benches and stools for the rest. The surviving table and benches at

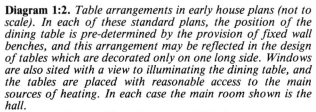

a   b

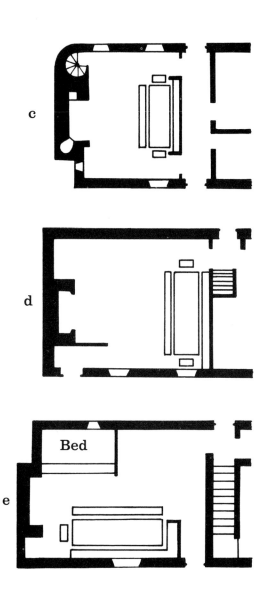

Diagram 1:2. *Table arrangements in early house plans (not to scale). In each of these standard plans, the position of the dining table is pre-determined by the provision of fixed wall benches, and this arrangement may be reflected in the design of tables which are decorated only on one long side. Windows are also sited with a view to illuminating the dining table, and the tables are placed with reasonable access to the main sources of heating. In each case the main room shown is the hall.*

a). *Gentry house, fifteenth century. This is a cross-passage plan, with entry to the hall via two doorways in the screen. On the right of the screens passage are the kitchen and buttery, with separate doorways. The hall has a central hearth, flanked by a pair of long tables with fixed and movable benches. The dais runs across the western end of the hall, and is furnished with a narrow table and great chair.*

b). *Gentry house, c.1500. This hall has a number of refinements which are improvements on the plan in* **a),** *notably a large wall fireplace. The overall plan is very similar, but the tables are now of different sizes to accommodate the hearth space. This plan was still widely used in the seventeenth century, and survives in a number of houses, colleges, schools and livery-halls (see the Drapers' Hall, Shrewsbury, Diagram 2:2).*

c). *Farmhouse, sixteenth century. Still using a cross-passage plan with screens, though on a smaller scale, the fixed bench is here attached to the screen itself. The single large table is provided with a movable bench and stools, and the fixed bench has heavy shaped bench-ends.*

d). *Farmhouse, seventeenth century. Here the front entry is in the south-west corner, and the interior is protected from draughts by a short 'spere' screen. The long bench is fixed to a heavy screen which forms the room division, and the screen also supports a simple staircase with a primitive form of ladder stair opposite the rear entry.*

e). *Farmhouse, seventeenth century. Here the return section of the L-shaped fixed bench is attached to the 'spere' screen, and the rest of the bench lies along the south wall. The built-in cupboard bed is provided with its own small window, and a fixed bench is attached to the front of the bed close to the fire.*

A great deal of further research is needed to find out more about the conventions of siting both fixed and movable furniture in this period, at all levels of society.

c

d

e

Bed

the Drapers' Hall in Shrewsbury are fine examples of this arrangement still *in situ* (Figure 2:7 and Diagram 2:2). Tables made for this conventional use are normally carved on one side only, and may be mistaken for side tables when they are found out of context. The fixed benches are attached either to structural walls, or to the heavy post-and-panel wooden partitions which divide up the rooms. Early building accounts sometimes make provision for 'benching-about' the hall, as in the case of Hengrave Hall in Suffolk; and the benches are still to be found in various houses such as Ockwells Manor, Bray; Forde House, Newton Abbott; or Ty Mawr, Conwy. In earlier houses evidence may be seen of fixed stone benches, as at Great Chalfield Manor in Wiltshire.

> 1594...all the benchboards or seats placed to the sides and walls
>   of the hall and kitchen to sit on, or for other uses or
>   services...
> 1597...a long joined table in the hall, a long fixed settle, and a
>   little settle...

Other conventions relate to the placing of furniture in habitual relationships with other pieces. The most obvious of these are the chair and stools around a table, but since these relationships are quite transitory, we have to look for documentary evidence of their frequency and currency. Significantly, the table and chairs (or stools) are usually mentioned as it were in the same breath in inventory lists, and we may assume that they were standing together when recorded. But occasionally we are lucky and the compiler may note "...one oaken table and one oaken chair that standeth at the table's end..." (1594). Hundreds of wills and inventories refer to chests placed "at the bed's feet", or "at the stairshead", and these must both represent common practice. The chest at the foot of the bed was especially useful for the safe storage of valuables at night.

Most houses, except the very poorest, contained a reasonable range of furniture types (a chair, a large table, a serving table, stools or backstools, chests for storage, a cupboard or two, beds, etc.), and the average inventory gives us a balanced view of the spread of furniture to be found in houses. Randle Holme gives a rather grand list of furnishings for both a dining room and a bedchamber (Appendix II), and in a very positive letter to her husband, William, Lady Compton gave a comprehensive glimpse of the 'necessities' in an early seventeenth century home:

> "...I will have all my houses furnished, and all my lodging
> chambers to be suited with all such furniture as is fit; as beds,
> stools, chairs, suitable cushions, carpets, silver warming pans,
> cupboards of plate, fair hangings, and such like. So for my
> drawing chambers in all my houses I will have them delicately
> furnished both with couch, canopy, glass, carpet, chairs.
> cushions, and all things thereunto belonging..."

The phrases 'suitable to' and 'thereunto belonging' are very common in inventories, though it is not clear whether this always means that the items described are necessarily matching or *en suite* with each other in the modern sense. Certainly, furniture was made in matching sets from an early date,[1] and examples are known (notably at Knole House); but it is rare today to find groups of pieces with matched decoration, such as table and stools.

The last aspect we must consider here before passing on to the actual construction of furniture, is the question of the symbolism which surrounds several forms of furniture, and in particular the age-old preoccupation with

---

1. In inventories, it is usually only the upholstery coverings and hangings which are 'suitable', and the phrase rarely seems to be used with reference to the woodwork and its decoration.

social precedence. The chair is far and away the most obvious, for in times when chairs were relatively scarce, only the most important man present was accorded the privilege of using a chair. In the earliest times this would have been an X-stool, but by the end of the Middle Ages an armchair served the same purpose. This seat of authority could be supplemented by further potent symbols. It might be placed on some form of elevated platform or dais which raised the sitter physically above the level of the rest of the company; it might have a footrest, in the form of a fitted footboard or a separate foot cushion (enabling the legs of the chair to be made longer than usual); it might be provided with a high back or 'dosser', on which could be displayed some costly fabric or the arms of the sitter (or the current Royal House); and lastly it might be surmounted by some form of canopy. The same symbols were adapted for use at altars and in the dining halls of the rich and powerful, and may be seen today in traditional settings such as college dining halls, or the courts of law. In the sixteenth century these arrangements declined in domestic use, though the importance of the chair remained, and the bed and dresser retained their backboard and canopy.

Figure 1:10. *Mural painting, from the parlour of a farmhouse at Ashdon, Essex. c.1600. The colours are dark green, white and a dull rose-red, freely handled without resort to stencils. The whole work is loosely carried out as an imitation of wall-panelling, and should be compared with the painted wall panel in Plate Four. Even the proportions of the panels follow current joinery practice (cf. Diagram 2:16c).*

Chapter Two

Makers and Methods
The Practical Context

THE FURNITURE-MAKING TRADES

THE CARPENTERS WERE the first of the woodworking trades to establish themselves as a guild in London, and the crafts were at first dominated by the Guild of Master Carpenters. The first Ordinances of the Brotherhood of Carpenters was granted in 1333, though the first Charter was not secured until 1477. They were the heads of the allied building trades, and normally acted as contractors for the whole operation of constructing and finishing a timber-framed building; or the roof and floors for stone (or later brick) structures. The better class of fitted woodwork and integral furniture was sub-contracted to the joiners and ceilers, and other decorations to the appropriate plasterers, pargeters, painters, gilders, etc. Within the Carpenters' Guild, the most important members were the sculptors or 'ymagers', whose work is sometimes proudly recorded in accounts where a table or cupboard is noted as "carven wt. ymagrie". These were closely followed in precedence by the carpenters themselves — in reality the house-wrights. Lastly came the hutchmaker, who was responsible for all manner of boarded furniture, but who was bound to observe only those regulations concerning the correct cutting and seasoning of timber. His constructional methods were apparently his own concern in earlier times, and for the most part these consisted only of nailed boards, usually strengthened with iron bands. The Carpenters' Company of London is unique in having an off-shoot in America, in the form of the Carpenters' Company of the City and County of Philadelphia, which dates from 1724.

The turners were perhaps among the first to organise themselves into some cohesive group, and one Warner le Turner is mentioned in the Pipe Roll of 1179-1180. But, despite the ancient origins of their craft, and the early and frequent mentions of their activities, the Worshipful Company of Turners of London did not receive a successful incorporation until 1604.

The joiners likewise had an early but ignominious beginning in the shadow of the carpenters. One William le Joynier is mentioned as early as 1239, but for most of the fifteenth century they were somewhat disguised by their affiliation to the religious guild of St. James Garlickhythe, which dates from 1375. The 'Mistery of the Joyners of the City of London' was a semi-independent body by 1400, when they were allowed to elect two wardens with power of search; but their first Charter was not granted until 1570, when the 'Faculty of Joyners and Ceilers or Carvers of London' was incorporated. This act of incorporation confirmed the severance of the joiners and ceilers (who were united by their common use of framed and panelled construction, q.v.) from the carpenters, and lent an increased pace to the perennial round of arguments and recriminations which characterised the relationships between the various trades.

Demarcations

The catalogue of demarcation disputes which arose between the assorted interests is very informative in terms of the way in which each trade interpreted its own function. However, we must regard most of the decisions and legal rulings as applicable largely in the realm of theory. The rules which developed, by a process of litigation and compromise, were very strict and precise; but there is a suspiciously large number of complaints about infringement, and so we are forced to assume that many of the rules were habitually broken. Theory does not relate entirely to the facts as they sometimes present themselves, and so we can only interpret who *should* have made what. The wardens and governors of most trades tried to apply rigorously their powers of search and punishment, but their efforts were always limited by the ingenuity of recalcitrant members and (especially in London) the sheer size of the problem. London was a warren of small backstreet workshops; and besides, the wardens' jurisdiction was confined to London itself and a very small area around; whilst the impenetrable labyrinth of Southwark, with its supply of highly-skilled immigrant artificers, produced a huge output of fine-quality furniture throughout the sixteenth century and later.

The principal quarrels developed because of the distinctions between the constructional techniques of the carpenters and joiners, and after 1550 turned decoration became such an integral feature of joined furniture that the turners had to watch out for trespasses on their domain. Even *within* their own company, the London joiners had to specify that the carvers were *not* joiners who specialised in carving, and that apprentice carvers should be set under a master carver and not taught to make mortice and tenon joints.

The carpenters regarded the joiners as an offshoot of their own trade, and became very jealous of the rising importance of joinery during the sixteenth century. Matters came to a head in 1632, after certain joiners were imprisoned for trespassing on the work of the carpenters. The London Court of Aldermen was called in to arbitrate in the dispute, and their committee attempted to settle the problem once and for all, by finding that "...these workes next following doe pperly belong to the Joyners:

1. Imprimis all sorts of Bedsteads whatsoever (onlie and except Boarded Bedsteads and nayled together).
2. Item. All sortes of chayres and stooles which are made with mortesses and tennants.
3. Item. All tables of wainscoate wallnutt or other stuffe glewed with fframes mortesses or tennants.
4. Item. All sortes of formes framed made or boards with the sides pinned or glewed.
5. Item. All sortes of chests being framed duftalled pynned or glewed.
6. Item. All sortes of cabinetts or boxes duftalled pynned, glued or joyned.
7. Item. All sortes of cupboards framed duftalled pynned or glued.
8. Item. All sortes of presses for wearing apparrell Merçers Silkemen Haberdashers Gouldsmiths Milleners or Napkin presses being pannelled duftalled pynned or glued.
9. Item. All sortes of wainscott and sealing of Houses...
10. Item. All sorts of shopp windows that are made for ornament or beautie...
11. Item. All sorts of doores framed pannelled or glued.

12. Item. All hatches edged framed or glued.
13. Item. All pewes pulpitts and seates with the desks belonging to them framed pannelled or glued.
14. Item. All sortes of frames upon stalls being framed or glued.
15. Item. All frames for picturs...
19. Item. All carved workes either raised or cutt through or sunck in with the Grounde taken out being wrought and cutt with carving Tooles without the use of Plaines."[1]

Significantly, the carpenters were forbidden the use of glue under most circumstances, and their structural form is defined as "boarded and nayled together". The joiners were allowed the free use of glue and various joints, and whilst the better sort of shop fittings were their prerogative, the carpenters were restricted to work benches and cheap tables for "...Drapers...Taverners, Victuallers, Chandlers, Compting House Tables and all other Tables made of Deal Elme Oake Beeche or other wood nayled together without glue..." Item 19 reinforces the view that carvers should associate with joiners, at least in London.

Forty years later, this ruling was again invoked when the joiners petitioned the Court of Aldermen that the carpenters were unrepentant over their latest trespasses on the joiners' craft. The carpenters made reply that the whole trade had originally been theirs and if the joiners, who "...were formerly but limbes members and a part of the Carpentry and Branches taken from them...", so chose to cut themselves off, then they must take the consequences without protection or favour. The Court took no further action than to remind both parties that their former order was still a by-law between them.

The year after the joiners' victory over the carpenters, in 1633, the Court of Aldermen was involved in another dispute, this time between the joiners and the turners. In a report of 1630 to the Turners' Company, it was noted that "...divers refractory and disobedient members...do work and turn in the shops of Joiners within and without the City of London and do teach and instruct joiners in the art of turnery..." The turners complained to the Court that joiners "...assume unto themselves the art of turning..." They observed that in their eyes the arts of turning and joining "...are two several and distinct trades... and they...conceive it very inconvenient that either of these trades should encroach upon the other..." They had found that some joiners habitually did their own turned work such as bed-posts and stool legs, and that they had even employed some out-of-work turners in their own shops, and had learnt from them the art of turning. The renegade turners were fined the huge sum of 10s. per week, for every week they continued to associate with a joiner.

The Provincial Trades

The London Guilds and Companies were somewhat unique in maintaining such a fierce insularity and independence between the trades. The reasons for it are clear, of course, with competition for business between large memberships, with large numbers of apprentices to regulate, and with the threat from a high immigrant population. Such conditions also applied in some measure to the larger provincial cities, especially Norwich, but generally the trades lived in greater harmony outside the capital. Chester, for example, had a Company of Joyners Carvers and Turners, whilst in York the joiners and carpenters were united. Each town evolved a set of rules to suit its own circumstances, but in practice these were broadly similar. Many smaller towns, which were still nevertheless large enough to

1. Quoted by E.B. Jupp, *Historical Account of the Worshipful Company of Carpenters,* London, 1887.

Figure 2:1. *The Joyners' Hall, St. Ann Street, Salisbury, Wiltshire. Early seventeenth century. The facade of the building is barely altered from its original state, and still retains the grotesque bracket figures and carved fascia board, which are attributed popularly to the hand of Humphrey Beckham. The building was one of the first to be acquired by the National Trust in 1894, but by then the rich panelled interior described by Hatcher in 1843 had disappeared without trace.*

support their own trade companies, had only one company to serve the building and allied trades.

It is instructive to choose one small city, Salisbury in Wiltshire, to examine the make-up of its guild, and to look at some of the demarcation disputes which *did* arise between different interests within the membership of the society. The Salisbury Carpenters' Guild was first referred to in the Corporation Ledger in 1440. Its membership then included "Carpynters, Bowiers, Coupers, Masones, Hellyers, Lymbners, ffletchers, and Skynners." The orders of the Craft Guilds were later revoked by Elizabeth I, and during their reconstitution the joiners made their new importance manifest, and we find the trade company constituted as the "Companye of the Joyners, Whellers, Worsteed Makers, Bookbinders, Carpenters, Millwrightes, Coopers, Free Masons, Rough Masons, Paynters, Instrumente Makers, Ropers, Turners, Saweyers, and Bellowe-makers, within the Cittye of Newe Sarum."[2] A rag-bag of trades by London standards, but one which combines the essential furniture and building trades. In 1612, the upholsters, for reasons known only unto themselves, had joined the new Grocers' Company, having previously belonged to the Mercers' Guild. After several false starts, the Joyners' Company received its constitution from the Mayor and Corporation in April 1617. At about the same time the Company occupied its fine new Hall (Figure 2:1), which still stands in St. Ann Street (then Tanner Street).

As with the London Companies, attempts were made to codify the limitations of each craft, but in a far more casual manner. Nevertheless, the joiners took advantage of the occasion to write in and award themselves formal concessions in the new Charter of 1617, taking liberties which would have been unthinkable in London, or in competition against a brother company:

> "It shall be lawfull for all and every person which is a freeman
> of this Company and have served out their apprenticeship in the
> art or mystery of a joyner to use and excercise all and every the
> arts and mysteries of joyning, carving, inlaying and such turn-
> inge as such joyners do use, and as they shall have been brought
> up to within this Cittie."

But despite the relative freedoms of their laws, the various trades within the Company could not live entirely in harmony. Amongst the various complaints was one that carpenters were including painting in their estimates, and another that a brewster was employing coopers to make barrels in his own workshop. Quarrels between the carpenters and joiners grew to such a pitch that in 1621 the Corporation ordered that "... at the next com'n Counsell, the company of Carpenters shall or may be severed from the company of joiners ..." In the following year, the order was repeated more specifically "... that the company be mended, Joyners, Paynters, Ropemakers, bookebynders, to be of one companye; and the carpenters and others to be of the other companye..." This would have had the effect of dividing the joiners and painters on one hand, from the carpenters, turners and sawyers on the other, producing an interesting scission of the trades. Yet, this is probably a reflection more of the personalities involved, than of any meaningful craft demarcations. The trades must have found some way of living at peace, for when the new Charter was issued under Charles II in 1675, it included the same trades as in 1617, with the addition of bricklayers and plumbers.

One result of the laxity and generosity with which by-laws were interpreted in provincial towns, was that many men were free to practise two or

2. Quoted by Charles Haskins, *The Ancient Trade Guilds and Companies of Salisbury*, published by subscription, Salisbury, 1912.

Plate Three. *Joined armchair. English; probably Leeds area, South Yorkshire. Oak, with inlay of coloured woods, mid-seventeenth century. This is one of a large group of cupboards, chests and chairs with similar decoration, which emanated from an urban workshop in the Yorkshire Clothing Dales area; probably in the large and rich city of Leeds itself (see Chapter Four, Figures 4:113-122).*

Plate Four. *Painted wall panel, from a run of low-level dado panelling. English. Oak, early seventeenth century. The usual coarse handling of the brushwork in decorative paintwork of this period is clearly seen here. This is closely paralleled both on other examples of wall panelling and on items of movable furniture such as the chest of drawers in Plates Five and Six. Mural paintings on plaster also reflect a similar approach.*

more trades. This was particularly true of the turner, whose basic tool, the turning-lathe, led him into the realms of the pumpmaker, wheelwright, bowl-turner and chairmaker, besides working on contract for the joiner, and supplying parts for many other trades. The will of Thomas Quilter of Great Dunmow, Essex, describes him as both joiner and turner.[3] He instructs his elder son to teach his younger brother "joining and turning in the best manner he can."

In the Colonies skilled labour was in such demand that little distinction was made at first between the various grades of woodworker. From the start, the greatest need was for skilled men able to turn their hands to all that was needed. Joiners and carpenters contributed to all aspects of their crafts, and did not discriminate between housebuilding, furniture making, and even the building of wagons, bridges and ships. In the early days of colonisation (1634), William Wood wrote of Massachusetts that what was needed in every district was "...an ingenious Carpenter, a cunning Joyner, a handie Cooper, such a one as can make strong ware for the use of the countrie..." The demands of a hostile environment forced the craftsman to turn his thoughts to the solutions for survival, and forget the niceties of inter-disciplinary disputes. But as the City of Boston established itself, and the numerous townships of New England acquired a more settled way of life during the second half of the seventeenth century, so systems of craft organisation developed which mirrored the forms and procedures which had worked so well in England. Trade companies of furniture makers were never formed as such in New England, but furniture production became stabilised to the extent that the forms produced relate very closely in structure and decoration to the range of their English prototypes.

Marketing Procedures

Despite the great volume of production of domestic furniture before the eighteenth century, we know very little of the daily marketing methods of the time, and of the exact nature of the relationship between the maker and his private customer. This is especially true of the middle and labouring classes, though the latter no doubt largely bought secondhand, or made it themselves. Certain diarists make reference to the fact that they had bought items of furniture, but it is rarely clear whether they had done so in the comparative anonymity of the public shop, or whether there was normally some closer relationship with the vendor, as was clearly the case with Samuel Pepys and Sympson the Joyner. How *did* the man-in-the-street go about the business of buying furniture?

The existence of shops or warehouses selling ready-made furniture, at least in London, is evinced by the fact that a lady of the Verney family had great difficulty in buying a new cradle after the Great Fire of 1666, "...as all their stores are burnt..."

During times when bespoke orders were slow in coming forth, the workshop master would undoubtedly engage his men on speculative pieces such as were always in demand by the casual customer — stools, tables, cradles, etc.; or with luck and good management he might have standing orders for his regular lines from a local or London retail merchant, who would undertake to buy his surplus production. Local market days must have provided an important outlet for many small craftsmen, while the trade companies usually undertook to buy at a fixed price from any members who were laden with unsold stock. The Ward rate book for 1648 includes an assessment for the "Stocke of Furniture" held at the Salisbury Joiners' Hall. It may be that the Hall served as a shop, offering goods for sale on behalf of the members (Figure 2:1).

Figure 2:2. *The interior of an early retail shop. English woodcut, c.1600. It is not clear how the marketing of furniture was organised at this date. Possibly only a very small proportion of items was sold over the counter in this manner, in separate retail premises. The only piece of 'furniture' to be seen here is the small framed mirror, and it seems likely that many larger and more expensive items were ordered direct from the makers.*

3. Quoted by F.G. Emmison, *Elizabethan Life, Home, Work and Land,* Essex Record Office, Chelmsford, 1976.

Diagram 2:1. *Unfinished date and inscription. Spaces are reserved for a set of marriage initials and the final date number.*

Occasionally, as in Diagram 2:1, one comes across a piece of furniture where a space in the run of carving on the frieze has been reserved for the later insertion of a customer's initials, and where this was never completed. The diagram is a typical example of a piece made 'off-the-peg', intended that the initials and date be completed after sale, and before delivery to that customer. Many initialled and dated pieces must have been prepared in this way, though most received their appointed inscriptions.

But the evidence more strongly demonstrates that most provincial workshops occupied themselves as far as possible on the production of specific orders, designed and constructed to the exact requirements of the customer. Almost anything might be guaranteed a ready sale in a great market such as London, but a poor country joiner. could ill afford to risk the use of expensive timber on an item which might subsequently lack a purchaser. There is ample evidence in contemporary accounts that the customer often paid the joiner for the *making* of the piece only. In 1482 for example, one John Clyff was paid 6d. "for making one chest" for Ashburton Church, Devon, whilst John Soper was paid separately for the sawing of the timber for the chest.[4]

The account for the 'New Cubborde of Boxes' at Stratford-upon-Avon, rendered by Richard Ange and Abraham Sturley, itemises separately for payments to Lawrence Abell (joiner?) and Oliver Hickox (blacksmith?) and costs for timber, nails and glue. It may be assumed that the customer (Stratford Corporation) thus bought all the materials on their own account, and submitted them to the joiner for assembly, since the only payment to him is for his time at sixteen and a half days:

> The accomptes of Richard Ange and Abraham Sturley Chamberleyns for the XXth day of December 1594 for one whole yeare then next followinge...
>
> The New Cubborde of Boxes.

Item for III hundred of boardes............	XVIs	
And a XI foote.........................		VId
Item for nayles and glue...................	IIIIs	
Lawrence Abelles worke XVI dayes and a halfe	XVIs	
Item for Iron, hinges, lockes, keys and skrewe pinnes.................................	VIs	VId
Item pd to Oliver Hickox for three payre of great hinges, III lockes and keyes, five score great nayles, XII ringes and staples, III payre of skrewes.................................	XVIs	IId
Total.... £3.	0.	8½.

4. Quoted by Fred Roe, *History of Oak Furniture,* Connoisseur, London, 1920.

In the Royal Accounts of Elizabeth I for 1560, are records of a payment to the upholsterer, John Grene, for the supply of an upholstered sleeping chair. The complicated iron stays, springs and ratchets for adjusting the back are the subject of a separate payment to the smith, William Hoode. Similarly, the account for the purchase of the deed chest at the Drapers' Hall, Shrewsbury, itemised the payment for the ironwork separately from the bill for the joiner, Francis Bowyer (see p.54). Presumably the blacksmith, Thomas Gratie, delivered the locks and hinges to Bowyer at his workshop, but applied direct to the Drapers' Company for payment.

Timber specifically for use in furniture was sometimes left to beneficiaries in wills, such as the following Elizabethan items:

> 1573... to my son, three boards to make him a chest...
> 1602... 3 planks and timber sufficient to make a frame and table...
> ... 3 planks and as many quarters wch. shall make a frame with six feet...[5]

A similar custom of separate provision is found in the building of great houses, where the builder/patron contracted separately to supply the mason with stone, brick, timber, etc. This was usually effected by buying stone from a quarry owner; buying or leasing a quarry for the duration of the job; opening a quarry on the estate; or by hiring a brickmaker to set up kilns or clamps on the site. Timber was often taken from the estate, or supplied by a neighbour.[6]

The whole system whereby the customer supplies all necessary materials to the maker, argues a closer and more satisfying involvement in his purchases for the new owner, and provides him with the opportunity for a thoughtful selection of processes which is entirely absent in modern marketing.

Workshop Set-up

The standard procedures of apprenticeship and the regulation of processes followed by the majority of trade organisations are outlined in Chapter One, and the woodworkers were no exception to these patterns. Having completed his training, the apprentice submitted himself for examination by the Guildmasters, who sought to satisfy themselves as to his skill and achievement in the craft by a process of questioning and judging the merits of his 'master-piece'. On passing these tests, the newly-qualified artisan was able to hire himself out as a journeyman in the workshop of a master or, if he could raise the capital, he might set up a workshop himself and become his own master, or else one day hope to do so.

In the villages and small towns that might not be such a difficult achievement. In the Worcester Record Office is the probate inventory of just such a small-town joiner, Edward Bickerton of Evesham, Worcs. (d.1668).[7] His circumstances at his death may be taken as typically those of a mildly prosperous small workshop owner, one of the few artificers to aspire to yeoman status. Although his belongings totalled a respectable £101 6s. 6d., over £68 of that was taken up by his working capital in the form of his tools and various standing and cut timber ''in his house and abroad''. In common with most men of his time, the modest house is furnished in an adequate but sparse manner. He illustrates, perhaps, that class of men who had managed to avoid being trapped in the restrictive world of declining subsistence wages which was the lot of the employed artisans. He was of the lower reaches of that middle class of small manufacturers and traders who had begun to rise in the sixteenth century,

5. Quoted by F.G. Emmison, op. cit.
6. cf. Malcolm Airs, *The Making of the English Country House 1500-1640,* The Architectural Press, London, 1975.
7. Quoted in full by John West, *Village Records,* Macmillan, London, 1962. See Appendix IV.

and who had managed to accumulate a little capital, security and comfort.

For the bulk of our period, and certainly outside the larger towns, the majority of small shop-masters lived at much the same physical and domestic level as the men they employed, and were hardly distinguishable from them in the matter of class. The master-craftsman worked with his men, taking a full share in the production of the shop and all the responsibility for its quality. The provincial master-joiner rarely employed more than a handful of journeymen and apprentices; but increasingly in the seventeenth century there were some who had become suppliers in bulk — no longer brother craftsmen but now merchants engaged in the business of buying and selling. In this manner the trade of the cabinet maker/upholsterer gradually developed until many of them became not furniture makers, but shopkeepers and designers.

In the villages, where most crafts coexisted in a small way to fill purely local needs and markets, the furniture maker usually employed little or no journeyman labour, and may even have shared his tools and facilities with another craftsman such as a cartwright or basketmaker. Extreme specialisation was still a matter for the towns, and for the future. Most villages of any size harboured a variety of crafts from bootmaker and clothier, to blacksmith and tanner, but most men had at least a working knowledge of crafts other than their own. In slack times it is likely that the village carpenter would boost his income by turning his hand to other work with a ready sale, and by selling the surplus produce of his garden.

Most of the great houses, colleges and cathedrals maintained estate workshops, often established during the original building operations, to administer to the various repairs and furnishing needs occasioned by the daily life in such establishments. The larger estates employed a range of craftsmen from masons and blacksmiths, to joiners and wainwrights. They were responsible for repairs, alterations and additions to the fabric of the houses, cottages, farm buildings, walls and bridges; for the making of all but the finest domestic furniture for house, servants and tenants; for making and servicing carriages, wagons and fences; and for making domestic and farm implements. Many houses and colleges still contain furniture made by the estate craftsmen, usually from timber cut and prepared in the home parks. They often take the form of uniquely designed movable or fixed constructions, suitable only to one place or function. Others are simply the standard furniture of the day, of such quality as to be indistinguishable from furniture of commercial production. The most obvious examples of identifiable estate-made pieces are the great dining tables used in the early communal hall. The tops of these tables, when of one length of plank, are often of such great size, that to have carried the timber far over early roads would have been an impossible task. Whether we are to believe him or not, Robert Plot described an oak tree grown in the New Park at Dudley, which was "...of prodigious height and magnitude, out of which a table all of one plank could be cut, twenty-five yards three inches long, and wanting but two inches of a yard in breadth for the whole length..."[8] The table of forty-two feet in Figure 2:162 is a perfect example of an estate-made piece.

Anonymity

One curious and elusive aspect of the whole period of joinery construction in the British Isles is the almost complete anonymity of the makers of specific works. Apart from the fixed woodwork of some major buildings, and other rare instances where documentation survives to name the makers of extant furniture (mostly still in their original settings), the

Figure 2:3. *Joined pulpit. The London Charterhouse. Oak, 1613. The accounts of the rebuilding of parts of the Charterhouse, on the occasion of its conversion for Thomas Sutton's Hospital, show that the chapel pulpit was made by two joiners, Thomas Herring and Edward Mayes, and that it was carved by Francis Blunt. Such precise records are unfortunately rare.*

8. Robert Plot, *Natural History of Staffordshire*, 1686.

51

names of makers are not identifiable. True, many names of men who are described as joiners, carpenters and turners are known from their wills, tax returns, business accounts and other local archive material, but few actual pieces are attributable to them. Early furniture is never signed by makers in the way that, for example, metalwork so often is. Pewterers, silversmiths, armourers and a host of other trades were obliged to sign their work with a mark or initials, in order that it might subsequently be identified, and on pain of severe penalties for default. But for all their concern with the quality of their members' products, and the accountability of individual makers, signed work was never insisted on by the furniture guilds.

It would seem that English furniture makers might have been thought presumptuous to put their names to items destined for private ownership.

Figure 2:4. *Mary Allyns Chistt Cutte and joyned by Nich. Disbrowe. Handwritten inscription found on the back of a drawer in a chest of 'Hadley' type, now in the Bayou Bend Collection, Museum of Fine Arts, Houston, Texas.*

A tantalising instance of signed work occurs in the case of an American chest now in the Bayou Bend Collection at the Museum of Fine Arts, Houston. This is a chest of the 'Hadley' type, made in the Hartford area of the Connecticut river valley, at the end of the seventeenth century. It caused a stir of interest in 1923 when it was discovered and published,[9] for on the back of the lower drawer is the following inscription: "Mary Allyns Chistt Cutte and joyned by Nich. Disbrowe" (Figure 2:4).

Nicholas Disbrowe was a migrant English joiner, born the son of a joiner and trained in Saffron Walden, Essex. He emigrated to Hartford in 1639, and worked there until his death in 1683. Mary Allyn was the daughter of Colonel John Allyn, Secretary of the Connecticut Colony, and a resident of Hartford. Mary was born there, and married in 1686; so the assumption was that the chest was made as a dower chest for her by Disbrowe, shortly before his death, when she was twenty-five or twenty-six years of age. The facts seem to fit very neatly, but the inscription is now generally regarded as a fake, largely on the unsubstantiated grounds that the chest was later reported as having been seen for sale in New York earlier in 1923, *without* the inscription. The fact that the signature is such an extravagant exception to the general rule must serve to strengthen doubts over its authenticity.

The New Englander's obsession with his ancestry, which at times amounted to a form of ancestor-worship, led to an inveterate concern over the history of family heirlooms. Wild claims were accepted as fact, until a whole mythology built up around the Pilgrim Fathers and their associated possessions. A modern cartoon lampooned the arrival of the *Mayflower* laden with furniture, with chests and chairs swinging from the yard-arms. Notwithstanding various false leads, such as the mass of work hysterically attributed in pre-war years to Thomas Dennis of Ipswich, Mass., American scholars have recently been able to achieve some highly successful results in the area of accurate attributions to makers. Family groups of joiners, such as the Symonds family of Salem, are now seen to be more influential than

9. By Luke Vincent Lockwood, *Bulletin of the Metropolitan Museum of Art*, Vol. 18, No. 5, May 1923. Also discussed by Patricia E. Kane, *Arts of the Anglo-American Community in the Seventeenth Century*, ed. I.M.G. Quimby, Winterthur Conference Report, 1974.

Figure 2:5. *Enclosed chest. English; Shrewsbury. Oak, 1637. Made for the Shrewsbury Drapers' Company by Francis Bowyer, joiner, for a total cost of £4. 7. 8. . This is a most interesting piece, which raises points of importance at several levels. Although made by an English joiner, it is not of framed panel construction. Stylistically, it belongs to the 'Laudian' group of post-1628 (see Figure 4:41), echoing support for the High Anglican movement, which was later dashed by the Puritan Administration in the 1640s. The form of the piece is also unusual, housing removable drawered boxes, and having a shallow box top.*

Figure 2:6. *The Drapers' deed chest opened. Access to the interior is by a series of concealed locks. The plank construction of the door is very clear, and should be compared with the doors in Figure 4:42. The iron hinges are inset into the wood to strengthen the frameless panel of the door. The form of the high foot is unusual, but quite original, and reflects (like the rest of this remarkable cabinet) the stylistic vocabulary of topical Flemish pattern-books and woodwork.*

individual makers, and indeed their position and influence in the life of local trades was probably more akin to that of the trade company in England.

A great deal of further research is needed to establish confirmed attributions on early and provincial English furniture. For some reason, English historians have shown little interest in the authorship of our furniture. This is partly due to apathy, but the situation has no doubt been aggravated by a severe lack of research funds, and the fact that the survival of relevant documentation for existing pieces is rare. The antique trade has been transporting and exporting furniture for over a century, with little thought to spare for conserving provenances intact. If the right facts could be established, no doubt English candidates such as Humphrey Beckham of Salisbury would emerge as craftsmen of some stature; and more shape would be given to our present meagre knowledge of workshop groups and regional styles.

In view of the rarity of documented survivals, it is pleasing to be able to publish here the small collection of furniture and relevant accounts which have remained at the Drapers' Hall in Shrewsbury since the middle of the seventeenth century. The Drapers' Company still has nine pieces of furniture and a framed portrait which were mentioned on the extant inventory of 1664. Some of these are also on the earlier inventories of 1653/4, but more importantly, the purchase of six of them are recorded in the Account Book, with specific payments to named joiners, Francis Bowyer and Richard Ellis (Burgess of Shrewsbury 1661). The 1664

Figure 2:7. *Joined long dining table and benches. English; Shrewsbury. Oak, 1632 or 1635. Made for the Shrewsbury Drapers' Company by Francis Bowyer, joiner, for a cost of £2. 15s. 0. or £3. 0. 0. The stool originally supplied for the narrow end of the table is missing. The original benches are orientated with plain ends which come together, and buttressed ends to the outside. The turned legs of the benches are scaled-down versions of those on the table, and the carved nulling of the frieze is common to all three, and no doubt the stool was matched accordingly. The blind side of the table has a simple channel moulding, as is usual on dining tables of this type, where only one side is shown to the room (see comments in Chapter Three: Tables). The remaining two sides of the table are served by a bench which is fixed to the wall-panelling.*

Diagram 2:2. *Sketch-plan (not to scale) of the probable seating arrangements at Drapers' Hall in 1662. This is an idealised scheme, since the second of the large tables seems to have been removed to the garret at the same time as the purchase of the armchair and the withdrawing table. Prior to 1662, the dais table was supplied with a bench instead of an armchair. Surviving movable furniture, and the fixed wall bench, are shown in solid line, and further documented pieces in broken line. The surviving long table with its matching benches, the wall bench and panelling may be seen* in situ *in Figure 2:7 (above).*

10. Quoted in full by Michael Peele, *Transactions of the Shropshire Archaeological Society,* Vol. 52, Part 2 (1948).

inventory is rather long and complete, but it is worth extracting the references to the existing furniture and the picture:

> An Invintory of the goods belong to the Company in the drapers hall & in the Almshowses taken the 4th day of Aprill 1664.
> * In the hall Inpr. one Cubboard of drawing boxes with three locks & 3 keyes and a box on the topp with lock & key.
> * it. one long drawing table & frame 17 foote.
> * it. one long table & frame 17 foote.
> * it. 4 Joyned formes answerable to the table. (3 surviving)
>   it. one short table & frame 9 foote.
>   it. one Joyned forme to it.
> * it. one large picture and frame of K. Ed. 4...
> * it. one new wainscot chayre.[10]

As may be expected after a lapse of over three hundred years, there is a slight discrepancy (in the identification of the benches), but the major items are clear enough and accord exactly with their descriptions. Those marked with an asterisk may be described further:

a). The "Cubboard of drawing boxes" is the deed chest of the Drapers' Company (Figure 2:5), and is noted in the 1664 inventory as containing "...evidences leases and writings in the boxes..." Its purchase is recorded in the Account Book for 1637:

> pd. Francis Boyer for the Chest presse wch is in the hall
> 03. 01. 00.
> pd. Thomas Gratie for lockes and hinges   01. 06. 8.

It has already been noted that Bowyer and the blacksmith were paid separately for their work. The form of the chest is interesting, comprising as it does a shallow chest top, above a pair of doors which enclose three removable nests of boxes (Figure 2:6). It is most instructive to compare the 1664 description. The locks are concealed behind a removable central column, the keys having been held by the Master and Wardens.

b). The long table and its benches (Figure 2:7) were also supplied by Francis

Bowyer, but there are two records of such a purchase:

1632... pd. for A new table, w'th three new formes to fcs: bayer
02. 15. 00.

1635... pd. for A new Table w'th A frame & 3 Joyned formes to francis Bowyer Joyner
03. 00. 0.

Presumably, a similar table was supplied for the opposite side of the hall, as was common practice, though there is now no trace of this. The 1653/4 lists both mention *two* seventeen foot long tables, one of which was replaced by the withdrawing table in 1662 and consigned to the Garret Chamber (now lost). Two benches now survive to match the table (see illustration), and the third was probably a simple stool to fit at the head of the table. The table still occupies its original position, and is supplied with fitted benches integral to the wall panelling. A simple plan of the hall describes the layout (Diagram 2:2).

The following items are a little later in date, both having been acquired new by the Company in 1662:

c). The withdrawing table (Figure 2:8) is used as the dais table, and was paid for along with certain other disbursements: "1662...Pd Mr. Richard Ellice for the drawing table & other worke 003. 10. 00." It is noted in the inventory two years later at its extended length of seventeen feet, but when closed the length is nine feet. It has a standard six-legged frame. The decoration of the table is very similar to the armchair, especially in the profile of the mouldings, the small applied pear-shaped turnings, and the unusual flat-turned panel in the frieze. The texture and colour of the timber, and the light patination, are likewise identical.

Figure 2:8. *Joined withdrawing table (detail). English; Shrewsbury. Oak, 1662. Made for the Shrewsbury Drapers' Company by Richard Ellis, joiner. This is a six-legged table, with a closed length of nine feet and an extended length of seventeen feet. It serves as the dais table, for which purpose it was no doubt intended.*

Figure 2:8a. *Detail of withdrawing table. A flat-turned panel is set into the frieze at this halfway point, matching the profile of the surrounding mouldings. The edges of the top and the drawing-leaf are clearly seen above (cf. Figure 2:10 overleaf).*

Figure 2:9. *Joined picture frame. English; Shrewsbury. Oak, 1660. Made by the joiner Richard Ellis for the portrait of Edward IV which had been supplied to the Drapers' Company by Thomas Francis in the same year. In 1659 the Assembly of the Company agreed that a "picture of king Edward the 4th shalbe p'cured to be drawne at large to the life in a fayre Table or frame, & under it to be written what he hath donne for this Companye...and that the waynscott that is new in the Drap's hall among the old shalbe putt into the Cullour of the old wainscot". The following year the Company received a bill from the painter-stainer Thomas Francis for "Making the King's picture in the hall collo'ring the wainscott & put Scutcheons on 25 buckettes..."*

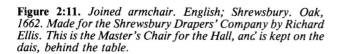

Figure 2:10. *Detail of armchair. The upper back and cresting-rail of the Master's Chair, showing the flat-turned panel which is identical to that on the frieze of the withdrawing table (cf. Figure 2:8a, previous page).*

Figure 2:11. *Joined armchair. English; Shrewsbury. Oak, 1662. Made for the Shrewsbury Drapers' Company by Richard Ellis. This is the Master's Chair for the Hall, and is kept on the dais, behind the table.*

d). An Assembly of the Company agreed in 1659 that "...the picture of king Edward the 4th (whom they regarded as the 'Royall founder of their Companie') shalbe p'cured to be drawne at large to the life in a fayre Table or frame, & under it to be written what he hath donne for this Companye..." This was carried out to the letter, and the Account Book for the following year (1660) notes that Thomas Francis was paid for painting the picture, and "Mr. Ellice" was paid, amongst other things, for "...a frame for the picture in the hall..." The portrait has several times been "...beutified at ye Company's charge...", notably in 1695 and 1721, but the frame remains as Richard Ellis made it in 1660 (Figure 2:9). The applied decoration is of a simple character, but the small pear-shaped turnings are found likewise on the preceding withdrawing table and the armchair; whilst the small bosses are to be found on the spandrels of the table.

e). These decorative similarities are helpful in determining Richard Ellis as the maker of the armchair (Figure 2:11), since he is not named in the Account book: "1662...pd for 9 bedsteeds for the Almshowses with boarded bottoms fixt and a chayre for drap's hall 003. 14. 00." This is the present Master's Chair, and is the "new wainscot chayre" of 1664. Despite the similarities, it was not made to match the withdrawing table, since the turnings are a different profile. The chair is significant in retaining its full original height to the seat of twenty-three inches. It has a richly moulded back panel, carved crest, and remains of black paint on many of the flat 'fields' of the back. Black and red painted detail is found similarly on the furniture of Cheshire (q.v.) slightly further North. This is the only aspect of decoration in the Drapers' furniture which might suggest some regional factor. The great table and benches are in an undifferentiated vernacular style; whilst the construction and decoration of the deed chest are in conventional Laudian taste, suggesting that Francis Bowyer may have been trained in London or Oxford.

Ownership Marks and Inscriptions (Figures 2:12-26)

Discussion has flickered for many years over the exact interpretation and significance of the sets of small branded initials found so frequently on items of early furniture. It has often been assumed that they are maker's marks, representing the initials of the craftsman who made the piece. It is not impossible that makers did occasionally thus sign their work, but in the very few cases where it is possible to attribute the branded marks to a known source, they prove in each instance to be the initials of *owners*, not of *makers*. It seems most likely that the marks were applied by branding irons in the course of taking an inventory of property; both for the purpose of recording ownership, and to aid identification in the event of a robbery. This would account for the frequent cases where more than one set of initials is found on a piece, the later and subsequent sets normally being in a more modern typeface (Figure 2:16). Occasionally such inventory marks are

Figure 2:12. *Joined armchair (later converted to a carrying-chair). Welsh. Oak, c.1680.*

found in the triangular form of marriage-initials, as A^CB. This must reinforce the *ownership* proposition. Many brands are of quite late date, and indeed the practice is still occasionally used, as in the case of some government departments. In an age when people were prepared to brand human beings as slaves or felons, the thought of branding one's furniture raised no objections.

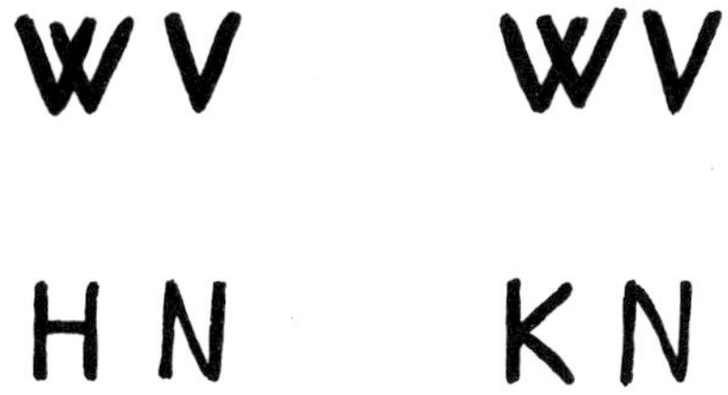

Of the few examples where inventory marks can be related to a known history of ownership, the unprepossessing armchair in Figure 2:12 is a prime and instructive example. This chair is now at the Welsh Folk Museum, and came from the family collection at Nannau, Llanfachreth, Merioneth. The rear uprights of the chair bear the following branded initials seen in Diagram 2:3:

WV   WV
HN   KN

Diagram 2:3

Family history provides the clues to their meaning: Colonel Huw Nannau (HN) was the younger brother of Gruffydd Nannau (see Figure 2:23), and succeeded on the death of his brother in 1689. The following year he married Katrin (KN), daughter of William Vaughan of Corsygedol. Huw Nannau died in 1701, which provides a close dating for the chair of 1680-1700, which is agreeable to its style. He was the last Nannau male to hold the estate. His daughter Catherine married another William Vaughan of Corsygedol (? her cousin), who was MP for Merioneth from 1734-1768. This marriage took the estate to the Vaughans, and the chair with it. It is not clear to *which* William Vaughan the WV refers: whether the father of Katrin, who may have given it to Huw in dowry; or to the husband of Catherine. Later in the eighteenth century, the estate (and the chair) was in the hands of their descendant Sir Robert Williames-Vaughan, 2nd baronet of Nannau, MP for Merioneth for many years, who died on 22nd April, 1843.

He was returned to Westminster thirteen times between 1792 and 1835, a

Figure 2:13. *Joined box-stool. English. Oak, c.1650 (see also Figure 3:110). The name R. Draiton is branded several times over the back of this stool. The hinges are not original, and the feet have been cut down to the level of the stretchers.*

VƧTOИE

Diagram 2:4

Figure 2:14. *Detail of enclosed chest of drawers in Figure 4:48. The name G:TAYLOR is branded on a side-rail of this piece.*

and the years are recorded beneath his initials (RWV) on the back-panel of the chair. In 1792, by now old-fashioned and consigned to a lumber room, the chair was brought out and converted into a sedan-chair by the estate blacksmith. Sir Robert was carried through the streets in celebration in this chair after each successful re-election.

It is rare to find a full name branded on a piece of furniture, but one instance was noted by Fred Roe.[11] He found a table at the Savoy, Denham, Bucks., which bore the branded inscription: 'Instone' (see Diagram 2:4). The Instones were a yeoman family residing in the neighbourhood during the seventeenth century. Their descendants disposed of the table c.1863.

I am able to illustrate here two further full-name inventory marks: one is a box-stool with the name R. Draiton applied several times; and the other is an unusual chest bearing the name G:TAYLOR (Figures 2:13 and 14).

There are several examples of royal furniture bearing brand marks, all of which support the *ownership* theory. Though all early furniture has long since left royal ownership, several examples remain in the hands of old families who received them as perquisities. At Knole, for instance, are some chairs marked with a crowned WP for Whitehall Palace; whilst others have the mark HC1661 (see Figure 2:130). The latter were taken from Hampton Court by the 6th Earl of Dorset soon after 1688 who, as Lord Chamberlain to William III, had rights over certain state furniture owned by the previous monarch. The chairs, which date from the reign of James I, no doubt received their marks during the taking of the inventory of the Royal Palaces after their repossession by Charles II. A pair of leather backstools in the collection of the late Thomas Bagshawe, curator of Luton Museum, have a crowned AR. It is assumed that they were in the possession of the Royal Household under Queen Anne (Anna Regina).

Institutional furniture frequently carries inventory marks, and a good provincial example is the set of ten leather backstools surviving in the vestry of the church of Sarum St. Thomas, Salisbury. They each bear the brand STP, for Saint Thomas' Parish (Figure 2:15). They are recorded in the ownership of the church at an early date, though two are now lost, and the full set of twelve appear on the plan of the church for 1745 (Diagram 2:5). The Account Book of the Shrewsbury Drapers' Company also records the use of ownership marks on five items purchased for the Hall in 1585:

> Itm. payed for foure trestles for the use of the Corporacon wiche are m'ked with our marke upon them all   iijs viijd.
> Itm. payed to hughe Evans for a table boord for the hale for thuse of the Corporacon wch hathe our m'ke upon the syde of it   Vs.

11. Fred Roe, op. cit.

59

Unfortunately, the trestles and table board have not survived to show us which form the mark took.

But if the branded inventory mark is a *restrained* method of denoting property, plenty of less subtle devices are found to proclaim the pride of original owners. One of the most vivid is the delightful panel of Sarah Ward's dower chest, now at the Welsh Folk Museum (Figure 2:19). The inscription boldly and proudly proclaims 'Sarah Ward Her Chest 1722'. The whole execution is coarse and lively, with two little birds eating from fruit trees or vines. Another well-known chest with an inscription of the same ilk, is in the Victoria and Albert Museum and bears the legend "THIS·IS·ESTHER· HOBSONNE· CHIST·1637" (Figure 2:20). These are two uncommonly concise statements. More usual is simply a name and date, or initials and the date. Figure 2:21 shows a small group of North Country items with full names. On a large piece such as a bed or cupboard, a marriage may be commemorated with the names of both husband and wife, and the year of the marriage. This may be rendered as pairs of intials as: AC BC; or more commonly in the triangular form as: A^{C}B or A$_C$B. In this arrangement the left-hand intial is for the husband, the right-hand for the wife, and the centre is the man's family surname: perhaps Amos and Beatrice Carter. In the panel Figure 2:22, a further set 'IT' has been

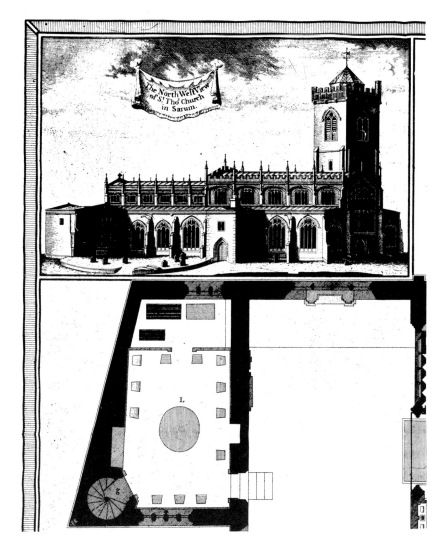

Diagram 2:5. *Detail of 'A Plan of St. Thomas Church: in the City of New Sarum, exactly taken by John Lyons. 1745'. Published 4th September, 1745. The plan is of the vestry house at the extreme north-east corner of the church, which may be seen in the left hand side of the accompanying view of the church. In the vestry itself are shown the large gateleg table and set of twelve chairs, from which only two chairs are now missing. The chairs are each branded STP for St. Thomas' Parish (Figure 2:15), and two are shown in Figure 4:245.*

Figure 2:15. *Detail of chair in Figure 4:245. The initials STP here stand for Saint Thomas' Parish (Salisbury). The original iron nails which tack down the leather cover at the back of the chair may also be seen, and are in sharp contrast to the neat brass nails on the front.*

Figure 2:17. *Detail of chair in Figure 4:160. The initials WF are branded on the rear of the semicircular cresting-rail.*

Figure 2:16. *Detail of stool. English. Oak, c.1680. Two sets of initials appear on this piece. The earlier set (TH) is in marked contrast to the design of the later set (CW).*

12. I am grateful to Arwyn Lloyd-Hughes, Archivist at the Welsh Folk Museum, for his help in ascertaining some details of the life of Gruffydd Nannau.

included to complicate the issue. Perhaps these are of the bridegroom's father, who may have donated the cupboard as a wedding present.

Once again, the *identification* of ownership initials is all too often lost. The knowledge of the original owner of such a personal thing as a chair or marriage bed lends much interest and life to inanimate objects, and renders the piece infinitely more valuable and important as a social document. We may turn again to the Nannau furniture at the Welsh Folk Museum to find a child's high chair inscribed 'GN 1669' (Figure 2:23). This was the chair of Gruffydd Nannau. This particular Gruffydd, the fourth of that name, was born shortly before 1669. He died, unmarried and without issue, in 1689. In that year he had been made High Sheriff of Merioneth, not an unusually early age for one of his class and time. Little is known of him, other than that a poem was composed in his praise by Siôn Dafydd Las in 1687, the last poet to receive the traditional patronage of the Nannau family. Two elegies were also composed on his death in 1689, one by Las and the other by Owain Gruffydd.[12]

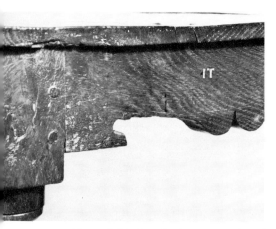

Figure 2:18. *Detail of court cup-board in Figure 3:250. The initials IT are branded into the side frieze.*

Figure 2:20. *Detail of chest. English. Oak, dated 1637. This inscription occupies the upper front rail, and reads 'THIS · IS · ESTHER · HOBSONNE · CHIST · 1637'.*

An important form of identification used on furniture and other woodwork was the coat of arms and other family or trade badges. These are not always strictly accurate in heraldic terms. Details may be altered or omitted to suit the demands of space or materials, and in unpainted examples the lack of colour (or *tincture*) may lead to confusion. Several examples are illustrated in these pages, but the most important single group would seem to be the Scottish armchairs, particularly those associated with Aberdeen.

Of the wide variety of textual inscriptions, from commemorative to cautionary, both conventional and otherwise, the most usual are pious proverbs or epigrams. They are not so common in furniture as in needlework or metalwork, but among those found on furniture may be listed the following:

> FERE GOD TO LOVE GOD
> THE LORD IS MINE INHERITANCE
> REMEMBER THE POOR WHEN THOV OPPENES THIS
> AND FORGET NOT
> A Harelome To This Hous For EVER 163-
> UNTO US A CHILDE IS BORNE * YE XXV DAYE OF
> JANUARIE 1640
> REPENT·THE·LORD·IS·AT·HANd * WATCH·ANd·PRAY
> * LIVE·WEL·ANd·dIE·WEL·1659

Inscriptions occur in other native languages, of course, notably in Welsh (as well as the more fashionable Latin). Welsh examples are:

> KYFFARWTH AIGWNA HARRY AP GR(uffydd)
> KOFIA DY DDECHRE 1594
> HEB·DDUW·HEB·DDIM·DIW·A·DICON 1609
> BVDD:DRVGAROG:YN: OL DY ALLV 1689

Figure 2:19. *Detail of chest in Figure 3:399. This bold central panel bears the proud inscription 'Sarah Ward Her Chest 1722'. The panel is original to the chest, and the crisp matting of the ground is seen as a sharp contrast to the coarser finish of Figure 2:22.*

Figure 2:24. *Detail of stool (top). English. Oak, dated 1699. Inscribed 'RL ML EL 1699'.*

Figure 2:25. *Detail of press cupboard. English. Oak, c.1640. An unusual pierced form of inscription, 'IW', in a cupboard with other pierced detail of an ornamental nature.*

THE CONSTRUCTIONAL TYPES

The need for furniture is one of the most basic requirements for even a moderately civilised existence, and the maintenance of an organised domestic life. At first, primitive man must have made do with the adaptation of ready-made objects, such as stones and logs, to provide the convenience looked for in seating, storage and sleeping facilities. However, the ready adaptation of found materials is severely limited, and it must have been very early in man's development as a social creature that he started to construct furniture using shaped parts and simple techniques, to some predetermined form. The remarkable stone furniture at the neolithic settlement of Skara Brae, in the Orkneys, is certainly the earliest survival of purpose-made furniture in the British Isles. This small group of houses was occupied c.1500 B.C., and the furniture consists of a limited variety of built-in bed nooks and dressers which are made from roughly-shaped slabs of the local flagstone. The beds consist of rectangular compartments hedged in by stone slabs, which were no doubt filled with grass and wool for bedding. But most remarkable are the shelved dressers, which have stone slabs supported by vertical bearers (see Diagram 2:6, below).

Diagram 2:6

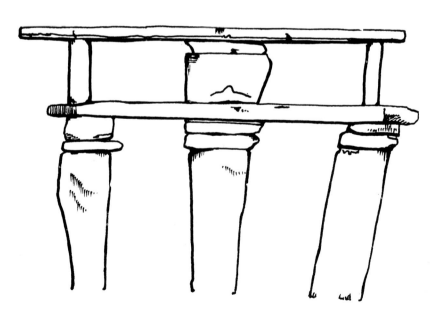

Figure 2:26. *Carved mortar. Welsh. Oak, painted grey-green, dated 1694.*

In areas where timber was freely available, simple constructional techniques were doubtless current from a very early date. The most primitive forms of wood construction have survived in common usage, alongside more developed and sophisticated techniques, up to and including the present day. I propose to discuss here three elementary forms of furniture making, which survived well into the modern age, and which represent almost the only form of true peasant furniture until the advent of Windsor chairs and cheap painted pine furniture during the course of the eighteenth century. Broadly, the original cost of new furniture is in direct proportion to the cost of time, skill and materials expended on its production; and so the social and financial standing of the original customer can be roughly gauged from such considerations as construction and decoration. Each trade retained its own rigidly-defined procedures, resulting in a catalogue of furniture types which accurately reflects the structural, material and stylistic preoccupations of the various groups:

Elementary
- i). Woven Basketwork.
- ii). Dug-out Furniture.
- iii). Primitive Construction

Subsequently, more efficient and sophisticated techniques are explored, consequent on the usual divisions of the furniture making trades:

- iv). The Turner.
- v). The Carpenter.
- vi). The Joiner.
- vii). The Coffermaker and the Upholder.
- viii). Trade Alliances in the Eighteenth Century (The Rise of the Cabinetmaker/Upholsterer).
- ix). Related Trades.

i). Woven Basketwork Construction (Figures 2:27-34)

The traditional systems of stiff woven construction are all known collectively as 'basketwork', since they are most commonly seen in the various domestic basketwares which are still so familiar today. There is an endless list of indigenous materials from which baskets, beehives, furniture, chair seats, carpeting and matting may be woven; these may be taken to comprise chiefly rushes, osier reeds, corn straw, grasses, sedges, willow withies (wicker), and vegetable ropes. In contemporary descriptions these are usually referred to indiscriminately as 'twiggen' or 'wanded', but sometimes a more specific allusion is found to materials:

1576...one twigged stool...
1588...one close little chair of rods...
1601...a twiggen chair...a wicker skreyne...
1608...In the Chamber over the hall...1 twiggen chair...
1642...2 withen chaires...
1671...3 wicker chairs 12s...
1673...1 twige chayer...
1676...one great straw chayer...
1694...a little wanded firescreen 1s...

Sedge leaves must be one of the cheapest of all materials, and the sparse inventory of William Nicholls, a poor cordwainer of Bedwardine, Worcs., includes "...one Segg chayre and one Segg stool..."[13]

Rush-seated, or 'matted', chairs were amongst the usual range of products made by the turner/chairmaker from the Middle Ages to the

13. Quoted in full by John West, op. cit.

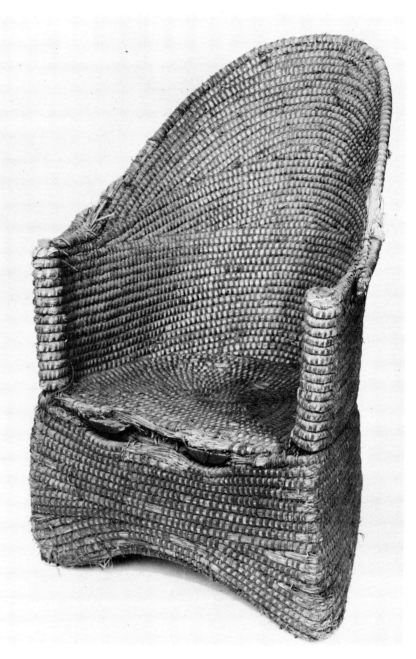

Figure 2:27. *(Above) Lipp-work armchair. Welsh. Ash frame, with cover of straw ropes bound with peeled holly-bark, early nineteenth century. This is the most typical and ancient shape for basketwork chairs, from Roman times and probably earlier. Wicker, straw and other woven furniture is often mentioned in English inventories from the Middle Ages onwards, and many of these items must have resembled this and the following specimens. No example is known to have survived from before the nineteenth century, owing to the impermanence of the material.*

Figure 2:28. *(Above left) Lipp-work canopied chair. Welsh; Monmouthshire. Ash frame, with straw cover, reinforced with leather, early nineteenth century. These hooded chairs were made in most areas, but seem to have survived later in Monmouthshire and the Severn area.*

Figure 2:29. *(Left) Lipp-work canopied chair. Welsh. Elm and ash frame and seat, with straw canopy and sides, early nineteenth century. This is essentially a wooden chair with lipp-work coverings, similar in principle to chairs still made in the Orkneys.*

Figure 2:30. *Lipp-work armchair. Welsh. Straw and peeled holly bark, early nineteenth century. This and the following chair are not supported by a wooden frame, but stand entirely by virtue of the stiffness of the weave.*

present day, but of greater interest here is the range of types either wholly or substantially made from wicker or straw, of which there are significant modern survivals. Almost the only items of furniture habitually made in this way were chairs and cradles, in addition to various storage baskets or hampers. Amongst surviving examples, none of which can be said to date earlier than the nineteenth century, two distinct techniques are noticed: lipp-work, which consists of straw ropes bound together with strips of bramble bark or holly bark; and wickerwork, in which the usual material is young prepared willow shoots (called withies). Woven furniture was made from very early times, and the chairs are familiar from Roman illustrations of daily life. The limitations inherent in the craft and materials impose restrictions on the forms and designs available. Thus, Roman examples are remarkably similar, in shape and decoration, to the nineteenth century country-made versions which are illustrated here. By extension, it may be assumed that basketwork chairs of the seventeenth century and earlier were also of very similar form. Indeed, contemporary Dutch paintings of interiors provide further evidence to bear out this assumption.

It is difficult to draw any conclusions on the regional distribution of basketwork furniture. Many late specimens survive in Wales and the Border Counties, and it would appear that they may have been common in many areas, especially the West Country and East Anglia. In fact they are mentioned in inventories from most areas, and a traditional variation is still to be found on the North Sea beaches of Holland and Germany.

Lipp-work

The chair in Figure 2:27 is perhaps the archetypal form of basketwork chair, and is certainly one which closely resembles Roman and Romano-British prototypes. It achieves its rigidity by means of a basic framework of

Figure 2:31. *Lipp-work armchair. Welsh. Straw and peeled holly bark, early nineteenth century.*

Figure 2:32. *Lipp-work cradle. Welsh. Straw, on oak rockers, early nineteenth century.*

Figure 2:33. *Wickerwork cradle. English; Lancashire. Willow, nineteenth century.*

Figure 2:34. *Wickerwork child's armchair. English; Wiltshire. Willow, modern.*

14. J.C. Loudon, *An Encyclopaedia of Cottage, Farm and Villa Architecture and Furniture,* London, 1833.

ash poles, around which the straw shell is woven. Of the five chairs shown here, the last two do not have some form of supportive wooden frame. The canopied chairs are apparently a regional type from South-East Wales (there is a further, better, example at the Brecon Museum), which fact was underlined by J.C. Loudon in 1833,[14] when he noted that "...In Monmouthshire easy chairs with hoods, like porter's chairs in gentlemen's halls, are constructed of straw matting on a frame of wooden rods, or stout wire, and chairs are made entirely of straw in different parts of England in the same way as the common beehives..."

The hooded chairs exemplified here certainly existed in seventeenth century England, for Randle Holme described them exactly (mid-seventeenth century):

> ...There is (a) kind of these chaires called Twiggen chaires because they are made of Owsiers, and Withen twigs: having round covers over the heads of them like unto a canapy. These are principally used by sick and infirm people, and such women as have bine lately brought to bed; from whence they are generally termed Growneing chaires, or Child-bed chairs...

The reference to 'Growneing' is surely more satisfactorily explained by the noise put up by such chairs as one sits in them.

Lipp-work beehives were very common, and the technique was also used for other apparatus such as seed-lipps, corn-measures, trays, baskets and agricultural hats. Apart from chairs, cradles or 'bassinets' were a common form of basketware furniture, and these are found in illustrations of domestic scenes over a very wide period. Figure 2:32 is of the usual timeless form, with a raised hood and wooden rockers. There is no record of the production of basketwork furniture *as a separate trade* before the nineteenth century, and no doubt they formed part of the range of products of the jobbing basketmaker.

Wickerwork

The growing of willow shoots, or withies, for basketmaking is still a thriving business both in Somerset and Norfolk. The beds are arranged in rows, alongside the irrigation canals of the low well-watered marshlands. The cut rods are boiled and dried to a state where they can be bent and woven without cracking. The cradle and chair of Figures 2:33 and 34 are typical products which can still be bought today — their form dictated by tradition and the limitations of the technique. The pied colouring of the chair is a traditional conceit, the darker colour being provided by the unpeeled bark, and may be seen in early Dutch interiors.

The modern wicker hamper had its prototype in the medieval wicker travelling chest (*coffre d'osier*), which might be both leather-covered and iron-bound for protection.[15]

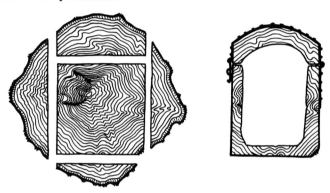

Diagram 2:7. One method of dissecting and hollowing a log for a dug-out chest, such as that at Orton Church, Westmorland, in Figure 2:35.

ii). Dug-out Furniture (Figures 2:35-42)

The light, mobile chests and chairs produced by the basketmakers exist in stark contrast to those hewn from the solid log. In a primitive or peasant culture, simple but laborious answers are frequently offered to solve technical problems. The tree-trunk chest is most certainly a case in point. The technique of hollowing out a tree, to produce a boat or a chest, is incredibly wasteful of man hours, timber and labour; yet it is a common solution where wood is plentiful and labour cheap. Primitive societies which have not developed techniques for constructing and covering a light framework (or who have not leap-frogged the process of development by adopting civilised methods at secondhand from Western man) still hollow out their canoes by a routine of alternately burning the timber and chopping with an axe or adze.

Figure 2:35. Dug-out chest. English; Orton, Westmorland. Oak, medieval.

15. For discussion, see Penelope Eames, *Furniture in England, France and the Netherlands from the Twelfth to the Fifteenth Century*, Furniture History Society, London, 1977.

Figure 2:36. *Dug-out chest. English; Wolverley, Worcestershire. Oak, probably early sixteenth century.*

Figure 2:37. *Dug-chest. Detail of Figure 2:36.*

Figure 2:38. *Dug-out chest. Detail of Figure 2:36.*

Despite its clumsy and very elementary nature, this technique was still used in medieval Britain, and there is evidence to suggest that it may even have persisted until the seventeenth century in isolated cases. Surviving examples are normally associated with churches, and this provides a clue to their particular usefulness. Obviously, the resultant chest is extremely heavy and difficult to carry, so that the chest and its contents would be difficult to steal. Early references mention chests being used in churches to collect alms for charity and donations for the Crusades. They are nearly always bound with iron straps, partly for security, but also to contain the splitting of the wood which is an inevitable result of using timber in this way.

The manner of making a dug-out chest is extremely simple. The log is first dissected with four saw cuts, the top plank being retained to form the lid of the chest. Diagram 2:7 shows the cross-section of a dug-out chest. The natural rounded shape of the top was also often retained, and it is from this feature that the name 'trunk' came to be applied later to any rounded-lid chest, even the lightly-built travelling box made by the coffermaker.

The body of the log was hollowed out with axes, perhaps aided by fire, to achieve the final form. The lid is attached with strong iron hinges, which are usually extended in straps to wrap around the carcase of the chest, and fitted with locks or staples for padlocks. Figure 2:35 is a Westmorland example, of indeterminate medieval date, which answers this basic description exactly. In another chest from Bishop's Cleeve church, Gloucester, the lid is constructed as a plank, and is settled into a rebate to render it flush with the body of the chest (see Diagram 2:8). Sometimes the space hollowed in the log is quite small in relation to the bulk of the log. These were probably intended purely to contain valuables or offerings. A fine variant in the church at Calne, Wiltshire, has a separate iron-bound boarded box seated into a huge log, the box being nailed to the log from the inside. Under the lid is inscribed a notably late date, and an unidentified name: Q:E:R· XXI   1579   IOHN WELSTED (Diagram 2:9).

Diagram 2:9. *(Above and right) 'Q:E:R: XXI 1579 IOHN WELSTED'. This large strong chest at Calne Church, Wiltshire, consists of an iron bound elm box which is seated into a deep well excavated in the oak log. The inscription under the lid probably signifies the date of manufacture, but the identity of John Welsted remains a mystery. Welsted is a common name in the Parish Registers at Calne, and he may have been the donor of the chest in 1579. The inscription is rendered with a series of straight and curved section chisels. 'Q:E:R: XXI' means, of course, the twenty-first year of the reign of Queen Elizabeth Regina.*

The double chest in Figures 2:36-38 has another character entirely. Here the huge log has been cut to an amazing thinness. Two adjacent sections of the same tree were used to create two receptacles. The log was accurately squared and the inside excavated to leave walls of only three inches average thickness. Even the central divisions are cut from the solid, having remarkably thin walls. As at Bishop's Cleeve, the lids are set into rebates and do not overlap the edges. The double form is original and may have been utilised for ease of handling during construction, since the overall length is nearly eight feet. The join was finally concealed with an iron band, giving the appearance of one chest. The lids were always independent of each other, and the double-lidded device was not uncommon with large chests, where a heavy lid would make access unreasonably difficult. Separate lids also allowed independent access to each compartment.

The chest is furnished with a total of nine locks (one is double), and six heavy strap-hinges. Each lid has a lifting-handle, and the ends of the main body are also bound with iron straps. The centre front strap, which once concealed the cleft between the two sections, is now missing. The entire chest was finally set into the stonework of the church (at Wolverley, Worcs.), which fact accounts for the extreme extent of rot at the lower rear edge (evident in Figure 2:38).

Figure 2:39. *Dug-out armchair. English. Ash, with elm seat, c.1760-1800.*

Figure 2:40. (Left) *Dug-out chair. Side view of Figure 2:39.*

Figure 2:41. (Right) *Dug-out chair. Rear view of Figure 2:39.*

The end view shows very clearly the annual rings of the log, and the radial direction of the shrinkage cracks. The prominent growth-rings should, in theory, allow a positive assessment of dating by means of dendro-chronology, especially since the front lower edge still retains a fragment of bark and a clear band of sapwood. This indicates exactly the year in which the tree was felled, and so the stage at which growth ceased.

In the absence of a positive dendrochronological conclusion, and the loss of any documentary provenance, it is extremely difficult to put an accurate assessment on the date of the chest. All the ironwork is extremely plain, and provides no stylistic or technical clues. In common with most dug-out chests, there is no decoration; and as we have seen, the type is found throughout the Middle Ages until possibly *after* 1700. Only the standard of finish may give us some meagre leads: the thinness of the walls has been noted, and the whole piece is accurately and cleanly cut; it does not show the summary (even clumsy) workmanship of most known medieval examples; the moulded edges on the front and top suggest a later, rather than an earlier, range of dating. These four factors lead me to suggest a date somewhere in the first half of the sixteenth century (say 1480-1540).

Tree-trunks were also used to make chairs; but, at least in the type shown here, the process of conversion was rather less laborious than in the hollowing of a chest. It was a simpler matter to find a hollow tree, the inside of which had rotted away, leaving a fairly thick shell. This was cut to a suitable profile, the spare material trimmed from the inside surface, and a separate plank inserted to form a seat.

Figure 2:43. *Woodcut illustrations from Randle Holme,· 'Academie of Armory,' 1649.*
"74: ...a countrey stoole, or a planke, or Blocke stoole, being onely a thick peece of wood, with either 3 or 4 peece of wood fastned in it for feet..."
"75: ...a round three footed stoole, or a countrey stoole made round with three feete..."
This simple construction was used throughout the Middle Ages and up to the present day.

The simplicity of this procedure no doubt accounts for the survival of the technique into the nineteenth century, accompanied by an element of somewhat self-conscious rusticity. There can be no doubt, however, that such chairs were part of an honest and genuine tradition, and do not necessarily fall into the realm of rural novelties. One example, recently on the market, has a perfectly genuine date of 1617 cut into the centre of its back. Dated specimens are extremely rare, but most chairs of this type are of eighteenth or nineteenth century date, like the two illustrated here (Figures 2:39 and 42).

Figure 2:39 is the larger of the two, and possibly the earlier. The shaping of the sides is precisely as found on contemporary plank-ended settles, cut to a profile that resembles the winged easy chairs of more affluent type. The arm-rests are conveniently provided with carrying-holes, whilst the seat is shaped and dished like that of a Windsor chair, for greater comfort. A sense of finish is achieved by the use of chamfering and the shaped cross stretcher. All these factors suggest a date of c.1760-1800. The second chair (Figure 2:42) is more dramatically evolved from the curve of an oak trunk, with elaborate use made of shaping and faceting on the upper back.

Figure 2:44. *Primitive three-legged stool. Welsh; Bridgend, Glamorgan. Elm, c.1800.*

Figure 2:45. *Primitive four-legged stool. English; Marnhull, Dorset. Elm, early nineteenth century.*

iii). **Primitive Construction** (Figures 2:43-56)

The most simple forms of wooden furniture which can be said to be constructed, are of the types which involve a simple wedged joint. They are not the product of any formal trade procedures, and in fact most examples can truly be said to be home-made. This is true European peasant furniture at its most typical, and the form survived until modern times, even when the decoration became fairly suave (e.g. in the carved and painted pine chairs of South Germany and the Alpine regions). This is such a familiar form of construction that a vocabulary of terms has hardly been found to describe it, but some early inventories seem to refer to it as 'staked', or 'with stake feet'. Added to this is the fact that it has been largely ignored by serious furniture historians, though its place in the development of furniture design is so important that it is hard to account for this neglect. It is variously known as the Windsor type, or peg-leg construction; but the epithet primitive is as descriptive as any.

The main factor in primitive construction is the way in which legs and other members are dependent on a central structural stabiliser, usually the seat board. Holes are bored through the seat board, and the other members are rammed home, normally to be secured by a wedge in much the same manner as an axe-handle is fixed to the head (see Diagram 2:10).

This must be by far the most common form of constructed furniture, since it has been found at all times, and over a wide geographical area. It has received little mention in literature or written documents, being unremarkable and most valueless; yet tables, stools and chairs are frequently to be seen in the background of medieval and later engravings and manuscript illustrations. Such furniture must have been a familiar adjunct to daily life. Almost the only *specific* reference which it is possible to find are two small engravings from Randle Holme's *Academy of Armory,* reproduced here (Figure 2:43). He describes them both as country stools, the one square with four feet, the other round with three feet. These correspond almost exactly with my Figures 2:44 and 45. They may be seen as the traditional milking-stool, carried afield by milkmaids since time immemorial, and a familiar accessory on the cottage hearth stone. The term 'cricket' is discussed with reference to these stools in Chapter Three. Another item constructed in this way, and found in most country homes until the early years of this century, was the low 'pig-bench', on which the family pig was killed and prepared in readiness for the winter. Farm, dairy and other workaday furniture was frequently of this type.

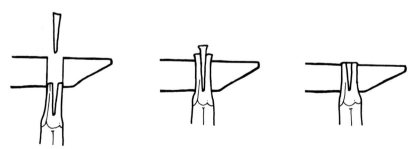

Diagram 2:10. *Primitive, or 'staked leg' construction. This is the simplest way of fitting a leg or some other member to a seat board, and was perpetuated in the eighteenth and nineteenth centuries through the popularity of the Windsor chair. The top of the leg is rammed through a hole in the seat board, and then wedged securely. The top is finally cut off flush with the seat.*

Figure 2:46. *(Left) Primitive backstool. Welsh borders. Elm, with ash legs, early nineteenth century. The first and most simple development from the primary stool, here with a single narrow vertical board acting as a backrest. An extremely rare type, but commonly plagiarised in reproductions, and referred to as a 'spinning-chair'..*

Figure 2:47. *(Right) A simple wooden backstool with late Gothic tracery decoration to the back and primitive 'staked' legs, a typological predecessor of the later Welsh chair in Figure 2:46. From an early sixteenth century German engraving,* The Last Supper *by Wendel von Olmutz (Graphische Sammlung, Albertina, Vienna).*

The provision of three legs, instead of four, may rightly be regarded as a manoeuvre to overcome the problems of uneven earth or stone floors, and is also a feature of many (more sophisticated) turned chairs and even some joined furniture. Three feet will stand with greater stability on an irregular surface, but it nevertheless takes a certain amount of skill to sit comfortably in such a chair, since it is easily overbalanced.

The simple stool was developed by the addition of a back. Figure 2:46 is a Welsh backstool of the type in which the back comprises a simple shaped board, socketed into the seat. This is related in form to the Italian *sgabello,* or more closely to the early sixteenth century German version in Figure 2:47, but this solid-back chair was never popular in the British Isles and examples are rare. Much more typical here is a back constructed of a series of struts supporting a cresting-rail (Figures 2:48 and 49), and known as a comb-back chair. Figure 2:50 has an Irish chair in which the principle is extended to provide arms. Note that the construction of the arms is not joined across the back, as in the more familiar Welsh armchair of Figure 2:51. Here the arms consist of a heavy yoke supported on struts, which provide a more comfortable structure for the sitter. The next progression is to extend a frame upwards from the yoke for further support, as seen in the fully-developed bow-back armchair of Figure 2:52. This chair also has stretchers which brace and strengthen the legs.

Here we reach a significant point, for this chair represents the true ancestral prototype of the Windsor chair of the eighteenth century. The type should have appeared in early times in the British Isles, since it is such an elementary idea, but there is no real evidence of its appearance before c.1720. It is clear that the generic term 'Windsor' should not be applied to the primitive forms illustrated here, since although Windsor-type construction is dependent on the unifying seat-board, it is characterised by more sophisticated forms of turned and cut decoration. The family of Windsor furniture is discussed more fully in pp.533-535.

True primitive furniture is almost completely devoid of real decoration, except of the most elementary kind. The workmanship is coarse and usually lacking in finish. Seats are sawn to shape and finished, like the legs and struts, by chopping or shaving with a draw knife or axe. Most pieces appear to have been finished with a coat of paint, usually red, green, blue or yellow, in various shades. Elm is the usual timber for seat-boards, since it does not split easily under pressure. It is easily sawn into boards, and is available in broad widths in country districts. Ash is normally used for legs and struts, since it cleaves easily into poles, can be bent to shape by steaming, and is tough and resilient in use. Other woods commonly found for various parts are oak, beech, sycamore, yewtree and fruitwood. It is impossible to provide accurate dates for specific examples of this type of furniture. All that can be said is that a piece *appears* to be old, or not. They were made as late as fifty years ago, especially in Wales and Ireland, but most examples of some age are of the eighteenth or early nineteenth century. All the pieces shown here were chosen for a sense of timelessness, as representatives of almost any period.

The chair in Figure 2:56 is a primitive form of slightly different concept. Here the stabilising element is not a seat-board, but the halves of a blackthorn branch which is split longitudinally to form the sides of the seat

Figure 2:48. *(Left) Primitive three-legged comb-back backstool. Welsh. Ash, early nineteenth century.*

Figure 2:49. *(Right) Primitive four-legged comb-back backstool. Welsh. Ash, with elm seat, early nineteenth century.*

Figure 2:50. *Primitive comb-back armchair and cricket table. Chair: Irish. Ash and elm. Table: Welsh. Ash. Both with original red paint, early nineteenth century. The fad in recent years for removing the (often) original painted finish from such pieces has resulted in an enormous loss of information on the painted furniture used in cottage interiors before the twentieth century..*

Figure 2:51. *Primitive three-legged yoke-back armchair. Welsh. Oak and ash, late eighteenth century.*

Figure 2:52. *Primitive bow-back armchair. English; West Country. Ash, with sycamore seat, and original green paint, early nineteenth century.*

Figure 2:53. *Primitive low-back settle. Welsh. Ash, early nineteenth century. An extremely rare type for the British Isles.*

Figure 2:54. *(Above) Primitive shove-halfpenny table. English; Marnhull, Dorset. Elm, early nineteenth century. Originating in a public house in this Dorsetshire village, from the same room as the stool in Figure 2:45.*

Figure 2:55. *(Right) Hybrid armchair. Welsh. Oak, with ash seat, late eighteenth century. Inscribed 'G^{E}LL'. The construction is of somewhat mixed type, since although the legs are wedged through the seat in true primitive style, the upper part is of quite sophisticated form and is secured with true mortices and tenons.*

and back. It is apparently a form which answers the problem inherent when wide planks are not available to provide a seat-board, as in Northern Scotland.[16] The seat was no doubt provided with a loose cushioning of heather, furze or fleeces; or the cross-slats may even have been woven with a fixed padding of rushes or similar material.

Figure 2:56. *Primitive armchair. Scottish; Sutherland. Hawthorn or blackthorn, early nineteenth century.*

Figure 2:57. *Turned pricket candlestick. Anglo-French. Sycamore or beech, painted copper-green, early sixteenth century.*

16. I.F. Grant, *Highland Folk Ways*, Fig. 21a, p.171. A similar chair is illustrated as a 'Sutherland type'.

iv). The Turner (Figures 2:57-106)

The Craft

The role of the turner is normally considered only in terms of his secondary function as a decorator of joined furniture. The demarcations between the turner and the joiner helped to create the essential character of so much joined furniture, in which the aesthetic statement of the turner is quite distinct from the structural contribution of the joiner. Yet, a major aspect of the turner's work was the production of an independent range of items which included furniture, spinning wheels, mortars, cups, bowls and dishes, rushlight bases, tool handles, lace bobbins, carriage wheels, boxes, sieves, toys, pulleys, ships' tackle, buttons, seals, scales, pumps and a thousand and one items from the check list of domestic and commercial trivia (Figures 2:57-68), made from a variety of materials including wood, metal and ivory.

> 1777... the Turner, sitting over the Treddle, turneth with a
> Throw, upon a Turner's Bench, Bowls, Tops,
> Puppets, and such like Turners work...

The bulk of their domestic trade was in the manufacture of the innumerable wooden table implements now classed as 'treen', in demand before the days of universal china. In middle class homes, pewter had ousted wooden utensils by the end of the sixteenth century; but in the homes

Figure 2:58. *Turned socket candlestick. English. Oak, c.1700.*

Figure 2:59. *Turned candlestick and rushlight holders. English. Left to right: chestnut, fruitwood, fruitwood, elm, early eighteenth century. Rushlight bases were made in a wide variety of shapes by the turners.*

of the labouring poor, wooden trenchers, bowls, cups and spoons were still to be found two hundred and fifty years later. Specific local needs were sometimes served by a concentration of tradesmen, such as those based in Wymondham, who produced spindles for the nearby textile trade of Norwich, as well as supplying the domestic needs of the region: "Wyndham was once celebrated for the manufacture of wooden spindles, spoons and other turnery ware..."[17]

Figure 2:60. *Turned rushlight holders. English. All fruitwood, early eighteenth century. The wrought iron stems are found in a wide variety of shapes and adaptations. .*

17. White, *Survey of Norfolk,* 1845, p.443.

Figure 2:61. *Turned posset-service. English. Sycamore, 1580-1620. This great standing cup is, in reality, a complete treen service of interlocking parts, consisting of a goblet, various boxes for spices and lemons, and a box of ten trenchers. The whole set is finely and delicately turned, with a simple scratched decoration.*

Figure 2:62. *The posset-service dismantled and laid out for use.*

The principle of turnery, which consists essentially of shaping a piece of wood with chisels whilst it revolves around an axis between the jaws of a lathe, was laboriously but precisely defined in the seventeenth century: "...Any Substance, be it *Wood, Ivory, Brass,* etc., pitcht steddy upon two points (as on an Axis), and moved about on that Axis, also describes a Circle concentric to the Axis; And an Edge-Tool set steddy to that part of the Aforesaid Substance that is nearest the Axis, will in a Circumvolution of that Substance, cut off all the parts of Substance that lies further off the Axis and make the outside of that Substance also Concentrick to the Axis...This is a brief Collection, *and* indeed the whole Summ of *Turning*..."[18]

The use of the turner's lathe, as with the potter's wheel, represents the earliest form of shaping machinery employed by man. Indeed, the two crafts share many common principles and many words in their descriptive language. The very terms 'turner' and 'thrower' mean precisely the same thing. The turner (Lat. *tornare,* OE. *tyrnan*) is classical and southern; the thrower (O.Ger. *drahan,* OE. *thrawan*) is Teutonic and northern. When we talk of 'throwing a pot', this has nothing to do with the potter's action of forcibly dropping the clay lump on to the wheelhead. It refers to the spin of the wheel (as with the spin of the lathe), and to the manner in which the thrower forms the pot, exerting a pressure in opposition to that exerted by the inertia of the spinning clay. Thus, the classic turned chairs are described in English inventories as both 'turneyed' and 'thrown'.

Experiments were made at various times with sources of mechanical power to drive turners' lathes, but even into the present century the most common source of motive power for country turners was provided by the turner's own foot operating the treadle of the simple pole-lathe, or the energy of an enthusiastic apprentice turning a geared fly-wheel by hand. With the pole-lathe, the work was spun first one way by the downward kick of the operator, then it spun back under the return pull of a supple pole or sapling (Figure 2:71). This meant that the chisel could be applied to the work only on the down stroke. But despite this inherent inconvenience, the

18. Quoted by W.A. Thorpe, *The Prosody of the Turner,* Antique Collector, December 1952.

83

Figure 2:63. *Turned standing cup. English. Sycamore, dated 1611. One of a series of extremely fine standing cups, mostly having steeple covers, and decorated with a very accomplished series of armorials and inscriptions. See Edward Pinto, 'Treen, and other wooden bygones', pp.34-37.*

pole-lathe remained the most popular device for the small workshop until recent times, and represents the machine on which the turned parts of most early English furniture were formed.

Because of the nature of the craft, certain woods tend to be more suitable than others. These are chiefly the non-porous hardwoods, with fine straight grain and few knots. For furniture, the turner's favourite wood was ash, with its close texture and wiry, supple strength. But whenever they could be got, he was happy with walnut, beech, hornbeam and the fruitwoods. Yewtree is of a beautifuly close texture, but so hard and irregularly grained as to make turning it a problem. Sycamore and maple, being smooth and tasteless, are the best for bowls and trenchers; hickory and box for tool handles. Elm does not turn well. Similarly, oak is not easy to turn, with its coarse, open grain; but since it served the joiners so well for their furniture, the turners made a speciality of it with a careful eye and sharp tools. Lignum vitae from the West Indies, a fine and heavy hardwood, was

Figure 2:64. *Turned money box. English. Ash, bound with iron, painted red, mid-seventeenth century.*

Figure 2:65. *Turned spice box. Welsh. Ash, eighteenth century. This box is made in three parts, with a mill or grater in the base, and compartments for nutmegs, etc.*

Figure 2:67. *Turned bowl. English. Ash, eighteenth century. This footed bowl is more complex in form than is usually the case with domestic wooden bowls.*

credited with magical curative powers, especially of the venereal diseases, and found a popular application for apothecaries' mortars.

Like stone and marble, most woods are at their crispest and most workable state when they are still fairly green. In his *Sylva* of 1662, the diarist John Evelyn noted that "...the greenest Timber is sometimes desirable for such as carve and turn...", though he could not recommend it for panelled work. Turners must often have worked with unseasoned wood for that reason, and this would account for the pronounced oval cross section often met with in early turnings, which have shrunk across the grain. It seems likely that turners must have habitually turned up sets of legs and posts for sale to neighbouring joiners, for use at a later date, *after* the wood had seasoned.

Figure 2:66. *Turned weighing scales. English. Ash, with sycamore bowls and base, eighteenth century. Probably used in the dairy or kitchen.*

This marginal shrinkage of timber across the grain seems to have been adopted as a device for tightening the joints in turned chairs. An examination of the *structural* posts of these chairs shows that the major cross members are invariably tenoned into the vertical members. Thus if the vertical posts are turned and assembled in the green state, they will shrink around the seasoned tenons of the cross members and achieve a very tight joint.

Trade Aspects

The London Turners' Company obtained its charter in June 1604, with the intention of uniting a brotherhood of lathe workers "under the government of the Company". They embraced a combination of trades which included pulley makers, seal makers, wheelwrights, chairmakers and joiner/turners. Over the next century they engaged in a series of running battles with other trades to secure rights of practice to the various processes which they regarded as their own.

In Salisbury, the local turners disputed before the Corporation in 1621 that the trade of a pumpmaker should be exclusively theirs, and the Corporation found in their favour that "...the trade occupacion or misterye of a plompe-maker doth onlye belong unto a turner, and not to a

Figure 2:68. *Turned apothecaries' mortar and pestle. English. Lignum vitae, late seventeenth century.*

Figure 2:69. *Turned table. English. Elm, with ash feet, c.1700.*

carpenter or joyner..."[19] Such decisions at local levels certainly reinforced general trade attitudes, for even in far away New Haven, Connecticut, the inventory of Ezekiel Sanford (a turner, d.1685) included tools and parts for both chairs and pumps.[20] The list includes "...a parcell of rounds for chayrs..." and it is interesting to speculate on whether these were parts for turned chairs, or if they were made for sale to a joiner.

One notable aspect of the turners' trade is the relationship between the chairmaker and the wheelwright. Not only do both trades use the lathe, but it seems that there was a closer link. Country turners would put their hands alternately to furniture, wheels and other work as the occasion demanded. Randle Holme, in talking specifically of turned stools and chairs, noted that they were "...made by the Turner, or wheele wrighte all of Turned wood..." This relationship extended into the Windsor chair era, for we find one John Pitt (d.1759) of Slough near Windsor, described on his trade label as 'wheelwright and chair-maker'. The label is affixed to the seat of a Windsor armchair, and a similar chair bears the label of 'Richard Hewett Chair Maker at Slough'. In the parish records of Upton-cum-Chalvey, Slough, is recorded the burial in 1777 of 'Richard Hewett, wheeler'.[21] There is no reason to doubt that this is the same man, described in both aspects of his trade. There can be little doubt that the frequent references to chairmakers before the eighteenth century, normally meant makers of *turned* chairs. Joined chairs were part of the standard production of the joiners.

19. Charles Haskins, op. cit.
20. Quoted in full by Patricia E. Kane, *Furniture of the New Haven Colony: The Seventeenth Century Style,* The New Haven Colony Historical Society, New Haven, Connecticut, 1973.
21. Both quoted by John Stabler, *Two Labelled Comb-back Windsor Chairs,* Antique Collecting, Vol. 11, No. 12.

Figure 2:70. *Turners' cupboard. English. Ash, with oak shelves, late seventeenth century. This spindle cupboard is constructed entirely without a joined frame, unlike most cupboards of similar form (cf. Figure 3:311).*

Figure 2:71. *The interior of a turner's workshop. English woodcut. Eighteenth century. The turner is working at a pole-lathe, the action of which is clearly visible. As he kicks down with his right foot, the work is rotated on the lathe before him; and as he releases the pressure at the end of the stroke, the pole fixed to the ceiling springs back into place. From Joh. Amos Comenius, 'Orbis Pictus, or The Visible World', ed. 1777.*

Turned Furniture

The *range* of furniture permitted by the somewhat limited structural facility of the turners is very small. It is effectively restricted to little more than small tables, open wall cupboards, baby walkers, stools and chairs: forms which do not employ squared tenons or other joints which might infringe the joiners' prerogatives. The table and cupboard in Figures 2:69 and 70 illustrate the point. Though widely differing in form, both are constructed from turned parts without a joined frame. In the cupboard, the three boards are held together with a series of turned spindles, and the doors are hinged by extending the inner spindle of each door *through* the boards to form a swivel pin. This form of hingeing is also found on open cupboards of joined construction. The tripod table, with its turned and dished top, dates from c.1700, but must resemble very closely the sort of table produced by turners over the preceding century or more, examples of which have not survived. The kinship between these two items, and the following chairs, is immediately apparent.

The Chairs

Stools and chairs are by far the most important aspect of turners' furniture. Curiously, no stools seem to have survived from before the mid-eighteenth century, though armchairs (and later backstools) are fairly numerous. The earliest appearance of English turned chairs is lost in time, but they were certainly common throughout medieval and post-medieval Europe; became the standard cottage/farmhouse chair in eighteenth and early nineteenth century England; were a popular form in Colonial and later New England; and are still manufactured today in huge quantities in various countries of the world.

They have formed an important family of furniture, yet modern furniture historians have consistently refused to take them seriously. Few of the standard works on early furniture have ever illustrated more than two or three specimens.[22] Percy Macquoid came up with a specific, but unfounded, theory that turned chairs were originally introduced into Northern Europe from Byzantium "by the Varangian guard", and then to England by the Normans.

Figure 2:72. *Woodcut illustration from Randle Holme, 'Academie of Armory', probably 1649.*
"73:...a Turned stoole...This is so termed because it is made by the Turner, or wheele wright all of Turned wood, wrought with Knops, and rings all over the feete..."
Strangely, no English specimens of this once-common type have survived.

22. A notable exception was Wallace Nutting, *Furniture of the Pilgrim Century*, Old American Company, New York, 1924 (and also in other works by Nutting). A recent valuable work was Richard D. Ryder, *Three-legged Turned Chairs*, and *Four-legged Turned Chairs*, Connoisseur, December 1975 and January 1976.

Figure 2:73. *Turned armchair. English. Yewtree, with oak seat, mid-seventeenth century. This is a very fine and mature expression of the simpler triangular chair. The wood has patinated to an excellent colour, and there is no restoration.*

Whatever the true story of their early development may be, the most respectably-ancient survivals of turned chairs are to be found in Scandinavia, notably those from the churches of Rusby, Aspö and Herrestad (Sweden), Vallstena and Husaby (Gotland), and Baldishol (Norway). Some remarkably early dates are ascribed to these chairs, and to other turned furniture such as the benches at Alpirsbach (Germany), in the Black Forest. Current authority regards them all as dating from before 1300. The only comparable English chair is the remarkable specimen at Hereford Cathedral, known as King Stephen's Throne (Figure 2:83).

Largely as a result of academic disinterest, and the fact that few private collectors would claim any real *liking* for them, there has been little attempt to classify these chairs and to investigate them properly. Yet, the lack of interest would seem to be as much a *result* of this neglect, as the cause of it.

In fact, a primary analysis is a fairly simple job, and in form they would seem to break down into the following groups:
a). Three-legged chairs. i). Low-back (Figures 2:73 and 74).
                                             ii). High-back (Figures 2:76-78).
b). Four-legged chairs. i). Raked-back (Figures 2:79-82).
                                             ii). Straight-back (Figures 2:83-105, 3:145 and 4:253-259).

However, this elementary classification is deceptively simple, since there are a large number of detailed differences between individual early chairs, and in the whole family of typological descendants. Also, it cuts across at least one apparent workshop group (Figures 2:78, 79, and 3:485); and moreover must exclude the important group of three-legged stools which have not survived (see Diagram 2:11, page 94).

The principles of construction used in turners' chairs are relatively simple. All the parts are formed on the lathe (except for the obvious boards of the panel seats, the woven seats of matted chairs, and the slats of ladderbacks), and the main joints are a simple round version of the mortice and tenon. The tenon is formed by retaining a thick projecting finger on the end of turned cross-members, and the mortice hole is bored to receive it. The joint may be secured by a transverse peg, or simply be wedged home. In some chairs, the long tenon is seen projecting right through the mortice.

The most significant feature to look for in identifying the work of the turner is the absence of rectangular tenon-blocks at the main joints. These are only present on joiner's work.

The seats of turned chairs were constructed in four different ways:
i). The fully panelled-in seat is found on both three- and four-legged chairs. Here the seat panel is set all around into grooves in the seat-rails.
ii). In some four-post examples the plank seat is lodged into grooves only in the front and back seat-rails, and is not supported at the sides.
iii). In some four-post examples the seat consists of a row of plain turned

Figure 2:74. *(Left) Turned armchair. English. Ash, with oak seat, late seventeenth century.*

Figure 2:74a. *(Above) Rear view of Figure 2:74.*

Plate Five. *(Left) Joined chest of drawers. English. Oak, walnut, elm and pine, painted in colours, c.1675. This is a very rare and complete survival of this class of English polychrome furniture. The vigorous, yet coarse, handling of the paint (see Plate Six) suggests that this chest was made for the home of a small town merchant or yeoman farmer, perhaps in Wiltshire, where the chest was first noted.*

Plate Six. *Detail of Plate Five. The texture and condition of the paintwork is very clear in this detailed view, and note should be made of the typical manner in which the paint has flaked at various points, particularly on those edges exposed to wear. The palette of colours is varied but harmonious, and the surface condition remarkably clean.*

Figure 2:75. *(Above) Joined armchair. English. Oak, late seventeenth century. Similar in form to the turned three-legged chairs, but made by a joiner. A crude form.*

Figure 2:75a. *(Right) Rear view of Figure 2:75.*

spindles, supported by the front and rear seat-rails. These were, of course, intended to support cushions.

iv). In the majority of four-post examples the seat consists of a woven mesh of rushes, osiers, withies, rope, or similar material. This is the standard 'matted chair' found throughout history, and so described in inventories and trade cards in the seventeenth and eighteenth centuries. This seat was apparently never used on triangular chairs:

> 1594... three chairs with bottoms of bullrushes...
> 1778... plain matted chairs, white and coloured, turned
>   matted chairs, white and coloured, from eight to
>   forty shillings per dozen... in ash and elder...

Three-legged chairs were possibly the most numerous type during the sixteenth century, but the four-legged groups were longer lived and more successful in terms of fostering a popular and varied tribe of descendants. It is too late now to attempt any systematic study of regional types, even if regional differences *did* exist as such during the seventeenth century. Differences are more likely attributable to workshop groups, though there is a slight pattern of consistent preferences between chairs from Britain, and American examples. But such differences are minor, being confined chiefly to the shapes of finials, and the construction of the arm. It appears that three-legged chairs were *not* made in America.[23] Turned chairs have been noted from most areas of England and Wales, but especially the Welsh Borders, the Midlands, East Anglia, Devon and South Wales. Figure 2:86 has a Cumberland provenance, which is unusual. Perhaps this indicates a survival of the type from medieval Norwegian settlement in the area, amongst a confessedly conservative people. A rare London turned chair is noted in Figure 2:87, but the records of the London Turners' Company

23. cf. S. Dillon Ripley, *An American Triangular Chair?*, Antiques Magazine, January 1964. This optimistic article must be regarded as over-hopeful. The chair in question is made largely of white oak, which could be English or American. The only positive American wood is a strip of red oak in the seat, which is probably a repair. Having said that, there is certainly no reason why three-legged chairs should not have been made in New England.

92

indicate a high production of furniture, and they include references to furniture made as proof pieces:

> 1609...a high chair for a child...
> 1609...a small stool for a woman...
> 1614...a man's arm stool...

Distinctive varieties of rush-seated chairs were produced during the eighteenth and nineteenth centuries, especially in the North of England (see Figures 4:256-259), and in America by the Shaker communities.

a). Three-legged chairs

Tripod furniture has a highly-respectable classical history, whilst at the opposite extreme the *primitive* three-leg stool occupies the lowest stratum of universal peasant furniture. Triangular turned chairs probably reached their final form of development during the late Middle Ages, and manuscript illustrations of the fourteenth to sixteenth centuries frequently include simple stools (often in use as tables or basin stands), backstools, and later armchairs. Under the heading "...Tryangle stolys for my Lord...", an early sixteenth century inventory of the Earl of Northumberland included "...It'm, xij thre fottyde stolles, torned, the scetts of them of blake lether..." The three related forms of stool, backstool and armchair are graphically demonstrated in Diagram 2:11. The sources for each type are common in European paintings from the mid-sixteenth century onwards,

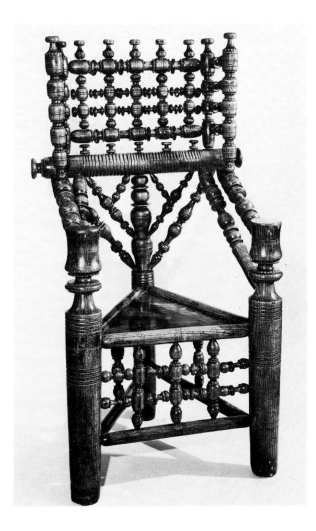

Figure 2:76. *(Left) Turned armchair. Welsh; from Ty'n-y-cymer, Porth, Glamorgan. Ash, seventeenth century. Another very fine chair, in remarkable original condition. The grain of the wood is particularly well-marked.*

Figure 2:77. *(Below) Turned armchair. English; probably Devonshire/Somerset. Ash, seventeenth century. A heavy specimen, and the turnings not very well articulated.*

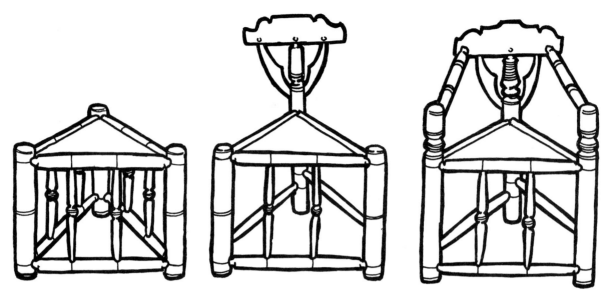

Diagram 2:11. *This sketch illustrates the close structural links between three-legged turned stools, backstools and armchairs. Early examples of the first two do not seem to have survived, though the armchairs are still reasonably common.*

Figure 2:78. *Turned armchair. English or Welsh. Ash, possibly early seventeenth century. This chair is virtually identical to chairs at Wells Cathedral and Harvard University.*

24. e.g. by Cescinsky and Gribble, *Early English Furniture & Woodwork*, Vol. II, p.187, Routledge, London, 1922.

e.g. the roundel by Pieter Brueghel the Younger (c.1564-1638) illustrating the proverb 'Falling between two stools'. This shows both a stool and a backstool, whilst the armchair may be based on an extant chair at Leycester's Hospital, Warwick. The *developmental* level shown here is compatible with what is known of the sixteenth century, in which the cross-post of the back is formed by a board. In later English chairs the cross-post is developed more comfortably as a *turned* member (Figure 2:73).

No early example of an English triangular turned stool has survived, and so we are fortunate to have Randle Holme's little engraving (Figure 2:72) and his description to record their use here. In referring to this class of furniture he notes that they were made by turners and wheelwrights "...all of Turned wood, wrought with Knops, and rings all over the feete, these and the chaires, are generally made with three feete..." Similarly, there are no English triangular backstools, but the low-back armchair is fairly common. This type was also made in a crude joined version, but examples are comparatively rare (Figure 2:75).

A more important effect is achieved by the high-back triangular chair. This has a rectangular superstructure imposed upon the rear cross-post, and this arrangement is supported by an extra pair (or a group) of turned spars which connect it with the front uprights to lend stability and strength. The cross-post may be supported by a low or a high rear leg, and this leads to variety in the arrangement of the backs of different chairs (Figures 2:76-78). The first of these three, from South Wales, is perhaps the best specimen of its type in existence. It is in mint condition, and the quality of the turning and general execution is excellent.

It is important to note that triangular chairs were *not* designed to stand in the corner of the room, and so the flat back does not contradict any such intention. This unfounded criticism has often been levelled by detractors of turned chairs.[24]

b). Four-legged chairs

i). The raked-back four-legged chairs are directly related to the high triangular chairs, the only difference being that the rear cross-post is supported on two legs instead of one, providing a rectangular seat instead of a triangular one. The rake of the back, which stems from level of the cross-post, is intended to offer greater comfort to the sitter, and is a factor which cannot be achieved in the numerous class of four-post chairs which follows.

Like the triangular chairs, the raked chairs have panelled-in seats, and the decorative scheme follows the same themes. Although some chairs are fairly plain, a superabundance of elaborate turnery may be found on the highly-decorated versions, enriched by applied knobs and spindles. "...loaded with turnery...", wrote Horace Walpole admiringly. Loose rings turned from the solid, and other technical fireworks, contribute to the sense that these chairs were often approached as an exercise in virtuosity. Like the potter, the turner could often get carried away by his own dexterity and produce deft confections, sadly lacking in modesty. But then, modesty was probably *not* a quality possessed by that class of people who patronised such wares.

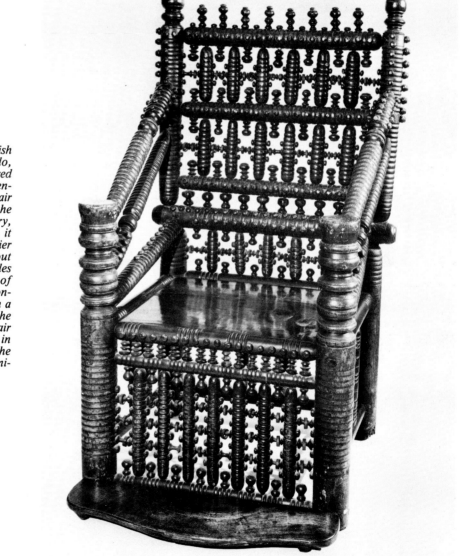

Figure 2:79. *Turned armchair. English or Welsh; from Tregib, Llandeilo, Carmarthen. Ash, with faded red paint, probably early seventeenth century. This is a very important chair which most authorities assign to the middle of the sixteenth century, abetted by family history. However, it is difficult to support a date earlier than 1600 until more is known about its history, and the general principles of dating turned chairs. The profile of the uprights, and minor factors of construction, seem to place this chair in a group with others which include the previous figure, the child's high chair in Figure 3:485, and the chair in America which is known as the President's Chair at Harvard University.*

The attribution of dates to these chairs is a very great problem. We can see that the type persisted over a very long period, probably with very little stylistic change. Yet if we apply the principle of a predictable rate of survivals (by comparison with the survival of other types), we are forced to the conclusion that most examples of early type must date from (say) 1640-1740. Yet certain chairs have a *tradition* of being much older. Family traditions can be contradictory and misleading, especially when we are faced with a case such as the famous 'Llandeilo' chair (Figure 2:79).

This chair came to the Welsh Folk Museum from Tregib, a house at Llandeilo, Carmarthen. Hughes family history calls it the 'Justice's Chair', not unlike other family chairs of similar type, such as Justice Popham's chair at Littlecote, Wiltshire. If the tradition is correct, and if we are to verify the official date of c.1550, then we must find the Justice to whom the chair originally belonged. There are several contenders among the Chief Justices and Sheriffs of Carmarthen, but we do not know exactly how long the chair has been associated with Tregib. There are several alternatives: If the chair has *always* been at Tregib, then it must have belonged to the Gwynne family, who descended from the Parrys (ap Harry) of Tregib. There was a multitude of Gwynne Justices from 1550 onwards, starting with Dafydd Gwynne ap Hywel ap Rhydderch. A little later Justice Morgan Siôn ap Harry of Tregib (d.1602) was Sheriff of Carmarthen. The Hughes family *now* of Tregib, donors of the chair, married into the Gwynnes of Tregib shortly before 1800. *They* may have brought the chair with them from their family home, Penmaes.

Figure 2:80. *Turned armchair. English, probably Devonshire. Ash, dated 1685. A rare dated specimen, and thus important in the chronology of turned furniture. Inscribed 'George Shillibeare'. There are certain stylistic parallels between this chair and a specimen at Dunster Castle in North-West Somerset, which suggests a stylistic group centred on Exmoor or the Devon/Somerset borders.*

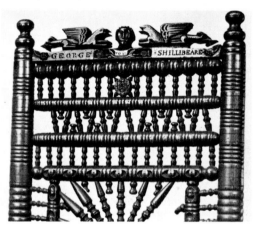

Figure 2:80a. *Detail of Figure 2:80. The date appears in tiny figures under the central carved head. The use of carved decoration on turned furniture is rare, which may help to account for the lack of dates on pure turned examples.*

As so often, we are left little the wiser. Very little factual material is known about the chair. It is a very fine and important specimen, and must have been the property of a man of considerable standing in his community. Yet, these are opinions, not facts. It is one of a small group of chairs which seem to be the products of a single workshop. This observation is based on comparison of details such as construction, and the profiles of various turned parts: in particular, the front uprights. The group includes this chair, Figures 2:78 and 3:485, the great three-legged turned chair at Wells Cathedral, reputed to have belonged to the last Abbot of Glastonbury in 1539, and the chair known as the President's Chair at Harvard University. The Harvard chair is identical in almost every respect to Figure 2:78 and the Wells Chair, and is (perhaps correctly) reputed to have been taken to New England by the Mather family at an early date.

In his contribution to the 1974 Winterthur Conference,[25] Christopher Gilbert observed that "any precisely datable thrown chair would be a welcome landmark for historians of vernacular furniture." Genuine dated

25. Christopher Gilbert, *Regional Traditions in English Vernacular Furniture,* Winterthur Conference Report, 1974.

parallels are an important component in assessing the dates of any furniture type, and his comment underlines the importance of the two chairs in Figures 2:80 and 81, since dated turned chairs are virtually unknown.

Nothing is known about George Shillibeare and his chair, before it was purchased for the collection of Sir William Burrell, except that it had recently come from South Molton, Devon. The date of 1685 is quite late in the history of ornate chairs, and the use of carved detail extremely unusual. The carved motifs include a cresting with two dragons centring on a human head; a rose and a thistle either side of the tiny date; below that a boss with a tiny coat of arms; and a sun-head in the centre of the panel of spindles. The scale and execution of the carving do not suggest the work of a professional carver. The following chair is even later at 1718.

Figure 2:82 is an American raked-back chair from the New York area, which is otherwise related to the straight-back types. A similar chair in the collection of the Connecticut Historical Society has a panelled-in seat, and that must have been the original arrangement on the present chair. Such a seat would relate it more closely to the preceding English chairs. In England, the joined armchair is far more common than its turned counterpart; but in New England the reverse is true, and joined chairs are rare in the seventeenth century. Many American thrown chairs survive from the period 1650-1750, though it must be said that few of these can

Figure 2:81. *Turned armchair. English; probably Devonshire/Somerset. Fruitwood, dated 1718. Another rare dated specimen, which brings elaborate turned furniture firmly into the eighteenth century.*

Figure 2:82. *Turned armchair. American; New England. Ash and hickory, 1680-1720. The matted seat probably replaces the original panelled-in seat.*

Figure 2:83. *Turned armchair. English, Hereford. Oak, medieval or sixteenth century. Another important chair which is usually assigned a great antiquity. It is reputed to date from c.1300 or earlier, but the evidence is very tenuous. Stylistically, the possibilities are broad (see text pp.98-101).*

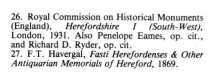

Figure 2:83a. *One of many medieval manuscript drawings which support the stylistic possibilities of a medieval date for the Hereford chair. Flemish, c.1340, from the* Romance of Alexander *(MS Bodley 264, f.68ᵛ, Bodleian Library, Oxford). The king is seated before his councillors in a turned four-post chair complete with its footboard, which is strikingly similar to the Hereford chair. However, the conservatism of the turners was so strong that the chair may well be an archaic production of a much later date — possibly as late as 1600.*

26. Royal Commission on Historical Monuments (England), *Herefordshire I (South-West),* London, 1931. Also Penelope Eames, op. cit., and Richard D. Ryder, op. cit.
27. F.T. Havergal, *Fasti Herefordenses & Other Antiquarian Memorials of Hereford,* 1869.

confidently be assigned within the seventeenth century itself (particularly in view of the late example of our dated English specimens). The enthusiasm of many American scholars has led them to offer an optimistically early date spectrum for some of these chairs, but there can be very few made before 1680.

ii). The straight-back four-legged chairs are by far the most numerous and long lived of the family of turners' chairs, appearing over a period from the early Middle Ages to the present day. They are characterised by having both front and rear posts formed each of a single length, without any join to provide a rake to the back; and are more easily referred to as four-post chairs.

The earliest English survival would seem to be the so-called King Stephen's Throne at Hereford Cathedral (Figure 2:83). Popular tradition has it that this was the chair used by Stephen on Whit Sunday 1142, but most modern opinion regards the chair as belonging to the thirteenth century.[26] The chair was certainly intended as a seat of honour. It is very large and well-constructed in oak (unusual amongst thrown chairs). It was fitted originally with a footboard, which is evidence of some exalted use, possibly in this case for a Bishop of Hereford. Havergal noted, in 1865,[27]

Figure 2:84. *Turned armchair. English. Ash, late seventeenth century. A highly elaborate version.*

Figure 2:85. *Turned armchair. English. Ash, late seventeenth century. Note the seat composed of turned spindles (type iii).*

Figure 2:86. *Turned armchair. English; Cumberland. Ash, late seventeenth century.*

Figure 2:87. *Turned armchair. English; London. Ash, late seventeenth century. Until 1902, this chair served the President of the Placemen at the London City Cornmeter's Office. This might be thought an archaic form for a London origin at such a date, and may have been brought from outside.*

that there were still traces of old vermilion paint and gilding in evidence on the chair, though these cannot now be seen. The central portion of the back is missing, but it would seem likely that the space was filled with a pair of round-headed arches, similar to those still present at the front of the chair; or that the series of concentric rectangles was completed, as in other chairs of the type seen here.

Any theory regarding the date of the chair is difficult to substantiate with facts. Chairs of this type *are* seen in early medieval sculpture and manuscript paintings (cf. Figure 2:83a), and the round-headed arch *was* a feature of early medieval architecture. But, stylistically and structurally, the chair is very difficult to pin down, and there are a number of conflicting observations which may suggest a later date:

* The round-headed arch, of which two survive below the front seat-rail, is a feature of Romanesque buildings; but I must question the assumption that its use here *necessarily* indicates an early medieval date. The shape of the arch derives from the constructional techniques employed by the maker, and not from any particular intended allusion to contemporary architectural themes. Such a conceit would be in the province of the carver, not the turner. The arch is semi-circular simply because it was made from a bisected ring of wood, fashioned on the lathe. It would have been difficult for the turner to have made any other shape, even if he had wanted to.

* The turnings are of types found commonly on chairs and other work, even into the eighteenth century (e.g. the rear top rail may be compared *exactly* with the stem of the candlestand, c.1680, in Figure 3:191).

* The seat, which is completely original, is made from two

Figure 2:88. *Turned armchair. English. Ash, painted red, late seventeenth century.*

Figure 2:89. *Turned armchair. English. Ash and fruitwood, with later wicker seat, c.1700.*

Figure 2:90. *Turned armchair. American; New England. Hickory and ash, 1660-1700.*

Figure 2:91. *Turned armchair. American; New England. Ash and maple, with rush seat, 1660-1700.*

Figure 2:92. *Turned armchair. American; New England. Maple, with rush seat, 1660-1700.*

Figure 2:93. *Turned child's high chair. American; New England. Ash, with rush seat, 1660-1700.*

Figure 2:94. (Left) Turned armchair. American; New England. Ash and oak, with rush seat, 1660-1700.

Figure 2:95. (Right) Turned armchair. American; North Carolina. Cherrytree, with rush seat, 1680-1730.

Figure 2:96. Woodcut illustration from Randle Holme, 'Academie of Armory', probably 1649.
"69:...a Turned chaire...without Armes..."

28. Quoted by F.T. Havergal, op. cit.

planks which are lodged into rebates in the front and rear seat-rails (Type ii). This is a weak method sometimes employed in armchairs and backstools of the seventeenth to nineteenth centuries. For this seat to have survived intact over seven hundred years would seem to stretch the bounds of credibility.

* Indeed, the chair is in a remarkably fine state of preservation, having suffered only the loss of some spindles in the back, the footboard and its sub-structure, and a little height from the feet. The amount of wear and worm damage is negligible.

* There are no facts surrounding any early record of the chair at Hereford. The earliest evidence of its existence is apparently an account of 1827,[28] describing it in the Lady Chapel (where it had been brought from the Bishop's Palace).

Such a confusion of imprecise and conflicting evidences makes an accurate dating impossible. Whereas a date c.1300 seems possible, it cannot be discounted that the chair may be an archaic product of the sixteenth century. At the very least it represents a type which was current throughout the Middle Ages, but which are now extremely rare. Another famous example is the Erasmus Chair at Queen's College, Cambridge, which (if the attribution is correct) must date from shortly before 1500.

Whatever the early history of four-post turned chairs, a consistent form had developed by c.1600. The elaborate chairs of the seventeenth century are represented here by Figures 2:84-87. They are directly in the tradition of the earlier chairs, with an abundance of rings, reels and balusters. Three have seats of turned spindles (Type iii), and wing-pieces which project out from each rear upright, in similar manner to the upholstered easy chair.

By the end of the seventeenth century, popular styles are reflected in chairs of progressively simpler design. This is not to suggest that simpler

Figure 2:97. (Left) Turned backstool. English. Ash, with rush seat, eighteenth century.

Figure 2:98. (Right) Turned backstool. American; New Haven, Connecticut. Ash, with rush seat, eighteenth century.

Figure 2:99. Turned armchair. English. Ash, with rush seat, 1660-1700. The form of the back is a curious hybrid of the two standard types, viz. the preceding group of spindle-back chairs, and the following group of ladder-backs, or 'slatted' chairs. Both types were current from the Middle Ages, or even earlier, and were made over a span of at least five centuries.

Figure 2:100. Turned armchair. English. Ash, with rush seat, 1680-1720.

Figure 2:101. (Left) Turned armchair. American; New England. Pine and ash, with rush seat, 1680-1720.

Figure 2:102. (Right) Turned armchair. American; Connecticut. Maple and hickory, with rush seat, early eighteenth century. The enlarged flat finials to the front uprights, appropriately known as 'mushroom finials', are peculiar to American chairs, being turned from a single block with the leg.

Figure 2:103. Turned armchair. American; Connecticut. Maple and ash, with a splint seat, early eighteenth century.

chairs are necessarily of later date, since a cheap form of turned and rush-seated chair had been in common production ever since the Middle Ages; but it is true to say that by 1720 the demand for elaborate versions was in decline, and the simpler versions remained as the standard chair in poorer homes. These were of two basic types: the spindle-back, which featured a series of turned spindles in different combinations; and the ladder-back, which consisted of a row of horizontal slats of various profiles. The latter appear to have been termed 'slatted chairs' in the eighteenth century and perhaps earlier. Examples are given here of each type, from both the British Isles and America. The earlier models are distinguished by elaborate finials to the rear posts, but during the eighteenth century the importance and prominence of the finials declined. Also, the earlier chairs are often more heavily built, but it would be wrong to adopt the rule-of-thumb (as Wallace Nutting did) that "heavier means earlier."

In America, popular mythology classified turned chairs as 'Brewster' or 'Carver' types, according to whether or not they are fitted with rows of spindles beneath the seat and arms. This is by way of association with two of the Pilgrim Fathers who are supposed to have owned such chairs: William Brewster (Ruling Elder, d.1644); and John Carver (first Governor of the Plimoth Colony, d.1621). This distinction is in fact meaningless, since it has no significance with regard to the constructional form, date, or regional origins; and the same makers made both types. The most noteworthy regional feature in the construction of American four-post chairs lies in the form of the arm. In Northern chairs (New England), especially before c.1700, the arm is morticed *between* the front and back posts, so that the upright normally rises above the level of the arm and terminates in a rounded knob or ball. In Southern examples (Carolinas, Virginia, Maryland) the arm usually passes *over* the front post. Both methods are found in England.

Figure 2:105. *Turned backstool. English. Ash, with rush seat, late eighteenth century.*

Last shown is a highly-traditional turned stool of c.1820. The form of the turnings corresponds very closely with earlier chairs, and the material is the turner's favourite ash. Some distinctive turned chairs of the eighteenth century are discussed in Chapter Four. During the nineteenth century, the craft of the country turner suffered heavily from competition by increasing industrialisation in furniture production, at such centres as High Wycombe (Bucks.), Worksop and Rockley (Notts.), and Macclesfield (Derbys.). But when it seemed that the turner/chairmaker would disappear entirely, an interest in the craft was revived by the Arts and Crafts Movement. Around 1890, Ernest Gimson spent some time at the workshop of Philip Clisset, a traditional ash chairmaker of Bosbury, Herefordshire. In 1893, probably encouraged by William Morris, Gimson and the Barnsley brothers moved to the Cotswolds to begin making a range of hand-made furniture which heavily influenced non-commercial design in the twentieth century.

Figure 2:104. *(Left) Turned armchair. English. Ash, with rush seat, eighteenth century.*

Figure 2:106. *(Right) Turned high stool. English. Ash, with elm seat, early nineteenth century.*

v). The Carpenter (Figures 2:107-119)

The work of the carpenter was primarily that of the housewright. He "...squareth Timber with a Chip-axe, ...and saweth it with a saw, ...Afterwards he lifteth the Beam upon Tressels, by the help of a Pully, fasteneth it with Cramp-irons, and marketh it out with a Line. Then he frameth the Walls together, and fasteneth the great Pieces together with Pins..."[29] This is an account of the carpenter constructing a timber-framed building with the use of pegged mortice and tenon joints, but we have already seen that by the end of the sixteenth century the joiner had successfully ousted the carpenters from the privilege of using tenon joints in the making of furniture. The 1632 ruling of the London Court of Aldermen simply confirmed the *fait accompli.* Naturally, the carpenters were bitter about this since for centuries theirs had been the premier trade, and there were further and continual squabbles. There can be no doubt that both trades poached on each other's territory, but *officially* the carpenters' furniture was limited to simple nailed boards — "Boarded and nayled together."

29. Joh. Amos Comenius, *Orbis Pictus, or the Visible World,* trans. from the Dutch by Charles Hoole, 1658 (ed. of 1777).

Such a consideration severely limits the range of forms which furniture is able to take. Almost the only basic structure is that of a four-sided box, which in turn is limited to a size governed by the maximum width of the planks used. The only variation which can be accommodated is in the shaping of the flat planks to allow a diversity of decoration and function.

Figure 2:107. *Boarded chest. English. Oak, bound with iron, remains of original painted finish under the lid, 1340-45. Known as the Richard de Bury chest (see text, pp.200-203 and Plate Eight).*

Figure 2:107a. *General view of Figure 2:107, closed. The condition of the iron banding is very complete, the bands over the lid terminating in fleurs-de-lys.*

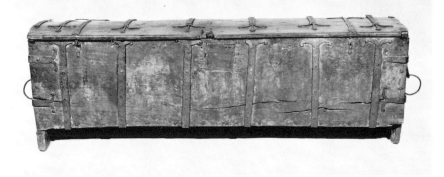

Figure 2:108. *Boarded box. English. Oak, bound with iron, early sixteenth century. The locks and hasps of various dates.*

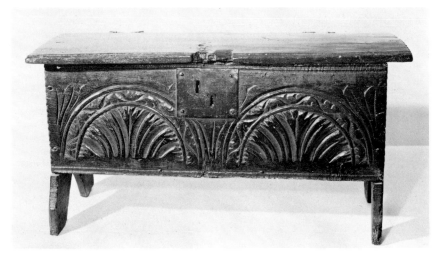

Figure 2:109. *Boarded chest. English. Oak, mid-seventeenth century.*

105

Figure 2:111. *Boarded chest. American; New England. Pine, dated 1673.*

Figure 2:112. *Boarded chest with drawer. American; New England. Pine, dated 1702.*

Figure 2:113. *Boarded chest. English. Oak, 1650-1700. The large, original spandrel-brackets are a good feature.*

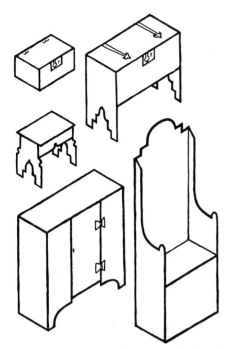

Diagram 2:12. *This isometric sketch illustrates the range of relatively simple forms to which carpenters were restricted by the nature of nailed board construction. All these pieces employ a rectangular box-like shape, and decoration is limited to simple two-dimensional shaping of the flat boards for feet, arms, spandrels and crests. Further decoration may be applied in the form of carving, painting or shaped ironwork.*

Schematically, the variety of box-like forms is limited to six-plank chests and boxes, five-plank stools, benches and armchairs. The armchair may be lengthened into a settle. Cupboards are normally limited to a three-plank width, though four or five-plank widths are known. The American boarded press cupboard (Figure 4:228) is representative of an ornate version found in New England. With a little ingenuity, a good deal of decorative variation can be introduced, but this rarely extends further than shaping the feet, banding with ironwork, or covering surfaces with carved or painted designs. Turned decoration is very rare in any form on boarded furniture (Diagram 2:12).

One of the intrinsic problems of boarded furniture is the manner in which the timber will shrink across the grain as it dries out. No matter how well-seasoned the board may be, it will always shrink further when it is put into a domestic atmosphere. If the boards are firmly held together by nails or pegs, this will inevitably lead to splitting of the boards owing to the tensions set up within them. This is an inherent problem for the carpenter, and in heavier work the normal solution was to bind the boards around with wrought-iron straps. The hinges of boxes and chests were extended to wrap completely around the piece to provide strength and stability.

Like other simple types, the use of boarded construction remained current over a very long period, certainly throughout the Middle Ages and into the nineteenth century. Also like other simple types, its usage gradually descended in the social scale after the end of the Middle Ages, until in its later phases it is found only amongst peasant cultures, or for strictly utilitarian items. Great boarded chests, such as the Richard de Bury chest of c.1340 (Figure 2:107), made for a Bishop of Durham, were valued and honoured possessions in the semi-public homes of the wealthy. During the early sixteenth century, the rich turned to joiners' work for their better pieces, and the rising yeomanry acquired a taste for the better sort of boarded furniture. But, by the seventeenth century it is rare (though certainly not unknown) to find a boarded chest or cupboard with fine carving, or some other expensive decoration. Figure 2:110 is a prime exception to that slightly perforated rule.

Figure 2:114. *Boarded chest with drawer. Welsh. Oak, mid-eighteenth century. The base plinth with bracket feet are typical features of the eighteenth century, and should be compared with the form of the spandrel-brackets in the previous figure.*

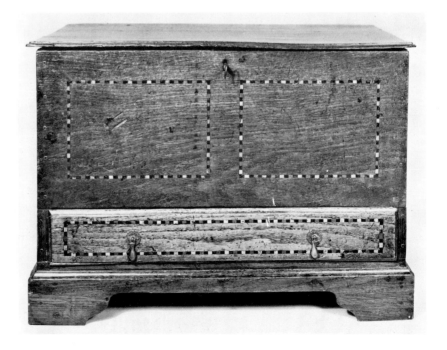

Figure 2:115. *Boarded stool. English. Oak, early seventeenth century.*

Figure 2:116. *(Right) Boarded armchair. English; probably Salisbury. Elm, early seventeenth century.*

Figure 2:117. *Boarded child's armchair. English. Pine, c.1800.*

30. Illustrated by Fred Roe, op. cit, Pl. LXXV.

Such factors make carpenters' furniture very difficult to date in the absence of specific decoration or inscriptions. The chests appear over a period of four hundred years or more, and some pine or elm examples are dated as late as 1830. Certain trends are significant: earlier specimens are usually of heavy construction, often with thick strong ironwork; later examples are of thinner boards, without iron banding; the greatest number of oak chests survives from the seventeenth century; eighteenth century chests are typically of squat proportions, and may have a plinth and bracket feet in imitation of cabinetmakers' work (Figure 2:113).

Boarded stools are often assumed to be of sixteenth century date, but in fact they must have been made throughout the next century also. An example at Midhurst, West Sussex, is inscribed 'MIDHVRST PARISH CHVRCH' and dated 1689.[30] There is no reason to assume that the date is a later addition. Only those with specific features should be considered especially early (see Figure 3:73).

Large boarded settles are relatively common from the later period (say, 1760-1860), but single armchairs of any period are extremely rare. They are identical to the settles in construction, but being potentially prone to damage, very few have survived. Figure 2:116 is an early and relatively sophisticated version, within the context of such simple construction. Much more common are children's chairs (Figures 2:117, 118 and 3:482-483).

Figure 2:118. *Boarded child's armchair with tray. Welsh. Elm, probably made by Isaac Lewis, carpenter of Bryngwyn, Monmouthshire, d.1830.*

Figure 2:119. *Boarded chest. English. Oak, late seventeenth century. Decorated with counterfeit panels, in imitation of superior joiners' work.*

The chest in Figure 2:119 is presented as evidence of the contemporary regard for joined furniture, as superior to the products of the common carpenter. This is, in fact, a boarded chest; but the carver (probably the carpenter himself) has taken the trouble to excavate part of the front in order to counterfeit the effect of a pair of framed panels. The imitation frame is complete with its chamfers, and the run of carving is laid out exactly as it might be on a frame of rails and stiles.

vi). The Joiner (Figures 2:120-125)

The Company of Joiners and Ceilers or Carvers of London received its charter in 1570/1, but the first *physical* evidence of their existence as a trade appears in the construction of certain chests some three hundred years earlier.

In order to overcome the two main drawbacks of carpenters' furniture (its great weight, and the tendency to warp and split), it was necessary to devise a technique whereby thinner boards could be joined by a method which allowed the wood to 'move' and shrink more freely without much change in overall dimensions, and where the use of iron nails and bands could be eliminated. Further, the new technique must not lack in strength or stability.

The problem of iron nails was sometimes overcome by the substitution of wooden pegs on boarded work, but the main answer was provided by the reintroduction of two distinctive features: the mortice and tenon joint; and the framed panel. These had both been known in the classical world, and their adoption in England (at different stages) revolutionised the making of wooden furniture.

> 1703... Mortess. Is a square hole cut in a piece of stuff to entertain a tennant fit to it...

The use of the framed panel enabled the joiners to make quite large pieces of furniture (no longer restricted to the width of single boards), and to cover the walls of houses in a manner which provided a suitably decorative structure with flat areas and edges inviting further decoration, which was light in weight, and free of the problems of warping and splitting which were the usual results of the rigid nailing together of planks.

Mortice and Tenon Joints

This is essentially a technique to *join* two pieces of wood together at right angles to each other. The mortice hole is cut into the *side* of one piece, and a tongue (the tenon) is cut from the *end* of the other. The tenon is seated tightly into the mortice, and the two are secured in place by means of a wooden peg (formerly called a 'trennell' — a colloquial contraction for 'tree-nail'). These pegs were always made from *riven* wood, not sawn, since this was less likely to break. They were cut to shape with a chisel, or whittled with a knife, so that they usually assume a slightly square or faceted cross-section. This helps them to grip the sides of the hole when they are driven home, unlike the modern smoothly-turned dowel. In order to ensure a tight fit at the shoulder of the joint, a technique called the 'draw-bore' process was commonly used. In order to achieve this, the peg-hole in the tenon is bored slightly nearer the shoulder than is the hole through the mortice. As the peg is hammered home it has the effect of drawing the tenon-shoulder tightly against the face of the rail, ensuring a neat and close join.

On the outside, the head of the peg is left standing slightly proud of the surface (in old work this is only *partially* due to the shrinkage of the surface). Inside a chest or cupboard the protruding point of the peg is usually cut or snapped off flush; but under seats or tables where the protrusion cannot be seen, the point is often left (Figure 2:120a).

The development of the tenon-joint apparently took place in two stages in England:

a). The earliest manifestation of joined work is the so-called 'clamped-front' chest, which seems to have first appeared in England early in the thirteenth century. This type was also common in Germany and France. The joint was used for uniting wide boards, and took the form of a long mortice-groove down the edge of one board, into which an equally broad tenon fitted from the end of the other board. The front of such chests consists of wide vertical stiles, or 'standards', with one or more horizontal boards clamped between. The ends of the chests are normally formed from vertical boards set into rebates behind the stiles (usually with a slight inward slope). On this board is often superimposed a framework of rails made with simple halved joints, and giving only the *appearance* of framed panelling (Figures 2:121, 122 and Diagram 2:13). The top rail of this end-frame is detached, and forms the side batten under the lid. The rear end of this batten acts as a pin-hinge for the lid (Diagram 2:13a and b).

The status of the joiner is not clear at this transitional stage, but it seems that for many years the makers of such chests were still considered as hutchmaker/carpenters. Separate status for the joiners did not come until the full development of framed panelling.

As the family of clamped-front chests developed during the fourteenth century, so a richly-carved form appeared, with architectural tracery sprinkled with a lively and naturalistic detail; or with a formalised sculptural scene, framed within the central board (Figures 2:123a and b).

Figure 2:120a. *Oak, mid-seventeenth century. Under view of a mortice and tenon joint. This is a detail of a standard open-frame joined table. The faceted pegs which secure the joints can be seen clearly projecting through the joint. The marks of the pit saw are visible on the inside surfaces of the apron pieces. Each cut is made at a slightly different angle, the grain being ripped open on each down stroke of the saw. The small holes on the underside of each apron piece, near the leg, are the exit holes of the pegs which secure the top, and which were drilled through from above. If left, the protruding pegs would have been visible from outside, so they were snapped off.*

Figure 2:120b. *Outer view of a framed mortice and tenon joint. The lower front junction of a chair leg with the stretcher. Note the angles and degree of wear on the stretcher and turnings, in this perfect demonstration of genuine wear, as it should appear. Note also the change of colour at the base of the leg, just where it meets the damp floor and kicking shoes.*

The construction is clear in these photographs, as is the quality of the carving.

The clamped-front form survived well into the seventeenth century in the form of the 'ark'. Figure 2:124 is a typical example of these archaic chests, which are characterised by having a lid with a canted or arched top. They were the usual domestic grain bins of the sixteenth and seventeenth centuries, and the lid is normally removable and can be turned over to form a kneading trough (or with the help of two poles, a hand barrow). They are more fully discussed on pp.356-358.

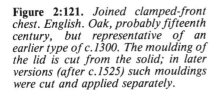

Figure 2:121. *Joined clamped-front chest. English. Oak, probably fifteenth century, but representative of an earlier type of c.1300. The moulding of the lid is cut from the solid; in later versions (after c.1525) such mouldings were cut and applied separately.*

Figure 2:122. *Joined clamped-front chest. English; Winchester, Hants. Oak, c.1300. The false framed ends of these chests are clearly demonstrated here. The previous example never had such an applied frame.*

b). Clamped-front chests still inherit the basic problems associated with the use of wide boards. Since the board is still *fixed* across the entire width, it is liable to crack on shrinkage. The answer was to contain the board as a panel within a frame, and to set the panel within grooves where it would be free to 'move' without constraint. In order to do this, the joiner had to develop small mortice-and-tenon joints which were efficient enough to construct a stable framework of rails and stiles (Diagrams 2:14 a and b). The technology was now available for the proper development of framed panelling. The panel is set into a rebate or groove which is run around the inside of the frame, and to accommodate this the tenon is slightly modified (Diagrams 2:14 c and d). Since it is more efficient to allow the panel-groove to run out at the top of the stile, a haunched tenon is normally used to fill the space which would otherwise result (Diagram 2:14e).

From the earliest days of framed panelling, the edges of the framework were customarily provided with a decorative edge-moulding. Immediately, these gave technical problems, since the only way in which mouldings may be run successfully together at adjacent corners is to form them with a 45-degree junction, or mitre. At first, the joiners copied the form of the mitre from that used by the stonemasons. This consists of cutting the mitre from the solid, in the rail containing the mortice (Diagram 2:15a). However, this clumsy arrangement was overcome by the development of the true mitre (Diagram 2:15b). This innovation probably first appeared c.1540, but the mason's mitre is often found on furniture as late as the middle of the seventeenth century (for example in Aberdeen). With the true

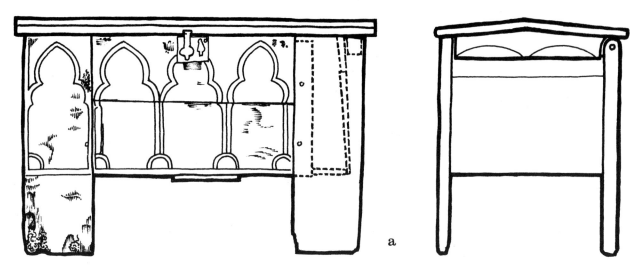

Diagram 2:13a. *Clamped-front chest at Graveney Church, Kent. Thirteenth century. The decoration is in the form of lightly incised Gothic tracery of an early type. The applied framework is missing from the end of the chest, but the side batten is still present under the gabled lid, and it is clear where the rear end of this batten is pinned through to act as a hinge.*

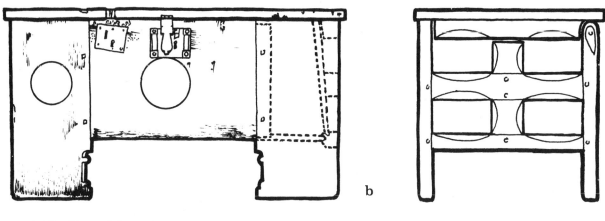

Diagram 2:13b. *Clamped-front chest at Stoke d'Abernon Church, Surrey. The decoration is in the form of three chip carved roundels similar to those in Figure 4:1. Here the applied framework is still present at the ends. The pin hinge is covered with the original kite-shaped iron plate.*

Diagram 2:13c. *The feet of clamped-front chests are finished with a variety of shaped and carved ornament. These are some of the patterns noted on late thirteenth and fourteenth century examples.*

Diagram 2:13d. *Grain chest or 'ark'. Late sixteenth or seventeenth century. This is a highly traditional form which retains the clamped-front construction of three centuries earlier. Such chests are usually constructed from coarse riven planks, and the lid is detachable to act as a kneading trough or hand barrow.*

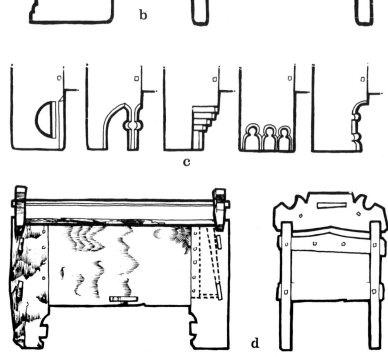

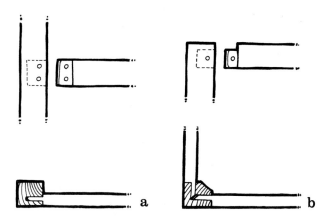

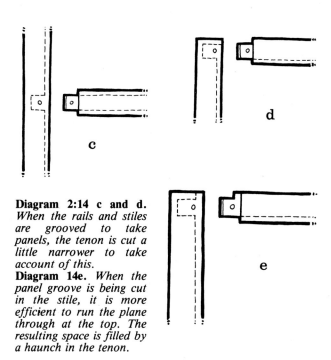

Diagram 2:14a. *The mortice and tenon joint enables two rails to be joined at right angles to create a framework. The joint is held secure by one or more pegs which are driven through to secure the tenon in place.*

Diagram 2:14b. *At the top of the framework a simple stepped tenon is used, so that the joint will not be visible at the top end of the vertical stile. Note in the plan views, how the rails are invariably fitted so that they are flush with the outside surface of the stile, a point often ignored by the makers of fakes and reproductions.*

Diagram 2:14 c and d. *When the rails and stiles are grooved to take panels, the tenon is cut a little narrower to take account of this.*
Diagram 14e. *When the panel groove is being cut in the stile, it is more efficient to run the plane through at the top. The resulting space is filled by a haunch in the tenon.*

mitre, the tenon-rail is set *into* the mortice-rail, so that the mouldings actually *meet* at the line of the mitre (Diagram 2:15b).

Other, and simpler, methods of dealing with the problems of mouldings were also developed, and several different methods are frequently found on one single piece of work. One way was simply to avoid having an edge-moulding on the mortice-rail (c), or else the moulding of the mortice-rail could be run out before it met the joint (d). A different approach entirely was to make the mouldings as separate strips, and to glue or pin them in position after the panelling is assembled (e). This is not a very permanent or satisfactory technique, and was not commonly used until after 1660 (Diagrams 2:15 c, d and e). At the base of the panel (i.e. the top edge of the rail), it was normal to provide a straight chamfer or splay instead of a moulding. This is obviously desirable, since a complicated moulding can harbour dirt and dust, and the chamfer is normally referred to as the 'dust-chamfer', or 'dusting-splay'. This also provides a problem at the junction with the moulding, and the earlier method of dealing with this was to stop the chamfer short of the joint, either with a plain or shaped stop (Diagram 2:15f). Alternatively, in later work the chamfer might be run straight through at the joint, and the shoulder of the tenon is then lapped over it. If the chamfer is continued all around the frame, then a very neat and simple effect is obtained (Diagram 2:15g).

To return briefly to the date at which framed panelling first appeared in England.[31] Reference has been made to the Medieval habit of applying a counterfeit framework to such areas as the boarded ends of clamped-front chests, so that the *idea* of framed panels is implicit quite early on. True panelling first appeared on the Continent probably c.1400, and must have reached England soon after. The earliest datable English survival would seem to be that of a built-in cupboard of c.1457 at the Vicars Choral, Wells, in Somerset.[32] The frame of this cupboard is heavily built, with a form of moulding commonly found on contemporary architectural beams, in which the moulding is stopped-off with a sharply curved taper (Diagram 2:16a).

31. Valuable comments are to be found in Penelope Eames, op. cit.
32. Penelope Eames, op. cit.

The plain panels are characteristically long and narrow, being made each from a single plank. This form remained current for many years, and the panels of the first half of the sixteenth century are typically rather narrow in relation to their length. Later in the same century, the panels were made more square by using wider boards, or by the simple expedient of joining two widths (Diagram 16c).

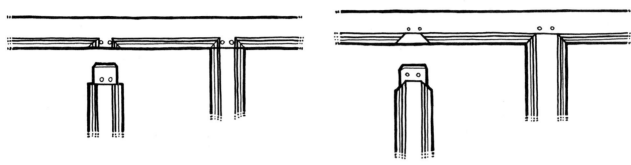

Diagram 2:15a. *Masons' mitre. Mainly sixteenth century.*

Diagram 2:15b. *True mitre. After c.1540.*

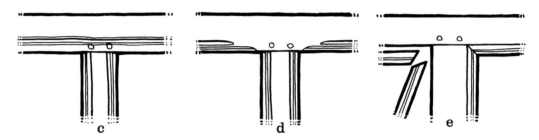

Diagram 2:15c. *Here the mortice rail does not have an edge moulding, so the tenon rail meets it in a simple flat-faced joint. Instead the mortice rail has a channel moulding set back from the edge.*

Diagram 2:15d. *The edge moulding of the mortice rail may be cut with a scratch stock, enabling the moulding to be run out before it meets the junction.*

Diagram 2:15e. *Edge mouldings may be applied separately to the inner edge of the framing, secured with nails or glue.*

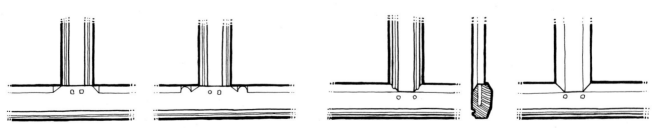

Diagram 2:15f. *Here the dust chamfers are stopped off around the joint. A variety of simple and complex stops were used.*

Diagram 2:15g. *Here the chamfer is run straight through on the mortice rail, and the shoulder of the tenon is lapped or 'scribed' over the chamfer.*

Figure 2:123a. *Detail of joined clamped-front chest. English. Oak, c.1400. A rich display of Gothic tracery fills the panel, whilst the end stiles have a cycle of grotesque animals. (Detail of Figure 4:3).*

Figure 2:124. *Joined clamped-front ark. Welsh. Oak, 1550-1650. It is very difficult to offer a categorical date for such long-lived traditional furniture.*

The earlier panels were not chamfered behind, but instead the edge of the panel was stepped to meet the groove in the frame. Later panels *were* chamfered behind, both to create a thinner edge, and to improve the lightness and strength. At the end of the seventeenth century, this process was reversed, and the chamfer was set on the front of the panel, in the standardised fielded panel of post-1660 (Diagram 16d). As a decorative device, fielding was known in the sixteenth century, but it was not as common as it became after 1700.

It is perhaps appropriate to explain here the various technical terms for the parts of the joined panel-frame: the horizontal members are known as 'rails', whilst the main vertical members are referred to as 'stiles'. Secondary vertical members are known as 'muntins', though this rather clumsy term is not much used today. Perhaps this latter case is unfortunate,

Figure 2:123b. *Panel of joined clamped-front chest. English. Elm, early fifteenth century. These sculptural panels usually carry complicated scenes from standard tales such as* St. George and the Dragon, *or scenes of jousting. In this case the subject seems to be identified with the Pardoner's Tale from Geoffrey Chaucer's* Canterbury Tales. *The vitality and sense of movement are very striking.*

Figure 2:125. *Joined chest. English. Oak, with black painted detail, c.1620. The standard joined chest of the seventeenth century.*

Figure 2:125a. *Rear view of Figure 2:125. Note the original wire staple hinges, the tops of which are seen in the previous figure.*

Figure 2:125b. *Under view of Figure 2:125. The bottom planks are hidden by the lower rail at the front, but exposed to the rear. Note the discoloration around the nails, and the fine dry texture of the wood.*

33. Penelope Eames, op. cit.

for 'muntin' would seem to be the seventeenth century term for the size of timber generally used for framing-members:

> 1649...The Rome well wanscoted about...with Moontan and panells...
> 1595...200 of quarters, 200 of ½-inch board, and 100 of mountains...

The generic term for panelled work, in use during the sixteenth and seventeenth centuries, was 'ceiling' (variously spelt). This referred to any area of framed panel, and might be used to describe wall-panelling, bedsteads, or even chairs. It is a more specific term than the comprehensive 'joined', but the latter is far more commonly applied to furniture in contemporary accounts:

> 1580...Contract at Chatsworth with Christopher Sedgfeld to...seall the parloure about with French panell...also, two parlours to be...scelyd to the heyght of the door...
> 1587...the walls of our houses on the inner sides...are seeled with oke...
> 1584...a seeld bedsted of wallnutree...
> 1626...j seild bedstead wth tester...
> 1671...In the new chamber over the Bruehouse...three back seiled stools...

The Ceilers were particularly makers of wall-panelling and screens. Since their work was largely architectural, they were somewhat at the mercy of the housewrights, and so they must have been pleased to retain their protective alliance with the joiners in 1570. This gave the joiner/ceilers a large measure of independence, and a stronger bargaining position with the contracting housewrights.

Framed-panel Furniture

One of the earliest surviving examples of English free-standing panelled furniture is the chest at Brasenose College, Oxford, of 1500-15.[33] This is

Plate Seven. *Painted and panelled interior of the Kederminster Library at Langley Marish Church, Slough, Buckinghamshire, c.1620. Recent restoration has shown that the oak panelling was possibly re-used from another site, but the scheme of painting is original to this room and of one date (1617-22). This is a rare survival of the sort of closet or library which could have been found in many manor houses at this date. The book presses contain Sir John Kederminster's library of books, which he made available for local ministers in 1623. The overmantel features a gilded ground over a large oval boss, bearing a potted pedigree of the Kederminsters and surrounded by symbolic and allegorical figures. The library table and small bench (Figure 3:501) are original to the room, and both are painted with a rough form of wood graining, though the walnut table top has been stripped in recent years to leave an incongruous pale colour. The room is seen here in much the same state as John Milton knew it in the middle of the seventeenth century.*

The library is approached from the Kederminster Pew (right), and may be seen in this view looking down the length of the enclosed pew. The exterior of the panelled pew (see Figure 2:230) is similarly decorated with a scheme of marbled paintwork and texts (see detail of panel in Plate Fourteen), and further details such as coats of arms and the 'Eye of God'.

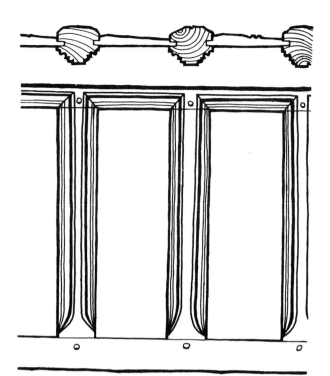

Diagram 2:16a. *Early form of post-and-panel, based on cupboard of c.1547 at Wells. Room partitions were often constructed in this way until a fairly late date, e.g. the well-known series from North Wales dated in the last third of the sixteenth century (see Archaeologia Cambrensis, vol. CXXIV 1975). Here, the construction is typified by a long narrow panel and thick framing stiles, which are tenoned into top and bottom rails.*

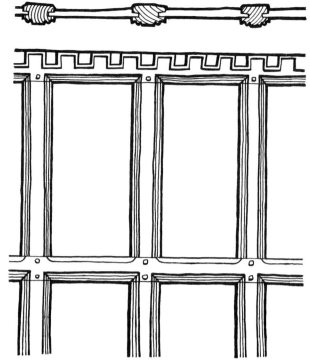

Diagram 2:16b. *1500-1570. The long narrow panel persisted through the early part of the English Renaissance, but with a lighter framework for furniture and wall panelling. True mitres were often used after c.1540, and the panels might be decorated appropriately (e.g. Figure 4:23).*

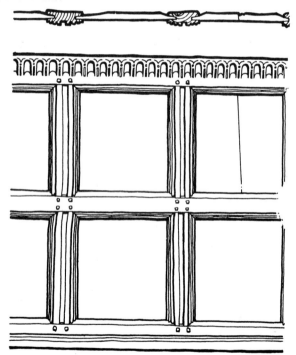

Diagram 2:16c. *1540-1740. This is the standard 'square' panel used throughout the Elizabethan period and the seventeenth century, and even later in country districts. The panels were made from riven boards, sometimes using two narrower widths glued together, and were usually roughly chamfered behind to give thin edges. A wide vocabulary of decoration was available to the joiner, and the framed panel system could be used to construct a wide range of enclosed furniture types. Large areas of panelling would serve for wall panelling, settles, bed heads and testers. Through most of this period, framed panels were referred to as 'cieled work'.*

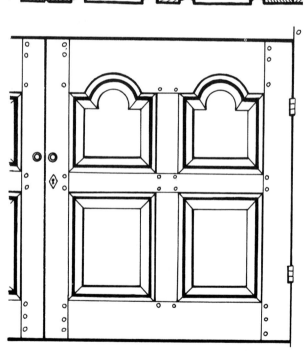

Diagram 2:16d. *1660-1830. After the Restoration, panels with deep fielding and simple frame mouldings became popular, following architectural fashions. This became almost the standard form in provincial joined furniture of the eighteenth century, and fielded panels may be seen at their best in dressers, 'deuddarns' and corner cupboards from North Wales. The joinery on such pieces is often heavy, and more finely engineered than the earlier work in 2:16c.*

118

entirely panelled with a large single panel, including the lid, and is of a massive and strong construction. The edges of the frames are mainly finished with a simple chamfer, with mason's mitres, and the joints display a somewhat irrational pattern of distribution (Diagram 2:17).

The variety of forms allowed by panelled construction is confined to chests, box-chairs, cupboards and similar enclosed pieces (as well as others which are made up from flat areas of panelling, such as beds). The feet of early pieces are invariably formed as continuations of the major vertical members, or stiles. The chest in Figure 2:125 is a representative example of the mature panelled work of c.1620, and is typical of such work over the following one hundred and fifty years. The front, sides and back are all constructed from framed panels. The back displays the customary lack of finish to the surfaces, which retain their pristine saw marks exactly as they left the saw pit. On good-quality work, the inside and back framing may be finished with edge-mouldings, but it is rare to find an item with a full scheme of decoration to the rear. When this *was* done, the piece was obviously intended to stand in the middle of a room (cf. Figures 3:367 and 3:370).

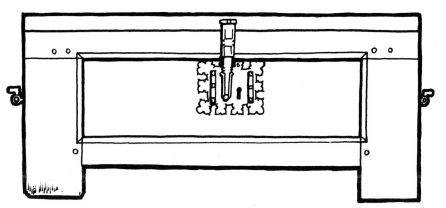 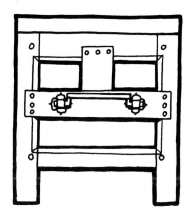

Diagram 2:17. *Joined and panelled chest at Brasenose College, Oxford. 1500-15. The chest is shown here as it appeared before the addition of two locks in 1516. The framing is heavy and somewhat eccentric, but the advanced form of the jointing should be compared with the clamped front chests in Diagram 2:13 a, b and d. The frame of the panelled lid has mitred corners.*

Open-frame Furniture

It is by no means clear when the idea of an open joined frame evolved, but it was almost certainly subsequent to the panelled frame. It probably first appeared as an attempt to provide a lighter form of chair, by omitting the panels to the frame below the seat (cf. Figures 3:21-24), soon after 1500. The idea quickly extended to tables (which had hitherto been of the trestle type, or with enclosed bases), to cupboards, and to stools.

Around the middle of the sixteenth century, the convention first appeared of decorating the legs of open-frame furniture by turning. At first this was an alternative and subsidiary to carving, but by 1600 turned legs and supports had become the standard adjunct to joined open-frame furniture.

The Rise of the Cabinetmaker

Besides tenoned frames and the use of glue, the London Aldermen's arbitration of 1632 (pp.42 and 43) specifically allowed to the joiners the use of dovetail joints. This simple joint is used to join two boards together, normally at right angles, across the end-grain in the manner of Diagram 2:18. The effect of this is to create a boarded box, in similar vein to carpenter's work, but with superior characteristics. The splayed shape of the dovetail tongue makes a very strong union possible, whilst the (theoretical) absence of nails makes for longer-lasting results in an acid timber such as oak. Dovetail joints were normally used by the English joiner only for small-scale work such as drawers, boxes and small cupboards (especially spice-cupboards).

Drawers (drawing-boxes or 'tills' as they were originally called) had made their appearance in case furniture before the end of the Middle Ages, but throughout the sixteenth century their construction was comparatively crude. In very poor work, the drawer runs on its bottom, supported underneath by either a bearing strip or simply the frame of the chest. But the most satisfactory arrangement is the side-hung drawer. Here the drawer is supported on side runners, fitted to the frame of the chest, which engage in a slot rebated into the thickness of the side of the drawer itself. These have the advantage of smooth operation, combined with the facility that the runner is easily replaced when it is worn (in theory the runner should be made of softer wood than the drawer).

Diagram 2:18. The dovetail joint is used to join boards at right angles across the end grain, by means of a mutually interlocking series of tongues.
a). Through-dovetails. Here the tongues project right through to the outer surfaces, and the end grain is visible on both surfaces.
b). Lapped-dovetails. Here the tongues are not carried through the full thickness of the outer board, thus maintaining a clean show-surface.

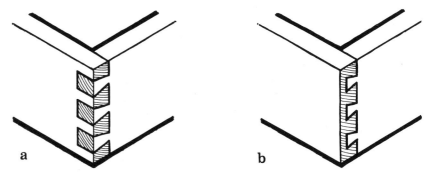

There was no completely standard method of constructing drawers. Cruder forms are often simply butted together and nailed. In early drawers, and in later country-made items, the dovetail may consist of only one large tongue, and that usually held with a nail. The popular use of applied mouldings as a decoration on drawer fronts is explained by the common use of the through-dovetail, which is hidden by the moulding. Increasing popularity of the chest of drawers after 1660 led to improvements in technique, and the lapped-dovetail was developed which did not show at the front of the drawer. Diagram 2:19 shows drawer construction.

The technique of joining large boards together by means of dovetails, to form a box, may be referred to as 'cabinetwork'. Although it formed part of their legal prerogative, large-scale cabinetwork was not a popular technique amongst the English joiners during the sixteenth and early seventeenth centuries. Instead, it seems to have been practised here mainly by immigrant Flemish joiners (*skrynemakers,* from the Latin *scrinium,* a chest). The main centres where these congregated were London and Norwich, and in particular Southwark harboured a great many 'stranger-artificers', most of them Dutch, Flemish, German and French. One class of work produced by them would seem to be the so-called 'Nonsuch' chests, and similar marquetry work such as the panels of the so-called 'Great Bed of Ware' at the Victoria and Albert Museum. These are all analogous to contemporary work from Cologne and the Rhineland.

The contrasting appearance of framed construction and cabinetwork may be demonstrated graphically (Diagram 2:20).

The chief method of decoration used with dovetailed board construction in England (apart from foreign marquetry) was the application of carved and turned pieces to the flat surfaces; in a manner quite alien to panelled work, in which the structural pattern of the frame dominates the aesthetic schemes of the joiner. A love of surface-pattern based on a grid-pattern of verticals and horizontals is a recurrent English theme, and is to be found in many other minor arts besides joinery; in needlework and woodcuts, for example.

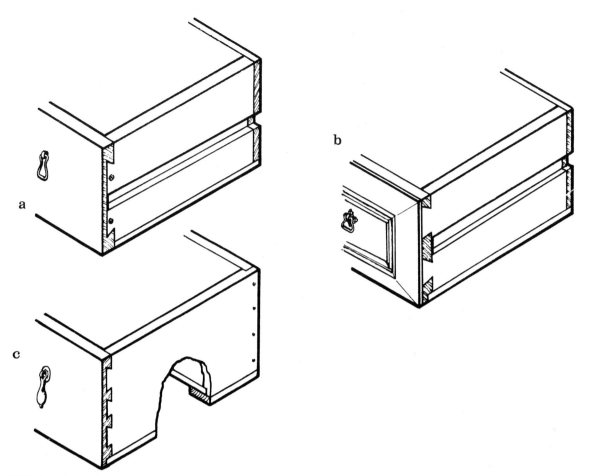

Diagram 2:19. *A wide combination of jointing techniques is found on drawers of the seventeenth and early eighteen century. The most common are a variety of dovetails and simple types of nailed butt joints, both of which are equally found on small boxes and chests. The base-boards were usually assembled with the grain running from front to back, but this was by no means universal, as is so often claimed. Especially in wide drawers, side-to-side grain was frequently used where the timber sizes proved more convenient. In the seventeenth century, most drawers of any quality were side-hung on runners notched into the carcase of the chest. The drawer was then seated on grooves let into each side. By 1700 it was becoming more usual to seat the drawer on bottom bearers, which slid over the horizontal divisions between each drawer.*

a). *c.1640. The drawer front is held with a large single lapped-dovetail, secured with nails. The sides and back are simply butted together and nailed. This and the following example have iron handles.*

b). *c.1680. The front is held here with through-dovetails, which are hidden by a scheme of applied cushions and mitred mouldings. This Anglo-Dutch fashion for glued and pinned surface decoration was extremely common on chests, low dressers and spice cupboards from the 1640s until well after 1700. In the eighteenth century, oak drawers tended to follow the walnut fashions for cockbeading, cross-banding, lipped edges, etc.; or they were given a splayed fielding to imitate the effect of fielded panels (see Figures 3:332-336).*

c). *c.1700. The front is held here with lapped-dovetails, and the rear board is nailed into a simple rebate. The base board is also rebated into the side, and the bottom bearer is glued and pinned over it.*

The immigrant skrynemakers and kistmakers may fairly claim to be the legitimate ancestors of the eighteenth century English cabinetmaker, who adopted both their constructional form and the twin techniques of marquetry and veneering. Yet, evidence of the growing interest in the smooth surface of cabinet construction amongst English joiners, even before the Civil War, is to be found in such pieces as the 1637 deed chest of the Shrewsbury Drapers' Company. The maker, Francis Bowyer, is evidently an Englishman, yet at this date such a piece might otherwise be attributed to the Anglo-Flemish workshops of London or Southwark. Similar work such as the 'Laudian' (Oxford) and 'Lime Street' (London) groups reflect the new Classical principles of Inigo Jones, and look forward to the finest work of a hundred years later.

After the Restoration, and animated by the spasm of re-furnishing which inevitably followed the Great Fire of London in 1666, veneered cabinet

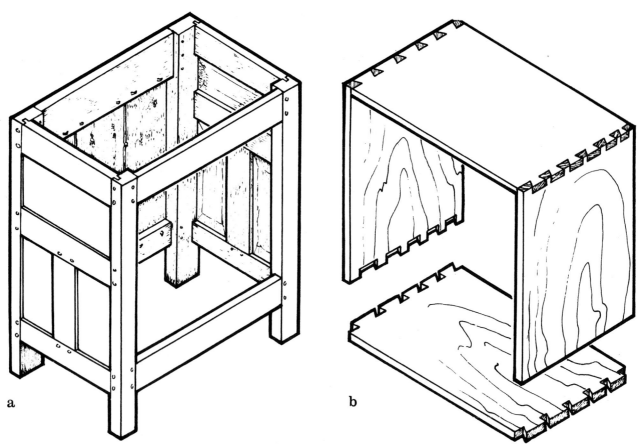

a

b

Diagram 2:20. a). *Framed-panel construction. The piece is assembled from a framework of rails and stiles which are united by mortice and tenon joints. The spaces may be filled with panels to create an enclosed space, or left as an open framework. This piece is envisaged as a small cupboard, waiting for the doors and top to be fitted. The back boards are simply nailed on over the broad rails, but in a better quality piece the back would be panelled. The main vertical stiles are carried down to form feet in the standard manner of joiners' work. This system of framing is highly flexible within its limitations, and is easily adjusted to provide a variety of forms such as seats, tables, cupboards, chests, bedsteads, or simply flat areas of wall panelling.*
b). *Dovetailed-board construction or 'cabinetwork'. Here the carcase is assembled from boards with flush surfaces, joined by dovetail joints (whether through or lapped). The through joints are then disguised in better quality work by applied mouldings or veneers. The whole piece (finished as a cupboard, chest or chest of drawers) is finally mounted on bun feet or bracket feet, or on a separate stand or plinth. Dovetailed-board construction was known and used in England since before the Middle Ages, especially for boxes and chests, but it did not become popular until after 1660, when it proved the ideal vehicle for the newly popular technique of veneering.*

construction was firmly established as *de rigeur* for the best case furniture. Joined panelwork continued to be used for another two hundred years in country-made furniture, but after this impetus of Continental influence the joiners' trade came increasingly under the control of the cabinetmaker, at least for any fashionable purpose. One effect of this was that the joiner sometimes tried to imitate the smooth and suave effects of cabinetwork design. This could be achieved in part by copying superficial ideas such as X-stretchers, twist-turning, and later cabriole legs. But attempts were also made to change the appearance of the panelling itself; first by enlarging the size of the panels, and later by fitting the panels flush with the surface of the frame. Other cabinetwork details also served to change the face of popular furniture design around 1680-1720 (such as architectural mouldings at the base and under tops, separate turned feet, and later bracket feet).

The effect of these subtle changes may be demonstrated in a series of drawings, based here on the end-views of typical chests of drawers (Diagrams 2:21 a, b, c and d).

To conclude, we have seen that although they were not amongst the trades most anciently concerned with furniture production, the joiners had established their supremacy over the other trades during the course of the sixteenth century, and had subsequently gained operative privileges at the expense of the other trades. The carpenters were still the dominant trade in timber house building, and the joiners sub-contracted to them for the supply and fitting of interior woodwork such as staircases, overmantels, panelling, doors and doorcases; and often for the furniture which was custom made for houses of quality. But for the independent production of furniture (the bulk of the market) the joiners were men of strength and self-determination.

This strength grew by means of legal battles between the trades, which often ended with advantage to the joiners. But in the end they were defeated by the dictates of fashion, in the form of a growing preference for the work of the cabinetmakers. By 1700 the London Joiners' Company was in serious decline, and this trend is reflected in many of the provincial companies. The new firms referred to themselves as 'Joiners and Cabinet-makers' (terms which now included a separate chairmaker).

vii). The Coffermaker and the Upholder (Figures 2:126-157)

Hard wooden frames and seats are not conducive to human comfort, and so it is not surprising that leather and fabric covers, draperies, and padded upholstery (whether loose or fixed) have long been associated with personal furniture such as seats and beds. There is no lack of evidence of the use of elaborate draperies and cushioned seats in classical times, but most indications are that the padding was in the form of stuffed, but separate, loose cushions. The cushions were put on the hard wooden seats, or on a base of slung leather, and occasionally behind the sitter.

In medieval Western Europe, exactly the same procedure is found. Manuscript illustrations show loose cushions used on turned or carved wooden thrones, though by 1400 some X-chairs may be seen which have slung leather or fabric seats, but with little indication of fixed upholstery.

It is not until after 1500 that the first suggestions of fixed padded upholstery are found in England. In 1546, for example, the ageing Henry VIII was being carted around Whitehall Palace in a chair called a 'tram', which was "...covered with tawney velvet, all over quilted...", and portraits of the middle years of the century often have in the background an

Diagram 2:21 *(right). A series of end views of typical chests of drawers 1680-1740. As the smooth-surfaced work of the cabinetmakers became increasingly fashionable after 1660, some joiners attempted to copy this rather bland characteristic within the limitations of their panelled work. At first they tended merely to enlarge the size of the panels, and the mouldings were omitted from the framework in order to reduce their visual impact. Later, after c.1720, they sometimes resorted to fitting flush panels which heightened the effect further.*
a). *c.1675. Traditional joiners' work built in two sections. The join is obscured by a heavy moulding across the middle, and the construction is fully panelled with edge mouldings to the framing-members.*
b). *c.1675. Fashionable cabinetmakers' work built in one piece. The smooth dovetailed boards are fitted with heavy top and bottom mouldings to enhance the architectural character of the piece, and with bun feet.*
c). *c.1690. Joined chest, still built in two sections, but with little visual emphasis on the framework. Heavy top and bottom mouldings are fitted, which hide the rails of the frame, and bun feet are adopted only at the front, where they will be seen to advantage.*
d). *c.1740. Joined chest mounted on bracket feet. The bland effect of the flush-panelled framework imitates the appearance of dovetailed boards very closely, if only at a distance.*

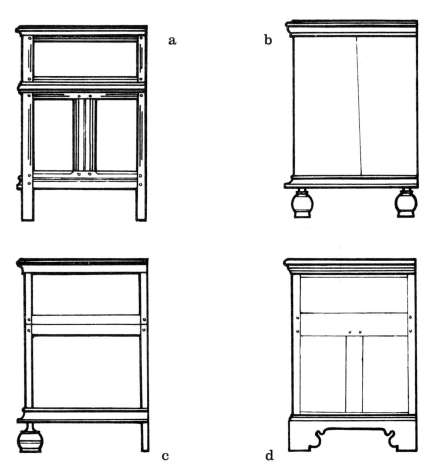

a   b

c   d

X-frame armchair, in which the seat is clearly of fixed upholstery, whilst the back is merely covered with matching fabric, and not padded. Where the subject is shown seated, then the back is normally softened with a loose cushion. This convention persisted well into the seventeenth century, and many later leather backstools and armchairs do not have padding to their backs.

Both chairs and beds were subjected to elaborate conventional forms of drapery during the Middle Ages. Perhaps the most significant was the canopy or 'celour' (later called the 'tester'), though the backcloth or 'dosser' (also at first called the 'tester') was also important in the formal scheme of things. A smaller conical canopy was known as the 'sparver'. These fabric drapes were used for beds, cupboards and chairs, but it is only in the case of beds and cupboards that they retained their significance when translated into wooden structures in the sixteenth century.

The wooden frames of earlier medieval beds were apparently of little importance, serving merely to support the draperies. By 1500, the frames were becoming the subject of more decorative attention, and it is from this date that the earliest carved beds survive. The standard wooden tester bed with two supporting posts, in which the draperies are nothing more than decorative curtains, was the chief form during the period 1540-1680 (Figure 2:126) but the upholstered bed again became more fashionable at the end of the seventeenth century.

Figure 2:126. *Joined tester bedstead. English; West Country. Oak, 1600-30. Here the bed is fully dressed with its full complement of valances, curtains, counterpane and pentes. In this case the high quality crewelwork embroideries are probably home-made, but the full set of bedding could be supplied by the professional upholder. In the seventeenth century, the pillows at the head of the bed would be piled up to a much higher level than in modern practice, obscuring the undecorated lower part of the headboard.*

Figure 2:127a. *Coffermakers' box. English. Pine carcase, covered with faded yellow-red velvet and various patterns of brass nails, c.1670.*

Figure 2:127b. *Woodcut illustration from Randle Holme, 'Academie of Armory', probably 1649.*
"66:...a Usurers Trunke, or coffer or Trunke or Caskett..."

Two distinct trades were associated with the manufacture of upholstered furniture.

The Coffermaker

Originally, the cofferer was primarily a worker in leather, and his name derives from the French *cuivrier*. His principal work was the manufacture of boxes, trunks, travelling-chests, cradles, close-stools and chairs in a technique which consisted of covering the wooden frames with leather, cloth, or painted paper. This covering was attached with glue, and finished with a pattern of decorative brass and gilt nails, though cheap or functional items would be finished with iron studs. Fine leatherwork was often finished with gilded stamps in the manner of bookbinder's work, and at the siege of Turwin the Earl of Northumberland had "...a stolle of eas...made like a booke, and covert with tawney lether..."

The small box in Figure 2:127a demonstrates the coffermaker's technique perfectly. It is made of pine boards which are covered with red velvet, now faded to a soft yellow, attached with both plain and stamped brass nails, and lined with marbled paper. Randle Holme illustrated a similar rounded lid box (Figure 2:127b) which he described as "...a Usurers Trunke, or coffer or Trunke or Caskett..." Travelling trunks continued to be made in the same way, even down to the domed lid, until very recent times. An engraved trade card of c.1760, for John Clements 'Trunk-maker' of St. Pauls,[34] illustrates a similar leather trunk, as well as a black jack and a fire bucket.

In the sixteenth and seventeenth centuries, the coffermaker probably made his own frames for the various boxes and cradles, since they are invariably of poor quality and inferior timber, usually beech or softwoods. Even the better made chairs are usually of beech, and consequently very few examples survive. All the quality was lavished on the exterior materials and finish, and almost the only difference between the cheapest and the most expensive varieties lay in the value of their coverings, and in the complexity of the nailed finish.

The Upholder

Before introduction of fixed upholstery, the upholders (later called 'upholsters', then 'upholsterers') were not involved in any process of the manufacture of furniture. Rather, they were concerned with the supply and manufacture of various fabric draperies and accessories, and in 1474 were

34. Illustrated by Ambrose Heal, *London Tradesmen's Cards of the XVIII Century,* Batsford, London, 1925. Pl. XCIII.

Figure 2:128. *Coffermakers' travelling trunk. English. Oak carcase, covered with leather, c.1580 (cf. chest in the Victoria and Albert Museum, possibly from the same workshop, bearing the arms of the Tudor Royal House).*

granted rights of search over feather beds, pillows, mattresses, cushions, curtains, etc. From early times a large portion of their trade was concerned with dealing in secondhand goods. John Stow, in his *Survey of London,* 1598, noted that "...from Birchover's Lane (in Cornehill Ward), on that side the street down to the stocks, in the reign of Henry VI, had ye for the most part dwelling Fripperers or Upholders, that sold old apparel and household stuff..."

The upholders' first involvement with furniture was in the supply of materials, stuffings, trimmings and finished cushions for beds and chairs.

During the reign of Elizabeth I, they became fully engaged in the production of upholstered seat furniture. Unlike the coffermakers, they seem to have bought their frames ready-made from the joiners, and finished them with fixed padded upholstery which consisted normally of an underframe of canvas webbing, a padded stuffing of various materials, and a cover of leather or cloth fixed with brass nails. By the end of the seventeenth century their output was tremendous. If it can be believed, a petition presented to Parliament by the Upholders' Company in about 1690 claimed an annual production of 5,000 dozen turkeywork chairs in previous years.[35]

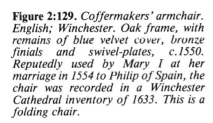

Figure 2:129. *Coffermakers' armchair. English; Winchester. Oak frame, with remains of blue velvet cover, bronze finials and swivel-plates, c.1550. Reputedly used by Mary I at her marriage in 1554 to Philip of Spain, the chair was recorded in a Winchester Cathedral inventory of 1633. This is a folding chair.*

35. Quoted by R.W. Symonds, Connoisseur, April, 1934.

Figure 2:130. *Coffermakers' armchair. English; made for Hampton Court. Joined beech frame, with velvet cover, early seventeenth century. This is the late form of X-chair, which is no longer made to fold. Branded 'HC 1661'.*

Figure 2:131. *(Right) Upholders' armchair. English. Walnut, with pine frame to the back, c.1685. There was a revived and nostalgic fashion for X-chairs after 1660, but survivals are rare owing to a basic weakness of the design as expressed here, and the usual materials (walnut, beech).*

Figure 2:131b. *Charles V of France, seated on a low-backed X-frame armchair. The slung leather seat has a fringed cushion, and the back-rest is formed by a slung strap with a similar fringe. Note the foot-cushion. The frame of the armchair is left uncovered.*

Upholstered Seat Furniture

For our purposes, the most interesting aspect of covered furniture lies in the complex history of upholstered seat furniture. We must not be misled by the apparent dearth of early upholstered chairs in modern collections. They were in fact quite common, and are frequently itemised in contemporary inventories. The low survival rate (particularly of textile covered chairs) is explained by the fact that the frames were usually discarded when the covers were worn out. It was generally considered not worth the cost of recovering the frame, which would in any case be old fashioned after some years of use, and so very few have survived intact.

During the sixteenth century the coffermaker's X-form armchair reached its mature form, and continued to be made until the time of the Civil War. The earliest extant examples are probably the chair at Winchester Cathedral (Figure 2:129), reputedly used by Mary at her wedding with Philip of Spain in 1554; and another somewhat similar at York Minster. As with other forms of coffermaker's furniture, the frames are completely covered with nailed fabrics. As here, the earlier X-frame chairs were made with *four* finials, to the front and rear uprights, so that the arm-rests are formed by the cross-posts morticed between front and back. With this construction, these particular chairs retain the original function of the X-chair as a *folding* chair. But by 1600 this function is forgotten, and most later X-form

Figure 2:132. *(Left) Upholders' armchair. English. Joined oak frame, 1580-1630, with later cover.*

Figure 2:133. *(Right) Upholders' armchair. English. Joined oak frame, mid-seventeenth century, with later cover. A small amount is missing from the height of the feet.*

armchairs are of fixed construction. These later coffermaker's chairs have arms which conform more closely to the scrolled form of joined chairs, and indeed the generally improved frames suggest that these were supplied by joiners.

The most important collection of early upholstered furniture is the remarkable group now at Knole, and two of the present examples are drawn from here (Figures 2:130 and 134).

The first appearance of upholder's chairs, i.e. using frames quite obviously supplied by the joiner, coincides with the general adoption of turned decoration to open-frame chairs, and the earliest survivals date from the very end of the sixteenth century (Figure 2:132). The turned legs and the general form of such chairs conform exactly to those of the panel-back and wooden seated varieties. The demarcated functions of the joiners and upholders are demonstrated not only by the obvious processes involved, but on the evidence of documentary sources; e.g. Nicholas Reade, Court Joiner to James I, was frequently paid for making and repairing the timber structure of various types of chairs, including X-chairs and chairs of estate. These must have been upholstered, yet nowhere is he credited with attending to upholstery work. On the other hand, his contemporary Ralph Grinder, the Court Upholster, was paid for work on various chairs, for example in 1623 for "...*covering* two chaires of state of crimson gould tissue, and for fustian, downe, girthwebbe and buckram, guilt nailes and bullion nailes...",[36] and for tasselled cushions and baize cases for the same. In turn, his bills do not specify work on the frames.

Apart from turnings, joined frames also allow other scope for decoration to the woodwork (such as carving, painting and gilding), as well as wider scope with the size and form of the piece. Following this flexibility, although chairs and stools were always the more common varieties, larger

36. Lord Chamberlain's Records, quoted by E.T. Joy, *Country Life Book of Chairs*, 1967.

pieces were developed. Various terms were used for these, such as 'couch' or 'day-bed' (later 'settee' and 'sopha'), but most of them were essentially upholstered settles. Several early seventeenth century examples survive at Knole (Figure 2:134), but they did not become common until after 1660.

Before 1600 there was a fashion in France which followed the Moorish custom of sitting on large cushions, instead of chairs. These might have leather bottoms, or they could be placed on low stools provided for the purpose. There is some evidence that this fashion was occasionally followed in England, e.g. at Knole c.1620, and at Ham House c.1670. At both houses there exist low stools which are usually thought to be footstools, but they may in fact be cushion stands which substitute for chairs (see Chapter Three — squab stools, cushion stools).

A variety of materials was used for the padding of stuffed upholstery (often referred to in early inventories as 'quilted' work). The best quality normally used feathers, down, sheep's wool or curled horsehair; but simple work was often stuffed with grass, chaff, leaves, straw or rushes. The by-laws of the Upholsters' Guild, in particular with regard to bedding, forbade the use of "...deers hair, goats hair, etc. which is wrought in grease and if foul give out, by the heat of a man's body, a savour so abominable and contagious that many are destroyed thereby..."[37]

Textile Covers

During the Middle Ages, rich textiles were always significantly more important than the simple wooden frames which supported them.

37. Quoted in *Dictionary of English Furniture,* ed. Macquoid and Edwards, Country Life, London, 1924.

Figure 2:134. *Upholders' settle. English; possibly made for Whitehall Palace. Joined frame, with later cover, early seventeenth century. This piece, at Knole House, Kent, is known as 'The Knole Settee', and was probably purloined from Whitehall by the 6th Earl of Dorset soon after 1688.*

Descriptions of beds and chairs in the homes of the wealthy normally omit any mention of the timber parts, but go into lengthy and imaginative details of the gorgeous embroidered drapes and covers. Mouth watering accounts of the fifteenth and sixteenth centuries attest to the important regard for these costly expressions of wealth and status. Rich fabrics such as velvet, silk damask, and even cloth of gold, often served as a vehicle for further embellishment with the needle:

> 1539...One folding cheyre of wallnuttre the seate backe elbowes of crymsen vellat embranderid with scallope shells and lettres frengid with golde silke with a foote stowle to the same likewise embranderid... One cheyre of wodde paynted, the seate back and elbowes coverid with riche cloth of golde reyzid with rooses of golde and fryers knottes of silver tissue...
> 1543...a Cheir covid with Crymsen vellat enbraudrid with Rooses and porte quillizes with iij litle pomells of silver and gilt... a Cheir of Russet vallat enbraudred with Rooses porteclooses & Sonne beames frengid wth White and grene silke...
> 1588...One ould overworne Chaire of watchet velvet with the seat and the upper parte of the backe wch remayneth laid one wth iij open bone laces of gould...

All these lavish descriptions bring to mind the expensive dresses worn by rich ladies of the time, and many a thrifty housewife saved the fabrics and trimmings from her outmoded dresses for conversion into cushions and upholstery covers.

Simple cloth covered chairs are frequently mentioned in inventories, especially for middle class homes, but surviving upholstery of middling quality is normally of some hard wearing form of needlework, such as tent- or cross-stitch, or turkeywork. Randle Holme illustrated a "...chaire made up by an Imbrautherer..." (Figure 2:135), but survivals of early embroidered covers are very rare. A set of back and seat for a backstool is shown in Figure 2:136. The arms are those of Roger Hill of Pounsford, Somerset, and his second wife Abigail Gurdon, who came of an East Anglian family. The covers were evidently worked for them (or by her), in tent-stitch, some time between their marriage in 1641 and his death in 1655. The covers remained unused until c.1670, the approximate date of the present walnut frame. This and other chairs have an all-over pattern of flowers and stems, and the repertoire of patterns must have related very closely to other contemporary needlework.

One pattern popular over a long period was known as Irish-stitch, but is now better-known as Hungarian point, or flame-stitch (see Figure 3:126):

> 1626...12 high stooles of Irish stitch with buckra covers...
> 4 low stooles of Irish stitch with covers...

Perhaps the most common and consistently popular fabric for chair covers was the ubiquitous turkeywork, also known as settwork, loomwork and carpetwork. This is a pile carpet material, made by knotting and trimming thick woollen threads through a woven canvas backing. The technique was developed in the sixteenth century, in imitation of imported Spanish, Turkish and Middle Eastern rugs. The Turkey Company, and later the Levant Company, imported rugs and carpets after 1580, and these were much admired for use on the floor, on tables and cupboards, and for wall hangings. English turkeywork was thick, tough, warm and hard wearing;

Figure 2:135. *Woodcut illustration from Randle Holme, 'Academie of Armory', probably 1649.*
68: "...This is a chaire made up by an Imbrautherer...of needle or turky worke...Some will say...a Turky worke Chaire...a stoole-chaire, or back stoole..."

Figure 2:136. *Upholders' backstool. English. Cover; tent-stitch, 1641-55. Joined walnut frame, c.1670.*

and mention is made of its use for foot carpets, table carpets, cushions, chair covers and wall hangings. It is often thought that turkeywork was not used for bedcovers or matching bedroom furniture, but at least one reference would seem to deny that conclusion:

1649... my posted settworke bedstead...

It is possible 'settworke' may here refer to another technique altogether — perhaps inlay or marquetry, e.g. an inventory of 1596 describes "a great Dansk chyste with settwourke." This could mean either that the chest was inset with coloured woods, or that it contained items of turkeywork.

Very little is known about the production of turkeywork, though it must have been produced on a widespread scale, on both a professional and an amateur basis. One of the centres of full scale production would appear to have been Norwich, but small factories must have existed in London and elsewhere. It was certainly exported to Scandinavia, Italy, France (*tapis d'Angleterre*) and New England. Some Italian walnut backstools of c.1640, now at Aston Hall, Birmingham, still have their original English turkeywork covers.

Figure 2:137. *Upholders' backstool. English. Cover; turkeywork, dated 1649. Joined oak frame (associated), late seventeenth century.*

Figure 2:139. *Upholders' stool. English. Joined oak frame, with turkeywork cover, c.1640.*

Figure 2:138. *Upholders' backstool. American; probably Boston, Massachusetts. Joined maple and oak frame, with turkeywork cover, c.1690.*

There is evidence to suggest that many ladies must have made turkeywork at home for their own use, or in poorer homes as a form of out-work for sale to merchants and upholsters. It was certainly practised as an aspect of domestic economy in the same way as needleworks, and there are scant references in inventories to looms and knotting frames, as well as mentions in wills to turkeywork panels and covers "of my own making". Likewise, upholsters' bills sometimes refer to the work of covering new chair frames with turkeywork "of your own making". In 1608, the inventory of Hall, a house near Fowey, in Cornwall, included "..one fram for an imbrotherer and a Turkey workeframe..." In the Boston area of Massachusetts, the Business Journal of one Samuel Sewall shows a credit to one of his customers for half a dozen turkey cushions and a carpet, the inference being that she was making them and selling her work to Sewall.[38] Turkeywork chairs were produced in Boston (Figure 2:138), using English or home-produced textiles, and other colonies also favoured the same taste, e.g. in 1657 Theophilus Easton of New Haven Colony owned "...4 high stooles of setwork 26s 8d...2 low stooles setwork 10s..."[39]

In England and Wales there is frequent mention of turkeywork furniture and carpets in inventories and accounts:

1594...six high stooles covered with loome work fringed...

1603...fower and twenty hye joined stooles, covered wth carpet work like the carpets, frynged with crewell...

1614...A cupboard of walnuttre wth a Turkie carpett, the ground redd...

1626...4 Turket carpetts for side cubberds and table...

1683...In ye room over ye Ketching...1 Carbett of turkie worke & 6 chaires of ye same...

1686...a Dozen and ½ of Turkey work chairs...

38. Quoted by Phillip Johnston, *Art in 17th Century New England*, exhibition catalogue, Wadsworth Atheneum, 1977. Source: Linda Baumgarten-Berlekamp, The Textile Trade in Boston, 1650-1700, M.A. Thesis, University of Delaware, 1976.

39. Quoted by Patricia E. Kane, op. cit.

Figure 2:140a. *Upholders' stool. English. Cover; turkeywork, c.1640. Joined oak frame (associated), late-seventeenth century.*

A measure of the contemporary regard for the qualities of turkeywork covers (hard wearing, comfortable, colourful, cheap), may be gained from the inventory of Hampton Court taken after the death of Oliver Cromwell, who was ever sympathetic to the tastes of the thrifty middle classes. He owned 138 pieces of such furniture there, though when he took over from his predecessor Charles I, there had been none at all. Middle class tastes are also reflected in the furnishings of public and semi-public institutions, such as the halls of livery companies, which were often let out for wedding receptions and similar functions. In London, for example, the Pewterers' Company purchased twenty-four chairs and two benches of turkeywork in 1660, from "Mr. Alder, the Upholster", for their hall in Lime Street. Six years later the hall was destroyed in the Great Fire, and in 1671 they bought a further sixteen chairs for the new hall, at a cost of 13s. each. In 1677,

Figure 2:140b. *Stool cover (detail of Figure 2:140a). English. Turkeywork, c.1640.*

furnishing *their* new hall, the Cutlers' Company bought seventeen turkeywork chairs and stools, and a large upholstered couch of the same material.

It is difficult to chart the stylistic development of turkeywork patterns, since very little survives from the sixteenth century, and in the following century very little is actually dated. But, by analogy with dated carpets, a few trends can be discerned. Earlier work, such as the cover of the armchair in Plate Two, usually had a plain background with regular repeats of stylised floral or other elements. This clarity of the individual elements is also seen in the cushion cover of c.1640 (Figure 2:141), and in the earlier needlework cover which follows. The rare dated chair cover of 1649 is at a transitional stage, where the individual floral elements are still fairly distinct, separate and well-formed. After 1660, the patterns become more repetitive and formal, possibly reflecting the introduction of organised production on a factory basis. The designs are confused and closely packed, and great use is made of black backgrounds. The black areas have nearly always suffered from the corrosive effects of the iron dyes, and late seventeenth century work usually has a slightly threadbare appearance because of this.

The angularity of the patterns and designs used in turkeywork is a result of the regular techniques of carpetwork, and is also a feature of Turkish, Persian and other Eastern rugs. Perhaps this quality contributed to the perennial English attraction for such work, and reflects in my earlier comments on the recurrent English regard for surface-pattern based on a grid of dominant verticals and horizontals (see p.120).

The practice of fitting loose covers, or 'cases', to upholstered furniture is an old one. In the sixteenth century and earlier, when valuable items were frequently carried around 'on progress' from one house to another, fine chairs were often supplied with a leather case, in which they would be packed away for the journey. But in more sedentary times, cloth cases were supplied in order to protect the fine fabrics from the effects of wear, grime and sunlight. The two extremes of practice were, on the one hand, to cover fine upholstery with plain cases; and on the other to fit fine cases over plain cloth-upholstered chairs when the occasion demanded. It is often claimed that normal seventeenth century practice was to fit fine cases over plain fixed covers, as in the famous set of twelve gilded dolphin chairs at Ham House (c.1665), whilst in the eighteenth century the reverse practice was followed. However, this is a misleading generalisation, and *both* fashions were used concurrently. At Hatfield Priory in 1626 were *inter alia:*

> 6 high Turkey chaires with buckra covers
> 2 high chaires of black velvet, laced wth covers
> 2 high chaires...embroydered wth cloth of gold, wth covers
> i low chaire of rushorne tawney velvet wth a cotton cover

Out of ninety-six pieces of upholstered furniture listed in the house, eighty-seven have their various covers of baize, cotton or buckram. It is not clear exactly on which occasions the covers would have been used, since even the great brass andirons and other chimney furniture were provided with cotton covers. Presumably these were all protective covers, brought out to cover the furnishings when the family was not in residence, or even when visitors were not expected. Rich covers, conversely, would be taken *off* when the family were away, no doubt for occasional cleaning and repairs, or simply safe storage.

Figure 2:141. *Cushion cover. English. Turkeywork, c.1640.*

Figure 2:142. *Cushion cover. English. Embroidered, wool and silk cross-stitch and long-armed cross-stitch, 1580-1600.*

Figure 2:143. *Leather cover (detail of Figure 2:155). English, c.1680. A typical sample of the thick quality of cowhide used in chair covers in the seventeenth century. The fine condition suggests that this is a piece of Russia leather, and it is fixed to the frame by the standard method of large headed brass nails, supplemented in parts by small headed iron nails.*

Figure 2:144. *Leather cover (detail of 4:245). English; Salisbury, Wiltshire. c.1685. Here the leather cover is partly fragmented, revealing the original stuffing of hay.*

40. Given by John W. Waterer, *Leather in Art, Life and Industry,* Faber & Faber, London, 1946.

Leather Covers

Frequent mention is found of leather covered chairs during the Middle Ages and the sixteenth century, but no English leather chair has survived intact from before 1600, and the vast majority must be dated after 1640. Leather is by far the most common survival of upholstery covers, and this speaks well of contemporary tanning methods. Mature leather seats are as tough and polished as the wood of the frame itself. The best quality chairs were made (or at least covered) by saddlers, but it is not clear which trade was actually responsible for the bulk of ordinary leather upholstery. The frames are always joiner-made, but the covers could be the work of upholders, cordwainers, or even the joiners themselves.

During the reign of Elizabeth I, a simple leather backstool became popular, based on a Continental type, and this pattern remained in common production throughout the seventeenth century and later (Figures 2:147-152). A great many have survived, owing to their sturdy construction and the fine tanning of the leather. Other variants include stools, armchairs and settles, and they were mainly to be found in the middle class homes of

Figure 2:145. *Under view of leather backstool. English, c.1680. The original canvas webbing remains under the seat.*

practical-minded yeomen and small merchants. A great many still have their original webbing and padding, the latter usually consisting of some natural material such as grass, hay or straw. The padding of the seat had a tendency to move about in use, so this was often secured by the simple expedient of sewing with strong thread through the seat and webbing. The resulting square or oval patch of stitching has the effect of tightening and quilting the seat, and may be seen most clearly in Figure 2:149.

Many inventories refer to such chairs as being covered with 'Russia' leather. Unfortunately there were many cheaper imitations of a more perishable nature, but real Russia leather was known for its qualities of suppleness and strength, its agreeable aromatic odour, and its resistance to insects and vermin. Russia leather was made from calf or cowhide, to a recipe said to have originated among the Tartars and imported by the Muscovy Company.

The method of production[40] was complicated, but produced a leather which improved in use. Many early pieces have outlasted inferior leathers

produced in the nineteenth century and even later. The raw hide was first steeped in a bath of rye or oat flour and yeast. This was washed off with running river water, and the hide again steeped in a liquor of willow or poplar bark. This was again washed out, and the surplus moisture was slicked out with smooth stones or rubbers. While the leather was still damp, a mixture of birch tar oil and seal oil was pummelled into the flesh side (or

Figure 2:146. *Joined leather stool. English. Beech frame, c.1700.*

Figure 2:148. *Joined leather backstool. English. Oak frame, c.1680.*

Figure 2:147. *Joined leather backstool. English. Oak frame, mid-seventeenth century.*

Plate Eight. *(Above) Boarded chest, or standard. English. Oak, painted with colours, 1340-45. Made for Richard de Bury, Bishop of Durham. The chest was originally painted all over the front, sides and lid, but now only the under surface of the lid is in anything like original condition. The painting was executed in a mixture of oil and tempera onto a ground of gesso, traces of which are found all over the wooden surface (see Figure 2:107).*

Plate Eight. *(Below) Joined chest. English; Dorset. Oak, stained with colours, 1650-55. The decoration of this chest is typical of a small group of chests and boxes from Dorset, some dated early in the 1650s. The designs are drawn out with a thinly incised V-gouge line, and the spaces coloured with a thin paint or stain. The red and blue-black stains are used only for accent, and much of the wood was left uncoloured. There seems in addition to be a thin original coat of clear varnish. The items displayed on the chest are all painted in various colours, and the red box may be seen in greater detail in Figure 2:227.*

Figure 2:149. *Joined leather backstool. English. Oak frame, c.1680.*

Figure 2:150. *Joined leather backstool. American; probably Boston, Massachusetts. Hard maple and oak frame, c.1680.*

Figure 2:151. *Joined leather backstool. American; probably Boston, Massachusetts. Maple and oak frame, 1680-1720.*

Figure 2:152. *Joined leather backstool. English. Oak frame, c.1680. Part of a set with the armchair right.*

Figure 2:153. *Joined leather armchair. English. Oak frame, c.1680. Part of a set with the backstool left. It is most unusual to see an English chair of any sort with turnings to the rear legs.*

Figure 2:154. *Joined leather armchair. English. Oak frame, c.1680.*

Figure 2:155. *Joined leather armchair. English. Oak frame, c.1680.*

sometimes both sides). A characteristic diaper pattern was produced by pressing the surface with a textured wood block whilst still damp. The most popular colours were brown, red, green and yellow, and the various colours were produced by dyeing with a mixture of brazil wood chips and such agents as cochineal, alkanet and santalred. Most old leathers are now patinated to varied tones of reddish-brown and black, with gradations similar to the patination of wood itself. No doubt, the methods of producing Russia leather varied greatly, but the best leather chairs were always qualified with the epithet 'Russia':

> 1672... foure Russia lather chaires...
> 1688... 6 new Rushey lether chairs...

The diaper was not the only pattern tooled into the surface of leather upholstery. Following Spanish practice, many patterns and symbols were punched with gilded stamps, though probably not to the same extent as on book bindings. Leather was also embossed and painted (following a Dutch fashion in wall hangings and carpets), and English examples survive from the late seventeenth century (Figure 3:62), but nothing now survives to compare with the following suite, owned by the Earl of Northampton:

> 1614... A cowche of crimson lether printed borderwise with silver and golde, one longe and two shorte (cushions) sutable to the same lined with hayre coloured velvett, and laced about with gold lace...

Figure 2:156. *Joined leather settle. English. Oak frame, c.1680. The adjustable side-flaps let down on iron ratchets.*

Figure 2:157. *Joined leather settle. American; Pennsylvania. Walnut frame, early eighteenth century. The back is covered with a single great piece of cowhide.*

AT the Old Collier *and* Cart, at Fleet-Ditch, *near* Holborn-Bridge, *Are good Coals, Deals, Wainſcote and Beach,* &c. ſold at reaſonable Rates, by John Edwards.

Figure 2:158. *Woodcut trade label. English, c.1700 (this specimen dated 1717 by hand, in use as a bill head). The range of goods supplied by John Edwards included prepared timbers.*

viii). Trade Alliances in the Eighteenth Century (The Rise of the Cabinetmaker/Upholsterer)

With the decline of the trade companies, the control of quality and standards passed into the hands of the new firms of 'Joiners and Cabinetmakers', and indeed of their patrons themselves. Although they were chiefly concerned with the following of new fashions, firstly in walnut (1660-1750), and then in mahogany (post-1725), they continued to advertise a wide range of domestic furniture in imported wainscot oak. In London and other major cities, these products were aimed chiefly at the middle classes, and for secondary and servants' rooms in wealthier houses.

By the middle of the eighteenth century, the term 'joiner' was completely superseded in fashionable circles, and many firms preferred to advertise themselves as 'Cabinet-makers and Upholsterers' in recognition of the increasing use of fabrics and upholstery in interior decoration and furniture. By thus combining, the two trades were able to offer a complete decorating and furnishing service from the one business. Many firms took under their wings a host of different trades, which in earlier days had valued their independence. Trade cards and makers' labels of the eighteenth century chart these new combinations, which commonly include joiner, carpenter, cabinetmaker, upholsterer, appraiser and undertaker (the last three being traditional aspects of the upholder's trade). Specific typical examples include:

c.1760... Henry Sidgier. Carpenter, Joyner, and Undertaker...Buys, Sells and Appraises all sorts of Household Goods, Pictures, China, &c. Likewise Cabinet and Upholsterers Work done, and Funerals Perform'd. NB, All sorts of Boxes & Packing Cases made.

1792... Robert Burr, Upholder, Cabinet-maker, Appraiser & Auctioneer... Funerals furnished.

140

Figure 2:159. *Joined chest. English. Oak, 1660-1720. A plain and workmanlike piece, of interest chiefly for the trade label of William Roper, of Cambridge, which is to be found glued under the lid.*

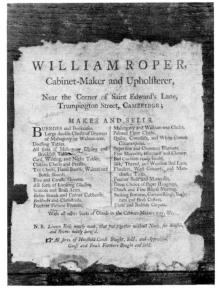

Figure 2:160. *Trade label. English, c.1760. Fixed under the lid of the chest in Figure 2:159.*

41. Quoted by R.W. Symonds, Antique Collector, January-February, 1948.
42. I am grateful to Robert Williams of Cambridge, for bringing this chest to my attention, and supplying the photographs.

At least one upholsterer advertised himself incongruously as a supplier of: "...organs, harpsichords and piano fortes. N.B.Dealer in coals..." Coals are among the stock-in-trade of the timberman John Edwards, whose bill heading of 1717 is shown here (Figure 2:158). He was presumably in the business of supplying timber to joiners and cabinetmakers. A list of the more common timbers in use later in the century is given in a book of 1796,[41] *Planting and Rural Ornament,* where it is noted that:

> The *cabinetmakers'* chief woods are MAHOGANY and BEECH: next to these follow DUTCH OAK (Wainscot), DEAL, ELM; and lastly WALNUTTREE, CHERRYTREE, PLUMTREE, BOX, HOLLY, YEW, and a variety of woods for inlaying of cabinets. In some country places, a considerable quantity of ENGLISH OAK is worked up into tables, chairs, drawers, and bedsteads.

Although oak furniture continued in common production during the eighteenth century, it is most unusual to find a trade label attached to a piece of joined oak furniture (other than depository tickets or dealers' labels of 1850-1950). The simple chest in Figure 2:159 is an exception. The label, glued under the lid, advertises the business of one William Roper, a cabinetmaker and upholsterer of Trumpington Street, Cambridge.[42] Roper had premises in this street from 1733-76, and in St. Edward's Lane from 1753-76. He died in 1783, and it seems likely that the label dates from about 1755-65. Another joiner named Edward Yorke set up shop in Trumpington Street in about 1755, and Roper may have had the label printed to differentiate this new business from his own.

It has been suggested that Roper was perhaps the maker of the chest, since such labels were in common use by box makers etc., and the label does list "clothes chests" among the range of wares; but another interpretation seems more likely. The chest, from its appearance and construction, would seem to date from 1660-1720. It is impossible with such a plain item to propose a closer dating, but such a piece can surely not have been made in Southern England as late as 1750. Also, whereas Roper specifically advertises his walnut and mahogany furniture, he does not mention wainscot, as do other cabinetmakers of the time.

Perhaps we should interpret Roper's description of himself as an upholsterer more literally within the broader traditional meaning of a secondhand dealer. No doubt the chest was acquired by him in the course of his trade, perhaps in part-exchange for new goods, and the label affixed by way of advertisement.

ix). Related Trades

A variety of tradesmen supplied essential goods and services to the furniture makers, but the most important are obviously those connected with the supply of raw materials and parts, in the form of timber and hardware.

Timber Preparation

Though we have noted that some customers supplied their own materials, many woodworkers kept large and sufficient stocks of prepared timbers for their foreseeable needs, and their wills often contain brief details of the timbers they held:

> 1585...all my boards, quarters and timber...
> 1587...all my timber, oak, ash, seasoned and unseasoned...
> 1588...my timber rough and wrought and made ware...
> 1592...my plank boards and joiner's stuff...
> 1608...plancks & tymber & wodd of all sorts...
> 1668...Item, Timber in his house and abroad...

Country craftsmen were able to buy their timber from their neighbours, while it was still standing. This doubtless made a good bargain for the buyer, but it demanded great insight and experience to predict the quality of timber before it was cut and seasoned. Perhaps the greatest gain for the joiner was the continuity of his involvement with his materials.

Edward Bickerton (Appendix IV) owned a good deal of timber "in his house and abroad", and some of the latter was no doubt still standing afield at his death, awaiting his instructions to the sawyer. In the larger towns, the sawyers found enough work locally to keep them in business, but in country areas they were an itinerant breed of men, travelling in pairs from job to job. Their task was the preparation of the felled timber, and no doubt some of the felling itself.

The differing characteristics of timbers, as well as the vagaries of individual trees, allow a variety of conversion techniques. The most common of these was to saw the log into appropriate scantlings with the great two handled pit-saw; but certain timbers (and oak in particular) will split readily down the line of the grain, and these allow the technique known as riving. Oak will split easily along the radius of the log, and the first action of the river is to hammer an iron wedge into this line, using a shaped wooden mallet known as a 'beetle'. A wooden handle is then inserted into the socket of the wedge, and the log is split open using the handle as a lever. A straight and even-grained log of wainscot oak can be converted into a series of extremely thin and wide boards, and these are ideal for panel stuff. Such boards show the beauty of the silvery 'figure' of oak to its best advantage, and were consequently highly-valued for this quality. Since they are formed from radial fissures, the individual riven boards are tapered in thickness from the outer to the inner edges, and this is often apparent in the finished work (e.g. see Chapter Three — the ark). Another characteristic of riven timber is its distinctive surface, in which the cleft grain may stand out in small ridges, and the surface will undulate gently in following the line of the grain. This is evident only on the rear and under surfaces of early work, since show-surfaces are normally finished smooth (Diagram 2:22a).

The marks of the pit-saw are likewise very distinctive and familiar to anyone who takes the trouble to inspect the rear surfaces of period furniture. They show a great variety in the depth and angle of the saw cut, unlike the regular and monotonous pattern left by a vertical machine-saw, in which the same cut is repeated every inch or so; or the regular curved line of the circular saw.

Pit-sawing is a filthy, strenuous and difficult job. Even so, it continued as the most commo method in English lumber yards until the second half of the last century. In Europe and America, water- and steam-powered sawmills were developed rather earlier. Industrial mechanical sawmills had been set up in Europe before 1500, but in England the pit-sawyers resisted the setting-up of mechanical mills until after 1800. In 1761, the Royal Society of Arts had presented a prize of £300 to one James Stanfield for the design of a mill which he had erected in Yorkshire. This was powered by a

Diagram 2:22. *Methods of converting logs into planks.*
a). *Most timbers will rive or cleave quite easily down the grain, and this tendency will allow the timberman to split the log into planks of tapering thickness. Oak splits most easily along the radius of the log, so a wedge may be driven in along this line and the plank cleaves off like a slice of cake.*
b). *The simplest way to saw a log into planks is merely to start at one side and saw in progressive parallel cuts until the log is finished; this process is known as slash-sawing or straight-sawing. In practice, the log is roughly squared first. Planks from near the centre of the log may be of very good quality, but those from the edges are prone to warpage on drying (see d below).*
c). *The best way to produce sound planks is the process known as quarter-sawing. All the planks are thus cut as nearly as possible from the radius of the log. This is somewhat wasteful of a certain volume of timber, but both riven and quarter-sawn planks have two prime advantages over straight-sawn planks; they are resistant to warpage, and the medullary rays appear in profusion at the surface, producing a strong and attractive figure.*
d). *In straight-sawn planks the annual rings lie roughly across the width of the plank. In drying out (seasoning) the rings attempt to pull themselves straight, causing the plank to warp. The average shrinkage in oak is five to eight per cent.*
e). *In quarter-sawn and riven planks the annual rings lie across the thickness of the plank. In seasoning the plank loses some weight and size, but there is no tendency to warp.*

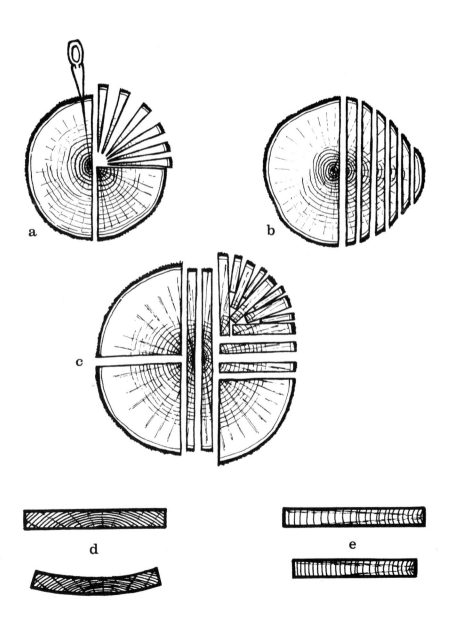

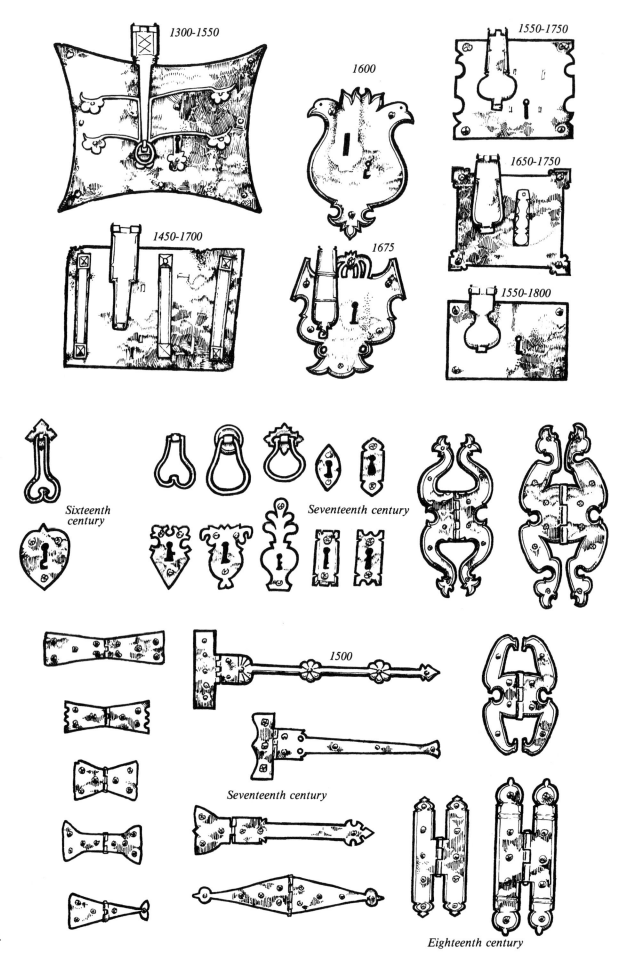

1300-1550

1600

1550-1750

1650-1750

1450-1700

1675

1550-1800

Sixteenth century

Seventeenth century

1500

Seventeenth century

Eighteenth century

144

water wheel, driving three frame-saws. Within a few years powered sawmills became a little more common, but like their brethren in the textile trades, the sawyers opposed the introduction of machinery for many years, fearing unemployment and loss of status.

The more responsible and experienced member of the pair of pit-sawyers was the 'top-sawyer', who positioned himself on top of the log. The 'bottom-sawyer' stood in the pit beneath the log, and his job was simply to provide the brawn and impetus for the down-stroke. The top-sawyer was responsible for guiding the saw, and thus ensuring the accuracy and regularity of the work. Most timber was converted into standard scantlings, such as ½-inch, 1-inch or 1½inch boards; 2-inch or 4-inch square-section; 1 by 3, 2 by 4, etc., etc. Many sizes were standardised under local guild regulations, and this can be confirmed by measuring extant work (allowing a certain tolerance for inaccuracies, planing and shrinkage).

The simplest and least wasteful approach to the sawing of planks is that known as slash- or straight-sawing (Diagram 2:22b), though this has certain inherent disadvantages. By this method the log is cut into vertical planks, working straight through from one side to the other. This wastes very little timber, but the outer planks have an unfortunate tendency to warp on drying (Diagram 2:22d). Only the centre plank avoids this defect completely, since the annual rings are at right angles to its surface. In order to retain this faculty, *all* the planks should be cut in this same direction. This can be done by 'quarter-sawing' the log.

Using this technique, the log is first cut down the centre (one or two wide boards can be cut at the same time), and then into quarters. Each quarter is dissected in such a manner that the planks follow the radius of the log (Diagram 2:22c). This is obviously a wasteful process, but quarter-sawn timber has a number of worthwhile properties, in common with riven boards. In practical terms, they have the mechanical advantages of resistance to warping, and the surfaces are more resistant to weathering than straight-sawn timber.

But the most obvious bonus is an aesthetic feature. Many timbers have a system of medullary rays which radiate out from the centre of the log (Diagram 2:25). Quarter-sawn and riven timber allows these rays to be fully exposed at the surface, in a very attractive manner. This is especially true of oak, in which the large, meandering rays appear as a silvery flickering 'figure' across the surface, a random feature which was much appreciated in the new timber, and is still highly valued in a patinated state. But other woods also have their figure, though on a smaller scale than oak. In most timbers the rays appear as fine shimmering flecks in the surface. They are a particular feature of the fruitwoods, especially cherry, but may also be seen to advantage in birch, beech and elm. Quarter-cut elm is extremely rare, but when it *is* found it presents a most attractive surface.

During the preparations for building a great house, the timber was chosen whilst still standing, and great occasion was sometimes made of ''choosing the Trees'' or ''veweinge of Timber'' by the chief carpenter.[43] Architectural timbers were often used in the green state, since they were easier to work, and subsequent shrinkage had little effect on the structure; but timber for furniture, floors, panelling, etc. had to be properly seasoned after the sawyer had done his job. Ideally, the logs or cut planks are first immersed for a time in running water, in order to wash out the acid sap. The planks are finally stacked in an open-sided shed, supported with battens between them, so that they may dry naturally. This process, still in common use today, was referred to in a letter of 1547[44] by Sir John Thynne (the builder of Longleat), when he ordered that the planks for his house should be ''laid

Diagram 2:23. *Wrought iron furniture hardware. A huge variety of original iron fittings are encountered on early furniture, and only the more usual varieties are shown here, from various dates. Lock-plates and hasps, key escutcheons, handles and hinges are the most common features, and some chests may have decorative bands for extra strength. It is difficult to determine how ironwork was originally finished, but most items were probably either polished bright, with a varnished or tinned finish, or else blackened.*

Fashions in ironwork changed very slowly, and most of these shapes appeared over a very long span of time.

43. See Malcolm Airs, op. cit., p.111.
44. Ibid, p.109.

Figure 2:161. *Wrought iron strap-hinge (from the spice chest in Figure 3:298). English, c.1670. Note the pitted and polished surface which is typical of iron fittings of this age. The hinge is held in place with three hand-made nails, and the lack of marks in the surrounding wood suggests that it has not been moved or altered.*

up drye with stikks betweene it so that it may season the better". He was much concerned that his timbers should be well-prepared, and only three days previously he had instructed his steward to be sure that "there be plancks sawen for my dores so that they may be seasoned in tyme". Like most patrons of his time, Thynne held his craftsmen responsible for the quality of the material they used, and he wrote of his joiners that if he should "finde any faut with the workmanship or the seasoning of their stuf they shall make it agayn".[45] The artificial drying of timber in a kiln or oven was also experimented with at an early date (for example at Kenilworth in 1571),[46] but this sophisticated procedure was not fully developed until modern times.

Hardware

One supply which no joiner or carpenter could manage without, was that of metal hardware and nails. Even though it is not desirable to use iron nails in the *construction* of oak furniture, it is impossible to avoid the use of locks, handles and hinges on almost every sort of chest, box, cupboard and folding table; and such hardware is always fixed with iron nails.

The huge variety of iron fittings were made and supplied, wrought on the anvil, by blacksmiths. There is also a good deal of evidence that furniture fittings were supplied by whitesmiths, with a bright tinned finish. This polished finish has almost always worn off, but where it does remain (e.g. inside chests or cupboards), the corroded layer of tin shows up clearly as a thin grey layer, like a coat of grey paint. Where original iron fittings are present, their condition should reflect the state of the surrounding wood. On patinated surfaces, the iron will be a rich glossy black, usually surrounded by a black patch of acid stain in the wood. On dry inside surfaces, the iron may be pale and dry, or lightly tinged with rust. Where the wood is heavily worn and weathered, the iron will be corroded and pitted with rust. Hinges and other moving parts will often have a light powdering of rust around the pivot barrel.

The presence of original ironwork on furniture is always interesting and important. Quite often, of course, iron fittings have had to be replaced because of past wear or breakage. There exists a bill of 1760 from Eliakim Smith (a joiner of Hadley, Connecticut), to one John Eastman, for making

45. Ibid.
46. Ibid.

146

"a pair of aiches for your bofet".[47] Such repairs must have been a common occurrence in more robust times, and are not always to be sneered at.

The nails used to secure iron (and sometimes brass) fittings are always the old hand-made type, which are now usually referred to as 'rose-head' nails. They were made with a series of hammer blows on the head, whilst the shank was held firmly in a special vice, and so the faceted heads are very irregular. No two nails are ever quite the same shape and size. Figure 2:161 shows three such nails holding a small strap-hinge on a spice cupboard of c.1670.

The form and decoration of wrought iron furniture fittings (Diagram 2:23) show many variations in detail, but general principles are few. The poorest are simply cut from flat plate and nailed roughly into place; the best are cut to complex fretted shapes, and are finely finished with filed chamfered edges and highlights, and sometimes stamped patterns. In the best work, the ironwork is also cut to fit in with carved or other decorative schemes in the woodwork, but inferior locks and hinges may often be found nailed over the carving in complete disregard.

The use of brass and gilt bronze hardware did not become popular in Britain until after the Restoration, though it may occasionally be found at an earlier date. In particular, early coffermakers' chairs often had fine gilt bronze and enamelled finials, and upholstered chairs of all sorts are usually finished with brass nails. But the use of brass drawer handles did not become common until the second half of the seventeenth century. The popularity of brass mounts seems to have originated with the import of Chinese lacquer cabinets early in the century, and by 1700 brass fittings were universal on cabinets and chests of drawers (where they are still most commonly to be seen).

Diagram 2:24. *Brass furniture hardware. Brass fittings are first found in the early part of the seventeenth century with the vogue for japanned furniture, but it was not until after 1660 that English-made brasses appeared in any quantities on walnut and veneered furniture. The mass-produced fittings were bought by joiners and cabinet-makers alike, so the same patterns may appear on furniture of widely differing qualities. Polished brass is particularly attractive against dark patinated oak, but original brasses are not encountered as often as one would like.*

47. Quoted by Rev. C.F. Luther, Antiques Magazine, September, 1929.

The metal, in its various forms, very quickly became popular; largely because of its attractive colour, and because it is soft and easily worked. It may be both cast and forged with ease, and may be chiselled with further decoration (chased), and polished to a bright surface. Two distinct trades were involved in bronze- and brass-working: the Founders, who made objects by casting metal into moulds; and the Braziers, whose work was carried out with hammer and forge. London still has an independent Founders' Company, but the Braziers were amalgamated with the Armourers in 1708.

Most brass furniture hardware was made by casting (Diagram 2:24), and the best items were then gilded. Cheaper versions were usually given a coat of clear lacquer or varnish, which might be tinted with an infusion of gamboge, alkanet, turmeric or saffron. The gilding or lacquer is now usually worn away with age and polishing, so that the exposed surfaces may be patinated to a greater or lesser degree. In the early part of the eighteenth century, brass industries were established in the Bristol area for the manufacture of furniture parts, candlesticks, etc., but they were soon eclipsed by the rise of Birmingham as a national centre of production. Fashions for brass handles and accessories followed thick and fast during the eighteenth century, particularly on fine walnut and mahogany case furniture, and most of these trends are reflected in the hardware to be found on their oak counterparts; whether these be country-made in English oak, or the secondary products of the cabinetmaker using imported wainscot oak.

MATERIALS USED IN CONSTRUCTION

Although household furniture may logically be constructed in almost *any* rigid or semi-rigid material (timber, stone, slate, marble, bone, ivory, metals, terracotta, bamboo, woven sticks, etc.), the vast bulk of English furniture has always been made of timber. The reasons for this are manifold, but the basic factor is the climate of these islands. On the one hand, the climate and soils are ideal for a profuse natural growth of fine timber trees; and on the other, the coolness of the climate generally inhibits the use of materials which are too cold to the touch.

The last factor effectively eliminates stone, marble and metals, all of which are found more commonly in Southern Europe. This is not to say that such furniture was unknown here. Early accounts frequently mention stone and marble furniture in rich households of the British Isles, but these were mainly provided for display. Indeed, there are even a few survivals, chiefly in the form of fixed thrones, wall benches, table tops and table supports (such as the Hexham 'frith-stool', and the fourteenth century fragments of a table excavated at Westminster Hall). Two oak-framed tables of c.1600, bearing thick tops of local granite, are in the collection at Trinity Hall, Aberdeen; and two stone pedestal tables of 1540 still occupy their original positions in tower rooms at Lacock Abbey. The most remarkable record of a single collection of marble-topped tables is the series of fourteen coloured drawings included in the Lumley Inventory of 1590. These were drawn and recorded by Lord Lumley's steward, John Lambton, in the course of an inventory of the contents of Nonesuch Palace, Lumley Castle, and two other Lumley houses at Stansted and Tower Hill.[48] Fine table tops of inlaid marble (*pietre dure*) and scagliola were imported from Florence and Rome to be borne on English frames, such as the fine example of c.1600 at Aston Hall, Birmingham. It is not until after 1700 that marble tops became common in England, and then not in vernacular furniture.

48. cf. Lionel Cust, transactions of The Walpole Society, Vol. VI.

1588... a square table layd in wth marble stone standing upon a
frame...

1592... a table made of a solid piece of black touchstone,
fourteen spans long, seven wide, and one span thick...

1614... a table of red coral (and watered marble, set in wood)
on the four sides of which are these sentences 'Virtutis
Laus Actio', 'Omnis Sapienta A Deo', 'Industriae
Formes Praemium', 'Regina Rerum Sapienta'...

English inventories frequently mention an item of equipment referred to
as an 'oyster table'. These were used in the parlour for the preparation and
eating of oysters, an everyday food in the seventeenth century. They are
never described in detail, but the tops were apparently of some water-
resistant material such as stone, slate or metal. Such tops would also be
useful for the preparation of the new hot beverages (tea, coffee and
chocolate), or for use as washstands after meals:

1600... An oyster Table lyinge upon a frame...

1641... an oke table covered with letaine (i.e. latten, or
brass)...

1688... one little table tinned over...

Iron and other metal-framed furniture (especially thrones and folding
stools) are noted in medieval accounts, but no English example would seem
to have survived. Likewise, there are no counterparts to the Northern
European habit of using large stoves made from terracotta or faience tiles,
frequently with integral seats and sleeping platforms. This is a surprising
omission in view of the recorded severity of occasional English winters, and
the complaints of discomfort to be found in the literature of the period. It
would seem that the English were never quite desperate enough to resort to
such expedients.

Timbers

The deciduous woodlands of medieval and Tudor England were the most
important of her natural resources. Wood for fuel and building materials
had been of increasing importance even in Saxon times, but the medieval
economy became heavily dependent on timber both as a source of domestic
and industrial energy, and as the raw material for buildings, furniture,
carts, bridges, ships and implements. The vast majority of town and
country houses and cottages were built of some form of timber frame, even
in areas rich in fine building stone, such as Gloucestershire,
Northamptonshire and Derbyshire. The only structures habitually built of
stone were those which survive today: churches, fortifications, castles, great
country houses, rich manors, the better town houses and major bridges.
Most towns, even as late as 1700, still consisted predominantly of thatched
box-frame buildings. Many of these towns were burnt in disastrous fires
during the course of the seventeenth century, which prompted their
reconstruction in stone or brick and tile. Individual timber structures still
survive in huge numbers behind the fashionable brick or stone facades
which updated them in Georgian taste only superficially.

Throughout the Middle Ages and later, the most popular and plentiful of
timbers was the native English oak. A wide variety of hardwoods was
available in England, but oak was the most highly regarded despite its
inherent disadvantages. There are instances of other woods being used in
building (notably chestnut, walnut, elm, ash, maple and pine, as well as
inferior timbers such as beech, willow, elder and sallow), but oak was

consistently preferred for its strength and durability, and in view of its great abundance. Most of the great forests were overwhelmingly of oak, and for hundreds of years these reserves were raided and diminished by the huge demand for timber supplies. Little thought was given to the need for conserving or replacing the slow-growing trees. Almost the only motive which inspired any thoughts of woodland conservation was a concern for the welfare of the chase, and the needs of game animals. Care was taken to preserve and control woodland cover in the many Royal and private hunting parks.

By 1500 a start had been made in forest husbandry by the development of a system known as 'coppice with standards'. By this method, the number of oak 'standards' was controlled (limited by law to twelve per acre in 1544). This allowed each tree to spread and grow in a healthy space, and the area beneath was planted with hazel 'coppice', from which hazel rods could be harvested for a number of purposes, especially basket and hurdle making.

But such thoughtful and effective therapy was too sporadic and belated to prevent the 'timber famine' which began to affect certain parts of the country during the course of the sixteenth century. Much has been made of the effects of such shortages, by both contemporary and modern writers, but the chief difficulties seem to have been fairly localised. A dearth of timber is first noted in Suffolk soon after 1500, yet many vestiges of the ancient oak forest were still virtually untouched in 1580 elsewhere in England. The Weald, Epping, Selwood, Sherwood, Dean, Arden and the New Forest still remained along with other smaller stands; but other areas less heavily blessed with woodland were beginning to feel the pinch. The four main reasons for the growing shortages were seen by contemporaries to be: the extravagant use of timber in buildings; the growth of the Navy and the mercantile marine; the prodigal consumption of firewood in emergent industries such as glass and iron production; and the spread of sheep farming with the consequent demand for pasture.

In his *Description of England* (see Appendix I), William Harrison estimated that in ten years of recent building, the English had used more oak than in the previous century. He ridiculed the wasteful amounts of timber used by the builders around him, and his feelings were echoed in 1618 by Robert Reyce, who complained of the "...carelesse wast of this age of our wonted plenty of timber..." Harrison also lamented the use of native timber in smelting products which could more cheaply be obtained from abroad; "...manie needfull commodities...are perfected with great cost (which may) with farre more ease and lesse cost be provided from other countries. I will not speake of iron, glasse and such like, which spoil much wood, and yet are brought from the other countries better cheepe than we can make them here at home..." The same sentiment was expressed by Thomas Fuller in an elegy to the native timbers sacrificed as fuel for smelting:

> Jove's oak, the warlike ash, veined elm, the softer beech,
> Short hazel, maple plain, light asp, the bending wych,
> Tough holly and smooth birch, must altogether burn,
> What should the builder serve, supplies the forger's turn.

Harrison's experience was particularly of Essex and the Home Counties, but elsewhere similar problems are seen. The matter was particularly acute in areas of traditional shortage, such as the Fens and Cornwall, but complaints may also be noted in Yorkshire, Lancashire, Wiltshire, East Anglia and the Weald. The latter seems a surprising case, but in 1607 John Norden felt moved to note depletions of Wealden timber, largely consumed in local glass production and iron smelting. Builders' accounts of the sixteenth and early seventeenth centuries frequently itemise the need to transport timber from a great distance for their projects.[49] It is not uncommon to find that timber was brought from sources up to thirty miles away or more, and sometimes secondhand timbers were used from earlier houses or barns. Re-used timbers are of course extremely common in lower class houses, and in less important parts of grander structures (though it is important to scotch all the old tales about re-used ships' timbers). Re-used timber is also occasionally found in furniture, but it is less clear here whether the motive is a shortage of new timber, or the cheapness of used materials.

At Plymouth, shortages due to the local ship building industry led to timber being imported from Ireland for the building of the Guildhall. But there is a long history of timber imports into England, and much of this was done from choice, and not in response to shortages. Pines and deals were imported from a very early date, especially large Baltic planks, and oak from the same area was highly valued (see Wainscot pp.155).

It is extremely difficult to assess accurately the effect of timber shortages on current furniture design, if any. It has often been said that a scarcity of timber, and the unquestionable rise in timber prices which followed, must have led to an increasing economy and thrift in the use of timber in furniture. This should be evidenced by corresponding perceptible changes in furniture design at the period in which these strictures were having their effect. Yet this is not the case. There is *no* apparent decrease in the lavish use of timber in the period 1580-1630, and indeed there was a tremendous *increase* in the volume of furniture production in these years, reflecting a rising prosperity and confidence among the middle classes. Such economies are not even suggested until the *end* of the seventeenth century, when timbers of lighter scantling come into play; but even then it is not clear whether the reasons for such changes are continuing timber shortages, or the mere vagaries of fashion in demanding furniture of greater flexibility and lightness.

Although it is customary to regard oak as the chief furniture timber of the medieval and post-medieval periods, that is until walnut (after 1660) and mahogany (after 1725) supplanted it as the more fashionable materials, it would be a mistake to assume that it was the only timber in use before 1660, or indeed that walnut and mahogany caused any appreciable decline in the proportion of oak furniture which continued to be made in their heyday. Rather, the popularity of oak furniture seems to have been a constant factor amongst the broad middle classes well into the nineteenth century. It is the more modish woods which suffer the aberrations of fashion, apparently in cycles of sixty to eighty years (during the second quarter of the eighteenth century, walnut and mahogany were equally popular, though mahogany has survived more completely from this period).

It is difficult to gain an accurate assessment of the relative popularity and proportion of the various timbers in use at different periods in the British Isles and the Colonies. Survivals are misleading, since they tend to represent only the most durable woods, or in some part the most valued by later generations (and therefore artificially preserved). Contemporary descriptions are similarly misleading, since they often single out for mention items which were unusual or novel, and therefore remarkable; whilst the commonplace often passed by unremarked into oblivion. Probate inventories and other accounts do not often mention the material from which furniture is made, especially in poorer homes, and the writers were rarely explicit, observant, or even literate. We may assume that where the

49. Malcolm Airs, op. cit.

wood *is* mentioned, this is either because the appraiser is particularly conscientious in his work, or the wood is unusual enough to attract his attention. Mentions of oak and wainscot are no doubt due to the former, but walnut and marquetry are often cited out of respect for the high quality and value which they imply.

Contemporary names for timbers occasionally differ from modern practice, and we can often make only an educated guess at the identity of such woods as Spanish wood, Norway timber, Jamaica wood, bois d'Ollande, bois d'Irlande, etc. The term 'wainscot' was often wrongly applied to English oak, since an imported timber would imply a superior product to the contemporary mind. As for the new woods imported from the New World, or used *in situ* by the settlers; some of these retained their native names in an anglicised form; others were named after their actual or supposed places of origin; whilst others were dubbed with familiar names on the grounds of the slightest resemblance of grain or colour to the oak, ash, cedar or pine of home, so that some American versions of English timbers are actually different species. Nevertheless, it is their aspect to the contemporary craftsman which must concern us here.

The timbers described in the following classification are only the more common varieties likely to be met with in practice or reference. Others were used, including further varieties of those given. It is often impossible to distinguish the actual species in use. An ability to recognise the respective timbers in their patinated state, inclusive of minor variations, can only come with experience and familiarity. The collector is urged to see and feel as many timbers as possible, and under a variety of conditions, since no

Diagram 2:25. *Cross-section of an oak tree. This is a section from a tree of slightly uneven growth, of about forty years old. The bark is the crusty outer layer beneath which the year's growth takes place. The young wood appears as a fairly narrow pale band of sapwood under the bark, enclosing the darker mature heartwood. The annual rings are revealed as a series of concentric lines with a pithy centre. The medullary rays lie at right angles to the annual rings and radiate out from the centre of the log. Where the rays emerge at a shallow angle to the cut surface of the plank, they provide the flecked silvery 'figure' which is so distinctive in oak, being larger and more pronounced than other timbers.*

written description can substitute for handling the real thing. Confusion can arise at several levels, and woods are not always easy to identify since grain patterns can vary even within species, especially when obscured by thick patination or paint. More especially, oak can be confused with chestnut or ash; walnut with chestnut; ash with hickory; sycamore with maple; yew with cedar; cedar with cypress; and the oaks, deals and fruitwoods bear close family resemblances within their groups.

The various cuts of timber reveal different grain patterns and figures, but the most decorative and sought after are the burrs and pollards. A burr is an excrescent growth rising in a mound from the surface of a tree, and usually results from disease or injury. Burrs can be extremely large on old trees, up to four feet or more across. They are likely to form on almost any species of tree, but are especially favoured on oak, walnut, elm, maple and yew. When sliced through, the pattern revealed is a contorted mass of curled knots and swirls, like a slice through an old tobacco-plug. The tight grain takes a high polish, and the resulting surface is the richest and most varied of all. Pollarded wood produces a similar result, though in this case the method of production is artificial. The crown and top branches of the young tree are removed, leaving the stem intact. Thereafter, the young shooting branches are trimmed away from the top after each growing season, until eventually a large club-shaped mass is produced. Like the burr, this can be sliced through and the resulting timber used in the solid or as a veneer. Years ago these knotty figures were referred to aptly and affectionately as 'plum-pudding.'

Another (rarely used) method of producing a rich and interesting surface was to compress a mass of wood shavings and glue into a block. This could then be turned in the solid as a pillar or spindle, or it could be sliced for use in veneer or inlay. When the wood and glue were stained in different colours, it seems to have been known as 'marblewood', and must have been very striking when new as indeed it is when patinated. It is worth looking very closely to distinguish marblewood from burr or pollard.

A Classification of Timbers (in common use in the British Isles and Colonies before c.1750)

All timbers are classified botanically under two basic categories: the hardwoods, and the softwoods. This distinction bears no relation to their hardness or softness in use, merely to their botanical form. The hardwoods are by far the largest group, and consist of the broad-leaved deciduous trees which replace their leaves annually. The softwoods are the conifers, most of which have leaves in the form of evergreen needles. Wood has a cellular structure which grows by creating a new layer under the bark during each successive year, so that the trunk thickens with age. The layers are normally quite distinct in timbers grown in temperate climates, and are called annual rings. The number of growth years in a piece of cut timber may easily be found simply by counting the number of growth rings present at the surface.

The cross-section of an oak trunk (Diagram 2:25) reveals the characteristics shared to some extent by all the timber trees. The annual rings are seen as a series of concentric circles which focus on a pithy centre. The bulk of the mature wood inside the tree is referred to as the heartwood, whilst the young and growing outer layers are defined as the sapwood. In many timbers the sapwood is a clearly-defined band of paler colour, which contrasts with a red-brown heartwood. In oak especially, the sapwood is very prone to attack by furniture beetle (woodworm). The medullary rays are well developed in oak, and are shown here radiating out from the centre of the log. The bark is a complex and important feature, but has no relevance in consideration of usable timber. The profile drawings given here indicate the normal winter appearance of typical specimens, and indicate the proportions of usable timber in trunks and branches.

In compiling the following classification, I have assembled the timbers roughly in order of importance, omitting some obscure examples and others of later significance in America, such as butternut and red gum.

Hardwoods	**Softwoods**
1). The Oaks	19). The Deals
2). Ash	20). Yew
3). Elm	21). Cedar
4). Beech	22). Cypress

Hardwoods

1). The Oaks
2). Ash
3). Elm
4). Beech
5). Walnut
6). Chestnut
7). Cherry ⎫
8). Pear ⎬ The Fruitwoods
9). Apple ⎪
10). Plum ⎭
11). Sycamore
12). Maple
13). Hickory
14). Hornbeam
15). Birch
16). Poplar
17). Elder
18). Willow

Softwoods

19). The Deals
20). Yew
21). Cedar
22). Cypress

Imported Exotics

23). Lignum vitae
24). Ebony
25). Rosewood
26). Mahogany

Hardwoods

1a). Common English Oak — *Quercus robur*
Q. petraea (sessile oak)

Like any other species, the timber produced by oaks will vary somewhat in accordance with the conditions of soil and climate in which the trees have grown. *Quercus robur* is the common North European oak, and is found in all countries of Northern Europe and the British Isles. Yet because of the wide variety of climates acting on their growth, the timber of British trees is different from European growths of the same species. The differences are subtle, but they are easily perceived with a little experience. The grain of English oak is fine and closed, with little show of deep grooving in the capillaries. The growth is often not very straight, so that there is frequently a great variety and interest in the markings.

On the other hand, European oak (imported into England as 'wainscot') is renowned for its straight and true growth. Wainscot oak has a coarse texture, often deeply channelled with open capillary grooves. The rays are normally more heavily accentuated than in English oak, and usually stand slightly proud of the surface. It is best studied at first hand in Dutch furniture, and the texture will then be more readily recognisable in English usage. The qualities for which wainscot oak was brought into England were these twin virtues of a straight reliable growth, and the showy, bright, well-figured grain. By comparison, English oak is unpredictable, yet it is strong and attractive. Certainly, far more English oak is to be found in use, though the imported timber tends towards the upper end of the market. The irregular crooks and knees of English oak were put to good use in the ship and house building industries, and William Harrison quoted a popular saying of his day, that "...no oke can grow so crooked but it falleth out to some use..."

Common English Oak — Quercus robur

Sessile Oak — Quercus petraea

Although it may not be the most impressive tree of the forest, the English oak has won for itself a position of traditional high regard in the minds and hearts of the people of these islands, no doubt fostered by long observation of its strength and reliability, in peace and at war. The 'Hearts-of-Oak' syndrome came to full flower on a flood of Victorian jingoism, and Loudon[50] felt inspired to compare it with the British Lion: "...The oak...has been represented...as holding the same rank among the plants of the temperate hemispheres that the lion does among quadrupeds, and the eagle among birds; that is to say, it is the emblem of a grandeur, strength and duration; of force that resists, as the lion is of force that acts...in one word, it is the king of forest trees..." But long before this bald analogy, Harrison had explored the same emotion in talking of oak as a building material: "...in times past, men were contented to dwell in houses, builded of sallow, willow, plumtree, hardbeame and elme...but now all these are rejected and nothing but oke any whit regarded..." And with the distorted nostalgia of an old man, he goes on to lament the passing of the fine young chaps of his youth: "...And yet see the change, for when our houses were builded of willow, then we had oken men, but now that our houses are come to be made of oke, our men are not onlie become willow, but a great manie altogither of straw, which is a sore alteration..."

Oak is frequently mentioned as a building or furniture material in early accounts, but rarely is the use of English oak distinguished from that of imported wood. The term 'wainscot' is frequently met with, but since the imported variety was so highly regarded it would seem that the word is used to refer to oak of all sorts, regardless of origins. The source and exact meanings of the word are not very clear, though most authorities would agree that it is a corruption from the Dutch. One school of thought favours the word *wagenschott,* a wagon shaft, signifying that the tough and straight oak was ideal for such a use; whilst another theory links it to the words *waeg,* a wall, and *schot,* a covering or panelling. Whatever its origin, the word quickly attained two distinct meanings in the English language:

a). The first, and more important, sense of the word refers to the timber itself. Oak was imported via the Hansa ports from Scandinavia, North Germany, and Holland, and later from Russia and Spain. There are very early references to the importation of 'Norway timber', but it is not clear whether these were in fact oak, or softwoods such as pine or spruce. In 1253 a Royal Warrant was issued for the purchase of "3000 Norway boards and half a hundred of great boards...to make tables" for Windsor Castle;[51] and over four hundred years later (1660) Evelyn was still referring to imported oak as the "...finer grain'd Spanish and Norway Timber, which is likewise of a white colour..." Harrison observed that "...wainescot is brought hither out of Danske..." and in 1803 Sheraton found that "...the oak used by Cabinet-makers is imported from Russia, Norway, Sweden, and the United States of Holland..."

b). The term 'wainscot' was extended in the sixteenth century (or earlier) to refer to the wall-panelling for which imported oak was commonly used. Medieval wall covering usually consisted of long vertical planks, for which purpose the straight riven boards were ideal. 'Wainscoting' is therefore identifiable with the early sense of 'ceiling' (see p.116). At Chatsworth, c.1600, one of the parlours was described as "...fayre waynescotted with white wood..." and in this sense the term has continued into modern use.

The imported riven or quarter-sawn oak boards were referred to by woodworkers and timber merchants as 'wainscots' or 'clapboards', and were brought in through London, Bristol and the North Sea ports. In 1525,

50. J.C. Loudon, *Arboretum et Fruticetum Britannicum,* London, 1854.
51. Penelope Eames, op. cit.

155

John Henryson of Kingston-upon-Hull left to his relative "...William Henryson, the carver, at the next comying of the hulkes oute of Danske, a c wayne scottes...",[52] and elsewhere among the raw materials of a joiner are listed "...rayles, sealinge-boards, wainscotte clappboardes and beddtymber..."[53] The term 'clapboard' still survives in reference to the outer sheathing of overlapped horizontal boards which are often applied as a weatherproof wall covering to houses in many areas including Kent, Essex, East Anglia, the Chalk Counties, New England and Virginia. Evelyn wrote of "Clapboard for wainscot", and in describing an oak cut down at Newbury in 1660, he described the grain as "...clear as any clapboard..." A varient recorded in Essex is 'clampole', and the Colchester Wages Assessment of 1583 mentions, among its list of trades, that of the splitters of "cloberd and clampbell".[54] Clapboard is still commonly pronounced as 'clabberd'.

> 1494...two celars of ooke, oon of them to be sette over the aulter...
>
> 1527...A new wainscot cupboard, with 2 ambreys and 2 tills, carved...
>
> 1588...a cupboard fastened to the wainscot...
>
> 1589...Itm. ij lyverie Copbords of Oke...
>
> 1596...2 settels of wenscote wth lockes and keys...
>
> 1600...A short thick oke planke for a Table lyinge upon two dormers...
>
> 1600...The Hall. The room wainscotted rounde aboute and a skreene of waynescott...
>
> 1600...A playne wainescotte courte cupboarde...
>
> 1608...In the Hawle...20 yardes of waynescotte, one waynescotte cupboarde...
>
> 1683...1 wenscoed bench...1 wenscoed Chaire...
>
> 1721...Wainscot-work of all sorts...
>
> 1735...2 Oval Wainscot tables, 12 Wainscot chairs...
>
> 1750...good Dutch oak well matched as to Colour & free from Sap...
>
> 1785...4 large Dutch Oak Dining Tables. 9:0:0...
>
> 1813...an oak desk and bookcase...

Although oak is known to reach a considerable age, a timber producing tree is in its prime after 150-200 years of growth. It is not a particularly large tree, though a specimen in Herefordshire is recorded as having reached a height of 150 feet and a girth of 12 feet; the usual height rarely exceeds 100 feet. This makes Plot's assertion (p.51) all the more remarkable, that a single plank of over 75 feet, by 34 inches in width, could be cut for a table top. In the event, the plank was too long for the hall at Dudley and it was shortened to 53½ feet. The longest single-plank table top known to the present writer was recently rediscovered at Cefn Mabli, Monmouthshire, having probably originated at nearby Tredegar Park. It is now in a sadly mutilated state, but was recorded in 1908 as being 42 feet long. A photograph taken at the same time gives a good impression of the length and thickness of the plank (Figure 2:162).

Oak is a timber whose sap is rich in tannic acid, which attacks metals such as iron, steel and lead which may come in contact with it. For this reason, the best constructional methods avoid the use of iron nails, though this is not always possible where it is necessary to fix hinges, locks and other hardware. Nails are often corroded by the acid, and ironwork generally

American White Oak — Quercus alba

52. Quoted by Wolsey and Luff, *The Age of the Joiner,* Barker, London, 1968.
53. Rev. P.H. Ditchfield, *The City Companies of London.*
54. F.G. Emmison, op. cit.

American Red Oak — *Quercus rubra*

stains the surrounding wood with a bluish-black patch, especially under damp conditions. The acid sap can usually be diluted by soaking the log in running water before seasoning, but it is not completely flushed out.

1b). American White Oak — *Quercus alba*

The white oak of the N.E. states is very similar to the European *Q. robur*, with a finely pronounced figure, and similar working properties. Much used and favoured by the early settlers, for obvious reasons. It is virtually indistinguishable in use from *robur*, even by microanalysis, and so it cannot be used for defining any American origin of furniture in which it is used (e.g. the stool in Figure 3:96).

1c). American Red Oak — *Quercus rubra* (Northern red oak)
Quercus falcata (Southern red oak).

The red oaks are somewhat similar in appearance to *alba*, but with often a reddish tinge to the heartwood, and a less pronounced figure. It is inclined to be brittle and coarse in texture, and was generally considered to be inferior to white oak. Fortunately for furniture historians, the red oaks *can* be positively identified by microanalysis; and since they are not found in Europe, their presence is a sure confirmation of American provenance.

Figure 2:162. *Joined long dining table. Welsh; Tredegar, Monmouthshire. Oak, c.1650. Photographed in 1908, the length of this remarkable single-plank top was recorded as 42 feet. The base had fourteen legs, but only those ten nearest the camera were turned, the other four being chamfered.*

Despite its poor reputation, red oak was frequently used in the seventeenth century.

2a). Ash — *Fraxinus excelsior*

This fine, flexible and versatile timber is much underrated. Found in the same regions as oak, its finest qualities are toughness and elasticity. Normally pale and close grained, ash has smooth and well defined markings, not unlike oak but without the ray figure. It is easily riven into thin boards and is highly regarded for turnery of all sorts. Its most universal application for furniture was in the wide variety of chairs made by the turners. Most of these chairs are made from ash (if not fruitwood or yewtree), and they cover a period from the Middle Ages well into the nineteenth century. Ash is also found in general use in Windsor chairs, since it can be steam bent for parts such as the bows of arms and backs. It is rare to find a mention of ash in inventories, but at Plas Cadwgan, Denbighshire, there was in 1586 "...1 drawing table of ash..." This is perhaps significant, since experience shows that the use of ash is rather more common in Welsh joined furniture than in English.

The heavily marked and convoluted grain of field grown ash is highly desirable in a patinated state, and indeed was used as a veneer in cabinet work of the eighteenth century. The remarkable grain of Hungarian ash was also imported for this purpose.

2b). American Ash — *Fraxinus americana* (white ash)
Fraxinus nigra (black ash)

Both American ashes are darker than the European variety, but the working properties and appearance are very similar. Commonly used for all the same purposes by colonists, especially turned chairs. In use, ash is rather similar to hickory, and may be confused with it.

3a). Elm — *Ulmus procera* (common English elm)
Ulmus x hollandica (Dutch elm)

Both these elms were common in England and Wales, but Dutch elm occurred throughout the British Isles. Dutch elm is tougher than English, and has a straighter growth, but otherwise they are similar. Elm has a crossed, fibrous and interlocking grain, which makes it very tough and difficult to cleave. The distinctive annual rings lend it a vivid well-marked grain, with an attractive pattern of fine zigzag markings. There is a marked tendency for planks to distort on drying since shrinkage is very irregular, so boards in seats and panels may assume quite a strongly-buckled appearance. Elm is mainly a hedgerow tree and is seldom found in forests, so it provided a readily accessible source of timber for village carpenters. It often grows to a hundred feet or more, so that it is occasionally found in large single-plank table tops:

> 1600...A long thick elme planke for a Table lying uppon iiij
>   dormers...
> 1642...on elmen Table-boarde...

By the mid-eighteenth century, elm had become the standard timber for Windsor chair seats, for which purpose its characteristics are perfectly suited.

3b). Wych Elm — *Ulmus glabra*

This has a straighter, finer and harder timber than the common English elm. It is harder to work, and so is found less frequently in furniture, even though it has a good grain and takes a better polish.

Ash — Fraxinus excelsior

Common English Elm — Ulmus procera

Wych Elm — Ulmus glabra

Beech — Fagus sylvatica

55. Quoted by Margaret Jourdain, *English Decoration and Furniture of the Early Renaissance 1500-1650*, Batsford, London, 1924.

3c). American Elm — *Ulmus americana* (white or soft elm)
Ulmus thomasii (rock elm)

Both found in N.E. states; the white variety has a soft woolly grain, whilst rock elm is the finest textured of the elm family, with a tough and resilient timber.

4a). Beech — *Fagus sylvatica*

This is one of the strongest of British timbers, but it is also highly susceptible to worm and rot. The straight even grain is marked with the flecks of a fine medullary ray figure and the colour is pale. It has a fine smooth texture, to the extent that it is quite dull and characterless. Because of this, the surface appears rarely to have been left without some sort of finishing or obscuring treatment. After 1660 it is seen as little better than a vehicle for counterfeiting other woods. It was stained or painted, often in imitation of walnut or ebony, and in provincial cabinet work of the eighteenth century it was stained red-brown to resemble mahogany.

Evelyn strongly disapproved of the use of beech, which he thought "...so obnoxious that I wish the use of it were by a Law prohibited all Joyners, Cabinet-Makers and such as furnish Tables, Chairs, Bedsteads, Cofers..." The close and regular texture renders it excellent for turning, and so it was popular for such products as cheap cane chairs, Windsor chair parts, bowls and trenchers, etc. But it is inferior to ash, and never competed for popularity as the material for turners' chairs.

One area in which beech did find extensive use was for the frames of coffermakers' chairs. In these chairs, all or most of the wooden surfaces were closely covered with nailed cloth or leather, and the perishability of beech accounts for the low survival rate of these once numerous chairs.

1588...A table of fine deale uppon a frame of beache...

4b). American Beech — *Fagus grandifolia*

Like the European variety, this is close grained and uniform in texture; prone to worm and decay, it appears little used in the seventeenth century.

5a). Walnut — *Juglans regia* (European walnut)

One of the most sophisticated of European furniture timbers, walnut is crisp and easily worked, even-grained, strong and light in weight. It carves and turns well, and takes a fine polish. The grain may be straight, or waved and rippled in a most attractive manner. The grain is one of the most varied of woods, but the finest figures can only be made best use of in veneers. The colour is a pale greyish-brown, but is apt to be streaked with grey, brown or black. This is often attractive in panels or veneers, but can be a disfigurement on turnings. It is prone to attack by furniture beetle and other pests, and can easily be stained in contact with iron nails and hardware. Patinated walnut sometimes fades to a beautiful grey tone, but this has been much despised by collectors in the past, and was often stripped off or stained over.

The tree was probably introduced into Britain by the Romans (the word 'walnut' is probably derived from the OE. 'wealh', meaning 'foreign', i.e. the nut from abroad, as opposed to the native hazelnut). However, some authorities feel that walnut timber was not grown here until after 1600, so that the walnut used extensively in sixteenth century furniture must all have been imported, probably via France. Certainly, some supplies were obtained from that quarter, for in May 1613 the Earl of Cork "...recd. out of France, 24 planck of walnutttree...",[55] but accounts of English trees suggest that large and old walnuts *were* growing here. For example, a huge tree cut down at Welwyn, Hertfordshire, in 1627 must have been growing

159

European Walnut — Juglans regia

for a considerable number of years, for from it "...were cut nineteen loads of planks...besides which there were thirty loads of roots and branches..."

Whether home-grown or not, by the middle of the sixteenth century walnut was well entrenched as a furniture timber in the homes of the rich and fashionable, and in much more widespread use than survivals would have us suppose. Many inventories contain a large proportion of walnut pieces (some imported ready-made), and its desirability is reflected in the fact that some furniture and panelling was "...peynted wallnuttree culler..." Imitation being a sincere form of flattery, such a practice is ample evidence of the esteem in which walnut was held. A large number of tables, chests and chairs were imported from France, Italy and Spain, but a fair proportion of sixteenth century walnut furniture is of undoubted English construction.

Walnut achieved a new status in English furniture after the Restoration of Charles II in 1660. He popularised a taste for the fine walnut furniture of his French and Dutch hosts-in-exile, and its suitability for crisp carving and light portable forms gave English walnut furniture a new lease of life. The foreign styles influenced many aspects of the continuing and concurrent tradition for furniture in oak and other native timbers, as may be seen in Chapter Four.

In 1664 Evelyn recorded the import of walnut from Grenoble, and black walnut from Virginia, and advocated their increased use "...instead of the more vulgar beech..." The severe winter of 1704 killed many of the walnut trees in Central Europe, and the corresponding shortage of the timber in following decades did much to accelerate the adoption of mahogany in England. By 1750 walnut had been ousted from favour by this more versatile and less perishable commodity.

1539...One folding cheyre of wallnuttre the seate backe elbowes of crymsen vellat...with a foote stowle to the same...

1588...A large foulded table of walnut-tree upon a faire frame, the posts whereof are conninglie wrought...

1590...Twoo fine walnuttree cupbords...

1626...j walnuttree drawing table...
j side table of walnuttree wth drawers...
j walnuttree court cubberd...
xij walnuttree high stooles...

1641...A French drawing table of walnut tree...
Nyne great Italian chayres of walnut tree with armes...

1735...2 walnut Tables with drawers...
Walnut draughts Table and Men...
2 walnut Card Tables...

5b). American Black Walnut — *Juglans nigra*

This is a fine furniture wood of varying colour and grain, according to growing conditions. Generally a little darker than its English cousin (hence 'Black'), it is also known in various forms as 'Red', or Virginia walnut. In seventeenth century America it was most commonly used in Pennsylvania, Virginia and the Southern states, but rarely in New England. Black walnut was imported into England from an early date, but it was probably not grown here until 1656, when it is mentioned in the catalogue of the Museum Tradescantium as growing in the garden of the younger Tradescant.

A similar timber is the American white walnut, or butternut *(Juglans cinerea)*, but this is less highly regarded than the black variety.

American Black Walnut — Juglans nigra

Chestnut — Castanea sativa

6a). Chestnut — *Castanea sativa* (sweet, Spanish, or edible chestnut)

Individual trees vary a great deal in growth, and in the character of the timber, but botanists appear not to distinguish them. In use, the softer forms of chestnut are very similar to the coarser varieties of walnut. But most chestnut used in furniture is of the harder type, which in its turn is easily confused with oak. Chestnut has a coarse annual ring marking which is very similar to that of oak, but it lacks the silvery medullary ray figure of oak. It is very difficult, as a result of this, to determine the proportion of chestnut used in early furniture, but certainly it is rare to find a positive identification of chestnut in furniture of the seventeenth century (only three pieces containing chestnut are illustrated in this study). Most reputed chestnut beams in old buildings turn out to be oak on inspection by microanalysis. On the other hand, Evelyn noted that "...Chestnut is (next the Oak) one of the most sought after by the Carpenter and Joyner..." We must assume that a large amount of chestnut furniture has perished, and Evelyn had to admit that it could not be recommended for strength or longevity, though he found it suitable for tables, chests, chairs, stools and bedsteads. In 1556, the furniture of Sir William More at Losely, Surrey, was recorded as being largely of chestnut.

The tree can grow to the respectable height of one hundred feet or more, though lesser in England, with sometimes an enormous girth. This can be misleading, however, for "... (contrary to the Oak) it will make a fair shew outwardly, when t'is all decay'd and rotten within..."

6b). American Chestnut — *Castanea dentata*

Like English chestnut, this timber is easily worked and must have been fairly popular for some uses, but the exact proportion is impossible to determine. It has a pronounced annual ring marking and is coarse in texture, but is inferior to the oaks in most respects.

7). Cherry — *Prunus cerasus* (sour cherry)
Prunus avium (Mazard, Gean or wild cherry)

This is the most versatile of the fruitwoods, since it shares all of their good characteristics, yet is found in larger sizes than most. It is found most commonly in country-made furniture, since it is easily available to country joiners, though we find cherry used as a fine cabinet wood in London and other urban centres in England and America. This popularity is partly due to a superficial resemblance to mahogany. The wood is tough and hard, but like all the sweet fruitwoods it is liable to attack by worm, and the planks are liable to warp. The grain is flecked with a fine pale ray figure, and as a result may be confused with walnut.

Cherry — Prunus cerasus

Cherry is especially fine for turning, and so is available for larger parts such as table legs and chair stiles. The heartwood is a reddish-brown, with a paler sapwood, though as with other timbers the American cherry is often darker. The patinated colour may vary from a rich red-brown akin to mahogany, to a pale faded creamy-yellow. Frequently used for inlay in the sixteenth and seventeenth centuries.

1776...8 Cheritree Chairs...

8). Pear — *Pyrus communis*

Up to the nineteenth century, most pears were grown on pear stocks, which produced larger timber than the modern practice of growing orchard pears on quince rootstocks, so scantlings were available which were large enough for furniture. Pear has a pinkish-brown timber with a fine even texture, and takes stains and colour readily. It also turns very well, and so was frequently used for the small ebonised bosses and spindles applied to furniture of the Anglo-Dutch taste.

Pear — Pyrus communis

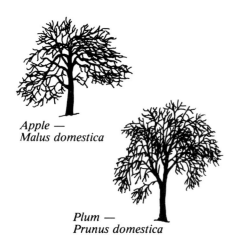

Apple —
Malus domestica

Plum —
Prunus domestica

Sycamore — Acer pseudo platanus

Left: Maple — Acer campestris
(European field maple)
Right: American Maple — Acer
saccharum (hard maple)

56. Malcolm Airs, op. cit.

1591...my leaf table of peartree...
1600...a peartree cubberd wt a presse in yt...
1750...peartree picture frames...

9). Apple — *Malus pumila* (also *M. domestica* — orchard apple)
Malus sylvestris (wild crab apple)

A hard and heavy wood, with a close, fine and varied texture, often dappled with tiny knots. The heartwood is pale brown or yellow, sometimes with a very pale and pronounced sapwood. Apple is excellent for turning, but generally is of a curved or crooked growth, so that planks may be quite long but narrow, with an irregular grain. Used for small furniture, spindles, drawer pulls, etc.

10). Plum — *Prunus communis* (also *P. domestica*)

A hard, heavy wood of brownish-red colour, not unlike cherry in many respects, but rarely found in other than small sizes.

1683...a little writing-desk of plum-tree wood...

11). Sycamore — *Acer pseudo platanus*

Akin to the maple, and very similar to the London plane, the true *platanus*. The wood is very white, crisp and close grained, with often an even rippled marking similar to tiger maple or the fiddle-back stripe of mahogany and walnut. Its pale colour made it very popular for white inlay and marquetry, whilst its readiness to take stains and colour made it ideal for the polychrome effects of the seventeenth century.

Sycamore is also particularly good for turning, and being tasteless in contact with food it was commonly used in the production of bowls, spoons, trenchers and other items of domestic ware. The timber is often available in particularly wide planks, and may frequently be found in the tops of farmhouse tables of various sizes. Here the scrubbed surfaces show off the hard creamy grain to best advantage; and the scoured tops of old tables may be deeply grooved where the softer parts of the annual rings have worn away.

12). Maple — *Acer campestris* (European field maple)

This is a fine, hard timber which both turns and wears very well. It is creamy-white in colour, sometimes with a yellow or red tinge, and the scoured surface can have the look of polished butter. It is often distinguished by different figures which arise from irregular growth, such as bird's eye (knotty), tiger (striped), curly, or rippled. It was used in inlay and veneers in England, but solid furniture was probably always unusual, and there seem to be no English turners' chairs of maple, which might have been expected. It appears very occasionally in inventories, and in builders' accounts as at Raynham Hall, Norfolk, and Redgrave Hall, Suffolk.[56]

1586...On court cubbert of maple tree Wood...
1588...3 square tables of maple inlaid and border'd with
        walnuttree wth frames to them...
1624...12 dozen of mapple trenchers never yet used...

12b). American Maple — *Acer saccharum* (hard, rock or sugar maple)
Acer saccharinum (soft or silver maple)
Acer nigrum (black maple)

The colonists of New England quickly recognised the importance and value of the vast maple forests, and maple survives as a furniture wood from the earliest period of American furniture making, especially in the form of turned chairs. Maple sugar, or syrup, was also their staple

Hickory —
Carya glabra

Birch — Betula pendula
(silver birch)

Poplar — Populus nigra (black poplar)

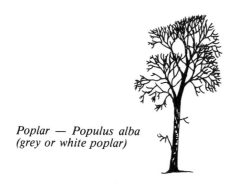

Poplar — Populus alba
(grey or white poplar)

57. Trade card illustrated by Pauline Agius, *Furniture History*, Vol. XII, 1976.

sweetener and a food, and is produced by boiling the sap of the hard maple. Each tree can provide up to 8lbs. of maple sugar in a season, though the average yield is about 2½lbs. Like European maples, the New World varieties have a bland and uniform grain, which may occasionally be enlivened by an interesting figure. Very tough and hard-wearing.

13). Hickory — *Carya glabra* (pignut hickory)
    Carya ovata (shagbark hickory)

Another timber of great value in colonial New England. Hickory is an extremely tough timber, which bears a close similarity to ash. These two are used in similar ways, but hickory is the stronger material. It is good for turning, and wears very well, but the grain is inclined to be very coarse. The high tensile strength renders it ideal for turned furniture such as chairs, and for tool handles. It is usually darker than ash, with a reddish-brown heartwood, but it has a distinct pale sapwood band.

14). Hornbeam — *Carpinus betulus*

This is a pale, hard, cross-grained timber; also not unlike ash in appearance, but tougher and with a smooth and bland grain. Extremely rare in furniture, but examples are known. More likely to be found in turnery ware, for which it is ideal.

15a). Birch — *Betula alba* (also *pendula* — silver birch)
     Betula pubescens (downy birch)

The grain of birch is white, rather soft and fibrous, and inclined to be a little woolly in the same way as beech. It turns quite well, and is most often found in small country-made cricket tables and chairs.

15b). Cherry Birch — *Betula lenta* (American)

This is a harder and stronger wood than the European, which turns well and takes a good polish.

16). Poplar — *Populus spp.* (esp. *nigra, alba*)

A whitish-yellow timber of hard, close-grained and even texture. It is occasionally found in medieval iron bound chests, where a section of the trunk acts as the lid. Commonly used in inlay and marquetry, sometimes stained in colours. Imported Dutch poplar, or asp, was sometimes used as a cheap substitute for ash, to the annoyance of the London Turners' Company. Black poplar was a fine, large timber tree; but the most familiar Lombardy poplar was not used in England for its timber.

17). Elder — *Sambucus nigra*

A white wood similar to holly, and generally used in inlay. Occasionally used in second-rate turned chairs; e.g. at the end of the eighteenth century, John Lacey, a "Cabinet and Chair-Maker" of Frome, Somerset, was advertising "...common, round, and quartered Ash and Elder Chairs, white and coloured, from eight to forty Shillings per Dozen..."[57] A Tudor chronicler referred disparagingly to the poor hovels which passed as cottages in his day as "...built of elder poles at every lane end..."

18). Willow — *Salix alba*

Another bland white timber, which is occasionally seen in cheap country-made furniture. A more important crop than the timber are the young shoots or 'withies' which are collected from pollards or coppice crowns. This is the main material for wickerwork basketry, and as such is occasionally used for woven furniture such as cradles and chairs.

Scots Pine —
Pinus sylvestris

European Larch —
Larix decidua

Norway Spruce —
Picea abies

Softwoods

19). Deals — *Pinus sylvestris* (Scots pine)

     Pinus strobus (American white pine)

     Pinus taeda (American yellow pine or loblolly)

     Pinus resinosa (American red pine)

     Larix decidua (European larch)

     Picea abies (Norway spruce)

Generally, softwoods have not been used for the better sorts of furniture, mainly due to their lack of resistance to wear, worm, and other forms of damage. They are rarely suitable for carving, though the harder and finer varieties such as yew and cedar generally produce good turnings. The latter have other exceptional qualities and so will be treated separately.

A great variety of resinous coniferous softwoods are used under the general title of 'deal', including pines, firs, larch, spruce, hemlock, etc. They have at various times been valued for their "faire culler" and their pronounced attractive grain markings. Softwoods may often grow to a very great size and age, as in the case of the Giant Redwood of California (up to 340 feet in height); or the Bristlecone Pine of Nevada, which may live up to five thousand years or more. Even the North European pines provided wide fast-seasoning planks, which were imported into England from a very early date. In 1252, Henry III specified Norwegian pine boards in an order for purchase at Southampton, to be used in wall-panelling at Winchester Castle.[58] A great deal of furniture and architectural woodwork in pine has survived from the late Middle Ages in the Alpine countries, but in England such survivals are rare. Notable examples are the two chests at All Souls College, Oxford, of c.1440,[59] and a standard of the same date at Hereford Cathedral.

Deal for panelling, and occasionally for furniture, was highly valued in sixteenth century England, and was specified by Henry VIII at Nonesuch Palace. In the eighteenth century, it was again popular both for fine panelling and for cheap furniture, but at this time it was almost always painted. The colonists of North America made full use of the wide pine boards available to them, especially for the tops of tables and chests. Many oak-panelled chests of seventeenth century American manufacture have single-plank pine tops, and these are one of their distinguishing features.

The origins of the word 'deal' are not clear, but it relates to both the Saxon 'thealu' — a plank, and the Saxon 'dael' — a portion. Sheraton defined it thus: "...from Deel, Dutch for a part, quantity or degree of. Hence fir or pine timber being cut into thin portions they are called deals..." This definition was cribbed from Samuel Johnson, but it is given life by Sheraton's experience with his trade. The word, then may be taken to refer to either the timber itself, or to the planks as imported. The various species, which between them may be classified as deals, are diverse in their character and origins, but broadly they have a pale yellow colour, with well-defined annual rings. They are mainly straight-grained and easy to work. The colour does vary somewhat, and they are sometimes called red, yellow or white.

  1588...a table of fine deale...

  1624...a litle fir table wth feet to fould up...

  1670...One firre table board...

  1688...1 great cheste of Spruce...

  1726...One deal dresser board with doors & drawers...

  1757...3 Old Deal Boxs's...

58. Penelope Eames, Furniture History, Vol. XII, 1976.
59. Penelope Eames, Furniture History, Vol. XIII, 1977.

Yew — Taxus baccata

Cedar of Lebanon — Cedrus libani

20). Yew — *Taxus baccata*

The timber of yewtree is so tough and resilient that those familiar with its qualities are surprised to find it classified with the softwoods, but it is in fact a conifer. It is hard and heavy, with a dark orange-brown heartwood that contrasts sharply with the yellow-white sapwood. The growth is often highly irregular, and the trunk is made up of multiple shoots which fuse together, often with air spaces between. As a result it is rare to find clean planks of any considerable width, eight inches or so being the usual maximum. The hard and irregular grain can be very difficult to work, since it may spelch out or tear under the plane, but clean timber often finishes very well and yew is ideal for turning. It takes a good polish, but is resistant to stains and paints. Yew is highly resistant to attack by worm, but such damage is not unknown in sapwood or softer heartwood. The bark, shoots, leaves and berries are highly poisonous to human beings and livestock. Yew grows to quite a considerable age, and English churchyard yews may be five hundred years old or more.

The great strength, elasticity and flexibility of yew made it the favourite timber for the medieval longbow, introduced into England from Wales, for which use it was officially promoted and protected. It appears occasionally in seventeenth century furniture, and in contemporary inventories as 'Ughe', though it does not fall into more common use until after the Restoration. Thereafter it appears both in the solid (chiefly as small tables and stools), and as a decorative veneer. Of all the woods which produce burrs, yew provides the finest and most attractive of burr figures, used either in the solid or in veneer.

The yewtree staircase at Llanvihangel Court, Llanvihangel Crucornau, Monmouthshire (c.1670), is an exceptional item on such a massive scale. A large number of cupboards in panelled yew were made in Ireland in the eighteenth century, but solid panelled yew is rare in English furniture. The greatest use for yewtree grew during the eighteenth century with the expansion of the Windsor chair industry. It was found that yew was ideal for the steam-bent bows and arms of these chairs, and some of the finest examples were constructed entirely from yew, apart form the universal elm seat.

1672...a little yew table, and a yew cupboard...

21). Cedar — *Cedrus libani* (Cedar of Lebanon — Middle East)
Cedrus atlantica (Atlas cedar —North Africa)

There are many varieties of the true cedars, and there was some importation of Mediterranean timber for use in sixteenth century England. Ready-made Italian cedar furniture was imported from an early date, and a great many chests still survive, usually with some form of pokerwork, penwork, or stamped decoration. Occasional examples are embellished with an English coat-of-arms, which suggests that they were sometimes ordered by noble tourists as souvenirs. The decoration is typical of Venice and the Adige district of Northern Italy.

Later, in the 1580s, some American false cedars were introduced to England, notably Spanish cedar (*Cedrela odorata*), and Virginia or pencil cedar (*Juniperus virginiana*). In Heriot's report on Virginia in Hackluyt's *Principal Navigations, Voiages, Traffiques and Discoveries of the English Nation,* cedar is described as suitable for "...chestes, Sweete and fine bedsteads, tables, deskes, lutes, virgenalles and many things els (of which there hath bene proofe made already)..." and he recommends it for further profitable importation into England.

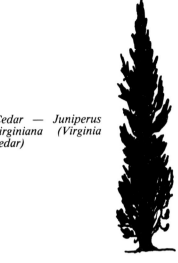

Cedar — Juniperus virginiana (Virginia cedar)

Cedar is a fine, pale, reddish-brown timber, a little soft in use, but valued for its fragrant and long-lasting aroma. It is particularly valuable for clothes chests and chests of drawers, because of its ability to repel moth, woodworm and other pests. Despite its softness, the resistance to worm and rot means that many very early examples have survived. The grain is not unlike that of the deals and pines, but it will be realised that pine of any great age is never free of the effects of woodworm, whereas cedar remains untouched. Sometimes the annual rings are fine and bland, and in such cases cedar may be confused with yewtree; but the growth of cedar is always more straight and regular than yew. For many years, the famous Hornby Castle chair now at Temple Newsam House (Figure 4:35, also Macquoid, *Age of Oak*, pl.IVb) was believed to be of yewtree, but it is in fact of cedar. The most common examples of English cedar furniture are chests of drawers of the second half of the seventeenth century; and from the same period, cedar parts are found in cabinets from Boston, Massachusetts, and New Haven, Connecticut. Cedar grows to a very large size, and there was no difficulty in obtaining large planks for table tops, etc.

> 1688...One great oval table of cedar and 12 Turkey-work
> chaires...
> 1689...Two cedar tables for ye Twilight (toilet)...

22). Cypress — *Cupressus sempervirens* (Italian cypress)

European cypress is similar in many respects to cedar. It has a straight, bland grain, and is of similar colour and softness. It is tempting to speculate that the frequent mentions of 'Cypruswood' in early accounts may sometimes stem from confusion with cedar, though cedar was preferred. Like cedar, cypress was much admired for use in musical instruments:

> 1539...Twoo faire paire of newe longe virgenalles made harpe-
> fasshion of cipres...
> 1617...a ciprus wodde cheste £5... (This indicates a very high
> value, since in the same inventory the table and forms in
> the Hall were valued together at only £1. This was
> presumably an imported chest with rich decoration.)
> 1624...a cyprus coffer...

Cypress — Cupressus sempervirens (Italian cypress)

22b). American Southern Cypress — *Taxodium distichum* (swamp cypress)

Southern cypress is restricted in its growth to the Southern Colonies, so early pieces are normally of Southern origin; Virginia or the Carolinas. The most northerly limit of common growth is the Dismal Swamp area of Virginia. Although the grain is occasionally rather bland, the annual rings are normally heavily marked (see the stool, Figure 4:252), and the wood bears little similarity to European cypress. The timber varies greatly in colour and intensity of grain markings, even in trees of the same locality. It is good for furniture and panelling, and takes a fine polish.

Imported Exotics

No imported timber figures importantly in the native tradition of furniture-making in England; but nevertheless, certain timbers make an occasional or specialised appearance, and four such are considered here.

23). Lignum Vitae — *Guaiacum officinale*

An extremely hard and heavy timber, imported into Europe from the West Indies since the earliest part of the sixteenth century. The grain is very tough and interlocked, with a streaked dark heartwood and a very pale sapwood. It was originally hailed as a powerful medicine, especially for the

Lignum Vitae — Guaiacum officinale

treatment of venereal diseases, hence its common name and other hopeful designations: the Wood of Life, the Holy Wood, Christ's Hands, the Blessed Wood. In Elizabethan vernacular it was less gloriously dubbed 'Pockwood'. In order to promote the supposed beneficial effects, there was much demand upon the turners to use it as a material for apothecaries' mortars. The turners soon diverted its unique physical properties to wider uses, and it served in mechanical functions such as self-lubricating pulleys, bearings, and other ships' tackle. Throughout the seventeenth century it headed the London Turners' Company list of timbers for supply to the Royal Navy.

It is rarely found in the solid in furniture (Figure 4:47 is exceptional), appearing more commonly as veneer after 1660. The most dramatic use is as 'oyster-shell' veneer, cut across the grain to make best use of the vivid sapwood.

24). Ebony — *Diospyros ebenum*

This is only one of many black hardwoods imported chiefly from the East Indies, and used as 'Ebeny'. They are mostly black streaked with brown, very hard, brittle and somewhat difficult to work. The most common application in England was for applied bosses, spindles and similar decorations in imitation of Dutch taste. Perhaps more significant in England and New England, however, is the manner in which ebony was imitated with black paints: on pearwood for applied bosses and turnings; and on beech for whole furniture such as chairs and tables.

25). Rosewood — *Dalbergia nigra*

Again, a common name for many similar woods, imported from South America and Honduras. The heartwood is heavy, and streaked with brown, violet, black and red. It is not clear how the term 'rosewood' came to be used, but it is found occasionally in English furniture from c.1560 onwards; though its greatest popularity was not until after 1800.

26). Mahogany — *Swietenia mahagoni*

The first introduction of mahogany to England is said to have been as a curiosity by Sir Francis Drake after his visit to the West Indies in 1597. The finest timber was the 'Spanish' mahogany from the Caribbean islands of San Domingo, Cuba, Jamaica and Puerto Rico. It is a crisp, strong wood of good red colour, impervious to worm and rot. In the eighteenth century, it was appreciated for its fine working qualities, and the exceptionally wide planks in which it was available, but before 1720 it appears only rarely, and then only as a novelty.

For many years it was known simply as 'Jamaica wood', and it was not until Walpole's Act of Parliament of 1721 abolished the hitherto heavy import duty on timbers from the Colonies (designed to increase supplies for the Royal Navy), that imports of mahogany began to proliferate. The mahogany chair of 1661 illustrated in Figure 4:105 is an extremely rare instance of a complete piece made from solid mahogany before the fashionable phase which began soon after 1710-15. The presence of mahogany in Aberdeen at this date is unexplained; but Aberdeen was an important port, in close touch with Spain and Continental Europe, so it is not surprising that a few planks of the timber might have come into the hands of Andrew Watson, a prominent tradesman, or of a joiner known to him.

Coincidentally, it was also in 1661 that the first reference to 'Jamaica wood' appears in the Royal Accounts. In that year Hampton Court was supplied with "...two Tables & five paire of Stands of Jamaica Wood, £18:0:0..."[60] The wood appears infrequently in small veneers or turned

Mahogany — Swietenia mahogani

60. R.W. Symonds, *Furniture Making in 17th and 18th Century England*, Connoisseur, London, 1955.

spindles applied to furniture of late seventeenth century date, but the word 'mahogany' does not appear in the Royal Accounts until 1724.

METHODS OF DECORATION

The importance of decoration, to the student of furniture, lies in the way it sets the pace of that indefinable quality which we call 'style'. Decoration, perhaps more than construction, is an essential guide to assessing the date, class, regional origin and merits of an individual piece. In considering ornamentation as a separate aspect of early furniture, we have to think largely of *joined* furniture in particular. The simpler craftsmanlike forms such as wickerwork relied on structural patterns for their intrinsic decorative effects; though it is often the case with primitive structural types that any decorative value is an unconscious bonus, and not the result of striven-after intentions on the part of the maker. At the other end of the scale, the cabinetmaker was normally concerned with the problem of *hiding* his structural forms under a cloak of veneers and mouldings. In his work, structural considerations are completely subservient to the dictates of decoration.

In its best expressions, the decoration of joiners' work is embodied as a *complement* to the structure, and generally makes full use of the form and tensions of the underlying skeleton. The composition of carved schemes, for example, is laid out within the confines of the framework of rails and panels, and rarely disregards the units of structure. Most decoration is of a fairly conventional nature, but within the apparently narrow framework is found an endless variety of motifs and execution, spiced-up with the occasional delightful touch of wit and observation.

The available practical methods of decorating wooden furniture are divided broadly into two natures, viz. the three-dimensional forms in which the interplay of light and shade are the dominant factors; and the two-dimensional forms which rely solely on responses to colour and tone, and the interaction of coloured shapes. They are considered here as follows:

- i). Carving
- ii). Turning
- iii). Mouldings
- iv). Inlay, parquetry and marquetry
- v). Paints and stains
- vi). Gilding and silver leaf
- vii). Finishes

i). Carving (Figures 2:163-210)

The Trade

The London Aldermen's Arbitration of 1632 significantly related the trade of the carver to that of the joiner (p.43). The Court viewed at least the simpler forms of carving as legally available to the joiner, viz. "...All carved workes either raised or cutt through or sunck in with the Grounde taken out..." A few years earlier, in 1617, a provincial company had taken the same view by allowing its joiner members the limited exercise of such carving "...as joyners do use..." (Salisbury Joyners' Company, p.45). Obviously, the standard of carving which might be expected from the hand of the average joiner was limited by the amount of time which he could spare for the practice, and by the limitations of his personal skill and inclinations, since few joiners received any intensive tuition at carving during their apprenticeship. For the sort of refined sculptural work which might be expected by a richer patron, the accomplishments of the specialist carver were required (see the notes on Humphrey Beckham, Appendix III).

Figure 2:163. *Carved angel. English. Oak, c.1500. The quality, and even some of the forms, of medieval carving persisted until a later date, as may be seen in the next figure.*

Figure 2:164. *Carved chair crest. English. Oak, c.1600. Some of the sense of form and decoration found in the imbricated feathers of the angel in Figure 2:163 may still be found in this carving of one hundred years later.*

Figure 2:166. *Joined chest. English. Oak, early seventeenth century. Supporting figures are often found used in this way, i.e. between arches in a panelled scheme such as chest fronts, bedheads and overmantels.*

The Golden Age of the woodcarver had been, of course, the Middle Ages. There had been a huge demand for secular and religious statuary and architectural woodwork before the Reformation, when the lavish decoration of roofs, panelling, pews and screens absorbed the time and energy of whole generations. We shall never know the exact extent of the achievements of the medieval 'imagers', since the vast bulk of their work was utterly destroyed in the iconoclastic fury of successive ages — whether

Figure 2:165. *Joined press cupboard (detail). English. Oak, early seventeenth century. These supporting figures were a favourite theme during 1570-1650 (and sometimes later). The male figures are correctly called 'atlantes', and the female 'caryatids'.*

Figure 2:167. *Carved architectural support. English. Oak, early seventeenth century. Here the paired figures are used in a free-standing form, probably once the supporting pillar of an open colonnade or arcade.*

Figure 2:168. *Joined withdrawing table. English; probably Yorkshire. Oak, early seventeenth century. The supports of the frame are formed as chimaerae, seated upon lions.*

under the reforming impulse of Henry VIII, the renewed zeal of Elizabeth I, the indignation of the Puritan Commonwealth, the ignorance and contempt of eighteenth century 'modernists', or the well-intended 'restorations' of the Victorians. We are left with but a fragment of the original wealth of carved woodwork with which England was blessed in the year 1520.

But the impulse which generated such a reservoir of creative energy could not be entirely subverted by a mere negative shift in motivation. Although the Reformation reversed the emphasis from religious decoration and dispersed the talents and skills of both monkish and lay craftsmen, the rest of the sixteenth century saw a rise in the market for private secular building on a lavish scale, and the creation of an entirely new middle class group which was anxious to keep up its end in the struggle to maintain outward appearances. Skilled carvers were turned to the embellishment of private houses and furniture, and to the public buildings which were the emblems of Elizabethan civic pride. It may be said that the standard of carving in Renaissance England declined when viewed against the yardstick of the High Middle Ages; but what it may have lost in painstaking thoroughness, it gained in brilliance and invention under the direct influence of foreign styles and craftsmen. The English carvers developed a whole new vocabulary of shape and form, moulded and adapted to suit their own particular abilities and materials.

The work of the carver was probably the most important element in furniture decoration during the first century of the English Renaissance, 1530-1630. During this time, carved and sculptural decoration was the prominent theme, and the carver achieved a position in the furniture trade which was not to be repeated until a century later. Samples of the work of the specialist are shown in Figures 2:163-178. His range of products included statuary and shop signs, but a large proportion of his work was done in co-operation with the joiner. This took the shape of relief panels, capitals, charges of arms, and a variety of supporters following the revived classical theme for figures which bear the weight of architectural stages. These usually took the guise of human figures or 'terms' (properly called 'caryatids' in the female form, and 'atlantes' in the male form, though the sexual identification is sometimes confused by the simultaneous sporting of beards and breasts!), known animals or birds such as the lion or eagle, or mythical creatures with diverse parts such as chimaerae or gryphons.

The form and content of much of the finest carved decoration seems directly inspired by foreign example; but most of this must have been gleaned from imported specimens, since only a surprisingly small proportion of carvers were listed by Benno Forman in his survey of Continental craftsmen living in London during 1511-1625.[61] Out of the 480 furniture makers listed (largely joiners and various boxmakers) only seventeen are described as carvers. Most of these men must have been involved to *some* extent on furniture decoration, but only *one* (Diricke Cornelys from Amsterdam, 1568) is specified as a "carver for joiners work", though three others are "joiner/carvers". Perhaps a large number of the 'strangers' present in England were leading an itinerant existence, travelling the country from job to job.

> 1504...a standing cubbourde carven wt. ymagry...price xiijs
> iijd...
> 1588...A large foulded table of walnut-tree upon a faire
> frame, the posts whereof are conninglie wroughte...

Figure 2:170. *Joined court cupboard (detail). English. Bulletwood (probably Mimusopps spp.), early seventeenth century. A highly professional piece of carved work, in the grandest style of James I, and inlaid with specimen marbles. The timber is a close-grained exotic hardwood; ideal for such crisp relief carving.*

Figure 2:169. *Joined court cupboard (detail). English; probably Suffolk. Oak, late sixteenth century. This boldly carved caryatid represents Judith carrying the head of Holofernes, whom she has just decapitated (detail of Figure 4:33).*

61. Benno Forman, Furniture History, Vol. VII, 1971.

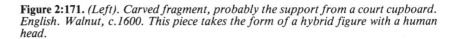

Figure 2:171. *(Left). Carved fragment, probably the support from a court cupboard. English. Walnut, c.1600. This piece takes the form of a hybrid figure with a human head.*

Figure 2:172. *(Below left). Carved fragment, probably the finial of a staircase newel post. English. Oak, c.1600. In the form of a gryphon.*

Figure 2:173. *(Below) Relief carved panel. English. Oak, early-sixteenth century. A simple and expressive work, illustrating the Crucifixion and the Instruments of the Passion.*

At a simpler level, we have seen that the less sophisticated forms of carving could be managed by the joiner himself, without resort to specialist aid. Seventeenth century vernacular furniture, in particular, displays endless repetitions of simple formal patterns, which are adapted in a regular manner to fit into almost any available space or surface. The formula is often predictable, but rarely monotonous, since most genuine period work is relieved by a sense of vigour and spatial confidence. The flat rectangular areas of joined and panelled construction seem to invite such simple but effective treatment, and in the most sensitive compositions the carved areas are balanced by plain areas.

The Techniques

The complexity and finish of carved work depends as much on the variety of tools available to the carver, as on his skill, experience and imagination. The simplest tools (available to any joiner or carpenter) are the range of V- and U-section gouge chisels, which will cut channels of corresponding section, and are made in a choice of widths and radii. If the carver has only a limited number of tools available, then he can make only a restricted range of shapes (though a series of deceptively simple chisel cuts *can* produce quite complicated results). But if the work is to be truly sculptural, then he will need a good selection of chisels, supplemented by extra tools such as rasps and stamps (or punches).

The carving of plane surfaces usually takes one of four basic forms (usually differentiated as 'incised', 'sunk', 'relief' and 'pierced' carving), though more complex work will use combinations of these. In its simplest form, incised work is simply 'drawn' into the surface of the timber, using a

Figure 2:174. *Relief carved panel. English. Oak, early seventeenth century. Adam and Eve, with the Serpent in the Tree of Knowledge, were popular subjects in many different media.*

V-gouge to form a narrow channel. Such linear work is at best of a perfunctory and superficial nature, often wrongly referred to as 'scratch carving', and is commonly found on the poorer sorts of boarded work made by the carpenter. If this is combined with the use of U-gouges, then a more rounded and satisfying finish can be achieved. Rather more satisfactory is sunk carving, in which the background is taken out from the plane surface, leaving the design in relief against a 'matted' ground. The background is finished in this way with a matting punch, which leaves a non-reflective surface to contrast with the polished flat areas of the design. The flat, raised motif may then be elaborated by the use of stamped or punched marks (usually stars, flowers or crosses), or by further sculptural carving. Figure 2:184 is a particularly sensitive and finely-conceived version of this relatively simple technique. Here the drawing and angles of the surfaces are subtly varied, and the shapes well-articulated, so that the result has a suave but somewhat fussy appeal.

Relief carving is usually of the finest quality, and involves the greatest cost in time and wastage of material. The original panel or block is sometimes very thick, and the ground is chopped away all round the motif, to leave it standing boldly out of the surface (see Figures 2:173 and 174). This process may be imitated or supplemented by gluing extra thicknesses to the surface of the original panel or rail. The practice of piercing patterns completely *through* the panel is normally done for a specific reason, and as such it is confined to use on screens and food cupboards; the one to admit light, and the other for ventilation.

173

Figure 2:175. *Relief carved armorial panel. English. Oak, dated 1665.*

Figure 2:176. *Relief carved armorial panel. English. Oak, late sixteenth century. The Royal Arms of England, with the Tudor supporters, the Lion and Dragon.*

Figure 2:177. *Cast lead panel. English; probably Bristol, dated 1620. The Stuart Royal Arms. This and the following figure are taken from a large lead garden cistern, originally from the Van, Caerphilly, Glamorganshire. It was probably made in Bristol, and the master blocks for the panels (which are repeated several times) were cut from wood by a woodcarver.*

Figure 2:178. *Cast lead panel. The style of this floral arched panel is typical West Country work.*

174

Figure 2:179. *Detail of joined arm-chair. English; Yorkshire. Oak, dated 166? This crude and lively rendering of the Royal Arms is inscribed: 'IH GOD BLAS THA KING AND SAND HIM LONG TO REAN 166-'. The earpieces are in the form of primitive warriors.*

Figure 2:180. *Detail of joined press cupboard. English; West Country. Oak, c.1640. Note the incoherent mixture of chisel cuts and motifs seen here. The quality of the carving varies from part to part, but this is not necessarily indicative of later additions. Such inconsistencies are familiar in middle-class work of the seventeenth century, though it is not to be admired.*

Figure 2:181. *Detail of joined press cupboard. English. Oak, dated 1673. This is a sensitive, articulate expression of middle-class provincial carving, but somewhat fussy in the small scale of the detail.*

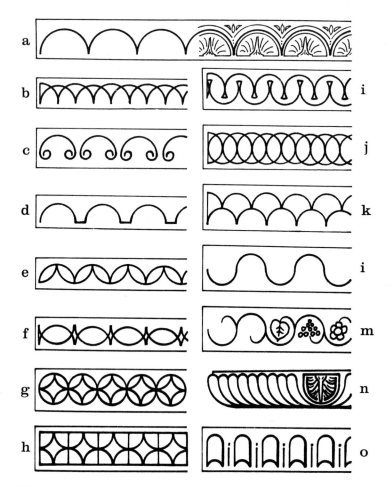

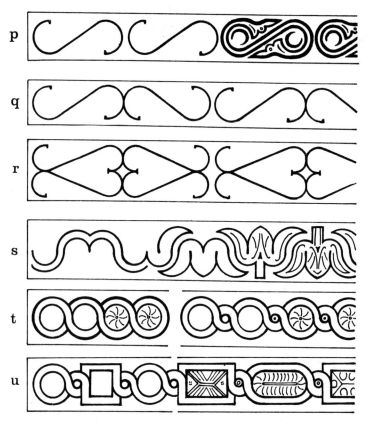

Diagram 2:26. *Sequential designs for carved ornament on rails and stiles in joined furniture. Most of the conventional forms of running ornament are found to be composed of simple repeated units. These are laid out initially with scribed lines by means of rule and compass, and the decorative detail filled in with chisel cuts. The three most common types are based on lunettes or C-curves (a-o); scrolls or S-curves (p-s); and the linked classical guilloche (t,u). The drawings given here represent a few of the basic schemes in which these may be used, but the final details of execution are capable of almost infinite interpretation and variety. Most of these motifs are self-explanatory, but the following have popular names:*

a). *Lunettes. Part of the band is shown with a common form of infill.*

m). *This branching trail is usually completed with leaves, flowers, bunches of grapes, etc. It was popular in Gothic and Renaissance work as 'vine trail', and was much used in embroidery of the seventeenth century.*

n). *Gadrooning. Based on a series of fleshy curves in full relief, and centring on various details. Common in seventeenth century silverwork.*

o). *Nulling. Based on a series of small concave arches.*

t,u). *Guilloche. Like many conventional patterns, the guilloche is found in ancient and classical work, and is capable of predictable variations.*

Diagram 2:27. *The standard forms of decorated panels. The basic patterns are expanded and enriched with a wide vocabulary of decorative infill. This is by no means an exhaustive list, but most of the conventional forms of panel are depicted here. These designs are subject to small variations in practice, and several may be combined for further effect. The dates are an approximate range:*

a). *Gothic tracery, before 1540.*
b). *Simple parchemin, 1450-1550.*
c). *Enriched parchemin, 1450-1550.*
d). *Early linenfold, 1450-1530.*
e). *Late linenfold, 1500-1580.*
f). *Romayne, 1520-1580.*
g). *Heraldic, all periods.*
h). *Vase and flowers, or 'flowerpotte', 1550-1750.*
i). *Cartouche, 1550-1700.*

j). *Arch, 1550-1750.*
k). *Circle, 1500-1700.*
l). *Diamond, 1550-1750.*
m). *Oval boss, 1580-1680.*
n). *Classical knot pattern, 1580-1680.*
o). *Celtic interlace, 1550-1750.*
p). *Saltire, or 'St. Andrew's Cross', all periods.*
q). *Quatrefoil guilloche, 1580-1700.*
r). *Double S-scroll, 1580-1750.*

s). *Double heart, 1580-1700.*
t). *Inner-frame moulding, 1560-1750.*
u). *Heavy edge-mouldings, 1560-1700.*
v). *Raised fielding, flat edge, 1560-1800.*
w). *Raised fielding, splayed edge, 1650-1800.*
x). *Raised fielding, splayed edge, arch top, 1675-1800.*
y). *Raised fielding, splayed edge, ogee top, 1700-1800.*

It is perhaps interesting to note that in this survey fashions have made a full circle from Gothic to Gothick Revival, and it is with the various revivals of the eighteenth and nineteenth centuries that the organic developments in traditional work finally lost their impetus.

Figure 2:182. *Detail of panel from joined chest. English. c.1600. Informal grotesque monsters are a common motif in sixteenth century carving. This leafy creature with a leonine head is displayed against a matted ground.*

Figure 2:185. *Detail of joined chest of drawers. English. Oak, c.1680. Here the tulip shapes are cut out with a fret-saw, and set into the cushioned frame of the drawer moulding. The ground behind the frets seems to have been finished originally with a coat of red paint, which would highlight the shapes to good effect.*

Figure 2:183. *Detail of joined press cupboard (Figure 3:271). English. Oak, mid-seventeenth century. Formal strapwork arabesques, defined by a sunk and matted ground. The richly moulded frame is also of interest.*

Figure 2:184. *Detail of joined table. English; Salisbury, Wiltshire. Oak, c.1630. A very simple form of incised carving, executed with a V- and a U-section gouge, and enlivened with punches.*

It would be a lengthy and somewhat futile exercise to attempt to classify *all* the variations of motif and form which may be found in period carving, since the possibilities are so wide and subtle; yet it may be valuable to look briefly at some of the elements which lie behind the more common forms of repeat patterns used on rails and panels. The simple principle for such work is the logical repetition of a single unit. Conventional names are given to the most familiar motifs, though these names owe more to modern invention than to any respectable ancestry. Most running ornament is based on sequential repeats of the units itemised in Diagram 2:26. The expanded details of line, form, infills, etc., will vary enormously according to factors such as date, class, quality and regional preference. Likewise, the execution and workmanship may vary from a broad and expansive gesture to a fine and fastidious rendering.

There is a small number of conventional panel types which occur at predictable dates. Once again, the variations are enormous, but it is worth analysing the format of the usual types (Diagram 2:27). These standard types are best examined with reference to specific examples, and they will mostly be found in the various photographs. Although carved decoration is extremely common in furniture of the English tradition, it is rarely mentioned specifically in inventories, perhaps because of this very familiarity:

> 1541...a small table or cupboard of waynscot wth a carved bottome...
> 1552...A fayer drawing table of wallnuttree uppon iiij carved pillors...
> 1569...one four-foulding table wth carved legs...
> 1581...In the Hall. A Karved cubbord 1£...
> 1590...on ambreye carved...
> 1594...a bedsteade of cutwirke...
> 1600...a lyvrie cupboarde of wallnuttree carvede...

Figure 2:186. *(Left) Boarded chest. English. Oak, early sixteenth century.*

Figure 2:187. *(Below) Boarded chest. English. Oak, early sixteenth century.*

Chip-carving (Figures 2:186-195)

There is a long and respectable history behind the simple form of all-over carving (lately the work of amateurs) referred to as chip-carving. The ground to be chip-carved is first marked out by compass point and scribe, into a series of simple geometric patterns based on circles within squares and rectangles. Then, using a simple sharp knife such as most men habitually carried at all times until recent years, the surface is whittled or 'chipped' away to leave cavities of triangular form, which relate as elements of the complicated overall effects. In medieval boarded and clamped-front chests, the most usual motif is the single roundel or 'Catherine wheel'.[62] More refined examples may include crude varieties of Gothic tracery (cf. Figures 4:1 and 2), but since chip-carving is associated firmly with carpenters' work at this date, sophisticated versions do not exist.

From the middle years of the seventeenth century are found a large number of small chip-carved boxes, frequently dated between 1640-70, the decoration of which follows a collective theme. It is possible that some were carved by professional boxmakers; but since the thematic persistence of chip-carving is so strong in the Welsh love token tradition of the following two hundred years, I am forced to the conclusion that much of this work was carried on boxes which had been purchased in the plain state, and then carved to serve as gifts. This impression is borne out by many of the inscriptions which may be found, since they often carry the name of a girl, or a simple message such as 'WIL THIS PLEAS YOU'. Some of the designs evidently figure as lovers' knots, and hearts are a frequent inclusion.

62. The attribute of St. Catherine, who was broken upon the wheel.

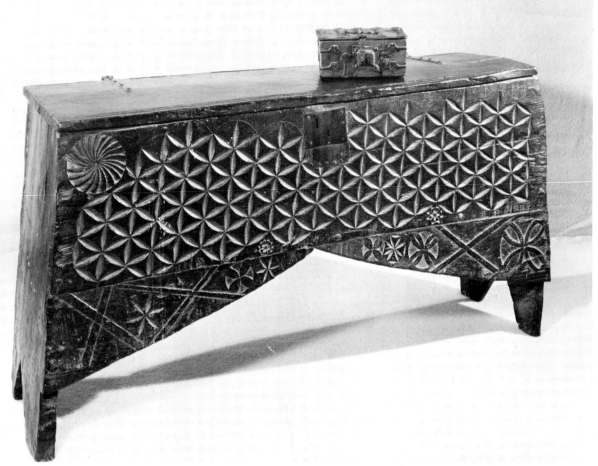

Figure 2:188. *Boarded chest. English. Oak, mid-sixteenth century. This post-medieval chest is free of the conventions of the late medieval forms in the two previous illustrations. The whole piece displays a remarkable sense of the casual enjoyment of surface pattern, and lacks any formal symmetry.*

Figure 2:189. *Boarded box. English. Oak, mid-sixteenth century.*

This mid-seventeenth century group of boxes seems mostly to be of English make, but there is apparently some regional polarisation, for later boxes and love tokens decorated in the same manner (such as spoons, stay busks, miniature furniture, etc.) are usually of proven Welsh origin. Chip-carving is also found in Spain, the North Sea coast of Europe (especially the Friesian Islands), and in Colonial America. A desk box similar to Figure 2:193 appears in the American Index of Design, and the appearance of chip-carving is normally associated with a peasant culture. The rushlight holder in Figure 2:195 is apparently Welsh, and is of exceptionally high quality for such a down-to-earth item. It might be assumed that rushlights were used

Figure 2:190. *Boarded box. English. Oak, mid-seventeenth century. This is a complicated structure, with numerous sliding compartments, chip-carved all over.*

Figure 2:191. *Boarded box. English. Oak, dated 1650. Inscribed 'THOMAS BEAMENT MADE THIS'. These boxes appear to be love tokens, carved by amateurs. This is an extremely rare instance of a piece actually signed by its maker.*

Figure 2:192. *Boarded box. English. Oak, mid-seventeenth century.*

only in poorer homes, but there is some Welsh precedent for the purchase of prepared rushes; at Tredegar House, Monmouthshire, in 1732. In this great house at least, rushlights were presumably used for secondary lighting, since the same account which records the purchase of three and a half dozen rushlights (probably from Bristol Fair), also includes forty-eight dozen candles.[63]

Profile Shaping (Figures 2:196-198)

A simple but effective technique much used in the seventeenth century and at other times, was to cut flat boards into a decorative shaped profile. This is most commonly found in the underside of horizontal rails, particularly the seat-rails and aprons of stools, chairs and tables, Such profiles are normally of a simple conventional variety, but sometimes a more unusual example is found, as in the tulip heads of the table in Figure 2:197. Major structural parts are sometimes shaped in this silhouette form, and the most obvious areas for such treatment are the crestings of chairs,

63. Quoted by M.R. Apted, The Monmouthshire Antiquary, Vol. III, Part II.

Figure 2:193. *Boarded desk box. English. Oak, 1648-60. This box bears the arms of the Commonwealth, consisting of the Cross of St. George and the Irish Harp, thus confirming a mid-seventeenth century date. In common with most other chip-carved boxes, it is covered all over with decoration, as the rear view (Figure 2:194) shows.*

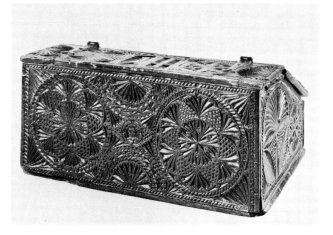

Figure 2:194. *Rear view of Figure 2:193.*

181

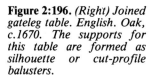

Figure 2:195. *(Left) Chip-carved rushlight holder. Welsh. Oak, dated 1763. This is an unusually fine specimen for a rushlight, which are normally mundane objects, designed for common usage.*

Figure 2:196. *(Right) Joined gateleg table. English. Oak, c.1670. The supports for this table are formed as silhouette or cut-profile balusters.*

Figure 2:198. *Joined child's high chair (detail). English. Oak, c.1675. An early expression of the taste for splat-back chairs, here with two splats and a shaped profile crest of earlier type. Note the fielded panel of the seat.*

the arms of chairs, and the end boards of carpenters' chests and stools in which the feet are formed by shaping in this way. Similarly, the shapes cut through perforated panels are cut profiles of various types. This work is referred to as 'fret work', and is performed with a special fret saw.

Less common in the seventeenth century is the occurrence of vertical splats or supports treated in this way. Silhouette balusters are occasionally found as the supports of tables, dressers or press cupboards, and at the end of the century are found for the first time in the form of splats inserted in chair backs. In the eighteenth century, this idea became very popular, and the splat-back chair was developed (based on a Chinese model). The use of cut profile splats persisted until the present day in Windsor chairs, and was perpetuated in the supports of some eighteenth century dressers (q.v.).

Figure 2:197. *Joined side table (detail). English. Oak, c.1680. The apron of this table is cut to a decorative profile of stylised tulip heads.*

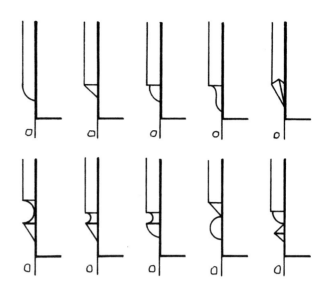

Diagram 2:28. *Stops for chamfers. A number of simple stops may be found on chamfered table legs, reflecting those found on architectural woodwork such as ceiling beams. The chamfer is stopped-off just short of the tenon which joins leg to stretcher.*

Figure 2:199. *Joined long dining table. English. Oak, second half of sixteenth century. A heavy and early example of a stop chamfered leg. The sheer sense of age in the surface and design of this massive table should be studied for its own sake. The thick, flaking patination combines with the worn edges to suggest generations of hard use. The rough construction and the use of stopped chamfers of architectural pattern may indicate here the work of a housewright.*

64. Quoted by R.W. Symonds, Connoisseur, Vol. CXIII, No. 491.

Chamfers (Figure 2:199)

The sharp edge or corner of a piece of squared timber is not only plain and uncomfortable in appearance, but it is bad practice to leave it so, since it will split and tear along the grain in use. For this reason, the exposed edges on furniture timbers are not left square and true. The corner is shaved off with a plane, to produce a splayed bevel or chamfer. For practical purposes this need only represent a tiny amount (⅛in. or so), but the chamfer is often made larger for decorative reasons. The chamfers on table legs, etc., are run out before the junction with the joint, and are usually finished with a decorative stop (Diagram 2:28). Even after the general introduction of turnings for legs, the use of the chamfer persisted in country-made furniture.

Perhaps the most common appearance of a chamfer is at the bottom edge of framed panels (see Diagram 2:15f and g). By far the majority of panel frames are finished in this way, since the chamfer is more easily cleaned of atmospheric dust than is a complex moulding. For this reason it is usually referred to as the 'dust chamfer', or 'dusting splay'.

Cut Balusters (Figures 2:200a and b)

A rather more sophisticated expression than the straight chamfer is the idea of imitating turnings by carving a baluster shape, but with a square or octagonal cross-section. This became popular in the late sixteenth century, and may be found on joined open-frame furniture such as tables, chairs and stools, and on staircase balusters. The profiles of such work almost always follow the shapes habitually used by the turner.

Carved Turnings (Figures 2:201-210)

During the second quarter of the sixteenth century, carving was firmly established as the prime means of decorating the legs and supports of open-frame furniture, especially tables and beds. Genuine survivals of this phase are extremely rare in unaltered condition, and so the evidence for it is largely documentary (such as the drawing-table "upon iiij carved pillors", mentioned in an inventory of 1552[64]), and fragmentary restored examples are known which bear out the observation.

Such all-carved work is invariably of square or octagonal cross-section and so it is not surprising that the carvers seized for novelty upon turning as an expedient for making a circular master block, which they could then embellish further by carving. This would seem to be the first manifestation

Figure 2:200a. *Joined stool. English. Oak, 1580-1630. This is a good-quality version of cut baluster work with an octagonal cross-section. The paired and reversed balusters are an early Italian type, much used in turnings, but rarely in furniture.*

Figure 2:200b. *Joined stool. English. Oak, 1680-1720. In this chamfered-leg stool, the suggestion of a baluster is merely hinted at by the slight knop reserved half way up the leg. The chamfers are finished with decorative stops.*

of turned decoration used in English joined furniture, and in the absence of precisely datable evidence, it seems likely that the step was taken during the decade 1550-60, at or before the beginning of the Elizabethan era. Pure turnings of Italian design had been used in the Italian-made choir stalls at King's College Chapel, Cambridge, in c.1535, but this was an isolated case which apparently did not affect English furniture until fifteen to twenty years later. A privately owned tester bed, securely dated 1565, is one of the earliest manifestations of turned and carved decoration in a piece of joined furniture.[65]

A series of conventional types of carved turnings developed during the latter half of the sixteenth century, and these are reviewed briefly in Diagram 2:30, and in Figures 2:201-210. Such features are extremely problematic to date accurately, since although the initial impetus for them was finished soon after 1600, they frequently reappear throughout the seventeenth century. A fluted baluster table of Dorset manufacture, for example, is dated 1638[66]; whilst a six-legged table at the Treasurer's House, York, has the remarkably late date of 1686 — remarkable because the leg is of exactly the same pattern as the magnificent trestle in Figure 2:202. In the absence of the date, it would have been tempting to suggest a date some sixty to eighty years earlier for the York table.

Figure 2:201. *Fragment of turned and carved bedpost. English. Oak, c.1580. The shape is first formed on a lathe by the turner; then the carver adds his decoration, leaving only a turned collar for accent. This vigorously interpreted version of the Roman Composite capital is typical of the originality of the early English Renaissance. The shaft of the column is covered with an inter-linked guilloche.*

Figure 2:202. *Joined trestle (detail of Figure 3:152). English. Oak, early seventeenth century. A large version of the cup-and-cover form. The deeply carved reeding of the bulb catches the light in a rich and positive way.*

65. See Sotheby Parke Bernet catalogue, 28th February, 1969, Lot 89 (illus.).
66. Illustrated by Anthony Wells-Cole, Furniture History, Vol. XII, 1976.

Figure 2:203. *Detail of joined withdrawing table. English. Oak, 1575-1625. A heavy and compact cup-and-cover, with a variety of reeding and palmate carving, surmounted by an Ionic capital.*

Figure 2:204. *Detail of joined long dining table. English. Oak. 1575-1625. Contrary to popular myth, there is no evidence that the heavier examples are necessarily of earlier date than lighter designs such as this.*

Figure 2:205. *Detail of joined dining table. English. Oak, c.1600. A richly carved baluster with fine and interesting details. Note the angles of the wear on the stretcher, and the unusual way in which the stretcher is set into the block of the leg. The apparent misalignment between the top of the leg and the frieze is, in fact, correct classical practice, as may be seen in Chippendale's engraving of 1754 (Figure 2:211), where the frieze is set back from the moulding of the capital. See also the following figure.*

Figure 2:206. *Joined stool table (detail of Figure 3:115). English. Oak, early seventeenth century. A finely drawn fluted baluster, complemented by heavily moulded stretchers and a shaped apron.*

Figure 2:207. *Joined stool. English. Oak, early seventeenth century.*

Figure 2:208. *Detail of joined table. English; Salisbury. Oak, c.1630. The partly-carved turning, here with simple fluting and a crisp stiff leaf.*

185

Figure 2:209. *Joined court cupboard (detail of Figure 3:248). English. Oak, c.1630. A partly-carved turned baluster, complemented by deep spandrels, a turned pendant and moulded stretchers.*

Figure 2:210. *Detail of joined armchair. English. Oak, mid-seventeenth century. A rare form of carved column, not related to any conventional type.*

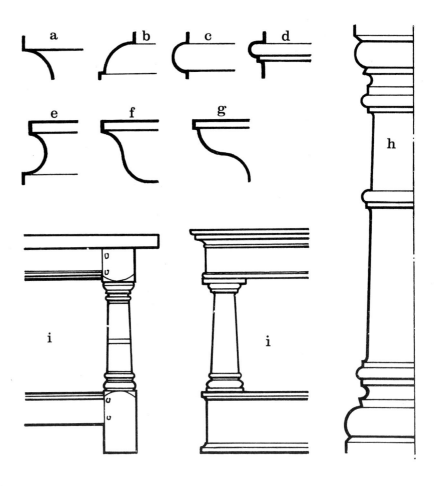

186

ii). Turning (Figures 2:211-217)

Following an initial subservience to the needs of the carver, through the latter part of the sixteenth century turned decoration was increasingly appreciated in its own right as a suitable means for decorating joined furniture. We have already seen that the turners were to a large extent autonomous in the production of thrown chairs and tables, and a whole range of domestic and commercial wares; and throughout the seventeenth century and later, turned decoration was to become an indispensable component of joined furniture; used for legs and other supports in particular, as well as feet, handles, panels of spindles and applied split spindles. No doubt many country joiners did their own turning, just as they did their own carving, but as a rule the standard of turned work is so good as to suggest that much of it was performed by professional turners who had served a thorough apprenticeship. The high standard is seen not only in the quality of craftsmanship, but also in a general comprehension of classical form and detail.

Herbert Cescinsky once wrote that "...classical sections are almost unknown in Jacobean or Stuart oak..."[67] but observation of the facts shows this to be patently not true: although they are frequently misunderstood or imperfectly interpreted, classical profiles are in fact the very *essence* of the design of mouldings and turnings throughout the whole of the post-Gothic period. Nowhere is this more true than in good-quality joined oak furniture, though it must equally be stressed that *true* classical proportion and detail was not fully understood in England until Inigo Jones and the Laudian period (q.v.), and the expansion of the cabinetmakers' trade in the eighteenth century.

It is therefore not amiss here to reproduce two late but definitive expressions of the classical orders, based on the Roman models of Vitruvius and Vignola. Figure 2:211 is the engraving used in the 1754 edition of *The Gentleman and Cabinet-maker's Director,* by Thomas Chippendale; and is followed by a fine model of c.1780, made for Queen Marie Antoinette by Robert Arnould Drais. The perfect representations contained in these will serve in part to illustrate the defects which exist in earlier English vernacular interpretations; but they also contrast with the originality and vitality of much of the earlier work, which did not feel obliged slavishly to copy pure classical form. There are two sides to the English coin; in that, whilst our native craftsmen were interested in the disciplines of classical conventions, they also felt free to interpret and modify within their own limitations, and to their own satisfaction.

The detailed breaks and profiles used in the best turned and moulded work are based on the simple classical formulae of alternating flat, convex and concave surfaces, broken with sharp ridges and fillets, which are used in combinations to produce the overall designs. Some of these are given in Diagram 2:29, but many novel and unconventional forms are used in vernacular work, which are 'classical' only by association. Mouldings and turnings are closely allied in the use of these details of profile, which are designed to catch and elaborate the contrasts of light and shade. Classical rules also indicate specific carved enrichments (such as egg-and-dart, anthemion, etc.) for specified profiles, but it is very rare that these are *correctly* used in early English work.

The turned members of joined open-framing are turned down from the original square-sectioned block, and as an aesthetic rule the swellings of the shape are generally carried to the full thickness of the original block. This helps provide a rich and sturdy appearance with no sense of weakness at the

Diagram 2:29. *(Left) The classical mouldings. In their simplest form, as here, these are the basic units which make up the vocabulary of classical moulded and turned profiles. They are assembled in various combinations and proportions, interspersed with fillets and shoulders, to make up a sequence of related shapes. These profiles rely on light and shade for their effect, but in old furniture the result is heightened by the colouring of patination.*

a). *Cavetto (concave).*
b). *Ovolo (convex).*
c). *Torus (convex, semi-circle).*
d). *Astragal, or bead (a small torus, sometimes with extra emphasis).*
e). *Scotia (concave, asymmetric semi-circle).*
f). *Cyma recta (concave above, convex below).*
g). *Cyma reversa, or ogee (convex above, concave below).*
h). *An example of a simple turned column with capital, base, and the shaft punctuated by an astragal. The column is made up with combinations of torus, scotia and astragal. In sophisticated work, the allusions to classical architecture may be carried to very great lengths.*
i). *Even in simple provincial joinery, the forms of the classical orders are followed very closely. The turned column is divided correctly into a shaft with base and capital. It sits on a pedestal or plinth (stretcher and tenon-block), and supports an entablature (frieze or seat-rail). The top overhangs in the manner of a cornice, and on some pieces the use of applied edge-mouldings is also copied literally.*

67. Herbert Cescinsky, *English Furniture from Gothic to Sheraton,* Garden City, New York, 1937, p.101.

Figure 2:211. *The Classical Orders.*
Engraving from Thomas Chippendale's
'The Gentleman and Cabinet-maker's
Director', 1754. From left to right:
Tuscan, Roman Doric, Ionic,
Corinthian, Composite.

Figure 2:212. *The Classical Orders.*
Model by Robert Arnould Drais,
c.1780.

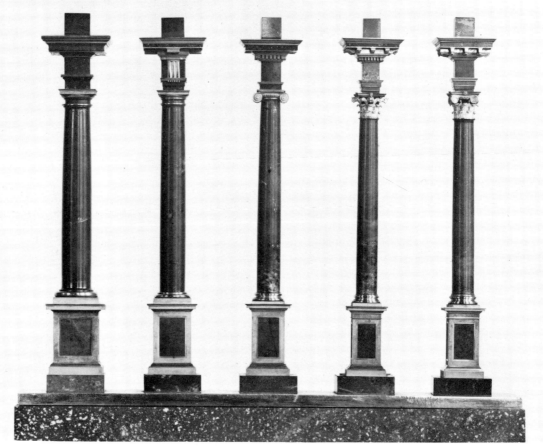

Figure 2:213

Figure 2:214

Figure 2:215

Figure 2:216

Figures 2:213, 214, 215, 216. *Joined stools. English. Oak, c.1630. Various treatments of turning and carving create different effects on the same basic item. The stool is a relatively simple piece of furniture, but is capable of infinitely varied treatment.*

knees, though it does mean that small inconsequential 'flats' are sometimes left at the extremities which mark the original surface of the block. During the course of the seventeenth century, the turners developed a rich vocabulary of plump and appropriate shapes; and though the variety to be found 'in the flesh' is almost limitless, most of the fashions in turnings which came and went between 1560 and 1740 are seen to fall into four broad groups, which may be determined by analysis (see Diagram 2:30). They are:

a). Turned and carved
b). Columns and balusters
c). Repeat forms
d). Post-Restoration varieties

As with any other feature, it is extremely difficult to give a general guide to the dating of specific types of turning. Nevertheless, most of them had a fairly short popular life, and can reasonably be assigned to within a period of forty years or so, though the classic forms of columns and balusters are found over a much broader range. Bearing this in mind, we may attempt to assign them to a reasonable date spectrum:

a). Turned and Carved

We have seen that the use of carved turnings originated soon after 1550, and by the end of the century all the basic variations had evolved. Most of the carved enrichment offers a vertical emphasis, and takes the form of fluting (concave channels) or reeding (convex ribs), though a great deal of floral, leafy or jewel-like ornament is also found. Decorated capitals are usually Ionic, or a simplified Corinthian. Richly-carved styles in this manner are usually associated with the reigns of Elizabeth I and James I, but there is plenty of evidence that they persisted after 1660, by which time they must be regarded as an archaism. The partly-carved turned leg which is sometimes found after c.1630 is possibly a vestigial form of the earlier taste for fluting and reeding.

Figure 2:217. *Detail of press cupboard (cwpwrdd deuddarn). Welsh; Denbighshire. Oak, dated 1729. A particularly large version of an applied split spindle, matching the turned supports of the cupboard. Note how the panel and frame of the door (on the left) are proportioned to match that of the fixed panel on the right. This meticulous attention to joinery detail is one of the most pleasing aspects of North Welsh furniture in the eighteenth century.*

b). Columns and Balusters

The simple form of column found in English furniture is closely based on the Tuscan or Roman Doric, or it is occasionally provided with an Ionic capital. In its extremes, the architectural allusions are carried forward in a literal manner, and the top frieze may be treated as an entablature (and sometimes even the bottom rail as a plinth or pedestal). Even in its restrained form, the standard columnar leg relates very closely to the classical format of pedestal — base — column — capital — entablature. Early in the seventeenth century a range of patterns developed, and remained popular over a considerable period. Column turnings frequently employ the Greek device of 'entasis', a slight swelling in the shape which helps avoid a mean, ungenerous look.

The baluster was also a classical device, the taste for which was imported to England from Italy. In its simple form, it is essentially a rising or falling S-curve, though the English turners also commonly used a rather inarticulate version with parallel sides. The rising baluster has a lightness and grace which is missing from the bottom-heavy inverted form, and as a result the former is the more usual. It is very rare to find the reversed (or paired) balusters in English furniture, though they are common enough in architectural woodwork such as staircases.

c). Repeat Forms

Probably during the decade 1630-40, there arose a fashion for a series of turnings based on sequential repeats of single units. It is by no means clear exactly when these first appeared, but they were certainly in common use during the Civil War period, and for this reason they are closely associated with the Puritan ethic. In fact they continued in very common usage until well after 1700, and by far their most frequent appearance is in provincial furniture of 1660-1740. The most usual form is the single repeated ball turning, and this may be alternated with fillets or other mouldings which are iterated rhythmically. At their best they represent a satisfying gleam of patinated shapes. At their worst they are dull and spiritless.

d). Post-Restoration Varieties

Following the high fashions set by walnut, and later mahogany, furniture after 1660 (and augmented by the haste to refurnish after the Great Fire of London in 1666), a series of modish turnings were foisted on provincial turners. Working in oak, fruitwood or yew, they attempted to reproduce the fashionable forms of the day, with variable degrees of success. The results may often lack the flair and verve of the original, but the country-made versions often have a spirit and strength of their own. Following closely on their reputable models (but with an obvious time lag), the shapes which appeared include the spiral, the inverted cup, the pad foot, and even the cabriole leg. Balusters continued in use, but in more complicated and attentuated versions. Such developments were accompanied by changes in the form of the stretchers, and later the complete omission of stretchers on pad foot and cabriole legs. This is quite alien to joined traditions, but it was made possible by improved techniques in the making of major joints, and made necessary by the particular form of the turned parts.

iii). Mouldings (Figures 2:218-219)

The profiles and cross-sections used in the design of mouldings follow the same basic rules of detail as do turnings. They are made in several ways, according to the size and nature of the job. The simplest technique is to use a shaped piece of flat steel, which is cut to a profile in reverse of the desired

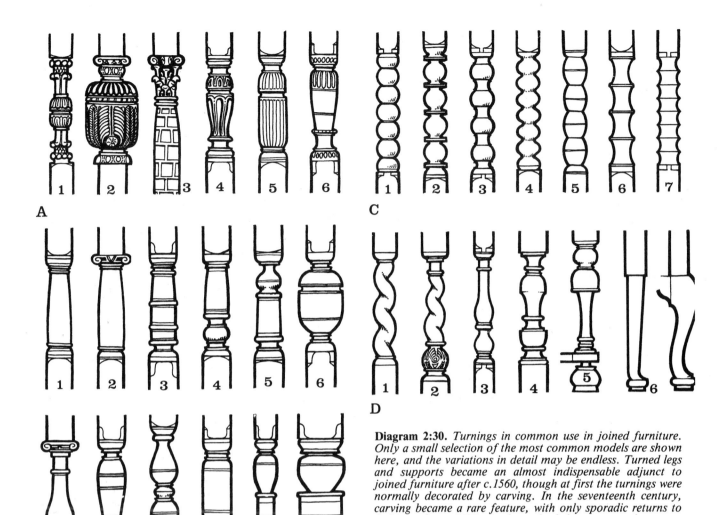

A

C

B

D

Diagram 2:30. *Turnings in common use in joined furniture. Only a small selection of the most common models are shown here, and the variations in detail may be endless. Turned legs and supports became an almost indispensable adjunct to joined furniture after c.1560, though at first the turnings were normally decorated by carving. In the seventeenth century, carving became a rare feature, with only sporadic returns to fashion after c.1625. At the end of the seventeenth century many of the shapes used echo those developed for walnut furniture, and after 1720 simple cabrioles and pad foot legs are found in oak and country timbers such as elm, fruitwood and yewtree.*

A). Turned and carved
1). *Embryonic cup-and-cover, c.1560.*
2). *Cup-and-cover, 1560-1680 (rare after 1640).*
3). *Corinthian capital, after 1560 (here with rusticated column, though other patterns were used, such as guilloche).*
4). *Fluted baluster, 1560-1640.*
5). *Reeded baluster, 1575-1640.*
6). *Vestigial fluted baluster, c.1630.*

B). Columns and Balusters
1). *Doric column, 1560-1800.*
2). *Ionic column, 1560-1680.*
3). *Column enriched with astragals, 1580-1740.*
4). *Column and ball, 1600-1740.*
5). *Column and baluster, 1600-1740.*
6). *Cup-and-cover, 1580-1680.*
7). *Classical baluster, with Ionic capital, 1580-1680.*
8). *Rising baluster, 1580-1800.*
9). *Paired, or reversed, balusters, 1580-1700.*
10). *Parallel-sided baluster, or marrow-leg, 1620-1740.*
11 and 12). *Baluster and peg, 1580-1700 (this popular pattern is shown in two sizes, scaled for a matching table and stool).*

C). Repeat forms (all after c.1640)
1). *Ball.*
2). *Ball and fillet.*
3). *Ball and reel.*
4). *Flattened ball.*
5). *Egg.*
6). *Reel.*
7). *Fine reel.*

D). Post-Restoration varieties (all after 1660)
1). *Single-bine spiral, or barley-twist, 1660-1725.*
2). *Tapered spiral, with carved ball, c.1680.*
3). *Elongated compound baluster, 1660-1800.*
4). *Peg-shaped baluster, 1675-1725.*
5). *Inverted-cup baluster, 1675-1700.*
6). *Pad foot, with tapered leg, after 1720.*
7). *Cabriole leg, 1720-1800.*

shape. The steel (which has a sharp burred-over cutting edge left by the file) is scraped along in the required position, eventually leaving a scratch moulding of the required section (Diagram 2:31). The steel scratch-plate is sometimes held in a wooden tool handle, known as a scratch stock. This is the simplest way to cut mouldings, and very large-scale work, such as ceiling beams, was often roughed out first by axe, to be finished with a series of basic profiles.

As mouldings became more conventionalised, e.g. on late seventeenth century chests of drawers, a series of moulding planes were evolved with shaped blades of the required profiles. A very complicated shape, such as a cornice, would be worked up with several blades.

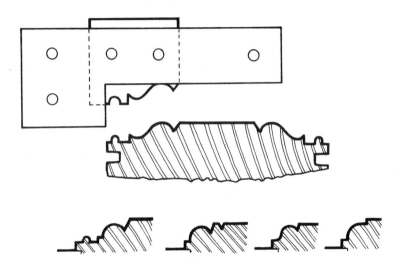

Diagram 2:31. *Scratch-plate and scratch-stock. The scratch-plate may be used to produce both edge-mouldings (as here) and channel-mouldings of simple type. The shaped plate is scraped along the work, leaving a decorative moulding. Several variations of profiles are shown, and it will be noted that, using this technique, it is not possible to under-cut the shape. The scratch-plate may be held in the hand or in a wooden stock (top) for ease of handling.*

Figure 2:218. *Joined chest. English. Oak, early seventeenth century. Heavy mouldings combined with applied split-spindles.*

Figure 2:219. *Joined chest. English. Oak, early seventeenth century. Heavy edge-mouldings are used to frame the panel.*

192

The rich variety of edge mouldings, channel mouldings and applied mouldings which may be found on period furniture, owe their effect to the same optical devices as do turnings, i.e. the control of light and shade into areas of line and tone. In old furniture, the patinated surfaces further enhance this effect by the contrasts of pale highlights over the darker recesses which lie between. Mouldings are used as visual frames and boundaries to control and enclose the overall composition of structural areas, particularly the edges of frames, tops, seats and drawers; and to enliven areas such as panels. In an architectural sense, they may be used as cornices, pediments and bases, to provide visual extremities to height and other dimensions. When used with imagination and flair, mouldings can provide sufficient decoration on their own, or in combination with turnings.

Figure 2:220. *Inlaid panel. English. Oak, with mastic composition, probably 1539. The arms are those of Lady Kingston, and others in the series bear the arms of her husband, Sir William Kingston, Constable of the Tower of London (d.1540).*

68. Lindsay Boynton, *The Hardwick Hall Inventories of 1601*, Furniture History Society, London, 1971, plate 15, and room 30, p.31.

iv). **Inlay, Parquetry and Marquetry** (Figures 2:220-226)

Each of these techniques involves the decoration of plane surfaces with combinations of parti-coloured woods or other materials; but due to frequent confusion of the terms, it is perhaps expedient to attempt a definition of the three processes and the 'grey' areas between them. Unfortunately, the modern uses of the terms do not always agree with early usage, since inventories before 1660 normally refer indiscriminately to 'marketree' or 'inlayed' work, yet the majority of early examples are of inlay. Conversely, the German marquetry chest which survives at Hardwick, was referred to in the 1601 inventory as a "great inlayde Chest" in Lady Shrewsbury's own withdrawing chamber.[68] In order that we may know what we mean, the different processes should be distinguished as follows:

Inlay: With this elementary technique, thick veneers or slips of timber (up to ¼in. thick) are cut to shape and *laid into* corresponding hollows which are chopped out of the solid surface of the panel or framing rail which is to receive the decoration. The whole scheme is glued securely into place, and the surface is then cleaned off with a plane or scrape. Such a crude technique limits the intricacy of possible designs, and as a result, inlaid work has a directness and vitality of its own. Elaborate curves or scrolls can be bent to shape, but complex elements are not possible.

Parquetry: This is a slightly more developed and sophisticated process, normally used for broad bands or areas of formal geometric pattern, or

193

Figure 2:221. *Joined press cupboard. English. Oak, inlaid with bog oak and fruitwoods, early seventeenth century.*

Figure 2:222. *Joined chest of drawers. English. Oak, inlaid with bone and boxwood stringing, c.1680. The small trundle wheels are a rare feature on furniture other than truckle beds, but it is not clear whether these are entirely original, or a slightly later addition. Compare the decoration with that in Figure 3:421.*

simple pictorial work. By this method combinations of coloured pieces are laid together, as a mosaic, into recesses cut in the solid. It is not clear whether the compositions were normally assembled *in situ,* or whether they would have been glued together first and then laid down as a parcel. Parquetry normally concedes a broad and coarse effect, like inlay, and the scale of the work is limited. In this case, the solid surface of the panel or rail is left to form a frame or surround to the parquetry section, but it does not form a ground *inside* the design as with inlay.

Marquetry: This is altogether a finer and more sophisticated approach, which plays almost no part in English work before 1660. Marquetry furniture was certainly produced in England from the sixteenth century onwards, but usually by immigrant craftsmen (especially Germans) working in centres such as Southwark or Norwich, and wholly in foreign styles. Groups of furniture such as the 'Nonsuch' chests fall within this attribution, as well as very fine individual items such as the 'Great Bed of Ware', and Hugh Offley's chest in Southwark Cathedral. It is largely impossible to be sure which of these pieces were actually *made* in England and which were imported as new, but certainly immigrant craftsmen *were* exercising such techniques in England. True marquetry is a cabinetmaker's technique, which consists of assembling patterns to form a complete veneer panel. This is finally laid down over the entire surface of the carcase (normally dovetailed boards, of course), obscuring the joints between boards and structures. Thus, the carcase or frame forms no part of the visible decorated surface.

Figure 2:223. *Joined chest of drawers. Anglo-Dutch. Oak, veneered with ivory and partridgewood, 1650-1680. Note particularly the use of machine-made rippled moulding and the contemporary obsession with small perspective views, here seen as a black and white paved corridor in the central panel.*

Figure 2:223a. *Portrait of a Young Man, by Pieter Fransz De Grebber, in original frame. Dutch, mid-seventeenth century. The mitred and engine-turned mouldings of the frame are exactly as found on contemporary Anglo-Dutch cupboards and chests of drawers, such as Figure 2:223.*

Figure 2:224. *Joined chest of drawers. English. Oak, veneered with ivory and various woods, c.1680*

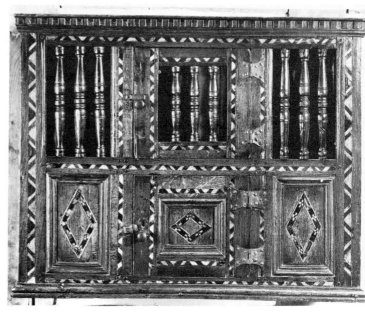

Figure 2:225. *Joined food cupboard. English; Yorkshire. Oak, inlaid with parquetry bands of bog oak and sycamore, mid-seventeenth century.*

Marquetry, and the related practice of veneering, was used in Europe as early as the fifteenth century. Inlay and parquetry both appear in England around the middle of the sixteenth century; but one of the earliest examples (the panel of c.1539 in Figure 2:220) uses not wood, but some form of mastic composition, which is used as a coloured ground to the enriched charge of arms. A similar mixture is found in small amounts at various periods, but the usual materials for inlay are hard substances such as woods, bone, ivory, metals, marbles, stone, slate, tortoiseshell and mother-of-pearl. Various woods are used for their natural colours, such as the pale holly, sycamore, poplar and maple; the medium browns of box, walnut and the fruitwoods; and the deep blacks of bog oak and ebony. Other colours such as red, green and yellow were obtained by the use of artificial stains; whilst textures were introduced with the use of burrs, pollards, and an artificial mixture of glue and wood shavings akin to marblewood (p.153).

Aristocratic inventories of the later sixteenth century frequently mention marquetry and inlaid furniture, but these were not always of English manufacture. Inlay appears in vernacular work of the seventeenth century, especially in Lancashire and Yorkshire (q.v.), and occasionally in America. Parquetry, as now, was used for geometric patterned floors, and according to Aubrey,[69] the drawing-room of a house at Chelsea was laid out with a chequered parquetry floor of "...Box and Ewgh panels of about six inches square..."

> 1582...A fair square chest inlaid wth white bone, wth the Talbot and FS...

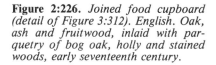

Figure 2:226. *Joined food cupboard (detail of Figure 3:312). English. Oak, ash and fruitwood, inlaid with parquetry of bog oak, holly and stained woods, early seventeenth century.*

69. Aubrey, *Natural History of Wiltshire.*

1601...a drawing table Carved and guilt standing uppon sea dogges inlayde with marble stones and wood...
a little desk of Ibonie, inlayde with white...

1614...An ebony cabinett inlaied with mother-of-pearle...
A large Trunke of Mother of Pearle with two drawers...

1679...One inlaid Table, one Large Looking-Glass and 2 Stands of ye same...

Figure 2:227. Boarded box. English. Oak, painted red, c.1680 (see Plate Eight).

Figure 2:227a. Interior view of Figure 2:227 showing original red combed paper lining.

v). Paints and Stains

Modern terminology generally distinguishes between paints and stains, in that the former are usually opaque and form a separate skin over the surface; whilst the latter are transparent and do not obscure the grain of wood. Stains may be used as a film of coloured varnish, or they may be used in such a way as to penetrate the surface and stain or dye the fibres themselves. To some extent these divisions reflect medieval usage, for the Painters were concerned with painting on wood, stone, plaster and other hard surfaces; whereas the Stainers were chiefly concerned with painting on cloth (in the form of hangings, flags, banners, etc.), and it is reasonable to assume that their colours might often be transparent. In medieval London, it was found that the interests of the two trades were closely allied, and this led to their combination in 1502, and the eventual incorporation of the Worshipful Company of Painter-Stainers in 1581. The Company was in perpetual dispute with the College of Heralds throughout the seventeenth century and up until 1738, over the contested right to paint coats-of-arms. Partly as a result of this hostility, several painters were jailed by the Court of Chivalry for the wrongful painting of arms.

The use of painted surfaces on furniture and woodwork is of great antiquity, and seems to have been popular in England at all times. The very low survival rate of early painted furniture gives a somewhat different impression, but medieval accounts often describe painted items and interiors, and a great many surviving pieces from before 1550 retain traces of their original polychrome or single-colour decoration. This is usually found as minute traces in crevices of the carving or the grain of the wood, and is usually underlain by a thin coat of gesso, acting as a grain filler and ground for the paint. Apart from the protection afforded to the timber by a suitable coat of paint (especially on chests which might be used for travelling), there were two other reasons for the popularity of such treatments: firstly, the sheer love of colour in an age in which colourful clothes and interior decorations formed a large part of the background to everyday fashionable life; and secondly for the proper identification and advertisement of coats-of-arms on furniture and other goods belonging to the wealthy.

The emphasis on painted furniture declined with the second half of the sixteenth century, though a consistent core of items was still decorated in this way until after 1700. Colour is found on aristocratic furniture, especially in connection with armorials, and sporadically in complete schemes in middle-class furniture such as the fascinating chest of drawers in Figure 2:235. Painting did not return as a fashionable expression until the later eighteenth century.

Paints were not supplied in a modern ready-mixed form until the early nineteenth century, when experiments began with lead tubes as containers. Before this innovation, the painter-stainer processed most of his ingredients for himself and his training included the necessary tasks of refining his oils, the grinding and mixing of colours, and making his own brushes. Most early colours were derived from natural ingredients, the availability of which were greatly enhanced by the expansion of overseas trade in the seventeenth century. The most common colours used to decorate woodwork were somewhat limited in comparison to the sophisticated and often expensive materials used by portrait and landscape painters. They consisted of various reds (red lead, iron oxide, red ochre, vermilion-cinnabar); blues (woad, smalt, indigo); greens (verdigris, green earths); yellows (yellow ochre, lead-tin yellow); blacks (lampblack, bituminous earths); with white lead as the usual cheap white. Actual shades and tones varied enormously with natural inconsistencies in the materials. Many of the pigments used and experimented with must have proven impermanent or fugitive, and a great many painted schemes have no doubt been lost on account of fading, crackling, flaking and other integral faults in the materials used. Paint technology was still in its infancy up to the nineteenth century, though many significant advances had already been made, such as the use of oil as a medium in the fifteenth century. Even relatively unsophisticated paints used a variety of media, binders and drying agents; but the most simple ingredients were the age old egg white, glue size and various gums, using water or oils as media.

The functions of the average painter-stainer were varied within the craft, and might include the production of hangings ("stayned cloths"), house-painting and interior decoration, sign painting and lettering, simple portraits, landscapes and other easel pictures, hatchments and other coats-of-arms, as well as decorating furniture, panelling and statuary. Apart from the laying down of flat colour and decorative compositions, the painter-stainer was required to be conversant with techniques such as priming, scumbling, gilding, wood graining and marbling. Little is known of the daily life and work of the jobbing painter, though they are occasionally mentioned by name in bills of work and other transactions, and their work is occasionally to be found in houses, churches and other institutions. In 1591, for example, the widow of a painter-stainer listed all his "frames with painted pictures or stories in them, together with all (his) stones, colours and frames, and all other things belonging to the art, mistery, science or occupation of a painter".[70] In America, where painted furniture is found as a more consistent theme after 1700, we find that the 1727 inventory of Charles Gillam of Saybrook, Connecticut, included "...ochre...umber...a painted chest with drawers...a parcel of collours...", as well as partially completed furniture and woodworking tools.[71]

Painted Furniture (Figures 2:227-237)

The most habitual remains of original paintwork are the single or self-colour paints found frequently on country-made furniture, especially of the eighteenth and early nineteenth centuries. The small box in Figure 2:227 is a particularly early and complete example of red-lead paint, which is complemented by the red combed paper which is still inside. The coarsely-ground texture of the pigment is quite clear in the photograph, and is a feature of this class of work. It would seem that the bulk of primitive and utility furniture was originally finished in this way, both for protection of the wood and to brighten cottage interiors. Another possible motive was to give simple furniture a homogeneous and 'finished' look, since they were often constructed from a disparate mixture of timbers. Such an illogical combination of timbers may often be taken as an indication that the piece was intended from the start to be given a unifying coat of colour.

In the eighteenth century, Windsor chairs were frequently used as garden furniture by the wealthy, and they may sometimes be seen used as such in fashionable family portraits, resplendent in their original green paint. In April 1730, John Brown "at the Three Chairs and Walnut Tree in St. Paul's Churchyard" issued an advertisement which included reference to his "Windsor Garden Chairs, of all sizes, painted green or in the wood." Several greens are found, including emerald, a dark bottle-green, olive, and a bright grass-green. Other colours include vermilion, red-lead, yellow ochre, a creamy yellow, a chalky blue, black and white. Apart from self-colour paints, imitative finishes are often found, such as marbling and wood graining (usually copying such distinctive timbers as oak, rosewood or bird's-eye maple). The combed paint of the desk box in Plate Eleven is a particularly vivid version, reminiscent of Staffordshire slipware pottery. In early eighteenth century New England, several local expressions of painted furniture are seen to develop (especially in Hadley, Massachusetts; Guilford and Saybrook, Connecticut; Taunton, Massachusetts; and Hampton, New Hampshire), but these are largely local impulses which owe little or nothing to English models or traditions (see also pp.512-516).

We must turn to a few scattered fragments in order to see English medieval painted furniture at its earliest stage. *Any* remains of such pieces are bound to be incomplete or at least heavily restored. Some are very well known, such as the restored altar chest at Newport Church, Essex; but others still await proper cleaning and investigation. Such a piece is the Lillebon panel of c.1315, in Winchester Cathedral. Although sections of the woodwork are missing, much of the original polychrome decoration is still in good state. If this piece were to be properly cleaned, its importance might be more fully appreciated. The panel was presented to the Cathedral before 1320 by Sir William de Lillebon, of Milton Lilbourne, Wiltshire.

One of the most important survivals of medieval painted decoration on furniture is the celebrated chest of Richard de Bury, now in the Burrell Collection at Glasgow (Figure 2:107, Plate Eight). This large, iron-bound

70. F.G. Emmison, op. cit.
71. Quoted by Dean A. Fales Jr., *American Painted Furniture 1660-1880,* Dutton, New York, 1973.

Figure 2:228. *Alabaster panel, in original oak hanging box. English; Nottingham, fifteenth century. The painting of the box lids is perhaps indicative of the quality of the better painted furniture of the later Middle Ages, examples of which have entirely disappeared.*

boarded chest or standard is datable by its heraldry to 1340-45. Unfortunately, the decoration which must have carried over the front, sides, and possibly the outer surface of the lid, has long since disappeared; and we are left with only the evidence of the remarkably well-preserved oil and tempera paintings under the lid.

The shields link the ownership or patronage of the chest to Richard Aungerville de Bury, Bishop of Durham (d.1345), and his associate Ralph, 2nd Lord Nevill of Raby (d.1367), a representative of the Crown. The two men were good friends, and are known to have been associated in various commissions between 1340 and 1345. If we could have known the nature of the lost decorations, we could perhaps be more specific in dating the chest, since it seems likely that there were other shields of arms, perhaps representing other members of a travelling commission for whose use the chest may have been supplied. One possibility is the occasion in April 1340, when de Bury and Nevill were appointed, with Henry de Percy and Geoffrey le Scrope, to travel to York to arrange tax collections and payments to the King's Army in the North and to make other payments for the defence of the Realm.

Certainly, the blue lion rampant, seen at the left hand end of the lid, was the badge of Henry de Percy; but the others (a brown dragon striped with blue, a belligerent centaur in a yellow hood, and a yellow dragon striped with red) are not identified, and may not have had any heraldic significance. If this conjecture is correct, then the front of the chest, or the outer lid, may have borne the arms of Percy and le Scrope, and perhaps others. The four existing shields are, left to right: D'Aungerville, an augmentation of D'Aungerville, the Royal Arms, and those of Nevill. The chest, which *does* have its original carrying handles, would have been provided to hold the documents, banners and other accoutrements of the commissioners on their journey to York, and may also have acted as their treasury.

Figure 2:229. *Joined staircase and arcade. Knole House, Kent. Oak, painted in colours, 1604.*

Until 1855, the chest was held at the Court of Chancery of the Palatinate of Durham, whence it was purloined by a building contractor. It subsequently went through several hands until Sir William Burrell acquired it from the collection of Capt. N.R. Colville of Penheale Manor, Cornwall. In the 1960s the paint was found to be in a seriously dry, dirty and flaking state (just compare the difference between Fred Roe's watercolour of 1902,[72] and the present colour plate), and so the paint was cleaned and consolidated at the Stenhouse Restoration Centre of the National Trust for Scotland.[73]

Two chests of slightly later date (1357-61) are held in the Public Record Office in London, and these both have painted armorials on the *outside* lids and fronts, not unlike the Richard de Bury chest. Coincidentally, one of these[74] also bears the same shield of Ralph Nevill. He had been with the company that captured King David Bruce of Scotland at Nevill's Cross, Durham, in 1346. Bruce was held in the Tower of London until 1357, when he was ransomed under the Treaty of Berwick. This Record Office chest held documents relating to the ransom and release of the Scottish king, and other shields relate to those involved in the affair.

The vast body of medieval painted furniture has passed into obscurity, and so it is all but impossible to gain an accurate idea of the general *quality* of workmanship. Illuminated manuscripts give some idea of the effect of a medieval painted and hung interior, but we are left with no impression of the actual handling of paint on furniture. Much of it was no doubt applied in a bold and carefree manner, but the box in Figure 2:228 is perhaps representative of some of the best work. Here, the paint is handled in a precise and confident way, using a restricted palette. The box is the original container for the Nottingham alabaster panel which it still holds, and was designed to be hung on the wall as a household shrine. The paint has been protected by the closure of the box, so that the colours are near pristine.

It is not until the end of the sixteenth century that survivals of original paintwork begin to appear in appreciable numbers. Even at this date it is sufficiently rare to give the mistaken impression that painted furniture was uncommon in its day. This low survival rate is accountable for several reasons, not the least being its fragile nature. The layer of paint represents an extremely thin membrane, which may be easily scratched or faded. Once this happens, the details of the decoration become indistinct and untidy, and the whole piece loses its appeal in the eyes of the proud householder. For such reasons a great deal of painted furniture must have been scrapped, scraped down or repainted after very few years of service. Those which have endured must owe that fact either to luck, or to negligence.

Since painted furniture is so susceptible to the cruelties of time, it is valuable to be able to turn to comparable work in order to gain some impression of its appearance. Architectural woodwork does not often receive the same hard wear as portable furniture, and in a few instances certain fireplaces, staircases and wall-panelling have retained their original schemes of paint (albeit retouched or cleaned). Two examples of the early seventeenth century are shown here, and it may be taken that their finish was typical of the lost painted furniture of their time. Figure 2:229 is the principal staircase at Knole House, Kent, which was inserted by order of Thomas Sackville, 1st Earl of Dorset, in 1604. The broad polychrome effects pick out the details of the carving, and create their own *trompe l'oeil* in the strapwork panels which fill the flat areas of plasterwork. The *real* balusters of the staircase handrail are imitated in paint on the inner wall, balancing the whole composition.

One of the most brilliant jewels of early seventeenth century interior

72. Fred Roe, *Ancient Coffers and Cupboards*, Methuen, London, 1902.
73. A full resumé of available information on the chest was given by William Wells, Scottish Art Review, Vol. 10, No. 4, 1966.
74. Celia Jennings, *Early Chests in Wood and Iron*, HMSO, 1974, Chest 1, p.2, Fig.1.

Figure 2:230. *Joined facade of the Kederminster Pew. Langley Marish Church, Buckinghamshire. Oak, painted in colours, probably 1622.*

decoration is the Kederminster Library, which nestles hidden in suburban Slough, like a pearl in a grey oyster, at the church of Langley Marish, Buckinghamshire. In 1613, Sir John Kederminster applied for a licence to build an "Ile or Chappell" on the south side of the church in his manor of Langley. This was duly granted, but Sir John vastly exceeded his brief. He annexed the entire south porch and a small chapel, and in 1617-22 rebuilt them as a library with its own fireplace, and communicating with a new enclosed family pew in the south aisle. From the body of the church, the only visible work is the panelled and shuttered exterior of the Kederminster Pew (Figure 2:230), resplendent in its original marbled paintwork and surmounted by a strapwork cresting and carved pinnacles.

The privacy of the interior is guarded by pierced grilles and hinged shutters, including some re-used panels of Gothic tracery of c.1500, and some remarkable (original) fretwork panels of complex geometric patterns, similar to the glazing patterns published by Walter Gedde in his *Booke of Sundry Draughtes* of 1613. One such panel is seen clearly at the top of the door, flanked by the diapered and hinged shutters. The blind panels of the screen and door feature imitation oval marble bosses (Plate Fourteen), and this theme is continued inside, with the addition of nine armorial panels of Kederminster and their alliances, and the ubiquitous 'God's All-Seeing Eye'.

Figure 2:231. *Joined tester bedstead. English; probably Somerset. Oak, painted in colours, early seventeenth century. The arms are those of Cooper, Gilbert and other families; the upper register carved and painted, whilst the lower are painted on flat panels.*

Looking down the pew a glimpse is caught of the library itself (Plate Seven), and the only entrance is through the door from the pew. The library is lined with panelling from floor to ceiling, with an elaborate mantelpiece. The panelling consists partly of a series of hinged doors which conceal a number of book presses, containing the original library of books presented by the founder (complete with the original framed catalogue of 1638). The subjects on the panels consist of cycles of complicated cartouches, saints and local views (including Windsor and Eton), whilst the inside surfaces of the cupboards can boast representations of opened books and the likenesses of Sir John and Lady Mary Kederminster themselves. The furnishings consist of the (apparently) original painted oak and walnut square table, and a painted beech child's bench (Figure 3:501) used as a mounting stool to reach the higher bookshelves. The fixed bench in the pew also matches these items very closely, and is painted in imitation of red figured marble.

The books and Library still survive substantially as when they were made available for the use of the ministers of Langley and the District, in 1623. One of the early visitors was the poet John Milton, who used the Library regularly whilst he was living nearby at Horton. In 1939 the entire group of Library and Pew had reached a shabby and neglected state, and subsequently a full and sympathetic cleaning and restoration was carried out.[75]

The close relationship between the painted finish of movable furniture and architectural woodwork is borne out by examination of actual examples. Midway between the two are large musical instruments, such as the chamber organ at Hatfield House, which was painted in 1611 by

75. The Kederminster Library and Pew are discussed in several published works: Royal Commission on Historical Monuments (England), *Buckinghamshire (South),* Vol. I, HMSO, 1912; Margaret Jourdain, op cit. (illus.); Charles Latham, *In English Homes,* Country Life, n.d.; John Harris, Country Life, 1st December, 1977; Church booklet, *The Parish and Church of Langley, Bucks.,* n.d.; H. Avray Tipping, Country Life, 31st July, 1909; E. Clive Rouse, Records of Bucks, Vol. 14. The actual dates of the building and provision of the Library are not clear, but 1622 seems the most likely year of completion of the work. The gift was officially acknowledged in the following year, and the catalogue of 1638 suggests that the books were in wider use by that date.

Rowland Buckitt (later Master of the Worshipful Company of Painter-Stainers in London in 1630). Musical instruments, especially large keyboard instruments such as organs and virginals, were often the object of delicate painted decoration, as in the case of the virginals (Plate Ten, also shown in Figure 3:237) by Thomas White of London, probably of 1644.

Amongst the list of work carried out by Rowland Buckitt for the Earl of Salisbury at Hatfield, may be found the following items:

> 1609/10 Feb.20 Mr. the Earle of Salsbury; by me Rowland Buckitt painter.
> Imprimis for the gilldinge & workeing of one grete Bedsted with floweres birdes & personages annswerablle to the furneture therof
> Itam for the gillding & workeing of on grete Chayre answerablle to the same Bedsted
> Itam for the gillding & workeing of to hie stolles & to lostolles answerablle to the Reste at 26s. 8d the on...[76]

This suite of furniture, in which Buckitt was of course responsible only for the painted decoration, must have presented a very grand appearance; but painted furniture was also found at a less elevated level, as shown by the tester bed in Figure 2:231. This carved and painted bedstead is conceived and executed on a restrained architectural scale, and the composition of the headboard recalls similar treatments often found in mantelpieces of the same period (such as the painted fireplace at Yarnton Manor, near Oxford).

Such an approach usually consists of enhancing the carved work with colour, a process which has considerable classical and medieval precedence; or the coloured scheme may be conceived in its own right, to be executed on a flat prepared ground; or sometimes the wooden surface is retained as a ground, and the painted design is rendered in such a way as to imitate a more expensive coloured inlay or marquetry. The latter appears on a tester bed at the Red Lodge, Bristol, and on the armchair in Figure 2:232. Here the two painted panels are treated as a black-and-white counterfeit of the imported 'Nonsuch'-type marquetry.

At a middle-class level, painted furniture of the seventeenth century displays a relaxed and homely approach. The paint is often thick and coarse; the colouring strong, bright and warm; and the handling summary, or even a little careless. All these qualities are similarly reflected in tempera wall paintings of the period, which survive in large but fragmentary numbers all over the country, especially in small manors, inns and chapels. Unfortunately, examples of comparable furniture are infinitely more rare, and those which *do* exist are anything but well known (except for American specimens). A securely dated group of chests survive in isolation at Winchester Cathedral. These are not items of domestic furniture, but were made as reliquaries to contain groups of the bones of individuals important in the early history of the Cathedral. Eight of these chests were made and set up in 1525 (though an account of 1635 records ten). In 1642, a troop of Parliamentary Dragoons under Sir William Waller smashed two of the chests before being stopped by the "Outcry of the People". In 1661, the two chests were replaced by slightly inferior copies of the Renaissance originals, and the following year all the chests were repainted by one Jerome the painter, whose name is frequently found in the Cathedral Accounts.

Although they were retouched in 1820, Jerome's handiwork survives intact as a sample of mid-seventeenth century painted woodwork. His rough-and-ready handling of the brush is seen in the details of the shields which surmount the chests, and is reflected in the paint of other items

Figure 2:232. *Joined armchair. English. Oak, two panels are painted in imitation of 'Nonsuch' marquetry, early seventeenth century.*

76. Old Furniture, January, 1929.

(Figure 2:235 and Plate Four). His scheme includes picking out the carved details in colour, marbling the more prominent mouldings, and gilding certain details. These eight chests present a tantalising image of the high quality of English Renaissance painted and carved furniture, the like of which barely exists anywhere else in such a complete state.

We find ourselves more firmly in a domestic setting with the chest of drawers in Figure 2:235. Although it is not dated, the form of this chest is typically that of the years c.1650-80, with cushioned geometric mouldings to the larger and deeper drawers, and a simple applied edge moulding to the upper drawer. It is made in two sections for ease of transport, and the frame is articulated with a series of split and applied lengths of ball turning. The entire chest is constructed from a diverse mixture of woods (including oak, walnut, elm and pine), which lends credence to the assumption that it was intended from the outset to be finished with paint (Plates Five and Six).

The great attraction and importance of this piece lies in the unusually complete and unrestored state of its painted finish. Of course, the surface has suffered a little from the effects of worm and abrasions, but there can be very few comparable items in existence. The scheme of the painting is largely independent of the underlying form, except where the mouldings and split turnings are picked out in colour. There is an undercoat of pale grey which is revealed in worn patches; and the top coat consists of a freely handled medley of dark and light grey-blues, dark green, scarlet, yellow ochre, black and white. The rosy cheeked atlantes enjoy a very realistic flesh tint, and further motifs include a virile mixture of dragons, baskets of flowers, and floral arches.

Unfortunately, nothing is known of the origins of this chest until its appearance at Burderop Park, Wiltshire, early in this century. At the sale of the contents in 1974, there was a painted tester bed in a somewhat similar palette of colours, but the two were not stylistically related.

An American chest of drawers is shown in Figure 2:236, which is superficially comparable to the Burderop chest, but conversely this Massachusetts piece carries a very full provenance. Two of the drawers are

Figure 2:233. *Joined reliquary chest. English; Winchester, Hampshire. Oak, painted in colours, 1661/2. Inscribed 'HAC IN CISTA ADo 1661 PROMISCUE RECONDITA SUNT OSSA PRINCIPUM ET PRAETATORUM SACRILEGA BARBARI DISPERSA AoD 1642' (In this chest AD 1661 were promiscuously re-interred the bones of princes and prelates scattered by sacrilegious barbarity AD 1642).*

Figures 2:234a and 234b. *Details of Winchester mortuary chests. Shields from the 1542 chests, repainted by Jerome the painter in 1662. The coarse handling of the paint is repeated in similar work of the period, as next, in a domestic chest of drawers of similar date (Figure 2:235). Retouched in 1820.*

inscribed respectively with the date and initials 'ISM' and '1678' (which makes it the earliest dated American chest of drawers). The chest was an heirloom of the Staniford-Heard families until 1930, and was originally purchased as the marriage chest of John and Margaret Staniford of Ipswich, Essex County, who married in 1678. The Stanifords were friends and close neighbours of the Ipswich joiner Thomas Dennis (q.v.) , and this fact has led to the rather hasty conclusion that he must have been the maker of this chest and a whole related group.[77]

Stylistically, the Staniford chest is part of a regional group based in Essex County, but it has the best preserved and most varied scheme of paint in the whole group (see pp.510-514). The character of this chest is, in detail and conception, quite different from its English cousin described above. The range of colours is limited to black, white and red; the *independent* painted motifs are restricted to simple plant-like linear scrolls and dots; and the colour decoration is altogether more closely related to the underlying form of the carved, moulded and turned fabric beneath. The disposition of the drawers has been in dispute for many years, but the present layout would seem to be correct, since the Winterthur Museum has found that they fit better this way.

Painted and stained decoration is seen to have been a very popular feature in American furniture of all periods, though a great many early pieces lost their original paintwork during the irrational craze for 'Golden Oak' in the early days of American collecting after the Centennial of 1876. Whether or not painted furniture was equally popular in the British Isles, we cannot now tell. The existence of pieces such as the Burderop chest suggests that painted decoration was only one of the several themes imported into the Colonies by immigrant craftsmen, to take root there and flourish. Too few English examples have survived to provide an accurate touchstone. Several West Country cupboards and boxes have carved and painted sunk-work panels similar to work from Eastern Massachusetts; but until a specific and comprehensive study is carried out, too little is known on the matter. The box dated 1691 in Plate Eleven is a case in point. This is *seemingly* an American box, related to both the Hadley (Connecticut) and the early Essex County groups — yet it was found in Devonshire, England. Do we have an English prototype for the American groups; or (assuming

77. Irving P. Lyon, *The Oak Furniture of Ipswich, Massachusetts, Part IV, The Small-Panel Type,* Antiques Magazine, April, 1938, Fig. 25.

Figure 2:235. *Joined chest of drawers. English; from Burderop Park, Wiltshire. Oak, walnut, elm and pine, painted in colours, 1650-80. A rare unretouched example of original paintwork (see also Plates Five and Six).*

Figure 2:236. *Joined chest of drawers. American; Ipswich, Massachusetts. Red oak, painted black, white and red, dated 1678. Inscribed 'I*S*M' for John and Margaret Staniford, of Ipswich.*

Figure 2:235a and 235b.
Details of Burderop chest of drawers, 1650-80.

the date of 1691 is correct) is it a wanderer, metaphorically washed up on foreign shores? The problem is discussed further on p.507.[78]

As a contrast to the rare all-over schemes of paint noted here, a more restrained system is commonly found in which single elements of the decoration are picked out in a single colour (usually black, but sometimes red and blue). The use of black stains has already been noted on split turnings in the Dutch taste, but it is also found used to emphasise carving and mouldings. It is often difficult to recognise the use of black paint under a dark patination, and it is certainly difficult to get any impression of the original impact of ebonised parts against the fresh oak surface of *new* furniture. For that reason alone, the American press cupboard in Figure 2:237 is of interest. In a misguided moment, an earlier owner has stripped the surface down to the bare wood, and repainted the turnings and mouldings in new black paint.[79] The only advantage this has given is to provide an impression of the rich articulation of the ebonised members, conveying some indication of the appearance of such a piece shortly after it first came into use. Black accents of this type are most commonly found in Anglo-Dutch furniture, and in certain regional groups from Lancashire, Cheshire and New England. The fashion for cane chairs after c.1665 was accompanied by a taste for painting the entire beech frame in black, in imitation of ebony.

> 1434... a litel tabel peynted trestelwise...
> 1539... one cupborde of waynescott colloured green and redd...
> One cheyre of wodde peynted, the seate backe and elbowes coverid...
> A chayre of walnuttree culler peynted with a trayle of white...

Figure 2:237. *Joined press cupboard. American; Connecticut Valley, possibly Wethersfield. Oak and pine, black painted details, late seventeenth century. The raw appearance of this piece is due to a complete refinishing carried out early in the present century, leaving an over-all impression of newness (cf. Figure 4:213).*

78. See also Patricia E. Kane, op. cit., Winterthur Conference Report, 1974.
79. See Walter A. Dyer, *The Tulip-and-Sunflower Press Cupboard,* Antiques Magazine, April, 1935, Fig. 5. He notes that Charles H. Tyler of Boston acquired the cupboard in c.1905, from the Hathaway family, previously of Hartford, who had owned the piece for several generations. He then blandly announces that "...except for splicing the feet *and refinishing the surface,* no restoration was necessary..." It is astonishing to the present generation of English collectors that such extensive refinishing should be thought "necessary".

1547...In the Hall. A Cobberd Joyned paynted grene...

1552...ij chaires th'one red th'other greene...

6 stoles of walnuttree painted...

1569...the hutch that is painted with a St. Catherine wheel...

1584...a bedsted of walnut tree, toppe faschion, the pillars redd and varnished...

1588...A felde bedstede of walnuttree, toppe fashion, the pillors and bedshead carved and garnished, parcell-guilte, my lo. armes painted therein...

A field bedsted of wallnuttree, painted red and guilt...

A fayre, riche, newe, standing square bedsted of walnuttree painted over with crimson, and silvered with roses...

1610...Item a wainscott table coulered redd and varnishedd...

Item a fayre court cubbered soe coulered...

1622...a newe read bedstedd...

1651...a halfe headed bedstead wth blew pillars...

a livery Cupboard coloured blue...

1654...a Green desk for a woman...

Japanning (Figures 2:238-240)

During the second half of the sixteenth century, the Dutch and Portuguese explored the possibilities of trade with the Far East, and began to import into Europe a number of commodities such as spices, raw materials and manufactured goods. Included among the latter were articles of furniture, boxes, screens and other items of lacquerware. The "most excellent varnish" of these goods, which soon reached London via Amsterdam, was instantly admired by the English (always on the lookout for novelties), and the interest of collectors and householders was much aroused. In 1598, an English translation of a Dutch work[80] described the production of "...Bedsteddes, chairs, stools...desks, Tables, Cubbordes, Boxes, and a thousand such like things...covered and wrought with Lac of all coloures and fashions..." Geographical descriptions were used very loosely, and lacquerwares were described vaguely as emanating from India, China and Japan.

In 1600 the British East India Company was founded in London with the express intention of trading in Oriental commodities. The earliest imports were probably largely from Japan, such as the "...Japanese wares, as ritch Scritores, Truncks..." etc., which arrived on the East India Company's ship *Clove* at London, in September 1614.

In the same year, the inventory of the Earl of Northampton included a dozen or so pieces of furniture of Oriental type. Some are described specifically as "Chinaworke", and most have gold or coloured patterns on a black ground. It is not clear whether these were Oriental products, or European copies; but certainly by this time lacquer furniture was being copied in Europe in a painted version which came to be known as 'japanning". The two cabinets illustrated here are typical of this work (Figures 2:238 and 239), whether of English or Dutch manufacture. The workmanship and style of the metalwork are ambiguous, but there is good reason to assume that some of it *was* made here, even if by a Dutchman. A set of japanned roundels or trenchers in the Victoria and Albert Museum are inscribed with English verses published in London in 1611, and confirmation of this date spectrum is provided by the dated ballot box of 1619, made originally for the Court of the British East India Company in London (and bearing their arms) which now belongs to the Saddlers' Company.

80. Jan Huyghen van Linschoten, *Navigatio ac Itinerarium,* London, 1598.

Figure 2:238. *Japanned cabinet. Anglo-Dutch. Painted in the 'Indian' style in gold and silver, on a black ground, c.1620.*

Figure 2:238a. *The cabinet in Figure 2:238, shown opened.*

212

Figure 2:239. *Japanned cabinet. Anglo-Dutch. Painted on a black ground, c.1620, the decoration owes little to Oriental styles.*

Figure 2:239a. *The cabinet in Figure 2:239 shown opened.*

The decoration of the ballot box is closely related to the cabinet in Figure 2:238. Both have similar flowing foliage on a black ground ("of a feathery description"[81]), and with gilded mouldings to the drawers. The general style of the painting of this cabinet is more akin to Indian and Persian originals than to Chinese or Japanese styles. Could it be that contemporary writers were making genuine distinctions between these styles when they referred to 'Indian' and 'China' work? The figures and their backgrounds owe a little to Oriental influence, but the costume is securely European. The decoration of the second cabinet (Figure 2:239) owes a *little* to Indo-Portuguese conventions, but otherwise it is a North European product, with its floral borders and cornucopian 'flowerpottes'. Faithfully copying the spirit of their Oriental prototypes, many of the European cabinets are finished inside with a coat of Chinese (or Cardinal) red. They do not however imitate the range of coloured grounds found in true Oriental lacquer, for these early painted versions almost always have a black ground decorated with gold and/or silver. The more ambitious coloured and sparkled grounds were not attempted until later in the seventeenth century.

Figure 2:240. *Cabinetmakers' bureau. English. Japanned in gold and silver, on a black ground, late seventeenth century. This is a mature and well-informed expression of the chinoiserie style.*

81. As Clifford Smith so nicely put it in The Burlington Magazine, Vol. XXXI.

After 1659, under a new charter from Cromwell, and later with the new outgoing policies of Charles II, trade with the East flourished and English cabinetmakers began to improve their techniques in copying both the *appearance* of lacquer and the Chinese styles of decoration, or *chinoiserie* as the French were calling it. In 1688 John Stalker published his *Treatise of Japaning and Varnishing,* whereby secrets of the trade were made available to amateurs, and the taste for all things Oriental was confirmed.

> 1614...A large square Chinaworke table and frame of blak varnishe and golde...
> one blak field bedstead painted with flowers and powdered with golde...
> a china guilte cabonnette upon a frame...
> 1641...A large cubbord fashioned Indian cabinett...
> a lowe Indian table...a little blacke Indian table...
> 1661...two very fine chests, covered with gold and Indian varnish...
> 1680...rich Japan cabinets, of which I think there were a dozen...
> 1725...seven Japan'd Windsor Chairs...

Inks and Penwork (Figures 2:241 and 242)

The North Italian cedar and cypress chests which were imported (and which still survive) in great numbers during the sixteenth century, were mostly decorated in a similar conventional manner. The often elaborate scenes of classical subjects and formal infill were first delineated by cutting away the background and matting this sunken surface. The details of the foreground were drawn in by one of three methods, which are rarely found in combination. In the earliest work (late fourteenth and fifteenth centuries), the drawing is punched with ready-made dies or inscribed with the point of a sharp tool. Later, a method was evolved of drawing the design with the point of a hot tool, a process generally referred to as 'pokerwork'. Latterly, probably after c.1540, the designs were drawn onto the surface with sepia-black ink, using pen and brush.

This last technique would seem to have been the inspiration for similar brush- and penwork decoration occasionally found in English joined work. The panels in Figure 2:241 belong to some built-in spice or salt cupboards in the chimney stack of a house at Marlborough, Wiltshire, of 1654. The oak

Figure 2:241. *Built-in joined salt cupboards. English; Marlborough, Wiltshire. Oak frames, with cedar panels, probably 1654. The panels have a faded ink-drawn imitation of floral inlay.*

Figure 2:242. *Detail of chest of drawers. English. Oak, with brushed ink decoration on maple or birch veneer, c.1670.*

frames and arches are conventional West Country work of this date, but the cedar panels are unusual in having a penwork decoration in imitation of floral inlay. The main design is drawn in sepia-black ink, and there are faded traces of green and red in the leaves and flowers, possibly with white-painted highlights. The frames also carry the remains of black and white geometric bands of counterfeit inlay. The panels do not fit the frames very well, so it seems possible that they are of Italian manufacture, re-used in this provincial English context.

Pen and brush drawing seems often to have been used for imitating other materials, perhaps because in itself the effect is thin and insubstantial. Heavily-marked veneers, such as rosewood or tortoiseshell are obvious candidates for this treatment. Figure 2:242 is a detail from a chest of drawers in which the markings of tortoiseshell are crudely reproduced by brush and ink on a veneer of maple or birch. The much finer chest in Figure 3:409 uses a similar effect in penwork, executed as a texture of fine calligraphic flourishes.

vi). Gilding and Silver Leaf

The use of true gilding plays very little part in *extant* English-made furniture from before 1660. Royal and aristocratic accounts often recorded items with gold or silver embellishments, but these have almost completely perished, and others were almost certainly imported. Some of Henry VIII's beds, for example, were "...peynted redd and parcell guilte...", and a cupboard "...olde and guilted..." appears among the goods of Sir R. Cromwell at the same date. The "...oval table painted with silver and colours..." found at Hampton Court in 1649, was typical of Charles I's taste; but these have all disappeared, and where gilding or silvering *is* found on furniture of the English tradition, then it is usually a later embellishment or replacement. Thin sheets or plates of worked silver were sometimes laid over the wooden frames of small tables and stands, as in the extant set at Knole, but such an extravagance was rarely mentioned before 1660. Traces of gilding may occasionally be found on the iron or brass hardware of some early pieces of good quality, with the undoubted intention of both decorating and protecting the metal from corrosion.

> 1641...One marble table inlayed uppon a gilt frame square...
> 1641...a silver Table and frame all layed over with silver...
> 1648...ye guilte cabanett that was your mother's...

vii). Finishes

Contemporary information on wood finishes before 1660 is almost non-existent. We have seen the tantalising references to beds and cupboards which were stained "redd and varnishedd", but no word is given of common English workshop practice of the day. Craftsmen learned their techniques by experience through the process of apprenticeship, and it was not thought necessary or desirable to publish such information for the benefit of all and sundry. A polished surface has both visual and practical benefits which are difficult to ignore. Not only is the surface sealed and protected against impregnations of dirt and discolouring agents such as grease and ink spillage, but a coat of varnish or polish adds depth and lustre to the grain of the wood, and the glint of reflected light adds life to carved and moulded decoration.

Varnishes of one sort or another were certainly known in the sixteenth century, but recipes have not come down to us. The probable constituents were a solvent, such as linseed oil or spirits of wine, and a resinous gum such as copal. These and other ingredients were certainly in common use at the end of the seventeenth century, as is confirmed by the recipes and advice published at that time by authors such as John Evelyn and John Stalker. Evelyn refers to "...Joyners Vernish..." and "...Japan and China vernishes...which infinitely excels linseed oyl..." The latter were based on spirits of wine and gum lac, and were possibly imported from the Orient ready-made. It is impossible to be sure, even on a pristine piece of furniture, whether any varnish present really is part of the original finish, or a subsequent application. Most pieces have been varnished at some time, since owners have always been in the habit of refurbishing their belongings from time to time, and a coat of varnish has long been the cheapest and quickest way of obtaining the desired effects. Varnishes have gained a very poor name for themselves in recent years, particularly in the wake of the obnoxious dark, sticky substances marketed in the last eighty years, but in fact old varnishes (suitably polished by years of wax and friction) form the bases of the most desirable forms of patination.

Friction polishes such as oil (linseed, nut, poppy, etc.) and beeswax were certainly applied at all times, and their use must ante-date that of varnish. Their introduction probably extends from attempts to preserve furniture timbers from decay and abrasion. Beeswax in particular can give a soft and lustrous gloss by rubbing with a soft cloth or a handful of rushes, and is the traditional basis of furniture polish. It is often difficult to interpret contemporary observations on polishing methods, since the words 'varnishe' and 'politure' were used indiscriminately to refer to any means of obtaining a shiny surface.

Books published earlier in this century engendered a still-current theory that an original application of oil to the surface of oak will have had the effect of darkening the surface of the wood by a process of oxidisation; and that an original application of beeswax will have had the effect of retaining the light colour of the wood.[82] But in fact such a proposition is completely groundless. The present state of colour and gloss in the surface of individual pieces of old furniture is due to a far more subtle blend of circumstances than the simple question of the original finish. All traces of any original application will normally have disappeared generations ago. Most wood

82. For example: *Dictionary of English Furniture,* 1927, Vol. III, p.48; Percy Macquoid, *The Age of Oak,* 1919, p.34.

surfaces are now darker than their original state, owing much to a combination of dirt, grease, friction, oxidisation and accumulations of discoloured (or even coloured) polishes. Many pieces received, in addition, a coat of black stain during the last century, and this has often settled down or worn off to a greater or lesser extent. A pale surface is normally the result of excessive recent (localised) wear, of undue exposure to strong sunlight, or to an artificial stripping of the surface at some time in the comparatively recent past.

It is not clear how far the publishing of recipes affected workshop practice in country districts at the end of the seventeenth century. It seems likely that traditional-minded provincial joiners (who certainly continued to make traditional forms of furniture) might not be swayed into using novel finishes in their everyday work. As with every other aspect of the craft process, we have to consider the importance of the apprenticeship system as an organ for propagating the continuance of the old ways. The trained journeyman found himself channelled into a groove of high standards and thorough craftsmanship, from which he would not find it easy to deviate.

Chapter Three

Form and Language
The Functional
Types and Nomenclature

THE LANGUAGE OF EARLY FURNITURE

THE WORDS USED to name and describe items of furniture are extremely important, for in using them we are compiling a mental image of their forms and associations. If we use the wrong words in a given context, then we will fail to convey exactly what is meant or implied; and by attributing the wrong names to things, we may confuse their precise significance, or even lose sight of it altogether. Such is the problem of human communication, and the difficulties are only intensified when we try to understand what was intended by a writer of three hundred years in the past. Not only may the very words he uses be different from ours, but he may intend a very different interpretation when he uses the *same* words. Unfortunately, many common words such as *cupboard, stool* and *table* have changed the breadth and direction of their meaning in the last three centuries; and a proper grasp of their original meanings will help us understand not only their immediate implications, but also precise lines of developments in different furniture types.

It has long been evident to serious students of furniture that the *lingua franca* of modern trade and collectors' jargon leaves much to be desired in the accuracy of the terms which are used to describe the forms and functions of early furniture.

Current misnomers may take many forms. We often use designations which were dreamt up in the quite recent past, reflecting (mainly) Victorian obsessions with some vague clerical or monastic Golden Age (Glastonbury chair, monk's bench, credence table, refectory table, coffin stool, mortuary chair, bible box); or a fanciful quasi-Elizabethan/Jacobean milieu (farthingale chair, yeoman's bed, rapier chest). In other cases made-up terms are used which do not reflect an accurate description of things, and distort their true context (mule chest, Cromwellian chair, Welsh dresser, coaching table, altar table); whilst terms which are perfectly accurate in one context, may be used incorrectly, whether too widely or too narrowly, in another, because there is confusion over their exact meanings (*court* cupboard, *wainscot* chair, *joint* stool, *four-poster* bed). Foreign words are too often used to describe typical English pieces when an English word would serve better, though sometimes there is no English equivalent and the foreign word was always used here (buffet, caqueteuse, tridarn, bureau, scrutore).

The distinguished furniture historian R.W. Symonds attempted to set a few of these matters right in a 1948 article entitled *The Renaming of Old English Furniture*.[1] The measure of his success (or the lack of it) can be gauged from the fact that out of the six terms (relevant to this study) which he tried to debunk, five are still in common use. The only one which has

1. The Antique Collector, July-August 1948. See also *The Language of Oak*, Victor Chinnery, *Antique Collecting/Finder*, July 1977.

219

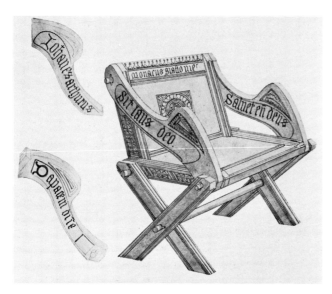

Figure 3:1. *Ink drawing of 'The Glastonbury Chair', by H. O'Neill, 1822. Commissioned by the Bristol collector George Weare Braikenridge. The chair was apparently made for John Arthur Thorne, the last Treasurer of Glastonbury Abbey, before his death in 1539.*

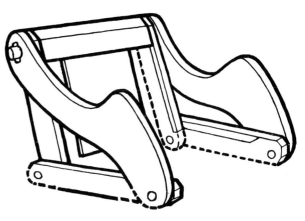

Figure 3:1a. *Sketch to define those parts of the Glastonbury folding chair which seem on inspection to be original work of pre-1539 (viz. the arms, side seat rails, side rear uprights, cresting rail and centre portion of back panel). The decoration of these parts also seems to be original work, and there seems no reason to doubt the authenticity of the ownership inscription referring to Iohanes Arthurus, Monacus Glastonie.*

now almost entirely faded from use is the absurd term 'dinner wagon' for a court cup-board.

Perhaps these other terms are now too firmly entrenched, after only three or four generations, ever to be dislodged. Nevertheless, we may examine them for some signs of justification; though in most cases the associations are entirely spurious and imagined, and serve only to obscure the truth.

Glastonbury Chair (folding or turned chair)

There are two candidates for the honour of being *the* eponymous 'Glastonbury chair', both of which are owned and exhibited by the Bishop of Bath and Wells at the Bishop's Palace, Wells Cathedral, Somerset. The most usual is the venerable chair shown in Figure 3:1, and discussed in p.232-233. This is a folding or X-base chair of early sixteenth century date, which seems reliably related to the abbey at Glastonbury which was dissolved in 1539 (and is thus one of the few relics with *genuine* pre-Reformation monastic associations). This much-copied antiquity was first popularised by the engraving of it published in Henry Shaw's *Specimens of Ancient Furniture* in 1836, since when the reproduction furniture trade has never looked back. It must seem that the vast majority of churches in the English-speaking world are possessed of one or more copies of it. The design is still in production today, though it is not clear *why* it should be thought so appropriate for church use, since the concept is entirely a secular one. Objections to the use of the term 'Glastonbury chair' apply only to the very rare *period* examples, and must be based on the fact that it offers no clarification to our understanding of folding chairs in general, and of this typological group in particular (see Figures 3:2 and 3).

The other candidate which is sometimes called 'Glastonbury chair' is a great turned chair which is reputedly associated with Richard Whiting, the last Abbot of Glastonbury, who was executed on 14th November, 1539. There seems no basis in fact for this connection, since the first record of the chair is at the end of the eighteenth century, when it was found to have been in the Archdeacon's house at Wells "since time immemorial." Whiting is reputed to have sat in the chair at his trial in the Palace in 1539, but an honest assessment of the date of the chair (which is a very fine specimen) would put it at c.1600. It is identical in almost every detail to Figure 2:78. This chair has led to the whole family of triangular turned chairs being referred to wrongly as 'Glastonbury chairs.'

There is no reason *as yet* to link either of these chairs to Somerset as regional types, though the folding chair of John Arthur Thorne self-evidently *was* made for his personal use at Glastonbury.

Brewster and Carver Chair (New England turned armchair)

The renewed interest in American Colonial history, which was especially stirred up by the Centennial Celebrations of 1876, was most heavily focused on the original Pilgrim Fathers and their journey in the *Mayflower* of 1620. More especially, a good deal of interest was aroused by possible survivals of the furniture which they might have actually brought with them from England and the Netherlands, or which they might have made in their first few years of life in the New World. In fact, interest in the Pilgrim Fathers was already active early in the eighteenth century, and contributed to the preservation of a number of supposed relics of the *Mayflower* passengers, such as the candlestand in Figure 3:192, which was thought to have belonged to Peregrine White (born on the Mayflower at Cape Cod Bay). Two particular items, received from descendants in the nineteenth century by the Pilgrim Hall at Plymouth, Massachusetts, were two turned armchairs. These were supposedly the actual chairs owned originally by William Brewster and John Carver, both prominent members of the original group which founded the Plimoth Colony and signatories of the Mayflower Compact. We must ask ourselves if it is not too good to be true that at least five chairs have survived with attributions to these and other Pilgrims (viz. Miles Standish, William Bradford and John Churchill). Were the eighteenth century historians particularly fortunate in their finds, or just optimistic?

Be that as it may, twentieth century collectors have taken the Brewster and Carver chairs to be significant of a stylistic difference in New England turned armchairs; in which the 'Brewster type' is fitted with spindles below the arms and seat, whilst the 'Carver type' is not. This distinction offers no meaningful basis for any typological allocations, since the differences between the individual chairs are less simple than this would suppose (Figures 2:90-94).

Wainscot Chair (joined panel-back armchair)

We can detect here a far too restrictive use of the word 'wainscot'. In the sixteenth century, the term meant two different things: either that particular grade of oak timber which was imported from the Baltic, Northern Europe and (sometimes) Spain; or wall-panelling in oak or other timbers. Thus, to describe a chair as 'wainscot', might imply that it was made from imported oak, or that it incorporated framed panel. Both these qualities apply to a far wider range of chair types than simply panel-back armchairs.

Mortuary Chair (Yorkshire-Derbyshire backstool)

The particular type of backstool which is closely associated with South-West Yorkshire and Derbyshire often incorporates a small human mask in the central decoration of the cross-splats of the back (see Figures 4:139-150). In the nineteenth century, this was taken to be a muted patriotic reference to the decapitated head of Charles I. The term 'mortuary chair' was coined to describe them by a death-obsessed generation; a supposition which is entirely fanciful.

Farthingale Chair (upholstered joined backstool)

This inappropriate conjunction grew out of the hasty supposition that upholstered backstools were invented around the year 1600, a theory which is still very popular. The idea was conceived that there was some connection between the popularity of the wide farthingale dress and the 'new' armless chair, and the theory was explained in many ways:

> "...Between 1580 and 1630, large town and country houses were furnished with...small chairs with upholstered backs and seats. These small chairs were originally designed to accommodate that extravagant garment, the farthingale. They were without arms, so that ladies encircled by that spreading cartwheel of fabrics could sit without discomfort. This was one of the first examples of the direct influence of costume on furniture design..."[2]

Unfortunately this neat and popular theory does not hold up to scrutiny, for backstools have actually been in use since the very earliest times (q.v.), and the upholstered backstool was only one of a long development of upholstered seats. The fact that they are convenient to a wearer of farthingales is purely coincidental, and of no conceptual significance (Figures 2:136-138).

Cromwellian Chair (joined leather backstool)

The leather-upholstered backstool, which was extremely popular throughout the period 1640-1740 (and had certainly appeared in England at least fifty years before that), was not in any way typical of the Commonwealth period, nor particularly acceptable to the taste of Cromwell himself. He seems to have preferred the more urbane and comfortable turkeywork, as shown by the 138 pieces of turkeywork furniture to be found at Hampton Court after his tenure. Most surviving examples date from long after the Commonwealth, and so the popular association between leather chairs and the Puritan ethic would seem to be largely mythical. The term is also, occasionally, used for the type of joined backstool which has extensive turned decoration (Figure 3:138), but since most of these are also datable after 1660, there seems little reason in it.

Coffin Stool (joined stool)

Another manifestation of Victorian morbid obsessions was the tendency to suppose that anything of great age must have been made with a religious or liturgical purpose. Since, in country churches and in the home, joined stools were often used to support a coffin when the occasion demanded, Victorian sentiment could not avoid the suggestion that this must be *the* purpose for which they were made. In fact high stools were the common everyday domestic seat until the second half of the seventeenth century, when they were gradually superseded by backstools. Certainly, they *were* used to support coffins, but this was hardly their primary function. In a Vestry Book entry of 1641, payment was made for "...two short fourmes to set a coffin upon...",[3] but most (pairs of) stools must have found their way into churches at a much later date when unfashionable oak furniture was being doled out by the local worthies. The practice of laying-out the coffin in the home, prior to removal for the burial service, was noted by Pepys in 1661 when he visited his uncle's house in Huntingdonshire and

2. John Gloag, *British Furniture Makers*, Collins, London, 1946, p.13.
3. Margaret Jourdain, *English Decoration and Furniture of the Early Renaissance, 1500-1650*, Batsford, London, 1924, p.245.

found the corpse in a coffin "...standing upon joynt-stools in the chimney in the hall..."

The continued use of the term 'joint' stool, though a perfectly accurate use of contemporary language, is not really desirable. It represents little more than a patronising enjoyment of the foibles of 'picturesque' early spellings. As we all know, the correct modern adjective for the products of the joiner is 'joined'.

Monk's Bench (chair-table and settle-table)

Beloved of the 'Tudor Oak Co.' mentality of Stockbroker Britain. For some reason a host of misinformed admirers came to regard the chair-table as the typical furniture of monastic England, though most examples date from the seventeenth century or a little later. Equally mysterious was Percy Macquoid's contention that the settle-table was invented by the Commonwealth Government,[4] out of some sort of spite for human comfort. He was quite wrong to suggest this, of course, since they were known from a much earlier date, and besides the lack of comfort can hardly be intentional. In fact, they are not so much uncomfortable as inconvenient.

Refectory Table (long dining table)

A further expression of the gratuitous indulgence of our whimsical notions about pre-Dissolution England. No dining table exists which might have graced a monastic refectory, though there are a great many which are associated with secular refectories in colleges and other institutions, such as Winchester College. Yet, most so-called 'refectory' tables are the ordinary domestic dining tables of the seventeenth century and later, and may be supported on trestles or a joined frame.

Credence Table (folding or falling-leaf table)

During the nineteenth century, many domestic folding tables of seventeenth century date (Figures 3:203-210) were taken into use in churches, to serve beside the altar for the purpose of holding the bread and wine before consecration for the Holy Communion. The name 'credence' was apparently used in the nineteenth century to refer to this function[5] (O.E.D.). By a typical process of confused double-think this term has been adopted by collectors to describe this early type of table, preferring the spurious ecclesiastical precedent to the genuine and simple domestic description.

Coaching Table (folding table)

Very few items of seventeenth century furniture were made or designed to fulfil only one restricted function. Except in rich homes, space and materials were expensive and therefore rare commodities, and so most pieces were expected to accommodate a variety of uses wherever possible. They were designed with a view to maximum adaptability and efficiency (within the limited meaning of the latter word which might have been understood at the time). A perfect example of such an intention is the group of small tables which may be folded completely flat (Figures 3:225 and 226), to be stowed away against the wall or in a cupboard. That jaded term 'occasional' table is perhaps a perfect description of them. Our recent ancestors fondly imagined that these tables were designed to be stowed away in highway coaches, to be brought out and set up for use at *alfresco* roadside meals. No doubt, such was occasionally the practice, but their

4. Percy Macquoid, *The Age of Oak,* p.217. His exact words: "...an uncomfortable and economical effort of Cromwellian inspiration..."
5. The term 'credence' was originally applied to the custom of a nobleman's food and drink being tasted by a servant, as a precaution against poisoning. By extension, the side table used by the priest for preparing the sacrament also became known as a 'credence table.'

Figure 3:2. *(Left) Joined folding armchair. English. Oak, early seventeenth century, cf. Figure 3:3.*

Figure 3:2a. *(Right) Joined folding armchair. Side view of Figure 3:2.*

primary purpose was for use in the home, to ease the all too familiar problems of having too many children and too little space.

Altar Table (dining table or side table)

The continuing wish to place as much early furniture as possible into an ecclesiastical context still leads to many perfectly ordinary domestic dining tables being thought of as 'altar tables.' Several clues are spuriously held up as 'proof' of this identification, such as the table being particularly high, or being unfinished (or partly finished) at the back. In fact it is impossible to tell whether a table was originally intended to serve as an altar table or *mensa,* unless there is documentary or other circumstantial evidence of such an intention. After the Reformation, the medieval type of stone altar slab was removed by Royal Order, and substituted with a wooden table. Elizabeth's order of 1564 specifically noted that the "...Parish provide a decent table standing on a frame, for the Communion Table..." and that the table should be brought forward from the chancel into the body of the church for the duration of the Communion service. It was not until Archbishop Laud's order of 1634 that the table was required to be kept at the head of the chancel, and to be railed in. These provisos meant that most altar tables were indistinguishable from domestic tables, and many must have been acquired by the parish from the ordinary stock-in-trade of the local joiners. Some of the non-conformist and Puritan churches even went so far as to treat the communion table exactly as a dining table, and so to conduct their services in the form of a communal meal.

Rapier Chest (long boarded chest)

Any long and narrow chest may possibly have been used at some time in its life to store swords, rapiers, or any other sort of weapon; but to infer that such a chest must have been constructed purposefully for the storage of

Plate Nine. *Joined chest with drawer. American; Essex County, Massachusetts. Oak and pine, painted black and red, 1690-1705. A small group of chests with identical details are dated between 1693 and 1701 (cf. Figures 4:221 and 222). In the present example, the panels are painted with an unusual combination of vertical and horizontal stripes to produce a tartan-like effect.*

225

such specific contents is nothing more than a blatant exercise in wish-fulfilment. The relationship between oak furniture and early armour and weapons, dates from the time when both interests were pursued by the same small group of collectors (as they sometimes still are). In dealers' advertisements in collectors' magazines of pre-1940, few illustrations of armchairs were thought to be quite complete without a rapier leaning nonchalantly against the arm of the chair, or a helmet sitting on the seat (waiting as it were for instant action).

Mule Chest (chest with drawer)

This a most ugly term, which was coined to suggest a supposedly hybrid stage in the development of the chest of drawers. The incorporation of one or more drawers in the lower section of a lidded chest was a sensible step in reducing the inconvenience of access to clothes, books or other items which might be otherwise difficult to reach or find in the bottom of a deep chest.

The chest with drawer is also sometimes referred to as a 'dower chest'. Whilst this is not an inappropriate term for a piece which *might* be used to store the linen and other goods belonging to a prospective bride (in New England the same piece was called a 'hope chest', or in poorer homes the spinster had her 'bottom drawer'), this is far more a description of *usage* than of *form*. The term is best reserved for examples which are specifically known to have been provided for a young unmarried girl, as was probably the case with Sarah Ward's chest in Figure 3:399, or that of Mary Pease in Figure 4:205, and which might not have a drawer.

Bible Box (various small table boxes)

Although the ownership of books was not a common phenomenon, according to early inventories, the most usual book to be found in simple homes was a copy of the Holy Bible (as might be expected). A great many small boxes have survived from the sixteenth and seventeenth centuries, yet there is no reason to put the two together and assume that small boxes (or indeed boxes of any size) must have been made to hold bibles. Bibles are rarely recorded as being kept in boxes, and the term 'bible box' certainly does not appear. If the contents of boxes are mentioned, they are usually an assortment of papers, letters, deeds, etc., and usually referred to as 'evidences.' In addition, small boxes might be used to store any kind of private or practical paraphernalia, such as writing materials, knitting wools and needles, smoking equipment, gloves and lace, or even bibles.

The term is used indiscriminately to refer to any size of flat-lidded boxes, which were kept usually on shelves, tables or cupboards; and is particularly unsuitable for the sloped-lidded writing boxes known as 'desk boxes' or 'writing slopes.' Sometimes, even box stools are clumsily referred to as 'bible box stools'.

Court Cupboard (press cupboard)

This is a subject over which there has been a very great deal of discussion, yet the evidence seems fairly conclusive. Following a practice established (if not initiated) by earlier writers such as Percy Macquoid, Ralph Edwards, Herbert Cescinsky, Fred Roe and Margaret Jourdain, it has become common practice to use the term 'court cupboard' to describe the great standing *enclosed* cupboard of the seventeenth century, of which many examples are extant (e.g. Figures 3:266-280). But it would seem from certain evidence that this is a wrongful use of the term, and that the true 'court cup-board' (which I propose to distinguish with its hyphen) is in fact the less common *open* type (as in Figures 3:247-256).

The early term 'cup-board' has its origins in the Middle Ages, when it described a side table of one or more tiers for holding or displaying valuable plate and food, or for serving from during meals, i.e. literally a *board* for *cups*. This sense of a cupboard being an *open* side table persisted well into the seventeenth century, and so for many years it was the open cup-board which was known as a 'court cup-board.' The origin of the term 'court' is much disputed, but it possibly *is* connected with the French for 'short', since almost without exception they stand lower than the average eye-level, so that the top planks have to be finished with a smooth surface and a moulded edge. In inventories, they are usually noted as having a cupboard cloth lying on top, often of some rich material, and of course there would be no point in providing this if it were above eye-level. Even if the cloth is placed on a lower shelf, this still indicates an open piece of furniture.

Certain contemporary illustrations show open side tables described as 'court cup-boards,' laden with food and plate[6], and Randle Holme refers among the necessities for a dining room to "...side tables, or court cubberts, for cups and Glasses...Spoons, Sugar Box, Viall and Cruces for Viniger, Oyle and Mustard pot..." The sense of a cup-board being a side table is strengthened in the following reference, where the third piece is certainly an *enclosed* cupboard:

> 1590...two cubbordes one that the plate standes on and a nother that the virgenalles standeth on on cobberd ther in the manner of an ambery...

The sense of a cupboard being an enclosed piece with hinged doors had begun to develop in the middle of the sixteenth century, when the terms 'press' and 'cupboard' began to supplant the old word 'aumbry.' But for at least another hundred years, 'cupboard' was ambiguous in its meaning, whereas 'press' was not.

But to return to the great standing cupboard...what should we call *that*? This piece is useful for the storage of a large number of small items, such as crockery, cutlery, napery, etc., and is seen at its most useful in such living rooms as the hall, parlour and dining parlour. Further, it is normally quite a high piece, and unlike the court cup-board its top is above eye-level and is finished with rough boards and (sometimes) an applied cornice moulding which obscures the rough edges. These characteristics all lend credence to some of the old names, like 'hall cupboard', 'parlour cupboard' or 'standing cupboard.' Doubtless, there were several terms which were all popular in different parts of the country, and which are now difficult to identify. In Essex inventories, for example, 'press cupboards' are frequently mentioned in living rooms (often the hall or the parlour), and it must seem very likely that this description must refer to the standing enclosed type. In the absence of better suggestions from other sources,[7] I would suggest that 'press cupboard' is a most suitable term, and is readily distinguishable from other varieties such as the 'clothes press' (q.v.). In the majority of inventories, private rooms such as the hall and parlour almost always have at least one piece which is referred to simply as a 'cupboard', with no form of distinguishing adjective.

Four-poster Bed (tester bedstead)

This term is often used to describe the typical 'tester' bed of the sixteenth and seventeenth centuries, which has in fact only *two* posts. These posts support one end of the roof or 'tester', whilst the other end is supported by the headboard.

6. E.g. an engraving in *Perspective Practical*, 1672, cited by R.W. Symonds in an article *The Dyning Parlour and its Furniture,* The Connoisseur, January 1944; and another engraving in *The Institution, Laws and Ceremonies of the Most Noble Order of the Garter,* by Elias Ashmole, also 1672, given by Peter Thornton in Furniture History, 1971.
7. E.g. in her study of Oxford inventories of 1568-1699, Pauline Agius did not find a single reference to 'press cupboards', but neither did she find a possible alternative other than one 'double wainscott press' of 1671. Furniture History, 1971.

Plate Ten. *Virginals on stand. English; by Thomas White of London, probably 1644. The underside of the lid is decorated with a scene of 'Orpheus taming the Wild Beasts', with the music of his lyre. The same casemaker and painter were doubtlessly used by several instrument-makers, since very similar virginals are known by other makers such as Gabriel Townsend (1641) and John Loosemore (1655). The stand here is of cedar, and the oak-cased instrument sits loosely upon it (see Figure 3:237). The cased virginals was easily transportable between houses, and would be set up for use on any convenient table.*

Prior to this, during the late Middle Ages, there was indeed a vogue for a tester bed in which the roof was supported by *four* posts, with a low panelled headboard between the head posts. This design virtually disappeared by c.1550, after which greater decorative emphasis was placed on the large headboard. This form persisted for the next two hundred years, under various guises which finally culminated in the great fabric-covered beds of the late seventeenth century and after. In the eighteenth century a return was made to a lighter form of four-poster bed with a tester of stretched fabric. The survival of the term 'four-poster' is no doubt a hangover from the latter type, which was also highly popular throughout the nineteenth century.

Yeoman's Bed (half-headed bedstead)

A cheaper and simpler form of bedstead than the tester type, was the 'half-headed bedstead', which was usually provided with a low panelled headboard and simple terminal footposts. This closely resembles the modern form of bedstead and is frequently mentioned in inventories, though genuine survivals are rare. Joined beds of this type are usually found in middle class houses of the period, though in fact tester beds are mentioned just as often, if not more so. Boarded versions are usually found in poorer homes, or in servants' quarters. There is no reason to think of the 'half-headed bedstead' as predominantly a yeoman preference.

Welsh Dresser (high dresser)

The original form of the 'dresser' was that of a side table, usually of some length and often of several tiers (closely related to, if not even identifiable with, the court cup-board), used primarily for the final dressing and serving of food in the dining parlour. In one form or another (q.v.) the dresser persisted into the eighteenth century, whereupon its usage descended into all levels of society, including especially the yeoman farmer and cottager. In Wales, the use of the dresser was especially common, being found in almost every home until quite recent years. Accordingly, when the old furniture trade began to expand in the nineteenth century, they found that Wales was a convenient and fruitful source of high quality dressers of all sorts. Despite the fact that dressers are found all over England and Ireland (though with variable frequency), the trade reference to 'Welsh' dressers was adopted as a generic term for the family of dressers as a whole. The richness and variety of dressers to be found in Wales is one the distinctive regional features of the Principality, though not exclusive to it.

Perhaps it is a pity thus to do away with much of the romantic nonsense which has long clung to popular ideas about old oak furniture, yet the real romance of history must surely lie in its truths, not in its fictions; and besides, much of this nonsense has actively damaged our accurate perception of things.

Having, perhaps, cleared away some of the dead wood, it may now be possible for us to examine the form and development of various pieces in the light of a more accurate terminology. All furniture types are conceived initially for some practical function, which they fulfil to a greater or lesser degree of efficiency, and it is within these functional groups that I propose to consider them next.

Unfortunately, the issue is by no means as clear cut or simple as it may at first appear. Furniture designs develop over the years in a slow but positive imitation of organic growth, punctuated from time to time by a burst of startling innovation. In England, such points of innovation are often linked to some political or trading contact with Europe or the East (usually the Netherlands, Flanders, France, Italy and China), and only the *interpretation* of trends has a native English character. The adherence to traditional forms is remarkably strong, and so functional typology is not always a useful guide to the dating of objects, since many pieces will demonstrate a sort of arrested development. In this way, a boarded chest of (say) 1650 belongs to a sequential stage of evolution which originated at a point several hundred years in the past; whereas a joined chest of drawers of the same date is in the forefront of its own branch of sequential developments. An individual piece can only represent a single fossilised moment in terms of its form, construction and decoration; but in the minds of men there is a wider picture of a continuing process of selection and growth. The mutations which furniture types undergo reflect an evolutionary response to changes in social demands. The forces which operate within one generation are not necessarily those which operate within the next; and although the basic requirements of mankind are perpetual and universal, their solutions to everyday problems are not.

Unfortunately, contemporary writers had little to say about furniture before the days of diarists and pattern books which followed the Restoration and the slow expansion of literacy. Most of what we know is gleaned from the erratic evidence of extant items, from the occasional throw-away comments to be found in literature and letters, from the all too brief descriptions in dictionaries and chronicles, or from occasional gems like Randle Holme's *Academy of Armory*. He makes some useful distinctions, but he is largely preoccupied with heraldic significances, and like many of us he is rather less than infallible. Inventories, wills and workshop accounts normally constitute mute lists of chattels, but they can be used in various ways to gain an insight into the character and disposition of many items. The language and spellings are not always easy to interpret, and dialect terms are often misleading. Some of these have no doubt actually changed their meanings with time and geography, while others have simply gone out of use. We must bear such words in mind and some could be re-adapted to modern use, though it would be wrong to suggest a conscious and artificial revival of archaic terms for their own sake since language loses its vitality under the dead hand of such a process. The genuine old vernacular names are invariably more direct and graceful than many of the fictional terms in current use, and there is surely good reason to refer to a piece by the name with which it was originally known. If we can determine a set of terms which are intelligible to the modern observer, yet accurate and pleasing in relation to the original usage, we shall not be too wide of the mark.

A CLASSIFICATION OF THE FUNCTIONAL TYPES

  i). Seat Furniture
 ii). Tables and Cup-boards
iii). Cupboards
 iv). Dressers
  v). Chests and Boxes
 vi). Chests of Drawers
vii). Desks and Bookcases (Library Furniture)
viii). Beds
 ix). Children's Furniture
  x). Miscellanea

i). Seat Furniture

The origins and relative importance of the chief forms of seating (seats of authority, communal seating and personal seats) are closely bound up with English social history and the development of social conventions. The use of a symbolic seat as a badge of power (throne, *cathedra,* folding stool, etc.) is found throughout both secular and ecclesiastical law, and is reflected in the widespread habit of assigning the most important seat to the most important person present on given occasions. At the highest extreme, gods, kings, bishops and judges are all seated upon thrones of one sort or another; and even in more lowly circumstances the same principal is adhered to. The chairman of a committee, the schoolmaster, the auctioneer and *paterfamilias* all have their seats of authority. In formal situations, such a seat may be physically elevated above the rest by being placed on a platform or dais, or by having a high cushion and a footrest; or it may be given importance by the provision of a high back and/or a canopy. It is a common misconception that chairs were necessarily rare in the Middle Ages, and that only the great could aspire to the use of an armchair. In fact the principle is one of relativity, so that in his own home or local community even the yeoman or peasant could be (and was) allowed the use of a chair. In France, even as late as the eighteenth century, etiquette strictly controlled the apportionment of chairs and stools (*tabourets*), but in England such conventions were a little more relaxed.

In Renaissance England, the armchair became firmly established as the seat of (relative) authority, and the stool or bench as inferior to it. During the seventeenth century, armchairs became increasingly common, and back-stools eventually replaced stools as a more comfortable alternative. Nevertheless, at most periods there were cheap and comfortable seats available to even the lowest classes, in the form of wicker chairs and rush-seated turned or plain matted chairs.

It has been said with good reason that "the chair predominates in any study of English furniture"[8], and this view is perpetually underlined by the range and subtlety of form and type which may be detected in chairs of all significant periods. Many changes appear first and most characteristically in chairs before any other furniture type. As a result, we can chart the importance of chairs in regional studies too, for not only have armchairs survived in large numbers, but they also seem to embody that which is most typical in the spectrum of local preferences (see Chapter Four).

The words used in English to describe the various forms of seat furniture have a complex history, deriving as they do from such varied sources; North European (*stool*), French (*chaire, bench*) and Latin (*sedilia, cathedra*). Up until the eighteenth century, stool and chair were largely interchangeable, in that either of them could have arms and a back. But in order to introduce some clarity, we should adhere to the modern stipulations as follows:

Armchair . . single seat with back and arms
Settle . . . . . . communal seat with back and arms
Backstool . . single seat with back
Stool . . . . . . single seat without back
Bench . . . . . communal seat without back
Chair . . . . . single seat with back or back and arms (the generic term)

The anthropomorphic impulse is very strong in mankind, and this has led to the naming of furniture parts with a set of terms which also applies to the human body, and nowhere more obviously than with chairs. Both chairs

8. Edward Joy, *Country Life Book of the Chair,* London, 1967.

Figure 3:3. *(Left) Joined folding armchair. English. Oak, early seventeenth century, cf. Figure 3:2.*

Figure 3:3a. *(Right) Joined folding armchair. Side view of Figure 3:3.*

and men have legs, arms, shoulders, seats, ears, elbows, knees, feet, toes and backs. Most of these terms were in use in the seventeenth century, though there were alternatives in that the seat-board might be referred to as a 'lift', while the legs were generally referred to as 'feet': "...(1633) the turning of Bedposts Feet of tables joyned Stools do properly belong to the trade of a Turner and not to the art of a Joyner..."

The X-Seat (Figures 2:129-131, 3:1-4)

In the ancient world, and persistisng through most of the Middle Ages, the X-form chair or stool was held in awe as a potent symbol of authority. Deriving from the ancient portable seat of office (such as the Roman *sella curulis,* which could be set up by a judge or bureaucrat wherever his intervention was timely), the folding stool (*faulxdesteuil* or *faldstool*) was used in medieval Europe as a symbol of kingly or ecclesiastical dominance. The X-form base was retained in upholstered chairs and stools until a very late date (see Figure 2:131), though in many examples from the fifteenth century onwards the ability to fold had been abandoned, and the X-form was merely retained as a decorative and structural device. By the sixteenth century, the familiarity with upholstered X-chairs had probably lessened the impact which had once been generated by the imperial *faldstool,* but many examples were still associated with royalty or high office.

Whether or not *the* 'Glastonbury chair' (figure 3:1) figured as such a symbol of office is now a matter of conjecture. It was made for John Arthur Thorne, a monk and the last Treasurer of Glastonbury Abbey, some time before 1539. The chair is inscribed with the monastic name of its original owner and some formal prayers:

Iohanes Arthurus — Monacus Glastonie — Salvet eum deus —
Sit laus deo — Da pacem domine.
(John Arthur — Monk of Glastonbury — God save him —
Praise to god — Lord give peace.)

232

Figure 3:4. *Turned folding stool. English. Walnut, with later fabric seat, c.1675.*

Figure 3:4a. *A king seated in a high-back X-frame armchair from the fifteenth century Flemish 'Bible Historiale'. The back and seat are of stretched fabric or painted leather (though the joined wooden frame is not covered), and the ritual cushion is provided as a footrest. At this stage in the development of manners, the provision of a high back and a footrest were of great significance to the dignity of the sitter. Other manuscripts show similar chairs with a fitted canopy extending forward over the head of the sitter. Compare the form of this chair with Figures 2:129-131.*

9. E.g. two chairs illustrated by Dr. Hermann Schmitz, *Encyclopaedia of Furniture,* Ernest Benn, London, 1926, p.80.

What a pity that Thorne did not instruct the joiner to include the date of making, or is it just possible that the chair was made as a memorial to Thorne soon after his death? Soon after 1539, the chair was apparently in the possession of Elizabeth Whiting (sister of Abbot Richard Whiting, who was executed alongside Thorne). She married a member of the Geanes family of East Pennard. Later one John Bowen, an antiquarian and Priest-Vicar of Wells Cathedral, married an Elizabeth Geanes and thus acquired the chair. In 1824, Bowen officially presented the chair to Bishop Law and his successors.

Despite the extensive repairs to the chair (which are not hinted at in O'Neill's drawing of 1822 in Figure 3:1), the important parts of the chair are genuine and original, and no doubt the replacements follow exactly the original parts. It is easy to be sceptical about the authenticity of the chair, but close inspection reveals that an early sixteenth century date is quite feasible, and that the inscriptions and decoration are perfectly genuine. Henry Shaw also drew attention to a similar chair which had lately (1836) been removed from Southwick Priory, Hampshire.

Folding chairs of this (and the upholstered) type were the earliest form of lightly built open-base chairs to be used in England, though possibly not made by joiners. Two later chairs of identical type are also shown here, (Figures 3:2 and 3) but it is difficult to see just how they fit into the scheme of English furniture. That they are English-made can be of no doubt, for the decoration (and the panelled back of Figure 3:2) is entirely English in conception; yet their form follows closely on Venetian models of the fifteenth century[9]. It is clear from the general design that they were originally designed either to fold or to be taken apart for travelling, and

233

early inventories frequently mention such chairs as being supplied with a leather case into which they were packed for the journey. The joints are normally held in place by small removable wooden pegs, though the pegs in Figure 3:2 are of a more permanent nature. Although modern copies of this type are very familiar, genuine examples are extremely rare, a fact which has not aided research into their history, typology or derivations. There is no suggestion that they were the products of a specific region or workshop, and it seems that they were never especially popular in their time. Perhaps they were limited by law or custom to a specific use, the nature of which eludes us at present. Certainly, the similarities between chairs of such diverse dates is a remarkable feature.

> 1541...a spanishe folding chair...
> 1552...In the little Dynyng Chamber...2 folding stoles...
> 1559...one foulding cheyre of wallnutre...

During the seventeenth century a highly portable form of X-stool was popular, sometimes made to fold, which seems to have been commonly used for temporary seating in churches and other public places. Many churches still had open-floored naves without fixed seats of any sort. Members of the congregation could bring their own stools with slung fabric seats, as in Figure 3:4, or they could be hired at a small cost. An engraving of 1637, published in London, shows the riot which ensued in St. Giles Cathedral, Edinburgh, when the Arch-Prelate of St. Andrews tried to use the new Service Book. Several stools of this type are seen in flight, thrown by the congregation who bombarded him with a variety of "...Cricketts, Stooles Stickes and Stones..."

The Settle (Figures 3:5-13)

If X-stools provided the most flexible and adaptable form of seating, settles did quite the opposite; yet their antiquity and basic usefulness are equally venerable, and their provision is intimately linked with such

Figure 3:5. *Hearth place with fixed flanking settles. Welsh; Abernodwydd Farm, Llangadfan, Montgomeryshire. The settles and their plank-panelled backs are integral with the seventeenth century timber-framed chimney canopy, which was inserted as a later addition to this sixteenth century house.*

Figure 3:6. *Wood engraving, showing a fixed wall settle of late Gothic character in situ in the Green Dragon Inn at Combe St. Nicholas, Somerset. From Parker's 'Domestic Architecture of England', 1859.*

elementary human needs as warmth, sleep and cooking. The earliest and most primitive forms of benching were closely associated with the central hearth or 'fire-place'; and in the Saxon communal hall, this took the shape of low benches or sleeping platforms, ranged about the hearth and butting against the walls. Here the inner life of the homestead was centred, and the inmates would cook, eat, talk, sleep and tell their stories on these integral platforms.

With the general adoption of wall chimneys in the sixteenth century, the importance of the fixed fireside bench or settle was in no way diminished. Fixed seats were often provided within the area of the hearth (the estate agents' beloved 'inglenook'), or movable settles were arranged closely flanking it. Until recently, such settles frequently doubled at night as beds for servants (or for the householders themselves), and some settles are contrived with sloped headrests for this purpose. The hearth in Figure 3:5 is provided with fixed flanking settles, which are integrated with the support-framing of the chimney canopy itself. Only one side is provided with a (rather high) arm-rest, but the pair of seats are very positively orientated around the hearth, which was the hub of life in a traditional house of this sort.

The term 'settle' is one of the earliest English words related to seats, and derives from the Latin *sella* and *sedilia*. At Durham Abbey in 1454 was a bench referred to in the Account Rolls as a *langsedile,* literally rather dog-eared Latin for a 'long seat'.[10] In later inventories, this is anglicised to 'langsettel', or 'longsettle', a term which still survives in the North Country. Eventually, over most of England and Wales, the term finalised as 'settle' (*setl* in Welsh). Inventories frequently note the settle as situated in the chimney corner; but they might also be used elsewhere, especially in

10. Quoted by Penelope Eames, Furniture History, 1977, p.201.

Figure 3:7. *Joined wall settle. English; from a farm near South Molton, Devon/Somerset border. Oak, early sixteenth century. In its present form, this piece has been wrongly re-assembled though the general disposition is correct (see footnote 11, opposite. This settle is illustrated by Adams-Acton as Figure II).*

summer, perhaps sited to act as a room divider or to contain a small area as a self-contained booth with a table.

The earliest development of the settle was that of the fixed type. Though primarily related around the hearth in smaller houses, fixed benches or wall settles were also to be found in the larger halls and inns, and these were often sited behind the long dining tables in exactly the manner of the surviving bench and table of the seventeenth century at the Shrewsbury Drapers' Hall (Diagrams 1:2, 2:2, Figure 2:7).

An early regional expression of this type of wall settle, closely associated with wall-panelling, is a series of settles from Devonshire and Somerset (Figures 3:6-10). These form a fairly distinct group with broadly similar characteristics, and seem to date from a period set largely within the first half of the sixteenth century. Many of them were discovered in the present century as fixtures in inns and farmhouses, and so the exact sources of some are recorded. An early (if unreliable) illustration of such a piece *in situ* was

Figure 3:8. *Joined wall settle. English; from Orchard's Farm, Monkleigh, Devon. Oak, early sixteenth century.*

Figure 3:9. *Joined wall settle. English. Oak, c.1540.*

Figure 3:10a. *Joined wall settle (detail). One of the cresting-panels seen in Figure 3:10, here with a formalised profile portrait of the 'Romayne' type.*

Figure 3:10. *Joined wall settle. English. Oak, mid-sixteenth century. The form of earlier examples is retained here, but the decoration assumes an entirely new character. The linenfold panels have been abandoned in favour of a larger plain panel, with Renaissance decoration concentrated in the cresting-panels.*

11. Illustrated by Murray Adams-Acton, *Wall-seats and Settles of the 16th Century,* The Connoisseur, March 1948, Fig.IV.

the woodcut of 1859 from Parker's *Domestic Architecture in England* (Figure 3:6). This settle was formerly in the Green Dragon Inn at Combe St. Nicholas, Somerset, and was graced with a particularly fine bench end, sporting a hammer beam of sorts with a carved shield bearer. The scale in the woodcut is too large, and the tracery cresting was already missing from between the finials. By the time it was photographed for *The Connoisseur* of March 1948, the settle was in a further delapidated state.[11]

Though differing greatly in detail and execution, these wall settles are similar enough in general conformation to suggest a cohesive local preference for them, and many derive from isolated Exmoor farmhouses, or busy wayside inns. In the article cited above, Adams-Acton showed a dated example of 1544 from an unnamed Devon church. In domestic halls, when the trestle tables were turned up and packed away after meals, the wall settles would still serve for the use of onlookers. They were often reserved for the elderly and infirm, and in churches the provision of wall benches often took the form of low stone ledges at the base of pillars and side walls. Resort to these is thought to be the origin of the phrase 'to go to the wall'.

Figure 3:11b. *Woodcut illustration of a domestic scene. Probably English, early sixteenth century. From Gringoire's 'Castel of Laboures'. The man of the house is taking his meal at a simple trestle table, seated on a panelled low-back settle not unlike the previous example in Figure 3:11a.*

Figure 3:11a. *Wood carving of the Virgin and Child with St. Anne, seated on a panelled low back settle. Probably Flemish. Oak, early sixteenth century. This is the form of light, movable settle which became extremely popular in the fifteenth century, and is seen in many contemporary illustrations of interiors.*

Most of the West Country settles in this group have linenfold panels, and a distinctive cresting panel which is slotted into the top rail and held on only three sides, between the finials. This is also a feature of other late Gothic and Renaissance panelled furniture, such as box-chairs, cupboards and wall-panelling. The seats of the settles are constructed as separate planks supported on crude brackets, which are curiously out of keeping with the fine standard of the framed panelling. That this is the original construction, is shown by two of Adams-Acton's illustrations, where he was able to photograph them in their original settings (*his* Figures II and X, correspond to *my* Figures 3:7 and 10). There are many extant examples of wall-benching in houses of the sixteenth and seventeenth centuries, and early building accounts sometimes note a provision for 'benching-about' hall or parlour (see pp.37-9).

Although she recorded this latter practice, Margaret Jourdain[12] made the following curious observation: "...settles of the late sixteenth and early seventeenth century do not appear to exist..." In fact, a brief investigation brings to light several examples of this period, such as the marvellous pair in the porch of Breamore Church, Hampshire, which are dated 1617 and bear the initials of the churchwardens who presented them. For a much earlier example, one could turn only a few miles away to the remarkable and huge Gothic settle in the South Transept of Winchester Cathedral. Indeed, we are very well supplied with medieval settles in the shape of the huge surviving number of fixed and movable church pews in Devon, Cornwall, Somerset, Suffolk and other counties, some of which represent the finest and most vigorous expression of medieval carved furniture. Many churches had no form of general seating whatever until the introduction of box pews, but in the richer counties and parishes fine and heavy bench pews were provided as

12. Op. cit., p.246.

Figure 3:12. *Joined settle. English or Flemish. Oak, early sixteenth century.*

early as the thirteenth century (such as those at Dunsfold, Surrey, and Clapton-in-Gordano, Somerset).

The earliest extant movable domestic settles are high-backed examples of around 1500, though contemporary sources frequently illustrate low-back types in use in interiors (Figure 3:11b). There is no conceptual basis for the popular and convenient theory that box-base settles and armchairs first developed from the chest, by adding a back and sides for comfort.

Figure 3:13. *Joined multiple seat or stalls. French or Flemish. Oak, early sixteenth century.*

Certainly, box-base settles are very similar in construction to contemporary panelled chests, but the association is no deeper than that. The idea of a long seat is just as old as that of a chest (though it is true both that chests were occasionally used as seats; and that a box-base is a very useful adjunct to a chair, providing storage space where there would otherwise be none).

Stylistically, settles are simply wider versions of the armchairs of the same period, as is amply demonstrated by Figures 3:12 and 13. The latter is akin to the ecclesiastical choir-stall, and is not offered as an intermediate stage in the evolution of the armchair, but as an intermediate idea between the long-seated communal settle and the single armchair. Here a multiple row of single seats is provided in one piece of furniture — movable, but hardly mobile — yet it clearly links the kinship between settle and armchair.

> 1454...1 scamnum voc. langsedile...
> 1571...a lang settel...
> 1585...two wainscot settles standing in and about the hall...
> 1596...2 settels of wenscote with lockes and keys to them...
> 1600...a bench settell with two chests and two lydds, having too lockes...
> 1638...one settle with 3 boxes in it...

The Armchair (Figures 3:14-66)

Randle Holme hinted (as late as 1649) at the relationship between the settle and the heavy form of enclosed-base armchair when he described such a piece as a 'settle chair', and elaborated further "...this is the old way of makeing the chaire...some term it a settle chaire, being so weighty that it cannot be moved from place to place, but still abideth in it owne station, haveing a kind of box or cubbert in the seate of it..." The chair in his woodcut (Figure 3:17) is not built of framed panels, but rather of coopered

Figure 3:14. *(Left) Joined armchair. French or Flemish. Oak, early sixteenth century. Gothic detail.*

Figure 3:15. *(Right) Joined armchair. Possibly English. Oak, c.1540. Gothic detail in the top panel of the back.*

Figure 3:16. *(Left) Joined armchair. Possibly English. Oak, c.1540. Renaissance detail in the top panel of the back.*

Figure 3:16a. *(Right) Joined armchair. Rear view of Figure 3:16. The extremities of the feet are missing.*

Figure 3:17. *Woodcut illustration: Randle Holme, 'Academie of Armory', 1649.*
"70:...a settle chaire...haveing a kind of box or cubbert in the seate of it..."
The construction of this piece is something of a mystery.

13. Discussed under 'Chests', pp.355-356.

or overlapped planks, like the chair from the collection of the Duke of Leeds in Macquoid's *The Age of Oak,* fig.116.

No English panelled chair exists from before the beginning of the sixteenth century, and indeed for the first fifty years it is very difficult to discern English work from Flemish or French of the same date. Probably, a great deal of the earliest joined work was done in England by immigrant joiners, and a large amount of furniture was imported at this time from a number of European sources. There are many references in inventories of the time to 'fflaunders' chests and chairs, as well as others, such as 'Danske' and 'Cyprus'.[13] These references are so common that contemporaries must have understood exactly what the terms meant, and each must have been easily distinguishable from the other. Yet their meanings are lost to us, and so we can only conjecture. A good deal of discussion has been generated, but with few tangible conclusions. In view of the fact that a good deal of panelled furniture was imported from Flanders, especially in the early days when joined construction was a novelty in England, might it not be possible that the epithet 'Flanders' was used at first to distinguish panelled chairs and chests from indigenous carpenters' and turners' work?

Throughout the Middle Ages, the only available forms of lightweight open-base seats were the X-seat and turned chairs or stools. Around the end of the fifteenth century and in the first part of the sixteenth, the joiner was experimenting with the omission of panels from the frames of chairs, in order to produce a lighter and more flexible arrangement. Partially enclosed chairs continued to appear over a long period (Figures 3:21-24), perhaps with a view to restricting the effects of draughts on the sitter; but the standard form was soon to emerge as a completely open base with a panelled back (Figure 3:26 *et al*).

241

It is by no means easy to ascertain the date at which open-frame joined armchairs first appeared in the British Isles, since extant chairs of this period are extremely rare and difficult to date precisely. Because of these problems, the chair of Sir Rhys ap Thomas (Figure 3:28) must be regarded as highly significant[14]. Sir Rhys had been largely instrumental in bringing Welsh support to the aid of Henry Tudor, and was knighted by the new Henry VII for services rendered at the Battle of Bosworth in 1485, and elevated to the Garter in 1505. Thereafter he was a virtual ruler in South-West Wales, working from his seats at Carew Castle and Dynefwr, Carmarthenshire. He died at the ripe old age of seventy-six, in 1527.

The chair bears the personal arms of Sir Rhys ap Thomas, encircled by the Garter, which are also to be found on the remains of his bed of c.1505, seen in Figure 3:27b). His arms were held subsequently by the family, but apparently with additions, and so the chair would seem reliably to date from after 1505 and before 1527. But the question still remains of the nationality of the chair, and in this respect it is related to the well-known *caqueteuse* armchair of Devonshire provenance (Figure 3:29). This

Figure 3:18. *(Right) Joined armchair. English. Oak, 1520-40.*

Figure 3:18a. *(Below) Joined armchair. Rear view of Figure 3:18.*

14. This is one of a pair of armchairs, recently deposited on loan at the Welsh Folk Museum. The second chair was restored c.1670, being fitted with scrolled arms, twist-turned legs and a new seat. The timing of this restoration is very interesting, since it coincides with a time when Sir Rhys's exploits were being elaborated by family historians. No doubt family pride caused a renewed effort to conserve the relics of Sir Rhys which still survived at Dynefwr, including these chairs and the bed in Figure 3:452.

Figure 3:19. *Joined armchair. English. Oak, 1520-40.*

Figure 3:20. *Joined armchair. Scottish; Aberdeen. Oak, dated 1574. This chair was presented to the Incorporated Trades of Aberdeen by 'JEROME BLAK', a cooper, and bears his name and the arms of Blak. The carving is painted in colours.*

Figure 3:21. *Joined armchair. English. Oak, mid-sixteenth century. A partially-enclosed form which persisted for many years (see Figure 3:23).*

Figure 3:22. *Joined armchair. English or French. Oak, early sixteenth century. Another partially-enclosed form which persisted for many years (see Figure 3:24). The authenticity of the front stretcher is obviously questionable, though the fact that it is rebated into the legs follows closely on French joinery practice (cf. Figures 3:29, 33, 34).*

Figure 3:23. *Joined armchair. English. Oak, dated 1631.*

Figure 3:24. *Joined armchair. English. Oak, c.1620.*

Figure 3:25. *(Left) Joined armchair. English. Oak, c.1540.*

Figure 3:26. *(Right) Joined armchair. English. Oak, c.1540.*

conjunction is also interesting from another point of view, since the two forms (perhaps) represent the types of armchairs normally occupied by a rich husband and wife in the early sixteenth century. Sir Rhys ap Thomas spent a good deal of time in France, and it is possible that his chair was commissioned and made for him there. Yet, stylistically, both chairs have parallels in fixed English woodwork of the period, and no closely comparable examples are known in France[15]. Apart from the differences in form, these two are very similar in details such as the mouldings of the arms, the character of the carved decoration, and the setting of the back panels within the framing members (with a stepped rebate). Perhaps they represent an aristocratic or courtly taste, which carries the suggestion that they may have been London-made. The *caqueteuse* was discovered in Colyton, South Devon, in c.1900; Sir Rhys ap Thomas's armchair is from Carmarthenshire; and a similar chair with a portrait panel was found in a cottage in Shropshire during the nineteenth century (Figure 3:31). Another *caqueteuse* of similar form, but coarser execution, is seen in Figure 3:32.

The *chaire caqueteuse* or *chaise de femme* appeared at first in France, as a lightly-built armchair or backstool, often upholstered, which was supposedly ideal for use by women (the term means literally 'gossiping chair', but there is no exact English equivalent). Today the word is used to refer to an armchair which is exemplified by its narrow back, wide front, and trapezoidal seat. In order to accommodate these proportions, the arms are set flat and are canted or curved outwards, often with an extra support under the angle. During the period of French influence in sixteenth century Scotland, the *caqueteuse* became the standard form of armchair in Aberdeen and other East Coast regions. Sometimes the form and decoration are copied direct from French originals (Figure 3:35), but in others the influence of indigenous (or even English) decoration is seen (see

15. See *English Chairs*, Victoria and Albert Museum Large Picture Book No. 10, HMSO, 1970. pp.1-2.

Figure 3:27a. *Joined armchair. Detail of Figure 3:28. The arms of Sir Rhys ap Thomas. Note the use of the mason's mitre at the joints. The light and confident handling of the carved panel looks forward to English Renaissance translations of French styles, in striking contrast to the heavy and formal hexagonal guilloches beneath the seat-rail (see Figure 3:28).*

Figure 3:27b. *Carved bed post. Detail of 3:452. The arms of Sir Rhys ap Thomas. Though differing in scale and execution, this and the previous example are of the same description, encircled by the Garter.*

Figure 3:28. *Joined armchair. Anglo-French. Oak, before 1527. An early example of the open-frame joined chair, bearing the personal arms of Sir Rhys ap Thomas of Dynefwr, Carmarthenshire. The spiral twist of the arm supports is hand cut, and may be compared with the cupboard of similar date in Figure 4:21. This is an important link in the appearance of the 'modern' movable chair.*

Chapter Four). The majority of English examples are largely unrelated individuals. This is a fairly rare type in England, and only Salisbury seems to have exhibited a consistent taste for this form of chair.

Turned decoration first appeared in open-frame joinery around the middle of the sixteenth century, and after this date *most* English armchairs have turned legs, and arms which scroll forward in (what was then) the Spanish fashion. The backs are normally panelled, or sometimes openwork with some form of carved or turned infilling. This basic form of chair survived in traditional use throughout the seventeenth century; and in remote areas such as Wales and the North Country very late examples are encountered, such as the armchair of 1742 at Townend, Troutbeck, Westmorland (or the even later Yorkshire settle of 1756 in Figure 4:138), which are still essentially in the style of the preceding century.

Figure 3:29. *Joined caqueteuse armchair. Anglo-French. Oak, c.1530. This chair may perhaps be regarded as the feminine counterpart of the previous example. Both chairs tend towards the Court style of Henry VIII, and it is possible that both were made in London at about the same time.*

The use of armchairs is rarely described specifically as such in the inventories (they are usually covered by the term 'great chair'), but the standard type of chair is clearly intended by the following entry in the Ingatestone inventory of 1600:

> "...In the hall...A high joyned chaire with armes and carved at ye back...

The faithful Randle Holme also had a few words to say on the matter:

> "...if the chaire be made all of Joyners worke, as back and seate then it is termed a Joynt chaire, or a Buffit chaire. Those which have stayes (*i.e. arms*) on each side are called Arme chaires or chaires of ease..."

Figures 3:30a and b. *(Left and right) Joined armchairs. Rear views of Figures 3:28 and 29. Though differing slightly in form, these chairs are of remarkably similar construction and execution. They represent some of the earliest appearances of the Renaissance style in English furniture. Sir Rhys ap Thomas enjoyed close connections and favour with the Tudor court, and the caqueteuse was doubtlessly made for a similarly exalted household; probably at the same time and place.*

Figure 3:31. *Wood engraving after a drawing by C.B. Birch, nineteenth century. This chair was apparently discovered by Birch's father in a Shropshire cottage in the early nineteenth century. The similarity to Figure 3:28 is unmistakable, and suggests a similar origin.*

16. It is often assumed that the cresting-rail was never set *above* the uprights until after c.1630, but the chair of 1585 from the Council House at Salisbury (Figure 4:58) demonstrates otherwise.

Open-frame joined chairs differ greatly in detail and character, though the basic format of construction is very similar whether they are decorated or not, upholstered or not. The differences are mainly those of proportion and decoration, reflecting the techniques favoured by different workshops or regions; and responding to the demands of the original client, whose choice would indicate his wealth and his social standing or pretensions.

Slight differences in construction between individual chairs are found particularly in the form of the cresting-rail. We have seen that in medieval chairs this often took the form of a cresting-panel, held on three sides by the top rail and finials. The most common form throughout the sixteenth to eighteenth centuries was for the top rail to be set quite simply *between* the main upright, elaborated by shaping of the rail or supplying finials to the uprights. By c.1580[16] a variation was introduced whereby the cresting-rail was set *above* the main uprights, elaborated by often quite complex shaping and spandrel brackets or ear pieces which support the overhang of the rail (Figures 3:43 a and b). A compromise was found (mainly in Scottish chairs) whereby the elaborated cresting-rail was stepped around the uprights, so that it both surmounted them *and* and was tenoned between. This is best seen by examining Figures 4:102-109.

Another (rare) variation in construction is found in a small group of chairs (Figures 3:54-58), in which the arm-supports are carried up to finish in a turned knob or finial, and the arm itself is tenoned into the block from behind. Many of these chairs have certain other characteristics in common (such as the form of the crest, the use of parquetry bandings, etc.); and it must seem likely that they originate from one locality (probably an urban centre in the West Country, such as Bristol).

A further rare feature which is occasionally met with may be seen in Figures 3:59 and 60 and 4:54 and 55. This takes the form of a secondary support which is superimposed upon the inner section of the main arm. The function of such an attachment is by no means obvious, but probably has to do with extra support for cushions which may be placed around the sitter,

Figure 3:32. *Joined caqueteuse armchair. Probably English. Oak, 1525-50. Though of coarser execution and finish, there are evident similarities between this chair and Figure 3:29.*

Figure 3:33. *Joined caqueteuse armchair. French. Walnut, late sixteenth century.*

Figure 3:34. *Joined caqueteuse armchair. French. Walnut, late sixteenth century.*

Figure 3:35. *Joined caqueteuse armchair. Scottish; probably Aberdeen. Oak, early seventeenth century.*

Figure 3:36. *Joined caqueteuse armchair. Scottish; probably Aberdeenshire. Oak, chestnut and pine, mid-seventeenth century. A country-made version of the previous chair, as evidenced by a simpler design and the mixture of timbers.*

Figure 3:37. *Joined caqueteuse armchair. English; West Country. Oak, c.1600.*

Figure 3:38. *(Left) Joined caqueteuse armchair. English. Oak, c.1600. This chair retains certain features of French influence, such as the stepped-forward front stretcher and the moulding of the arm, but the construction is entirely English. The seat, in particular, should be compared with the chairs from Salisbury (Chapter Four).*

Figure 3:39. *(Right) Joined caqueteuse armchair. English, mid-seventeenth century. A vernacular English version of restrained conventional type.*

Figure 3:40. *Joined caqueteuse armchair. English; Salisbury. Oak, elm panel, c.1700.*

Figure 3:41. *Joined caqueteuse armchair. American; New Jersey. Maple and oak, originally painted pumpkin yellow, c.1700.*

Figure 3:42. *Joined armchair. English; Yorkshire. Oak, with inlay, c.1640.*

Figure 3:43a. *Joined armchair (detail). A very fine example of a pierced chair-crest, set above the uprights and supported on either side by scrolled ear pieces. English. Oak, with inlay, early seventeenth century.*

and secured in place by ties or ribbons. These 'wings' are reflected in the rather similar projections to be found on certain turned chairs (Figures 2:84-86 and 4:259). The idea of a side rest of this sort was carried out more fully in the upholstered and winged easy chair of the later seventeenth century (see p.256).

An early manifestation of the upholstered winged form is seen in the leather easy chairs in Figures 3:61 and 62. The first is one of those rare semi-mechanical contraptions known as a sleeping chair. The back is hinged to the frame, and the angle of repose is adjustable about an iron ratchet. Easy chairs were often used for sleeping by our ancestors, and a chair specially adjustable for the purpose was not a new idea after the Restoration. John Grene had made a similar chair for Elizabeth I, which was probably not unique: "...one great stoole of walnutre with one large pillow covered with cloth of golde...withone staie for the back of the Queen...with staies, springes, and staples of iron to set the same higher and lower with apillow of downe..." William Hoode, a blacksmith, supplied separately "...ij pillers with xxvij holes and one brode flatte plate full of holes ij square boltes with lowpes staples..." The Duke of Lauderdale had a very grand pair of sleeping chairs at Ham House in 1679, which were probably made for him by John Pauderine, the Royal Chairmaker. The chairs are still at the house, complete with their original covers.[17]

> 1466...a chaire of tymber of astate, covered wt blue cloth of
>   gold...a case of lether thereto...

(Armchairs are rarely specified as such before the seventeenth century, since *joined* backstools were comparatively rare and there was no need to differentiate between stools and chairs.)

> 1614...one man's arm stool...
> 1673...one great armed chaire...
> 1677...one elbow chair, & one litle chair...
> 1679...Two arme Chayres, carved frames, of walnut tree...
>   2 sleeping Chayres, carv'd and guilt frames...
> 1689...in the hall of his dwelling house, 2 boarded chaires...
> 1693...one two armed chaire...
> 1694...one 2 armed chaire...

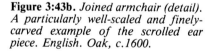

Figure 3:43b. *Joined armchair (detail). A particularly well-scaled and finely-carved example of the scrolled ear piece. English. Oak, c.1600.*

17. Another "...Sleeping Chayre of Crimson velvet..." which was in the Duke's Closet in 1679, is now in the collection of Lord Tollemache at Helmingham Hall, Suffolk, and was brought there by inheritance.

Figure 3:44. *Joined armchair. English. Oak, with inlay, early seventeenth century. The fan-shaped crest and scrolled finials are very distinctive, the former being highly reminiscent of the headings to important doorways of the same date, such as that of Exeter Guildhall.*

Although the majority of pieces conform to a large degree with the standard products of their age, occasionally a design or variant appears which is startlingly novel in the context in which it is found. Such a design was the remarkable set of chairs produced by Francis Cleyn for use at Holland House, Kensington, in about 1625. Cleyn was a German, a native of Rostock, who had worked and studied first in Italy and then in Denmark. In 1623 he joined the staff of the Mortlake tapestry factory as a designer, and shortly afterwards designed the white and gilded panelling for the Gilt Room at Holland House (destroyed in World War II). The room was furnished with a set of armchairs similar to Figure 3:63, though it is not clear if this actual chair was part of the Holland House set. There are several extant examples of this type (e.g. the pair at Aston Hall, Birmingham), and although the general form is identical, differences in execution suggest a different maker and different sets. Holland House was probably also supplied with a number of matching backstools, since a set of six backstools survives at Lacock Abbey, Wiltshire (in 1795, William Davenport Talbot of Lacock married Lady Elizabeth Fox-Strangways of Holland House, and the chairs are noted at Lacock for the first time in the inventory of 1800).

The Holland House chairs were painted white with gilded enrichments to match the scheme of the Gilt Room, though the six at Lacock were repainted some time in the eighteenth or early nineteenth century. The fan-shaped shell-back, and the general form and decoration of the chairs, derives from Cleyn's experiences in Italy.

Figure 3:45. *Joined armchair. English. Oak, c.1630.*

Figure 3:46. *Joined armchair. English. Oak, c.1630.*

Figure 3:47. *Joined armchair. English. Oak, c.1630. Note a late use of the mason's mitre in the joints of the panel frame.*

Figure 3:48. *Joined armchair. English; probably South Yorkshire. Oak, dated '1678 FM'.*

Figure 3:49. *Joined armchair. English; probably Westmorland. Unidentified timber of beautiful amber-like colour, seventeenth century.*

Figure 3.50. *Joined armchair. English; North Country. Ash, oak panel, c.1700. The seat is formed by a mesh of ropes which supports a cushion, unusual in single chairs, being more usually a feature of settles.*

Figure 3:51. *Joined settle. English; Lancashire. Oak, late seventeenth century. In terms of its construction, this type of open-frame settle may be seen simply as a longer version of the single-seat armchair, and is more closely related to chairs than to the generic family of fixed settles seen earlier in this chapter (Figures 3:5-10). Note once more the late use of mason's mitres in side uprights.*

Figure 3:52a. *Joined armchair. English; probably Shropshire. Oak, mid-seventeenth century. The rich turned and carved decoration of this chair is typical of a small group of similar examples which deserve further investigation (see Figure 3:53).*

Figure 3:52b. *Joined armchair. Further view of Figure 3:52a.*

Figure 3:53. *Joined armchair. English; probably Shropshire. Oak, mid-seventeenth century. Compare the details of construction and turnings with those on the previous example.*

Figure 3:54. *Joined armchair. Side view of Figure 3:55, demonstrating the joint between arm and the arm support, in which the latter ends with a turned finial.*

Figure 3:55. *Joined armchair. English. Oak, c.1600.*

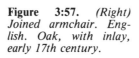

Figure 3:56. *(Left) Joined armchair. English. Walnut, with inlay, early seventeenth century.*

Figure 3:57. *(Right) Joined armchair. English. Oak, with inlay, early 17th century.*

Figure 3:58. *Joined armchair. English. Oak, with inlay, late sixteenth century. An unusual and aristocratic chair in several respects, with a good deal of Flemish inspiration in the design.*

Figure 3:59. *Joined armchair. English. Oak, c.1625. The vigour and enthusiasm behind the carving compensate for any lack of quality and finesse.*

Figure 3:60. *Joined armchair. English. Oak, c.1625. The details and characteristics of this chair are so similar to the previous example as to suggest a common origin and source.*

Figure 3:61. *Joined sleeping chair. English. Walnut, leather upholstery, wrought iron fittings, c.1680. The wrought iron extensions from the arms are provided to support a reading-desk. The hinged back, and the ratchets to set the angle of the back, are clearly seen.*

Figure 3:62. *Joined easy chair. English. Oak and ash, painted leather upholstery, c.1680.*

Figure 3:63. *Boarded armchair. English; similar to a set designed by the German artist Francis Cleyn for Holland House, Kensington, near London. Oak and elm, painted white and gilded, c.1625.*

Figure 3:64. *Boarded armchair. Rear view of Figure 3:63. The construction as seen here is derived directly from Italian types. The extensions to the rear foot are not original.*

Figure 3:65. *(Above) Boarded armchair. Detail of the shell back in Figure 3:63, similar to contemporary Italian chairs.*

Figure 3:66. *(Left) Boarded armchair. Detail of front base of Figure 3:63, similar to contemporary Italian chairs.*

257

Figure 3:67. *Joined chair-table. English; Gloucestershire. Oak, c.1630. Shown turned down for use as a table.*

Figure 3:68. *(Right) Joined chair-table. Another view of Figure 3:67, here with the hinged top thrown back for use as an armchair.*

Figure 3:69. *(Left) Joined chair-table. English. Oak, c.1640. The back panel is treated just as if it were a normal framed chair back.*

Figure 3:70. *(Right) Joined chair-table. English. Oak, c.1630. This version has an octagonal top, and incorporates a drawer beneath the seat.*

The Chair-Table (Figures 3:67-71)

Even in very great houses, in the Middle Ages and later, it was common for household officials and retainers to be assigned only one room for their personal living quarters; or at best a pair of rooms which consisted of a parlour and bedchamber. Inventories frequently refer to such rooms by the name of the occupant (...In the Clerks Chamber...In Mr. Matchettes Chamber...In Jonces' Chamber...In my cozen Amphilis's Chamber...In the Mayd's Chamber...In My Lord's Bed Chamber...etc.), and except in the last case the list of furniture is very short — usually a standing bedstead of some description, sometimes a truckle bedstead, a chair, a stool or two, a small table, a court cupboard or a clothes press, and some small personal items. Likewise in small private houses, especially in towns, rooms for everyday living were often very small, and it was imperative to make efficient use of the space available. It was doubtless under conditions such as these that the idea of a 'chair-table' was conceived, whereby the table could serve for use at small, private meals; and afterwards the top would fold back to accommodate a guest in conversation, or the master of the house for his pipe of tobacco (Figures 3:67 and 68).

Unfortunately, the reality is not quite so cosy, for rarely does a chair-table serve either as a comfortable chair *or* an efficient dining table. Consequently they are quite rare items in their genuine state. The longer version was referred to as a 'settle-table', and whilst the top normally consisted of one long board pivoted over the arms, the example in Figure 3:71 is divided into three tops which allow a greater flexibility of usage. This is especially practical in that it may be used as a seat *and* a table at the same

Figure 3:71. *Joined settle-table. English. Oak, mid-seventeenth century. This interesting piece incorporates three lockers beneath the seats, and three independently hinged tops. This allows greater flexibility of use, and is shown here set for a meal.*

Figure 3:71a. *Joined settle-table. Another view of Figure 3:71, here with tops turned down for use as a side or serving table. It would be impossible to use this as a dining table with any comfort.*

time; a highly successful device. Further, this piece provides storage in the form of three lockers under the seats.

1543...Item, a yoyned table, chayrewise...
1558...a round chaire table...
1639...one Chayer table...
1642...A chair uncovered with a falling back for a table...
1671...one Table-chaire, 2s...
1686...one table chaier...
1696...ane cheer or round table...

Figure 3:72a. *Boarded stool. English. Oak, late sixteenth/early seventeenth century.*

Figure 3:72b. *Boarded stool. Another view of Figure 3:72a.*

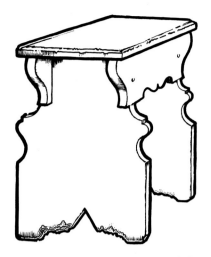

Figure 3:73a. *Boarded stool. English; Brede, Sussex. Oak, seventeenth century (after Fred Roe). Although this type of stool is usually associated with an earlier period, the classical shaped profiles used in this and similar stools suggest a date after 1600. This type of stool is surprisingly rare, considering the huge numbers in which they must have been made.*

Figure 3:73b. *Boarded stool. English; Midhurst, West Sussex. Oak, dated 1689 (after Fred Roe). There is no reason to doubt that 1689 was the year of manufacture of this stool, since the character of the construction and (minimal) decoration is entirely in keeping with contemporary rustic boarded chests.*

18. In inventories of the seventeenth century, stools are often referred to as 'short formes'. Dr. Johnson confirmed a modern interpretation by giving in his *Dictionary:* "...Stool. A seat without a back, so distinguished from a chair..."
19. This form of chipped edge was usually done on end-grain edges, and was effected by the use of a U-gouge chisel. It is normally found only on plank seats and chest tops, often in combination with a scratch-moulded side-grain edge.

The Stool (Figures 3:72-126)

Having established that, at least for modern purposes, a 'stool' is a single backless and armless seat[18] and a 'bench' (or form) is a multiple seat of the same type; we must now consider some of the variations which are differentiated by construction and name. It is perhaps as well to consider them under the following types:

    a). Boarded stools
    b). Joined stools
    c). Box stools, and other combinations
    d). Cricket stools
    e). Squabs and cushion stools

a). Boarded Stools (Figures 3:72-78)

Little is known about the various types of English medieval stools, since no reliable examples have survived. Manuscript illustrations show a variety of types, mostly three-legged versions of the turned or primitive 'staked-leg' types (see Chapter Two), and fairly simple boarded versions. Until recent years it was thought that some of the surviving carpenter-made boarded stools were of medieval date, but in fact none can be reasonably assigned to a period prior to the sixteenth century (and many must date from the seventeenth century). As an example, when Fred Roe showed a stool identical to my Figure 3:72 in his *History of Oak Furniture,* 1920, pl.XXVIII, he misleadingly described it as a "gothic joint stool"; yet in the same book he provided a drawing (pl.LXXV) of one of the pair of boarded stools from Midhurst church, which are dated 1689 (Figure 3:73b).

Boarded stools must have been made in enormous numbers over a very long period, being very cheap to produce in terms of time, materials and expertise. Yet the construction is intrinsically too weak and vulnerable to serve well for stools in the face of vigorous daily usage, and their popularity must have progressively given way to the more serviceable joined stools. They relate very closely in construction to the simple boarded chests of the same period, being composed quite simply of five flat shaped boards held together by nails or pegs; and many fakes have been made by the simple expedient of altering plain and comparatively valueless chests. Though not especially early, the stool in Figures 3:72 a and b is one of the most complete and satisfying examples that it is possible to find. The side boards are buttressed forward in the usual manner, and the apron pieces are arched to lighten the whole effect of the stool. The meaning of the incised cross is not satisfactorily explained, but is a familiar feature on certain types of sixteenth century furniture (though it is *not* necessarily indicative of a sixteenth century date).

Unlike Continental stools of the sixteenth century, English boarded stools (or at least those which survive) are usually rather plain in their execution, and decoration rarely consists of more than shaped-profile edges, simple pierced shapes in the aprons (Figures 2:115, 3:74 and 4:11), and the familiar chipped edge usually found on boarded furniture (Figure 3:75).[19]

An interesting set of heavy and very serviceable boarded stools survives at the London Charterhouse. Some wonderfully early dates have been ascribed for these stools, and it is still generally held that they were made for the original Carthusian monastery, which was finally dissolved and surrendered in 1537, after much trial and tribulation. Yet, if we look at the facts, we find that the Charterhouse was altered and put to use as a private house several times during the sixteenth century (notably after 1545 and in

Figure 3:74. *Boarded stool. English. Oak, sixteenth century. The pierced apron is one of the standard patterns.*

Figure 3:76. *Boarded bench. English or Welsh. Oak, sixteenth century.*

Figure 3:75. *Boarded stool. English. Oak, sixteenth century.*

Figure 3:77. *Boarded stool. English; London. Oak, probably 1614. Made for the Scholar's Hall of Sutton's School, at the London Charterhouse, Islington (see next figure).*

20. The term 'refectory' table is used correctly here.

1571). Finally, in 1613-14, the buildings were adapted and extensively refurnished for the founding of Thomas Sutton's Hospital and School. The stools in question (Figure 3:77), along with some similar long benches and some heavy refectory tables,[20] formed part of the furnishings of the Scholars' Hall. This was originally the School dining-hall, but was destroyed by incendiary bombs in 1941. There is no reason to assume that the stools were not provided new in 1614 for the Hall furnishings, having been made by one of a long list of carpenters who are recorded at work fitting out the School buildings. They are hardly of a character to have been retained among the furnishings of the very grand sixteenth century households (which included those of Lord North, the Duke of Norfolk, the Portuguese ambassador and the Earl of Suffolk). The massive and plain form of the stools, strengthened as they are with a heavy moulded stretcher, is entirely in accord with the specifications of other institutional furniture of this date, and suitable for the rough usage which might be expected from a complement of forty boys.

Figure 3:78. *The Scholar's Hall, London Charterhouse. This view of the hall was taken before its destruction in 1941. Some of the stools and benches are seen, with an original table nearest the camera. Barely visible at the far end, is a long wall-bench on turned legs.*

Figure 3:79. *Joined stool. English. Walnut, c.1575. A fine and early example of a high-quality walnut stool, such as are recorded in large sets at this time. The rich gadrooning of the frieze, and the simple fluted columns here make their first appearance in English furniture.*

Figure 3:79a. *Joined stool. English. Oak, late sixteenth century. An unusual tripod form, recorded in inventories as 'three-footed' or 'three-cornered'. The rather flimsy top is lobed in the form of a trefoil (cf. Figures 3:103 and 104).*

b). Joined Stools (Figures 3:79-104)

Before the middle of the sixteenth century, stools were made only by turners and carpenters, or were of the primitive home-made variety. The development of open-frame joinery made possible the introduction of the very light and strong joined stool, which became the standard form of individual domestic seating throughout the next two centuries (to be gradually superseded after 1650 by the backstool). Apart from the chest, which has been made over a considerably longer period of time, joined stools must have been by far the most common and familiar piece of furniture in seventeenth century England. They are very frequently mentioned in inventories, and only the poorest homes seem to be without. Some rooms contain as many as twenty or two dozen stools; but most frequently they are described in sets of six, in concert with the table, forms and a chair:

1585...my frame table in the chamber with 6 stools...
    ...the joined table and half a dozen joined stools belonging to it...
1586...great joined table, 6 joined stools, and one walnut-tree chair...
1594...*Great Chamber,* One drawing table of walnutte cutt and carved of thre leaves longe, and Xij stooles cutte and carved...
    Dyninge Parlor, One drawinge table of thre leaves, viij Buffet stooles...

Figure 3:80. *Joined stool. English. Oak, early seventeenth century.*

Figure 3:81. *Joined stool. English. Oak, 1580-1600.*

Figure 3:82. *Joined stool. English. Oak, 1580-1600.*

Figure 3:83. *Joined stool. English. Oak, early seventeenth century.*

Figure 3:84. *Joined stool. English. Oak, early seventeenth century.*

1615...In the Hall...one table bord, one forme, 5 stolles...

1681...In the parlor...One long table, eighteene joined stooles, two chaires...

1686...In the hall...One long table, eight joyne stooles, two joyne fourmes...

1693...one long tabel & 6 joynt stooles, 16s...

The comparatively low rate of survival among stools is due to a history of rough usage and the ravages of damp floors and woodworm. No doubt individual workshops made several dozens of each pattern, and sold them to customers in the desired quantities. They are very rarely found in sets today, though a few sets of six are known. Most stools appear singly, but pairs are not infrequent, since most church stools survive in pairs as coffin stools (q.v.).

The standard dining stool was made quite high (usually 23-24ins.) to match the height of the table, though many stools have now been shortened by the loss of the extremities of the feet. The 'toes' of stools, as with most joined-frame furniture, were formed either by simple downward extensions of the square-section tenon blocks (Figures 3:81, 86, 87, 99, etc.); or they were turned on the lathe at the same time as the rest of the leg (Figures 3:85, 91-93, 109, etc.). In many cases the turned toe has been eroded almost completely, and only the smallest vestige remains to announce its former presence (Figures 3:79, 83 and 84, etc.). Occasionally, all trace of the

Figure 3:85. *Joined stool. English. Oak, early seventeenth century.*

Figure 3:86. *Joined stool. English. Oak, early seventeenth century.*

Figure 3:87. *Joined stool. English. Yewtree, c.1640.*

Figure 3:88. *Joined stool. English. Oak, c.1640.*

heightened toe has disappeared and the stretchers are reduced to sitting on the ground (Figure 3:110), but it is important to realise that *no* joined furniture was originally made in this manner.

In order to provide extra stability, the legs of high stools are built with an inward slope or splay, so that the area of the top of the frame is less than that covered by the feet. The top overhangs the apron by a small amount, and is normally finished with an edge-moulding. A lot of nonsense has been talked about so-called correct and incorrect patterns of pegging for fixing the tops of stools; in fact three different patterns are commonly found, with

Figure 3:89. *Joined bench. English. Oak, c.1640.*

Figure 3:90. *Joined bench. English. Oak, mid-seventeenth century.*

Figure 3:91. *Joined stool. English. Oak, mid-seventeenth century.*

Figure 3:92. *Joined stool. English. Oak, c.1680.*

Diagram 3:1. *Methods of pegging the top of a joined stool. These are the three patterns in which tops may be found.* **a).** *is the most satisfactory, and* **c).** *is the least. Boarded stools often have pegged tops, but sometimes the uprights are tenoned through the tops and cut off flush with the seat.*

little or no distinction as to quality or region. The pegs are inserted through the top in one of the ways shown in Diagram 3:1.

Exceptions are *very* suspect, and should be looked on firstly with suspicion. a) and b) are more satisfactory than c), since with the latter technique the pegs are held only by the end grain of the legs, which provides less friction and grip than the side grain of the aprons, and therefore a less stable fixing.

In addition to the high dining stools (called 'buffet' stools in some parts of the country), a variety of low stools were provided for sitting, for the use of children, or as footstools. These do not usually have splayed legs, and may be confused with children's or other small tables, though tables have thinner tops with a greater overhang.

> 1552...6 stoles of walnuttree paynted...
> ...In the litle Dynynge Chamber...12 ioined stoles, 2 folding stoles, 2 squarre litle stoles, 1 fote stole...
> 1556...In the Great Chamber...One large deale table wt. his frame, 8 ioyned square stoles, ij fourmes, 12 new walnuttree corned stoles...
> ...12 stoles three corned ioyned, 2 loe fotestoles...
> 1594...Fower & XX hie stooles, viij loe stooles of ye same...
> ...The Dyninge Parlor...viij Buffet stooles...
> 1624...XII walnutree high stooles...
> 1685...In the Great Parlour...five join'ed stooles buffeded...

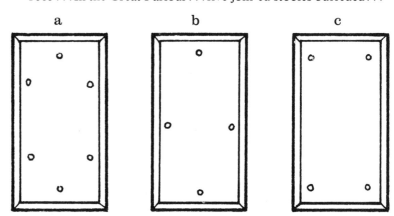

Figure 3:93. *(Left) Joined stool. English. Oak, c.1680.*

Figure 3:94. *(Right) Joined stool. English. Oak, c.1680 (the feet replaced).*

Figure 3:95. *(Left) Joined stool. English. Oak, dated 1681.*

Figure 3:96. *(Right) Joined stool. American; New England. White oak, c.1680.*

Figure 3:97. *Joined stool. English. Oak, c.1680.*

Figure 3:98. *Joined stool. English. Oak, c.1630. The centre stretcher is rare in stools, though common in benches.*

Figure 3:99. *Joined stool. Welsh. Oak, c.1680.*

Figure 3:100. *(Left) Joined stool. English. Oak, dated 1680. A square and low format, quite unlike the preceding high dining-stools.*

Figure 3:101. *(Right) Joined book press. English. Oak and wrought iron, c.1680. Here the stool format is adapted as a frame for a small book press. Bookbinders were common, even in small towns, since books were sold in their unbound state and the customer would have all his books bound to suit his taste and pocket.*

c). Box stools, and other combinations (Figures 3:105-119)

There were several attempts to make practical use of the space beneath the tops of stools, by providing some convenient form of storage, but with varying measures of success. Perhaps the least effective was the provision of a drawer (Figures 3:113-114). A stool is essentially a mobile piece of furniture, which may be carried around and set down at will. If a stool with a drawer is carried in a thoughtless or casual manner, then the drawer will easily fall out and smash on the floor, spilling its contents. Stools with drawers are understandably rare.

A more successful idea, and therefore more commonly met with, is the box stool. Here the seat-board is hinged to the seat-rail in the form of a small lidded chest, and the compartment is floored over and fitted with a lock. Such a piece might be used for storing almost any daily trivia, from

Figure 3:102. *Joined mortar stand. English. Oak, late seventeenth century. Here again, this stand is built as a joined stool frame, with special provision for holding a domestic mortar. Brass or bell metal mortars were used in almost every home, and mortar stands were familiar objects (see Miscellanea, Figures 3:510-513).*

Figure 3:103. *Joined stool. English. Oak, early seventeenth century.*

Figure 3:104. *Joined stool. English. Oak, early seventeenth century.*

Figure 3:105. *Joined box stool. English. Oak, early seventeenth century.*

Figure 3:106. *Joined box stool. English. Oak, mid-seventeenth century.*

Figure 3:107. *Joined box stool. English. Oak, mid-seventeenth century. The box top retains its original fitted boards which divide it into four compartments, and the original wire staple hinges are intact.*

Figure 3:108. *Joined box stool. Another view of Figure 3:107.*

269

Figure 3:109. *Joined box stool. English. Oak, c.1680.*

Figure 3:110. *Joined box stool. English. Oak, c.1680 (see rear view Figure 2:13).*

Figure 3:111. *Joined close stool. English. Oak, c.1680.*

Figure 3:112. *Joined close stool. English. Oak, c.1680.*

papers and small books to smoking or sewing materials. The stool in Figure 3:107 retains the original boards which subdivide the interior into four smaller compartments for some unknown purpose.

An enclosed space of this kind in any piece of furniture usually prompted the adjective 'close'; thus we find references to a 'close' chair or 'close' stool. But the latter usually implied a rather specialised purpose, in that it might be the container for a pewter chamber-pot. Other terms include rather shy and allusive references to the function of the piece by calling it a 'night' stool, 'necessary' stool or 'stool of ease' (though the latter might equally refer to a simple upholstered stool or chair). Though most extant close stools are of a fully-enclosed chest form (see Chests), some are raised on legs and stretchers (Figures 3:111 and 112), and space is provided for a padded interior seat by raising the lid slightly on thickly-moulded side pieces. Two-seater close stools are on record, such as that owned by Darnley in 1567; and in 1602 a portable privy was recorded in the shape of "...one house of easement which cost 40s...".[21]

Figure 3:113. *Joined stool with drawer. English; Salisbury. Oak, c.1630. Note the absence of tenon pegs beside the drawer, indicating that the drawer is an original inclusion. Note the unusually high positioning of the suspension groove of the drawer.*

Figure 3:114. *Joined stool with drawer. English. Oak, c.1680. Note the tenon peg which holds the original cross bar, supporting the drawer.*

21. F.G. Emmison, *Elizabethan Life: Home, Work and Land,* Essex Record Office, Chelmsford, 1976.

Figure 3:115. *(Left) Joined stool table. English. Oak, early seventeenth century. The leaves supported on lopers which pull out from the frame.*

Figure 3:116. *(Right) Joined stool table. English. Cherrytree, c.1650. The leaves supported on a crane gate.*

Figure 3:117. *Joined stool table. English. Oak, c.1650. The leaves supported on lopers which pull out from the frame.*

22. E.g. by Gertrude Jekyll, *Old English Household Life*, Batsford, London, 1925, Fig.109.
23. Pauline Agius, Furniture History, 1971.

1595...A litle coffer stoole...
1601...In a little roome within my Ladies Chamber: a Close stoole covered with blewe cloth stitcht with white...three pewter basons, a little Close stoole...
1624...one close stoole and pewter panne...
1650...a stoole with a locke...
1678...a litel wainscotte closestoole with a pispotte of tynne...

The basic stool might also be fitted with falling leave or flaps, which are raised for occasional use as a table (Figures 3:115-118). The raised top was usually square or round (though oval and octagonal examples are found), and the leaves were held in place with lopers, which are slid out from the frame. Others have hinged gates, like miniature gateleg tables; and with some it may be hard to decide if they really are stool-tables, or simply small tables. As a general rule, stool-tables have splayed legs, like stools. Figure 3:118 is actually a conversion of a joined stool into a stool-table, by the later addition of gates and leaves. The top of an ordinary high stool could also be enlarged by the addition of a separate (larger) board which was slid over the fixed top on runners, which loosely gripped the sides. Several examples have been illustrated,[22] and they are mentioned in inventories, e.g. in Oxford:[23]

1672...One little table on a joynt stoole...
1698...One table cover for a Joynt stoole.

Unfortunately, the stool illustrated here (Figure 3:119) has lost its fixed top, and the loose cover is now nailed down; but the grooved runner is clearly seen, and it gives a good impression of such a top in use, though other specimens may be larger.

d). Cricket Stools (Figures 3:120 and 121)

The term 'cricket' or 'cracket' still survives in the North of England and in parts of Scotland, to describe a small stool such as a footstool or a child's stool. The use of the term was much more widespread in the seventeenth century and earlier, and there has recently been a good deal of speculation over exactly what type of stool the word referred to. In fact, contemporary evidence is conflicting, and lends itself to the suggestion that any small stool could be called a 'cricket'. Mention has already been made of the print of 1637 (p.234) in which a crowd is shown using "Cricketts, Stooles Stickes and Stones" as missiles in a disturbance at St. Giles Cathedral, Edinburgh.

271

Figure 3:118. *(Left) Joined stool. English. Oak, c.1680. At a later stage, perhaps c.1740, the stool was converted into a stool table by the addition of leaves and folding gates.*

Figure 3:119. *(Right) Joined stool with loose extra top. English. Stool: oak. Top: elm.*

The print clearly shows both folding stools (cf. Figure 3:4) and three-legged primitive stools (cf. Figure 2:44) in use, and it is tempting to interpret the three-legged variety as the 'Cricketts'.[24] However, when Randle Holme showed a similar three-legged stool only a dozen years later (Figure 2:43) he made no mention of the term. Instead he described a further type (Figure 3:120) as a cricket. This is shown as a low stool consisting of a top board raised on a simple shaped underframe with integral feet. He also described it as a "nursing stoole... low stoole, or a childs stoole", and a simpler stool of identical form is used as a perch by a child at the dining table in the woodcut in Figure 3:162. No examples of this type would seem to have survived from the seventeenth century, but the same article must often have been used by adults as a footstool, and may even be identifiable with the squab stools discussed below.

1559...one litill crekett stole 4/-...

e). Squabs and Cushion Stools (Figures 3:122-126)

Like other forms of upholstered seats, stools were generally referred to by the material with which they were covered, and we find references to leather stools, cloth stools, Turkey stools, Irish stools (Irish-stitch), etc. But occasionally they are called more specifically 'cushion' stools, and reference is also made to 'squab' frames.

The former is almost certainly a stool with fixed upholstery, whilst the latter was probably a stool or frame designed to hold a loose cushion. At Paget Place, London, in 1552 there was "...a quoishen stole, with a long quoishen of checker silk...",[25] but a more explicit description is found in the inventories of Sir Thomas Fairfax of Gilling. In 1594 he had *inter alia* "...iij little stooles covered in green clothe and frindged with green silke..." By 1624 these had apparently been removed to Walton, for there we find "...one of the old greene cushion stooles, and two of ther frames without covers...", suggesting that the first mentioned cushion stool still retained its *fixed* upholstery of green cloth.

1686... In the chamber over the parlor...six joyne stooles, four cushion stooles...

24. Especially in view of the suggestion that the game of cricket may have evolved from the use of such a stool as a wicket, and that three stumps are still used as a wicket. A three-legged table is still referred to as a 'cricket' table (q.v.), but this usage is of doubtful antiquity.

25. There were also, inexplicably, a "...litle quoishen table ... a ioyned quoishen cupboard...a ioyned quoishen table wt. a quoishen of checker silk..." Unless there is some confusion over the use of terms, these may relate to the recorded habit of keeping cushions on top of cupboards (see Chapter One, p.34).

Figure 3:120. *Woodcut illustration: Randle Holme, 'Academie of Armory', 1649.*
"76:...a nursing stoole...In some places it is called a crickett, or low stoole, or a childs stoole..."

Figure 3:121. *Woodcut illustration, early seventeenth century (detail of Figure 3:162). The child is standing at a dining table, perched on a low stool or 'cricket'.*

1667...standing in the parler...4 Joynd stooles and a cushing stoole...

It has often been proposed that buffet stools were upholstered,[26] but the evidence suggests otherwise, for at Walton there were also "...six high buffet stooles...all these stooles have wooden covers (i.e. seat-boards)..." Randle Holme also made it quite clear that (at least in Cheshire) joined and buffet stools (and chairs) are synonymous:

"...If the chaire be made all of Joyners worke, as back and seate then it is termed a Joynt chaire, or a Buffit chaire...
...A Joynt stoole...is so called because all made and finished by the Joyner, haveing a wood cover: In most places in Cheshire it is termed a Buffit stoole..."

Figure 3:122. *Joined cushion stool. English. Oak, with turkeywork cover, c.1680.*

26. This theory is mentioned in the *Dictionary of English Furniture*, 1927, vol.III, p.165. No evidence is raised to support such a theory, and indeed the only quotation given is by Randle Holme, which denies such a conclusion.

Figure 3:123. *Joined cushion stool. English. Oak, with later cover, c.1680.*

Figure 3:124. *Joined squab stool. English. Oak, c.1680.*

273

Figure 3:125. *Joined squab frame. English. Oak, c.1640.*

It is also worth noting at this point a further item at Walton, which demonstrates an interesting practice:

> "...six high stooles covered with leather seates and covers of green clothe and fringe on them, which may be taken off at pleasure..."

Many early inventories record the copious provision of loose cushions covered in various fabrics and needleworks, especially in the parlour and other private rooms. These are normally placed on chairs or settles to soften them for daily use, and indeed most wooden seats are too uncomfortable to use without cushions; but occasionally special mention is found of a stool or frame provided for the express purpose of supporting a loose cushion, known as a 'squab'. The panel seats of many late seventeenth century chairs are specially dished to receive a squab, as is the stool in Figure 3:124. It seems likely that such a piece might have been referred to by contemporaries as a squab frame, though all such references seem to be found in somewhat grander circumstances than this obviously middle-class stool. At Ham House in 1679 there were (and still are):

> "...In the Gallerie...Four Squobbs with Cases of purple and white Sarsnet...In the Green Closet...Two squobb frames, two seats upon them covered with green damask...
> ...In the Queens Bedchamber...Two small squob frames carv'd & guilt..."

The latter small gilded squab frames (now in the Queen's Closet) are very similar in form and size to many low stools which were previously considered to be footstools (e.g. several at Knole, and the stool accompanying the chair of Archbishop Juxon at the Victoria and Albert Museum), but it now seems likely that some of them were used to support one or two thick cushions, probably as seats for ladies. In 1689, John Hervey noted in his Book of Expenses: "...Due to ye joyner who made the chairs, stools & squobs for my wife, £19..."

The four squabs with cases mentioned at Ham are still in the Long Gallery, and are identical in form (though not decoration) to the earlier long

Figure 3:126. *Joined squab frame. English. Walnut, with Irish-stitch cushion, c.1675.*

squab frame or 'gallery' stool in Figure 3:125. This latter piece has been interpreted as a truckle or servant's bed; but the view of it as a day-bed or squab stool is more convincing, in regard to its quality and the lack of wheels which a truckle bed should in theory have (q.v.). In his *Dictionary,* Dr. Samuel Johnson did indeed define a squab as "...a kind of sopha or couch: a stuffed cushion..." Contemporary distinctions between the exact definitions of the settee, sopha, couch and day-bed are confused by modern ideas, and a lack of clarification in early accounts. The term 'settee' is certainly identifiable with the upholstered settle (though 'settee' was apparently not used in the seventeenth century), and the 'couch' seems likewise to have often been a piece with fixed upholstery, but not with the fixed back and arms of a settle. In its original Eastern context, the 'sopha' was a rather magnificent stand for sumptuous loose cushions, and perhaps inspired the idea of a squab frame; whilst the 'day-bed' also seems to have had loose cushions, and one or two raised ends for supporting the sitter (Figure 3:127). All four are now considered as long seats, which might accommodate several people at once, or one person reclining.

Figure 3:127. *Joined day bed. American; Virginia. Walnut and cypress, cane seat, c.1720.*

Figure 3:128. *Joined settle, with adjustable ends. English. Oak, early eighteenth century.*

Figure 3:129. *Primitive backstool. Welsh. Ash, rope seat; probably eighteenth century, but of timeless form. Chairs of this type (known as 'plain matted chairs') have certainly been made in the British Isles since the Middle Ages, and possibly earlier. See also Figure 2:105 and Diagram 3:2 c and d.*

27. R.W. Symonds, *Coffer-makers and Upholsterers' Chairs,* The Antique Collector, January-February 1950.

In many inventories, the main living-room has a bedstead in it, which is partly explained by the illness of the testators, in that they may often have wished to serve out their final illness downstairs. But this is only a partial reason, and it must seem likely that even in the poorer homes the bed was often used for sitting on during the daytime — a curious survival of the medieval custom.

1582...One Cowche of Curled ashe wth the appurtenances...

1614...a cowche of crimson leather...

1624...the fringed couch-chaire with half a dozen sutable cushions for it fringed ready to cover stooles with all...

1626...1 coutch of russet and silver tabines...

1688...In My Lady's Chamber...a couch-chaire wth a cushion...

1695...In the Large Olde Eating Roome...a couch two squabbs & two boulsters...

1743...a cane couch and squab, six cane chairs, one elbow ditto...

1594...lulling on a lewd day-bed...

1600...from a day-bed where I have left Olivia sleeping...

1700...un sopha à six places...

The Backstool (Figures 3:129-146)

It has long been a popular theory that the single armless chair with a back first appeared in England (as if at a stroke of divine revelation) somewhere around 1600, or even a little later. Some writers have even been so precise as to say "c.1614", or "in the time of James I", a contention which no doubt appeared in order to justify the absurd term 'farthingale' chair (q.v.). In fact the stool with a back, or the armless chair, is a very simple conception and was a familiar ob·ect in Egypt and the classical world (e.g. the Greek *klismos*). They were certainly known in medieval Europe (and why not England?), and throughout most of English history have been referred to as 'backstools'. The late R.W. Symonds found a documentary reference to a 'bacstowyll' as early as 1436;[27] and the term persisted in use until the end of the eighteenth century or later. Alternative terms were used of course: they might be referred to as simply as 'chairs', or 'dining chairs', whilst the upholstered variety were called after the fabric of their covers. The faithful Randle Holme wrote of "...a stoole-chaire, or back stoole...when it is

Figure 3:130. *Joined 'salt box' back-stool. Welsh. Walnut and oak, early eighteenth century.*

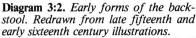

Diagram 3:2. *Early forms of the back-stool. Redrawn from late fifteenth and early sixteenth century illustrations.*
a). *Four-legged chair with 'staked' legs, and a carved solid back-board which is tenoned through the seat-board.*
b). *Three-legged turned chair with a curved T-post backrest.*
c). *Four-post matted chair with square members, the back filled with a lattice of nailed laths.*
d). *Four-post matted chair with square rear posts and turned front legs.*

made up of needle. or turky worke...some will say onely, a Turky worke Chaire..."

The antiquity of backstools in the present context may be demonstrated graphically in Diagram 3:2. Here various backstools are redrawn from contemporary illustrations of the fifteenth century. Most were fairly crude and serviceable items, made by carpenters and turners, which cannot be expected to have survived. Figure 3:129 is a primitive rush-seated chair which stands directly in this tradition. Plain and turned 'matted' chairs of this type were produced consistently for a cheap market by turners and other woodland craftsmen "since time out of which no man's mind runneth to the contrary" (cf. Figure 2:105, and comments in Chapter Two).

1685... six chaires bottom'd with rushes...
1729... six black rush bottom chairs 5s...

The only grain of credibility in the 'farthingale' chair idea is that the earliest *survivals* of upholstered backstools certainly do start to appear after c.1615. A simple walnut backstool at the Victoria and Albert Museum, with its original blue cloth covers, dates from about this time; but such early specimens are rare. The chair in Figure 3:131 is of the same period, though its original coverings are lost. Leather backstools occasionally appear in Elizabethan portraits — such as that of Dorothy Arundell, Lady Weston, in the Getty Collection at Sutton Place — but little is known of them until c.1640, after which date they enjoyed a century or more of consistent popularity.

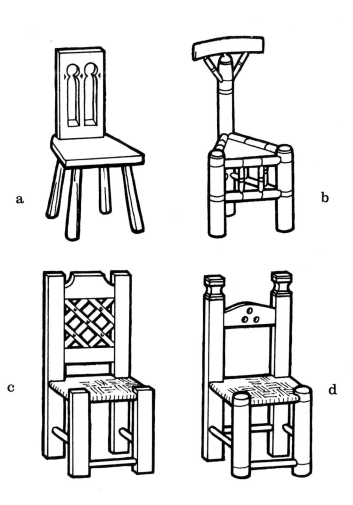

a

b

c

d

Figure 3:133. *Joined backstool. English. Oak, mid-seventeenth century. The heavy Anglo-Dutch style is more familiar from cabinets of the period.*

Figure 3:132. *Joined backstool. English or Scottish. Oak, fruitwood back spindle, mid-seventeenth century.*

Figure 3:131. *Joined upholstered back-stool. English. Oak, later leather cover, c.1620. This early specimen has a seat height of 23ins., the same as contemporary dining stools. Later chairs have lower seats, usually 18ins.-20ins. The low front stretcher is also a consistent feature of backstools of the earlier type. Later in the century the front stretcher was usually fitted in a higher midway position.*

The earliest of the chairs shown here (Figures 3:131-137) demonstrate the low front stretcher which continued in use in the traditional way, and the often very high seat to conform with contemporaneous stools and tables (e.g. the seat of Figure 3:131 retains its original height of 23ins.). After c.1660 the front stretcher was placed higher in the midway position, and this became the standard method thereafter.

Very little is known about the early appearance of non-upholstered joined backstools before c.1630. One fact which does emerge with surprising clarity is the positive regional polarisation of backstool types, in that all-wooden backstools are extremely rare in the South of England; to the extent that there is no standard variety which is indigenous to any of the Southern counties. Obviously, open back or panelled backstools must have been made in the South, but not with sufficient consistency as to develop a distinctive regional type. It would seem that only the upholstered backstool found any real favour in the South.

Conversely, all the standard varieties of joined backstool are closely identifiable with the North Country and the North-West Midlands. This is especially true of South Yorkshire, Derbyshire, South Lancashire and the Cheshire Plain. The earliest expressions of some of these distinctive types are given here in Figures 3:134-137, whilst their descendants of the second half of the seventeenth century are treated more fully in Chapter Four. Many of the characteristic features are already apparent in these chairs: the pyramid finials of Lancashire-Cheshire; the paired-leaf crest of the Yorkshire Clothing Dales; the crescent-shaped cross-splats of South Yorkshire; and the open arcaded back of the Yorkshire-Derbyshire type.

Figure 3:134. *Joined backstool. English; Lancashire-North Cheshire. Oak, c.1640.*

Figure 3:135. *Joined backstool. English; South Yorkshire. Oak, c.1640.*

Figure 3:136. *Joined backstool. English; South Yorkshire. Oak, c.1640.*

Figure 3:137. *Joined backstool. English; South Yorkshire-Derbyshire. Oak, c.1640.*

Through the second half of the seventeenth century the variations in joined backstools proliferated, as they became more popular and gradually ousted the use of stools at the dining table. Sets of chairs are associated with the increasing use of gateleg tables, and so the height of seats is increasingly made lower to conform with the tables. Late seventeenth century backstools tend to have higher backs, and are more flimsily constructed, to conform with fashions set by the walnut chairs favoured by a higher social level of patronage. It is perhaps worth mentioning at this point that *no* backstool or armchair was made *in the joined tradition* with an upholstered seat and a wooden back. Chairs were either made *entirely* of wood by the joiner, *or* he supplied unfinished frames to the upholder who covered both seat and back with stuffed leather or fabrics. The market for joined backstools was eclipsed in the course of the eighteenth century by the increased availability of the cheaper, lighter and more convenient forms of turned and Windsor chairs (Figures 3:145 and 146).

1436...a bacstowyll...
1578...my oaken stool with a back...
1588...lowe stoole wth a backe thereto...
1612...a little French backed and buffet chair...
1649...twenty four wooden stooles with Backes painted and guilt...
1658...five Jointe stools and Eight bucket (backed) stools...
1683...12 back stooles with cane bottoms, japanned...
1791...six back stools at £4. 15s...

Figure 3:138. *Joined backstool. English; Oak, c.1675. Note the introduction of the high front stretcher, which becomes very common after 1660. This chair, with its extensive turned decoration, is of a type often wrongly associated with the Commonwealth, but in fact is more common later in the century (cf. the child's high chair in Figure 3:493).*

Figure 3:139. *Joined backstool. English. Oak, c.1680. The panel back.*

Figure 3:140. *Joined backstool. English. Oak, c.1690. The slat back.*

ii). Tables and Cup-boards

The earliest origins and forms of the table in the British Isles are far more obscure than is the case with chairs or chests. There seems to be little by way of classical derivations influencing either the form or the manner of using tables in the Middle Ages, though the word itself seems to derive from the Latin *tabula*. But the restricted meaning now attached to the word 'table' is a comparatively modern innovation. In the sixteenth century and even later, a 'table' could also mean a picture or its frame, as well as several other forms of rectangular surface, such as a chess board; some sense of which is still retained in the modern form as 'time' tables or 'mathematical' tables.

> 1539... Item. A Table wth the whole stature of the Kynge's Maiestie stayned uppon a clothe...
> Item. A Table of the buryall of oure Lorde all of sondrye woodes ioyned togithers...
> 1620... Fifteen English pictures, hanged in tables att the upper end of the Galerie...
> 1659... the picture of King Edward the 4th...in a fayre Table or frame...

The modern sense of a table as being a piece of furniture with a flat top was more usually expressed by the specific term 'table board', accompanied by another specific mention of the form of underframing which served to support it in position (usually a pair of trestles, or after 1550 a joined frame). This dual concept of the table board as being distinct from its supports, is an important point to understand in reading early inventories and accounts; for reference is sometimes found to boards, cup-boards or

Figure 3:141. *Joined backstool. American; New England. Ebonised maple, c.1700.*

side-boards which are supported on an enclosed form such as an aumbry, as well as the more usual open trestles or frame. The 'cubberd' is only the top, which might have any form of support. An illuminating variety of side tables and dining tables is to be found in the inventory of William Gray of Alnwick, Northumberland (1590), including one with an enclosed base*:

> ...a cubborde with the trossels...
> a cubbord with a frame...
> two cubbordes one that the plate standes on and a nother that the virgenalles standes on...
> *on cobbord ther in the maner of an ambery with lock and Kye...
> a long table with formes belonging to it...
> a little round table with tresels...

Note that the term 'cubborde' is used here with specific reference to the side tables, whilst the long and round tables are centre tables, used for dining. The cup-board was literally a side table or board for the display and storage of cups, and in this sense belongs to the family of tables, rather than the enclosed cupboards. A side table with two or more boards or tiers (known as 'desks') was referred to as a 'court cup-board', though the meaning of the term is in dispute.

Broadly, the functions of tables may be divided into two distinct groups: *Centre tables,* which are used in the centre of the room, independent of the walls; *Side tables,* which are used at the side of the room, backed by the walls.

Figure 3:142. *Joined backstool. English. Oak, c.1700.*

Figure 3:143. *Joined backstool. English. Oak, c.1700.*

Figure 3:144. *Joined backstool. Welsh. Oak, 1720.*

Figure 3:145. *Turned backstools. English. Ash, with rush seats, eighteenth century.*

Figure 3:146. *Windsor chairs. English. Ash, elm seats, late eighteenth century.*

Figure 3:147. *Trestle table. English. Ash, pine top, c.1700.*

Figure 3:148. *Trestle table. American. New England. Oak, pine top, c.1700.*

Figure 3:149. *Trestle table. American; New England. Oak, pine top, c.1700.*

This dichotomy would seem to be fairly central to the ways in which tables were used and viewed in most periods, and is *always* reflected in the modes of construction and finish of individual tables. Side tables are always left unfinished and undecorated on the rear side, since the back was never intended to be seen. The workmanship may vary here from rough sawn to quite smoothly finished surfaces, but the decoration is never carried around onto this fourth side. Centre tables are a little more complex, in that most of them are finished identically on the four sides; except for a small group of dining tables which were intended for use against a fixed wall bench or other seats placed against the wall (e.g. Figures 2:7 and 3:163; see also Chapter One). Here, only one side of the table is on permanent view to the room, so this is fully decorated, and the rear side is finished with a simple moulding. The centre table could, according to its size and disposition, be used for a number of functions which include eating, gaming and working; but the side table is largely restricted to display of plate and finery, and for serving at meals, in which sense it must be seen as an ancestor of both the cup-board and the dresser/sideboard.

Centre Tables
Trestle Tables (Figures 3:147-154)

Although side tables might also be supported on trestles (or 'dormants',[28] as they were sometimes called), these movable supports are usually listed with the main dining board. Throughout the Middle Ages, trestles supporting a board were almost the only form of long dining table available, though there are accounts of long chests being used for this purpose. The principle behind their use is that a long board may be supported at two or more points along its length, and that the board and

28. The usual interpretation of the phrase *table dormant* is to presume a fixed and permanent arrangement with a joined frame or support; but the references given here to table boards with *dormants* suggest the use of trestles, and a flexible pattern of usage. Each of these references is from Essex, so the term may be confined to London and South-Eastern England.

trestles may be easily turned up and put aside when the space is needed for other purposes. The medieval custom was to sit at only one side of the table for dining, so that the diner could sit with his back to the wall and be served easily across the table. In manuscript illustrations this is nearly always the arrangement, and the tables are made correspondingly narrow for ease of service.

The trestles usually take one of two basic forms, although no example has survived of the earlier type as usually seen in medieval illustrations. These take the form of a simple high bench-like structure with splayed legs, as in Diagram 3:3. Unfortunately the tables in these pictures are always draped with a tablecloth for dining, and so it is never possible to see either the table-board or the top of the trestles, but it is easy to imagine that the splayed legs must support a heavy cross-bar or board, on which the table top may rest. The majority of trestles thus depicted are very plain and functional (as in Figure 3:11b), but occasionally a more decorative carved, or even turned, version is seen. The benchlike form of these early trestles recalls an interesting point, in that Randle Holme recorded "...a Bench, a Forme, or a Tressell..." as alternative names for the same piece of furniture, viz. a long stool or seat. This latter observation must throw some question on the exact interpretation of the common inventory reference to "a table with the trestles" (does this really mean a trestle table, or a table with accompanying benches?).

Diagram 3:3. *Medieval forms of splayed-leg trestles for dining tables. Redrawn from illustrated manuscripts.*
a). *Turned trestle with sledge feet. German, fifteenth century.*
b). *Simple trestle with square members and a strengthening brace. French, fifteenth century (cf. Figure 3:11b).*
c). *Trestle decorated with a Gothic cusped arch, carved and painted. English, fourteenth century.*

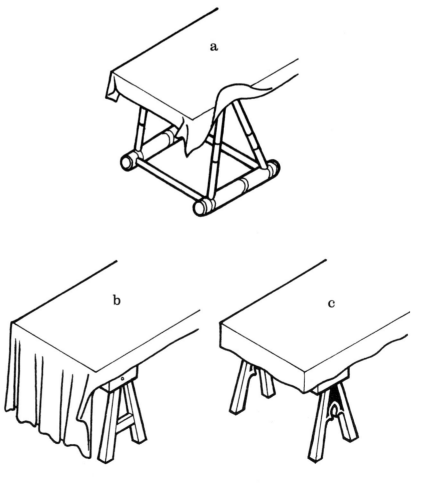

Figure 3:150. *Joined trestle table. English. Oak, late seventeenth century.*

Figure 3:151. *Joined trestle table. English. Oak, late seventeenth century.*

Figure 3:152. *Trestle table. English. Oak, early seventeenth century. Here the trestles are of the free-standing pedestal type, a survival of medieval practice. One trestle may be seen in detail in Figure 2:202.*

Figure 3:153. *Joined table of trestle form. English. Oak, walnut top, mid-seventeenth century.*

Figure 3:154. *Joined table of trestle form. English. Pine, early eighteenth century.*

The alternative form of trestle, which persisted far longer in use, was provided with only one central pedestal leg or pillar, and either a cross-bar at top and bottom (Figures 3:147-151) or a cruciform foot (Figure 3:152). The cruciform pedestal trestle was obviously able to stand free of any extra support, and any number could be used in tandem to support tops of varying length; but the cross-bar trestle was not free-standing, and so was normally linked with one or more others by a system of pegged stretchers. This was generally a temporary arrangement in that the stretchers were secured by removable pegs; but sometimes the whole assembly was locked together in a permanent arrangement, which amounted to a form of joined frame with only the *appearance* of demountable trestles (Figures 3:150, 151 and 153 and 154).

    1434... a litel tabel peynted trestelwise...
    1522... a tabill and the trostells...

1539...ij tabills & ij formes with ij peyer of trossellis...
1568...too littell tables upon Trestells...
1582...a table lying on too trustles...
1586...an elmen table or plank and trestles, wt a litle fourme to ett...
1592...a table with a pair of dormans...
1597...a table borde standinge upon a paire of trestells...
1601...a playne tabel upon trestalles...
1603...In the Hall. An old plank table standing upon dormans...
1638...In the hall. one Plank Table wth the Dorments...
1648...a table borde lyinge uppon Antique tresstles...
1660...in the chichin — one table upon darmans...
1672...In ye Kitchin. One planck Table & tressell-frame...

Figure 3:155. *Joined counter table. English. Oak, c.1540. The lid is hinged in the manner of a chest.*

Figure 3:156. *Joined counter table. English. Oak, c.1540. The arms are those of Scarborough and Ghisburn, Yorkshire.*

Framed Tables (Figures 3:155-180)

The development of efficient frame joinery in the fifteenth century made possible the adoption of secure and permanent underframes for tables of all sorts. The standing enclosed cupboard was probably the first joiner-made item to be used as a side table, and their distinctive construction was adopted in the earliest joined centre-tables, in that they retained the enclosed cupboard- or chest-space beneath. They took the form of shallow panelled chests or cupboards (aumbries) with extended legs, and were mostly *not* fitted with stretchers (Figures 3:155-158). The term 'counter' frequently appears in early inventories, and has been equated with this form of table; though usages of the word are so varied that it is difficult to draw any precise conclusions.

The term apparently originated with the 'counter board', a table or cloth panel used in the medieval 'counting' house, an office which was attached to the shop or residence of most merchants and men of substance. The cloth, or the table top itself, was marked out with a series of lines and squares, and used for calculating accounts in much the same way as an Oriental abacus. The markers and counters used in calculations took the form of imitation coins (tokens, or 'jettons'), and the total format must

Figure 3:157. *Joined table with enclosed cupboard. English. Oak, early sixteenth century.*

Figure 3:158. *Joined withdrawing table with enclosed cupboard. English. Oak, 1540-50.*

have influenced very closely the design of various board games such as draughts and tric-trac. It is not clear whether a counter table was a specific form of table, or whether the name simply denotes a particular usage of any table. The latter must seem more likely, since there are references to both long and square counters, and even one habitually used as a dining table, as well as others which have no apparent connection with trade.

The term continued in use throughout the seventeenth century also, though it is not clear if the meaning remained the same. It still survives today, of course, in the shop counter, which is in essence nothing more than a long table over which monetary transactions are passed and received. By the middle of the seventeenth century such a piece was increasingly referred to as a shop board, but the term counter nevertheless remains with us.

1407...To Willyam my sone the counter that I ete apon...

1560...a counter table in the hall and a counter table in the parlor...

My long counter table standing in the hall...

1566...an counter board...

1665...In the Milke House...a counter presse

(a glover) In ye Shopp, one shopp-board, several plancks & boards...

Figure 3:159. *Joined withdrawing table. English. Walnut, late sixteenth century.*

Figure 3:160. *Joined withdrawing table. English. Oak, early seventeenth century.*

Figure 3:161. *Joined withdrawing table. English. Cedar, early seventeenth century.*

Figure 3:162. *Woodcut illustration, early seventeenth century. A simple family meal is in progress at a long dining table. The arrangements are very basic, with the parents seated at stools and children standing.*

1671 . . . (a grocer) two Counters 10s . . . In the Shopp, One old Counter . . .

1677 . . . In the shopp . . . tow counters, a nest of drawers & 5 Shelves, 3 pair of scales and waights, one pestile and mortar . . .

1678 . . . (a tailor) a shopboard table and forme . . .

Some modern opinion suggests that the true counter table, of the early sixteenth century and later, should be identified as the type fitted with a loose top which slid on bearers from front to back. When monetary transactions (such as the payment of rents, debts or purchases) were completed, the accountant would slide forward the loose top and sweep the money back into the well or space beneath (Figures 3:155 and 156). Most

Figure 3:163a. *Joined long dining table. English. Oak, c.1630. This table was intended for use with a fixed wall bench. The present front is accordingly decorated with a run of carving, whereas the back (Figure 3:163b) is finished with a simple channel moulding (cf. Figure 2:7 and Diagram 1:2c, d and e).*

Figure 3:163b. *Joined long dining table. Rear view of Figure 3:163a.*

289

Figure 3:164. *Joined long table. American; Salisbury, Massachusetts. White oak, c.1660. Supposedly made as a communion table for the meeting house at Salisbury, where it was found early in this century. It may have started life as a domestic table, however (see Altar Table, p.224).*

Figure 3:165. *Joined long dining table. English. Oak, dated 1581. A magnificent eight-legged table, with a single piece top. An unusual feature in the construction is the use of round tenon blocks at the feet.*

surviving tables of this type now have their tops replaced, or the original top may be fixed down or hinged for convenience.

Whether such terms in early use were really limited to a narrow specification of physical type, or more broadly to modes of usage of differing forms, is a matter which urgently requires more intense research in the coming years. Unless the table top has to be marked or covered for a particular use, as for example with gaming tables, almost any table can be put to a variety of uses, though many inventories and accounts specify the functions of tables which they describe. Such tables might be distinguished by their form or materials, but more often the usage described is simply that to which the table is habitually put:

> 1536...a little round table for oysters...and a moulding table...

Figure 3:166. *Joined long dining table. English. Oak, mid-seventeenth century.*

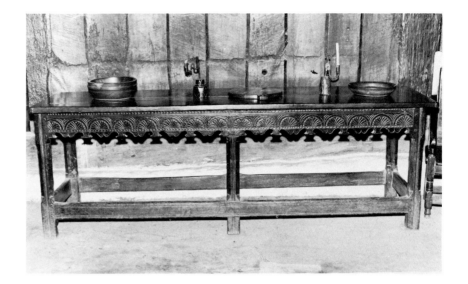

Figure 3:167. *Joined long dining table. Welsh. Oak, late seventeenth century.*

1544...a brekefaste table of walnuttree...
1600...an oyster table lyinge upon a frame...
1603...one little ioined borde, for oisters...
1624...a standing Table for tailours to work on...
1632...all Tables for (Drapers) Taverners, Victuallers, Chandlers, Compting House Tables and all other...
1663...In the Bakehouse, one Moulding boord...
1668...In the Milke House, Six shelves, one Cheese table...
1673...In the Kitchin, two dresser boards...
1681...In the Shop, fouer peeces of lether, one cutting bord, 8 dozen of lasts...
1685...In the Great Parlour, one livery boarde...
1693...In the Parlour, 2 livery cubbert tables...
a little wanscote table for tea, cards and writing...
1743...In the Best Room, one dressing table and glass...

The long dining board of medieval type remained popular throughout the sixteenth and seventeenth centuries, but the trestle underframing was gradually replaced in preference by the stronger open-frame joined base.

Figure 3:168. *Joined long dining table. Welsh. Oak, late seventeenth century.*

Figure 3:169. *Joined long dining table. English or Welsh. Oak, c.1700.*

Trestles remained in occasional use in farmhouses and other less fashionable settings until as late as the eighteenth century, but after 1550 it was the long joined table which assumed pride of place for the next century or so. The usual table for a small family was the four-legged variety, with an average length of seven or eight feet. The puritan family in the woodcut in Figure 3:162 are ranged around a rather plain version of just such a table, though their seating is far more simple than is suggested by most inventories. Here, the parents are seated on stools whilst the children stand at table (the little girl perched on a cricket, q.v.); whereas in most homes at this time, we find the great table is supplied with a full set of stools or benches, and an armchair.

In larger households, tables of great length were provided, sometimes in pairs as had been the practice in the medieval halls, ranged around the central hearth as at Penshurst Place in Kent. To support their great length, these tables were built with a large number of legs. Six legs are usual on

Figure 3:170. *Joined small centre table. English. Oak, mid-seventeenth century.*

Figure 3:171. *Joined small two-tier centre table. English. Oak, mid-seventeenth century.*

Figure 3:172. *Joined small centre table. English. Oak, c.1680.*

Figure 3:173. *Joined small centre table. English. Oak, c.1680.*

Figure 3:174. *Joined small centre table. English. Oak, c.1680.*

Figure 3:175. *Joined small centre table (one of a pair). English. Oak, c.1680.*

tables of average length, but longer examples have as many as eight or ten (see also shovelboard tables, below). The decoration of the legs and frieze display all the variations of turning and carving in contemporary use.

Small tables were produced for general use (Figures 3:170-174), and these were sometimes fitted with drawers (Figures 3:175 and 176), with a small enclosed cupboard (Figure 3:177) or with a box or chest top (Figures 3:178 and 179). Small tables for various popular games are frequently found amongst the contents of the richer houses throughout the post-medieval period, as well as in the furnishings of inns and other public houses. Tables for cards were rarely a specific provision before the eighteenth century, though at Hardwick Hall there is a square walnut table of c.1580 which has playing cards of each suite inlaid on the top, leaving no doubt as to its purpose. The high popularity of card games throughout our period is not in doubt, but cards may be played on any suitable table, especially if the top is covered with a loose cloth or a fixed fabric such as baize or needlework. Green baize, probably originating from the days when the game was first played in a grass-covered yard, is the traditional cover for billiards tables — a game which first appeared in the fifteenth century, and became more popular in England as the Renaissance progressed:

> 1588... a billyard bord covered wth a green cloth wth a frame of beache wth fower turned postes, thre billyard stickes and ii balles of yvery...
>
> 1603... one billiarde borde, wth two staves to it of bone, and ij of wood, and iiij balls...
>
> 1649... a Billiard Board covered in green cloth...
>
> 1697... Long Gallery... a square in the middle where stands a billiard table...

Another game which required a fairly large table (at least in its earlier forms) was of shovelboard, the modern shove ha'penny. Here, a well-polished table is marked across with a series of transverse grooves (optional); the object of the game being to slide a brass disc or counter

Figure 3:176. *Joined centre table with drawer. English. Oak, mid-seventeenth century. Most small tables which have drawers like this are actually side-tables, but here the decoration is carved all round, permitting this piece to be used in the centre of a room*

Figure 3:177. *Joined table with enclosed cupboard. English. Oak, c.1640. We cannot be categorically sure what use these tables were designed for. This is probably intended as a livery table, or as a serving table, if not simply for more general storage. In use, this is a far more practical arrangement than the following box-top tables.*

along the board, to score by coming to rest entirely within one of the divisions, or as close as possible to the end of the table. Those discs which overshot the length of the table were collected in a box or 'swallowing dish' fixed at the further end. Noblemen competed with each other over the quality of their shovelboard tables, and some fine examples still survive. One at Littlecote Manor, Wiltshire, has ten legs and an overall length in excess of 30 feet. A notable table of its day was described by Robert Plot,[29] which had a plain parquetry top made up of two hundred and sixty pieces that were "...so accurately joined and glewed togither, that no shuffleboard whatever (was) freer from Rubbs or casting..." This construction is echoed in a table at Aston Hall, Birmingham (originally one of a pair from Brereton Hall in Cheshire); and another still *in situ* at Astley Hall, Chorley, Lancashire. The latter table is over 23 feet in length, and is supported on no less than twenty turned legs. Enormous sums were won and lost at shovelboard, at all levels of society, and it was several times prohibited by law, especially under the Commonwealth. During the eighteenth century (by which time the tables were usually considerably smaller, *vide* Figure 2:54), the game lost favour with the gentle classes, though it has survived until the present day in public houses and as a children's game.

1604...one longe table for sholven borde...

1610...a Shovel-a-Board Table whereon meat never stood...

1656...mayntayning of an unlawfull game called Shovyll a Borde or Slyde grote contrary to Statute...

1681...My Lord cut down (an ash tree) and made a fair shuffle-board in his hall...

1724...In the Parlour. 1 shuffle-board table, i sett of shuffle-bord pieces...

29. Robert Plot, *Natural History of Staffordshire*, 1686.

294

Figure 3:178. *Joined centre box table. English. Oak, mid-seventeenth century.*

Figure 3:179a. *Joined box table. English. Oak, c.1680.*

Figure 3:179b. *Joined box table. English. Oak, c.1680.*

Other gaming tables were marked out, or provided with special apparatus, for the particular requirements of individual games such as chess and draughts, tric-trac (backgammon), troll madam (or trolle-my-dames), or a long-popular game called E.O. More often than not they would simply take the familiar modern form of a pair of hinged boards (called a pair of tables), which were simply laid on top of a conventional table for use, as in Figure 3:180; though some tables and chests were apparently painted or inlaid permanently with the appropriate graphics.

    1551...a paier of playeng tables VId...
    1552...a chesse bourd, ij pairs of tables...
    1556...a chesse boarde wth the men...
    1586...2 chests to play withall, one payre of tables...
    1594...a chess boord and chesse men...
    1624...a pair of white and black checkered tables...
    1626...i Troll madam...i Chesse bourd and Chesmen...
    1634...2 paire of playinge tables...
    1649...one table to play at Trolle Madame...a paire of playne
          (? playing) Tables of Ebony plated wth Iron, wth a pr.
          of Dice of silver, and thirty men...
    1735...Walnut draughts table and men...

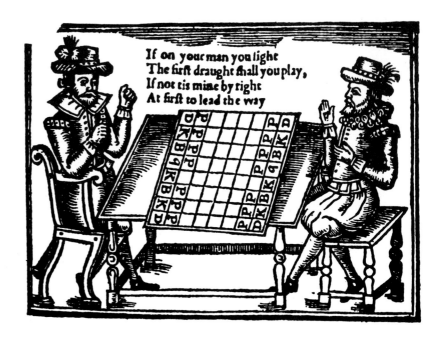

If on your man you light
The first draught shall you play,
If not tis mine by right
At first to lead the way

Figure 3:180. *Woodcut illustration, early seventeenth century. A game of chess in progress. The chessboard, or 'pair of tables', is laid across a joined table for the purposes of the game. One player is seated at an X-framed armchair, whilst the other occupies a joined stool which matches the table.*

Figure 3:181. *Joined cricket table. English. Oak, c.1670.*

Tripod Tables and Stands (Figures 3:181-201)

Domestic inventories are peppered with a wide assortment of small tables and stands, few of which have survived, owing to the vulnerability of such small and inexpensive items of furniture. After the middle of the seventeenth century, they begin to appear in increasing numbers and varieties. Some were made by the turners (*vide* Figure 2:69), but many were joiner-made with elaborate turned decoration. Most are contrived with three feet, since it was soon discovered that a small topped table, with a necessarily vertical emphasis in its proportions, is more secure when balanced on three feet only. This ensured a wobble-free stance and greater stability on uneven floors. Framed tables of this type were made over a long period (Figures 3:181-183) and are now generally termed cricket tables, presumably in deference to the three-legged stools of the same name.

Small pedestal tables, i.e. with a single pillar or support, were made with a spreading tripod or cruciform base. Larger examples are often fitted with a birdcage movement, whereby the loose top is fitted to the stem by a bearer which allows the top to revolve freely. The base of the cage holds the whole assembly steady, and a peg through the stem secures it in place (see detail Figure 3:185a). The earliest of these tables (1640-1720) have their legs shaped from a flat board and tenoned into the base of the stem, as here, but in later examples the leg is a full compound curve related to the cabriole leg (Figure 4:268). The increasing popularity of this type of table at the end of the seventeenth century and through the eighteenth, no doubt reflects the mounting consumption of tea and other hot beverages such as coffee and chocolate. This table thus played its part in the important bourgeois ritual of tea and chatter, and until recent years a great many were still to be found partnered with Windsor chairs in many of our more old-fashioned provincial tea rooms, the passing of which is much to be regretted.

During the reign of Charles I, people suddenly found it necessary to adopt the use of small topped pedestal tables as candlestands, though their ancestors had been quite content to place a candlestick on the nearest stool, ledge or table. These became very fashionable after the Restoration, when the finer examples were made *en suite* with a dressing table and a pier glass.

Figure 3:182a. *Joined cricket table. English. Oak, mid-seventeenth century.*

Figure 3:182b. *Joined cricket table. Under view of Figure 3:182a. Note the heavy cross brace under the top, which is a usual feature of triangular base tables of all periods.*

Figure 3:183. *Joined cricket table. English. Ash, with elm top, early eighteenth century.*

Figure 3:184. *Joined tripod pedestal table. English. Oak, c.1700. The large 'birdcage' is often a feature of earlier tables of this type.*

Figure 3:185a. *Joined tripod pedestal table. Detail of Figure 3:185b. A rather simpler 'birdcage' movement as commonly found.*

Figure 3:185b. *Joined tripod pedestal table. English. Oak, early eighteenth century.*

Figure 3:186. *Tripod pedestal table. American. Hard pine and soft maple, red paint, early eighteenth century.*

Figure 3:187. *Tripod pedestal table. English. Oak, early eighteenth century.*

Figure 3:188. *Joined pedestal lectern. English. Oak, early seventeenth century.*

Figure 3:189. *Joined pedestal table. English. Oak, c.1680.*

298

Figure 3:190. *Candlestand. Welsh. Oak, with elm top, c.1680.*

Figure 3:191. *Candlestand. English. Oak, c.1680.*

Figure 3:192. *Candlestand. American; New England. Hickory base, maple stem, pine top, c.1680.*

Figure 3:193. *Candlestand. American; New England. Maple and pine, c.1700.*

Figure 3:194. *Candlestand. English. Oak, c.1680.*

Figure 3:195. *Candlestand. English Oak, c.1680.*

The two candlestands with spiral stems (Figures 3:194 and 195) were made in imitation of their better walnut contemporaries. Vernacular examples were generally provided with a cruciform base and a simple turned or chamfered stem. Besides functioning as candlestands, other uses suggested themselves as noted by Randle Holme, and 'basin stand' would seem to be a suitable alternative term for them.

> 1649... two wooden painted frames to set candlesticks upon...
>
> ...a little round table, set upon one pillar, or poste, which in the foote branches itself out into three or foure feet or toes for its fast and steddy standing...it is used for to set a bason on whilest washing, or a candle to read by...

An ingenious series of simple small tables and stands made use of a screw-turned principle to provide an adjustable setting for the height of the top. They could be fitted with a flat table top, or with a holder for candles or rushlights, and then wound up or down to be set at a convenient height. A more conventional form of adjustment was the provision of a ratchet or trammel (Figure 3:201).

Figure 3:196. *Adjustable candlestand. English. Oak, ash and elm, c.1700.*

Figure 3:197. *Primitive adjustable rushlight holder. English. Ash, eighteenth century.*

Figure 3:198. *Adjustable betty-lamp holder. American; New England. Hickory base, with hard birch stem and cross-piece, c.1700.*

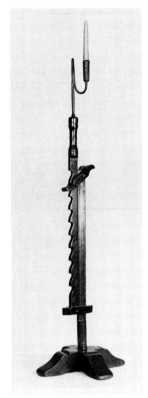

Folding Tables (Figures 3:158-161, 202-236)

The conflicting demands and competition for available domestic space led to early experiments in producing tables with variable tops, which might be enlarged when needed, and diminished or even eliminated when necessary. To a small degree, the demountable trestle table answered this need, but it was a clumsy thing to handle. Several hands were required to take down the top and remove the trestles, and there was still the problem of storing the board and trestles. The obvious answer was to hang one or more hinged leaves on the board, so that the top might be folded and made smaller; but a permanent solution could not be sought until the development of the rigid joined underframe which provided a stable base to counteract the leverage of the leaf.

Several early framed dining tables bear evidence that hinged leaves were once (? originally) hung at each end of the top board, as in the altered specimen of early sixteenth century date in the collection of the Shakespeare Birthplace Trust at Hall's Croft, Stratford-upon-Avon. These leaves would have hung down nearly to the ground, and were held up in place by heavy lopers which slid out from the underframe. There are a few intact tables of seventeenth century date which demonstrate a retention of this idea, but it was essentially a clumsy arrangement and was replaced by a more elegant solution in the form of withdrawing leaves.

The table in Figure 3:158 would seem to be possibly the earliest surviving example of a withdrawing table, since the top has every appearance of being the original. Despite its early date, it represents a fully-developed form which was followed in nearly every detail for the next one hundred and fifty years. The top board rests loosely on a vertical riser, which is guided

Figure 3:202. *Joined folding table. English. Oak, early seventeenth century. An otherwise normal rectangular table is fitted with falling leaves, supported on lopers, which rise to make an oval top.*

Figure 3:203. *Joined folding table. English. Oak, early seventeenth century. Here, the falling leaf is hung at the back, and is supported by a gate. One rear leg and stretcher are split to form the gate, in the Dutch manner. A box or compartment is also provided under the top, a fashion which was revived later in the century (Figures 3:235 and 236).*

through a narrow fixed transverse board beneath. Either side of the lower board, and lying under the main top, are the two withdrawing leaves. These rest on long cantilevered bars, by means of which they are drawn out and held in place flush with the main board, almost doubling the length of the

Figure 3:204. *Joined folding table. English. Oak, early seventeenth century. Fitted with two small drawers, one above the other.*

Figure 3:205. *Joined folding table. English. Oak, early seventeenth century. Fitted with an enclosed cupboard-space and a potshelf.*

302

Figure 3:206. *Joined folding table. English. Oak, c.1640.*

table. The date of this recently rediscovered table (it had formerly been in the Meyrick-Jones Collection at Woodlands Manor, Wiltshire) is most interesting, since it may antedate the earliest explicit inventory reference to a withdrawing table of 1552.[30]

1539...Item, a counter with one leefe, with an olde carpit on yt...

1552...a fayer drawing table of wallnuttree upon iiij carved pillors...

1558...a new joined drawing table...

1565...a short two-leaved table...

1570...my leaf table of peartree...

1582...a table shot with leaves...

1586...Imprimis. A table board to draw out at both ends...
...one drawing table of ash...

1594...one drawinge table of wallnuttree cutt and carved of three leaves longe...

1603...one long joined borde wt. a frame and a piece wt. a foote to enlarge it in length...

1671...In the Hall...one drawing Table & 5 stooles...

1687...one table, & one old table leaf...

The earliest extending table idea, that of providing a folding leaf hinged to the main board, was gradually refined and developed. It was not suitable for long tables since the withdrawing leaf was far more convenient; but a huge variety of small folding tables evolved in the seventeenth century. The alternative methods of construction were to provide leaves which either folded over on top (usually referred to as 'folding' tables); or leaves which hung down at the sides or back (referred to as tables with 'falling' leaves).

30. R.W. Symonds, Connoisseur, March 1948.

Figure 3:207a. *Joined folding table. English. Oak, mid-seventeenth century. Fitted with a cupboard and potshelf. The door boasts a fine selection of original metalwork.*

Figure 3:207b. *Joined folding table. Another view of Figure 3:207a, here shown open. Note the unusual rear leg, which slides out from the main structure*

Figure 3:209. *Joined folding table. English. Oak, late seventeenth century.*

Figure 3:208. *Joined folding table. English. Oak, early seventeenth century.*

Figure 3:210. *Joined folding table. English. Oak, early seventeenth century.*

Figure 3:211. *Joined folding table. English. Walnut, seventeenth century. The leaves supported on lopers.*

Figure 3:213a. *Joined folding table. English. Walnut, c.1680. Here shown closed.*

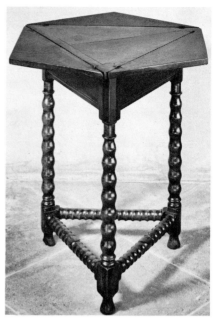

Figure 3:213b. *Joined folding table. Another view of Figure 3:213a, here shown open, the leaves supported by lopers.*

Figure 3:212. *Joined folding table. English. Walnut, seventeenth century. An identical table to Figure 3:211, here shown closed. The construction of the base should also be compared with the stool in Figure 3:79a.*

Some of the earlier examples were supported by lopers, but a more efficient form developed before 1600 in which the leaves were held open by strong framed 'gates' which swung out from the main frame. This latter type are now called 'gateleg' tables, a term which was unknown in the seventeenth century. Another form of leaf-support which was common in New England was a shaped flat board, known now as a 'butterfly gate' (Figure 3:231). This is often thought to be an American innovation, but the earliest examples (though rare) are probably English.

The earliest forms of folding tables to be provided with a gate (Figures 3:203-210) were fitted with a gate and leaf on one side only, and were so orientated that when folded up they could be pushed back against the wall to serve as side tables. In inventories, this type is sometimes referred to as a 'folding livery table (or cubberd)', and were used for the distribution of the livery of bread and wine to the houshold (see p.319-321). At Walton, for example, there was in 1624 a 'foulding livery cubberd', which should perhaps be identified as this type of table. Such a function is not far removed from the spurious 'credence table' idea (p.223), though it does place the tables in a correct domestic context.

1526...a small cubberd table wth falling leaves...

Folding tables were made with a very wide variation in the form of the base. Many were fitted with a platform or potshelf over the stretchers, and the space beneath the top was normally utilised for storage. In some examples, access to this space is via a cupboard door (Figures 3:205 and 207), whilst others were fitted with drawers (Figures 3:204 and 210). More rarely, the under-top was hinged to lift like a chest lid, revealing a shallow space beneath (Figure 3:203); an idea which was revived after c.1680 (Figures 3:235-236). The tops of folding tables were normally round or octagonal when fully opened, but some polygonal tops were made with as many as twelve sides (Figure 3:206).

1567...one table, foulded, three-leaved...

Figure 3:214. *Joined folding table. English. Fruitwood, c.1680. The falling leaves are supported on hinged flaps.*

Figure 3:215. *Joined gateleg table or stand. English. Oak, c.1680.*

Figure 3:216. *Joined gateleg table. English. Cedar, c.1680.*

Figure 3:217. *Joined gateleg table. English. Oak, mid-seventeenth century.*

Figure 3:218. *Joined gateleg table. English. Oak, c.1640.*

1587... one old folding table...
1598... a large foulded table of walnut-tree upon a frame...
a foldinge round table...

Gateleg tables were made in all sizes, from very small and low versions which doubled as stools (q.v.) and taller ones which were little more than folding stands (Figures 3:215 and 216); to huge oval tables with double gates (Figure 3:233), some of which were capable of seating sixteen or more persons at dinner. As if this were not enough, Pepys recorded a novelty in 1665: "...To Sir Phillip Warwick's to dinner, where abundance of company came in unexpectedly; and here saw one pretty piece of household stuff, as the company increaseth, to put a !arger leaf upon an oval table..."

The tops of gateleg dining tables are normally oval (though rectangular and octagonal are not unusual), and it is by this feature that they are described in inventories. The large oval dining table and its complement of

Figure 3:219. *Joined gateleg table. English. Oak, c.1680.*

Figure 3:220. *Joined gateleg table. English. Oak, c.1680.*

Figure 3:221. *Joined gateleg table. English. Oak, c.1680.*

Figure 3:222. *Joined gateleg table. English. Oak, c.1680.*

Figure 3:224. *Joined gateleg table. English. Oak, c.1700.*

Figure 3:225a. *(Left) Joined folding table. English. Oak, c.1680.*

Figure 3:225b. *(Right) Joined folding table. Another view of Figure 3:225a, here shown closed.*

leather or turkeywork chairs were to be found in many middle class homes; whilst after 1660 a fashion evolved in polite society for using several small gateleg tables in one dining room, to accommodate a large number of guests in small parties for intimate conversation.

The construction and decoration of gateleg tables vary only in detail, though many smaller tables were built with only one support at each end of the frame, which terminates in a shaped block or trestle foot (Figures 3:215-225); and occasional examples are made to fold completely flat in order to be stowed away when not needed (Figures 3:225 and 226). Here,

Figure 3:226a. *(Left) Joined folding table. English. Oak, c.1700.*

Figure 3:226b. *(Right) Joined folding table. Another view of Figure 3:226a, here shown closed.*

the single-piece gates are pivoted about the central stretcher, and the single top hinges about the same plane.

1587...a litle falling table...

1641...an ovall Table of wanscote with falling sides...
a great ovall table of wanscote with folding sides...

1674...a great ovell table, ten old Russia lether chaires...

1679...a very large strong ovall table with a double set of twisted pillars...

1687...Ovall wanscott Table 6ft.6in. long and 4ft.6in. broad with a Turned frame (the Table made to fould)...

Figure 3:227. *Joined gateleg table. English. Oak, c.1640. This early table has all-wooden knuckle joints to the gates, which can clearly be seen in this view.*

Figure 3:228. *Joined gateleg table. English. Oak, c.1660. A single-piece leaf, made from one width of board, is always a desirable feature on any table.*

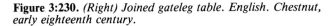

Figure 3:229. *Joined gateleg table. English. Cherrytree base, with ash top, c.1690.*

Figure 3:230. *(Right) Joined gateleg table. English. Chestnut, early eighteenth century.*

Figure 3:231. *Joined butterfly gate table. English. Oak, c.1690.*

Figure 3:232. *Joined gateleg table. American; Virginia. Walnut, c.1690.*

Figure 3:233. *Joined gateleg table. English. Oak, c.1680-1700. Such a large table needs double gates to support each leaf. The inverted cup turning is the fashionable shape for this date, supplemented by the equally modish moulded edge to the top.*

Figure 3:234. *Joined gateleg table. English. Oak, c.1680. A fine quality table with excellent detail and patination.*

Figure 3:235. *Joined gateleg table with box-top. English. Oak, c.1680.*

Figure 3:236. *Joined gateleg table with deep box-top. English. Oak, c.1690.*

311

Figure 3:237. *Joined side table/stand for a virginals. English, London. Cedar stand, oak virginals case, dated 1644 (the stand possibly contemporary). This is the virginals and stand shown opened in Plate Ten. The quality of the ironwork of the case is very high and reminiscent of earlier work.*

Side Tables

Small Side Tables (Figures 3:237-246)

The use of separately designated side tables is recorded in inventory form as early as 1436,[31] and no doubt reflects an earlier use of flat-topped chests for the same purposes — those of displaying fine plate and napery, and the holding of dishes and utensils for serving at dinner. Different functions of the side table are suggested by other common terms such as side-boards, side cup-boards and dressing boards. The appearance of side tables and boards in both living rooms and kitchens naturally suggests vast differences in form and decoration, which are usually reflected in comparative probate values. They must necessarily range from ornate vehicles of display to simple scrubbed kitchen work tables.

In the Middle Ages, serving tables were often built into the fabric of the house, in the form of elaborate arrangements of wooden or stone shelves, such as the sideboard which survives at Dirleton Castle, East Lothian.[32] The form of such stone tables is very similar to the many table tombs which are to be found in the walls of English parish churches.

31. *Dictionary of English Furniture,* 1927, Vol.III, p.254.
32. Illustrated by Eric Mercer, *Furniture 700-1700,* Weidenfeld and Nicolson, 1969, fig.51.

Figure 3:238. *Joined side table. English. Oak, c.1640.*

Figure 3:239. *Joined side table. English. Oak, c.1640.*

Figure 3:240. *Joined side table. English. Oak, c.1680.*

Figure 3:243. *Joined side table. American; New England. Ebonised ash, pine top (single plank 30ins. wide), c.1700.*

Figure 3:241. *Joined side table. English. Oak, c.1680.*

Figure 3:242. *Joined side table. English. Oak, c.1680. A fine-quality table. Compare the spandrels with Figure 3:234.*

Figure 3:244. *Joined side table. English. Oak, c.1700.*

Figure 3:245. *Joined side table. English. Ebonised walnut, c.1700.*

Figure 3:246. *Joined side table. American; East Virginia. Walnut, with hard yellow pine and poplar, c.1700.*

Long joined oak serving tables are sometimes to be found, dating from Elizabeth I or James I; and of course the court cup-board and later the dresser are both side tables with special characteristics. Since the use of the term offers so much variety of interpretation, we must first consider the side table as it is generally found today, i.e. as a single topped framed table, usually with a drawer, which is expressly designed to be placed against the wall. This generally implies the type of small table which became popular in the second half of the seventeenth century, though earlier examples are known. Almost the only developments were in the structural form of the base, and in modish alterations to decorative details such as hardware. Most have a simple fixed top for general uses, but some were specially adapted as stands for chests or musical instruments. The cedar side table/stand in Figure 3:237 supports a London-made virginals by Thomas White, of 1644, and is representative of other similar pieces. Virginals were easily transportable and were usually provided with a fitted velvet or leather travelling case, so that when set up at home they were often deposited on a side table:

> 1590...a nother (cubborde) that the virgenalles standeth on and
> a pare of virgenalles with locke and Keye...
> 1624...A frame on which stands a pair of virgenalls...

Side tables are frequently mentioned in early accounts and, though their functions are not usually specified, they are often associated with the dining parlour and serve as subsidiaries to the dining table. In this sense they were the tools-of-trade of the Steward of the Table, or Butler.

> 1480... salte selers shall be sette upon the syde-tablys...
> 1594... on litle side Table wth turned feete...
> 1626... one side table of walnuttree wth drawers, i side drawing
> Table of walnuttree...a side table, to draw out on the
> sides, 4 Turkett carpetts for side cubbards and tables...

1657... The Butler filleth strong wine out of a Flagon, into Cups or Glasses, which stand on a Cupboard, and he reacheth them to the Master of the Feast, who drinketh to his guests...

1686... one Side borde table, one litle sid board table, one sideboard cubbord, one liveri side table...

The Court Cup-board (Figures 3:247-256)

The principles which link the court cup-board to the family of side tables are self-evident. Here, 'cup-board' is used in its earlier sense as an *open* piece, without any enclosures by means of hinged doors. Perhaps the simplest working definition of a court cup-board is that of a side table with more than one open shelf or platform, some having two or four, though the usual number is three. Accounts are found of court cup-boards erected for special occasions, having many shelves for displaying plate and finery, but these have never survived.

The meaning of the word 'court' is discussed briefly in pp.227-229, but no satisfactory interpretation is available. Contemporary illustrations show pieces which range from a simple side table (covered with a cloth so that no details are visible), to a multi-shelved structure which incorporates a small enclosed cupboard.

Whatever the form it took, there can be no doubt that the court cup-board existed primarily as a vehicle for *display*. Randle Holme thought it one of the necessities for a dining-room, to hold cups, glasses and condiments; and William Harrison described in great detail the abundance of plate and valuables with which his contemporaries were wont to furnish their cup-boards. In inventories the cup-board is often described in the same

Figure 3:247. *(Left) Joined court cup-board. English. Oak, early seventeenth century.*

Figure 3:248. *Joined court cup-board. English. Oak, c.1640.*

Figure 3:249. *Joined court cup-board. English. Oak, c.1640.*

Figure 3:250. *Joined court cup-board. English. Oak, c.1640.*

Figure 3:251. *Joined court cup-board. English. Oak, c.1640.*

Figure 3:252. *Joined court cup-board. English. Oak, c.1640.*

Figure 3:254. *Joined court cup-board. English. Oak, c.1600.*

Figure 3:253. *Joined court cup-board. English. Oak, c.1600.*

breath as the plate which it bears, and likewise in literature the two are automatically associated:

> 1606... Here shall stand my court-cupboard, with its furniture of plate...
>
> 1611... you have your court-cupboards planted with flagons, cans, cups, beakers, bowls, goblets, basins and ewers...

In 1621, one Margerie Booth of Worcestershire had "...one payre of cobbards..." in her hall.[33] It would seem that this must describe a single piece of furniture with two shelves, i.e. a court cup-board (Figures 3:247, 248, 250 and 251).

The form and decoration of court cup-boards are closely linked to prevailing fashions for dining tables, and many were doubtlessly made *en suite* with the table which they were intended to accompany.[34] The chief departure from the conventions found in centre tables is, of course, that the *rear* legs of side cup-boards are usually not turned, but are made flat and square with a very simple decoration. They are frequently provided with drawers in the middle or upper frieze, to accommodate cutlery and other utensils. The standard form of three-tier court cup-board was probably established by the middle of the sixteenth century, and they continue to appear until the end of the seventeenth century:

> 1558... a courte cubberte, with 2 stayes of iron (? a folding serving table)...
>
> 1586... one court cubbart of maple tree Wood...

33. John West, *Village Records,* Macmillan, 1962, p.108.
34. Court cupboards were also noted in bedrooms, where they might be used for the display of plate under the watchful eye of the householder, or for the same purpose as a livery table or livery cupboard, i.e. to serve the night's supply of food and drink.

Figure 3:255. *(Above) Joined court cup-board. English. Oak, c.1640.*

Figure 3:256. *(Above right) Joined court cup-board. English. Oak, c.1700.*

Figure 3:257. *Joined standing livery cupboard. English. Oak, with sycamore turnings, ash and fruitwood, early seventeenth century.*

318

1594...the court cupboard in the chamber...
1597...my court cupboard in the great parlour...
1621...2 court cubbards wth two drawers...
1626...2 Court cupboards, i walnuttree, i wainscoate...
1677...one court cubard...with some potts & glasses & 2
       candlesticks...
1694...one cort cubberd & cloath...

iii). Cupboards

The earlier appearances of enclosed cupboards ('presses' or 'aumbries') is discussed elsewhere, for it is more interesting at this point to pursue the theme of the incorporation of enclosed compartments within the existing form of the open cup-board; since we can divine there parallel developments both in the form of the standing cupboard, and in the meaning of the word 'cupboard'. The partially enclosed cup-boards in Figures 3:257-265 are all variations on a common theme, which is best interpreted as a court cup-board of which the major part is enclosed by a compartment with doors. This description is echoed exactly by some early inventory descriptions:

1527...A waynscott cupborde wt. too aumbries...
1552...my new cubbarde with ye presse in yt...
1565...one littell cobord with a loker...
1600...A ioyned livrie cupbourde with two close cupbourdes in
       it...

In the earlier of these, the term 'cupboard' is still used in the sense of a side table, with lockers as extra fittings; but by 1600 the word was beginning to mean also a doored compartment (replacing the earlier term 'aumbry'). This confusion lasted through much of the seventeenth century, but later the 'cupboard' assumed its restricted modern meaning of only a doored compartment. In addition the word 'press' survived in meaning the same thing.

Livery Cupboards (Figures 3:257-265)

A good deal of thought and energy has been expended in attempts to identify the exact meaning of the term livery cupboard, which is very frequently met with. Most furniture historians have assumed a livery cupboard must necessarily have been a recognisably distinctive form of cupboard in its own right; yet it does seem rather more likely that 'livery' is an expression of a particular usage of any suitable piece of furniture. There are also references to livery tables, as we have already seen, and any item thus described is probably habitually used for the household distribution of wine and bread, or some similar purpose (see p.334-336, food cupboards). Those writers who have sought to identify a livery cupboard by its form alone have generally chosen the present partially-enclosed standing cupboard as the most likely candidate,[35] emphasising its suitability to hold both food and related utensils such as ewer and basin. In fact most of the conditions attached to a livery cupboard are also applicable to a court cupboard; though Wolsey and Luff suggested that the former may have been used for food and drink, and the latter for cups and dishes. Whilst none of these arguments are entirely convincing, there are no better alternatives at present, so we had best let their conclusions stand.

The construction of these standing livery cupboards is closely akin to the three-tier court cup-boards, except that the middle stage is entirely taken up by the enclosed compartment. This may have a single door and canted sides,

35. R.W. Symonds, The Antique Collector, June 1951; Wolsey and Luff, *The Age of the Joiner*, London, 1968, pp.38-40; Peter Thornton, Furniture History, 1971, pp.63-64.

Figure 3:259. *Joined standing livery cupboard. English. Oak, c.1640.*

Figure 3:258. *Joined standing livery cupboard. English. Oak, with birch panels stained in colours, c.1600 (the base renewed).*

Figure 3:260. *Joined standing livery cupboard. English. Oak, c.1680.*

Figure 3:261. *Joined standing livery cupboard. English; Gloucestershire. Oak, c.1630.*

Figure 3:262. *Joined standing livery cupboard. English. Oak, c.1630.*

Figure 3:263. *Joined standing livery cupboard. English. Oak, mid-seventeenth century.*

or two doors along a flat-framed front. Occasionally, the doors are recessed behind a shelf and pillars (Figure 3:261) as in a press cupboard. All these were equally popular in New England, and they represent some of the finest American pieces of seventeenth century date (Chapter Four). The cupboard from Virginia (Figure 3:264) is an extreme rarity in having the lower section enclosed and an open canopy above. Unfortunately, no other comparable pieces have survived to show whether this was in any way a local preference in the Southern Colonies. A very small number of such cupboards were also made in England, but not to such a degree that any consistent pattern is apparent.

Figure 3:264. *Joined standing livery cupboard. American; Virginia. Oak and walnut, with yellow pine panels, c.1680.*

Figure 3:265. *Joined standing livery cupboard. English; North Country. Oak, mid-seventeenth century. Evidently closely related to Figure 3:266.*

Figure 3:266. *Joined press cupboard. English; North Country. Oak, mid-seventeenth century. The turned pillars are missing from the top stage (compare with Figure 3:265).*

Figure 3:268. *Joined press cupboard. English. Oak with inlay, 1580-1620. A fine-quality example, one of the more expensive products of its time, intended to contribute towards the prestige of the original owner.*

Figure 3:267. *Joined press cupboard. English; Leeds area, Yorkshire. Oak, with inlay and parquetry, mid-seventeenth century. A fine, large cupboard with a drawer, decorated in the manner of a large workshop group (see Figures 4:113-122).*

Press Cupboards (Figures 3:266-280)

The process of completely enclosing the cup-board with doors resulted in the mature press cupboard or parlour cupboard. Its dependence from the court cup-board is clearly demonstrated by the invariable two-part form, which often physically comes apart in two sections for ease of handling. The upper part may have the canted-side compartment similar to some livery cupboards (Figures 3:257-260 and 267), but a recessed flat front is more usual. This is flanked by a pair of pillars of some form, or later these may be reduced to a pair of vestigial pendants. The lower part is entirely closed by doors, though their arrangement may vary; most convenient are the simple pair of large doors which close symmetrically (sometimes reinforced

Figure 3:269. *(Left) Joined press cupboard. English. Oak, early seventeenth century.*

Figure 3:270. *(Below left) Joined press cupboard. English. Oak, dated 1661 (see detail Figure 2:22).*

Figure 3:271. *(Below) Joined press cupboard. English. Oak, mid-seventeenth century.*

Figure 3:272. *Joined press cupboard. English; Yorkshire. Oak, c.1680. The wide, low proportions of this piece are common to many press cupboards from Yorkshire and other parts of Northern England.*

Figure 3:273. *Joined press cupboard. English; North Country. Oak, with fruitwood spindles, c.1700. The overpowering effect of the turned bosses has destroyed the otherwise delicate presence of finer detailing.*

Figure 3:274. *Joined press cupboard with canopy. English; Westmorland. Oak, dated 1689. The canopy is entirely original to the cupboard. Similar specimens may be dated thirty-forty years earlier (cf. Aronson, Figure 548, which is dated 1659).*

Figure 3:275. *(Right) Joined cwpwrdd tridarn. North Wales. Oak and fruitwood, c.1680. Inscribed in English: 'REMEMBER THE POOR'.*

Figure 3.276. *(Above) Joined cwpwrdd tridarn. Welsh; Denbighshire. Oak, dated 1726.*

Figure 3:277. *(Above right) Joined cwpwrdd tridarn. North Wales. Oak, mid-eighteenth century.*

Figure 3:278. *Joined cwpwrdd deuddarn. Welsh; from Abermeurig, Teifi, Cardiganshire. Oak, late eighteenth century. The later persistence of the traditional press in North West Wales is recorded in the will of John Jones of Hafod y Porth, Beddgelert, Caernarvonshire: he left in 1782 "...to my son John Jones £50 also the Press Cupboard lately made by Rowland Griffiths the joiner..."*

Figure 3:279. *Joined cwpwrdd deuddarn. North Wales. Oak, late eighteenth century. The late date is suggested by the poverty-stricken pendants and the large side panels which lack any edge mouldings.*

Figure 3:280. *Joined cwpwrdd deuddarn. Welsh. Oak, c.1800.*

by a central fixed stile), though others have three or four smaller doors. The open lower stage of Figure 3:266 is a rare feature.

Apart from the tester bedstead, the great press cupboard was the most important and prestigious piece of furniture which many small households could boast. They are often dated and initialled in commemoration of a marriage, and their importance and regard has resulted in the survival of a great many examples. As a type, they first appeared in the second half of the sixteenth century, and continued to be made in North Wales and some other remote areas until the beginning of the nineteenth century. The two-part construction is reflected in their Welsh name, *cwpwrdd deuddarn* (lit. two-part cupboard). In some parts of North Wales and North-West England a third stage was added in the form of an open canopy, which served to display and protect such items as the best household pottery or pewter. The practice of displaying valued wares (even in a poor household) is derived from the medieval use of the cup-board for such a purpose, and was continued later in the high dresser with its rank of shelves (see Dressers, pp.340-347). This practice was recorded in an Essex inventory of 1705, where Elizabeth Eree of Writtle had in her hall "...a press cupboard &...earthenware upon the cupboards head..."; though her cupboard would not have had a canopy, unless it were at least two hundred years old. The canopied press cupboard was called in Welsh a *cwpwrdd tridarn* (lit. three-part cupboard), but there is no such neat term in English. The earliest surviving examples are from the Snowdonia area, and daround 1675; though many are dated one to two hundred years later. Sometimes the canopy is a later addition to a *cwpwrdd deuddarn,* but a large number do exist in which the canopy is original and contemporary.

The problem of identifying the correct name for this piece is compounded by the twin facts that few inventories add any sort of adjective to the ubiquitous 'cubberd', and that there must in any case have been local variations in the habitual name. Essex inventories, for example, are full of references to 'press cupboard', but in Oxford the only likely candidate was a "double wainscott Press" of 1671.[36] The terms which must frequently have referred to this type of cupboard are as follows:

> 1587. . . a presse wth certeine shelves in it. . .
> 1594. . . my greatest cupboard which standeth in the Parlour. . .
> 1623. . . the great standinge cupborde at the Hall syde. . .
> 1635. . . In the Hall, one oulde presse Cupborde. . .
> 1667. . . one Presse wth 2 drawers. . .
> 1672. . . In ye Hall. . . one standinge old Pres. . .
> 1685. . . In the Parlor. . . 2 old joyne press cupboards 10s. . .
> 1700. . . one great Cubboard wth drawers. . .

Standing Cupboards (Figures 3:281-289)

Of course, many of the references to standing cupboards must relate to types other than those intended for the parlour or hall. The term 'standing' is a common one, and is also used for other pieces of furniture such as bedsteads. It would seem to imply a large item which stands independently. With cupboards, the distinction generally applies between free-standing versions and those which are hung on the wall, i.e. mural cupboards.

The uses to which free-standing cupboards may be put are determined by their individual form. Some will contain a variety of enclosed compartments, of which several examples are illustrated. The earlier types of boarded or joined cupboards (or aumbries) are shown in Chapter Four, pp.415-416, though these simpler forms persisted in use throughout our

Figure 3:281. *Joined standing cupboard. English. Oak, early seventeenth century.*

Figure 3:282. *Joined cupboard with box top. English. Oak, c.1630.*

36. In the Essex inventories, F.W. Steer found no less than eighty-five references to 'press cupboards', out of 248 households covered, in the period 1635-1749 *(Farm and Cottage Inventories of Mid-Essex,* Essex Record Office, Chelmsford, 1950).

Figure 3:283. *Joined standing cupboard. English; North Country. Oak, c.1680.*

Figure 3:284. *Joined clothes press. English; Harpole, Northamptonshire. Oak, early seventeenth century.*

Figure 3:285. *Joined clothes press. English. Oak, mid-seventeenth century.*

Figure 3:286. *Joined clothes press. English; Westmorland. Oak, dated 1701.*

Figure 3:287. *(Left) Joined clothes press. English; Gloucestershire. Sycamore, original chalk-blue paint, c.1640.*

Figure 3:288. *(Right) Joined clothes press. English. Pine, with black painted detail, c.1700. A wide drawer is missing from the lowest level.*

Figure 3:289. *Joined clothes press. American; Southern (possibly Georgia). Hard pine, c.1700. This piece was originally fitted with bun feet.*

37. An interesting cupboard of c.1480-1500 survives in St. Mary's Church, Aylesbury, Bucks. Here the perches are fitted within the cupboard, and are hinged for access. Illustrated and discussed by Penelope Eames, in Furniture History, 1977.

period. Large plain cupboards were constructed for the storage of clothes, a type known as a clothes press. The word 'wardrobe' does not appear to have been applied to a piece of furniture until the end of the eighteenth century, and originally implied a room or office for the storage of documents or clothes. In the medieval bedroom, clothes were hung overnight on a horizontal pole or perch,[37] whilst more permanent storage was effected in a chest or trunk. The clothes press might also be called a hanging press, since the garments were hung in rows on wooden pegs, but this term is open to confusion since mural cupboards were also sometimes described as 'hanging' (on the wall). Many houses retain built-in closets for clothes storage, and for this reason clothes presses are not often recorded amongst the movable furniture in inventories.

1643...one wainscott press there to hang thereon clothes...
1651...one large press to hang cloths in...
1658...one large close cubbard for cloths...

Hanging and Mural Cupboards (Figures 3:290-329)

A huge variety of small mural cupboards were developed during the course of the seventeenth century, fulfilling a variety of small storage needs. Some were permanently built into the structure of the house, usually in the chimney. These were for the dry storage of salt and spices, valuable commodities which required a mild source of warmth to be kept dry and safe from mildew (Figure 3:293). Such cupboards are to be found in almost every region, but they survive in especially large numbers in Westmorland and the Lancashire Lake District. In Wales, salt was often stored in a box or a box-seat chair (Figure 3:130), which was stood by the fire for the same reason.

Most small cupboards were made to hang upon the wall, either by means of an iron hanger, or simply by being nailed through the back-boards. They could have been intended for almost any form of contents, but it seems that most were intended to hold either food or drinking glasses. The

Figure 3:290. *Boarded mural cupboard. English or Welsh; Border Area, possibly Monmouthshire. Oak, late seventeenth century. The construction of this, and the following two cupboards, is most unusual. The sides consist of a single riven plank of oak, which is bent around in a semi-circle and secured by nails. The cupboards are not fitted or sub-divided inside. A further example is to be seen at Cwmmau Farm, Brilley, Herefordshire (National Trust); and a simple version at the Welsh Folk Museum is dated 1716, and may be seen over the bed in Figure 3:449, found in the Gower.*

Figure 3:291. *Boarded mural cupboard. English or Welsh; Border Area, possibly Monmouthshire. Oak and elm, 1680-1720.*

Figure 3:292. *Boarded mural cupboard. English or Welsh; Border Area, possibly Monmouthshire. Oak, 1680-1720.*

Figure 3:293. *(Left) Built-in joined mural cupboard. English; Collinfield Manor, Kendal, Westmorland. Oak, dated 1674.*

Figure 3:294. *(Right) Joined mural cupboard. English; Gloucestershire. Oak, c.1630.*

construction of mural cupboards is necessarily light of weight, in order to avoid strain on the wall or on the structure of the cupboard itself. Accordingly, they are usually rather flimsily constructed of thin nailed boards, with much use of pierced panels both for lightness and ventilation.

Figure 3:295. *Boarded mural spice cupboard. English. Oak, mid-seventeenth century. This little chest must be one of the 'prettiest' pieces of oak furniture in existence. The delicate pierced and floral decoration combine with a fine colour and perfect condition, to create a marvellous object. The classical pediment encloses an incongruously Gothic motif.*

Figure 3:296. *Boarded mural spice cupboard. Figure 3:295 shown opened.*

Figure 3:297. *(Left) Joined mural spice cupboard. English. Oak, c.1640.*

Figure 3:298. *(Right) Joined mural spice cupboard. English. Oak, mid-seventeenth century.*

Their construction is very similar to small boxes of the same date, and it seems not unlikely that many were made by box makers (q.v.). Very few small mural cupboards incorporate any trace of joined framework, and some were evidently made entirely by the turners (Figure 2:70).

Cupboards for the storage of foodstuffs take two different forms; they either incorporate some provision for ventilation, or they enclose a series of small drawers for spices and other dry goods. As such, the latter are akin to the chest of drawers, but spice cupboards are normally enclosed by a door. The arrangement of the drawers varies only slightly from piece to piece, but the treatment of the exteriors differs greatly according to the date and place of manufacture (Figures 3:295-306). Spices and herbs were very important in English cuisine before the present century, whether as flavourings, preservatives or medicines, and a well-stocked spice cupboard was an asset to the conscientious housewife. The drawers sometimes still bear the old handwritten labels, but if not the different smells will often identify the original contents — nutmeg, pepper, cloves, cinnamon, allspice, cummin, ginger, aniseed, liquorice and many others. Each of these would be grated or crushed in a mortar for use as needed.

Plate Eleven. *(Top) Boarded box. English. Oak, stained in colours, mid-seventeenth century. The highly original sunburst design on this box is stained in panels of black and red, which alternate with unstained areas to produce a varied effect. Note the cheerfully unconcerned manner in which the (original) lockplate is banged on the front with complete disregard to the scheme of decoration underneath. Such casual approach is very common in other boxes of the period.*

Plate Eleven. *(Middle) Boarded box. (?) American; New England. Oak and pine, painted with colours, dated 1691. The red and blue-grey paints are the original colours, though the latter has been re-painted. The carved tulips are closely related to work from both Essex County, Massachusetts, and the Connecticut River Valley; but it is still not clear whether this is a true American piece, or an English prototype (from Devonshire) for the school of carving associated with William Searle, who was trained at Ottery St. Mary in Devon, and then emigrated to Ipswich in Massachusetts c.1661. If the latter theory is accepted, then the date of 1691 must be a later addition. See Chapter Four, Figures 4:194-198.*

Plate Eleven. *(Bottom) Boarded desk box. Welsh. Sycamore, painted in colours, early eighteenth century. The top coat of brown paint has been scraped with a comb when still wet, revealing the yellow undercoat. This simple method of imitating woodgrain has been popular for at least four centuries, and the bold effect obtained here is similar to the early Staffordshire combed slipware pottery of similar date.*

Figure 3:299. *Boarded mural spice cupboard. English. Oak and fruit-wood, original brown paint with yellow stripe, mid-seventeenth century. Shown with its accompanying nutmeg grater.*

Figure 3:300. *Joined spice cupboard. American; Essex County, Massachusetts. Oak, pine, walnut and maple, dated (16)79. Probably made for a member of the Hart family of Lynnfield, Mass.*

Figure 3:301. *Boarded mural spice cupboard. English. Oak, late seventeenth century. The design of this piece is highly reminiscent of contemporary clock hoods.*

Figure 3:302. *Boarded mural spice cupboard. English. Cedar, fruitwood and oak, with boxwood stringing, late seventeenth century.*

38. The interpretation of 'ark' probably varied from district to district (Randle Holme was a native of Chester).

The ventilated cupboards are another diverse and very interesting group. Some of these are glass cupboards, as we shall see, but many were apparently intended as food cupboards. There is a great need to clarify and identify the correct nomenclature and purpose of the different types, but certain conclusions are available now. The perforations may take several forms, from a series of tiny holes drilled in patterns (Figures 3:308 and 309), to more ambitious fretwork patterns (Figures 3:313, 316, 317 and 322), or the panels may be filled with rows of turned spindles or flat-cut slats. Sometimes food cupboards may stand on the floor, but more often they are suspended in some way to minimise access by vermin; rodents and flies being the biggest problems. The latter were usually eliminated by the simple expedient of nailing a piece of hair cloth behind the ventilation, so that early cupboards often retain traces of the cloth inside, and of the nails by which it was secured. Randle Holme identified such a piece as an 'ark',[38] and they are sometimes mentioned in inventories. Many were covered on the outside with hair cloth, but these have not survived for obvious reasons.

> 1649... an ark; a kind of little house made of wood and covered with haire cloth, and so by two rings hung in the middle of a Rome, thereby to secure all things put therein from the cruelty of devouring Rats, mice, Weesels, and such kind of Vermine. Some have the pannells made all of Tyn with small holes for aire, others of woode...
>
> 1666... In the Butery... one hare cuboard...
>
> 1726... In the Little Pantry... a keep cupboard covered with haircloth...

The form of suspended food cupboard described by Holme in 1649 is seen in the cupboard of 1671 in Figure 3:308, where the construction is of the latter type. Many slatted bread cupboards survive with this sort of suspension system, but few are so elaborately and conventionally panelled.

Figure 3:303. *Spice cupboard interior. Detail of Figure 3:298. Note the panelled door.*

Figure 3:304. *Spice cupboard interior. English. Oak and elm, mid-seventeenth century.*

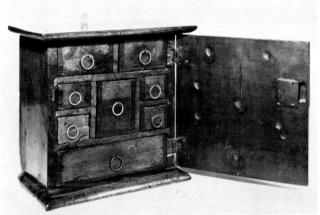

Figure 3:305. *Spice cupboard interior. Detail of Figure 3:302. Note the boarded door.*

Figure 3:306. *(Left) Joined spice chest. English. Oak, c.1740. Here the use of a door has been abandoned, and the chest is seen as a miniature chest of drawers, with full architectural treatment in the classical style.*

Ventilated food cupboards have been variously identified as both livery cupboards and dole cupboards, but the precise interpretations of these terms are, in fact, not very clear. The livery was identified from an early date as an allowance of food, drink and candles issued to members of a household, their guests and servants, usually at night. In the *Black Book* of 1483, it was laid down that each person should receive ''...for his Livery at night, half a chet loaf, one quart of wine, one gallon of ale; and for Winter livery...one percher wax, one candle wax...'' Edmund Spenser noted in 1596 that ''...the liverye is sayd to be served up for all night, that is theyr nyghtes allowance of drinks...''[39] From these and similar descriptions we may infer that livery tables and cupboards were used in connection with this domestic ritual, though it must be remembered that the term can give us no clue as to the actual form of the piece. Dole cupboards and dole shelves are concerned with a similar but more public act of charitable distribution.

39. Edmund Spenser, *View of the State of Ireland*, 1596.

Figure 3:307. *Joined ventilated food cupboard. English. Oak, with inlay, c.1620. This small, but very fine quality cupboard is designed to hang on the wall, probably to serve as a livery cupboard in the private parlour or bed-chamber of a rich house.*

Figure 3:308. *Joined hanging food cupboard. English. Oak, dated 1671. This cupboard was probably intended for kitchen use, and is suspended from the ceiling by means of ropes and pulleys.*

Figure 3:309. *Joined standing livery cupboard. English. Oak, mid-seventeenth century. The panels drilled with holes in formal patterns.*

Figure 3:310. *Joined standing livery cupboard. English. Oak, c.1680. The panels filled with turned spindles.*

They are to be found in churches and other public places, and were used for containing loaves for the parish poor. Many were provided under the terms of specific bequests, and some are still used for their original purpose. Sometimes a shelf or cupboard was provided in the doorway of a wealthy house, so that surplus food might be left there for the use of the poor. Such acts of charity were regarded as the righteous duty of any self-respecting Christian, and inscriptions to 'Remember the Poor', or to 'Pity the Poor', are found on furniture and metalwork of the period.

Inventories frequently note a livery cupboard in the bedchamber, and it was no doubt customary for the individual to store his livery here overnight. Our ancestors spent a good deal of their time in bed, especially in the winter, and a store of refreshment might be a great comfort in the long hours before dawn. The practice of distributing household liveries seems to have declined during the course of the seventeenth century, but the term 'livery cupboard' persisted in use.

> 1589...Itm. ij lyverie copbords of Oke...
> 1624...In the best chamber...a livery cubberd & turkey carpet on it...
> 1649...my posted settworke bedstead and livrey cupboard to it...
> 1663...In the buttery chamber...a fetherbed, 2 livery cubboards...
> 1672...One Joyne standinge bedsted, one livery cupboard of Juniper...
> 1708...In the parlor chamber...one bedsted wth curtains & valens, one livery cupboard...

Cheap and coarsely-made drinking glasses were fairly plentiful even in lower middle class homes in the sixteenth and seventeenth centuries, but owing to their fragile nature some special system of storing them was a

Figure 3:311. *Joined mural livery cupboard. English. Oak, mid-seventeenth century. The turned 'feet' are merely pendants, and the piece is not designed to stand.*

Figure 3:312. *(Right) Joined mural livery cupboard. English. Oak, ash and fruitwood, with parquetry of various coloured woods, early seventeenth century. For detail see Figure 2:226.*

Figure 3:313. *Joined mural livery cupboard. English. Oak and fruitwood, c.1640.*

Figure 3:314. *Joined mural livery cupboard. English. Oak and chestnut, c.1640.*

Figure 3:315. *Joined mural livery cupboard. English. Walnut, elm and oak, c.1630.*

Figure 3:316. *Joined mural livery cupboard. English. Oak and fruitwood, mid-seventeenth century.*

Figure 3:317a. *Joined mural livery cupboard. English. Oak and fruitwood, mid-seventeenth century.*

Figure 3:317b. *The same basic type of cupboard as Figure 3:317a. The informal Gothic tracery of this delightful cupboard suggests that the design may have been loosely copied by the maker from a fine window in his parish church. Whilst the lower register of arches and windows is simple and accurate enough, the more complex tracery of the higher level has been misunderstood and improvised.*

Figure 3:318. *Joined mural livery cupboard. English. Fruitwood, mid-seventeenth century.*

Figure 3:319. *Joined mural livery cupboard. English. Ash, mid-seventeenth century*

Figure 3:320. *Joined mural livery cupboard. North Wales. Oak and ash, early eighteenth century.*

Figure 3:321. *Primitive bread cage. Welsh. Fruitwood, with oak shelves, eighteenth century.*

Figure 3:322. *Boarded glass cupboard. English. Oak, dated 1693. The painted inscription (red on cream) reads: 'Maids i advise you have a Care, Glasses & Lasses are Brittle ware. 1693'.*

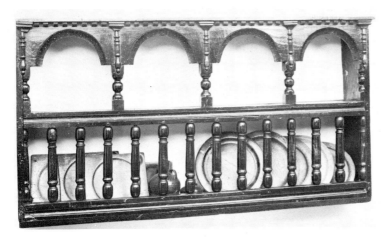

Figure 3:323. *Joined trencher case. English. Oak and fruitwood, mid-seventeenth century. This piece might be used to store a variety of items including treenware, glassware, pewter or horn mugs, and delftware.*

Figure 3:324. *Joined mural case. Detail of Figure 3:323. The door is shown opened, to demonstrate the construction, in which the innermost spindle is extended through the frame in order to provide a pivot.*

Figure 3:325. *Joined glass shelves. English or Flemish. Oak, c.1640.*

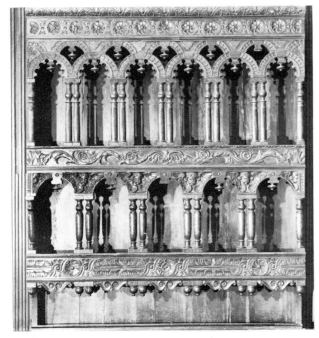

Figure 3:326. *Boarded glass case. English. Oak, dated 1655.*

Figure 3:327. *Boarded glass case. English. Oak, mid-seventeenth century.*

Figure 3:328. *Boarded glass case. English. Oak, mid-seventeenth century.*

necessity. The answer was a lightly-built case of shelves, known as a glass case, glass perch or glass cupboard, which first made an appearance toward the end of the sixteenth century. These were sometimes provided with doors in the same manner as a food cupboard (Figure 3:322), but the usual seventeenth century version has open shelves. Obviously, racks of shelves of this type might be used to hold all sorts of wares, and an inventory of 1666 (quoted below) notes a little glass case which contains books and trenchers.[40] Glass shelves are closely related to the dresser rack, and to the delft rack of the eighteenth century, and were in fact superseded by them.

> 1580... a Case for glasses, vjd...
> 1594... a glass cubberd...
> 1596... certeine shelves for vessells...
> 1603... At ye Great Chamber Dore one little joined boarde wt a
>   fast frame to it, to sett on glasses...
> 1620... In the Butterye... a glass cubberd...
> 1638... one glass case with glasses, a ltle glasse case...
> 1666... One glass Case and litell one with some bookes and
>   Trenchers...
> 1678... a glass peartch with sondrie glasses...
> 1700... one Glass Case wth six Drinking Glasses...

iv). Dressers

The universally familiar and archetypal farmhouse dresser of the eighteenth century is so well known that we tend to accept it unthinkingly, with little concern as to its origins, development and infinite variations of region and form. In fact, the different types of dresser are so diverse that they must be considered as different classes of furniture altogether. Added to the complexities of the differing forms of dresser is the question of quality — for the kitchen dresser is a very different thing from the dresser made for the dining parlour.

40. A late seventeenth century trencher rack at Great Chalfield Manor, Wiltshire, has a series of vertical slats to hold flat wooden trenchers, not unlike a Victorian plate-rack. Such items are recorded in inventories as a trencher case or dishes case; and this term might include another familiar form, the delft rack.

Figure 3:329. *Boarded glass case. English. Oak, mid-seventeenth century.*

Figure 3:330. *Joined dresser or buffet. French. Walnut, c.1500. This is a high-backed plate cupboard, designed expressly for the display of material wealth, and indicative of the status of its original owners.*

41. Not to be confused with the dressing table of the eighteenth century, at which a lady sat whilst dressing herself (Figure 4:279).

42. An attempt was made to unravel the complexities of the medieval forms of *dressoir* and *buffet* by Penelope Eames (Furniture History, 1971, pp.55-65), but the duplicity of meanings can only be solved by oversimplifying the matter. Dr. Eames decided to restrict the term *buffet* to describing the formal plate cupboard on display in public rooms, and the *dressoir* for the service furniture to be found in kitchens. This is a distinction of usage, rather than of form.

But to begin with the name itself, the term 'dresser' derived from the medieval Anglo-French *dressoir,* and the later English dressing board.[41] The *dressoir* took several physical forms, but its usage was primarily concerned with the display and preparation of food and plate,[42] which relates it to the English cup-board and sideboard. The dressing board was more usually an item of kitchen furniture, and as such was a simple work board or table for the menial task of cooking, in the same way as the later painted pine versions.

1485... A dressing bord of elmen for the larder of X fote...
A dressyng-borde of elmen for the Kytchin xij fote long...
1590... in the Kitching...two dressinge bordes...
1658... In the kitchin...a Dresser bord...
1672... In the kitchin...one dresser bord and shelves, Three Dozen of peuter plates, foure porringers and other small peuter...

The latter dresser and shelves, with its garnish of pewter, marks a significant point in the development of dressers in the British Isles. Here we see a revival of the medieval high dresser with a rack or canopy, which is quite a different thing from the low dresser or sideboard. In order to see dressers in a proper perspective, we must consider these two separately.

The High Dresser (Figures 3:330-343)

The display of plate and other valuables on a high canopied *buffet* or *dressoir* was an important facility in medieval social thinking. The ability to put on a good show of wealth on formal occasions was a source of great pride to a family which considered itself to be of any substance and account. Importance and precedence were announced by the number of shelves or stages (referred to as 'desks') which such a plate cupboard might boast, and on royal occasions they were constructed with six stages or more. Sometimes, they would consist of a free-standing rack of stepped shelves, but in less elevated circumstances a simple superstructure (possibly of a purely temporary nature) was provided on top of a standing cupboard. This was known as an 'hawt pace', a corruption of the French *hault pas*, a high step.

1505...a cowbourd wt an hawt pace. iijs. iiijd...
1547...A Cobberd Joyned paynted grene, wt a halpace...
1558...a joyned cubberte, wt a hall payse, and a deske for plate...
1580...a plate Cupborde wth a Deske...
1588...paid to the joiner of Maldon for the half pace...5s. 4d...

Figure 3:331. *Joined mural canopy. English, or Flemish. Oak, painted in colours, c.1500. The inscription below is the standard 'AVE MARIA GRATIA PLENA'. This piece possibly originated as an altar canopy, though it may equally have hung over some form of dresser or serving table, or even a throne chair.*

Figure 3:332. *Joined cwpwrdd tridarn. North Wales. Oak, early eighteenth century. The canopy is either a survival of the medieval form, or an unsophisticated revival of the same, and seems to have first appeared in the Snowdonia area shortly after 1660. The tridarn was made in Wales until after 1900.*

Figure 3:333. *Joined enclosed high dresser. North Wales; probably Denbighshire. Oak, early eighteenth century. The form is essentially that of a cwpwrdd tridarn, but the canopy here takes the nature of a shelved rack. In other examples, the turned pendants of the tridarn canopy are also retained (see Figure 3:334).*

Figure 3:334. *(Above) Joined enclosed high dresser. North Wales; probably Denbighshire. Oak, early eighteenth century. Here is the fully developed dresser-rack, but still retaining the turned pendants of the tridarn canopy.*

Figure 3:335. *(Right) Joined enclosed high dresser. North Wales; probably Denbighshire. Oak, early eighteenth century. The turned pendants here omitted from the rack, but the small side-cupboards are a feature of this area (Figures 3:334-336).*

43. From *The Newe Navigation and Discoverie of the Kingdome of Moscovia, by the North-East, in the yeere 1553*, published in *The Principal Navigations, Voiages, Traffiques and Discoveries of the English Nation*, Richard Hackluyt, 1598.

Representations of cupboards with stepped and shelved superstructures are fairly common in late medieval manuscripts, but they had probably ceased to be used by 1600, for a couple of years later Sir Thomas Kytson's steward could not even remember the correct word for such a piece, and the inventory he compiled contains the following descriptive entry: "1603...Itm. a thing made like stayrs to set plate on..." In English medieval descriptions, the term used for the stepped display stand was 'copborde', and the same term was used as late as 1553 in an English description of an identical piece seen in the Emperor's Golden Court at Moscow:[43]

> "...in the middes stoode a mightie Cupboord upon a square foote, whereupon stoode also a rounde boord, in manner of a Diamond, broade beneath, and towardes the toppe narrowe, and every steppe rose up more narrowe then another. Upon this Cupboorde was placed the Emporours plate, which was so much, that the very Cupboord itself was scant able to sustaine the waight of it..."

The fine French walnut dresser or *buffet* in Figure 3:330 has a simpler superstructure in the form of an upraised panelled backboard, and represents a group found on both sides of the Channel. The provision of a high back or a canopy was a powerful symbol in medieval terms, and was applied equally to cupboards, chairs and beds. High-backed dressers were used for everyday purposes in rich households, as serving cupboards and plate cupboards; but for special emphasis an overhanging canopy was an essential adjunct. Canopied cupboards are extremely rare in anything approaching original condition,[44] and so I have shown here a complete canopy which probably started life as an altar canopy or reredos. This is identical in form to the canopies over cupboards of the same date (early sixteenth century), but it shows no signs of attachment at the base. The overhanging canopy was known at this time as a 'sayling hance', and it served to emphasise the open display board area at "the cupboard's head," where rich objects were set out on a suitable cupboard cloth.

> 1504...a standing cubbourde carven wt a sayling haunce wt ymagry gylt...

As the sixteenth century progressed, the powerful symbolism of the canopied cupboard and chair declined, and by 1600 it survived only in formal usage. The favoured display vehicle was now the court cup-board, and the dresser survived in use only as a piece of service furniture. But the

44. Heavily-restored examples may be seen at Badminton House, Gloucestershire, and in the Burrell Collection (see Percy Macquoid, *Age of Oak*, plate III).

Figure 3:336. *Joined open high dresser. North Wales; probably Denbighshire. Oak, early eighteenth century. The potboard dresser is not usual in the North, and this example has other rare features, such as the long turned supports to the rack. Compare the general form with the later Southern dresser in Figure 3:341.*

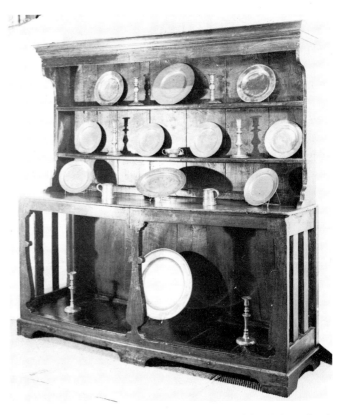

Figure 3:337. *Joined open high dresser. Welsh. Oak and ash, early eighteenth century.*

Figure 3:338. *Joined open high dresser. South Wales; probably Carmarthenshire. Oak and pine, mid-eighteenth century.*

Figure 3:339. *Joined open high dresser. Mid-Wales; from Cefngwifed, Tregynon, Montgomeryshire. Oak, chestnut and fruitwood, c.1780. The crudely rendered 'Georgian' architectural decoration is enchanting, especially the primitive fretwork capitals over the side-cupboards, and the Chippendale-like latticework frieze between them.*

45. Two important articles by Tom Crispin (Antique Finder/Collecting: Vol. 7, No. 8, and Vol. 8, No. 1), located the regional origins of some English and Welsh dressers, but a great deal of specific research is needed to fix both the areas of production and the direction of influences.

idea of the overhanging canopy was due for a revival, though at a much reduced social level. After the middle of the seventeenth century, at a time when the ruling classes were striving towards new forms and fashions, there was a small renewal of interest in the display canopy fixed on top of a cupboard. Curiously, this seems to have been concentrated amongst the yeoman farmers of remote North Wales and the English North-West (see press cupboards, pp.326-327). By far the largest number of press cupboards with a canopy are from North Wales (the *cwpwrdd tridarn*), and it is no coincidence that this area is also famed for the quality and early date of its dressers. This theme is typical of some of the archaic preoccupations of rural Wales in the period 1650-1850, and expresses the innate conservatism of its people.

Figure 3:332 is a standard tridarn from Denbighshire or Caernarvonshire, standing directly in the tradition of the medieval overhanging canopy, though now it serves to display a garnish of pewter or delftware instead of gilt and silver plate. It is a simple step to translate the idea of a canopy into that of a shelved rack, as in the dresser in Figure 3:333. Here the base unit, and the central unit of three small cupboards, are identical to the preceding tridarn; but the top canopy is provided instead with shelves. It is not suggested that the high dresser first appeared in this way, yet the correlation of ideas is an interesting one. However and wherever it may have reappeared from, the high dresser was an established form by 1700 or a little later. The best examples are often of Welsh type, but some areas of England also produced high-quality dressers in the eighteenth century.[45]

Figure 3:340. *Joined open high dresser. Mid-Wales; Trallwng, Montgomeryshire. Oak, with burr oak drawer-fronts and inlay of various woods, c.1780. The inlay consists of cockerels, a jug, a goblet, and geometric stringing. The ogee arches between the legs are a typical feature of the area.*

Figure 3:342. *(Right) Joined enclosed high dresser. North Wales or North West England. Oak, with mahogany cross-banding and pine backboards, 1780-1800.*

Figure 3:341. *Joined open high dresser. South Wales; probably Glamorganshire. Oak and pine, with bone keyplates, c.1800.*

Figure 3:343. *Joined open high corner dresser. South Wales; probably Carmarthenshire. Oak and pine, 1780-1820. The 'crooked dresser', as it was known, fitted into the corner of a room in order to economise on space.*

Specific regional differences between types of high dressers are better seen than described, but certain broad comments may be held as accurate: Welsh dressers fall into three main groups. In the North, they are usually of the enclosed type, following closely on the pattern of the contemporary *cwpwrdd tridarn* (fielded panels and drawers, integrated racks, fine quality joinery and timber, etc.). In the South, a lighter form of open-base potboard dresser was popular, more akin to the low dresser, in which the rack seems almost an afterthought. In Central Wales, especially Montgomeryshire, a very fine-quality potboard dresser was produced (Figure 3:339 and 340), which no doubt influenced the dressers of Shropshire and the English West Midlands. English high dressers were largely produced in the area West of the Pennines, in a broad band running from Shropshire up to Cumberland (see also Chapter Four), but during the nineteenth century such positive regional differences faded out and the built-in high kitchen dresser became a universal requisite.

> 1637...a dresser of five shelves...
> 1678...in the dairy...dressers & shelves...
> 1683...in the Keching...one table & dresser...
> 1727...in the Hall, One dresser and shelves, 3 pewter dishes & 12 pewter plates...
> 1743...In the pantry...a dresser...fifty five pieces of Delph & earthen ware...
> 1754...a dresser and shelves of wainscott...

Figure 3:344. *Joined open low dresser. English. Oak, 1650-80.*

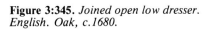

Figure 3:345. *Joined open low dresser. English. Oak, c.1680.*

Figure 3:346. *Joined open low dresser. English. Oak, 1680-1700.*

Figure 3:347. *Joined open low dresser. English. Oak and fruitwood, c.1700.*

The Low Dresser (Figures 3:344-353)

As an item of dining room furniture, the low dresser grew out of the various forms of side serving table (the court cup-board and the sideboard). Two distinct forms of low dresser developed in the second half of the seventeenth century, open and enclosed, and these are best treated separately.[46]

a). The Open Low Dresser

This is essentially a lengthened version of the side table with drawer, which developed stylistically along similar lines. The dressers have anything from two to five drawers; and the form of the legs and stretchers varies considerably from piece to piece. Some have no stretchers at all, since the depth of the drawer frame allowed sufficient strength in the construction. Most of the earlier versions have turned legs, but flat-cut legs are not unusual, and many eighteenth century dressers adopted the fashionable cabriole leg (see Figures 4:282-283).

46. It is impossible at present to make any detailed comments on the regional origins of English low dressers. Experience has shown that dressers of the type in Figure 3:351 are often associated with Yorkshire, but this is slender fare indeed. Thousands of farmhouse dressers have moved home in the past hundred years, and the time is fast running out when we can still call on the experience of the present generation of itinerant dealers to help classify the regional styles of the dressers they have handled.

Figure 3:348. *Joined open low dresser. English. Oak, c.1730.*　　**Figure 3:349.** *Joined open low dresser. English. Oak, c.1730.*

The style and construction of the drawer are the most significant guides to dating individual pieces. Throughout the second half of the seventeenth century, the most popular decoration was the same system of mitred mouldings as are commonly found on chests of drawers. In the early eighteenth century, the drawers were more plainly-finished with a variety of edge-treatments — fielding, overlapped moulding, cockbeading, crossbanding, etc. True low dressers were made without a high rack, but during the course of the eighteenth century many were fitted with later racks of shelves, though this normally results in an ungainly appearance on an open-based dresser.

1698...a Dresser with Drawers...

Figure 3:350. *Joined enclosed low dresser. English. Oak, 1670-80.*

b). The Enclosed Low Dresser

The fully-enclosed low dresser adopted a variety of arrangements, but most consist of a combination of drawers and cupboards. The earliest examples (say 1650-80, Figure 3:350) often have full banks of drawers, and may resemble two or three chests of drawers pushed together. Later, the drawers were concentrated in the top row, and the lower parts were enclosed by doors alone. Eighteenth century versions are closely akin to the base section of the high dresser and the *cwpwrdd deuddarn,* and the collector must be wary of the possibility that an alleged low dresser did not start life as either of these.

1727... one deal dresser board with doors & drawers...

Dressers of all sorts held a special place of affectionate regard in the hearts of yeoman farmers and cottagers alike until quite recent times. The perceptive eye of Thomas Hardy noted this phenomenon as late as 1889, when he described in *Tess of the d'Urbervilles* the typical house-moving ritual of the Dorset peasant. The system of tied cottages meant that each year, after the great Candlemas hiring fairs, thousands of families would up and move house on Old Lady Day, changing their homes with father's job:

> "...The day being the sixth of April, the Durbeyfield waggon met many other waggons with families on the summit of the load, which was built on a well-nigh unvarying principle, as peculiar, probably, to the rural labourer as the hexagon to the bee. The groundwork of the arrangement was the family dresser, which, with its shining handles, and fingermarks, domestic evidences thick upon it, stood importantly in front, over the tails of the shaft-horses, in its erect and natural position, like some Ark of the Covenant they were bound to carry reverently..."

Figure 3:351. *Joined enclosed low dresser. English; probably Yorkshire. Oak and fruitwood, c.1700.*

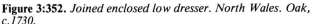

Figure 3:352. *Joined enclosed low dresser. North Wales. Oak, c.1730.*

Figure 3:353. *Joined enclosed low dresser. English; possibly Shropshire. Oak, mid-eighteenth century.*

In Wales, even in the industrial valleys of Glamorganshire, the high dresser sustained a special place in family life until almost the second half of the twentieth century. In some parts of rural Wales this pride of place is still maintained even today. The dresser is still seen as a necessary part of a young girl's dowry, and it will spend the rest of her married life in her parlour or kitchen, festooned with an array of brass knick-knacks, lustre pottery, willow-pattern plates and Staffordshire figures; or if she is particularly fortunate, a gleaming garnish of pewter.

v). Chests and Boxes

The generic term 'chest' may be regarded as proper to a whole family of lidded receptacles, which have always been the most common variety of storage furniture, though later overshadowed by the more convenient chest of drawers which developed from it in part. The word derives from the Latin *cista,* and is found throughout the British Isles in vernacular forms as 'chist' or 'kist'. The chest is differentiated from a box in that it has legs or some other integral support which raises it from the ground. A box always has a flat base and was intended from the start to sit directly on the floor or on top of something else (though a few boxes are formed as miniature chests, with feet of their own). The standard flat-topped joined or boarded chest made in huge numbers throughout the post-medieval period should always be referred to as a chest, and not a coffer. Randle Holme was only reflecting current practice when he noted in 1649 that "if it have a streight, and flat cover, it is called a Chest; which in all other things represents the coffer, save the want of a circular lid, or cover..." (cf. Figures 2:127 a and b and 3:363).

Yet real life is much more confused than such a simple formula would pretend. Students of inventories will have noted a dozen or more basic terms which describe chests of one sort or another, to say nothing of the many different uses to which they are attributed, or subtle combinations such as the 'coffer-standard' cited below. Many of the common terms are partly interchangeable in practice, but it is worth examining certain classes of chests in the light of such patterns as do happen to emerge.

Plate Twelve. *Small bureau or standing desk with drawers. English. Ash, with yewtree interior, mid-eighteenth century. A good, small desk of standard type, showing the finely-marked grain of English field-grown ash.*

Baggage Chests

The furniture-owning classes of the Middle Ages were an itinerant breed, and so much of their domestic furniture was carted from house to house when the household was 'in progress'. Chests, therefore, were useful items for they could be packed full for the journey and still serve as seats or cupboards when in residence. Certain chests were constructed specifically as baggage packs, often made of some lightweight material such as canvas, leather or wicker (the 'hamper'). These were known by specific names, such as 'malle', 'bahut', 'trussing cóffer' or 'sumpter chest' (the latter usually in pairs to be strapped either side of a mule):

> 1374... pour un coffre d'ozier, couvert de cuir, ferrez...
> (for a wicker coffer, covered with leather, with iron fittings)
> 1384... a pair of Trussyng-kofrers...
> 1411... my 'cofres' called 'Trussyngcofrez' and all my napery...
> 1502... Itm. a grete trusing basket...

Other common items, which might well have been travelling chests of some sort, were known as ship chests or *coffres de mer,* though surprisingly little is known about them. They are sometimes, but not exclusively, found among the effects of seamen and mariners:

> 1415... a shipchest att London wth yren...
> 1417... Unam cistam vocatam shipcofre...
> 1597... a great ship chest standing at the stair's head...

Standards (Figures 2:107 and 3:354)

Even if they were not constructed primarily as baggage containers, many medieval domestic chests were certainly constructed with such a purpose in mind. We have already seen the important Richard de Bury chest, which was probably made to contain the coin and documents for a Royal Commission of c.1340 (Figure 2:107, also pp.200-203), and which still has its original iron carrying handles whereby it was slung from a stout pole. Such chests are referred to in medieval accounts as standards. They are usually bound with iron straps, and may be either painted or covered with cloth or leather. Many of the medieval examples are quite large (the Richard de Bury chest is 6ft. 4ins. long), but others are small enough to be carried comfortably by two men in the required fashion. The adaptation for travelling is reflected not only in the provision of carrying handles, but also in the fact that most examples have either domed or gabled lids, so designed as to help throw off rain-water on a wet journey. In their materials and form, standards are seen to be closely akin to coffers and trunks, and the real distinction possibly lies only in the fact that the standard is the more heavily built of the three, and is not necessarily covered in cloth or leather.

> 1423... Item, III cofrestandard liez de ferr... (Item, 3 coffer standards bound with iron)
> 1466... stuff brought from Wingfield to Ewelme in a Standard...
> 1500... 5 standardes coverid wth lether & peyntid redd... a square standarde, and coverid with blaakletheir, and bowden wth yrne, wth 2 lokys...
> 1600... a flatte standerd bounde about with yron haveing two locks...
> 1713... one Large Strong Standard Trunk...

Figure 3:354. *Boarded standard. English. Elm, oak and walnut, with iron bands, c.1500. There are traces of coarse linen or velvet coverings under the iron. The two lock plates are original, as are the carrying handles at each end.*

Figure 3:355. *Boarded chest or ark. Scandinavian. Wainscot oak, c.1600. Inscribed 'HENRK'. Although this chest is in oak, it may possibly resemble the group of softwood chests imported from the Baltic areas, and known as 'Danske' or 'Sprews' chests.*

Imported Chests (Figures 3:355-358)

Even though not of English make, various types of imported chests were a vital element in the English interior because of the huge numbers in which they seem to appear; and their influence on the working methods of English craftsmen must not be underestimated. Furniture was imported from various European countries over a very long period, and this practice was often the cause of complaint and even suffering on the part of the English artisans. In 1483 the Guild of Cofferers petitioned that they were "like to be undone by the said wares" being brought from Flanders, and a hundred years later it was still possible to note that Dutchmen were bringing over "wainscot already wrought, as...cupboards, stooles, tables, chests". The Book of Rates of 1582, recording the import duties levied on various classes of goods, noted that chests were imported in batches or 'nests' of three. Some chests were also imported as packing for goods of different sorts, though the standard packaging of the period was in the form of coopered barrels.

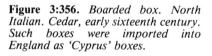

Figure 3:356. *Boarded box. North Italian. Cedar, early sixteenth century. Such boxes were imported into England as 'Cyprus' boxes.*

The most usual references to foreign chests in English homes are covered by the following terms:

a). 'Danske' chests. These were apparently imported from (or at least associated with) the Baltic port of Danzig (Gdansk), a trade which must have been aided by the efficiency and protection of the Hanseatic League. Attempts actually to identify a specimen of a Danske chest have failed, since we can only conjecture as to exactly what they were like, despite their very common mentions in inventories. The Baltic area produced both oak and softwoods for the English market, but since oak chests are often distinguished from Danske as 'wainscot', we must assume that Danske chests were of some softwood. Spruce and fir are both recorded, and this is of some relevance, for 'spruce' is a corruption of *Pruce* or Prussia, the area in which Danzig is situated. Softwoods were usually stained or painted, and some Danske chests are noted as inlaid.[47]

> 1569...a danske painted coffer...
> 1582...chests of spruce or dansk, the nest contayning three...
> 1586...3 chests of which 2 are flanders and one danske...
> 1587...a Dansk chest wherein my linen doth lie...
> 1590...one lardge Danske chiste with insett worke, ij Danske chistes of furr...
> 1614...a Danske cabonnett inlaid with coloured wood...

Figure 3:357. *Boarded chest. North Italian. Cedar or cypress, 1603-25. Chests of this type were made in great numbers for the English market, and were known as 'Cyprus' chests. This specimen bears the Stuart Royal Arms, and the initials J(ames) R(ex). The decoration is drawn on with a finely-incised line, and is related to similar chests and cupboards with poker work.*

b). 'Cyprus' chests. These were another group of imported softwood chests, likewise easily recognisable to contemporary compilers of inventories. In this case the wood was cypress or cedar, and they were imported in large numbers from Northern Italy, especially the areas of the Southern Alps, Venice, the Adige and Umbria (Figures 3:356 and 357, also Chapter Two, p.165-166). The woods (which are easily confused) were both valued as a protection against moths and other pests, and the chests were used largely to store clothes, linen and bed hangings. Extant examples may vary in size from huge standards of seven feet or more in length, to quite small table

47. This problem, and some conclusions, are reviewed by Peter Thornton in Furniture History, 1971, pp.66-69.

Figure 3:358. *Boarded 'Nonsuch' chest. Anglo-German or German. Oak, with marquetry of various coloured woods, 1580-1630. Chests of this type were imported from the Cologne area, via the Rhine, and were possibly the type known here as 'Flanders' chests. They also seem to have been made by the immigrant 'schreiners' who settled in Southwark and (possibly) Norwich.*

boxes such as that in Figure 3:356. Here, as so often, the decoration is of a traditional nature which derives from Byzantine and early Christian models, but many of the chests made specifically for the English market were decorated with more appropriate motifs. A travelling nobleman, for example, might order his personal coat-of-arms, whilst others were embellished with the arms of the reigning monarch (Figure 3:357).

> 1474...my wryghtyng box of sypresse...
> 1588...fower faier flatt Venetian chests...
> 1618...a sipresse cheast and a nother...

c). 'Flanders' chests. Reference has already been made to Flanders chairs (p.241), and the proposition that 'Flanders' furniture was simply a description of some of the earlier panelled furniture which was imported in the early sixteenth century, before the English joiners had fully established themselves. Certainly much of the first English joined furniture displayed pronounced Franco-Flemish characteristics; but the term must also have been used to distinguish pieces actually imported from (or via) Flanders and the Low Countries. A class of chests which must have come to England by just this route were the elaborate marquetry chests which we now know as 'Nonsuch' chests (Figure 3:358). Although they were later made in England by immigrant German joiners and inlayers (probably in Norwich and Southwark), they were originally imported from Cologne and the Rhineland via Antwerp and the Rhine Estuary.

> 1542...on Flaundres chayer, ij fflaundres kystes...
> 1572...my gret Flaunders chest...
> 1605...3 large Flanders chests, 1 short of waineskote...

Arks and Hutches (Figures 2:124, 3:359-362 and Diagram 2:13d, p.112)

Both these derive from ancient words for chests, the one from the Latin *arca,* and the other from the French *huche.* The connection between them is that both appear to have normally (though not exclusively) been used for the storage of corn, meal and bread. Unfortunately, it is not clear exactly to

Figure 3:359. *Clamped-front meal chest, called a 'hutch' or an 'ark'. English. Riven oak, sixteenth or seventeenth century. The lock and hasp are a later introduction.*

Figure 3:360. *Small hutch or ark. English. Riven oak, sixteenth or seventeenth century.*

which type of furniture each word was used to refer. 'Hutch' was sometimes used for a low cupboard, but both were certainly used for corn chests or grain bins of one sort or another. There is also some regional differentiation, for in the seventeenth century 'hutch' appears mostly in Southern England, whilst 'ark' is more usual in the North (where Arkwright still survives as a common surname). Randle Holme also used 'Arke' to describe a hanging food cupboard or meat safe. In Scotland a meal chest is still called a 'corn-kista'.

In order to arrive at an understandable use for the words, it is necessary to examine the usual type of corn chest as found in the sixteenth and seventeenth centuries. Four examples are given here, and another in Chapter Two. They represent an archaic survival of the medieval clamped-front chest, in which a wide horizontal board is clamped between two vertical stiles; in fact they are often represented optimistically as of fifteenth

Figure 3:361. *Great meal hutch or ark. Welsh. Oak, seventeenth century.*

Figure 3:362. *Great meal hutch or ark. West Wales. Oak, dated 1688.*

century date. The lids were not originally fixed to the base, though some have been fitted with hinges at a later date. Instead, the base acted as a corn bin, and the top could be removed to act as a kneading trough or a hand barrow. This interpretation is reinforced by Cotgrave's dictionary-like definition of 1611, where he gives a hutch as a "Binne, or kneading trough". Most of these arks are devoid of any decoration, and are roughly but soundly constructed from riven oak boards. In Wales, they were still made into the eighteenth century, and examples survive with fully developed fielded-panel construction.

> 1377...a chest called 'Cornencheste'...
> 1397...ij archae pro pane (2 arks for bread)...
> 1485...a grete binne to leye in otes...
> 1597...the hutch in the parlour to lay clothes in...
> the little hutch wherein I use to put my writings...
> the hutch that my evidences lie in...
> 1638...one Corne Binn...one Corn Hutch...
> 1691...In the Boulting House — a kneading trough, a meale
> hutch, a bran tub, foure sives...
> 1713...In the Mill House...a wheat hutch...

In the Midlands and elsewhere, the hutch was used to contain 'boultings' or sieved flour, and may appear as a 'boltying whitche' (1603), 'whitch' being a common rendering of 'hutch' in the Western counties.

Coffers and Trunks (Figures 2:127 and 128, 3:363)

Our ancestors appear to have had little problem in distinguishing between coffers and other forms of chests and boxes, though the nature of that distinction is not always clear to us. Inventory lists often include chests and coffers as clearly separate items. In theory, we know that coffers were made by the coffer maker, whose speciality was the manufacture of chests and trunks made of thin boards and covered with nailed or ironbanded leather or cloth. Yet sometimes, coffers are described simply as 'oaken', whilst others are more akin to iron strong boxes. The association between coffers and money or jewels is a long one. The post of Treasurer or 'Cofferer to the Household' is an ancient Royal Appointment, and Sir William Cope

Figure 3:363. *Coffer or travelling trunk. English. Beech carcase, covered with Russia leather, with brass and iron nails and fittings, late seventeenth century. This is one of the standard products of the coffermaker or trunk-maker, and should be compared with Figures 2:127 and 128. Similar trunks were made over a long period, and were covered in a variety of materials including leather, seal skin, horse hide, velvet, embroidered cloth, turkeywork and marbled, printed or painted papers. The interiors were usually lined with cloth or marbled papers.*

(d.1513), who was Cofferer to Henry VII, adopted as his arms that capacity a device with "three coffers sable".[48] These are shown as black (leather) boxes with gilt (iron) bands, and four green (cloth) straps which can be tied over the lid and sealed. Anyone tampering with the box and its valuable contents must leave evidence in the form of a broken seal (see accompanying drawing).

> 1471... Cofferer of the kinges houshold, wych taketh in charge all the receytes for the tresaurer of houshold, as of money...
> iiij floryns of gelde, fro his privy cofrers...

Randle Holme wrote very disparagingly of coffers and trunks, which he felt "...were first invented to be thus garded by old usurers, and covetous Misers, to keep safely that treasure committed to it...the token of negligence and niggardlyness by over much keeping of worldly pelse and muck..."

The English Cofferers' Ordinance of 1517 lists a variety of baggage chests, standards and trussing-coffers among their products; and although by the eighteenth century the name of the trade was more commonly that of 'trunk maker', the list of products had changed but little.

> 1384... Item un coffre ferré couvert de cuir...(Item an iron-bound coffer covered with leather)
> 1518... my black cofer in the newe chambur...
> 1561... a cofer of woode, carved, paynted, and gilt...
> 1605... one old okne chest with feate, 4 little okne coffers...
> 1634... the great blacke trunke at the bed feete...
> 1667... a great Russia lether trunke, lyned with sarcenett and quilted...
> 1678... a litle seale skynn trunke, to putt in mylady's thinges...
> 1760... Samuel Forsaith, Trunkmaker, London, Makes & Sells all Sorts of strong Iron bound Trunks for travelling in foreign Roads, Sumpters & Portmanteau Trunks, Covered Hampers, Saddle Bags, Jacks, Harvest Bottles; Cases for musical instruments...

One of the coffers in the arms of Sir William Cope (died 1513), from a contemporary drawing in the College of Arms. The straps are for tying and sealing to protect the privacy of the contents. A similar coffer or trunk appears in the portrait of Sir Anthony Mildmay (c.1600) at The Museum of Art, Cleveland, Ohio. See Furniture History, 1971, plate 18.

Figure 3:364. *Boarded chest. English; possibly Northamptonshire. Oak, c.1500. This chest should be compared with Figure 4:2, which still has the original spandrels (for which the peg-holes may be seen here).*

48. Reproduced by F. Gordon Roe, *History of Oak Furniture*, Connoisseur, 1920, p.60.

Figure 3:365. *Boarded chest. English. Oak, early seventeenth century. The absence of a lock is a most unusual feature.*

Figure 3:366. *Boarded chest. English. Oak, mid-seventeenth century. The large flamboyant spandrels are a particularly good feature.*

Boarded and Joined Chests (Figures 3:364-376)

The vast majority of surviving chests are of the simple boarded or the joined varieties. These were the normal form of household storage furniture throughout a considerable period of English history, and most houses possessed at least one chest. Rich households might be equipped with dozens of assorted chests, and even individual chambers are sometimes recorded with half-a-dozen or more.[49] The contents were usually in the form of clothes and linen, but chests were also used for other items which at a later date would have warranted other forms of storage, such as books, weapons and food. Smaller items were stored in a separate compartment or till within the chest (Figure 3:374a), and the till may also have served to hold fresh herbs or lavender bags to help sweeten the clean linen. This form of vertical storage is most inconvenient, since items at the top of the chest have

49. The Nettlecombe inventory of 1526 lists, in the Master's Chamber alone, fourteen chests of different sorts; whilst at Hardwick in 1601, Lady Shrewsbury's Bed Chamber contained twenty-one assorted chests and boxes. In all, her small personal suite of three rooms and the Maid's Chamber could boast no less than forty-seven chests, trunks, boxes, coffers, trussing coffers and standards, besides other 'trunckes' not numbered. The steward who compiled the inventory appears to have had no doubts in distinguishing these different types of receptacle, though his distinctions are largely a mystery to us.

Figure 3:367. *Joined chest. English. Oak, c.1540. This is the rear view of a piece which was intended to stand in the centre of a room, hence it is decorated on both front and back with linenfold panels.*

Figure 3:368. *Joined chest. English. Oak, mid-seventeenth century. The large single panel is unusual.*

Figure 3:369. *Joined chest. English. Oak, early seventeenth century.*

Figure 3:370. *Joined chest. English. Oak, mid-seventeenth century. This piece was intended to stand in the centre of a room, and is decorated on all four sides.*

to be disturbed in order to reach those further down. For this reason the chest of drawers was developed as a more suitable alternative.

> 1592...all that lynnen wch is used to be locked up in my cheaste...
>
> 1600...a long plaine chest wth 2 particions & 2 lockes & keyes...
>
> 1638...one ioyned chest 2 boorded chests, one box. 1£...
>
> 1648...a great chest of elming boarde standing in the lower gallerie for to put therein the bookes...
>
> 1659...one litle Chest Carved, 3s.4d.; one Chist with a lock above, 4s.6d....
>
> 1661...my apparel and bookes with the chest wherein the same are kept...

Figure 3:371. *Joined chest. English. Oak, with inlay, mid-seventeenth century.*

Figure 3:372. *Joined chest. English. Oak, 1580-1630. Heavy mouldings are the only decoration here, apart from the fine lockplate and hasp. Note the dropped centre panel, specially formed to accommodate the ironwork.*

Figure 3:373. *Joined chest. English. Oak, c.1640. Inscribed 'GODS:PROVIDENCE:IS:MINE:INHERITANCE'.*

Figure 3:374. *Joined chest. English; probably Gloucestershire. Oak, c.1630.*

Figure 3:375. *Joined double chest. English. Oak, late seventeenth century.*

Figure 3:374a. *Interior view of chest, showing the fitted till or box, with a very good shaped lockplate, indicating the storage of small valuables or private papers, since tills are not normally fitted with a lock. Other fittings to be found in chests may include small drawers or secret compartments.*

Stylistically, the decoration used on chests follows all the trends which may be found on other pieces of the same dates and regions, with no particularly special or differentiated treatments.

As a group, chests are still very commonly to be found in old country churches, though most of these are of domestic origin, and were deposited in churches in great numbers only during the eighteenth and nineteenth centuries, when the use of chests in the home was largely superseded by the chest of drawers. At least, such comment applies to the large number of seventeenth century joined chests to be seen; but in fact the provision of chests in churches was required by law from a very early date, and many of the medieval examples result from such instructions. In 1166, for example, a royal warrant ordered that a chest should be set up in every church in order to collect contributions toward the Crusades in the Holy Land. These were to have three locks, so that the keys might be held by three responsible persons, and the chest might only be opened in the presence of all three. This set a precedent for church practice, and most later church chests have three locks — one for the priest, and one for each churchwarden.

Figure 3:376a. *(Left) Joined close stool. English; South Yorkshire. Oak, 1650-80. The close stool is easily identified by the deep lid, which allows space inside for a padded or wooden seat.*

Figure 3:376b. *(Right) Boarded close stool or box. English. Oak, late seventeenth century. Close stools of this chest-like form were quite common. Others may be drum shaped, or covered in nailed leather.*

Boxes (Figures 3:377-395)

Small boxes and caskets were made in huge numbers at all dates, and in a fantastic variety of shapes, sizes and materials, though we are concerned here only with wooden boxes. Some were provided for special purposes, such as holding sewing materials, chessmen, writing materials (see Desks), jewels and other valuables; or for carrying objects like chalices (Figure 3:377) or clocks (Figure 3:393). But mostly they were made as simple wooden containers (usually rectangular, though not always), into which might be put goods of any description — gloves, linen, lace, deeds and letters, books, and all the clutter of everyday life.

The construction of most of the common sort of table box is of a rather flimsy nature, consisting of simple nailed or pegged boards. Joined and panelled boxes are quite rare (Figure 3:383), yet the box makers were an incorporation of the Joyners' Company in London, not the Carpenters'; a fact which may explain the high quality of carving to be found on some boxes and boarded chests.

Figure 3:377a. *Boarded chalice box. English. Oak, early sixteenth century. This heavy, solidly-made box has three cylindrical compartments to receive a set of chalices.*

Figure 3:377b. *Reverse view of the box in Figure 3:377a. On the gable end of the lid are four stamped silver marks, which no doubt correspond with the marks on the original contents.*

Figure 3:378. *Boarded box. English or French. Oak, early sixteenth century.*

Figure 3:379. *Boarded box. English. Oak, dated 1673.*

Figure 3:380. *Boarded long box. English, mid-seventeenth century.*

Figure 3:381. *Boarded box. English. Oak, c.1600.*

Figure 3:382. *Boarded box. English. Walnut, c.1640.*

Figure 3:383. *Joined box. English. Oak, dated 1636.*

Figure 3:384. *Boarded box. English. Oak, c.1630.*

Figure 3:385. *Boarded box. American; New England. Oak, c.1680.*

Figure 3:386. *Boarded box. American; New England. Oak and pine, c.1680.*

A box maker planing at his bench. From a mid-seventeenth century broadsheet illustrating various trades.

Figure 3:387. *Boarded box. English. Oak, mid-seventeenth century.*

Figure 3:388. *Boarded box. English. Oak, c.1680.*

Figure 3:389. *Boarded box. American; New England. Oak, c.1680. Compare with Figure 3:397.*

Figure 3:390. *Boarded box. American; Connecticut. Oak and pine, late seventeenth century.*

Figure 3:391. *Boarded box. English; South Yorkshire. Oak, late seventeenth century. An armchair at Conisborough Church has identical carving.*

Figure 3:392. *Boarded box. American; New England. Pine, late seventeenth century.*

Figure 3:394. *Block-printed wallpaper used to line a box. English. Early seventeenth century. The subject is the Royal Arms within the Garter, surrounded by a formal infilling of flowers based on 'blackwork' needlework designs.*

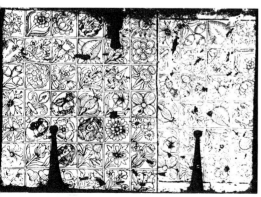

Figure 3:395. *Block-printed wallpaper used to line a box. English. c.1670. The heads of Charles II, Queen Katherine and the Duke and Duchess of York are combined in a diaper pattern with flowers, lions and other formal motifs.*

Figure 3:393. *Boarded carrying case for a clock. English. Oak, c.1675.*

Many of the boxes surviving from the seventeenth and eighteenth centuries still retain the original printed papers with which they were lined. These consist of single sheets printed with woodcut patterns and subjects, usually in black on white, which are pasted inside the box as a decorative lining paper (Figures 3:394, 395 and 403). Some were intended as wallpapers, and may be hand-painted or blocked with further colour. A trade card of c.1690, printed for Edward Butling of Southwark, offers a variety of patterned papers, including some in imitation of Irish stitch, wainscot, marble, damask and turkeywork. These papers may be found not only in boxes, but inside other pieces such as small cupboards and chests of drawers.

1547... a woode boxe wth xii payers of hawkes belles smalle and great, and a fawconer's glove...

1598... her boxe with ruffles and other accessories...

1619... a litle E.O. box, bilonging with the tables...

1620... a box for my Lords bouks...

1681... a long wainscoat box with a payre of sheets & other linnen in it...

Figure 3:396. *Joined chest with drawers. English. Oak, c.1640.*

The Chest with Drawers (Figures 3:396-401)

The box form was developed at the end of the Middle Ages to provide a sliding compartment then known as 'drawing boxes' or 'tills', now more familiar as 'drawers'. Banks of deep square drawers were provided for the storage of papers and document rolls, and several examples survive from the period 1450-1530 in the muniment rooms of certain institutions such as the Vicars Choral at Wells, and Winchester College.[50] They were also adapted for use in movable furniture at an early date, and the famous cupboard in the Burrell Collection, of the early sixteenth century, is perhaps the best and earliest English example from this date (Figure 4:7).

> 1527... A new wainscot cupboard with 2 ambreys and 2 tills,
> carved...

The adoption of drawers in the lower stage of chests was an important and convenient departure: convenient, because they did away with the task of delving right through to the bottom of an otherwise deep chest; and important, because such a step was one of the first stages in the confused lines of development which were eventually to result in the full 'chest of drawers'. The English 'chest with drawers' probably did not appear until c.1600, though foreign craftsmen had made them in England from an earlier date, as witnessed by the fine marquetry chest donated to Southwark Cathedral by Hugh Offley (c.1588-94). Offley was a prosperous London alderman and leather merchant, who died in 1594, though the arms on the chest fix its date of manufacture as probably 1588. He possibly ordered the chest from a German 'schreiner' living in Southwark. Similar chests (though not of such fine quality) are to be found in some English houses such as Hardwick, where a chest with two drawers in the lower portion was mentioned as early as 1568.

> 1599... a great chest or standerd, with drawing chests or boxes
> in it...
> 1601... a great Chest with tills...

50. These examples, and another at St. George's Chapel, Windsor, are discussed by Penelope Eames in Furniture History, 1977.

Figure 3:397. *Joined chest with drawer. American; New England. Oak and pine, c.1680. The carving of the top rail should be compared with the box in Figure 3:389.*

Figure 3:398. *(Right) Joined chest with drawers. American; Connecticut River Valley. Oak and pine, c.1700. The so-called 'Hadley' type.*

Figure 3:399. *Joined chest with drawers. English; North Country. Oak, dated 1722. This chest is entirely original, including the dated panel and the curious feet.*

Figure 3:400. *Boarded chest with drawer. American; East Windsor, Connecticut. Pine and oak, 1670-1730.*

Figure 3:401. *Boarded chest with drawer. Bermuda (English Colonial). Mahogany, c.1750. The decoratively shaped dovetails are a feature of the cabinetwork from Colonial Bermuda, and may also be found in Spanish Colonial Peru.*

Despite the great number of chests of drawers which appeared after the middle of the seventeenth century, the chest with one or two drawers in its base continued to be made in great numbers, especially at the lower end of the social scale, until well into the nineteenth century. Even in great houses, such chests remained in use as 'blanket chests', as witnessed by the examples in mahogany, or with japanned decoration.

vi). Chests of Drawers (Figures 3:402-415)

The fully-developed chest of drawers, i.e. fitted only with drawers, seems to have made its first appearance shortly before 1650. But in trying to trace its genealogy, we find a confusion of pieces which are provided with drawers, and which are difficult to classify. However, two main trends are discernible which have certain common characteristics, and which merge together by about 1675.

a). The first main line of development is the one which appears as a natural sequence to the addition of drawers at the base of a lidded chest. As the multiplicity of drawers increases, so the lidded compartment assumes a less important role, until eventually it is nothing more than a shallow box top (Figures 3:402-404). In its final stage, the box top is replaced by a drawer. These three early examples each take quite a different form. The first is of a very flimsy boarded construction which suggests that it was made by a box maker. The character and execution of the carving is very good indeed, and each stage is rendered with a different pattern. The joined walnut chest is of quite a different character, though the general conformation is the same.

b). The second main line of development derives from the practice of fitting drawers inside an enclosed cupboard or press. Such a piece might be called a "cobberd with tilles" (1601), and the most famous example is undoubtedly the "New Cubborde of Boxes" made for the Corporation of Stratford-upon-Avon in 1594 (discussed on p.49). We should perhaps call it a 'press with drawers'.

Such problems of semantics are not ours alone, for difficulties of nomenclature also beset the original owners of certain items of furniture. The Deed Chest of the Shrewsbury Drapers' Company (Figures 2:5 and 6, and 3:404) is a case in point. We see it now as an early example in the development of the chest of drawers, and when new it must have appeared

369

Figure 3:402. *Boarded chest of drawers with lidded top. English. Oak, c.1630. Probably made by a box maker. The feet are not original. At first glance, this unlikely piece of furniture may not look genuine, but proper examination proves it to be so. The carving is of very good quality, and was designed to accommodate both handles and lock plates.*

Figure 3:403. *(Right) Joined chest of drawers with lidded top. English. Walnut, c.1630.*

Figure 3:404. *Chest with lidded top, enclosing boxes of drawers. English; Shrewsbury. Oak, 1637. This is the Deed Chest of the Shrewsbury Drapers' Company, see Figures 2:5 and 6.*

as an unfamiliar object to its new owners, with the result that they did not quite know what to call it. It consists, obviously, of an enclosed cupboard, containing small removable chests of drawers, and fitted on top with a lidded compartment. When it was first purchased in 1637, the Accountant called it a "chest presse"; but when the new Wardens made their inventory of 1653, they called it a "Cubboard of drawing boxes...and a box on the top." Both phrases describe the piece adequately, but with different emphasis.

In the following piece (Figure 3:405) the drawers follow a more conventional system. Since they are enclosed behind doors, they are completely devoid of any decoration and are fitted with the usual simple iron handles. Original drawers of this type are usually in a very dry and clean state. In these late (1660-1700) enclosed examples, the upper drawer(s) is exposed and decorated in the same manner as the doors, and only the lower half is enclosed (Figures 3:405-407). Some chests of drawers of this date retain the traditional form of the foot, in which the main stiles are extended down to the ground; but a great many have adopted the Dutch/Flemish form of a separate turned ball or bun foot. This, of course, is only in accordance with the general adoption of Dutch fashions for applied decoration, which is almost universal on chests of drawers after c.1640.

One very singular development which seems to have appeared only in New England (examples are noted in Eastern Massachusetts and the New Haven area), was the large standing press cupboard with drawers. This takes the form of a conventional press cupboard in the upper half, having

Figure 3:405. *Joined enclosed chest of drawers. English. Oak and fruitwood, c.1670. Here shown open, revealing the three interior drawers in dry, pristine condition. Unlike the previous figure, the top compartment is also a drawer, not a box with a lifting top.*

Figure 3:406. *Joined enclosed chest of drawers. Anglo-Dutch. Oak, with fruitwood veneers, c.1670.*

Figure 3:407. *Joined enclosed chest of drawers. American; probably Boston, Massachusetts. Red and white oak, cedar, chestnut and black walnut, c.1670.*

Figure 3:408. *Joined press cupboard, with drawers. American; Plymouth, Massachusetts. Oak, pine and spruce, red and black paint, c.1670.*

Figure 3:409. (Left) Joined chest of drawers. English. Walnut and oak, with birch veneers, bone plaques and penwork decoration, c.1670.

Figure 3:410. Joined chest of drawers. English. Oak, c.1680.

Figure 3:411. Joined chest of drawers. English. Oak, 1660-1720.

Figure 3:412. Joined chest of drawers. English. Walnut and ash, 1660-1720.

Figure 3:413. *Joined chest of drawers. American; New England. Oak and walnut, 1680-1720.*

Figure 3:414. *Joined chest of drawers. American; Essex County, Massachusetts. Oak, with pine top, 1680-1700.*

51. One example is given in the *Dictionary of English Furniture* (1924, Vol.II, p.48, fig.I), but this seems to have started life as an open-base livery cupboard of c.1630, to which the over-lapped drawers must have been added about one hundred years later. Figure 4:48 is somewhat similar to the American examples, but the lower half is enclosed by doors.

recessed cupboards fronted by pillars and a shelf, but the lower half is fitted with drawers instead of doors (Figure 3:408, see also Chapter Four). There seems to be no precedent for this type in the British Isles,[51] even though it is a manifestly practical piece of furniture.

In all other respects, the English chest of drawers of ordinary type is remarkably similar to contemporary American examples, both conforming quite closely to the prevalent International Anglo-Dutch styles of 1660-1720 (Figures 3:409-415). Chests of drawers were amongst those items imported

Figure 3:415. *Joined chest of drawers. American; New York. Walnut, 1700-25.*

Figure 3:416. *Joined chest on frame, with drawer. American; Massachusetts. Oak, pine and maple, black paint, c.1680.*

Figure 3:417. *(Left) Joined chest on frame, with drawer. American; Massachusetts. Oak and pine, 1680-1700.*

Figure 3:418. *(Right) Joined chest on frame, with two drawers. English. Oak, 1680-1700. Compare with the side table in Figure 3:244.*

Figure 3:419. *Joined chest of drawers on frame. English. Oak, 1680-1700.*

Figure 3:420. *Joined chest of drawers on stand. English. Oak, black stained details, 1680-1720.*

via Boston at the end of the seventeenth century, though indigenous examples are to be distinguished by their uses of timber and certain regional characteristics (e.g. in the Ipswich-Salem groups, of Essex County, Massachusetts).

Chests of drawers are mentioned in accounts (with increasing regularity) from c.1645 onwards, though they rarely call for any special comment or description:

1661 . . . (Pepys) a fair chest of drawers . . .
1677 . . . a chest with six drawers 8s.6d . . .
1691 . . . a chest of drawers of olive wood . . .
1693 . . . one Wallnutree chest of drawers . . .
1739 . . . a chest of drawers of wainscott vernished . . .
1760 . . . a Chest of Oak Draws colored & varnished £5 . . .

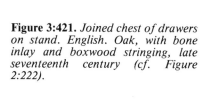
Figure 3:421. *Joined chest of drawers on stand. English. Oak, with bone inlay and boxwood stringing, late seventeenth century (cf. Figure 2:222).*

Figure 3:422. *Carved book lectern. English. Oak, with gilded decoration, early seventeenth century.*

The Chest on Frame (Figures 3:416-421)

Chests of all sorts were usually made to stand on feet which were either simple downward extensions of the framing members, or else they might be provided with separate ball feet which were inserted at the base of the stiles. Sometimes, however, the whole chest might be given more height and grace by raising the whole thing on a joined underframe with stretchers and turned legs of the conventional types. At first the frame was integral with the main structure (Figures 3:416-419), but later it was found more convenient to construct a separate stand, which might have one or more drawers of its own (Figures 3:420 and 421). In the eighteenth century, this idea was to culminate in the tallboy and the chest on chest.

vii). Desks and Bookcases (Library Furniture)

In the sixteenth century the possession of libraries of books, and therefore the necessity for furniture to house them, was almost exclusively the prerogative of the rich and the learned. Almost the only libraries

Figure 3:423. *Carved book lectern. English. Oak, c.1675. A very similar folding lectern is in York Minster.*

Figure 3:424. *Boarded desk box. English. Oak, late sixteenth century. There is a strong retention of Gothic sentiment in the carving, particularly in the spandrel at the side, which should be compared with Figure 3:377a.*

surviving from before this time are in the great colleges or the cathedrals, or similar establishments. Small libraries, the property of country gentlemen, became common later, but few have survived (the Kederminster Library of 1622 is a notable exception, see pp.204-205 and Plate Seven). Almost all the private libraries were extensively reorganised and enlarged in the later seventeenth century, and no self-respecting gentleman of the following century would have thought his house complete without his complement of bookcases and leather-bound volumes.

The high rate of illiteracy amongst the middle and lower classes is quickly evident on perusing their wills and inventories. Very few were possessed of books or writing materials, and the only book which appears at all frequently was, of course, the Holy Bible. Nevertheless, desks and bookshelves are sometimes to be found, sometimes accompanied by the pens, knives and paper necessary for writing. Books were often laid on a cushion for support whilst reading, but a more practical arrangement must have been a sloping wooden surface such as a lectern or the lid of a desk

Figure 3:425. *Boarded desk box. English. Oak, early seventeenth century.*

Figure 3:426a. *Boarded desk box. English. Oak, c.1650.*

Figure 3:426b. *Another view of Figure 3:426a. The run of carving is continued all around the box.*

Figure 3:427. *Boarded desk box. English. Pine, painted with imitation wood grain, c.1700.*

3:428a. Boarded writing box. English. Chestnut, c.1675.

Figure 3:428b. *Another view of Figure 3:428a, showing the fall front and fitted interior.*

box. The standing lectern to be found in churches is a familiar object (though early wooden examples are rare, see Figure 3:188), but a more practical folding table-model was used in the home (Figures 3:422 and 423). These are of an ingenious form of construction, being made from a single board which is cut down the centre and the hinge contrived from the solid. This form is also to be found in the Islamic culture of the Middle East, whence the idea possibly derived.

Desks (Figures 3:424-438)

The distinctive feature of a desk is the provision of a sloping surface on which a book or paper may be placed for reading or writing, usually with a rest at the bottom of the slope to prevent the book from sliding off. Medieval illustrations show book desks and writing desks of great variety, many of which are adjustable in height by some means or other. Almost all of the surviving desks from before c.1675 are of the desk box variety. These were designed to be placed on the lap of the sitter, or on the table before him, and are often of a convenient and portable size. Many are fitted inside with small drawers for pens and ink bottles, seals, wax and sand shakers, and all the varied equipment needed to write a letter in the days before

Figure 3:429a. *Boarded writing box. English. Chestnut, c.1675.*

Figure 3:430. *Boarded desk box. English. Yewtree, early eighteenth century.*

Figure 3:429b. *Another view of Figure 3:429a, showing the fall front and fitted interior.*

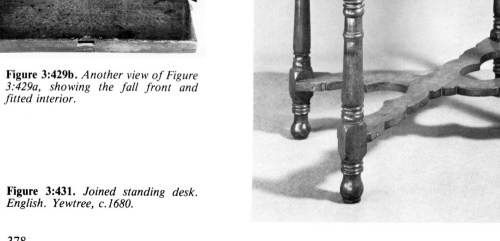

Figure 3:431. *Joined standing desk. English. Yewtree, c.1680.*

Figure 3:432. *Joined standing gateleg desk. Burr yewtree and oak, with inlay, c.1680.*

Figure 3:434. *Joined table with adjustable top. English. Oak, early eighteenth century.*

Figure 3:433. *Joined standing desk. English. Oak, c.1700.*

gummed envelopes and quick-drying ink.

Towards the end of the seventeenth century, desk boxes (or writing slopes) began to be made with their own integral underframing, in the form of the standing desk or desk on frame. In polite society the French terms *bureau* or *scrutoire* were readily adopted to describe this piece, but the old term 'desk' seems to have kept favour in more robust and provincial circles, and has survived until the present day in its workaday forms of school and office. In the earlier examples of standing desk, the concept of the desk box as a separate entity is retained, in the form of an overhang at each side (see Figures 3:431-433) which sets the box visually apart from its stand, even if they are structurally one unit.

1527...a deske coverid wth black velvette and garnished withe
       gilte nayles...
1547...2 deskes havinge a paire of sycssores a payer of compas
       and a penne knyfe...
1584...a littel holowe desk lyk a coffer, whereupon men do
       write...
1601...three Deskes covered with lether, whereof one a great
       one, a lyttle deske to write on guilded...
1632...1 Deske wth gloves, knives and other things in it...
1633...two Deskes, and a quire of paper...
1671...one deske, a litle Table and a book Shelfe...
1689...In the Hall...bookes, and a writing-deske...
1694...one inlaid Scrutoire, one Brass-Desk for Bookes...
1699...one bewroe from France...

1743...a wainscott bueroe and bookcase...
1762...one oak beaureau...
1768...A wainscot desk and bookcase, stained red and vernished...

The lids of desk boxes were always hinged at the top, so that the user needed only to lift it to a horizontal position, to be able to gain access to the interior without disturbing his writing paper. But the standing desk was a different matter. Here it was found more convenient to hinge the lid at the bottom, so that the user might fold it over towards himself. The open lid is supported on lopers which draw out from the frame, enabling the user to sit with his feet well clear of the stretchers, and providing a flat work surface. On some examples the lid is supported on gatelegs which swing out from the frame (Figure 3:432), allowing even more leg space.

The familiar fully-enclosed desk or bureau of the eighteenth century type made its appearance before 1700. This eminently practical piece of furniture provided a variety of storage in large drawers in the main carcase, and in small drawers and pigeon-holes behind the slope. Earlier examples also have a space or well beneath the desk top, which is reached via a slide. Others may be fitted with an enclosed bookcase which sits atop the main desk (Figure 3:436). A later development was the secretary drawer, which slides out from the main carcase, has a hinged front, and is fitted inside with smaller drawers and compartments. These are usually found only in chests of drawers or chests on chests (Figure 3:437), but an unusual example is shown here fitted to a low dresser (Figure 3:438).

Figure 3:435. *Joined (dovetailed board) desk. English. Oak, mid-eighteenth century.*

Figure 3:436. *Joined (dovetailed board) desk and bookcase. English. Oak, mid-eighteenth century.*

Figure 3:437. *Chest on chest, with secretary drawer. Oak, c.1780. The fitted drawer is designed to be used in the standing position and most examples have this fitment in the top level of the base half.*

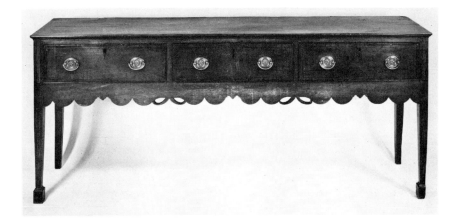

Figure 3:438a. *Joined low dresser, with secretary drawer. English. Oak, late eighteenth century.*

Figure 3:438b. *Detail of Figure 3:438a, showing the secretary drawer opened.*

Writing Tables (Figures 3:439-443)

The provision of special flat-topped tables for any purpose other than the most general was a rare thing before the Restoration, other than the games tables and oyster tables already mentioned. The appearance of writing tables and others at the end of the seventeenth century was indicative of a new sense of the social functions of furniture, though it is not always easy, at this distance in time, to divine the exact purpose of any given piece. By this token, the table in Figure 3:439 was evidently intended to be sat at, since the front stretcher is purposefully omitted; but we cannot be certain whether it was intended as a dressing table or a writing table. With the following example we are on firmer ground, for it is fitted with a standish-well and recesses for candlesticks.

Tables still survive which formed part of the original furnishings of pre-Restoration libraries, but like the table in the Kederminster Library (Plate Seven) they are not specially adapted in any way for the purposes of writing. But the library table in Figure 3:442 represents a novel departure from this principle. It is in the Bibliotheca Pepysiana at Magdalene College, Cambridge; and though it was not mentioned by Pepys at the time he bought the matching bookcases (q.v.), it was no doubt also supplied by

Figure 3:439. *Joined writing table. English. Burr yewtree, c.1680.*

Figure 3:440. *Joined gateleg writing table. English. Burr yewtree and walnut, c.1680.*

Figure 3:441. *Joined gateleg writing table. English. Oak, 1680-1720.*

'Sympson the Joyner' at the same time (August, 1666) or soon after. Here, the pedestal supports are in fact glazed bookcases with a series of false drawer fronts, but at a later date the form of the pedestal library table became very popular (Figure 3:443), fitted with real drawers.

1552...a joyned bourde to write uppon...
1697...a ffolding writing Table inlaid with white and covered with greene velvete...
1711...a Walnut Tree writing Table...
1767...a large wainscote Library Table...

Figure 3:442. *Joined library table. English; London. Oak, c.1666-70. Probably made by Thomas Sympson, a London joiner, for Samuel Pepys, the diarist.*

Figure 3:443. *Joined library table. English. Oak, c.1740.*

Figure 3:444. *The Bibliotheca Pepysiana, Magdalene College, Cambridge. The room contains the twelve bookcases and books which had originally occupied Pepys' own library at his house by the watergate at the foot of Buckingham Street in London.*

Figure 3:445. *Joined bookcase. English; London. Oak, probably 1666. This is bookcase no. 5 of the group of twelve at the Bibliotheca Pepysiana. They are virtually identical to each other in construction and decoration, and may be compared closely with other examples, such as Figure 3:446.*

52. The book presses at the Kederminster Library (Plate Seven) are rare examples of these in their original state. Some open bookshelves of c.1630, with carved cornices, may be seen in the Library at Winchester Cathedral. These were installed in 1669, and are thought to have been brought from Farnham Castle, a palace of the Bishops of Winchester.
53. Furniture History, 1971, p.98, and footnote 10.

Bookcases (Figures 3:444-447)

Allusion has already been made to the domestic convention of storing books in chests, though even poorer homes could sometimes boast a bookshelf; but in the great libraries it had long been recognised that the best way to store books was in cases of shelves or cup-boards, or in presses or aumbries which could be enclosed by doors or curtains. In this way, the books could be more effectively catalogued, and protected from damp, dust, light and wear. Like many of his contemporaries, Samuel Pepys was as much concerned with the safety of his fine bookbindings as with any other aspect of his library; and it was probably for that reason he commissioned the famous series of bookcases which now grace the Bibliotheca Pepysiana.

Earlier bookcases were either in the form of open shelves (called 'book desks'), or they were enclosed in panelled cupboards (referred to as 'book presses').[52] Pierced tracery panels had been used in a bookcase made for Archbishop Laud at St. John's College, Oxford, in 1636; but Pepys chose a very modern form of glazed doors for his presses. In July 1666 he spent a morning with 'Sympson the Joyner' discussing the design and fitting of the presses, and a month later they were installed in his house; which suggests that they were then a standard product of Simpson's workshop. Very similar examples are known from other houses, such as Cuckfield Park, Sussex, and Dyrham Park, Gloucestershire (Figure 3:446). These may well be from the same, or a neighbouring, workshop, In fact, Thomas Povey, many of whose possessions went to Dyrham after his death, was a friend of Pepys and may have used the same joiner.

'Sympson the Joyner' has been variously identified as both Christopher and Thomas, but Benno Forman notes that the only reference to a 'Simson' in the records of the London Joyners' Company at the time the Pepys bookcases were made, is to a "Thomas Simson, joiner and citizen of London", who is noted in an apprenticeship deed of 1657, and who was still alive in 1669.[53]

In the eighteenth century, large bookcases in heavy architectural styles were fashionable accessories in the country house, though oak examples are

Figure 3:446. *Joined bookcase. English; London. Oak, 1665-70. Now at Dyrham Park, Gloucestershire. Probably made for Thomas Povey, resident in London, and a friend of Pepys. It is virtually identical to those in the Bibliotheca Pepysiana.*

not common in a fully-fledged form. Figure 3:447 is at Leeds Castle, Kent, and is a fine country-made specimen of c.1750.

1480...the bookes...had been kepte dylygently in an almarye...

1684...6,000 volumes, in great order in wainscott presses...

1694...Six Wainscot Cases and Bookes in them...

viii). Beds

The remarkable stone bed-nooks at Skara Brae, in the Orkneys (c.1500 B.C.), set the scene for the earliest and longest surviving forms of built-in and enclosed bedsteads, which continued to be made in Western Britain, Scandinavia, Holland and Brittany until less than one hundred years ago. These wooden cupboard bedsteads, which might be either free-standing or built-into alcoves in the house, were designed to provide both privacy and warmth in harsher climates. In Britain, they are chiefly found in Wales and

Figure 3:448. *Joined built-in cupboard beds. English; Waitby, Westmorland. Oak, 1650-1720. The large pairs of doors, ventilated by panels of turned spindles, each enclose a bed space. This and the following examples are derived from a much older tradition of built-in beds.*

Figure 3:449. *Fireplace with joined built-in cupboard bedstead. Welsh; Kennixton, Llangenydd, Glamorganshire. The bedstead and its attached settle flank the fireplace in this farmhouse from the Gower Peninsula. Quilts and bedding can be seen inside the bedstead. Compare this arrangement with the house-plan in Diagram 1:2e.*

Figure 3:450. *Joined built-in cupboard bedstead. Oak, elm and pine, early eighteenth century. This is the bedstead from the previous figure, here shown closed.*

Figure 3:451. *Joined standing cupboard bedstead. Welsh. Pine, c.1800. The whole framework is designed to be easily dismantled for removal, being held together by iron hooks.*

54. This simplified nomenclature of the parts of a bed is complicated by at least one change in meaning: the headboard was known as the 'tester' in the Middle Ages, but the word was later used to refer to the canopy or 'celour'.

North-West England (Figures 3:448-451). They vary greatly in detail, according to date and locality, but from the outside they normally assume the appearance of a large cupboard, usually with some provision for ventilation in the form of pierced panels or open rows of spindles. The doors may be hinged in the normal way, or (more conveniently) they may be made to slide, as in the two Welsh examples shown here. The bed from the Gower has a very cosy arrangement whereby it is closely associated with the fireplace. The occupants have a good close view of the fire, and the front of the bedstead has an attached settle for daytime use (Figure 3:449).

1594... In the stable...a cubborde bedstede...

Tester Bedsteads (Figures 3:452-465a)

The need for warmth and privacy remained a prime consideration in the design of bedsteads right through to at least the eighteenth century, particularly in the great houses and even Royal Palaces. The middle class farmer or merchant was usually provided with a small self-contained bedchamber, but in the great houses most of the rooms were of a semi-public nature. This meant that, not only were they open to access by all and sundry, but the succession of lofty rooms which opened into each other encouraged draughts.

For these reasons, most bedsteads were enclosed, and the use of fabric curtains became standardised at an early date. The medieval great bedstead was perhaps the most important piece of furniture in the domestic scale, but it was typified more by its use of fabrics than by the wooden structure itself. The bed consisted essentially of three elements: the bedstock or base on which the bedding was laid; the dosser or headboard which stood up against the wall; and the tester or canopy which formed a horizontal roof over the bed.[54] Even at an early date, the tester might be supported by posts rising

Figure 3:452. *(Left) Joined tester bedstead. Welsh. Oak, c.1505. This is the great bed of Sir Rhys ap Thomas of Dynefwr, Llandeilo, Carmarthenshire (d.1527). Only the centre portions of the four posts and the three tester valances are original in this ludicrous rearrangement. The valances are shown in detail in Figures 3:453a, b and c.*

Figure 3:453a. *Tester valance (foot end). The holes drilled along the top to take bed ropes are a later addition, dating from the time when the valances were lowered to form a bedstock.*

Figure 3:453b. *Tester valance (side). The tenons which originally entered the tops of the posts are clearly visible, with their peg holes.*

Figure 3:453c. *Tester valance (side). The horseman with a lance near the extreme left may be tentatively identified as Sir Rhys ap Thomas himself.*

Figure 3:453a

Figure 3:453b

Figure 3:453c

Figure 3:454. *Joined tester bedstead. English; probably Central Lancashire. Oak, 1500-21. Made for Thomas Stanley, Earl of Derby (either the 1st or 2nd earl). This photograph shows the bed in its uncleaned and unrestored state. Some of the carving is spurious, and the arrangement of the bedstock has since been altered. It is thought that one of the griffin finials may be original. See Figure 3:457.*

Figure 3:455a. *Joined headboard, with pierced panels (detail of Figure 3:457). This is the present (cleaned) state of the bed, which reveals heavy traces of the original red and green paint.*

Figure 3:455b. *(Left) Detail of Figure 3:455a. The centre knop of the left-hand post, with the Stanley badge — an eagle preying on a swaddled child.*

Figure 3:455c. *(Right) Detail of Figure 3:455a. The centre knop of the right-hand post, with the badge of the Isle of Man (a Stanley tenure) — the Three Armoured Legs.*

Figure 3:456. *Fragments of the headboard posts from a tester bed. These bear the initials 'T' and 'S', and were perhaps from a bed which was initially the property of the Stanleys. They are certainly from the same workshop as the present Thomas Stanley bed.*

from the foot of the bedstock; but since so many medieval testers consisted only of fabrics, they were often supported by strings from the ceiling of the room.

But we are more concerned here with beds of the sixteenth century and later, and therefore with wooden bedsteads, in which the curtains and fabrics are a secondary consideration. The wooden tester and its supporting posts would seem to have made a return to favour around the end of the fifteenth century, though hardly any physical evidence remains to show us how they were constructed, or what they looked like. It seems likely that the first transition was a stage at which the fabric tester was retained over the bed, and carved wooden tester valances were placed at either side, supported by four posts (or two footposts and a headboard). This is perhaps a correct interpretation of the original form of the great bed of Sir Rhys ap Thomas of Dynefwr (Figures 3:452 and 453), whose armchair we have already seen (Figure 3:28 and details).

A few early sixteenth century bedsteads survive (such as Figures 3:457 and 458, and the bed at Saffron Walden Museum), but none retains clear traces of the original form of the tester. For this reason the Rhys ap Thomas bed is a valuable relic. The bed probably dates from about the turn of the century (1505-10), though only the three tester valances and the four posts are extant. It is shown here in the rather ludicrous form endowed on it by later seventeenth century and nineteenth century 'restorations', when the valances were put down to the base and the posts mounted above them. All the other woodwork is spurious and unrelated. We have to imagine the valances once again held up by the posts. The original nature of the dosser is not clear, but the posts are in their original form and they may have supported a fabric hanging more or less as shown. The decoration of the valances is most interesting, comprising some deep bas-relief carving of

Figure 3:457. *(Left) Joined tester bedstead. English; probably Central Lancashire. Oak, 1500-21. This is the Thomas Stanley bed, in its present restored state. See Figure 3:454.*

Figure 3:458 *(Above) Joined tester bedstead. English; probably Central Lancashire. Oak, 1500-30. This is the bed discovered by Shaw at Lovely Hall, near Blackburn. The form of the tester is completely conjectural. The knops of the posts are decorated with crosses, except for one, which bears the initials 'R' and 'J', conjoined with a lovers' knot.*

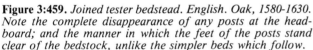

Figure 3:459. *Joined tester bedstead. English. Oak, 1580-1630. Note the complete disappearance of any posts at the head-board; and the manner in which the feet of the posts stand clear of the bedstock, unlike the simpler beds which follow.*

Figure 3:460. *Joined tester bedstead. English. Oak, mid-seventeenth century. A simpler and slightly later bed than the previous example, representative of the usual quality of bed to be found in middle class English homes.*

soldiers, horsemen and other figures, which probably depict some of the exploits of Sir Rhys and his friends. There would certainly have been some Welsh bowmen amongst his contingent at Bosworth, and the men shown in the carvings include longbowmen, crossbowmen and a diminutive harpist. The posts are divided into a series of diapers, which enclose variously the Tudor(?) Rose, heads, figures, and Sir Rhys's own coat-of-arms (Figure 3:27b).

By a strange coincidence of history, the following bed (Figure 3:454-457) was possibly made for a man who was also present at Bosworth in 1485, and in equal prominence to Sir Rhys ap Thomas. This was Sir Thomas Stanley, who personally stooped to pick up the crown that had fallen from the head of the dead Richard III, and placed it upon the head of Henry Tudor, henceforth Henry VII. Stanley, who must have been well acquainted with Sir Rhys ap Thomas, was immediately created the first Earl of Derby. The Stanley bed probably dates from c.1500-21, and bears many small armorial devices with the achievements of the Stanleys and their allies. These are to be found on the faces of each of the knops which punctuate the posts, giving fourteen devices in all.

The most important of these are the head-posts (Figure 3:455). On the middle stage is the Stanley badge itself, which they inherited from Lathom (an eagle preying on a swaddled child, see also Figure 4:53), and the three armoured legs of the Isle of Man (the Stanleys had their main estates in Lancashire and the Isle of Man). Below these are some initials: on the left is a letter 'T', which might stand for either the 1st or 2nd earl (both Thomas); and on the right is another 'T' which is conjoined by a lovers' knot to its companion (now unfortunately obliterated). The 2nd earl, grandson of the

Figure 3:461. *Joined tester bedstead. English. Oak, 1650-1700.*

Figure 3:462. *Joined tester bedstead. English. Oak, mid-seventeenth century.*

Figure 3:463. *Joined tester bedstead. English; Yorkshire. Oak, with inlay, c.1680.*

Figure 3:464. *Joined tester bedstead. Welsh. Oak, dated 1658, but probably earlier. The inscriptions read: 'DEATH' (over a scratch drawing of a figure with bow and arrow) and 'IAMES PRICE — MAY 4 — 1658'. The construction and decoration are both extremely crude, and the cut form of the posts is interesting.*

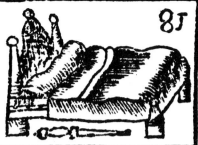

Figure 3:465a and b. *Woodcut illustrations from Randle Holme, 'Academie of Armory', 1649.*
"80 ...a Bed Royall, the vallance, curtaines (turned about the posts) and counter pane laced and fringed about: with a foote cloth of Turky worke about it: the Tester adorned with plumbes...
"81 ...this is a bed prepared for to lodge in, but having no Tester...In the base of this square ly's a Bed staffe, of some termed a Burthen staffe..."

1st earl (who died in 1504), is perhaps the more likely candidate for the original owner, which provides a closer dating of 1504-21 for the manufacture of the bed; though the possibility remains that the bed may have been made for the 1st earl, prior to his death in 1504.

The bed was bought in auction as a 'a pile of carved wood' some six years ago, after a chequered history. When first put together, it appeared as in Figure 3:454, complete with various nineteenth century additions and repairs. It has now been thoroughly cleaned (which revealed heavy traces of the original red and green paint), and now appears as in Figure 3:457. The tester has here been conjecturally restored as a simple cloth canopy, and no further clue may be obtained from a very similar bed (Figure 3:458), which was first noted by Henry Shaw in his *Specimens of Ancient Furniture* in 1836. Shaw noted that the original tester was then missing, and it has since acquired the present fanciful 'restoration'. This bed is known as the Lovely Hall bed (after the house near Blackburn, Lancashire, where Shaw drew it), and was discovered locally in Central Lancashire. This makes all the more interesting the similarities between the two beds, since they both belong to the same area (the Stanley bed is first tentatively recorded at Rochdale Manor). The similarities are so striking, especially in the details of the headboard, that they must derive from the same workshop, somewhere in Central or South Lancashire. The Stanleys may have had other similar beds, for in the Victoria and Albert Museum are the remains of identical posts (Figure 3:456), with initials 'T' and 'S'.

Whatever the form of their original testers, whether of wood or fabrics, the remaining parts of these beds are set very much in the form followed by tester bedsteads for the next one hundred and fifty years. The headboard is a solidly-made panelled construction, though it still has vestigial posts of the medieval type; the tester is supported by two foot-posts; and the bedding is laid on a bedstock made of heavy bars framed together. The fully-developed Elizabethan bed is exemplified in Figure 3:459. The vestigial posts on either side of the head are no longer present, and, as with all important beds of this class, the foot of the bedstock stands separately from the posts. In terms of decoration, this bed is more restrained than some, but it is none the less representative of the richer middle classes of c.1575-1650.

Harrison wrote eloquently of the general improvements in comfortable bedding in the middle part of the sixteenth century (see Appendix I), and it is in bedsteads of this type that the improved bedding might be found. The bedstock was provided with a series of holes, through which a tight mesh of ropes was strung. On this was laid a woven rush mat or mattress, and on top of this was laid a flock or feather bed. Pillows and bolsters were piled up at the head, so that the sleeper lay in a half-sitting position (this is why the lower part of the headboard is rarely decorated, since it would normally be hidden by bedding). On top of this, the sleeper was provided with a series of sheets, blankets, 'ruggs' and quilts. All these accessories were provided by the upholder, and the furnishing of the bed was not complete without a set of curtains, valances and (sometimes) lower valances or 'pentes'. The curtains hung from rails or wires which passed around the edge of the tester.

> 1509...a counterpoynt of popynjaye and blonkett, for a trussyng bed, and a trussyng bedstede...
>
> 1541...i trussing bed of wynscot wth iiii pillors carved...
>
> 1586...A grene fyelde bed of walnutt tree, with a canopy of greene Saye, 5 curtyns with gilt belles, a green Irish rugg coverlett, a matte, a fetherbed, a bolster, 2 pillowes, 3 white blanketts, 6 bedstaves...
>
> 1590...a turned trusinge bed corded with a teaster uppon the head and irones belonginge to it which the courtinges showld runne upon...
>
> 1601...a bedstead seeled with tester of wood and turned postes...
>
> a bedstead wth turned postes fluted...
>
> 1624...A bedsteade of cutwirke, A teaster and vallans of black and cremysine velvet and frindged with cremysine silke and golde, Curtaines of red and yallowe changeable taffitie, One downe bed, a bowlster, ij pillowes, and ij wollen blanckettes, One red rugge, one quilte of cremysine sarcenet...
>
> 1666...a very large Bedstead with embroidered curtains and valence of broadcloth, lined with carnation-coloured sarcenet, and 7 plumes in the bedtester...
>
> 1690...one featherbed and bedstead, one flock bed and matt, 2 blancets, one coverlid, curtains and valyants, 6 bed sticks...
>
> 1719...a carved bedstead, a feather bed, two bolsters, five pillows, three blanketts, one quilt, a sett of curtain rods...

Bedsteads are frequently referred to as 'trussing' or 'field' beds, though it is by no means clear what these terms mean. They may both be different kinds of travelling beds, which can be taken apart or folded for journeys (though in fact all large beds were designed to be taken apart when necessary. The major joints were held with removable pegs or iron hooks, and the roped base held the structure tight). We have met the term 'trussing' in relation to baggage chests, and Katherine of Aragon possessed not only a trussing bedstead, but also two suitable "lether cases to trusse it". A French-made campaign bed with a sloping tester, of the seventeenth century, which survives in the Nordiska Museet (Stockholm), may resemble earlier English models such as the "slope little bedsted for the fielde" owned by the Earl of Leicester in 1588. The frame of this travelling bed is completely collapsible, and the tent-like hangings pack up with the parts of the frame into a very small space. Most Elizabethan references to 'field beds' clearly indicate, however, something much more elaborate and permanent than a simple campaign bed.

One item of bedroom equipment which makes a frequent (if somewhat mysterious) appearance, is the group of six bedstaves. They are also referred to as bed sticks or burthen staves, but so far no example has been positively identified as such, and their usage is slightly problematical. Yet there seems no reason to doubt Dr. Johnson's definition of a bedstaff as "...a wooden pin stuck anciently on the sides of a bedstead to hold the cloaths from slipping on either side..." The huge pile of bedding and bedclothes in common use must have required some form of restraint. Many extant beds have a series of holes drilled in the upper side of the bedstock to receive the staves. Not all beds have them, but not all inventories mention bedstaves. They are normally only found in the chambers of rich or refined persons, who we might expect to be better supplied with soft bedding than the poorer classes. In 1586, the house of Sir Edward Littleton in Worcestershire contained nine bedchambers for the various members of the household and servants who were living-in. The contents are described in full,[55] but only the best rooms are provided with a complement of six bedstaves each. The servants' rooms (including a bedstead in the stable) have only simple bedding with no bedstaves. They would seem to have been made in both long and short versions, and the former were no doubt useful for beating and settling the great floppy feather beds. Randle Holme actually illustrated a turned bedstaff (Figure 3:465b), but failed to enlighten us as to its purpose. It is possible that the woodcut in Figure 3:468b gives us the only noted picture of a bedstaff actually in use, holding back the clothes on the great tester bed.

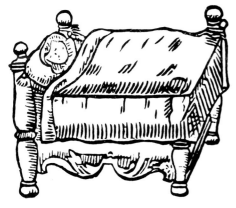

Figure 3:466. *Memorial brass, in Boxford Church, Suffolk. Inscribed to the infant David Bird, February 1606. He lies in a low bedstead with four turned posts.*

> 1586...a fyelde bedstede with a canopy...a fetherbed, a bolster, 2 pillowes, 2 white blanketts, a coverlette of tapestrye worke, 6 bedstaves...
> 1603...6 coloured turned bedstaves in a case of wood... 6 large turned bedstaves...
> 1626...all the furniture in the twelve poor scholars' chambers, yt is to say six bedsteads, sixe mattresses, six feather beds, three dozen bedstaves and six pewter potts...

Randle Holme also shows the seventeenth century habit of mounting the tester with finials or plumes of feathers (Figures 3:465a). This was especially prevalent with the great upholstered beds at the end of the century, but it was also found at an earlier date, the plumes being known as *panaches:*

> 1600...fower guilt topps for the iiii corners of ye bed teaster...
> 1649...a Bed Royall...the Tester adorned with plumbes ...Tester Bobbs of Wood...
> 1652...the pennaches or tufts of plumes belonging to one of her beds...

Half-headed Bedsteads (Figures 3:465b-467)

Although they were frequently mentioned in inventories, half-headed bedsteads are now quite rare in their genuine form. This is the low form of the bedstead, in which the headboard rises to no great height above the pillows, the footposts are restricted to simple turned or carved terminals, and there is no tester. It would appear that half-tester bedsteads had made

55. Quoted in full by John West, op. cit., pp.109-115.

Figure 3:467a. *Joined half-headed bedstead. English. Oak, dated 1669. Whilst tester beds were provided with expensive curtains (see Figure 2:126), a low bed such as this could not be, though in the seventeenth century many people questioned the wisdom of sleeping in a 'naked' bed.*

Figure 3:467b. *Joined headboard from a half-headed bedstead. English. Oak, c.1630. Despite some damage and repair, the form of the low headboard is clear.*

an appearance at an early date, but none have survived from the seventeenth century or earlier. Some quite highly-decorated versions of the half-headed beds were produced for elevated members of society (such as the bed made for Sir Richard Shuttleworth, which is still at Gawthorpe Hall, Burnley, Lancashire); but since the absence of curtains gave no opportunity for privacy or display, their use was largely restricted to the yeoman and lower classes. Many examples are extremely plain, and some have survived because of their use in almshouses and similar institutions (see the bedstead from Castle Rising Almshouses, now at Strangers' Hall, Norwich).

The two early cuts shown here (Figures 3:465b and 466) are the usual type, with simple turned posts and a low headboard. Unfortunately, Randle Holme's description is here slightly at variance with his illustration. He rightly says that it is "...a Bed...having no Tester...", but he goes on to say that they also termed truckle beds, though these must obviously differ in important details (see below).

1609...2 halfe headed bedds, 14s.; i halfe headed Joyne bed, 12s.6d...

1621...one join bedstead, one half bedstead...

1635...one halfeheaded bedsteddle with one small featherbed and feather boulster, one blanket, one ould coverlid, XXs...

1724...In the Garretts, 2 olde halfe headed bedsteads, 2 old flockbeds...

The last two beds were apparently relegated to the servants' use, and a great variety of bedding arrangements was to be found among the labouring and servant classes. Where they had bedsteads at all, these were either of poor and simple boarded construction, or they were sturdy old-fashioned relics handed down from their masters. Conditions among the poor (the majority of the population by some definitions) were such that bedding consisted at best of straw pallets laid upon the floor; whilst many servants and apprentices slept under the kitchen table, the shop counter, or their own work benches. In most houses of any size, the most important house servants had chambers of their own, whilst the menial grades slept in the attics and garrets. Farm hands and other outworkers were often provided with a bednook and straw in the stable loft.

> 1607... In the Manes Chamber, 2 borded bedsteads, 2 flock-
> beds,
> In the Maydes Chamber, 3 borded bedsteads, 3 flock-
> beds...

Household servants frequently made use of convenient chairs or settles on which to sleep, and we are reminded of the medieval habit of bedding down on large chests or tables; but in the eighteenth century, a number of folding beds were specially made which outwardly resembled desks or chests of drawers, and which were folded out for use at night. But these were not a Georgian innovation, for as early as 1601 there were at Hardwick Hall three "bedstedes to turn up like Chestes". These were kept beside Lady Shrewsbury's chamber door, and were presumably for the use of her personal maidservants.

Truckle Beds (Figures 3:468 a and b)

We are considering a period in which personal servants (valets and maids) enjoyed a very close relationship with their employers. A measure of this intimacy can be drawn from the fact that personal servants frequently slept in the same room as their masters, separate provision being made by the presence of a truckle bed (also called a trundle or pallet bedstead, or a wheelbed). The latter term pinpoints their essential feature, and although very few examples have survived, certain descriptions do agree on the form they usually took.

Figure 3:468a. *Joined truckle bedstead. Welsh; Gelli, Glamorganshire. Oak, seventeenth century. A pair of hinge stubs remain to show the former presence of a folding headboard. This rare survival was designed to roll sideways under a high bed.*

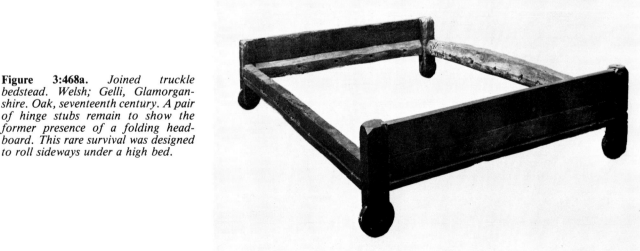

Figure 3:468b. *Woodcut illustration from a mid-seventeenth century broadsheet. English. The amorous couple are seated on a truckle bed or wheelbed, the wheel of which is clearly visible. Despite the high headboard, it is apparently intended to be stored away under the great posted tester bed on the left. (Could that be a turned bedstaff stuck into the frame of the tester bed, holding back the bedclothes to give the bed an airing during the day?)*

The bedstead in Figure 3:468a must be quite typical of this simple piece of furniture, which consists of a low frame set on wheels. The truckle was stored under the high bed during the daytime, to be wheeled out at night on its wooden castors. In 1662, Pepys recorded on one occasion that he went "...to bed all alone, and my Will in the truckle bed..." When staying at Brampton in 1669, he recorded that the maid, Deb Willet, slept in the truckle bed and he and his wife in the "high bed" in the same room. In the light of the rare occurrence of any reference to children's beds, we may also infer that children often slept in their parents' room on a truckle bed. The relationship between the truckle and the main bed is confirmed by the frequency with which they are found together:

1586...A fyelde bedstede wth a canopy, a truckle sheet to lay under a bed...

1608...In the Hall Chamber, 1 joined bed, 1 joined trundle bed...

...In the Seller (? solar), on joynd bedd wth. a joynd Trocle bedd...

1611...a greate posted bedsteadle, a trundlebedsteadle to it...

1617...One joined bedstedd, one truckle bedstedde...

1638...One Bedstead wth featherbed & trundlebed With Furniture belonging...

1649...Such are termed Truckle beds, because they trundle under other beds...

1657...One testerbed with a fetherbed and furniture thereto belonging,
One trundellbed with a flockbed and furniture thereto belonging...

1660...little trundel beds under the greate beds, which were for the gentlemen's men...

1679...a wheilbed, corded, with a flockbed...

1690...Two joined bedstedes with mattes & cordes; two payer of curtaines with valliantes & curtaine roddes, one pallet bedsted...

1763...a Trundlebedstead 60/-...

ix). Children's Furniture

Modern child psychology has shown that young children have consistent and positive characteristics of their own, and that in order to grow up as normal adults they have to pass through a process of maturation which involves complicated rituals of learning and development. But in the sixteenth and seventeenth centuries a far less sophisticated view was commonly taken of the place occupied by children in the greater scheme of things. It was generally held that children are nothing more than miniature adults, who need only the edifying process of moral and practical instruction in order to fit them for their place in the world. Of course, a great many loving parents treated their offspring with greater affection and sympathy than such a harsh comprehension might suggest; but this simplistic view is amply reflected in children's books and clothing, and in the furniture provided for their use in the seventeenth century.

Apart from the more obvious physical limitations of size and dexterity, early children's furniture makes few concessions to childish needs. The decoration of such items as cradles and high chairs follows the normal fully-developed styles to be found on adults' furniture; and with the sole exception of cradles, almost all early children's furniture was designed with an educational purpose in mind, though such education was somewhat severely limited to an introduction into the habits and customs of adulthood. The childish need for play (for both recreation and manipulative learning) was barely catered for, though most small girls must have had a doll or two (Figure 3:469), and simple toys were common enough.

A room specially set aside as the nursery was to be found in only the more affluent households of the Middle Ages and later, and even if the room was not so-called, it might be recognised by its list of contents:

Figure 3:469. *Carved doll. English. Oak, mid-seventeenth century. Probably made by a professional furniture carver, perhaps as a regular item of his stock-in-trade.*

> 1434...a litel tabel peynted trestelwise; also a litel joyned stoll for a child, & a nother joyned stoll, large for to sitte on whanne he cometh to mannes state; also a litel cofur to putte in his smalle thynges...
>
> 1567...The Nursere. One trussing bedd (? for the nurse), One trundle bedd wth a fetherbedd, a mattres, ij blankette, ij shetts...
>
> 1601...In the Nurserie: too mattrisses, too fetherbedes being little ones...

More usually, items of children's furniture are noted in the rooms used by their parents, such as "...the childrens dynyng table, and 2 squarre little stoles..." in the 'Litle Dynyng Chamber' at Paget Place in 1552.

Cradles (Figures 3:470-474)

We have already seen the flat-bottomed wicker cradle or bassinet (Figure 2:33) which was intended to sit flat upon the floor, but mothers have always found it advantageous to be able to rock the cradle whilst engaged in more productive tasks. If the mother is occupied with knitting or spinning, she is easily able to maintain the momentum of the cradle with a nudge from her elbow or foot. Two methods of mounting cradles were commonly used: they might be suspended between two posts, so that the cradle is free to swing (Figures 3:470-472); or they might be mounted on wooden rockers (Figures 2:32, 3:473 and 474). In both types the movement is intended to pacify the infant and help it sleep contentedly.

Both types were known in the Middle Ages, but the swinging cradle in Figure 3:470 is probably the only English medieval example in existence. As

Figure 3:470. *Hanging cradle. English. Oak, originally painted and gilded, c.1500.*

Figure 3:471. *Hanging cradle. Welsh. Oak, c.1700.*

Figure 3:472. *Hanging cradle. American; New England. Pine and maple, painted reddish-brown, early eighteenth century.*

56. Most recently by Penelope Eames in Furniture History, 1977.

with later versions, it consists essentially of a pair of upright posts mounted on trestle feet. The uprights are supported by heavy Gothic brackets, and the body of the cradle is a simple box of heavily moulded boards. This famous cradle has been much discussed,[56] and was long the object of various fanciful legends. The most persistent of these declared it to be the cradle used by the infant Henry V (born 1388), though its actual date must be c.1500. It is known to have come from Courtfield, near Monmouth, in the eighteenth century. The young Henry V was sent here from his birthplace at Monmouth Castle to be nursed, which accounts for the romantic attribution of the cradle. From various collections in West Gloucestershire, it passed to a series of Bristol collectors which included George Weare Braikenridge. In 1908 it was sold at Christie's to Edward VII, and has since 1911 been on loan to the London Museum.

Rocking cradles survive in quite large numbers from the mid-seventeenth century onwards, and their decoration is very similar to contemporary chairs and chests. Late seventeenth century joined examples are often highly decorated, and are usually inscribed with dates and initials, but later examples tend to be much plainer, with the usual fielded panels of their time (Figure 3:474). Cradles of different sorts were made by all the major furniture-making trades, including joiners, carpenters, coffermakers, and even turners; as well as the ubiquitous basket makers, whose wares are found at all periods. Like their armchairs, the coffermakers' cradles were entirely covered with leather or fabrics, nailed and fringed; and a solitary example survives from the early seventeenth century at Badminton House, still with its original crimson velvet and trimmings.

Figure 3:473. *Joined rocking cradle. English. Oak, dated 1685.*

Figure 3:475. *Portrait of a young boy with a red coral rattle. English. Mid-seventeenth century. He is standing in a turned and painted baby walker, the use of which is clearly demonstrated.*

Figure 3:474. *Joined rocking cradle. English or Welsh. Oak, 1680-1740.*

Figure 3:476. *Turned baby walker. English. Yewtree and beech, c.1700.*

Figure 3:477. *Turned baby walker. English. Elm and syca-more, painted green, c.1700.*

Figure 3:477a. *Detail of Figure 3:477, showing the method of opening the top frame for access by the child.*

Figure 3:478. *Joined walking frame for a child (detail). English. Oak and elm, early eighteenth century. The child is placed in the hole in the sliding board, and is restricted to walking up and down the length of the frame. A tray is provided for playthings.*

Baby Walkers (Figures 3:475-478)

As soon as the child is ready to learn to walk, he is able to use the device which has been variously known as a baby walker, go-cart, going stool, baby trotter, baby cage or standing stool. These were almost invariably made by the turners, since they needed to be of light yet sturdy construction. The child is held standing by a hoop or ring of wood which encircles the waist, and which is held in turn in one of several types of frame. The most mobile versions are mounted on a set of four or six wooden castors, by means of which the child is able to propel itself vigorously around the room. The waist ring is hinged for access, and the child is secured in place by an iron hook which closes through an eye on the frame. This device has been reintroduced in recent years, after maintaining its popularity up until the end of the nineteenth century. Medieval examples are known only through illustrations, and it is unlikely that any examples now survive from before the middle of the seventeenth century. Such is the approximate date of the charming but anonymous painting in Figure 3:475. The little boy is holding a red coral and silver rattle, and standing in a turned and painted baby walker with four castors. Later examples are more commonly hexagonal, with six wheels (Figure 3:476).

In another variety, the child is held through a plank, which is free to slide along the length of an open frame (Figure 3:478). These are usually about four to six feet long, and often incorporate a tray for toys and baubles. In yet another type, with equally restricted movement, the child is held at arm's length from a vertical pole, which is pivoted at top and bottom into ceiling and floor, so that the child may travel only in a circle with the pole at its centre.

Figure 3:479. *Portrait of Thomas Smyth. English. Early seventeenth century. He is standing with his new little joined and velvet-upholstered armchair, with its matching low table. Both table and chair have the fashionable fluted baluster-turned legs of the period. The armchair should be compared with Figure 2:132.*

Figure 3:481. *Joined child's armchair. English. Oak, c.1680.*

Figure 3:480. *Joined child's table. English. Oak, c.1680.*

Tables and Chairs (Figures 3:479-484)

The majority of surviving children's chairs are high chairs (q.v.), but a certain number of low chairs are to be seen which are quite faithful miniature versions of the chairs made for adults (Figures 3:481 and 482). Thomas Smyth is provided in his portrait with a little velvet-upholstered armchair and a matching table, by which he proudly stands (Figure 3:479). He wears his best lace-edged gown, perhaps on the occasion of his second or third birthday. It would be interesting to know if chairs were presented to mark such an occasion, since chairs are obviously of little use during the first year.

Children's tables are very difficult to identify positively, since, like the one in little Thomas's portrait, they are very similar to the usual low square stool provided for adults (Compare Figure 3:100). The only real distinction (if it was in fact intended) is that the tables have thinner tops, with a wider overhang than the stools. That in Figure 3:480 seems to be a child's table, though the wear on the top testifies that it has often been used as a stool. The table and armchair in Figure 3:480 and 481 are perhaps later versions of those used by Thomas Smyth, though they do not actually belong together. Boarded low armchairs are much more common than their joined counterparts, especially from the eighteenth century, when they were often home made from oak, pine or elm boards. The chair in Figure 3:483 is firmly within this mould, and is decorated with hearts and patterns which are entirely within the traditional framework of the Welsh love-spoon carver.

Figure 3:482. *Boarded child's armchair. English. Oak, c.1680. Compare this example with the adult's armchair in Figure 2:116.*

Figure 3:483. *Boarded child's armchair. Welsh. Pine, painted black, c.1800. The carving of the back strongly echoes the contemporary tradition of love-spoon carving in Wales.*

Figure 3:484. *Turned doll's armchair. American; New England. Birch, with splint seat, painted black, c.1800.*

Figure 3:485. *(Left) Turned child's high chair. English or Welsh. Ash, 1600-30. This chair is in fine original condition, complete with all its parts including the foot-board, and must surely be the best surviving example of its type.*

Figure 3:485a. *(Right) Rear view of Figure 3:485.*

402

Figure 3:486. *Joined child's high chair. English. Oak, dated 1620.*

Figure 3:487. *Joined child's high chair. English. Oak, c.1640.*

Figure 3:488. *Joined child's high chair. English. Oak, c.1640.*

Figure 3:489. *Joined child's high chair. English. Oak, c.1640.*

High Chairs (Figures 3:485-497)

Turned high chairs for children may be seen in fifteenth century paintings, but surviving English chairs are no earlier than the end of the sixteenth century. Figure 3:485 is perhaps the finest of these, and may be seen in the collections of the Shakespeare Birthplace Trust at Hall's Croft, Stratford-upon-Avon. Despite being made of ash, it is in perfect and original condition, and even retains the original footboard.

Most of the joined oak high chairs show some evidence of having been provided originally with a footboard, but these are normally missing. Sometimes there are a series of holes for adjusting the height of the footboard, while some late seventeenth century examples are provided with a step in the frame which supports the footrest (Figure 3:490). High chairs in the seventeenth century were probably not provided with a bar across the arms in order to keep the child in its seat (this feature seems to be a later invention, and therefore in the nature of an alteration to earlier chairs). Instead, the heavy table top served to retain the child, or he would be tied about the waist with a broad sash or belt. The legs of the chair were often, but not invariably, splayed inwards to provide greater stability (cf. Figure 3:489 with Figure 3:491 and others).

As sets of dining chairs became more popular at the end of the seventeenth century, so a high chair was sometimes included to match the rest of the set. Two of the high chairs shown here have styles of backs which are commonly found in backstools (Figures 3:494 and 495), and it is more than possible that they both started life as part of a set.

403

Figure 3:490. *Joined child's high chair. English; South Yorkshire. Oak, with inlay, dated 1680.*

Figure 3:491. *Joined child's high chair. English. Oak, with leather upholstery, c.1680.*

Figure 3:492. *Joined child's high chair. English. Oak, with leather upholstery, c.1680.*

Figure 3:493. *Joined child's high chair. English. Oak, c.1680. The all-over turned decoration is characteristic of this group of furniture. Even the seat rails are turned, and should be compared with Figure 3:138.*

Figure 3:494. *Joined child's high chair. English. Oak, 1690-1720.*

Figure 3:495. *Turned child's high chair. English; Lancashire/Cheshire. Ash and fruitwood, c.1800.*

Figure 3:496. *Turned child's high chair. American; Connecticut. Hickory, stained red, eighteenth century.*

Figure 3:497. *Child's primitive high chair. Welsh; Carmarthenshire. Oak and ash, painted imitation wood grain, c.1800.*

Stools (Figures 3:498-501)

Low stools and footstools were commonly provided for adults, and it must be said that many of these have passed as stools for children, and have been used as such. An honest child's stool, like other pieces of children's furniture, should somehow possess a miniature character. It should have been actually reduced in scale, and not simply have been made a little lower than usual. The three stools and the bench shown here all have this characteristic. They have retained the proportions of their adult counterparts, yet are significantly smaller. The bench in particular has a sort of chubbiness, which makes it almost childlike, and which the full scale of the joints and timbers serve only to emphasise.

Chests and Presses (Figures 3:502-507)

The storage of clothes and toys is a major problem with young children, and small chests and presses were provided for such purposes. These not only served to segregate small clothes which might get lost in the parental clothes' trunk, but a child would be encouraged in tidy habits if he had a chest of his own. Once again it is often difficult to be certain if a small chest was actually intended for the use of a child, but with very small pieces it is reasonable to assume so. There can be no such doubts in the case of the marvellous clothes press of 1712 (Figure 3:507), built as it is in the form of a dolls' house, and enclosing hanging space, shelves and a variety of drawers.

Figure 3:498. *Joined child's stool. English. Oak, c.1630.*

Figure 3:499. *Joined child's stool. English. Oak, c.1650. Note an amusing feature here, in that the joiner has assembled one leg the wrong way up.*

Figure 3:500. *Joined child's stool. English. Oak, c.1650.*

Figure 3:501. *Joined child's bench. English; Buckinghamshire. Beech, painted imitation wood-grain, c.1625. This little bench forms part of the original furnishings of the Kederminster Library at Langley Marish Church.*

Figure 3:502. *Boarded child's chest. English or Welsh. Oak, c.1680.*

Figure 3:503. *Boarded child's chest. English. Oak, c.1680.*

Figure 3:504. *Boarded child's chest. English. Oak, c.1680.*

Figure 3:505. *Joined child's chest. English. Oak, c.1640.*

Figure 3:506. *Joined child's chest. English. Oak, c.1640.*

Figure 3:507. *Boarded child's clothes press. English. Oak and pine, dated 1712.*

Figure 3:507a. *A further view of Figure 3:507. It is inscribed 'Edmund Joy 1712'.*

Figure 3:508. *Birdcage. English. Oak, with iron wires, dated 1697.*

Figure 3:509. *Beer coaster. English. Oak, with leather jug and horn mugs, late eighteenth century. The coaster is mounted on wooden wheels, whereby the beer is passed along the dining table for each to serve himself.*

Figure 3:510. *Carved mortar stand. English. Walnut, with white marble mortar, c.1620. The high quality of the carving suggests an original use in a high class apothecary's shop.*

Figure 3:511. *Turned mortar stand. English. Elm, with bronze mortar, dated 1720. Possibly from the kitchen of a great house or an apothecary's shop. The stand is 25ins. high.*

x). Miscellanea (Figures 3:508-515)

The regular forms of furniture for sitting, eating, sleeping, reading, writing and storage, as already discussed, were not the only types of movable furniture to be found in the average home. Unlike the modern furniture manufacturer, the early joiner or turner could adapt his products to suit the needs of the individual customer, or he could produce some entirely novel piece to fulfil a particular purpose. Many such custom-built pieces were made by estate joiners, but they could be found in the ordinary home as well. Often, such specific pieces are built into their original locations, but when a movable piece is removed from its original context it often fails to make any practical sense.

The list of wooden objects (classed together as treen) which formed part of the equipment of the late seventeenth century household is almost endless, but it is worth listing and illustrating here some of the larger items which have not already been covered: mirror and picture frames, birdcages, mortar stands, bellows, clock cases, beer coasters, napkin presses, cutlery boxes, salt boxes, candle boxes, spinning wheels, chimney boards and musical instruments, as well as a whole host of other small household items.

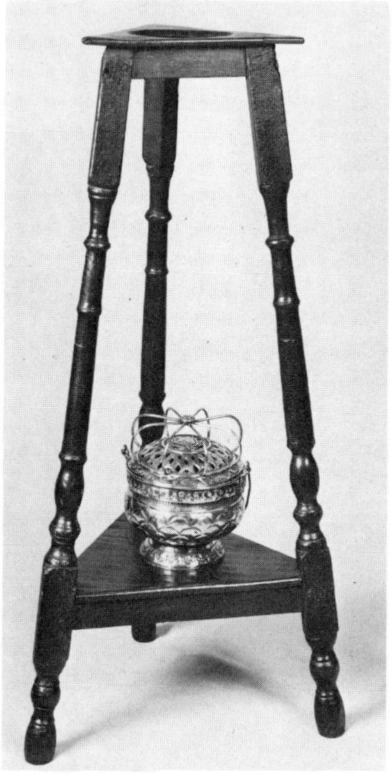

Figure 3:512. *Joined mortar stand. English. Oak, c.1730. For a small domestic mortar.*

Figure 3:514. *Boarded corner spoon rack and cutlery tray. English. Oak, c.1750.*

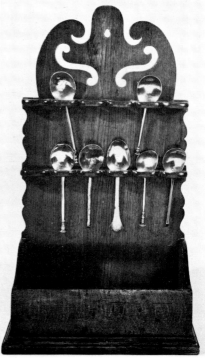

Figure 3:515. *Boarded spoon rack and cutlery tray. English. Oak, c.1760.*

Figure 3:513. *Tripod mortar stand. English. Oak, c.1750.*

Chapter Four

The Stylistic Themes
A Decorative
and Regional Chronology

THE TECHNICAL AND functional characteristics of early furniture, as they have been discussed so far, serve in only the most generalised way to define the actual time and place in which an individual piece of furniture might be supposed to have been made. We can define some of the timescale and geographical limits within which certain features of construction and form are known to appear, but outside of any strokes of luck such as a specific date, provenance or inscription (or a comparable specimen with these attributes), we have to rely more largely on the aesthetic character of a given item to provide clues as to its origin. Decorative types are as consistent as any other aspect of early furniture, and the nature and treatment of decoration often provides a secure basis for the recognition of social and regional types, as well as for the assessments of dates of manufacture. For this reason, very plain and undecorated furniture is often extremely difficult to 'place' in terms of date and regionality.

Even where decoration is present, the characteristics are often subtle and difficult to read in the poor light of such little knowledge as is available to us. In comparison with other fields such as ceramic history, where actual kiln sites may be excavated and objects such as moulds and wasters may be retrieved for comparison with extant wares, the information available on furniture typology is often rather flimsy, and interpretations may be at best only intuitive.

Even so, well informed intuition may be a powerful instrument if used sensibly, and the furniture historian should develop a 'feel' for early furniture which can sometimes be used to supplement the all-essential hard information which is available. To this end, we should develop a sensitivity to the 'stance' and proportion which is common within many groups of furniture. In this way, one can recognise the 'handwriting' of a workshop or regional group, in the same way that a connoisseur of porcelain can recognise the products of a known factory.

The examples presented here as illustrations have been selected for the way in which each may be considered in terms of the affinities which it shares with others of the same group. Some groups are very specific, such as the regional groups from closely-defined geographical areas or towns; but others are more amorphous and may reflect the preferences of an ill-defined social conformation, such as the yeoman farmers of the early eighteenth century. One of the most interesting aspects is the way in which emigrant joiners and other craftsmen carried their traditional forms and techniques with them to their new homes in the townships of New England. It may be argued that one of the most endearing peculiarities of the English tradition of furniture making in this period is that each piece possesses a strong flavour of individuality which transcends any conformity to the group. This is certainly true, but as we peruse the specimens presented here we find that each piece also bears the unmistakable definitions of kinship with other members of its group, however loosely knit that group may be. Purely superficial similarities can be very misleading in identifying apparent group affinities, and we must be sure that correlations are traceable in the small details of handling and execution, and not merely in the broadest gestures.

The prime motive behind any attempts to analyse the stylistic content of furniture decoration is the wish to place individual examples firmly within a comprehensible framework of stylistic developments, and thereby to assign a realistic date of manufacture. In recent years it has also been thought important that the *place* of manufacture should be understood, though in the British Isles at least this is still a very young and stripling area of study.

The range of furniture production which we have chosen to study here (broadly, the tradition of furniture making in oak and other native materials before 1800) is a curiously rich and varied body of work. Examples range on one hand from the finest aristocratic work of international quality, down to peasant craftwork whose interest is largely ethnographic. Between these bounds lies a complex variety of styles and forms which have, in the past, been crudely classified together as 'Jacobean' or 'Stuart', both of which are entirely inappropriate as descriptive terms.

The hard core of surviving furniture from this period is found in the form of middle class joined oak pieces of basic domestic type. The bulk of such work dates from the century 1620-1720, and represents the products of a sturdy vernacular craft system. The vocabulary of this tradition is largely derived from an overlying stratum of more fashionable work, though in more backward regions a deeper influence is felt from the folk memory and ancient peasant motives. In considering the various styles of decoration, we have to look largely at *joined* furniture, where the large areas of flat surface offered ample attraction to the carver, painter and inlayer. The 'style' of decoration is more often a result of the inherent characteristics of the craft process, than a conscious imposition of any striven after effect; yet there are nevertheless certain persistent themes which run through it all, and which stamp a strong feeling of time and place on the products which we see.

In an attempt to impose some sense of order on an apparently bewildering array of styles, and to continue with a loosely-woven thematic thread which emphasises the importance of the social classes, we may consider the various progressions under three main headings. The first of these will acknowledge the importance of the ruling classes in medieval and post-medieval England; the second and major section will chronicle the rise of the new middle class, and the establishment of conventional styles which were to persist well into the eighteenth century; and the third will chart some of the influences which filtered down into yeoman furniture from the grander levels of post-Restoration developments:

Gothic and Renaissance, before 1640.
The Mainstream of the Middle Classes, 1580-1750, (including
    regional styles).
'Country' Furniture, 1660 and later.

GOTHIC AND RENAISSANCE, BEFORE 1640

The Middle Ages (Figures 4:1-21)

By far the greatest surviving body of English medieval woodwork and furniture (both fixed and movable) is to be found scattered piecemeal in our many parish churches and other ecclesiastical institutions. As a result, the

Gothic decoration which is found in medieval furniture and architecture is inextricably linked in our minds with the church and with religious sentiment, an association which was heavily underwritten by Victorian obsessions with the Gothic dream. Yet, apart from items such as choir-stalls and pulpits, there is never any reason to assume that *any* item of Gothic furniture was *necessarily* made for church use. It may have been, or it may not, for the Gothic style was in current use for architecture and furniture of all designations, whether religious, secular or domestic. By far the most numerous item which has survived in this context is the chest. Several hundred medieval chests are still in existence, and many of these owe their continued existence to the common medieval habit of depositing chests with valuable contents for safe-keeping in churches and ecclesiastical institutions. Allied to this, of course, is the fact that churches were at various times obliged to provide a chest for the storage of parish records, alms collections, etc., and that many of these have survived from very early times. Conversely, other items which were also commonplace in the Middle Ages, such as cupboards, chairs of various types, stools, large and small tables and beds (all on the evidence of illuminated manuscripts and written accounts), have largely if not entirely disappeared. The present rarity of all these items has led to the myth that they were also very scarce during the Middle Ages, though the hard evidence of inventories and visual sources would suggest otherwise. Though not over-furnished by modern standards, the average well-to-do household of the Middle Ages was supplied with a reasonable variety and quantity of furniture.

In considering the decorative nature of medieval furniture, we must necessarily be concerned with those items made for a relatively affluent class of burghers and merchants. The furniture of the most numerous classes, the peasantry and minor yeomanry, has almost entirely disappeared, and any which may have survived is largely unrecognisable as such by virtue of its sheer simplicity and a similarity to later primitive types which have survived in large numbers. Medieval illustrations which do happen to show the activities of peasants and artisans leave the impression that workaday furniture of this sort was not essentially any different from the eighteenth and nineteenth century pieces shown here in Figures 2:39-51.

Any study of medieval furniture is severely hampered by the great rarity of surviving pieces other than chests. Genuine and unaltered furniture pre-dating the Dissolution (say 1540) is extremely rare indeed. Far more rare, in fact, than the optimistic authors of sixty years ago would have us believe. In his *Age of Oak* published in 1919, Percy Macquoid filled the first two chapters with a number of pieces which were supposed to be of Gothic or Early Renaissance date, but when some of these appeared on the market in recent years they were sadly unconvincing. In the wake of the Victorian passion for anything medieval, it seems that collectors of the time were ready to delude themselves with a blind faith in their pet purchases. Most fakes are successful because the prospective purchaser wants to believe that they really are what they only pretend to be. This disease is still with us, and continues to cloud our perceptions over a good many issues in the field of antiquarian collecting and scholarship.

There have been few serious and objective attempts to isolate and define English movable furniture of the period 1480-1540,[1] with the result that we still find it difficult to be sure which pieces of this period are securely English in character, or even to know if it is possible to draw any real distinctions. Some of the simpler forms, such as the clamped-front chests (Figure 4:1) or the boarded cupboards (Figures 4:8-10), are easier to define

1. The large and valuable study by Penelope Eames, Furniture History, 1977, stops tantalisingly short at the end of the fifteenth century, just when actual survivals of English furniture start to appear in significant numbers and greater variety. This is frustrating to one seeking comparative information on late medieval and early Renaissance transitional pieces, such as the early open-frame joined armchairs in Figures 3:28 and 29.

Figure 4:1. *Clamped-front chest. English; London or Home Counties. Oak, c.1300. This characteristic use of chip-carved roundels is found on a series of medieval chests associated with churches in South-Eastern England.*

because of their frequent appearance in English sources; but it is not good enough to subscribe to the traditional view that fine quality pieces found here are necessarily of Continental manufacture. The quality of carving to be found on fixed English woodwork equals the best in Europe, and it is inconceivable that a similar quality was not lavished on the most important movable furniture. This is not the place to undertake any extensive survey, since this period is not central to the task in hand. A small number of late medieval items are illustrated elsewhere in this volume, and I propose here to view only briefly the basic principles of the late medieval stylistic vocabulary.

The Late Gothic Style (Figures 4:2-13)

The decoration of much English furniture of the thirteenth and fourteenth centuries is characterised less by its *style,* than by the actual *techniques* of decoration which are variously employed. These techniques tend each to impose a form and aesthetic quality of their own, rather than

Figure 4:2. *Boarded chest. English; probably Northamptonshire. Oak, c.1500. A later use of chip-carving, in a mature Gothic style, though of intermediate quality (cf. Figures 2:188 and 3:364).*

Figure 4:3. *Clamped-front chest. English. Oak, c.1400. A fine chest, using the fully-developed Gothic style in an architectural manner (see detail, Figure 2:123a).*

bending to accommodate the details of any preconceived schematic arrangement. Thus, painted furniture such as the Richard de Bury chest (Plate Eight, Figure 2:107) is seen to follow the designs found in other forms of painting such as fresco or manuscript illumination. Here, it is the technique of painting which is important, and the chest itself is used simply as a vehicle for the decoration. The various elaborate iron-bound chests are used in the same way. The wooden boards, and the form of the chests, are entirely plain, and the wrought iron bands are free to writhe at will over this wooden ground. Even the chip-carving on the chest in Figure 4:1 is largely unrelated to the form of the chest. With a typical medieval disregard for the rules of symmetry (so important to later generations), three different roundels are placed at intervals across the face of the chest. This motif is characteristic of a group of similar clamped-front chests from South-East England, which include the famous examples in the churches at Earl Stonham, Suffolk; Stoke d'Abernon, Surrey; and Climping, Sussex. The later boarded chest in Figure 4:2 continues with chip carving as a technique, but here it is used in a more sophisticated manner, incorporating formal motifs such as a row of Gothic crockets and a running trail of simple vine leaves, and representing a regional group from Northamptonshire.

Throughout most of the Middle Ages, the greatest decorative emphasis in furniture was placed, not on the wooden structure itself, but on the rich hangings which were normally used to drape such items as beds, plate cupboards and chairs of estate. But in the fifteenth century this emphasis was gradually reversed, and greater thought and attention was devoted to decorating the wooden surfaces of such pieces.

Chests were an exception to that rule, of course, since they were never ideal subjects for draping with fabrics, and so the decoration of the front surface was an important area from the start. The complex architectural style which we now know as Medieval Gothic was by far the strongest unifying theme in the spectrum of medieval decorative styles. It is important to think of Gothic as only one of several styles current in the later medieval period, and not all medieval furniture is actually Gothic. The Gothic style became the established norm in architecture in the twelfth century, and was no doubt very quickly adapted for superficial application to furniture. It may be seen used in scant fashion in the early chest from Graveney Church, Kent (p.112). The chest in Figure 4:3 is a more mature expression of the use

Figure 4:4. *Carved door from a cupboard. English or Flemish. Walnut, c.1400.*

Figure 4:5. *Joined plate cupboard (detail). Probably French. Oak, c.1480. This piece, which dates from an early stage in the development of panelled construction, uses the Gothic style in a purely decorative manner, not in any sense as the structural device for which it was conceived by architects. Note in this piece and the cupboard below, that the doors are made from single planks, not framed panels.*

Figure 4:6. *Joined armchair. Scottish; Aberdeen. Oak, 1507. This is a very valuable piece for assigning dates to comparable work. The panels and framework were taken from the choir-stalls of an Aberdeen church and made into a chair in c.1560. A contract is on record for the original construction of the stalls by John Fendour in 1507.*

Figure 4:7. *Joined press or aumbry. English. Oak, c.1500. The tracery decoration is closely related to the preceding examples.*

Figure 4:8. (Left) Boarded press or aumbry. English. Oak, early sixteenth century. A very rare example of a simple two-door cupboard. As with all genuine cupboards of this type, there is evidence that cloth coverings were originally nailed behind the traceried openings.

Figure 4:9. (Above) Boarded press or aumbry. English, early sixteenth century. This, and the following example, have each lost their lower half. It is a matter for conjecture whether they were originally of single- or two-door form, but they must certainly have had shaped feet in the same manner as Figure 4:8.

of the Gothic style at the end of the fourteenth century (see also the detail in Figure 2:123a).

Superficially, the significant elements of the Gothic style consist of a schematic use of the pointed arch, with an infilling of supplementary details such as cusps and crockets. But more importantly, Gothic is an architectural system which uses a highly sophisticated interaction of thrust and counter-thrust to produce a self-supporting skeletal structure. The infilling between the structural ribs is not important to the stability of the structure,

Figure 4:10. Boarded press or aumbry. English. Oak, early sixteenth century. This cupboard was discovered in the ruins of Ivychurch Priory, at Alderbury, near Salisbury, Wiltshire.

Figure 4:11. Boarded stool. English. Oak, early sixteenth century. The pierced tracery of the apron is very similar to those on contemporary cupboards. The rear apron is missing.

Plate Thirteen. *Carved armorial panel. English. Oak, painted in colours, c.1600. The arms are those of Jeffreys-Fulthorpe, and the panel may once have formed part of an overmantel in their possession.*

Figure 4:12. *Boarded press or aumbry (detail of door). English. Oak, early sixteenth century. This St. George and dragon are a particularly lively example of the folk art of this period. This is the original door of a much-restored cupboard.*

Figure 4:13. *Joined press or aumbry (detail of panel). English. Oak, early sixteenth century. A pierced panel, similar to preceding examples, with traces of the original nails which held pieces of haircloth behind the perforations.*

and so for the first time it became possible to provide a huge area of glazed windows in a building. Highly complex designs could be built up using the basic stylistic elements, and a huge variety of treatments may be seen in the tracery designs of the period.

In furniture, these principles can normally be followed in only a superficial and small-scale manner. The designs of blind and perforated tracery, as they are executed on a wooden panel, have no structural reality as they have in a full-scale masonry edifice. Nevertheless, many items of furniture were conceived as miniature buildings and, even in fairly crude examples such as the boarded cupboards in Figures 4:8-10, the ventilations are presented in imitation of the windows of a building. In more sophisticated work, all the pinnacles and buttresses of a real building are also included, though surviving English work cannot rival the excesses of its French counterparts.

The real charm and vitality of English medieval furniture often lies in the small details of carved work, such as is so often found on church bench-ends, but more rarely in furniture. The fragmentary cupboard door in Figure 4:4 can only hint at the delight taken by the medieval carver in the inclusion of grotesque or humorous figures in his work. Gothic carving is almost always very crisply and finely executed, in true regard to the monkish and devotional traditions which motivated so much of late medieval artistic life.

The 'Linenfold' Style (Figures 4:14-21)

The formal beauty of folded drapery in clothes and hangings was a constant source of appreciation in medieval art, and was probably seen at its most exaggerated in Flemish panel paintings of the fifteenth century, where the complex folds of fabrics could often supply a major element of the composition. An extension of the same theme is seen in the delight taken in the heavy parallel mouldings so often found in architectural timbers such as ceiling beams and fireplace beams, where the sharp interplay of light and shade produces a rich striped pattern. Both these features are used to clever effect in the late and fully-developed panel typified by Figure 4:18b. The fabric drapes which were such an important adjunct to medieval wooden furniture, are finally (in a sense) translated into the substance of the wood itself.

A good many theories have been advanced as to how the idea of the linenfold panel originated, and through which stages it must have passed in its evolution. Obviously the visual characteristics of pleated and draped linen were a primary inspiration, but this seems to have had more effect on the details of treatment than on the origins of the idea itself.

Let us first consider the simpler form (Figures 4:14-16), which is not really a linenfold at all, but has more appropriately been referred to as *parchemin* or parchment-fold. In the simplest version, shown in Figure 4:14, it amounts to little more than a pronounced central ridge which is finished at either end with a straightforward ogee arch. This was a very common pattern in late medieval furniture from Western Europe (cf. Figure 3:11a), and is often seen in early woodcuts and other representations. Two theories are advanced with regard to its original appearance:

i). That early panels were often covered with a sheet of parchment glued to them (either for mechanical strength, or as a ground for painted decoration). Being of a greasy nature, the corners and edges of the sheets would often have lifted and curled back as the glue failed to hold them down, and this effect might be copied by the woodcarver as a decorative novelty, which later became a widely-used convention.

Figure 4:14. *Joined wall-panelling (detail of a cupboard door). French. Oak, c.1500. The simple form of parchemin panel, finished at both ends with an ogee arch.*

Figure 4:15. *Joined press or cupboard (detail of door). Flemish. Oak, early sixteenth century. An enriched form of the parchemin panel.*

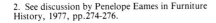

Figure 4:16. *Specimen panel. English. Oak, early sixteenth century.*

2. See discussion by Penelope Eames in Furniture History, 1977, pp.274-276.

ii). The central ridge may have been arrived at as an exaggeration of the usual joiners' technique of chamfering the edges of a panel, a process which adds to the mechanical strength of the panel. Very wide chamfers will tend to meet in a ridge down the centre of the panel.

Parchemin panels are also seen in highly-enriched versions (Figures 4:15 and 16), usually with distinctive Gothic details which suggest a date before the middle of the sixteenth century. In England, this work is mostly associated with the South-East and East Anglia, particularly Norwich, which at this period had a separate existence from the rest of East Anglia being the second city of early Tudor England. Such work was, no doubt, also popular in London. *Parchemin* panels would seem to have originated a little before 1550, and were popular for one hundred years or so.[2]

True linenfold appears in some accounts after c.1450 as *lignum undulatum* (literally 'wavy wood'), but this may not always refer to the joined and framed panels with which we are now familiar. The earliest form of wall-panelling, and a type which continued in use until a very late date, consisted simply of vertical planks of deal or clapboard which were linked with a long tongue-and-groove joint in the same manner as modern match boarding. The long vertical joints were obscured by decorative edge mouldings run down the length of the planks, and these were frequently multiplied across the face of the planks, producing a series of vertical ribs which hung like the folds and pleats of linen or woollen wall hangings. Such a similarity would be too much for the woodcarver to resist, and examples are known in which the carver has copied the cords, tenterhooks and cow-horn rings which were the normal means of suspension for domestic hangings. No doubt some panellings were also painted in colours to

complete the illusion of painted cloths or tapestry. The door in Figure 4:17 may once have been *en suite* with a room of panelling carved in this manner, or it may simply reproduce the curtains which were also hung in doorways. It consists of three planks, and the term *undulatum* is seen to be fully justified.

Figure 4:17. *Joined door and frame. English. Oak, early sixteenth century. The decoration of the door clearly imitates cloth hangings, and the carver has even reproduced the tenterhooks and cow-horn rings from which the curtain hung on cords. No doubt the door was originally painted in colours to complete the illusion.*

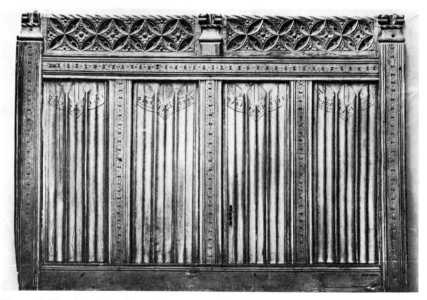

Figure 4:18a. *Joined wall-panelling (originally the back of a wall-settle, cf. Figures 3:6-10). English; from Kingstone, Somerset. Oak, early sixteenth century. The panels reflect the earlier type of linenfold, in which the 'curtain' hangs down to the ground, with a formalised decorative edging only at the top.*

Figure 4:18b. *Joined bed-head (detail of panel). English. Oak, c.1540. The later form of linenfold panel, folded like a napkin with formalised decoration to both top and bottom.*

Figure 4:19. *Joined chest. English. Oak, c.1540. The linenfold is full, curly and rich.*

Figure 4:20. *Chest of hybrid construction. English. Oak, mid-sixteenth century. The linenfold is stiff and formal, lacking in imagination. Note the hybrid construction of this piece, which has a panelled front attached to a boarded carcase.*

Figure 4:21. *Joined standing cupboard. English. Oak, early sixteenth century. The linenfold used both vertically and horizontally. The slow spiral twist of the front supports may be usefully compared with those on Sir Rhys ap Thomas' chair in Figure 3:28.*

Whether or not this is the first manner in which the linenfold style was expressed, cannot now be determined with accuracy; but it does seem the most logical precursor to the next stage, in which the folds at the top are rendered in a formal way, and the bottom is simply cut off straight. Perhaps the earliest surviving example of this is in the clapboard panelling of the porch at the Lavenham Guildhall, Suffolk (? mid-fifteenth century); and the same stage is evident in a framed panel bench back from Somerset (Figure 4:18a). Here the lace or embroidered edge of linen is also simulated, a convention which became general in the first quarter of the sixteenth century. The earliest precise date at which true linenfold appears in England would seem to be 1492, the date at which the surviving linenfold doors were installed in the Audley Chapel at Hereford Cathedral, but they must have been known for some forty or so years previously. Several examples are given in Chapter Three of chairs of 1520-50 which have linenfold panels, and it seems that the style may still have been used as late as the early seventeenth century, though it is rare after c.1560.

Marking their descendency from clapboarding and post-and-panel work, the earlier panels are often of a long and narrow proportion, but by the middle of the sixteenth century they were generally made broader and shorter. Also, in view of their derivation from hanging linen, the earliest panels were generally assembled with their folds set vertically; but this convention was soon laid aside when the panel shape dictated otherwise, so as an example we find the linenfold set horizontally on the drawers of the cupboard in Figure 4:21. In the earlier stages, linenfold panels are often combined with Gothic details in a definitively medieval manner; but after c.1525 a new sense of lightness and informality is increasingly evident as the more graceful elements of a new style are slowly absorbed into the English vocabulary. A brief comparison of the two chairs in Figures 3:15 and 16 will underline the new feelings at this essentially transitional stage.

Figure 4:22. *Joined clothes press. Flemish. Oak, c.1520-40. A full, rich rendering of the romayne panel, which inspired a great deal of similar English work on wall-panelling.*

Figure 4:23. *Joined wall-panelling. English; from Waltham Abbey, Essex. Oak, c.1530. These panels lack the decorative flair of the previous example, though the carving is vigorous and humorous. Note the lingering Gothic details in the crocketted tops of the upper row.*

Figure 4:24. *Specimen panels. English. Oak, c.1530-40. This beautiful pair of panels, which show clear signs of the original framing, are doubtlessly portraits of man and wife. A strong sense of pattern may be discerned in the man's beard and his wife's neckpiece.*

The English Renaissance (Figures 4:22-44)

We now refer to this new 'quickening of the pulse' of English design as the Early English Renaissance; but it must seem that the field of furniture design is the one that least justifies the application of such an optimistic concept, at least in the earliest stages. Until c.1560, that is the beginning of the reign of Elizabeth I, the so-called Renaissance style in English furniture

Figure 4:25. *Specimen panels. English. Oak, c.1550. These portraits of the boy-king Edward VI (1547-53) and King Solomon were probably from a set of 'Ancient and Modern Worthies'.*

424

is little more than a decorative cloak applied to the conservative substructure of still-Gothic forms. Certainly, there are some real innovations which appear during the generation of 1520-70, but these are largely the reflections of greater social changes, to which the adaptions of furniture designs are in the nature of a practical provision (lighter forms of seating, more flexible storage, an increasing variety of furniture types, greater privacy for the family, etc.). Furthermore, these changes were largely restricted to the circumstances of the rich and the minor gentry. The domestic condition of the poor changed hardly at all from the Middle Ages until the Industrial Revolution, and then usually for the worse. The early sixteenth century saw a faint stirring in the fortunes of the yeomanry and small merchants, but it was not until later that they developed a consistent furniture style of their own; and innovations were always initiated by the ruling classes, though usually following the inspiration of foreign sources, and the example of imported pieces and craftsmen.

Figure 4:26. *Boarded chest. English. Oak, 1530-80.*

The 'Romayne' Style (Figures 4:22-28)

The influence of Gothic design lingered for many generations, both in construction and in the details of rustic decoration, though the school of Gothic carving died a real death with the Dissolution of the Monasteries and the subsequent Reformation of the Church of England. In this sense, the Gothic style represented the old order of spiritual sentiment, whilst the new 'Renaissance' was guided by a more secular impulse. Although the Reformation denied the power of the Roman Church, it was an Italian aesthetic (interpreted via Flanders) which came to dominate the new styles in England. The Italian Renaissance, which had flowered as a revival and a renewal of Classical learning in the fourteenth century and later, had a much belated effect on the conservative English. It was the young Henry VIII who, after c.1510, encouraged an influx of Italian sculptors and decorators who undertook various important commissions, using and instructing English artificers in the process. They introduced the stock elements of the Italian taste — the classical columns and pilasters, the strapwork and the grotesque animals, the curly arabesque foliage, and the framed profile heads recognised by the English as 'Romayne', or Roman.

Romayne panels are perhaps the most distinctive feature of the new style, aside from the classical architectural scheme within which they are properly

Figure 4:27. *Joined chest. English. Oak, c.1600. A late and provincial version of the romayne panel in use. Possibly a later chest incorporating panels of this date. Details of the panels are shown below.*

found; since they combine both the portrait head itself, and a typical accompaniment of secondary decorative detail. The Flemish cupboard in Figure 4:22 demonstrates the pure variety of interpretation normally found in France and the Low Countries. The carving of the details is highly accomplished and handled in a very sensitive manner, whilst the heads are applied in almost full relief, projecting boldly from the surface of the panel.

By contrast, the English panels in Figure 4:23 are more clumsily handled, but with a boldness and humour which links them directly to the Gothic tradition which was still very much alive around them. They came from a house in Green Yard at Waltham Abbey, in Essex, and may have been associated with the Abbey of Waltham Holy Cross itself. The Abbey was not dissolved until the very late date of March, 1540, which post-dates the probable date of the panels; though the relationship between the Abbey and the panelled room, of which these six form a small part, is not proven. Other panels have a variety of armorial bearings and, though very similar throughout, they may in fact derive from different sources. This possibility is underlined by a difference in emphasis found in the panels, and seen here between the top and the bottom rows. The top panels each have a Gothic cresting, composed of an ogee crocketted arch, whilst the others are entirely in the new spirit. Despite this discrepancy, the six panels shown here are certainly from the same hand, and probably of the same date within a year or two around 1530.

The heads are typically framed within a roundel, but other shapes are not unknown, such as a square or a diamond (e.g. Figure 3:29). They can rarely be seen as actual portraits of individual persons, and are more usually stylised representations of named or anonymous quasi-classical heroes and beauties. But if the rendering of personal features is particularly strong, as in Figure 4:24, it may safely be assumed that portraiture is intended. Here we have, presumably, a husband and wife taken from a panelled room or cupboard of which they were once the proud owners. The heads are carved in full relief, and the handling is strong and accomplished, if without the delicacy we might have expected from a French version. They are none the less admirable for that.

The subjects contained in this format are not limited to human heads, in profile or otherwise, but will often include armorials, badges and animals. The chest in Figure 4:26 has a dolphin and a snail, perhaps badges of the original owner, with the motto 'IN VIRTUTE IN ULTIONE'. In one form or another, panels with profile heads continued in use until the mid-seventeenth century, though they are more associated with room panelling than with movable furniture.

The 'Elizabethan' Style (Figures 4:29-40)

The most significant step forward in the design of English furniture-decoration came in c.1550-60 with the adoption of turning as an important aesthetic element of joined furniture. This opened up a wider range of potential for the joiner, whose decorative vocabulary was hitherto almost completely restricted to carving and mouldings. At first, turnings were used

Figure 4:28. *Joined overmantel (detail of panel). English. Oak, c.1600. This picaresque little portrait may be of the original owner.*

Figure 4:29. *Joined press cupboard. English. Oak, with inlay, c.1575. An aggressive, yet competent, piece of work, which must be taken to represent the most expensive type of wooden furniture of its day.*

Figure 4:31. *Joined centre table with folding top. English. Oak and walnut, c.1580.*

Figure 4:30. *Joined court cupboard. French. Walnut, c.1575. Furniture of this kind was imported for use in rich English households, and influenced the style of English work such as the stool in Figure 3:79, or the table in Figure 4:31.*

Figure 4:32. *Joined court cupboard. English. Oak, 1580-1600. The feet have obviously been altered.*

Figure 4:33. *Joined court cupboard. English; Suffolk. Oak, 1580-1600 (see detail Figure 2:169).*

only as a basis for further carving, but the inherent beauty of pure turning was soon grasped and exploited and eventually became a prominent feature of seventeenth century joined furniture.

But, inasmuch as the major trends of the Elizabethan period are linked with the thoughts and actions of a virile and ambitious aristocracy, the most important feature of the age is an exaggerated emphasis on richly-carved and coloured ornamentation. Under Elizabeth I, England enjoyed a period of artistic and economic expansion, which is amply reflected in all areas of the decorative and domestic arts. English self-confidence encouraged a cult of theatrical heroism, in which the themes of the Renaissance were given full play. Elizabeth herself, perhaps inheriting some of the thrift of her grandfather Henry VII, eased her household expenses by travelling the countryside with all her company, and staying alternately as the guest of different hosts. In order to recieve these 'Progresses' in a seemly manner, many a courtier was encouraged to commission new schemes of architecture and furnishings. The inventories of great houses of the time conjure up a rich picture of walnut and marquetry furniture, of embroidered silk and tapestry hangings and upholstery, of rare and costly 'foot carpets' of turkeywork or gilded leather, and of gleaming garnitures of gold and silver vessels displayed on cup-boards for all to wonder at.

For the modern observer, the usual effect is one of visual indigestion, but it is important to interpret such extravagance objectively in terms of the contemporary view. When a patron orders a piece in a particular taste, he is expressing in equal measure both his social aspirations *and* his financial limitations. A confection such as the press cupboard in Figure 4:29 is not only a piece of storage furniture, it is a statement of the view held by the original owner as to his position in society; and by displaying such a piece in his home, he must have hoped to elicit due respect from his guests and his staff alike.[3] Whether or not the result is attractive, such a piece of furniture is a costly production. The structure is intricate and (for its time) relatively novel, and the decoration is complex and well-executed.

The 'Elizabethan' taste persisted virtually unchanged throughout the following reign, and surviving aristocratic (wooden) furniture of the period 1575-1630 underlines the taste for extravagant display. There is an often monotonous repetitiveness about the way in which the stock elements of the designs are used again and again, though this is relieved by the quality and vitality of the workmanship. English carvers built up a vocabulary of decorative motifs which were only loosely based on Italian, French and Flemish originals. The classical origin of such decoration is sometimes quite heavily disguised in a welter of fluted or reeded columns, caryatids and atalantes, swags and brackets, and heavy mouldings. A number of devices were invented or adapted to fill the long spaces on rails or friezes, such as the favourite medieval form of the running vine, or repeats using single elements in the form of lunettes, nulling, gadrooning, arabesques, guilloches, imbrication, rustication and a dozen others.

Aristocratic furniture rarely displays any *regional* or *local* characteristics of design or decoration, for the simple reason that the aristocracy was rarely involved in the artistic life of the provinces. In matters of taste, they took their cue from the Court and from London. Life in the great country houses was largely self-sufficient, and the work of builders and furniture makers was rarely drawn from the provincial towns. For mundane works, the estates maintained their own joiners and stonemasons; whilst for special commissions, skilled artisans were drawn from London, or from an itinerant pool of specialists. An interesting exception may be cited in the case of a small group of chairs associated with the Conyers family, of

Figure 4:34. *Joined armchair. English; Chester, Cheshire. Walnut, dated 1603. The marquetry panel bears the arms of Sir Peter Warburton of Chester, a Justice of the Common Pleas, for whom the chair was made. The chair was later in the collection of Horace Walpole at Strawberry Hill, and was sold in the 1842 sale as lot 117.*

3. In other words, not only was costly furniture the means by which the ruling classes expressed and advertised their importance, it was also in part the means by which they maintained their position in society.

Figure 4:35. *Joined armchair (the Temple Newsam chair). English. Cedar, early seventeenth century. This is the best chair in this small group, bearing the arms of Conyers of Hornby Castle, Yorkshire. Stylistically, the carving is related to examples from North-West England and Kircudbrightshire. The feet and stretchers are replaced.*

Hornby Castle, Yorkshire. Though of rather 'grand' design, and bearing the arms of this influential family of Northern landowners, the chairs are somewhat coarse in execution and have decoration of a regional type (Figures 4:35-40).

The exact relationships between each chair, and their original purpose, are not entirely clear at present. Although they are broadly similar, there are significant differences, and there is no common factor in their known history (further hindered by some extensive restorations). The decoration is related to similar examples in North-West England and South-West Scotland;[4] and since the Conyers family held land here, it may well be that the chairs were made locally for certain of their properties. The heavily-knobbed nail-head decoration common to each of the chairs is seen in a fragment from Threave Castle, Kirkcudbright (Figure 4:38); the interlace pattern on the Burrell chair (Figure 4:36, detail 4:39) is seen in both Kirkcudbrightshire and the Lake District; and the guilloche decoration of the rails and stiles have unexplained parallels in certain chairs from Aberdeen (Figures 4:101-104). The Conyers group dates broadly from the first quarter of the seventeenth century, and a similar chair still at Norton Conyers Hall is dated 1603.[5]

4. See discussion by Anthony Wells-Cole in *Oak Furniture from Lancashire and the Lake District,* Temple Newsam, Leeds, 1973, pp.viii-xi.
5. I am indebted to Christopher Gilbert for this information.

430

Figure 4:36. *(Left) Joined armchair (the Burrell chair). English. Oak, early seventeenth century. This is the least reliable of the chairs, owing to heavy restoration, including the crest and stretchers. The carving is otherwise largely original.*

Figure 4:37. *(Right) Joined armchair (the Rous Lench chair). English. Oak, early seventeenth century. The general form is very like the Burrell chair, but this one retains the original stretchers which conform to the seat rail.*

Figure 4:38. *Joined wall-panelling (detail). Scottish; from Threave Castle, Kirkcudbrightshire. Oak, early seventeenth century. The heavy cabled nailhead carving is similar to that on the Conyers chairs.*

There were probably never a great many elaborate wooden chairs of this type made for the great houses at this time, since inventories show a greater preponderance of upholstery. The emphasis was placed on rich and elaborate fabrics and trimmings rather than carving. Perhaps the largest surviving corpus of elaborate wooden furniture is in the state beds to be found in various houses and collections, though a number of tables, chests and cupboards also survive in the same taste. Unfortunately, there was also a comparable taste for heavily carved furniture in the several phases of 'antiquarian' interest of the last two centuries; and a great many amateur 'improvers' took it upon themselves to add further decoration to existing, and otherwise genuine, furniture. Many of these 'improvements' are readily apparent to the modern observer, but nevertheless any heavily-decorated example should be scrutinised very carefully for additions or alterations; some pieces may even combine both genuine and spurious elements in the carving and structural parts (see comments in Appendix VI).

In parallel with this taste for an elaborate anglicised version of the Renaissance, was a very much simpler and more purely classical appreciation of French and Italian walnut furniture. Such furniture was imported in large numbers during the sixteenth century and later, and the refined shapes were copied by English joiners, using oak, walnut or cedar. Beds, chairs, tables and cupboards were the usual vehicles for this simplified approach, though surviving examples are rare. A typical example is the walnut table in Figure 3:159, which has an unusually pure version of the Tuscan column, and a chaste architectural form. Though a certain few well-travelled and intelligent members of the aristocracy must have appreciated the reticence of this French style, it was not sufficiently demonstrative or 'showy' to become generally acceptable to rich English patrons at this date. Instead, this form of understatement appealed more readily to the puritan ethic which was growing during the reigns of Elizabeth and James, until the Puritans emerged as a real political force against the threatening absolutism of Charles I and the high ecclesiastical rule of Archbishop Laud.

The Laudian Style (Figures 4:41-44)

A new and sudden element of maturity was brought to English Renaissance architecture with the appointment in 1615 of Inigo Jones as Surveyor of the King's Works. Before this date (and in the mainstream of provincial building works, for a long time after), English architectural design remained a successful pastiche of Medieval and Renaissance detailing and structure. Jones had been a prominent designer of theatrical masques at the court of James I, but when he returned from his Italian trip of 1613-14 he had acquired a unique first-hand knowledge of Roman monuments and an enthustiastic admiration for the work of Andrea Palladio (1508-80). Palladio had successfully combined the ideas of pure Roman architecture with those of the Early Italian Renaissance, and though true Palladianism did not sweep England until after 1700, the works of Inigo Jones of 1615-42 constituted its first public airing in England.

Such radical buildings as the Queen's House at Greenwich (1616 and c.1630) and the Banqueting House at Whitehall (c.1620) pose something of a problem for the furniture historian, for the main furniture styles in vogue at the time are not sympathetic to the daringly original interiors. The Italianate rooms were bare and chaste, and quite unsuited to the sturdy and phlegmatic joined furniture available here. So, how were they furnished? Did they use some of the fine inlaid furniture available from Southwark, or did the architect arrange for suites of Italian furniture to be imported? The chairs designed by Francis Cleyn in c.1625 (Figures 3:63-66) would have been eminently suitable, and since the evidence suggests that several sets were made, might it be that some were used at Whitehall or Greenwich?

Figure 4:39. *Detail of the Burrell chair (Figure 4:36). The interlace pattern at the centre is common in North-West England and South-West Scotland.*

Figure 4:40a. *(Left) Detail of the Temple Newsam chair (Figure 4:35). This was the model for the restoration of the Burrell chair.*

Figure 4:40b. *(Right) Detail of the Rous Lench chair (Figure 4:37). The most complete of the chairs.*

Figure 4:41. *Cabinet on stand. English. Oak, c.1630. A most remarkable and forward looking piece of work for this date. An early example of cabinetmakers' work, in the Laudian taste, and possibly made for Laud himself when Bishop of London (1628-33).*

Another suggestion lies with a group of furniture and architectural woodwork, some of which is directly associated with William Laud (Bishop of London 1628-33, Archbishop of Canterbury 1633-40, executed 1645). Laud was the founder of the High Church party under Charles I, and his persecution of Puritanism was to become one of the chief causes of the Civil War which destroyed him and his King. Laud's taste is seen in several works which he commissioned at Lambeth Palace and at his college, St. John's, Oxford. These are characterised by a very pure architectural form, and Roman-Italianate decoration, very much in the style expounded by Inigo Jones in his contemporary Royal buildings. There can be little doubt that Jones furnished his interiors with similar furniture; and indeed there survive some designs by him for cabinets which may have been made, but which have perished with the rest of Charles's property.

Figure 4:41a. *Interior view of the Laudian cabinet on stand. It would seem to have been constructed as a collector's specimen chest, perhaps for a 'cabinnett of curiosities,' then so much in vogue.*

The cabinet in Figure 4:41 is perhaps the best and most complete example of 'Laudian' furniture now extant. It is almost identical to a cedar cabinet (now at Arbury Hall) which was actually made for Laud himself during his tenure as Bishop of London. Very similar woodwork survives in St. John's College, and the Victoria and Albert Museum has a group of panels and fireplaces in similar vein (Figures 4:42 and 43), which derive from the Lime Street area of London. As may be seen from the interior view, this Laudian oak cabinet is a true product of the early Anglo-Flemish cabinetmaker. The construction is of dovetailed boards, and is remarkably akin to the rather less sophisticated Deed Chest of the Shrewsbury Drapers' Company (Figures 2:5 and 6 and 3:404), which was made by Francis Bowyer in 1637. It may be surmised that Bowyer had picked the elements of the style and construction a few years earlier in London or Oxford, since there can be little possibility of his having copied them from documentary or pattern book sources.

Apart from the architectural basis, and the free use of flat pilasters with applied decoration, the most distinctive element in the design is a complex

Figure 4:42. *Joined over-mantel. English; London. Oak, 1620-40. Taken from a house in Lime Street, in the City of London. The elements of the 'Laudian' style are very clear here, and should be compared with Figure 4:41.*

Figure 4:43. *Section of joined wall-panelling. English; London. Oak, 1620-40. Taken from a house in Lime Street. A further example of the 'Laudian' taste, which compares with Figures 2:5 and 4:41.*

Figure 4:44. *Joined cabinet. English. Oak, 1635-75. The design is an architectural exercise, conceived as a miniature classical building. The use of splay-fielded panels may confirm a date after 1650.*

435

framed cartouche in the centre of the largest panels; all of which foreshadow the 'Anglo-Dutch' style which will be discussed later. Many of these are closely copied from designs for mirror- or picture-frames, taken from the pattern books of Flemish engravers such as Vredeman de Vries; whilst another very common motif is an oval frame punctuated by four keystones. The architectural theme is taken to its ultimate conclusion in the cupboard in Figure 4:44, which is conceived entirely as a miniature building. The facade consists of two storeys of orders, topped by a pair of broken pediments. At the base, approached by steps, are a pair of perfectly scaled doors. It is extremely difficult to date this piece exactly, since it could have been made either shortly before, or a little after, the Civil War. Either way, it bridges the literal beginnings of the Palladian movement, and the later developments of the post-Restoration period, at least in the area of so-called high-style furniture.

THE MAINSTREAM OF THE MIDDLE CLASSES, 1580-1750
including regional styles

The simplest rule-of-thumb that we can apply as a definition of middle class furniture is that it will be of middling quality, and somewhat restrained in execution. The slickness and facility of such an obvious statement may tend to hide a basic fact — that the forces which affect matters of taste are, in part, economic. The householder must buy such furniture as he can afford, or stretch his purse to such as he would like his neighbours to think he can afford (the latter has always been a prime factor in bourgeois thinking). It follows, then, that the furniture of the yeomanry and the minor gentry will be a little less costly than their aristocratic counterparts, and by the same token better than the simple products in the

Figure 4:45. *Joined press cupboard. English. Oak and fruitwood, mid-seventeenth century. A hybrid version of the Anglo-Dutch taste, combining traditional carving with geometric mouldings and applied split-turnings. This piece may usefully be compared with some of the American items from Massachusetts, especially Figures 4:213-217.*

Figure 4:46. *Joined enclosed chest of drawers. English. Walnut, with ivory paterae and exotic veneers, c.1670.*

Figure 4:47. *Joined court cup-board. English. Walnut, with lignum vitae turnings and veneers, c.1670. A rare piece, but very closely related to the previous figure in terms of construction and decoration. A detailed comparison is most rewarding.*

homes of the labouring classes. This coarse view is open to many exceptions, but it may provide us with a yardstick with which to operate certain distinctions. A middle quality piece will not employ such expensive devices as sculptural carving, flamboyant inlay or exotic timbers; yet it will be well constructed in a competent and workmanlike manner, and decorated with care and skill.

Another powerful influence on expressions of personal taste is best described as socio-political. There were, especially in the first half of the seventeenth century, very strong religious and political forces at work in middle class life. The conflicts arose as a result of extremist opinions amongst such disparate groups as the Puritans and Royalists, the Levellers and the Anglo-Catholics. The plain and strong furniture which has been narrowly associated with the short period of the Puritan Administration (the Commonwealth of 1649-60) is in fact the expression of much wider puritan convictions which were found throughout the seventeenth century and later. Political and religious sympathies with Dutch Protestantism led to a revival of trade in the 1650s, which led in turn to a wider taste in England for Dutch styles. The importations of Dutch and Flemish furniture in the Mannerist taste influenced an acceptance of an Anglo-Dutch style in both England and New England.

Figure 4:48. *Joined enclosed chest of drawers. English. Oak, c.1670. An unusual form, with cupboards in the upper half, and enclosed drawers below. Superficially resembles a small press cupboard. See detail of branded ownership mark in Figure 2:14.*

Figure 4:49. *Joined stool. English. Walnut, with fruitwood appliqués, 1650-80.*

Figure 4:50. *Joined armchair. English. Oak, with fruitwood appliqués, 1650-80.*

This is characterised by a rather plain style of joinery, on which may be lavished a profusion of applied decoration in the form of mitred mouldings, small split-turnings and areas of veneer. The effect is emphatically architectural, and first appeared in this country in the 1640s in the form of a series of chests with elaborate inlay of bone and mother-of-pearl. It is often difficult to distinguish Dutch workmanship from English, though an English provenance is very clear in the huge number of chests of drawers which survive from the second half of the century. This taste was also very popular in New England, especially in Eastern Massachusetts. It would seem to have been imported into Boston and Plymouth direct from England, rather than having derived from the Dutch in New Amsterdam (New York). Figures 4:45-52 will help to define the style. In English and American work, the geometrical nature of the applied decoration is often integrated with more traditional carving and turning, so that the result may be something of a hybrid.

But the prime task in hand here is to look at the overwhelming influence of the joiner in middle class furniture of the seventeenth century; and the way in which purely traditional forms persisted until a surprisingly late date in some Northern and Western areas of England and Wales. The majority of the items illustrated in this book are products of this same tradition, at one stage or another. Essentially, the individual motifs used in the carved ornament (and to a lesser extent in the turnings and inlay) are derived and simplified from those developed in the aristocratic furniture of the Elizabethan period; though we can be sure that the bourgeoisie lagged only very slightly behind in the process of aping their masters. From this, we may be sure that a mature provincial vernacular 'style' had begun to establish itself by c.1580. This was rapidly propagated by the foundation of powerful

439

Joiners' Companies in London (in 1570) and the major provincial centres, who promoted a policy of sound craftsmanship underpinned by a rigorous system of apprenticeship, and paid for by an expanding capacity in the middle class market.

One of the most interesting aspects for the modern student is the manner in which provincial furniture of the period 1580-1760 can be demonstrated to display consistent variations in design and ornament. Such differences are largely related to the various natural regions and provincial centres in the British Isles and New England; but in considering the character of the many regional styles, it is important to note the existence of smaller workshop-groups within the larger regional groups. Whilst these are certainly local in character, they may not reflect styles which were otherwise current within their locality. On the other hand, some workshop-groups are seen to follow the local style with great fidelity, and are recognisable only by distinctive features of treatment and handling of details, wholly *within* the general conformities of that style. Unfortunately, the detailed study of local groups of seventeenth century furniture is still very much in mid-infancy, and little more can be done here than to report briefly on the work which has been achieved, and to provide further typical examples.

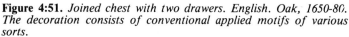

Figure 4:51. *Joined chest with two drawers. English. Oak, 1650-80. The decoration consists of conventional applied motifs of various sorts.*

Figure 4:52. *Joined chest of drawers. English. Oak, with ash appliqués, late seventeenth century. The original flat bun feet are noteworthy.*

Pieces From an Unidentified Workshop (Figures 4:53-55)

Let us first look at a small group of pieces which display such a strong kinship that they must have been made by the same hand. They are now very widely scattered, but each was seen by this writer at various times in recent years, and the similarities recognised.

The standing chest and two chairs were evidently made for a customer of some idiosyncracy, who can tentatively be identified as William Stanley, a younger son of the Earl of Derby. He was born in 1640 and died unmarried in 1670. The Dowager Countess of Derby wrote of him in 1660 that ''my son is with his master (Charles II) who they tell me does him the honour of liking him...'' His support for the exiled king may be alluded to in the curious devices which are to be found on the furniture. Most of these symbols are now rather meaningless, but at least two of them appear as

Figure 4:53. *Joined standing chest. English; possibly Lancashire. Oak, dated 1659. The form of this high chest is very rare, with its sloped lid, superstructure and framed legs; but comparable examples are not unknown in North-West England.*

Figure 4:53a. *Detail of standing chest in 4:53. The total inscription reads: 'REPENT·THE·LORd·IS·AT·HANd· WATCH·ANd·PRAY LIVE·WEL·ANd·dIE·WEL·' The initials 'WS' refer to William Stanley, a younger son of the Earl of Derby. The centre panel is the badge of Stanley and Lathom. The horse and rider panel also appears on the 1659 chair (Figure 4:55), and the unicorns appear on the 1656 chair (Figure 4:54). The reader may trace many further similarities for himself.*

Figure 4:54. *(Left) Joined armchair. English; possibly Lancashire. Oak, dated 1656.*

Figure 4:55. *(Right) Joined armchair. English; possibly Lancashire. Oak, dated 1659.*

Figure 4:54a. *Detail of armchair in Figure 4:54. Compare the unicorns and other details with those in Figure 4:53a.*

Figure 4:55a. *Detail of armchair in Figure 4:55. Compare the horse and rider with that in Figure 4:53a.*

badges on the earlier Stanley bedstead (Figures 3:454-457). These are the deer (or hart) and, more importantly, the Stanley/Lathom badge of an eagle preying on a swaddled child. Other devices include a horse and rider, a peacock with sunflowers, a unicorn, a horse, an ostrich and a camel. The crude design and execution of each piece is possibly accounted by the low fortunes of the Royalist Stanleys under the Commonwealth.

The structural and decorative similarities between these three items are self-evident, but they owe no allegiance to any known regional style. The Stanleys were essentially a Lancashire family, and the curious form of the standing chest is not unknown in the North-West; but we have no other clues as yet.

Regional Styles of the British Isles and New England

The potential value of regional furniture studies has been evident to furniture historians for many years. As early as 1912, Arthur Hayden realised that the secondhand furniture trade would soon be responsible for obscuring much of the indigenous evidence which then still survived. He wrote:[6]

"...The study of local types affords considerable scope for critical study. It is essential that such pieces should be identified and classified before it is too late. Rapidly all cottage and farmhouse furniture is being scattered over all parts of England..."

Yet for many years, the only interest expressed in English regional stylistic types was in a number of throw-away comments by some of the

6. *Chats on Cottage & Farmhouse Furniture,* 1912, p.233.

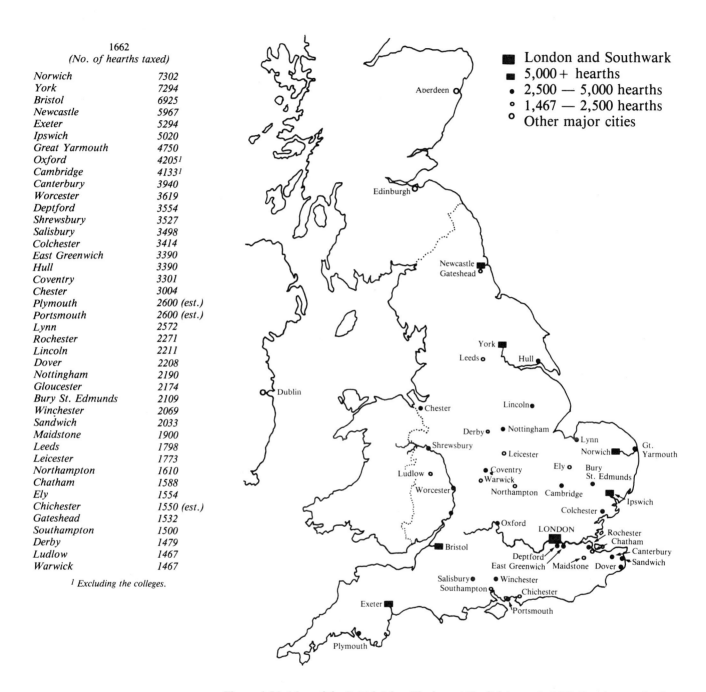

1662	
(No. of hearths taxed)	
Norwich	*7302*
York	*7294*
Bristol	*6925*
Newcastle	*5967*
Exeter	*5294*
Ipswich	*5020*
Great Yarmouth	*4750*
Oxford	*4205¹*
Cambridge	*4133¹*
Canterbury	*3940*
Worcester	*3619*
Deptford	*3554*
Shrewsbury	*3527*
Salisbury	*3498*
Colchester	*3414*
East Greenwich	*3390*
Hull	*3390*
Coventry	*3301*
Chester	*3004*
Plymouth	*2600 (est.)*
Portsmouth	*2600 (est.)*
Lynn	*2572*
Rochester	*2271*
Lincoln	*2211*
Dover	*2208*
Nottingham	*2190*
Gloucester	*2174*
Bury St. Edmunds	*2109*
Winchester	*2069*
Sandwich	*2033*
Maidstone	*1900*
Leeds	*1798*
Leicester	*1773*
Northampton	*1610*
Chatham	*1588*
Ely	*1554*
Chichester	*1550 (est.)*
Gateshead	*1532*
Southampton	*1500*
Derby	*1479*
Ludlow	*1467*
Warwick	*1467*

¹ Excluding the colleges.

Figure 4:56. *Map of the British Isles: The largest English towns in 1662. London was by far the biggest city, with a population in the region of 460,000. This map shows forty-two other towns and cities. The figures are based on the Hearth Tax Returns for 1662, which do not provide accurate tables of capitation, but which are nevertheless closely comparable for relative sizes of populations. (After Hoskins; and Meekings, Public Record Office. See also Appendix V.)*

major authors, and in random illustrated advertisements put out by provincial dealers. Certain chair types were correctly identified by this process, notably those of South Yorkshire and Lancashire, but no real pattern emerged.

In 1948 and again in 1957, R.W. Symonds published two isolated articles[7] which attempted to put some of his wide experience into shape. In the first of these he expressed the idea that the strong parochial nature of the provincial Joiners' Companies must have contributed greatly to the growth of local styles, and went on to define a group of Gothic chests from Northamptonshire (which included the present Figures 3:364 and 4:2). He also considered a group of Lancashire/Yorkshire cupboards from the same source as the present Figures 3:267 and 4:113-122.

In the second article, his conclusions are a little more tenuous, and he attributed a Gloucestershire armchair (similar to Figure 4:87) to a Yorkshire origin, solely on the grounds that the dragons "...suggest the emblem of Saint Hilda of Whitby and, if so, this could be an indication of Yorkshire origin..."

It was soon realised that regional attributions would have to be based on a much more secure form of evidence, though the chances of collating examples which still remained in their original locations were becoming more and more slender by the year. As F. Gordon Roe noted:[8]

"...There are, of course, cases in which one can be certain — or reasonably so — that furniture has never been more than the proverbial stone's-throw from the place of discovery, though the chances of finding such pieces are greatly decreased, and the scientific study of local types is correspondingly hindered and complicated..."

If surviving items were to be of any use as samples of local styles, then at least one of several factors must pertain in order to confirm a provenance. The trade in old oak furniture has been active since at least the early part of the nineteenth century, and so any purely circumstantial evidence should predate this era. The sort of evidence which does provide the essential leads may be briefly summarised as follows:

* Documentary evidence of origins, in the form of accounts or bills of purchase, early inventories, contemporary descriptions, illustrative material, etc. These are very rare for vernacular furniture, or indeed for any item of early date.
* Confirmatory inscriptions or heraldry which declaim a positive association with the site or district.
* A known history of long association with the site or district.
* Close correlation with fixed woodwork from the same site or district.
* Close correlation with other examples from the same site or district.

The establishments which have proven fruitful in the provision of the correct sorts of evidence are such as the ancient parish churches, old family houses, and the public, private and ecclesiastical institutions which are so strong in our provincial capitals and cathedral cities. These are often the receptacles of some fascinating items, though suitable scepticism should be exercised over pieces which carry an unsubstantiated family history.

Armed with these principles, it has been possible in recent years to publish a small series of studies which have successfully defined some of the distinctive regional types of certain areas, viz: Yorkshire, Westmorland, Lancashire, Gloucestershire, Somerset, Dorset and the Salisbury District.[9] This short list has only scratched the surface of a large task, but it is hoped that the total of current knowledge (1979) is reflected in these pages.

7. *The Regional Design and Ornament of Joined Furniture*, Connoisseur, June 1948; and *A Study of English Regional Furniture Design*, Connoisseur, June 1957.
8. *English Cottage Furniture*, Phoenix House, 1949, revised 1961, p.31.
9. *Oak Furniture from Yorkshire Churches*, by Christopher Gilbert, Anthony Wells-Cole and Richard Fawcett, Temple Newsam, Leeds, 1971. *Oak Furniture from Lancashire & the Lake District*, by Anthony Wells-Cole Temple Newsam, Leeds, 1973.
Oak Furniture from Gloucestershire & Somerset, by Anthony Wells-Cole and Karin Walton, Temple Newsam, Leeds, and City Art Gallery, Bristol, 1976.
Early Oak Furniture of Salisbury & South Wiltshire, by Victor Chinnery, Antique Finder/Collecting, September 1976.
Oak Furniture in Dorset, by Anthony Wells-Cole, Furniture History, 1976.
Anthony Wells-Cole is currently planning a national survey of early furniture on a regional basis.

Figure 4:57. *Two joined chests, with broadly similar treatment of the West Country double-heart motif. Top: English; West Wiltshire. Oak, c.1650. Bottom: Anglo-American; Guilford, New Haven Colony. White oak, painted red, 1650-80.*

In order to provide some guide towards future activities, a map is given here (Figure 4:56) of the major provincial towns of Britain in 1662. These towns are all likely to have fostered a strong urban tradition of their own, sometimes with the influence of an independent Joiners' Company; and they are also likely to have been the major influence in their immediate rural districts. This urban approach has certainly proven effective in the case of Salisbury and Aberdeen, and it is suggested that other towns would reward fuller investigation. In the case of London itself, such complex factors are seen to operate that a simple regional-orientated study is probably impossible. Nevertheless, the capital might repay some serious research, for our ancestors seem to have had little trouble in recognising London work, if some inventory references are anything to go by:

> 1597...London chest covered with black lether and banded with Irone...
> 1607...One new London table, wth a court cupboard belonging to the same...
> 1610...a fayre bedstead...of London Worke...

The vernacular furniture of the Eastern United States was largely influenced by the native styles of the parent countries which controlled the various areas, and by the pattern of later immigrations. Thus Delaware displays a tendency towards Swedish forms; whilst New York, New Jersey and Eastern Pennsylvania are broadly Dutch or German. These influences are often modified by complex cross-currents from other immigrant groups within the colonies, though the whole of the Eastern Seaboard was firmly under British control by the beginning of the eighteenth century. The areas which received the most consistent English influence were Virginia and New England, though the former chose to rely fairly heavily on supplies from England, and so no consistent pattern of furniture making emerged here. In New England, however, a very different trend was revealed, since the settlers intended from the first to carve out a new and independent life for themselves.

The seventeenth century furniture of New England strongly reflects the styles of their late sixteenth and seventeenth century English prototypes, and they will be viewed here as a legitimate aspect of English regional furniture design — in fact, as English provincial furniture. Most of these pieces were made, if not by emigrant Englishmen, then by first or second generation Americans. After all, the colonists were still nominally 'Englishmen' until 1776, and thought of themselves as provincials for much of this time. As a result, the influence of English styles and forms is often very direct, a fact which is underlined by the chests in Figure 4:57. Here are very similar renderings of the familiar double-heart motif, as found in Wiltshire on the one hand and in the New Haven Colony (Connecticut) on the other. The English sources for some specific American regional types have already been investigated to some extent,[10] and the future development of English regional studies will help to pinpoint these sources with more accuracy.

The fact that we are looking at the continuance of an *existing* tradition of turners' and joiners' work, planted afresh in the soil of the New World, is not to suggest that American Colonial designs suffer from any lack of originality or identity. On the contrary, furniture makers responded to the challenge of new conditions and materials, and Boston and the small townships in Massachusetts and Connecticut quickly developed strong stylistic instincts of their own during the second half of the seventeenth

10. E.g. by Patricia E. Kane, and by John Kirk (see his article *English Sources for American Furniture,* in Antiques Magazine, December 1965).

century. Although the area was actively colonised from 1620 onwards, with especially heavy migrations of Puritans under the Laudian persecutions before 1640, it must seem likely that no surviving American-made furniture can with real confidence be dated to before 1650.

American scholars have a far better track record of interest in their own regional traditions than is the case in Britain. A fascination with all things Colonial was bred by the Centennial Celebrations of 1876, and although the ensuing period encouraged a good deal of fatuous mythology, it also gave rise to some serious collecting and research of early American furniture. An important milestone in scholarship was a series of articles on the furniture of Ipswich, Essex County, Massachusetts, by Dr. Irving Lyon.[11] Many of his theories have been drastically revised, especially his generous attributions to the hand of Thomas Dennis, but Essex County furniture remains today a fertile theme of American scholarship. Since 1960, a great deal of valuable work has been achieved in the fields of regional typology, craft conditions and the identification of makers; achievements which have inspired efforts on the part of English furniture historians.

Although it is recognised that any regional survey must be far from comprehensive in the limited terms of present knowledge, it is proposed to consider here only the most distinctive features from a few specific areas. Such facts as we have will undoubtedly be added to and revised in the coming years, and it is hoped that the identities and products of specific makers will be revealed with some accuracy. The conclusions offered here are derived from various published works, articles and catalogues, the records of provincial museums, and the combined experience of a number of respected curators, dealers and collectors whose itinerant habits over recent years have given them an unparalleled opportunity to see and handle regional furniture *in situ*. It will be found that chairs, and more especially armchairs, are the predominant furniture type to be shown. The reasons for this are several, but chiefly because chairs display the strongest variations in regional character. They are to be found in large numbers in controlled situations (such as churches), and so they provide a catalogue of panel types and other details which can be related to other pieces such as cupboards, chests, beds, pulpits, wall panelling and other fixed woodwork. Certain decorative details are helpful in the task of dating provincial furniture, but it must be recognised that the date of 1660, which is such an important divide in the sequence of metropolitan and aristocratic furniture, is of no consequence whatever at a vernacular level. This is especially true of Northern England. In the South, most of the distinctive types are manifest well before 1650; but in Yorkshire and the Lake District most items are dated after 1650, and often well into the eighteenth century.

The choice of the ancient City of New Sarum (Salisbury) for a sample study of this nature was a purely random one, governed by the fact that this writer happens to have lived there and knows it quite well. Any of the major provincial cities of the seventeenth century, as exemplified on the map in Figure 4:56, should be able to provide the leads for a similarly rewarding exercise. The choice of a county for a regional study is often an unsatisfactory one, since county boundaries are in the main an artificial concept which often bears little relation to the geographical realities of terrain and natural regions. In real life, the direction and spread of local preferences was more closely governed by such factors as the ease of communications along major river valleys or across lowlands. In lowland areas, the stylistic centres are easily identified as the major market or cathedral towns; and it must be questionable whether a significant school of joinery was ever able to thrive in a purely rural environment, outside the

11. *The Oak Furniture of Ipswich, Massachusetts* (six parts), Antiques Magazine, November 1937-August 1938.

Figure 4:58. *Detail of armchair in Figure 4:60. The initials on the cresting-rail are for Robert Bower, Mayor, who presented the chair to the Corporation of New Sarum in 1585, for use in the new Council House. The coat of arms is that of the city (Salisbury), and was newly-granted in that year.*

Figure 4:59. *Detail of armchair in 4:61. The initials on the cresting-rail are for Maurice Greene, Mayor, who presented the chair to the Corporation of New Sarum in 1622, to match the existing chair of 1585 in the Council House. The design and execution of the panel and crest of this later chair are far better than the earlier one.*

12. Quoted by Penelope Eames, Furniture History, 1977, p.201.
13. The chairs must have been rescued from the disastrous fire of 1780, and are still the property of the City Corporation.

supportive activity of an urban market. The Trade Companies were certainly centred in such places, and in most regions the Joiners' Company must have served as the fount of any sophisticated impulse.

In rural areas such as Wales and the Lake District, both of which have the additional problem of difficult terrain, a different set of circumstances will apply. The rural joiner or carpenter, without the advantage (?) of metropolitan contacts, cannot do else but work in a style closely derived from the folk traditions of his family and neighbours. His market may be poor and widely scattered, and his life semi-nomadic as a result. In an age of poor communications, it must be expected that the remote areas of the North and West would conserve the old ways for the longest, and that the roots of those ways would stretch back the furthest.

In order to provide a balance between time-progressions and geographical logic, the regions will be treated in the following sequence:

1). Salisbury and District, 1580-1650
2). Somerset, 1600-1680
3). Gloucestershire, 1600-1680
4). Aberdeen, Scotland, 1580-1700
5). Yorkshire, 1630-1720
6). Lancashire and the Cheshire Plain, 1640-1720
7). Westmorland and the Lake District, 1650-1750
8). Wales and Ireland
9). New England, 1650-1720

1). Salisbury and District, 1580-1650 (Figures 4:58-78)

Perhaps the earliest reference to locally-made furniture in Salisbury was the 'chair of Sarum make' noted in the Principal Chamber, in the 1440 inventory of the Old Deanery,[12] in the same year as the Carpenters' Guild was first mentioned in the Corporation Ledger. But the earliest datable piece with an undoubted Salisbury provenance is the Council House chair of 1585 (Figures 4:58 and 60), which was donated for use in the new Council House of that year by the incumbent Mayor, Robert Bower. His initials are on the cresting-rail of the chair (Robert Bower, Mayor); and the back panel bears the arms of the Corporation of New Sarum. The other initials are those of other city officials. The fact that the chair is made of walnut suggests a special commission, and the carving is highly competent, but unremarkable. A few years later, in 1622, a companion was made for this chair to the same design; but the second chair is the work of a rather more gifted carver (Figures 4:59 and 61 and frontispiece). This is also made of walnut, and was the gift of Maurice Green, Mayor.[13]

The finest features of the chairs are their sculptural crests, with rather plump *décolletée* ladies supporting date-tablets between them. The back panel of the 1622 chair is exceptionally well-conceived and executed: the design fills the space extremely well, and the carving is crisp and balanced. The relationship between these two chairs is extremely interesting, for although they are separated by a space of thirty-seven years, the later chair is a remarkably close copy of the other; to the extent that their form and style were probably long-standing preferences in Salisbury, and in 1622 neither would have been considered old fashioned. Indeed, the dates are broad enough to act as parameters for other chairs of similar style from Salisbury, and we may deduce that this was a consistent local fashion of the years 1580-1630. Several stools and tables in local churches display identical features to the 1622 chair, exemplified by the stool in Figure 4:62. Similarities may be traced exactly in the treatment of the turned legs, in the

Figure 4:60. *Joined armchair. English; Salisbury. Walnut, dated 1585. This and the following chair are still in use in The Guildhall.*

Figure 4:61. *Joined armchair. English; Salisbury. Walnut, dated 1622. Probably made by Humphrey Beckham, a joiner and carver (1588-1671).*

Figure 4:62. *Joined stool. English; Salisbury. Oak, c.1620. The joinery and decoration are sufficiently similar to that in Figure 4:61 to suggest an attribution to the Beckham family workshop.*

14. See Appendix III.

handling of the simple cabled frieze, in the standard timber sizes, and in the profiles of various mouldings such as the seat edges.

These practical correlations help us to trace the work of a single, but (as yet) anonymous, joiner or workshop within the larger body of Salisbury pieces shown here. But the fine carving of the 1622 chair, and the sculptural parts of others such as 4:65 (crest), 4:66 (crest and panel) and 4:67 (crest), all prompt us to look for a specialist carver, who no doubt worked on regular commissions for several workshops in the city. In order to do this, he must be a full freeman of the Joyners' Company, and his skill would entitle him to a respected position in local society. Only one personality sports all the qualities of this definition, in the shape of Humphrey Beckham, who was Chamberlain of the Joyners' Company in 1621. He was enough of a 'character' to have made a strong impression on local folklore, aided no doubt by the large-breasted figures on the facade of Joiners' Hall which are popularly attributed to his hand. He was apparently given to story telling and flights of fancy, so much so that until recent years a braggart of the town was commonly faced with the retort "Aye, you be a Beckham".

Humphrey Beckham was born in Salisbury in 1588, into a family of clothiers. The family was closely associated with joinery in the town, since Reynold Beckham appears as a joiner in the St. Thomas Churchwardens' Accounts for 1573, and John and William Beckham are both recorded as members of the Joyners' Company (1615-22). Humphrey displayed a talent for carving and modelling at an early age,[14] and was subsequently apprenticed as a painter-carver to a Mr. Rosgrave of Salisbury. His early work and repute as a joiner and carver are noted in several accounts (see Appendix III), and during the nineteenth century a good deal of carved

Figure 4:63a. *Joined pulpit (detail of panel). English; Great Durnford, Salisbury (three miles). Oak, dated 1619. This is one of the few dated components which confirm an early seventeenth century date for this class of local joinery. The handling of the construction and carving is identical to most of the chairs shown here.*

Figure 4:63b. *Joined armchair (detail of Figure 4:71). English; Salisbury. Oak, 1580-1630. This chair is typical of the middling class of joinery of this date, to be found in and around Salisbury. The central motif of the panel is known on at least two other chairs.*

work remained in Salisbury with Beckham attributions (correct or otherwise). The firmest attribution for the remaining examples undoubtedly belongs to his tomb panel in Sarum St. Thomas church (Figure 4:64), which bears the legend 'Here underlyeth the Body of HUMPHRY BECKHAM who died the 2nd day of February Anno 1671 Aged 83 Yrs. His own Worke.' The bottom row of carvings are merely associated fragments, but the main panel is a large and vigorous piece of work which lacks only the bottom edge of the framing. It is doubtful whether he can have executed such a large work in the last twenty years of his long life, so we must assume that the panel and frame were made (perhaps for an overmantel) some time before 1650. It can no doubt be identified as one of the two chimney pieces which figure in his inventory of 1671 (Appendix IV).

The best of Beckham's work must have been done between the time of his apprenticeship to Rosgrave (c.1605) and the Civil War, when "...Beckham lived to see it thought meritorious to destroy with more than Gothic barbarity, the statues of Saints and eminent men, and every remains of antient ingenuity..."[15] He would have been at the height of his powers and reputation (aged thirty-four) when the 1622 Council House chair was made, and it seems inconceivable that Maurice Greene would have entrusted the carving of his prestigious gift to any other hand. Unfortunately, the documentation which might confirm this has not yet come to light; and although we know that Beckham was also a joiner by trade, we cannot know whether he also constructed the chair. A close comparison between the details of the tomb panel and the best of the chairs (Figures 4:61, and 65-67) reveals similarities of content and handling which are more than superficial. Details which might usefully be cited are the general similarity of facial types, the treatment of hair and plumage, and the consistent reappearance of the Flemish scroll border (as exemplified by the cartouche in the lower half of the panel in Figure 4:59).

The presence of sophisticated metropolitan and foreign influences is only to be expected in Salisbury, which was a flourishing centre of the international wool trade before 1650, supplying undyed broadcloth to the European market via London and Antwerp. Salisbury merchants may even

Figure 4:64. *Carved tomb panel of Humphrey Beckham, in Sarum St. Thomas Church, Salisbury. Oak, probably 1620-40. This panel was set up by his family in 1671, and is probably to be identified as one of the 'chimney peeces' in his inventory (see Appendix IV). The inscription has been repainted several times, but there is no doubt that the lettering follows the original form.*

15. ibid.

Figure 4:65. *Joined armchair. English; Salisbury. Oak, early seventeenth century. Attributed to the Beckham workshop.*

Figure 4:66. *Joined armchair. English; Salisbury. Oak, early seventeenth century. Attributed to the Beckham workshop. This is one of only three recorded Salisbury chairs which are not of caqueteuse form.*

Figure 4:67. *Joined armchair. English; Salisbury. Oak, early seventeenth century. Attributed to the Beckham workshop.*

have brought back Continental furniture from their travels, which may account for the single most distinctive factor in Salisbury furniture — a marked preference for the *caqueteuse* armchair. Isolated examples of English *caqueteuse* chairs are not unknown (see Figures 3:37-40), but no other centre seems to show such a distinctive preference for them (Figures 4:60, 61, 65, 67-74). Out of about thirty-eight Salisbury chairs so far recorded (1979), only three are not of *caqueteuse* form. One of these is shown here (Figure 4:66), recognisable only by the typical treatment of the decoration and the details of the joinery.

The variations in quality which are found throughout the group indicate that several hands were responsible for their manufacture (joiners, carvers and possibly turners), though the similarities are close enough to suggest that only one important workshop produced them. This begs the question as to whether they represent a truly local style which several workshops adhered to, or whether they are the distinctive products of a single workshop.

The more mundane examples (Figures 4:68-74) are decorated in a simple and cursory fashion. Even these are not without some spectacular features, such as the crest of Figure 4:71 (which is cut from a single board with the cresting-rail), but in general the carving is performed with simple U- and V-gouges. The quality of execution is varied and inconsistent, though there is some use of sunk ground work with matting. The edge mouldings of panel frames are usually quite simple, with no recorded use of mitres at the corners. The two folding tables in Figures 4:77 and 78 share the same turned and carved forms as many of the chairs, though the use of applied split turnings has not yet been found on any chair. Most of the chairs show signs of having had turned finials to the uprights, but so far no example has been recorded with these finials intact. An unusual constructional feature which is shared by chairs and tables is the manner in which the legs are always cut from square-sectioned blocks, despite the fact that the side stretchers are jointed to them at an awkward angle. In most canted tables and chairs, the blocks are angled to allow the stretcher to meet the face of the leg with a right angled joint. This may be understood by comparing the Salisbury examples with Figure 2:209, where the conventional technique is clearly seen.

Another constructional feature, which serves to distinguish the Salisbury *caqueteuse* from French and Scottish examples (q.v.), is the manner in which the arm is always tenoned into the front face of the rear uprights; in foreign examples the arm normally connects at the side of the upright, or bridges the corner between both faces.

The form of construction used in the Salisbury chairs is remarkably consistent throughout the group. The only slight variation would seem to be in the placing of the rear stretcher. Except in the first (1585) chair, the arm supports do not end in a square tenon-block under the arm; instead the tenon is turned and housed in a drilled mortice-hole (evident in a number of damaged examples). The form of the arm is always the same (except in Figure 4:66 which is not a *caqueteuse*) and unlike the Scottish chairs the arms do not curve inwards to enclose the sitter. Most of the chairs have rear uprights which project above the level of the cresting-rail. The rear panels display a large variety of types (armorial, arch, diamond, vase-and-flowers, rosettes, etc.), and many of them feature a fielded ground with a moulded edge. The crests are likewise very varied, though the most consistent version is the large lunette, which is also found on a boarded armchair (Figures

Figure 4:68. *Joined armchair. English; Salisbury. Oak, 1580-1630.*

Figure 4:69a. *Joined armchair. English; Salisbury. Oak, 1580-1630. Almost identical to Figure 4:69b, except in minor details. The central motif of the panel is repeated in Figures 4:69b and 71. Compare also the general appearance of Figure 4:72 and others.*

Figure 4:69b. *Joined armchair. English; Salisbury. Oak, 1580-1630.*

452

Figure 4:70. *Joined armchair. English; Salisbury. Oak, 1580-1630.*

Figure 4:71. *Joined armchair. English; Salisbury. Oak, 1580-1630.*

Figure 4:72. *Joined armchair. English; Salisbury. Oak, 1580-1630.*

Figure 4:73. *Joined child's armchair. English; Salisbury. Oak, 1580-1630.*

Figure 4:74. *Joined child's armchair. English; Salisbury. Oak, 1580-1630.*

Figure 4:75. *Boarded armchair (detail of crest, Figure 2:116). English; Salisbury. Elm, early seventeenth century. This chair was discovered near Salisbury, and the style of the crest and its carved detail link it very closely to the group of joined armchairs.*

Figure 4:76. *Joined armchair. English; Salisbury or district. Oak, beech and fruitwood, mid-seventeenth century. Apparently a late survival of the Salisbury fashion.*

4:65, 66, 68, 70, 72, 73 and 75), and even on local pew ends, e.g. at Winterbourne Gunner Church. The form of the column turnings shows little variety, but the balusters are less consistent.

All joiners working in the City of Salisbury (except within the Cathedral Close) were bound by the ordinances of the Joyners' Company.[16] The jurisdiction of the Company ended at the City Boundary, but the influence of the Company was very wide throughout the region. The Company could be called on to recommend its members for various commissions, and in 1617 we find Edward Batten (a member of the Salisbury Company and of a large family of joiners) working on the great house at Chantmarle in Dorset, a distance of forty-five miles.[17] Chairs and tables of Salisbury type are to be found throughout Dorset, in churches and old houses; and they are the standard type throughout the settled river valleys of South Wiltshire, and even into South Somerset.[18] Further research into the activities of the Company will provide some answers to two interesting questions: To what extent were provincial Companies responsible for the quality of their members' work; and how far did their influence extend geographically?

2). Somerset, 1600-1680 (Figures 4:79-85)

If we are to maintain that the production of good joinery was largely an urban phenomenon, rather than a rural one, then we must look in each region for likely towns as centres of motivation — towns which had the means to sustain one or more workshops in a sufficiently active state for them to develop a house style of their own. We may assume that country

Figure 4:77. *Joined folding table. English; Salisbury. Oak, early seventeenth century. The turnings and joinery should be closely compared with chairs such as Figures 4:68 and 69 a and b.*

16. The organisation of the Salisbury Joyners' Company is discussed in Chapter Two, p.45, including a list of the other trades incorporated in the Company.
17. Dorset County Record Office MW/M4 f.23., quoted by Malcolm Airs, *The Making of the English Country House*, p.62.
18. E.g. Temple Newsam Catalogue 1976, No. 16., and Furniture History, 1976, plates 5a and 10a.

Figure 4:78. *Joined folding table. English; Salisbury. Oak, early seventeenth century. The simple carved decoration is identical to the arch panel and seat-rail of Figure 4:68, as are the turnings.*

Figure 4:79. *Joined armchair. English; Somerset. Oak, dated 1672.*

Figure 4:80. *Joined armchair. English; Somerset. Yewtree, mid-seventeenth century.*

Figure 4:81. *Joined armchair. English; Somerset. Oak, mid-seventeenth century.*

Figure 4:82. *Joined armchair. English; Somerset. Oak, mid-seventeenth century.*

churches and the smaller manor houses were equipped with their finer woodwork by the hands of joiners and carvers who were based in such regional centres. Such fine work was doubtlessly prefabricated in the urban workshops, and then transported for finishing and fitting on site. In the same way, movable furniture (of the better sort) was made in the towns and carted to the customer's home. Some of the finest church woodwork in Somerset, for instance, is the fine series of pews and other fittings of c.1616 at Croscombe, near Wells. The cathedral city of Wells was a thriving, but rather small, place at this time; and so we must ask whether the city was able to command and supply such fine joinery and carving, or should we look further for the makers, perhaps to the regional capital of Bristol itself? The potential market for good joined furniture was so thin on the ground in rural areas, that we must assume the larger towns to be the chief sources of supply.

In the great houses, such as Montacute in the south of the county, different factors were at work. Such establishments were like islands in the rural sea, sufficient unto themselves. The great builders did sometimes patronise masons and joiners from the immediate neighbourhood, but just as often they seem to have relied on a relatively small circle of itinerant specialists who travelled the country from job to job with their tools and patterns. They would have been little impressed by the successive vernacular traditions which they saw around them.

Somerset is a diverse county in its land forms. The southern half is largely taken up by the flat low-lying plain of the Somerset Levels, which are skirted by the old Tudor Post Road from London to Cornwall (via Salisbury and Exeter, now the A30). The west is part of the great highland of Exmoor; whilst the north is occupied by the limestone hills of the Mendips and the lower Cotswolds. Through the north of the county runs the old Great West Road from London to Bristol, via Bath. Both the old roads must be regarded as important cultural links with London and the other cities; but it is arguable that the major urban influence in this area must have derived from the great seaport of Bristol, with a hinterland that included not only the West Country, but also (by sea) parts of South Wales and Monmouthshire.

Figure 4:83. *Joined chest. English; Somerset. Oak, 1630-50.*

Figure 4:84. *Joined chest. English; Somerset. Oak, early seventeenth century.*

Figure 4:85. *Joined chest. English; Somerset. Oak, early seventeenth century.*

Figure 4:86. *Joined armchair (detail of Figure 4:87). The paired dragons of the crest are typical of Gloucester chairs, and are seen in the next four examples.*

Figure 4:87. *Joined armchair. English; Gloucestershire. Oak, dated 1640.*

The variety in the physical characteristics of the county is reflected in the variety of high-quality carved furniture to be found in the area, though county boundaries are seen to be no barrier to the availability and frequency of popular motifs. Many of the common Somerset motifs are found equally in North Dorset, West Wiltshire and Gloucestershire. The most obvious of these are the three most popular panel forms: the double heart (Figures 4:57, 83, 91); the quatrefoil (Figures 4:84 and 85); and the enriched arch (Figures 4:63a, 68, 78-82, 86-90 and 92). It is also possible to draw several other correlations. The use of inlay is noticeably absent in West Country furniture in general, except perhaps in Bristol itself (see the group of armchairs in Figures 3:54-57, which possibly originates in Bristol, or some other West Country urban source).

Somerset is the home of a series of richly carved armchairs and chests, which mostly seem to date from the first half of the seventeenth century. The chair in Figure 4:79 bears an unexpectedly late date of 1672, even though it is quite consistent with other local chairs. Another surprising feature (rare anywhere in England) is the long pair of side pieces which reach the full height of the back. The only immediate parallel for these is in the Thomas Dennis chairs of similar date from Ipswich, Masssachusetts (Figure 4:197). A common constructional feature in Somerset, as elsewhere in the West, is the deepened top rail on chests and chair backs (Figures 4:80-84), which is normally treated with a rich band of carving.

3). Gloucestershire, 1600-1680 (Figures 4:86-93)

The geological divisions of Gloucestershire are simpler than those of Somerset, but just as positive. Most of the south-eastern side of the county is taken up by the dip slope of the Cotswolds, where they run down to the Upper Thames Valley. Here, the old inhabitations are largely restricted to the small river valleys in the limestone, and the broad valley of the Thames itself. But the most rewarding area for our study is the wide trench of the Vale of Gloucester, and its extension as the Vale of Evesham (i.e. the Avon/Severn lowland which lies north-west of the Cotswold Escarpment). This valley allows easy passage between Bristol and the Midlands (through Gloucester, Stratford-upon-Avon, Warwick and Coventry, into Leicestershire).

An ancient obsession raises its head here in the form of the crests of paired dragons which are such a consistent feature of Gloucestershire chairs

Figure 4:88. *Joined armchair. English; Gloucestershire. Oak, dated 1631. Found at Edgworth Manor, Cirencester, Glos. The initials 'W_SW'supposedly refer to William and Sarah Wiggle, the ancestors of a local family which is still numerous in the Gloucester-Cheltenham area.*

Figure 4:89. *Joined armchair. English; Gloucestershire. Oak, 1630-40. The feet have been built up later in rather a curious manner.*

Figure 4:90. *Joined armchair. English; Gloucestershire. Oak, 1630-40.*

(Figures 4:86-90). Dragons are embedded very deep in the folklore of Western Britain, and may be found even in the eighteenth century in Wales, Lancashire and the Lake District (cf. Figures 4:115, 147, 148, 151, 163, 169-173, 175). Neither are they restricted to the West but may be seen in East Anglia (e.g. on a firebeam at Brundish Manor, Suffolk).[19] Nearer to Gloucestershire, they may be seen in the early seventeenth century oak frieze in the parlour at the Greyfriars, Worcester.[20] They also appear in pairs on the richly-carved chest in Figure 4:91; which has other characteristic motifs, such as the same fleshy plant tendrils as may be seen on the previous two chairs (Figures 4:89 and 90).

Figure 4:91. *Joined chest. English; Gloucestershire. Oak, 1630-40. The floral panel is closely related to the two previous chairs, with a characteristic straight central stem, thick fleshy scrolling branches, and raspberry-like bunches of grapes.*

19. See *Suffolk Houses*, Eric Sandon, Baron Publishing, Woodbridge, 1977, pl.69.
20. See Country Life, 27th November, 1969, p.1394, fig.9.

Figure 4:92. *Joined chest. English; Gloucestershire. Oak and elm, c.1680.*

In general, the carving on Gloucestershire furniture is less accomplished than that of Somerset and Devon. Much of the carving is done with large and expansive cuts of the chisel, producing a rather coarse and repetitive effect. The running leafy cable seen on the rails and stiles of the chest in Figure 4:93 is entirely typical of this area, and may be seen on the chair-table in Figure 3:68, as well as the seat-rails and lower panel-rail of the armchair in Figure 4:89. The regional character of carving is thus seen more clearly in the handling of detail, rather than in the frequency of popular motifs and panel-types. The general outline and character of chairs is often a strong indication of regional affinities, and the close family likeness of this group of Gloucestershire armchairs is immediately apparent. The shape of the arm is often a clear indication, and a telling feature here is the scrolled carving at the tip of the arm. Although the various details of arm-shapes are more or less universal, the actual character and conformation of the arm often has a local flavour. As in so many other instances, the reader may be left to draw further visual comparisons for himself.

Figure 4:93. *Joined chest. English; Gloucestershire. Oak, c.1640.*

Figure 4:94. *(Right) Joined armchair. Scottish; East Coast. Oak, c.1580. Strong French influence is seen in the architectural perspective of the panel, as well as the general form of the chair.*

Figure 4:95. *(Far right) Joined armchair. Scottish; East Coast. Oak, c.1600. This interlaced panel is a French or Flemish design.*

4). Aberdeen, Scotland, 1580-1700 (Figures 4:94-112)

During the period under discussion, Scotland was gradually reduced from the home of a proud and hardy aristocracy, to an extremely poor and discontented country. The lot of the poor had always been one of grinding oppression under a series of rapacious overlords, aggravated by an often harsh climate. The wealthy southern half of the country had been gradually laid waste by wars with the English in the course of the sixteenth century, and by internal troubles associated with the Scottish Reformation. In the middle of the seventeenth century, a great deal of money was squandered on futile efforts to help Prince Charles (later Charles II), to be rewarded only in the form of heavy fines from Oliver Cromwell. The last case of plague appeared in Scotland in 1648, but up until then it was virulent in many Scottish towns,[21] and sapped the strength of the nation.

Yet, despite this catalogue of woes, Scotland does not deserve the reputation it has acquired amongst Englishmen as something of a cultural desert in the seventeenth and eighteenth centuries. True, its great houses were usually built as castles until a later date than the rest of Britain, but they were by no means devoid of the arts of interior decoration (Figure 1:8). Dr. Samuel Johnson did nothing to soften the Scots' reputation in England when he wrote in 1773:[22]

> "...I know not whether it be peculiar to the Scots to have attained the liberal, without the manual arts, to have excelled in ornamental knowledge, and to have wanted not only the elegances, but the conveniences of common life..."

But these scathing comments were directed at the primitive conditions which still then pertained in Western Scotland, entirely in ignorance (it seems) of the rich Franco-Scottish culture of the East Coast cities. The

21. See *Man, Environment and Disease in Britain,* G. Melvyn Howe, Pelican, 1976, p.142.
22. *A Journey to the Western Isles of Scotland.*

Figure 4:96. *Joined armchair. Scottish; Trinity Hall, Aberdeen. Oak, dated 1621. The words and date 'conuiner 1708' are a later alteration, the chair having been presented in that year by James Simpson, tailor. The coat-of-arms is a spurious one, based on the attributes of Simpson's trade.*

Figure 4:97. *High contrast photography reveals a trace of the original inscription on Figure 4:96 (on left). Special treatment of this print has isolated the date of 1621 (right), though the rest of the original wording has been too efficiently obliterated to be readable (see comments on p.463).*

'Auld Alliance' between Scotland and France gave birth to a rich heritage of French influences in the furniture of Eastern Scotland, whose busy ports were in close contact with France and other European countries (see especially Figure 3:35).

The city of Aberdeen springs easiest to mind in this context, largely because of the existence of two important collections of armchairs from known sources in Aberdeen, supplemented by a number of similar chairs in country houses in the region (Aberdeenshire and Kincardineshire). The first and smaller collection (not illustrated here) is at Provand's Lordship, in Glasgow. This collection was assembled piecemeal during the present century, but it nevertheless contains some important documentary Aberdeen chairs.[23]

The second group (of twenty chairs) is a much older one, having been assembled mainly during the seventeenth century at Trinity Hall, Aberdeen, the headquarters of the Old Incorporated Trades of Aberdeen. This is a guild organisation of seven trades, not unlike the English Trade Companies, which comprises hammermen, bakers, wrights and coopers, barber-surgeons,[24] tailors, shoemakers, weavers and fleshers. The chairs were donated to mark their terms of office by Deacons of each trade, or by the Master of the Company (the Deacon Convener). An inventory of 1696 lists

23. See *Some Early Scottish Chairs,* Andrew Hannah, Scottish Art Review, Vol.V, no.3, Summer 1955.
24. The Barber-chirurgeons' (or Leechers') Incorporation is now extinct, but their Deacon's chair is still at Trinity Hall (Figure 4:99).

461

a total of twenty-three chairs, of which fifteen can still be identified. Not all the chairs are of local type, and so only the more significant ones are illustrated here. Of the fifteen chairs shown here, eleven are mentioned in the inventory:

> ...An inventory of the plenishings belonging to Trinity Hall, taken in the presence of Patrick Whyt, Deacon Convener, 1696:
>
> Hammermen.
> ane cheer gifted by Matthew Guild, armourer (Figure 4:6).
> ane cheer gifted by Patrick Whyt, hookmaker, Deacon Conveener, 1690 (Figure 4:100).
>
> Bakers.
> ane cheer gifted by John Middleton, baxter, Deacon Conveener, 1634 (Figure 4:103).
>
> Wrights and Coopers.
> ane cheer gifted by Jerome Blak, couper, 1574 (Figure 3:20).
> ane cheer gifted by William Ord, wright, Deacon Conveener, 1635 (Figure 4:104).
>
> Taylziours.
> ane cheer gifted by Thomas Cordyn, taylyer, Deacon Conveener, 1627 (Figure 4:101).
>
> Shoemakers.
> ane cheer gifted by Thomas Robertson, shoemaker, Deacon Conveener, 1633 (Figure 4:102).
> ane cheer gifted by Alexander Idle, shoemaker, Deacon Conveener, 1679 (Figure 4:106).
>
> Weavers.
> ane public cheer for their Deacon, 1684 (Figure 4:108).
>
> Fleshers.
> ane cheer gifted by Andrew Watson, Deacon (Figure 4:105).
> ane cheer marked WP coft to the Hospital (Figure 4:107).

Four further chairs are also illustrated from the Trinity Hall collection (Figures 4:96, 98, 99 and 109), but for various reasons they did not figure in the inventory, though each has a history of ownership by the Trades.

All the great seaports of Eastern Scotland supported thriving mercantile communities (Edinburgh, Stirling, Perth, Dundee, Montrose, Aberdeen), and the furniture produced in these centres is still to be found scattered in great country houses and castles throughout the region. Unfortunately it is not yet possible to analyse the nuances of individual local styles. A number of simple joined armchairs in oak and pine are known, such as Figures 3:36 and 4:110, 111, and two pine examples at Provand's Lordship from Stonehaven (Kinross-shire) and Lumphanan, Aberdeenshire (dated 1688). These are all suggestive of a vivid but crude tradition of furniture making in the countryside and the fishing ports, using the chief local woods; but the finer examples of Franco-Scottish type must all be associated with the urban workshops, and notably those of Aberdeen and Edinburgh.

The ancient city of Aberdeen was a rich and influential place at the beginning of the seventeenth century. It housed one of the four Scottish universities, and served a large hinterland in the north-east. Since Trinity Hall was the home of the major group of trade companies, it is only to be expected that the chairs used there would equal in quality the finest products then available in the city. No doubt, if it is possible to identify the makers of any of these chairs, they will be numbered among the members of the Wrights and Coopers Incorporation. A preference for *caqueteuse* armchairs had been firmly established in Scotland in the sixteenth century, more especially under the influence of cultural contacts made with France under Mary Queen of Scots (Figures 4:94 and 95).

The earliest dated *caqueteuse* at Trinity Hall is that given by James Simpson in 1708 (Figure 4:96). The original inscription and date (1621) on the lower half of the panel were roughly erased, and the words 'conviner 1708' were incised in their place. Fortunately, the removal of the original lettering was carelessly done, and although the words are now indecipherable, it has been possible to reveal the original date by means of special photography (Figure 4:97). The name 'IAMES SIMSON' is evidently original work of 1621, and it seems likely that the chair belonged originally to an ancestor of the Convenor Simpson of 1708, who simply altered the relevant date. The coat-of-arms is based on the appurtenances of Simpson's trade, that of a tailor (smoothing iron, pair of shears, a bodkin and vase of lilies). A rather similar chair at Crathes Castle, Banchory (near Aberdeen) is dated 1597, and the horizontal emphasis of the cresting is seen to be typical of the earlier chairs (1570-1630).

At least two major workshop groups of related chairs are evident at Trinity Hall, with close correlations at Provand's Lordship. The first of these is represented by Figures 4:98-100. The main similarity lies in the disposition of the back, which is split into two panels, and which is angled backwards from the level of the arms instead of the more usual method at the seat. The lower panel in each case is an enriched saltire; and the upper panels are armorial. The chair in Figure 4:98 is a damaged example which is important because of the date, 1627, which provides a guide for dating the others. Because of it, we are led to question the date of 1690 on Patrick Whyt's chair (Figure 4:100). To all appearances, Whyt must have caused the original back panel to be replaced with one of his own design; an

Figure 4:98. *(Left) Joined armchair. Scottish; Trinity Hall, Aberdeen. Oak, dated 1627. The coat-of-arms and the initials 'AF' refer to the family of Farquhar or Farquharson. The stretchers are wrongly restored.*

Figure 4:99. *(Right) Joined armchair. Scottish; Trinity Hall, Aberdeen. Oak, 1625-30. The coat-of-arms and the initials 'HG' refer to the family of Guthrie. This chair is the property of the Barber-Surgeons, hence the inscription 'CHIRURGIE(N)'.*

Figure 4:100. *Joined armchair. Scottish; Trinity Hall, Aberdeen. Oak, 1625-30. The panel is a replacement of 1690, when the chair was presented by Patrick Whyt, hookmaker. A similar panel in another chair is dated 1685.*

Figure 4:101. *Joined armchair. Scottish; Trinity Hall, Aberdeen. Oak, dated 1627. Presented by Thomas Gardine, tailor. The panel bears the initials 'TG', the arms of the Garden family, and their motto 'IN GOD IS MY TRUST'. The crest bears a pair of shears, an attribute of Gardine's trade.*

Figure 4:102. *Joined armchair. Scottish; Trinity Hall, Aberdeen. Oak, dated 1633. Presented by Thomas Robertson, shoemaker. The panel bears the initials 'TR', the arms of the Robertson family, and their motto 'GRACE ME GOD'. The crest bears a leather-knife, an attribute of Robertson's trade.*

observation which is fully confirmed by an identical chair at Provand's Lordship, which retains the original panel bearing the arms of Cockburn and Paterson, and the date 1629. By extension, both Whyt's chair and the chair of the defunct Barber-Surgeons' Incorporation (Figure 4:99) may be dated to c.1625-30. Unfortunately, it is never possible to give a very close dating with confidence, since many features appear over a wide timespan, and the crest of this latter chair is actually of sixteenth century type.

The next four chairs are very closely related, and are obviously by the same hand (Figures 4:101-104). The closeness of their dates (1627, 1633, 1634 and 1635) is matched by a similarity of execution and decoration. Although the details may vary, the handling is the same. The showy expertise of these four chairs (and of the following three) betray the hand of a skilled carver(s), perhaps a Frenchman working in Aberdeen. Out of the four donors of these chairs, only the last, William Ord (1635) is described as a 'wright' (a carpenter or joiner). There is no record of Ord's particular speciality of work, but if he was a skilled joiner, there would be every reason to assume that he made his chair himself, and so by extension the other three. The carving of the crests, turnings and panels is undoubtedly the work of a specialist, but the simpler ornament of the frame and seat-rails is more typical joiner's work. The crests, and the 1627 panel, are particularly accomplished, and display a clear mastery of French Renaissance design. As with so many of the chairs in this collection, the symbols of the trades are included in the decoration.

Figure 4:103. *Joined armchair. Scottish; Trinity Hall, Aberdeen. Oak, dated 1634. Presented by John Middleton, baker. The panel bears the initials 'IM', the arms of the Middleton family, and the motto 'MY SOUL PRAIS THE LORD'. The crest bears a peel charged with two loaves, attributes of Middleton's trade.*

Figure 4:104. *Joined armchair. Scottish; Trinity Hall, Aberdeen. Oak, dated 1635. Presented by William Ord, who is described as a 'wright'. If this really does mean a joiner, he may have been the maker of this chair and the previous three. The panel bears the arms of the Ord family and their motto 'IN DOMINO CONFIDO'. The cresting-rail bears a pair of dividers, a square and an axe, all attributes of Ord's trade.*

Figure 4:105. *Joined armchair. Scottish; Trinity Hall, Aberdeen. Mahogany, dated 1661. Presented by Andrew Watson, butcher. The panel bears the initials 'AW' and the arms of the Watson family. The crest bears a butcher's axe and three fleshing knives. This is a most remarkable appearance of mahogany at such an early date, and this chair must be the earliest dated piece of British-made mahogany furniture in existence. A few planks of the timber must have come into Watson's possession, or that of a joiner known to him, from a Spanish or French source.*

Figure 4:106. *Joined armchair. Scottish; Trinity Hall, Aberdeen. Oak, with bands of inlay, dated 1679. Presented by Alexander Idle, shoemaker. The panel bears the name 'A Idle', the date '30·of Nor 1679', and a leather-knife.*

Figure 4:107. *Joined armchair. Scottish; Trinity Hall, Aberdeen. Oak, c.1680. The panel bears the initials 'WP' and the arms of the Paterson family. The donor of the chair is not known, but it was included in the 1696 inventory of Trinity Hall.*

Figure 4:108. *Joined armchair. Scottish; Trinity Hall, Aberdeen. Oak, dated 1684. The panel bears the legend 'WEAWERS — SPERO IN DEO ET IPSE FACIT', and the crest bears the arms of the Weavers Incorporation.*

Many of the similarities shared by these four are evident in the next three (Figures 4:105-107), especially the first of these (1661). Despite a gap of twenty-six years, Andrew Watson's chair has the same carved turnings and 'personalised' architectural crest as before. Other details have been elaborated to an extreme, but there are nevertheless two close parallels at Provand's Lordship. The first of these is the most interesting, for it was also the property of Andrew Watson and bears the same coat-of-arms and initials 'AW (DE)ACON 1657'. The crest is simpler, but it shares the same elaborate arcaded underframe, carved turnings, fluted uprights and pierced panel-rail. Another chair shares most of these features, and is inscribed 'W^{M}C' and 'IF, 1667'. This was the marriage chair of William Chalmers, Professor of Divinity at Aberdeen University, and Isabella Forbes.

Yet, despite its extravagant design, Andrew Watson's chair has a greater claim to distinction in the very material from which it is made. This is probably the earliest dated piece of mahogany furniture of British make. The wood is extremely close-grained and hard, of a slight reddish hue, with a bright patination. Over the years it has taken a good polish,[25] and the wear has been slight but even. Oak and pine are the usual timbers in Scottish furniture (whether native or imported from Scandinavia), but the presence of mahogany in Aberdeen should not be a surprise at this date. 'Spanish' or 'Jamaica' wood was well known by the middle of the seventeenth century, and a few planks might easily have found their way into this busy port from Spain or France.

25. I am grateful to David Learmont for his confirmation of these observations. Mr. Learmont is Curator to the National Trust for Scotland.

Figure 4:109. *Joined armchair. Scottish; Trinity Hall, Aberdeen. Oak, dated 1690. Presented by George Gordon, tailor. The panel bears his name and the attributes of his trade, a bodkin and a pair of shears.*

The fashion for elaborate *caqueteuse* chairs is taken into the 1680s by the next two (Figures 4:106 and 107) with no condescension to post-Restoration styles, other than (perhaps) the thin turnings of the 1679 chair. Although this date is in a different hand to the rest of the inscription on the chair, there is no reason to doubt its accuracy (a dated chair of 1686, in a private collection, has the same crest and pierced panel-rail). These late chairs still exhibit the same spirited refinement of carving that is seen on the earlier chairs; but there is little to show that this excellence was carried beyond the seventeenth century. Chairs dated late in the century (Figures 4:108 and 109) show a decline in the former high traditions of carving in urban Aberdeen, though the joinery is still solid and well formed.

The Trinity Hall chairs bear witness to an accomplished and appreciative domestic life amongst the landowners and burghers of the Scottish east and north-east, which is in stark contrast to the lot of the poverty-stricken peasant highlander (cf. Figure 2:56).

5). Yorkshire, 1630-1720 (Figures 4:113-150)

Yorkshire is the largest and most diverse of the English counties, with several individual lowland regions in which schools of furniture were free to develop (see map, Appendix V). However, we are concerned here only with the Clothing Dales area of the West Riding, which was during the seventeenth century the bustling and affluent heart of the English clothing industry. This is essentially an area of densely settled valleys in the Pennines, which extend across the county border into East Lancashire. The major city in the seventeenth century was Leeds, but other important

Figure 4:110. *Joined armchair. Scottish, East Coast. Oak and pine, c.1680.*

Figure 4:111. *Joined armchair. Scottish; East Coast. Oak and pine, c.1680.*

Figure 4:112. *Joined armchair. South-West Scotland. Oak, dated 1681.*

Figure 4:113. *(Left) Joined armchair. English; Leeds area, Yorkshire. Oak, with inlay, mid-seventeenth century.*

Figure 4:114. *(Right) Joined armchair. English; Leeds area, Yorkshire. Oak, with inlay, mid-seventeenth century.*

centres were already present in Bradford, Halifax (Yorkshire) and Burnley (Lancashire). These prosperous towns and valleys create a complex pattern of relationships, but there is enough of a common theme in their decorative furniture to allow consideration as a cohesive region. The production of joined and carved oak furniture persisted until a very late date throughout the North Country; but Lancashire and the West Riding were both specially rich in surviving examples until very recent times. In the last eighty years or so, huge numbers of locally-made items have been collected from the area by the antique trade, with the result that Yorkshire/Lancashire furniture is heavily represented in collections all over Britain and elsewhere. Indeed, Yorkshire panel-back armchairs are certainly the most common single regional type available.

The problem of assigning dates to furniture from the West Riding is a very difficult one. The vast majority of dated specimens are securely after 1650, and sometimes a long time after. The settle of 1756 from Lotherton Hall (Figure 4:138) is admittedly an exceptionally late phenomenon, but the general range of dated examples prompts a date-spectrum of 1650-1720. Yet this conclusion is possibly deceptive, since it seems probable that the custom of dating furniture was not usual in this area until the second half of the century, and that many of the stock motifs and panel forms which appear with late dates were actually developed much earlier. Most of the chairs illustrated here have a broad similarity in certain features: notably in the form of the scrolled crests and earpieces; in a limited range of arm types; and in a limited range of panel types, such as the diamond or lozenge, usually enriched in a predictable manner (Figures 4:126 and 130). In addition to these broader similarities, much closer relationships are traceable in respect of a number of workshop groups. These groups, which are united by close parallels of form and handling, deserve far more penetrative analysis than is possible here, and scope is provided by the large number of examples still in large houses in the district.

Plate Fifteen. *Joined side table. English. Walnut, late seventeenth century.*

Figure 4:115. *(Left) Joined armchair. English; Leeds area, Yorkshire. Oak, with inlay, mid-seventeenth century.*

Figure 4:116. *(Right) Joined armchair. English; Leeds area, Yorkshire. Oak, mid-seventeenth century.*

A Workshop Group from the Leeds Area (Figures 3:267 and 4:113-122)

One group which is rather more conspicuous than the others is represented here by a number of chairs, chests and cupboards. They are characterised in almost every case by a rich variety of inlaid floral panels and bands of geometric parquetry ornament. In addition, the carving is distinctively formed, with a formal yet mobile sense of style. The joinery is extremely well made and carefully finished, unlike some other groups. The quality of the work suggests that it may have been done in the rich city of Leeds, though several surviving examples are located in houses and churches a little south-west of Leeds itself, in the Dewsbury/Batley/Halifax area.[26]

Figure 4:117. *Joined chest. English; Leeds area, Yorkshire. Oak, with inlay and parquetry, mid-seventeenth century.*

26. See Temple Newsam Catalogue, 1971, for further examples, pls.12 and 21.

Figure 4:118. *Detail of press cupboard in Figure 4:120. The various decorative elements seen here in detail are repeated on many other members of the group.*

Figure 4:119. *Detail of press cupboard in 4:120. The dragon on the right-hand stile is repeated exactly on the crest of the armchair in Figure 4:115.*

Figure 4:120. *Joined press cupboard. English; Leeds area, Yorkshire. Oak, with inlay, mid-seventeenth century.*

Even though this work is distinctly 'Elizabethan' in its character (with an extensive use of carved turnings, florid inlay and sculptural carving), there is no suggestion that any of it belongs to the sixteenth century. The chair types all correspond to the standard local products which are dated in the second half of the seventeenth century. In the absence of any precisely-dated component from this group, it is best to exercise a little caution and suggest a range around the middle of the century, say 1630-80.

The decoration of these pieces should perhaps be regarded as an archaic survival of an earlier taste, particularly in the case of the inlaid panels. These are decorated with a variety of plants which issue from a variety of flowerpots and mounds. As is usual with inlaid work, the panels were made in pairs so that the blacks from one can be reversed with the whites of the other; thus, the flower on one panel is the 'negative' of the same flower on the other panel. This is best seen on pieces which retain the pair of panels, such as the chest in Figure 4:117. The bands of geometric inlay and parquetry were apparently prefabricated in standard patterns (as later in the eighteenth century), since the same stock patterns are repeated time after time, and they are often cut off in mid-sequence to fill the allotted space. The usual patterns are fairly simple runs of dog-tooth or chequerwork, but a more ambitious motif is seen in the zig-zag parquetry of the centre panel in the chest in Figure 4:117, which is repeated on the top frieze of the press cupboard in Figure 3:267.

Figure 4:121. *Joined press cupboard. English; Leeds area, Yorkshire. Oak, with inlay, mid-seventeenth century. The verve and quality of earlier work is still present in this piece, which gives the lie to popular theories that the quality of carved work gradually declined throughout the seventeenth century.*

Figure 4:122. *Joined chest. English; Leeds area, Yorkshire. Oak, with inlay, mid-seventeenth century.*

The chairs of this group are fairly accomplished in their treatment (such as the shaped crests of Figures 4:113 and 114, and the paired dragons on the crest of Figure 4:115), but these distinctions are largely matters of detail, and in general they conform quite closely to the other chairs of the region. Figure 4:116 is a typical local product, though its affinities with the present group are demonstrated by the similarity of the proportion with Figure 4:115. It has the same arm profile as the preceding chair, and the same long earpieces, but the quality is otherwise much inferior. This may serve to demonstrate the broad range of products turned out by one workshop for customers of varying means; or it may be on a late and degenerate product of the same workshop in a declining phase. The former interpretation seems the more likely.

Armchairs (Figures 4:123-138)

The most distinctive 'signature' of the Dales armchair is the broad curly profile of the double-scrolled pediment crest, in which the scrolled earpieces are an integral part of the design. Within this simple formula is found a huge variation of infilling detail. Most of these chairs can be divided into workshop groups, but this would involve a highly complicated analysis. Many of the distinctive panels and carving styles appear on several joinery types, suggesting that the work of a limited group of carvers and inlayers was used by a wider group of joiners. Also, it would seem that joiners 'borrowed' designs for turnings and arm profiles from each other.

An earlier date than most is suggested by the carving and restrained crest of Figure 4:123. The delicate handling of the panels is remarkably similar to some of the minor panels on the Laudian (1634) screen of St. John's Church, Leeds, and suggests a date in that decade or soon after. The peculiar form of the turnings and the tapered scroll of the arm is reflected in other chairs, especially Figure 4:125 (dated 1661). The decoration of the earlier chairs is in a very smooth and accomplished metropolitan style, but

472

Figure 4:124. *Joined armchair. English; probably Leeds, Yorkshire. Oak, mid-seventeenth century.*

Figure 4:123. *Joined armchair. English; probably Leeds, Yorkshire. Oak, c.1630-40. The bulk of Yorkshire chairs seem to date from after the middle of the seventeenth century, though this is possibly a misleading assumption derived from the fact that dated specimens occur almost entirely after 1650.*

Figure 4:125. *Joined armchair. English; probably Leeds, Yorkshire. Oak, dated 1661.*

27. Temple Newsam Catalogue, 1971, p.11.

after c.1660 a bolder and often simpler vernacular sense asserts itself (this is not to say that 1660, and the Restoration, should in any way be regarded as a significant date in this area, since many of the vernacular impulses are seen in fixed woodwork of an earlier date; e.g. further north in a family pew of 1631 at Kirkby Malham).[27]

Most Yorkshire armchairs must be dated in the period 1660-1720, and a great many of these are still extant. One very distinctive group of chairs is represented by Figure 4:126, which is exactly paralleled by an identical armchair at Bolling Hall, Bradford. The panel (repeated here on a chest from Bradford, Figure 4:127) consists of a small diamond which is flanked by a series of heavily cross-hatched trilobes and lightly-incised *fleurs-de-lis*.

Figure 4:126. *Joined armchair. English; probably Bradford/Halifax area, Yorkshire. Oak, with inlay, 1650-1700. This chair is representative of a large workshop group with broadly similar characteristics, though they seem to include the work of several individual joiners and carvers, and some inlay work.*

The crest is especially persistent throughout the group, having a distinctive drooping pair of bifurcated leafy buds, set within the usual double-scrolled outline. The same device is seen with variations of treatment in Figures 3:490 (dated 1680) and Figures 4:134 and 135. The proportions, joinery and turnings of Figure 4:126 are also exactly paralleled by a dated chair (1689) at Rufford Hall, Lancashire. But in this case the carving has a very different character, which is matched here by Figures 4:128 and 129. Several similar chairs are known from the Burnley district, which raises the question of either a Lancashire provenance, or the work of several joiners and carvers who were itinerant within the district. It becomes impossible to describe these interrelationships in verbal terms alone, and a close geographical analysis will only become possible when a comprehensive photographic archive is available.

Figure 4:127. *Joined chest. English; probably Bradford/Halifax area, Yorkshire. Oak, with inlay, 1650-1700. The panel is of identical design to the previous example, but of sufficiently different character to suggest a different hand. The heavy cross-hatching of the trilobes is a recurrent feature of carving in this area, as in Figures 4:126, 129, 132, 139 and 140 etc.*

Figure 4:128. *Joined armchair (detail). English, south-west Yorkshire/East Lancashire, possibly Burnley area. Oak, 1680-1700. This is one of a group found throughout the Clothing Dales, in both Yorkshire and Lancashire. The general form is more characteristic of Yorkshire, but of course the county boundaries must be largely ignored in considering the distribution of furniture types. This, and the next two examples, show the typical fine linear carving of the group, with similar crests and bird-like earpieces. An example at Rufford Hall, Lancashire, is dated 1689.*

Figures 4:129 and 129a. *Two joined armchairs. English; South-West Yorkshire/East Lancashire. Oak, 1680-1700.*

Figure 4:130. *Joined armchair. English; Leeds, Yorkshire. Oak, with inlay, 1650-1700.*

Figure 4:131. *Detail of armchair in 4:130. This diamond panel with fluttering pennant-like terminals is highly characteristic of the Dales area, cf. Figures 3:376, 4:116, 133 and 134.*

It is quite rare to find a Dales armchair dated after 1700, though several are known; but the settle of 1756 from Lotherton Hall, near Leeds, is exceptionally late (Figure 4:138). Though superficially similar to Dales settles of fifty to eighty years earlier (cf. a settle of 1688 in the Burrell Collection), certain details confirm a mid-eighteenth century date for this piece. The fielded panels are wholly consistent with this date, as are the thin, stiff arms (supported by mean little turned stumps). The settle is dated only two years after the first appearance of Chippendale's *Director,* yet some awareness of contemporary taste is shown in the little band of strapwork fret on the rear uprights beneath each arm. Otherwise, all the decoration is a rather formal and archaic rendering of an earlier style of carving, none of which actually captures any of the spirit of the seventeenth century.[28] Assuming that the 1756 date is genuine, it is difficult to decide whether this piece is a bona fide last flickering of an out-moded tradition, or an early expression of eighteenth century antiquarianism. The slick romantic piety of the inscription would suggest the latter: 'DEUS:VIDET·Q·N·T·N·L·TAYTA:MEATA·' (God sees those thoughts which lie hidden in your soul at night).

28. Except, perhaps, for the two horizontal rails below the front of the seat.

476

Figure 4:132. *Joined armchair. English; South-West Yorkshire. Oak, with inlay, 1650-1700. A particularly lively specimen. Compare with Figure 4:113.*

Figure 4:133. *Joined armchair. English; Leeds, Yorkshire. Oak, 1650-1700. Compares closely with Figure 4:116.*

Figure 4:134. *Joined armchair. English; South-West Yorkshire. Oak, dated 1685. The raised and turned stretchers are most unusual.*

Figure 4:135. *Joined armchair. English; South-West Yorkshire. Oak and ash, 1650-1700.*

Figure 4:136. *Joined armchair. English; South-West Yorkshire. Oak, 1650-1700.*

Figure 4:137. *Joined armchair. English; South-West Yorkshire. Oak, 1650-1700.*

Figure 4:138. *Joined settle. English; Lotherton Hall, Leeds, Yorkshire. Oak, dated 1756. A curiously archaic design at this date, perhaps made for a customer with antiquarian tastes.*

Backstools (Figures 3:135-137 and 4:139-150)

Curiously, the distinctive backstool of the West Riding and South Yorkshire bears little stylistic affinity with armchairs from the same region. Whereas the armchairs which we have just seen are exclusively of panel-back construction, the backstools are always of the open-back variety shown here. Most of these have a pair of characteristic crescent-shaped

Figure 4:139. *Joined backstool. English; South Yorkshire. Oak and ash, 1670-1700.*

Figure 4:140. *Joined backstool. English; South Yorkshire. Oak and ash, 1670-1700.*

Figure 4:141. *Joined backstool. English; South Yorkshire. Oak, 1670-1700.*

478

Figure 4:142. *Joined backstool. English; South Yorkshire. Oak, 1670-1700.*

Figure 4:143. *Joined backstool. English; South Yorkshire. Oak, late seventeenth century.*

Figure 4:144. *Joined backstool. English; South Yorkshire. Oak, c.1700-20.*

Figure 4:145. *Joined backstool. English; South Yorkshire/Derbyshire. Oak and ash, late seventeenth century.*

Figure 4:146. *Joined backstool. English; South Yorkshire/Derbyshire. Oak, late seventeenth century.*

Figure 4:147. *Joined backstool (detail). English; South Yorkshire. Oak, 1650-80.*

Figure 4:148. *Joined backstool (detail). English; South Yorkshire. Oak, 1670-1700.*

Figure 4:149. *Detail of backstool in Figure 4:140.*

Figure 4:150. *Detail of backstool in Figure 4:143.*

cross-splats, enriched with scrolls and other details (Figures 3:136 and 4:139-144). A variant of this, which is more often associated with South Yorkshire and Derbyshire, retains the top cross-splat and has a row of spindles beneath (Figure 4:145); whilst another model has a fully-developed span of architectural arcading, supported on two turned spindles (Figures 3:137 and 4:146).

It is extremely difficult to give close dates for these various types of backstool, though most of them clearly belong to the last quarter of the seventeenth century and a little later. It seems likely that the earliest specimens may date from a little before 1650 (see Figures 3:135-137), and two later versions are actually dated 1680 and 1686. The position of the front stretcher is of no real help as a guide to dating, since a low stretcher was often used even at a late period; whilst repetitious turnings, popularly associated with the Commonwealth period, in fact persisted in everyday use until after 1700. The enriched scrolled finial to the uprights generally suggests an Eastern Pennine provenance, whilst the simpler scroll (Figures 4:160-162) seems to belong west of the Pennines.

The double cross-splat backstool (Figures 4:139-144, 147-150) is a firmly entrenched pattern in Yorkshire, with a wide variation in individual treatments as confirmed by the illustrations. Recent migrations, over the last one hundred years, have ensured that specimens are now scattered widely over the British Isles and further afield. This means that it is probably now too late to attempt to locate the original workshop centres, of which there must have been several. The position is a little more hopeful with armchairs, since many remain in local houses; but even so they have become scattered. For example, a West Riding armchair has been for many years in the chancel of Edington Church, Wiltshire. This might have been assumed to be a local chair, but enquiry eventually revealed that it had been purchased a long time ago from a well-known dealer in Ripon, Yorkshire. It is important to recognise and define intruders of this sort when involved in field investigations into regional types.

6). Lancashire and the Cheshire Plain, 1640-1720 (Figures 4:151-168)

Geographically, the county of Lancashire is broadly divided into the highland zone in the east, and a wide coastal lowland in the west, with a detached portion in the north forming part of the Lake District (q.v.). The furniture of East Lancashire is closely akin to that of the West Riding of Yorkshire, with the old centres of production apparently in such towns as Burnley and Rochdale. For furniture types which are distinctive to Lancashire, we have to look to the lowland area of Central Southern Lancashire and North Cheshire. This area provided relatively free access to outside influences in the seventeenth century, both overland and via the ports of Liverpool and Chester, and so much of the decoration shows an awareness of conventional national styles, especially in the first half of the century.

Yet in the middle of the century a distinguishable chair type, and a small range of panel types, began to appear in this area. Unlike Yorkshire, the armchairs and backstools both conform to the same pattern, with no real stylistic differences. The joinery is generally very neat and well-shaped, if sometimes a little thin, and the most obvious feature to look for by way of

Figure 4:151. *Joined armchair. English; South Lancashire/North Cheshire. Oak, c.1680.*

481

Figure 4:151a. *Joined armchair. English; South Lancashire/North Cheshire. Oak, 1650-1700. The seat is fitted with a drawer, which pulls out to the front.*

Figure 4:152. *Joined armchair. English; South Lancashire/North Cheshire. Oak, 1650-1700. The inclusion of a drawer under the seat, which here pulls out to the side, is not uncommon in chairs from this area.*

Figure 4:153. *Joined armchair. English; South Lancashire/North Cheshire. Oak, c.1680. The pattern of the blind fretted crest is repeated in the following two pierced examples, and the panels are closely related.*

identification is the little pyramid finial which almost always caps the rear uprights of chairs and settles (Figures 4:151-159, 163-165). Many of the backstools have a large lunette crest with floral or other formal infilling (Figures 4:158-166); and another type has a flatter scalloped crest, often with blind or pierced fretwork patterns (Figures 4:151-157). The blind frets, along with other details such as channel-mouldings or the backgrounds to sunk carving, are often picked out with black paint (though this may not always be obvious due to the obscuring effects of wear and patination). The panels are often framed with an applied moulding (Figures 4:151-156), though this is sometimes lost, leaving a blank border and tell-tale nail marks or scratched placing lines (Figure 4:154a).

The range of panel types is found equally on settles (Figure 3:51), chests and other items. The best of these is a widely varied combination of flowers and grapes, often centring on a fan-shaped flower head (as in Figure 4:154b). Another exciting subject is the stylised dragon which sometimes appears on chairs or chests. These may take the form of a fully integrated panel (Figure 4:163), or simply dragon-head finials incorporated into a larger design, as in the crests of Figures 4:113 and 151. A pair of backstools very similar to Figure 4:158 have been at Chetham's Hospital since the seventeenth century, in the old market town of Manchester. The backstool in Figure 4:159 is a common pattern of which several dozen are known. The detail of the carving (Figure 4:165) shows this to be cut in a very simple manner, with an elementary silhouette treatment of oak leaves, sketched in with an incised line.

The backstools with simple scrolled finials represented by Figures 4:160-162, are included here on rather more slender evidence. Certainly, the first of these bears decoration which is very typical of the Cheshire Plain

Figure 4:154a. *Detail of armchair in Figure 4:155. The applied moulding is missing from around the edge of the panel.*

Figure 4:154b. *Detail of backstool in Figure 4:156.*

Figure 4:155. *Joined armchair. English; South Lancashire/North Cheshire. Oak, 1680-1720.*

Figure 4:156. *Joined backstool. English; South Lancashire/North Cheshire. Oak, 1680-1720.*

Figure 4:157. *Joined backstool. English; South Lancashire/North Cheshire. Oak, late seventeenth century.*

Figure 4:158. *Joined backstool. English; South Lancashire, perhaps Manchester. Oak, 1680-1720.*

Figure 4:159. *Joined backstool. English; South Lancashire. Oak, 1680-1720.*

Figure 4:160. *Joined backstool. English; South Lancashire/North Cheshire. Oak, late seventeenth century.*

Figure 4:161. *Joined backstool. English; South Lancashire/North Cheshire. Oak, 1680-1720.*

Figure 4:162. *Joined backstool. English; South Lancashire/North Cheshire. Oak, 1680-1720.*

Figure 4:163. *(Left) Detail of backstool in Figure 4:158.*

Figure 4:164. *(Right) Detail of joined backstool. English; South Lancashire. Oak, 1680-1720.*

Figure 4:165. *(Left) Detail of backstool in Figure 4:159.*

Figure 4:166. *(Right) Detail of joined backstool. English; South Lancashire/ North Cheshire. Oak, 1680-1720. Similar to Figure 4:161.*

area, but the distribution of the others is a little less certain. Perhaps they belong further South in Cheshire. In particular, Figure 4:162 represents a very common model, which is now very widely distributed in private and public collections, so that firm conclusions may never be possible.

From the North of Lancashire, where the lowland is reduced to a narrow coastal strip around Lancaster and Bowland, comes a series of cupboards and chests with a distinctive flat and finely-curled style of carving. They are represented by a late press cupboard of 1705 (Figure 4:168, which is said to have come from a farmhouse in the Trough of Bowland), and by a much earlier dated press cupboard of 1658 (Figure 4:167, which has no provenance). This very individualistic carving is found over a very long period, extending from the middle of the seventeenth century (at least) until well after 1700. A chest of 1706 at the Church of St. Mary, Lancaster,[29] has very similar panels and runs of carving to the present cupboard of 1658; and a clothes press of 1717 at the Welsh Folk Museum has carving which relates exactly to the press cupboard of 1705, from Bowland. Other dated examples, with little variation in their decoration, range from 1667 to 1712,[30] though the largest number of dated examples are concentrated at the

29. See Temple Newsam Catalogue, 1973, no.10.
30. ibid.

485

Figure 4:167. *Joined press cupboard. English; North Lancashire, Lancaster area. Oak, dated 1658. Identical carving is found in this area and further north, from before 1650 until after 1720, evidence of a strong continuance in local traditions.*

Figure 4:168. *Joined press cupboard. English; North Lancashire, Lancaster area. Oak, with inlay, dated 1705. Similar cupboards are often dated between 1690 and 1720, and many have yewtree facings to the drawers.*

latter end of the range. Fixed woodwork of 1678 and 1684 in the parish of Over Wyresdale confirms both the date range and the geographical location of this school of carving;[31] whilst a little further north, similar carving is seen on a fixed cupboard of 1675 at Collin Field Manor, and a press cupboard of 1694 at Dallam Tower (both Westmorland).[32]

7). Westmorland and the Lake District, 1650-1750 (Figures 4:169-183)

The road north from Lancaster (to Carlisle and into Scotland) was in the seventeenth century the only major land route through to the Lake District, and it is inevitable that this mountainous area was largely isolated from the rest of Britain until the coming of the railways. Only in the nineteenth century was Lakeland opened up to the influx of tourists, appreciative for the first time (at least, on a wide scale) of the magnificent and picturesque scenery. Before then, the north-west of England was an introspective and parochial area, bound up in its own traditions and an instinctive awareness of its own long history. The departure of the Romans in the fourth century was succeeded by a series of invasions and settlement by sea-borne outsiders, first Saxons, then Danes and (as late as the tenth century) the Viking Norsemen. Through most of the Middle Ages the area was unsettled by border raids from the Scottish moss-troopers, but after the Union of 1603 these were forcibly suppressed by James I.

31. ibid.
32. Royal Commission on Historical Monuments, *Westmorland,* 1936.

486

Figure 4:169. *Joined armchair. English; Lake District, Westmorland. Oak, probably late seventeenth century. Dated chairs with this characteristic crest are seen from c.1630 until 1742, indicating an exceptionally long persistence of this single feature. This makes it very difficult to assess the date of undated specimens.*

Figures 4:170a and 170b. *(Above and below) Two joined armchairs (details). English; Westmorland. a). Barbon Church. Oak, dated 1662. b). Burton-in-Kendal Church. Oak, dated 1712.*

33. See R.W. Brunskill, *Vernacular Architecture of the Lake Counties,* Faber & Faber, London, 1974, p.50.

34. Two extremes are seen in a chair of 1633 which was recently on the market, and another of 1742 at Townend, Troutbeck, Westmorland (National Trust), both of which have essentially the same form of decoration. A dated chair of 1623 from Ings (Westmorland, illustrated in Temple Newsam Catalogue, 1973, no.14) should be looked on with some suspicion. The style of the arms, the turnings, and the generally thin joinery are more indicative of a date nearer to 1723. Indeed this chair closely resembles my Figure 4:174, of 1705.

The seventeenth century saw an opportunity for the development of a more settled agricultural system in Westmorland and the neighbouring parts of Lancashire (Furness) and North Yorkshire. This is reflected by a sudden appearance in the mid-seventeenth century of a permanent form of yeoman farmhouse in the Lake District,[33] which is paralleled by the increased production of dated furniture from the middle of the century onwards. The furniture of this area has a distinct and cohesive style of its own, which first appears in isolated examples dated as early as the 1620s and 1630s, and persisting as late as the 1740s.[34] The long persistence and the late appearance of conservative styles of decoration on carved and joined oak furniture are seen as two of the hallmarks of Lakeland and the surrounding area. The custom of inscribing dates and initials on furniture and architectural woodwork was especially common here in the second half of the seventeenth century and a little later, and many examples still survive. Unfortunately, dated examples are of little use here in the task of assigning approximate dates to undated pieces, in view of the broad periods which they indicate.

Plate Sixteen. *Desk and bookcase. English. Oak, c.1730.*

Figure 4:171. *(Left) Joined armchair. English; Westmorland. Oak, late seventeenth century. A plain and sturdy farmhouse chair, very similar in squat proportion to the following example.*

Figure 4:172. *(Right) Joined armchair. English; Westmorland. Oak, dated 1680. The inclusion of a plain panel is unusual, though the form of the crest is typical.*

Figure 4:173. *Joined armchair. English; Westmorland. Oak, dated 1685.*

The Eden Valley is the only sizeable patch of lowland in the county of Westmorland (which stretches from the Lake District in the west to the Pennines in the east), and so settlements are largely restricted to the valley floors, upland villages and farmsteads, with a few small urban centres such as Kendal. We can therefore discount any major urban influences on local styles other than Lancaster, or perhaps Penrith and Carlisle in the north. A certain amount of sophisticated furniture must have been imported from these towns for use by the gentry, but in the main the local carvers seem to have turned inwards to the indigenous folk cultures for their themes and inspiration. The Norse invasions of the early Middle Ages had been largely peaceful and entirely successful, to the extent that the North-West was the seat of an extensive Scandinavian subculture, and the Norse language was spoken here throughout the Middle Ages.

One of the favourite decorative motifs (amounting almost to an obsession) of both the Celtic and the Scandinavian peoples was a complex strapwork interlace, often with naturalistic and fantastic animal and human details. This is freely used in Anglo-Viking stonework in the North-West, and, though there is no real evidence of a direct link through medieval carved woodwork, the interlace pattern is found to be still a common theme in the seventeenth century (Figures 4:170a, 173, 174 and 177). Interlace patterns were also introduced into England from Renaissance sources, and may be found on sophisticated furniture (especially in inlays, see Diagram 2:27 n and o); but in south-west Scotland, Western England and Wales they spring from an altogether deeper native past. The links between the Lake District and North Wales are possibly closer than it may seem, even in the seventeenth century, and certain correlations need exploring more fully (such as the use of interlace patterns, the appearance of the 'tridarn', the use of built-in furniture, the late appearance of conservative forms, etc. Some of this can be explained by the shared Celtic heritage, but it also suggests close maritime links in the seventeenth century).

489

Figure 4:174. *Joined armchair. English; Westmorland. Oak, dated 1705.*

Figure 4:176a. *Joined wall cupboard. English; Longsleddale Church, Westmorland. Oak, dated 1662.*

Figure 4:175. *Joined child's high chair. English; Westmorland. Oak, dated 1720.*

Figure 4:176b. *Joined salt cupboard. English; High Underbrow, Strickland Roger, Westmorland. Oak, dated 1676. Compare the interlace panels with those in the upper stage of Figure 4:182.*

Figure 4:177. *Joined chest. English; Westmorland, Lake District. Oak, dated 1669. The frieze and panels are all comparable with others shown in these pages; and the two outer panels have small worm-like heads with hooked beaks, as on the chair-crests. Note especially, the continuing obsession with the ancient Celtic interlace patterns.*

Related to the interlace, but with generally a simpler format, is the fat serpent-like pattern seen in the main panels of Figures 4:169, 176b and 182. Whether or not this derives from more ancient zoomorphic forms cannot now be determined, for there is a lack of more specific detail, such as heads and tails. Plant-like forms are also common, as in the clear fern leaf elements of Figure 4:176a and many related panels, and in the common appearance of floral rosettes. Diamond panels are also popular, perhaps relating to those seen further south in Yorkshire, Lancashire and even the West Country.

The most curious and distinctive animal form to be seen lies in the very common use of a pair of snail-like creatures which so often adorn the crests of Lakeland armchairs (Figures 4:169, 170, 172-175). Occasionally, these are reduced to a stylised rosette (Figure 4:174), but usually they are very definite curled-up creatures with small heads and curved beaks. Dated examples are found over a span of 120 years or so, from the 1630s onwards, and their identity may possibly lie in the ancient North Country folk tales of

Figure 4:178. *Joined built-in press cupboard. English; Glenside, Trout-beck, Westmorland. Oak, dated 1634 (photographed in 1933).*

giant 'warms' or dragons which ravaged the countryside from time to time. Perhaps the most famous of these was the 'Lambton Warm' of County Durham.

There is a very extravagant use of light and shade in Lakeland joinery. The surfaces of panels and framing-members are deeply cut, or scored with channel-mouldings (Figure 4:176a is a rare exception to the latter), and turnings are balanced and well articulated. The whole effect is one of intense linear feeling, which is heightened by the fine dark colour and patination so often present on furniture from this area (provided by a combination of smoky interiors, generations of proud housewives, and, as the locals would have it, the occasional application of a polish compounded from bull's blood, vinegar and beeswax).

Figure 4:179. *Joined built-in press cupboard. English; Bitchfield, Firbank, Westmorland. Oak, dated 1682 (photographed in 1934). The left-hand lower cupboard opens into the parlour from which the photograph was taken, whilst the right-hand cupboard opens to the rear in the kitchen beyond.*

The Lake District still contains a large number of unspoilt yeoman farmhouses of seventeenth century vintage, despite the efforts of the 'Ideal Home' generation, through which may be traced a full catalogue of structural and decorative detail. One of the chief delights of these small vernacular houses is the very common use of built-in furniture such as beds (Figure 3:448), salt or spice cupboards (Figures 3:293, 4:176 a and b) and press cupboards (Figures 4:178-180). The latter are a special feature of Lakeland interiors, where press cupboards are frequently used as room dividers in farmhouses. Where this was always intended, the cupboard is made with two separate compartments, one of which opens into the parlour, and the other into the hallway or kitchen at the rear. The parlour side is usually finished and carved with the most care, and the rear is often a little less ornate (Figure 4:179). Other examples appear to have been made with the intention to stand freely, but have been built into the architectural fabric at some later date (Figures 4:178 and 180). These are constructed no differently from free-standing cupboards, and when removed from their places are often found to be fully finished at the sides, and not integrated with the building in any way.

Figure 4:180. *Joined built-in press cupboard. English; Ivy Cottage, Burton, Westmorland. Oak, dated 1708 (photographed in 1934).*

Figure 4:181. *Joined press cupboard. English; Westmorland. Oak, dated 1658.*

Lakeland press cupboards display a wide variation of door arrangements in the lower stage (the six shown here each have different patterns), but otherwise they show a fairly consistent character. Apart from heavily moulded framing-members, the decoration is usually confined to the upper panels and rails. Standard runs of carving and panel types are seen, and the importance of the press cupboard in family life is testified by the invariable inclusion of dates and initials. These are not always marriage initials, but may represent only the head of the household. No doubt the press cupboard held a place of symbolic importance in Lakeland life which is paralleled later by the dresser in Wales, but this aspect is not nearly so well chronicled, nor so well remembered by the people.

8). Wales and Ireland

Both Wales and Ireland are poorly represented here, and for very different reasons. The historical and social factors which have affected the production of furniture and chattels in each country are so different that each must be viewed in a separate light:

Ireland

Up to the seventeenth century, the Irish people were largely made up of loose associations of the old Celtic tribes, latterly ruled by an aristocracy composed of the old Anglo-Irish families such as the FitzGeralds of Kildare. The Reformation imposed by Henry VIII, and the consequent destruction of the monasteries (the only seats of learning in Ireland), was

Figure 4:182. *Joined press cupboard. English; Westmorland. Oak, dated 1681.*

Figure 4:183. *Joined press cupboard. English; Westmorland. Oak, dated 1685.*

only the first step in a policy whereby England was to gain control in Ireland. The possibility of Spanish intervention in Ireland was seen as a great threat by Elizabeth I, and the only way to prevent the Spaniards gaining a foothold which might threaten England was for the English to colonise Ireland first. The policy of subjugation in Ireland is one of the saddest and least forgotten chapters in the relationship between the two countries. The Irish peasantry was put down with great cruelty, and many areas were both exploited and laid waste. The native population hardened in its adherence to the Roman faith, in which they identified a passionate hatred of the English. The abolition of the Anglo-Irish nobility was begun in the sixteenth century, and their place taken by 'gentlemen adventurers' from England, who were awarded their lands in return for services rendered to the English Crown in Ireland, forming the basis of a new Protestant nobility with little sympathy for the Irish people.

This process, started by the Tudors and continued by the Stuarts, was completed by the new Republican Government under Cromwell and Ireton. The soldiers who fought in the Conquest were paid off in Irish land, and they remained in the most part as settlers and colonists. But it was only in Protestant Ulster that this new yeoman class retained a sense of British identity, whilst in the rest of Ireland they intermarried with the natives, or simply gave up and went home.

In the wake of such a disturbed history, it comes as no surprise that no evidence may be found of any developed furniture styles in seventeenth century Ireland. The furniture of the peasantry was the same as peasant furniture in any other time or place (see Figure 2:50), and the furniture used by the English intruders was no doubt crudely functional, or simply the same as they used at home. Dublin was the only city of any size (as it had been since 1170 when the citizens of Bristol were granted licence to take over from the Danes settled there), and as such it is perhaps the only centre where a traditional style of furniture decoration might be encountered. Whether for lack of evidence, or lack of effort, no such style has yet been isolated or recorded. Trinity College, then the only university in Ireland, had been founded in Dublin before 1600, and the city boasted a number of guilds and trade companies, but little now remains of pre-Georgian Dublin. It must be accepted as a general rule that the urban renewals of the last 250 years will have obliterated much evidence of seventeenth century furnishings, especially in the 'Georgianised' cities such as Dublin and Bath, and in cities of high post-industrial growth like Leeds, Manchester, Nottingham and Bristol; and so the search must be concentrated in those urban institutions which have miraculously survived (such as Trinity Hall, Aberdeen, and the Drapers' Hall, Shrewsbury), and in the surrounding countryside.

Unfortunately, initial indications are that almost all the Irish house interiors and furnishings of any consequence were destroyed in the Cromwellian wars, or later following the defeat of James II at the Boyne in 1690. It should still be possible to chart stylistic groups of later country-made dressers (of which several fine examples are known), and some other pieces, but much of the earlier culture of metropolitan Dublin has disappeared.

Wales (Figures 4:184-188)

The Principality of Wales is largely a mountainous country, though travel is made relatively easy by the numerous valleys and large fertile lowlands, such as the Vales of Clwyd and Glamorgan. Early settlement was largely concentrated in the rich river valleys and estuaries, with a broad scattering of upland villages and hill farms on less hospitable slopes. There were few towns of anything other than local importance in the seventeenth century, and at this stage it is impossible to pinpoint any native urban source of joinery. By contrast, the Welsh peasantry was never as depressed or bullied as their Irish or Scottish counterparts, and so a rich and varied rural folk culture evolved in the post-medieval period. There was also the opportunity for the rise of an expansive rural middle class of yeomen and minor gentry, though not on the same scale to be found in England.

Figure 4:184. *Joined press cupboard. Welsh; reputedly made at Harlech, Merioneth. Oak, early seventeenth century. This remarkable cupboard is only slightly short of 10ft. long.*

Figure 4:185. *Joined armchair. Welsh. Oak, dated 1609.*

Figure 4:186. *Detail of armchair in Figure 4:185. The inscription reads: 'HEB·DDUW·HEB·DDIM· DUW·A·DICON' (without God, without anything; God is enough).*

The alliances and estates of the land-owning classes were the single most powerful political force in the life of the countryside. Their mansion-houses still punctuate the landscape and many still contain important pieces of early furniture, with family provenances still intact. The old county families were closely interrelated, and their holdings and influences are the stuff of history in Wales (as in Scotland, New England and Virginia), and a good many pieces of furniture owe their survival to real or imagined connections with a revered ancestor.

The production of joined oak furniture continued in Wales until a very late date, in fact the tradition was maintained virtually unbroken into the early part of the present century. Yet, this tradition divides into two distinct aspects, which must be considered separately. The earliest phase is concerned with the sixteenth and seventeenth centuries. There is a rich harvest of furniture of this period in Welsh houses, much of it with secure provenances, but on stylistic examination many of these are seen to be of

English or Anglo-French manufacture. The chairs belonging to Sir Rhys ap Thomas (Figure 3:28) are a prime example of this; and another example may be cited in the great cupboard of Sir John Wynn of Gwydir Castle (c.1535, now in the Burrell Collection, see Macquoid *Age of Oak*, Pl.III). Despite restorations, this is possibly the most important piece of Welsh furniture in existence, but there is little to suggest that it was made by a local craftsman. Of somewhat later date is the armchair of 1609 in Figure 4:185, which has a familiar pious inscription: 'HEB·DDVW·HEB·DDIM·DVW· A·DICON' (without God, without anything; God is enough). But even here, the inscription confirms only a Welsh association, and not necessarily Welsh manufacture. Stylistically, the chair could be English. Obviously the original owner was a Welshman of some means, but he may have been an expatriate living and trading in England. Other confirmed Welsh furniture, such as the high chair of Gruffydd Nannau (Figure 2:23) or the Williames-Vaughan armchair (Figure 2:12), has a very limited sense of decorative identity which is of little use in defining national or regional characteristics. Even the presence of dragons in carved decoration (the Royal cognisance of Wales) is no confirmation of a Welsh provenance, since dragons are to be found in furniture decoration all over Western Britain.

The fact that few conclusions are yet available as to the precise character of Welsh joinery and carving is emphatically not to suggest that furniture of quality was not made in Wales before c.1680; only that it lacks a proper study. The only published book on Welsh furniture[35] gives no clue to Welsh stylistic preferences in the early period. Many items are shown on no firmer basis than having been recently collected in Wales, such as the pieces from the Maesrhyddid Collection (Monmouthshire), now at the Welsh Folk Museum. Several of these are of distinctive English types (e.g. my Figure

35. *Welsh Furniture,* by L. Twiston-Davies and H.J. Lloyd-Johnes, University of Wales Press, Cardiff, 1950.

Figure 4:187. *(Left) Joined armchair. Welsh. Oak, late seventeenth century.*

Figure 4:188. *(Right) Joined armchair. Welsh. Oak, late seventeenth century.*

4:136, and a Lakeland press cupboard of 1702). Other groups of furniture are found in the border areas of the Welsh Marches, and it is difficult to decide if they really are Welsh or English (see the armchairs in Figures 3:52 and 53, or the curious cupboards in Figures 3:290-292).

The second (and major) phase in the history of Welsh furniture begins with the last quarter of the seventeenth century, and continues throughout the next two centuries. This phase may be crudely classified as 'country-made' furniture, and as such it is considered later in this Chapter under Country Furniture. In fact, during the eighteenth century the numerous survivals of Welsh furniture are seen to make a very substantial contribution to the corpus of British country furniture. The demand for joiner-made furniture was more persistent in Wales than in England, and the most popular forms are often late versions of types which had virtually died out in the rest of the British Isles (such as the ark, the *cwpwrdd deuddarn* and the panel-back armchair). In addition, we find in Wales a continuing production of retarded peasant furniture on a scale not matched in England. Even though it may be typified by a kind of archaic traditionalism, Welsh oak furniture of the eighteenth century is very sturdily constructed and often very finely finished. For various reasons it has been thought more effective to show Welsh furniture in different aspects of this volume, and not to gather it together as a rather loose regional group; though examination will reveal a high proportion of Welsh pieces, even if the conclusions must be rather scattered.

It is important in Wales to remember the direction in which imported influences tended to work. In the earlier period, the only outside influences are seen in the furniture of the aristocracy. This was a truly international and much-travelled group, with great importance and presence in the Tudor and Stuart Courts. Much of their furniture was purchased in the course of travel to London and Europe, and not made locally. But at the lower social levels, local conditions were much more effective. There was little direct cultural contact between north and south, owing to the difficult nature of early roads. Instead, the contacts were largely with the neighbouring parts of Western England, so that Chester and Shrewsbury were important to North Wales, whilst Hereford, Worcester and Gloucester were important to Monmouthshire and the south. In addition, there was a good deal of sea-borne contact between South Wales and the English West Country, where Bristol and the North Devon ports maintained close trading links. There was an easy flow between rural Eastern Wales and the English counties over the border, but West Wales was more isolated by the mountainous geography. Here the coastal towns such as Tenby, Aberystwyth and Caernarfon served an important function; and in the eighteenth century (and probably earlier) furniture was brought into these ports from Bristol, Chester and Dublin.

9). New England, 1650-1720 (Figures 4:189-230)

A great deal of published material is available dealing with the earliest period of furniture making in New England; unlike the British Isles, where the abundance of seventeenth century furniture has led to it being treated as little more substantial than a group of picturesque chattels. Only in very recent years has British vernacular furniture been thought worthy of objective academic interest, whereas in the United States a greater concentration of scholarship has long been focused on this area.

It should come as no surprise to the English reader that a sufficient wealth of seventeenth century American furniture and documentation still

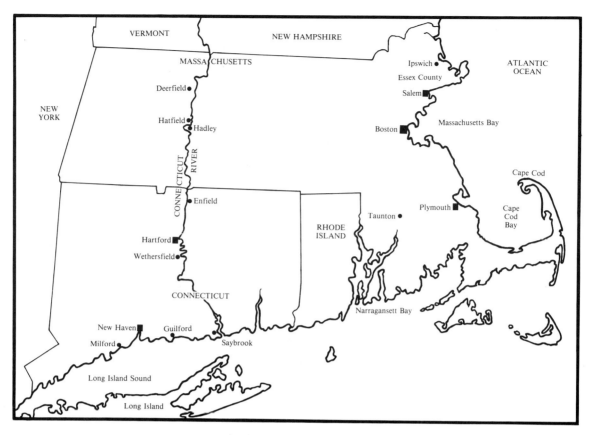

Figure 4:189. *Map of New England, showing the towns and main areas discussed in this book.*

remains for the subject to be studied at some depth, for by the year 1700 the American Colonies already had a long history of British interest and involvement. The Land of Virginia was so named in honour of Elizabeth I as early as 1584, and three years later the first English child to be born in America was likewise christened Virginia. Soon after, the Virginia Company and the Massachusetts Bay Company were founded in London with the expressed intention of earning a good percentage for the shareholders, and to create new markets for English goods in exchange for the raw materials of the New World. Potential colonists were invited to join them in a land reported to be flowing with milk and honey. The early wild expectations were soon dimmed by tragic failures to maintain even a foothold in North America; but after the planting of Jamestown (Virginia) in 1607, and the success against tremendous odds of the early Massachusetts Bay colonies (including the Pilgrim Fathers who founded the Plymouth Colony in 1620), English settlers began to flock to Virginia and New England. Between 1630 and 1640, the period sometimes known as the Great Migration, about 20,000 English souls settled in New England (Massachusetts, Connecticut and Rhode Island). By 1643 the Massachusetts Bay Company had invested £200,000 in settling New England.

The colonists themselves, most of whom consisted of underprivileged or ambitious members of the yeomanry and peasantry, were motivated by a variety of purposes. Some were seeking better prospects for themselves and

Figure 4:190. *Joined armchair. Anglo-American; Essex County, Massachusetts. Oak, 1650-80.*

Figure 4:191. *Joined armchair. Anglo-American; Essex County, Massachusetts. Oak, 1650-80.*

Figure 4:192. *Joined chest. Anglo-American; Essex County, Massachusetts. Oak and pine, 1650-80.*

their children, though the only real prospect faced by the first farmers and craftsmen was one of seasonal hunger and unremitting toil. Others were trying to escape from disadvantage or persecution they had faced at home. It is no coincidence that the Great Migration visibly diminished in the same year (1640) as the impeachment of Archbishop Laud.

Voluntary emigration declined somewhat at the outbreak of the Civil War, during which time some convicts and rebels were transported and sold into slavery in Virginia, until it was decided that only African negroes should be held in perpetual bondage. As the tobacco trade became established in Virginia the plantation-owning classes turned to England for supplies of furnishings and luxuries. The production of sophisticated goods was hampered by English law, by the rural form of the local economy and the lack of towns of any consequence, and by the 'Colonial mentality' of many leading Virginians which tolerated a reliance on the mother country. As a result, Southern furniture of the seventeenth century is very rare (see Figures 2:95, 3:232, 246, 264 and 4:252). Early letters from Virginia are full of requests for furniture and furnishings to be sent from England, such as that of Lt. Col. William Fitzhugh, who wrote to his London agent in 1681 requesting "...feather bed & furniture, curtains & vallens..." for his personal use.

Many of the puritan refugees settled in Massachusetts, which later became little short of a theocratic republic, in which the spiritual leaders often denied to others the religious freedoms for which they themselves had fought. But most men came for reasons of economic betterment, and their greatest prize lay in the freedom they gained from the iron grip with which the English landowner and the legislature had held them.

The New Englanders had come to build a new life and a civilisation in the wilderness, and furniture making appears to have become an established activity in the early days of settlement. Despite the extravagant claims about the *Mayflower* and other ships, there seems little reason to suppose that pieces of furniture were exported to New England in any numbers, other than chests and boxes which might be used for packing. Space was very valuable on these tiny ships, and it would be far more economic to transport a craftsman and his tools. This may help explain the popularity of turned chairs in the early colonies, since a turner could set to work immediately, without the need for a large store of seasoned timber which a joiner or carpenter would require.

In 1642 a trained joiner, Edward Johnson, was able to note of Massachusetts that "...the Lord hath been pleased to turn all the wigwams, huts and hovels the English dwelt in at their first coming, into orderly, fair and well-built houses, well-furnished many of them..." These houses were constructed in the same way as the small timber-framed farmhouses of England, with clapboard panelling within and a sheath of weatherboarding to keep out the harsh New England winter. They might have a single stone chimney, or a timber chimney-canopy not unlike that in Figure 3:5. The family lived chiefly in the small hall or 'keeping room', and the scarcity of space meant that rooms often had to be used for several purposes. Large houses were not unknown in some of the richer towns, but in 1688 Samuel Sewall of Boston noted that he had permitted a young couple of his acquaintance to be married in his bedroom, and a few years later he entertained eleven guests to dinner "...in my Wives Chamber at the great ovall table...", presumably for lack of space.

As the population started to grow in the new Colony, so new communities were founded in isolated pockets across the land. Overland

Figure 4:193. *Joined chest. Anglo-American; New Haven Colony, Connecticut. White oak and white pine, 1640-80.*

travel was difficult and dangerous, and so the coastal and inland waterways became the important links. The good harbours of Massachusetts Bay (Boston and Salem), Cape Cod Bay (Plymouth), Narragansett Bay (Rhode Island) and Long Island Sound (New Haven) all supported thriving ports; the broad Connecticut River Valley encouraged settlement in Connecticut and Western Massachusetts, and the rich farmlands around Boston (Eastern Massachusetts) soon made it the greatest city in the New World. Just as in England, the urban centres quickly established and supported consistent furniture-making conventions of their own, serving a wide rural market. The joiners and turners quickly adapted to a new range of timbers (red oak, hickory, maple, tulip, cedar and the wide planks of pine); though they took little advantage of their new characteristics, other than to use the unaccustomed broad widths of pine for single piece tops for chests and tables (Figures 3:243, 4:192 and 193). The turners found maple and hickory ideal for their purposes, though they continued to use a large proportion of the native American ash, in extension of practice they had learned at home.

Most of the first generation of Anglo-American craftsmen had served their apprenticeships at home in England, and they brought with them all the skills and traditions of provincial England. The earliest surviving examples of their products reflect very closely the style and construction of contemporary English furniture; though succeeding generations managed to develop a distinct character of their own within the general framework of Anglo-European trends. The earliest group (1650-80) rests entirely within the prevailing conventions of joined furniture decorated by carving and turning. Much of this furniture was originally painted or stained, a practice which seems to have been highly popular in New England, though increasingly rare in England (see Figures 2:235 and 236). The mixture of timbers found in American provincial furniture is a good indication that they were originally intended to be finished with a unifying coat of paint, and many examples retained this finish until stripped by the first generation of over-zealous collectors in the present century.

The progression of taste in the last quarter of the seventeenth century tended to move away from the provincial English preference for carved decoration, and towards the Anglo-Dutch style, with an emphasis on the use of applied geometric mouldings and split-turnings. This follows closely on trends in England, of course, and there is surprisingly little evidence of any direct Dutch influence in New England from New York, where Dutch styles were still to be seen long after the English took over in 1664.

The regional styles of New England have been well chronicled in recent years, and it is now clear that the two most important sources of early carved furniture are Essex County (Massachusetts) and the New Haven Colony, which was absorbed by Connecticut in 1665 (Figures 4:190-202).[36] Essex County occupies that part of the Massachusetts coastal lowland immediately north of Boston, lying next to the colony of New Hampshire. A number of items of the earlier period (1650-80) have been collected in this area, varying widely in quality of conception and execution. Most of this work is anonymous, but a small group of work has been attributed to two joiners, William Searle and Thomas Dennis, both of Ipswich. Searle was born in 1634 at Ottery St. Mary, Devonshire. Here he trained as a joiner, and in 1659 he married a local girl, Grace Cole. William and Grace Searle are next recorded in Ipswich, Massachusetts, in 1663, having left England as hopeful emigrants or Puritan refugees.

The English origins of Thomas Dennis are uncertain, but it is believed he came to Portsmouth, New Hampshire, shortly before 1663. He was working there as a joiner, but in 1668 he moved to Ipswich and married Grace, who was now William Searle's widow. No doubt he took over Searle's workshop, business, tools and stock of furniture and materials. A large group of similar pieces has been attributed to one or both of these makers (represented here by Figures 4:194-198), but there is little evidence whether the style is specifically that of the Searle-Dennis workshop, or an expression of wider preferences in the Ipswich area. Figure 4:196 was actually discovered in Portsmouth, which must prompt speculation that the style is wholly that of Thomas Dennis, who was working in this way before his move to Ipswich in 1668. The armchair in Figure 4:197 is arguably the finest American armchair in existence from the seventeenth century, and is one of several items with similar carving which have descended in the Dennis family. These have been attributed to the hand of Thomas Dennis, or to his predecessor William Searle. It is a great pity that no significant examples of the style are securely dated before or after Searle's death. Such evidence might have helped decide the balance of responsibility for this work between the two men. Thomas Dennis is the stronger candidate, in view of Searle's early death in 1667, but he was only one of many joiners working in Ipswich. The styles of furniture made in the area changed radically before his death in 1706, "Aged about 68 years," and it must seem

Figure 4:193a. *Joined chest. English. Oak, c.1640. This is one of many examples where motifs used in New England may be traced to an English source, though after c.1670 the influence is less direct (cf. with previous illustration).*

36. Essex County furniture has been the subject of much investigation and discussion by American scholars, over the last forty years or more. The New Haven Colony furniture was examined by Patricia E. Kane in an exhibition catalogue, *Furniture of the New Haven Colony: The 17th Century Style,* New Haven Col. His. Soc., 1973; and in an article of the same title in Antiques Magazine, May 1973.

Figure 4:194. *Joined chest. Anglo-American; Ipswich, Essex County, Massachusetts.* *Oak,* *1660-80.* *Attributed to William Searle or Thomas Dennis.*

likely that he changed his style of work at least a little in order to accommodate the shifting demands of his customers (see Figure 4:214).[37]

The richness and competence of the Searle-Dennis carving are only fractionally repeated in the New Haven furniture. The Ipswich pieces are carved with a rich and consistent series of leafy panels, which display a masterly control of space-filling pattern; but contemporary items from New Haven are significantly less ambitious. This is explained by the economic decline experienced by the Colony after 1650. The earliest years, following the founding of the New Haven Colony in 1638, were very successful, but the failure of a communal trading venture in 1646 reversed the colonists' good fortunes. In 1658 there was evidence presented that some wood-workers did not have sufficient employment to keep their apprentices busy,

Figure 4:195. *Joined chest. Anglo-American; Ipswich, Essex County, Massachusetts.* *Oak,* *1660-80.* *Attributed to William Searle or Thomas Dennis.*

37. A useful collection of various articles dealing with Thomas Dennis and Essex County furniture is given by Robert Trent in *Pilgrim Century Furniture,* Main Street/Universe Books, New York, 1976.

Figure 4:196. *Joined chest. Anglo-American; Ipswich, Essex County, Massachusetts. Oak and white pine, painted red, black, blue and white, 1660-80. Attributed to William Searle or Thomas Dennis.*

Figure 4:197. *Joined armchair. Anglo-American; Ipswich, Essex County, Massachusetts. White and red oak, 1668-80. Attributed to Thomas Dennis, to whose descendants the chair belonged until 1821. Another almost identical chair was also in family hands until 1872.*

Figure 4:198. *Boarded box. Anglo-American; Ipswich, Essex County, Massachusetts. Oak and pine, painted red, 1668-80. Attributed to Thomas Dennis. The treatment of the carved S-scrolls is very similar to those on the previous chair and other Dennis pieces.*

Figure 4:199. *Boarded box. Anglo-American; Guilford, New Haven, Connecticut. Oak and pine, 1650-80. The treatment of the S-scrolls is very similar to other New Haven Colony furniture, such as the following press cupboard.*

Figure 4:200. *Joined press cupboard. Anglo-American; Guilford, New Haven, Connecticut. Oak, red cedar and chestnut, 1650-80. Four other identical cupboards are known.*

Figure 4:201. *Joined armchair. Anglo-American; New Haven, Connecticut. White oak, painted green, 1650-80. Identical carving is found on other New Haven furniture.*

and it was suggested that they might be more gainfully employed in the Massachusetts Bay Colony.[38] Much of the furniture of this period from the coastal towns of Guilford and New Haven are characterised by a thin and repetitious use of a leafy S-curve (Figures 4:57, 199-201), which is repeated and conjoined in several different ways. Local turners would seem to have contributed to a vigorous group of turned chairs from Connecticut (Figures 2:90-94, 98), and to have supplied the joiners with turned accessories (Figures 4:200).

The earliest expressions of distinct and original native American styles in joined oak furniture, for which there is no close parallel in English work, may be seen in the two large groups of chests known as the Hadley type (Figures 4:203-209) and the Sunflower type (Figures 4:210-213). These are still generically of English form, and their prototypes may be found in England, yet they appear here as mature and novel designs. Both these groups derive from the Connecticut River Valley, and are concentrated in the last quarter of the seventeenth century or a little later. Stylistically, they represent an intermediate phase, making free use of both surface carving and applied split-turnings, though the latter are noticeably absent from the earlier Hadley chests.

The Hadley chests[39] represent the largest single group of American furniture of this date (with 126 recorded specimens), but they are the products of several workshops over a broad area from Hartford (Connecticut) to Deerfield (Massachusetts). They are loosely characterised by the use of a flat, two-dimensional overall pattern of tulip heads and

38. See Patricia E. Kane, op. cit., pp.6-7.
39. A comprehensive survey of Hadley chests was presented by Patricia E. Kane in *Arts of the Anglo-American Community in the Seventeenth Century,* Wintherthur Conference Report 1974, ed. I.M.G. Quimby.

Joined armchair. Anglo-American. New Haven, Connecticut. White oak, 1650-80. This was the Presidential chair of Yale Collegiate School, later Yale University, New Haven.

40. ibid., pp.81-86.

leaves; often supplemented by stars, hearts, pinwheels and other motifs. Many are inscribed with initials or (rarely) full names, which are usually identifiable with young women, suggesting that they were made as dower or 'hope' chests. Some are dated. In most examples, the carving is very simple, with plain sunk backgrounds and coarsely scratched details. Most of them seem to have been finished originally with a simple painted or stained colour scheme.

A great deal of speculation has been enjoined over the makers of the various sub-groups of Hadley chests, but with no convincing conclusions as yet. The names of several joiners have been put forward from towns such as Hartford, Hatfield and Enfield. For example, Mary Pease (Figure 4:205) was the daughter of John Pease, a carpenter/joiner of Enfield (Connecticut), who had moved there from Salem, Essex County (Massachusetts). The latter examples shown here (known as the 'Hartford' type, Figures 4:208 and 209) bear close formal similarities to the earlier Searle-Dennis carving of Essex County, particularly in the handling of the tulip-head, the use of U-gouged enrichment, and the three-dimensional quality of the stems.[40] The carved and painted box of 1691 in Plate Eleven is perhaps a significant link piece in this relationship. It was found in Devonshire, but seems to be of New England manufacture in view of its timber, its date, and the remarkable similarity it bears to both the Searle-Dennis and the Hartford carving. Perhaps these conformities are entirely coincidental and misleading, but further stylistic comparison may suggest otherwise.

The sunflower chests are almost as numerous as the Hadley type. Over a hundred examples are recorded, as well as a handful of related press cupboards. The decoration and form of these pieces do not vary a great deal, except in small details, as may be seen from those shown here (Figures 4:210-213). The usual three sunflowers on the centre panel (which gives the group its name) are to be seen in Figure 4:210, and on the press cupboard, but Figure 4:211 is slightly unusual in featuring a set of marriage initials

Figure 4:203. *Joined chest with drawer. American; Connecticut River Valley. Oak and pine, painted red, 1670-1710. Carving of the Hadley type.*

Figure 4:204. *Joined chest with drawer. American; Connecticut River Valley. Oak and pine, 1670-1710. Reputedly made for Mary Russell (1686-1738).*

507

Figure 4:205. *Joined chest with two drawers. American; Connecticut River Valley. Oak and pine, painted black and red, 1688-1714. Possibly made for Mary Pease by her father John Pease, a joiner of Enfield, Connecticut.*

Figure 4:206. *Joined chest with two drawers. American; Connecticut River Valley. Maple, pine, oak and sycamore, painted red, 1690-1710. The Hatfield type.*

Figure 4:207. *Joined chest with two drawers. American; Connecticut River Valley. Oak and pine, 1690-1710.*

Figure 4:208. *Boarded box. American; Connecticut River Valley. Oak and pine, c.1700. Carving of the Hartford type. Five chests are known in this group (including Figure 4:209), dated 1699-1701, and two other boxes.*

508

Figure 4:209. *Joined chest with drawer. American; Connecticut River Valley. Oak, pine and maple, dated 1699. Made for Prudence Kellog of Hadley, Massachusetts. There is a band of inlay between each pair of spindles.*

instead (S^WR). The tulip panel which also appears in almost every example is shown clearly in Figure 4:212, along with the usual two variations of applied split-spindles. The differences between individual pieces are so slight as to suggest strongly that they are all the products of a single craftsman or small workshop. The earliest member of the group with a reliable provenance is a press cupboard (identical to Figure 4:213) which was purchased in Wethersfield (Connecticut) by the Rev. Joseph Rowlandson in 1677 or the following year. Recent research[41] has attributed this group to a joiner called Peter Blin, who had settled in Wethersfield a few years earlier. Blin worked in the town for about fifty years, until his death in 1725. He apparently made most of the sunflower chests before 1700, for after c.1704 his work (if it *is* his) seems to change, with the introduction of painted instead of carved decoration.

Figure 4:210. *Joined chest with two drawers. American; Wethersfield, Connecticut. Oak, pine and maple, painted red with black details, 1675-1700. Attributed to Peter Blin.*

41. See Houghton Bulkely, *A Discovery on the Connecticut Chest,* Connecticut Historical Society Bulletin 23, 1958, pp.17-19.

Figure 4:212. *Detail of chest in Figure 4:211. The oak carcase appears to have been originally stained red, and the maple spindles painted black.*

Figure 4:211. *Joined chest with two drawers. American; Wethersfield, Connecticut. Oak, pine and maple, 1686-1700. Probably made for Samuel and Rebecca Wright, who were married in Glastonbury, Connecticut, in 1686. Attributed to Peter Blin.*

The main flat surfaces of most sunflower furniture show signs of having been painted or stained red, while the mouldings and turnings are invariably painted black. Both these characteristics are shared at the same date by the second generation furniture of Essex County, Massachusetts, though with far greater variety (Figures 4:214-222). There is still a large body of Essex County work dating from the last quarter of the seventeenth century, suggesting a very prosperous community and a large reserve of skilled joiners and turners. Much of this furniture was attributed to Thomas Dennis's workshop by Irving P. Lyon in his heady articles of 1937-38 (see p.447), though it is now quite rightly seen as the expression of a regional style, and a local version of the international Anglo-Dutch. No doubt Dennis did adapt his work to suit prevailing tastes, and Figure 4:214 is possibly an anonymous product of his workshop at this stage, since it bears bands of carving which relate very closely to the earlier Searle-Dennis carving. The combined use of carving with mouldings and turnings appears as a sort of transitional stage throughout the decade 1675-85, and is seen here in Figures 2:236 and 4:209-216.

Recent research has revealed hundreds of furniture makers working in the Greater Boston area in the seventeenth century,[42] many of them exposed to the influence of imported English furniture and the demands of a well-travelled clientele. Not surprisingly, most of the urban centres of Eastern Massachusetts produced Anglo-Dutch furniture after c.1670, and the pieces from Plymouth are another expression of this taste (Figures 4:223 and 224). The press cupboard with drawers is almost identical to one owned by Governor Thomas Prince of the Plymouth Colony at his death in 1673. The

42. See Benno Forman, *The 17th Century Furniture of Essex County, Massachusetts, and its Makers,* unpublished M.A. thesis, University of Delaware, 1968, and Robert Trent, *The Joiners and Joinery of Middlesex County, Massachusetts, 1630-1730,* Wintherthur Conference Report 1974.

Figure 4:213. *Joined press cupboard. American; Wethersfield, Connecticut. Oak, maple, pine and poplar, painted red with black details, 1675-1700. Attributed to Peter Blin.*

Figure 4:214. *Joined press cupboard. American; Ipswich, Essex County, Massachusetts. Oak and pine, 1675-85. Attributed to the workshop of Thomas Dennis.*

Figure 4:215. *Joined spice cupboard. American; Salem, Essex County, Massachusetts. Red oak, dated (16)76. Attributed to John Symonds. Probably made for Thomas and Sarah Buffington. Compare with Figure 3:300.*

Figure 4:216. *Joined press cupboard. American; Essex County, Massachusetts. Oak and pine, stained red and black, 1675-95. The carving of the middle drawer is almost identical to that in Figure 2:236.*

511

Figure 4:217. *Joined livery cupboard. American; Essex County, Massachusetts. Oak and maple, stained red and black, dated 1680. Perhaps made for Peter Woodbury of Beverly.*

Figure 4:218. *Joined folding table. American; Essex County, Massachusetts. Oak and maple, painted in imitation of wood grain and marble, late seventeenth century. This table continues the preference for bulbous turnings seen on the previous cupboards.*

kinship between this chest and cupboard is quite obvious, and they represent a group from an unidentified maker in Plymouth. This form of press cupboard, with three or four drawers in the lower stage, is virtually exclusive to New England. The New Haven area also produced some furniture with applied mouldings and turnings, represented here by some pieces from a Milford workshop (Figures 4:225-227). The joined press cupboard is a rare example of the use of glued veneers in New England, here arranged in a simple chequer and diamond parquetry. The form of the spindles and the heavy base moulding are repeated almost exactly in the following boarded chest. The two chests are of cheap nailed-plank construction, yet the fronts successfully imitate the more expensive joiners' work by a subtle use of applied decoration, heavily accentuated with red and black paint.

In this survey we have looked at the more sophisticated regional aspects of joiners' work in New England, but it would be wrong not to hint at the rich legacy of vigorous painted furniture made by country carpenters. Very little of this cheaper work survives from before 1700, but the rural artisans were hardly touched by the new fashions of the eighteenth century. They continued to make the traditional forms, though there is some evidence that the black japanned chinoiserie furniture made in Boston did have some influence on the palette of colours used by men such as Robert Crosman of Taunton, Massachusetts (Figure 4:230). Similar groups of sprightly painted chests are known from other areas, including Hadley (Massachusetts), Hampton (New Hampshire), and the Guilford-Saybrook region of the Connecticut Shore.[43] Most of these use a rather bland timber in their

43. These are reviewed and illustrated by Dean A. Fales Jr. in *American Painted Furniture 1660-1880*, Dutton, New York, 1973.

Figure 4:219. *Joined small chest with four drawers. American; Essex County, Massachusetts. Oak and pine, recently repainted, 1690-1705. The area of small panels, and the free use of applied spindles, are both hallmarks of a large group of pieces which includes Figures 2:236, 4:220-222 and Plate Nine. Some of these are attributed to the Symonds family of joiners in Salem.*

Figure 4:221. *Boarded box. American; Essex County, Massachusetts. Oak and maple, 1690-1705. Joined chest with drawer. American; Essex County, Massachusetts. Oak, maple and yellow pine, dated 1693. The chest should be compared closely with that in Plate Nine.*

Figure 4:220. *Boarded box. American; Essex County, Massachusetts. Oak and maple, dated 1694.*

construction, such as pine or tulipwood (also known as whitewood), but the delightful press cupboard in Figure 4:228 is fronted with boards of curly-grained tiger maple which shines out from the polished surface. From the very beginning of the eighteenth century, American joiners and cabinetmakers diverged more and more sharply from their dependence on English models. Although the most fashionable forms would always be closely linked to the trends from London, vernacular furniture quickly assumed a strong personal identity of its own, with marked regional variations.

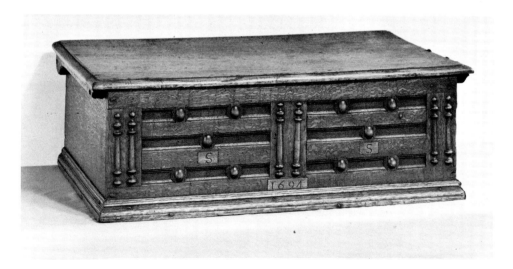

Figure 4:222. *Joined chest with drawer. American; Essex County, Massachusetts. Oak, maple and pine, painted red and black, 1690-1705. Some members of this group do not have the small-panelled lower drawer (e.g. Plate Nine), but the large spindles and the general form are quite typical.*

Figure 4:223. *Joined chest with two drawers. American; Plymouth, Massachusetts. Oak, pine and spruce, painted red and black, 1670-95. A number of chests and cupboards are known from this workshop (see Figure 4:224).*

Figure 4:224. *Joined press cupboard with drawers. American; Plymouth, Massachusetts. Oak, pine, cedar and maple, 1670-95.*

Figure 4:225. *Joined press cupboard. American; Milford, New Haven, Connecticut. White oak, black walnut, soft maple, chestnut and red cedar, 1670-1720. The use of parquetry is rare in American furniture of this period.*

Figure 4:226. *Boarded chest with drawer. American; Milford, New Haven, Connecticut. Tulip and oak, painted red and black, 1680-1720.*

Figure 4:227. *Boarded chest with drawer. American; Milford, New Haven, Connecticut. Tulipwood, painted red and black, 1680-1720.*

Figure 4:228. *Boarded press cupboard. American; Hampton, New Hampshire. Tiger maple and pine, c.1720. Possibly made as a dower chest for Sarah Rowell of Hampton Falls, whose initials are on the lower front apron. The painted decoration is in black.*

Figure 4:229. *Boarded chest with drawer. American; South Massachusetts. Pine and maple, painted white and yellow on a black ground, c.1720. Only the bottom drawer is real, the other three being simulated. The rear feet are cut from natural branches.*

Figure 4:230. *Boarded chest with drawer. American; Taunton, Massachusetts. Pine, painted white on a black ground, dated 1735. Attributed to Robert Crosman, 'drum-maker and carpenter.'*

Figure 4:231. *Joined armchair. English. Oak, with leather covers, late seventeenth century.*

'COUNTRY' FURNITURE, 1660 AND LATER

It is a widely-observed fact that the general movement of stylistic influence is to be seen working in a (socially) downward direction: new fashions are produced as novelties to satisfy the recurring demands of royal or noble patrons, and these same novelties are then adopted and passed down through the whole gamut of the rich urban middle classes, the rural gentry, and finally to the well-to-do farmers and yeomen (truly fashionable styles rarely passed any further than this). By this process, a single impulse which made its appearance in modish society at a given date may predictably be seen within a few years serving a useful purpose in less elevated circumstances. It may have been progressively modified or simplified, but not beyond recognition.

It is easy to imagine a provincial joiner having gained sight of some fashionable pieces in the houses of the local gentry, then rushing home to make notes for the adaptation of similar motifs into his own work. Before the widespread publication of pattern books in the eighteenth century, the transmission of most new visual ideas was effected by this sort of example. The very essence of fashion is bound up with the cribbing of ideas in one way or another, and by definition the 'man of fashion' is more concerned with conformity than with originality, even if he pretends differently. The illustrations given here (Figures 4:231-302) are concerned with the way that provincial artisans have 'cribbed' ideas from the beau-monde and (often successfully) incorporated them into a more traditional framework.

The restoration of the Stuart line to the English throne in 1660, in the person of Charles II, is regarded by the student of metropolitan styles as the most important single date in the history of English furniture, though in many ways the practical alternatives opened up by the Great Fire of London in 1666 are even more significant. Charles returned with a taste for French

Figure 4:232. *Joined armchair. English. Oak, dated 1681.*

Figure 4:233. *Joined armchair. Welsh. Oak, 1680-1740.*

Figure 4:234. *Joined armchair. Welsh. Oak, 1680-1740.*

Figure 4:235. *Joined armchair. Welsh. Oak, 1700-1740.*

Figure 4:235a. *Detail of Figure 4:235, showing drawer beneath seat.*

Figure 4:236. *Joined armchair. Welsh. Oak, 1700-1740.*

517

Figure 4:238. *Joined rocking chair. English or Welsh. Oak, early eighteenth century.*

Figure 4:237. *Joined armchair. English or Welsh. Oak, 1700-1750.*

Figure 4:239. *Joined backstool. English. Oak, c.1680.*

Figure 4:240. *Joined backstool. English. Oak, c.1680.*

Figure 4:241. *Joined backstool. English. Oak, 1680-1700.*

Figure 4:242. *Joined backstool. English. Oak, c.1700.*

Figure 4:243. *Joined backstool. English or Welsh. Oak, 1700-1740.*

and Dutch furnishings which injected a new impetus into the cycle of English styles, but it was the aftermath of 1666 that provided the opportunity to put all the theories of the new taste into practice. Besides the loss of 13,000 houses, a great many churches and public buildings were destroyed, including St. Paul's Cathedral, the Royal Exchange, the Guildhall and the halls of many City companies. Almost the whole of fashionable London was destroyed in the Great Fire, mercifully with little or no loss of life, but all those buildings and their contents would have to be replaced within a few short years if the importance and prestige of the capital were to be maintained.

In order to encourage the task of rebuilding the city, the Rebuilding Act of 1667 allowed 'stranger' joiners and carpenters to work in London for the next seven years without the constraints and impositions of compulsory membership of the trade companies. The feverish activity which ensued gave birth to a new balance in the furniture-making trades, in which the cabinetmakers rose to a new importance, ably supported by other specialist craftsmen in the form of the upholsterers, the chairmakers, the japanners and the marquetry-cutters. The Rebuilding Act also granted freeman rights for life to any artificer who took advantage of the seven-year ruling. This clause must have enabled a good many gifted immigrant *schrynmakers* to enter into the full competitive life of the City, where they had previously been excluded by the jealous Guilds. Their skills of carving, marquetry and dovetailed-board construction would enable them to offer just the right kind of workmanship demanded by the new taste, though it was not until the following century that the *schrynmakers* evolved fully into the mature firms of 'Cabinet-makers & Upholsterers'.

By 1685 these craftsmen were well versed in the new styles, and the names of immigrant craftsmen such as Gerritt Jensen (later a member of the Worshipful Company of Joiners) became closely associated with rich and royal patrons.

Figure 4:245. *Pair of joined backstools. English; Salisbury, Wiltshire. Oak, with leather covers, c.1685. Ten of these chairs survive from an original set of twelve, which were already in the church of Sarum St. Thomas before 1745 (see Diagram 2:5, and details Figures 2:15, 144).*

Figure 4:244. *Joined backstool. English or Welsh. Oak, c.1700.*

519

Figure 4:246. *Joined backstool. American; Boston, Massachusetts. Ebonised maple, with leather covers, 1700-1720.*

Figure 4:247. *Joined backstool. American; Boston, Massachusetts. Maple, with leather covers, c.1720. Note the 'bended' back.*

44. Following the example of Percy Macquoid in the 2nd volume of his *History of English Furniture*. For the sake of simplicity and a broad effect, he divided his study into the four Ages of Oak, Walnut, Mahogany and Satinwood. This classification has affected our view of English furniture ever since, for better or for worse.

The timber most closely associated with this new furniture is walnut, to the extent that the period 1660-1730 is sometimes referred to as the Age of Walnut.[44] But this title is something of an over-simplification, for a wide range of new techniques and materials were developed after 1660, all of which helped to diminish the old preferences for joined oak furniture. In addition to walnut, other timbers such as yewtree, cherry and ebonised beech were widely used, with pines and deals coming into common use for room panelling and the carcases of veneered case furniture. Floral marquetry (as opposed to inlay) became more popular, as well as quartered and burr veneers, and the 'oyster' veneers which exploited the end-grain patterns of certain variegated timbers such as laburnum, yewtree, olivewood, ebony and lignum vitae. Carving assumed a more refined and graceful sculptural quality, especially under the inspiration of Grinling Gibbons, who was "discovered" working in a "solitary thatched house" near Deptford by John Evelyn in 1671. Greater use was made of gilding and japanning, and simple polished surfaces were enlivened with brighter hardware by the wider use of brass or silver instead of wrought iron.

The English have always displayed an appetite for foreign novelties, and in Restoration England this was fed by a rapid widening of trading contacts with Europe and the Far East. Besides lacquerwork and the 'chinoiserie' style, China also provided such minor ideas as the cane-seat chair, the splatback chair, the 'bended-back' chair; and later the cabriole leg, which had been known in China at least since the Middle Ages. The more immediate European contacts introduced such novelties as spiral turnings, the fleshy Flemish S-scroll, Braganza or Spanish feet, bun feet, bracket feet and the flat X-stretcher. Cabinetmakers had been experimenting with new types of furniture even before the Civil War (witness the remarkable Laudian cabinet and stand of c.1630 in Figure 4:41), but it was not until after 1660 that English customers were ready to take with any enthusiasm to such innovations as glazed bookcases, scrutores, cabinets on stands, and topical set pieces like the ubiquitous "mirror, table and stands". In room panellings, the interiors of fashionable houses were revolutionised by the introduction of the large fielded panel, set into deep bolection-moulded

Figure 4:248. *Joined stool. English. Oak, early eighteenth century. The top is fixed with pegs, and has no edge mouldings. Instead, the edge is rounded-off in the same manner as Figure 4:250.*

Figure 4:249. *Joined stool. English. Oak, mid-eighteenth century. The top is fixed with screws from underneath, in the usual method for this date, though the stool is otherwise traditional in appearance.*

Figure 4:250. *Joined stool. English; Somerset. Oak, dated 1793. There is no reason to doubt this as the date of manufacture for this archaic stool, since the top is fixed with screws and the joints are secured with glue instead of the traditional pegs.*

frames. These seem to have originated in the 1650s at the instigation of architects (such as John Webb), and they became increasingly popular after 1660, despite the constructional problems which they presented to the joiner.

But the demands for novelties from an outward-looking and fashion-conscious clientele are markedly counterbalanced by the more static and consistent demands for traditional furniture, chiefly represented by the urban merchant class and the staid backbone of rural gentry and yeomen farmers. In the more remote areas, especially North-Western England, the demand for archaic joined and carved furniture continued unabated well into the eighteenth century; but there was a marked lessening in conformity to the old regional styles in the richer Midlands and Southern England, to the extent that hardly any regional flavour is discernible in the south after c.1675. Instead, the provincial joiners (and those working for the cheaper markets in London) adapted some of the motifs and forms from fashionable furniture, and evolved a sort of hybrid style which we now think of as 'country' furniture.

Figure 4:251. *Joined high stool. English or Welsh. Oak, with burr elm oval top, early eighteenth century.*

Figure 4:252. *Joined high stool. American; Charleston, South Carolina. Cypress, early eighteenth century.*

In many ways this is a meaningless term, since almost every firm of joiners and cabinetmakers in London and the provincial towns produced this cheaper range of goods in oak and other native timbers, quite distinct from their finer range in walnut and (later) mahogany. The real distinction between 'town' and 'country' furniture may lie not especially in any stylistic differences, but in the fact that the urban craftsman was able to lay his hands on a more predictable quality of imported timbers and selected native timbers. In their advertisements, urban suppliers emphasised the fact that their secondary wares were made from wainscot (imported oak) and selected grades of cherry and beech; whereas rural craftsmen had to be content with local supplies of native oak, fruitwoods, yewtree, ash, elm, sycamore and so on. At the bottom of the social scale was the huge class of labourers and servants, whose meagre furniture was either home-made

Figure 4:253. *Turned armchair. American; Connecticut. Maple and hickory, with rush seat, early eighteenth century.*

Figure 4:254. *Turned backstool. American; probably Connecticut. Ebonised hard pine, with rush seat, early eighteenth century. Despite their blocked posts, this and the following armchair were made by turners, probably imitating the finer joined chairs exported by the Boston coastal trade, and in their turn copied from English models.*

Figure 4:255. *Turned armchair. American; probably Connecticut. Ebonised maple and walnut, with rush seat, early eighteenth century.*

(from field grown or forest timber), secondhand or in the cheapest range of plain painted deal.

The broad middle range of oak country furniture adopted only the most obvious aspects of the patrician styles. Gilding, sculptural carving and veneering were largely ignored, though the latter sometimes found use in the eighteenth century in simple cross-banding on the edges of drawer fronts and table tops. Marquetry, as such, was too ambitious for most non-specialists, but it was frequently imitated by the use of inlay.[45] Floral and geometric inlay was very popular in Wales throughout the eighteenth century, especially in the Vale of Glamorgan. The spiral turning made an appearance at a vernacular level in about 1670. The armchair in Figure 4:232 is dated 1681, and is decorated in a purely traditional way, apart from the spiral turnings. At around the same date we find mentions of furniture with spiral turnings in rural inventories, e.g.

> 1679...a very large strong ovall table with a double set of twisted pillars £3.10s...
> 1686...A Lauderdal Table-Board for ye little Parlor 4 feet long, 3 feet Broad with twist-leggs all of Walnut-tree wood...

The latter table was owned by Dr. Ciaver Morris of Wells, Somerset, and was purchased locally by him in that year.[46] The execution of spiral turnings in oak varies from fairly crude (Figure 4:231-232) to fairly competent

45. Later in the eighteenth century, small workshops were able to buy ready-made lengths of chequer and other banding, as well as simple marquetry motifs. The most popular of these was the familiar shell set in an oval cartouche.
46. Quoted by Gabriel Olive, Furniture History, 1976, p.22.

Figure 4:256. *Turned armchairs. English. Ash, with rush seats, 1730-1830. The wavy ladderback pattern is generally associated with South Yorkshire, and the spindleback with South Lancashire and Cheshire. A great many variations in detail are found.*

(Figure 4:261), but rarely are they as finely made on a country piece as those on the stand in Figure 4:271. This very interesting cabinet on stand follows closely on the form of contemporary marquetry cabinets, yet retains all the idiom of joined wainscot furniture. It is progressive and forward-looking, to the same degree that the press cupboard of 1722 (Figure 4:272) is conservative and archaic.

Fielded panels were reasonably common in British joinery over many years, particularly after c.1580 (e.g. some of the Salisbury chairs and some from Aberdeen); but the introduction of fielded wall panels after 1650 led to their new popularity in furniture. Following the architectural example, these panels are designed with a deep chamfered splay, unlike the earlier

Figure 4:257. *Turned backstools. English. Ash, with rush seats, 1730-1830. These were turned out in huge numbers, with armchairs to match (see previous Figure). These patterns are still in continuous and unbroken production today.*

Figure 4:258. *(Left) Turned armchair. English; Cheshire. Ash, with rush seat, c.1800.*

Figure 4:259. *(Right) Turned armchair. English; Cheshire. Ash, with rush seat, c.1800.*

type which normally has a flat edge (see Diagram 2:27 v and w). The raised 'field' in the later type is often fitted so that it projects forward to the same level as the framing. Boldly projecting bolection mouldings are not often found on furniture, but instead the edges of the framing members are usually given a simple thumb-moulding, or ovolo. This simple system became very popular after c.1680, and may be seen on a huge variety of eighteenth century oak and fruitwood furniture, particularly from North Wales. The press cupboard of 1722 is a fine example of these panels in use, and even includes some very large versions on the main doors. This late type of fielded panel is usually considered as sufficient decoration on its own, supplemented with the usual simple edge moulding and a heavy cornice; but occasionally they are seen in concert with traditional carving and/or inlay, as in the North Lancashire press cupboard of 1705 (Figure 4:168).

Figure 4:260. *Joined long dining table. Welsh. Oak, 1680-1740. The frieze is interesting, as it simulates an elongated fielded panel, and is precisely indicative of this date.*

Figure 4:261. *Joined oval gateleg table. English. Oak, late seventeenth century. The turnings are a fine flattened double-bine twist.*

Figure 4:262. *Joined small oval gateleg table. English. Oak, 1700-30. The slim, elongated baluster turnings are characteristic of this date.*

Figure 4:263. *Joined corner gateleg table. English or Welsh. Elm, c.1720.*

Figure 4:264. *Joined side table. English. Oak, c.1680. The flat X-stretcher is a vernacular version of the more fashionable pattern in Figure 4:265. The drawer is a later alteration.*

Figure 4:265. *Joined side table. English. Oak, 1680-1720. This is the 'correct' Dutch version of the flat X-stretcher with separate bun feet. Compare with the American table in Figure 3:246.*

Figure 4:266. *Joined small table. English. Oak, early eighteenth century.*

Figure 4:267. *Joined small table. English. Oak, early eighteenth century.*

Figure 4:268. *Joined pedestal table. English. Oak, mid-eighteenth century. This model was produced in huge numbers throughout the eighteenth century.*

Figure 4:269. *Joined cricket table. English. Elm, late eighteenth century.*

Figure 4:270. *Joined cricket table with cupboard. Ash, with elm door, late eighteenth century.*

The introduction of the cabriole leg in around 1700 opened up new possiblities for the rural joiners, though the absence of stretchers was an alien idea to them. Chairs still demanded the strength and stability which were provided by stretchers, but oak dressers, chests, tables and desks all appeared with clean free-standing cabriole legs by c.1720. Some of these may be accounted a little rustic and clumsy, but many of them matched the elegance of walnut versions (Figures 4:277-284), though oak never had the strength to match some of the fine engineering which could be achieved with mahogany.

Wales and the North Country played a prominent role in providing the more personable and well-made examples of late joined oak furniture (1680-1800), though there is a real problem in trying to pin down regional variations in the decorative styles of eighteenth century country furniture. Most areas of the British Isles produced items with standardised fielded panels and simplified versions of turned, spiral or cabriole legs. Such variations as do exist are more likely to be found in different forms of furniture, such as the distinctive North Wales *cwpwrdd tridarn* (Figure 3:332) and dresser (Figures 3:333-335), or the North Country turned chairs (Figures 4:256-258). Otherwise, provincial furniture is fairly homogeneous, and is represented by a large number of old favourites in the form of tables, turned chairs, settles, clothes presses and press cupboards. After 1700, these were supplemented by new pieces such as dressers, corner cupboards, bureaux and Windsor chairs, which were to become old favourites in their turn.

Figure 4:271. *Joined cabinet on stand. English. Oak, late seventeenth century. A provincial piece, copying more fashionable models. Note that the rear legs are not spiral-turned, yet follow the general form of the front legs.*

527

Figure 4:272. *Joined press cupboard. Welsh; Denbighshire. Oak, dated 1722.*

Figure 4:273. *Joined hall cupboard. English or Welsh. Oak, mid-eighteenth century. This useful cupboard offers a variety of storage, including six drawers.*

Figure 4:274. *Joined corner cupboard. English. Oak, mid-eighteenth century. The upper compartment has the usual shaped shelves and shell-hood.*

Figure 4:275. *Joined corner cupboard. Welsh. Oak, mid-eighteenth century.*

Figure 4:276. *Joined hanging corner cupboard. Welsh. Elm, mid-eighteenth century.*

Figure 4:277. *Joined desk or bureau. English. Oak, c.1740.*

Figure 4:278. *Joined chest on stand. English. Oak, c.1740.*

Figure 4:279. *Joined dressing table or lowboy. English. Cherry, 1720-40.*

Figure 4:280. *Joined side table or lowboy. English. Fruitwood, c.1740.*

Figure 4:281a. *Joined side table or lowboy. English. Oak, c.1740.*

Figure 4:281b. *Joined folding tea table. English. Yewtree, c.1740.*

Figure 4:282. *Joined low dresser. English. Oak, c.1740.*

Figure 4:283. *Joined high dresser. English. Oak, 1720-40.*

Figure 4:284. *Joined armchair. English. Walnut, c.1730. The drop-in seat is covered with crewel-work embroidery. The plain bended-back splat derives from Chinese chairs of an earlier date. Note also the retention of stretchers to the legs, for strength and stability.*

531

Figure 4:285. *Windsor backstool. Welsh. Ash and oak, c.1800. Though of a very primitive type, this little chair is differentiated from true primitive furniture (see pp.75-81) by the use of turned decoration to the rear uprights, and the sparsely-shaped splat which echoes the finer English versions.*

Figure 4:286. *Windsor armchair. Welsh. Ash, with a solid fruitwood arm yoke, early nineteenth century. The use of three legs is fairly common with the more primitive chairs and stools.*

Figure 4:287. *Windsor armchair. English. Ash and elm, late eighteenth century. A simple, low-back armchair.*

Figure 4:288. *Windsor armchair. English. Elm, late eighteenth century. A simple, comb-back armchair with a perfunctory shaped crest.*

Figure 4:289. *Windsor armchair. Welsh. Ash and elm, c.1800. Note the unusual arrangement of the stretchers, with the medial rail running from front to back.*

Figure 4:290. *Windsor armchair. English. Ash and elm, late eighteenth century.*

Windsor Chairs (Figures 4:285-302)

Though we are all familiar with Windsor chairs, and what we mean by 'Windsor chairs', the actual origins of both the design-type and the term are lost in the mists of the early eighteenth century. It is probably safe to say that no extant Windsor chair can be dated to before 1725, though some of the more primitive examples of stick-back chair must represent an ancestral type which originated in the dawn of furniture construction (see Chapter Two, pp.75-81).

The term must derive from the appearance of these cheap, mass-produced chairs in the market at Windsor, Buckinghamshire. They were drawn here from the various centres of manufacture in that area of the Thames Valley, more especially from nearby Slough, where a steady supply of elm and beech was guaranteed from the chalk forests of the Southern Chilterns (Burnham Beeches). Curiously enough, the earliest recorded mention of Windsor chairs is in an American inventory of 1708, where three such chairs were owned by a Philadelphia merchant, John Jones.[47] Yet, there can be no certainty that this is a reference to the same type of chair that is now understood as a Windsor chair. Neither is this a unique instance where a chair type is referred to by the name of the town where it originates; e.g. in eighteenth century Connecticut, a distinctive group of splat-back turned chairs was imported via the coastal trade from New York, and referred to as 'York chairs'. When the local chairmakers copied the style, they still called them York chairs.[48]

In England, the term 'Windsor chair' is first encountered in a letter of 1724,[49] though rather disconcertingly the writer describes it as "like those at Versailles". Thereafter, Windsor chairs are increasingly referred to by name in accounts and inventories, and in 1730 a chairmaker called John Brown of St. Paul's Churchyard advertised his "Windsor Garden Chairs of all sizes, painted green or in the wood". Windsor chairs are often associated in the eighteenth century with garden, tavern or other recreational contexts, and an outdoor use is probably the reason why so many were given a painted finish when new. The usual colour is green of various shades, but other colours are also found.

Figure 4:291. *Windsor backstool. English; possibly Wiltshire. Fruitwood and elm, early nineteenth century. The design is a curious hybrid, in which the solid splat harks back to older designs (cf. Figure 2:47), yet has the baluster outline familiar from footmen's chairs in grand Georgian houses.*

47. Quoted by Esther Singleton, *The Furniture of Our Forefathers*, 1900.
48. See *The Crown and York Chairs of Coastal Connecticut and the work of the Durands of Milford*, by Benno Forman, Antiques Magazine, May 1974.
49. See *The Dating of 18th Century Windsor Chairs*, by Mark Haworth-Booth, in The Antique Dealers' and Collectors' Guide, January 1973.

Figure 4:292. *Windsor cricket table. Welsh. Ash and sycamore, early nineteenth century.*

Figure 4:293. *Windsor stool or table. Welsh. Sycamore and birch, early nineteenth century.*

Figure 4:294. *Windsor backstool. English; Yealmpton, Devon. Ash and sycamore, original green paint, c.1820.*

Figure 4:295. *Windsor backstool. English; probably Cambridge. Yewtree and elm, early nineteenth century. This pattern may be attributed to Robert Prior of Cambridge.*

Figure 4:296. *Windsor armchair. English; Home Counties, probably Surrey. Yewtree and elm, c.1800. The design of the back reflects current taste for the 'Gothick' style.*

Figure 4:297. *Windsor armchair. English; Home Counties, probably Surrey. Yewtree and elm, c.1800. Possibly by William Webb of Newington, Surrey.*

Figure 4:298. *Windsor child's high chair. English; North Midlands. Ash and elm, early nineteenth century.*

Figure 4:299. *Windsor child's low armchair. English; North Midlands. Yewtree and elm, early nineteenth century.*

Figure 4:300. *Windsor child's low armchair. English; Mendlesham, Suffolk. Fruitwood and elm, early nineteenth century. Possibly by Dan Day of Mendlesham. This type of chair is to be found in two distinct qualities. Fine examples incorporating fruitwood and with white stringing lines, and rather clumsier ones with no stringing lines. These latter have been attributed to Scott of Diss (a town ten miles from Mendlesham) who was working at the same time as the Days.*

Windsor-type construction is quite evidently derived from the primitive 'staked', 'peg-leg' or stick construction which has always been associated with the most elementary furniture used by the poor, and especially the rural labouring classes (see Figures 2:43-55). It would appear that, some time in the first quarter of the eighteenth century, this construction was adapted for the manufacture of a slightly more sophisticated type of chair with turned decoration to the spars and legs. It is this use of turnery, and a more formal approach to decoration, which sets the 'Windsor' chair apart from the primitive stick chairs. Windsor chairs are still dependent on a single seat plank, into which the legs and the superstructure are secured, but they are no longer home-made. Instead, turners and wheelwrights were able to produce a cheap, light and strongly-made chair which revolutionised cottage furniture in Georgian England. Windsor chairs were highly successful in competition against the heavy and expensive joined chairs, and even against their closer rivals in the form of the rush-seated turned chairs.

With a little organisation, Windsor chairs could easily be mass-produced on a factory system, and the Chiltern chair industry became focused around the town of High Wycombe, not far north of Slough and Windsor. Turned parts were made in the beechwoods by itinerant turners called 'bodgers', who set up their pole lathes wherever there was a supply of freshly-cut green wood. The legs and arm supports were stacked in the open to dry and season a little, then carted into the factories for assembly. The seats were adzed into shape by a 'bottomer', and the steam-bent parts were prepared by the 'bender'. The splats and other sawn parts were cut by a 'benchman', using fretsaws and files, and final assembly was carried out by the 'framer'.

But such a mechanised approach was not fully worked out until the onslaught of Victorian industrialisation. In the second half of the eighteenth century, Windsor chairs were still produced in small workshops

Figure 4:301. *Windsor armchairs of standard types. Both English; North Midlands. Yewtree and elm, early nineteenth century.*

scattered throughout the countryside. They are found in almost every region of the British Isles, though the more primitive versions are usually associated with Scotland, Ireland and rural Wales. For these areas, it may never be possible to define true regional styles, since so many chairs were the products of tiny local workshops, each with its own method of working. But in England the prospect is a little more hopeful, and a consistent pattern of styles may be defined,[50] at first in the Thames Valley and Surrey, and later more widely scattered through the North-East Midlands, East Anglia and the South-West.

Although they are more usually associated with the middle and labouring classes, Windsor chairs were quickly adapted for use in the best homes in the land — reflecting current tastes for a kind of antique pastoralism, in which ladies of quality spent their time playing at dairy maids and shepherdesses. In 1729-33 the joiner Henry Williams supplied St. James's Palace with "2 Mahogany Windsor Chairs, richly carved"; perhaps the first time in the history of furniture that taste has percolated up the social scale, instead of down.

Figure 4:302. *Windsor armchair. English; Yorkshire. Yewtree and elm, late nineteenth century.*

50. Some elementary conclusions, with special reference to named makers, are given by Thomas Crispin in *English Windsor Chairs: A Study of Known Makers and Regional Centres,* Furniture History, 1978. See also *'American' Windsor Chairs from Devon,* by Gabriel Olive, Furniture History, 1976. Significant centres of production are noted in the Slough/Windsor area (Buckinghamshire), Newington (Surrey), Yealmpton (Devon), Mendlesham (Suffolk), Rockley, Gamston and Worksop (Nottinghamshire), Boston and Grantham (Lincolnshire), Geddington (Northamptonshire) and Cambridge.

Appendix I

Extracts from *A Description of England, or a briefe rehersall of the nature and qualities of the people of England and such commodities as are to be found in the same,* by William Harrison (1534-93), B.D. Camb., Rector of Radwinter, Canon of Windsor. (1st edition of 1577 collated with 2nd edition of 1587 prefixt to Holinshed's Chronicle.)

As found in *Rev. William Harrison. Description of England 1577-87,* ed. F.J. Furnivall, published for The New Shakespeare Society by N. Trubner & Co. London, 1877.

Reference has been made in the text to the valuable and oft-quoted work of the English topographer, the Rev. William Harrison, who was born in London, studied at Oxford and Cambridge, was Rector at Radwinter in Essex, and in 1586 became Canon of Windsor. His studies, and his use of Leland's manuscripts, resulted in his fascinating observations first published as *A Description of England* in 1577, and then as *A Description of Britain,* written for Holinshed's Chronicle in 1587. Harrison's interests covered all of English life, and much of everybody else's, and his text is peppered with pertinent and impertinent observation and comment; often about the personal behaviour of others and the general conduct of affairs, and frequently returning to the (shocking) rate of inflation experienced by the Elizabethan economy. The latter is usually expressed as the rise in rents and commodity prices, and the effects of these on the agricultural community in particular. In addition to these delightful asides, there is the main intention behind his work — the provision of a pen-picture of England by an eye-witness to one of the most important periods of English development.

Although the *Description of England* has often been quoted in various works on furniture and social history, the text is little known apart from the obvious few extracts. Therefore, it is thought valuable to give here a more full excerpt from the work, so that the quotations may be seen in context. I have edited sections from three chapters, chosen for their relevance to the present study, omitting the more tedious and excursive passages, and modifying the original language only slightly to help the modern reader.

In reading the full text of Chapter 5, one is left with a strong impression (no doubt shared by many of his class) of Harrison's personal view of the system of social hierarchy of his time, viz: a formal and uncritical awe for the institution of nobility; a sceptical tolerance of the gentry, fired with a scathing contempt for the antics of its less reputable members and their servants; a similar scorn for parasitic merchants and lawyers; a slightly self-righteous recommendation of his fellow-clergy ("...now are they beloved for their painefull diligence..."); a profound respect for the backbone of the yeoman classes, whom he plainly admires as the salt of the earth; and a patronising regard for the honest artisans, always provided they do their work well and don't charge too much. Gentlemen's servants and vagrants are both equated and reviled.

In Chapter 12 Harrison chronicles a period of rapid change in the development of domestic comfort, bringing to bear as he does all the perspective of a man of advanced middle age. His reminiscences, and those of his older contemporaries, contrast remarkably with the increase of comfort in housing and furnishing which he sees around him in the later years of the sixteenth century. He enumerates those comforts, and the display of new bourgeois wealth, but he barely approves of them.

Chapter 5. Of degrees of people in the Commonwealth of England

We in England divide our people commonlie into foure sorts, as gentlemen, citizens or burgesses, yeomen, and artificers, or laborers. Of gentlemen the first or cheefe (next the king) be the prince, dukes, marquesses, earls, viscounts, and barons: and these are called gentlemen of the greater sort, or (as our common usage of speech is) lords and noblemen: and next unto them be knights, esquiers, and simple gentlemen; so that in effect our gentlemen are divided into their conditions...

The title of prince dooth peculiarlie belong with us to the kings eldest sonne, who is called prince of Wales, and is the heire apparant to the crowne...The kings yoonger sonnes be but gentlemen by birth (till they have received creation of higher estate, to be either viscounts, earles, or dukes).

The title of duke (was) in times past a name of office due to the cheefe governour of the whole armie in the Romane warres: but is now a name of honor...

In old time he onlie was called marquesse (who held a marcher province), but that also is changed in common use, and reputed for a name of great honor next the duke...

The name of earle (is next in precedence)...

...the viscont in time past governed in the countie under the earle, but now without anie such service or office, it is also become a name of dignitie next after the earle, and in degree before the baron.

The baron is such a free lord as hath a lordship or baronie, whereof he beareth his name, & hath diverse knights or freeholders holding of him, who with him did serve the king in his wars, and held their tenures for performance of such service...

Unto this place I also referre our bishops, who are accounted honourable, and whose countenances in times past were much more glorious than at this present it is, bicause those lustie prelates fought after earthlie estimation and authoritie with farre more diligence than after the lost sheepe of Christ, of which they had small regard...

Knights be not borne, neither is anie man a knight by succession, but they are made either before the battell, to encourage them the more to adventure & trie their manhood: or after, as an advancement for their courage and prowesse alreadie shewed, or out of the warres for some great service done, or for the singular vertues which doo appear in them...knights in England were chosen most commonlie according to their yearelie revenues or abundance of riches, wherewith to mainteine their estates...This neverthelesse is certeine, that who so may dispend 40 pounds by the yeare of free land, may be inforced into the taking of that degree, or otherwise paie the revenues of his land for one yeare...how soever one be dubbed or made knight, his wife is by and by called madame or ladie, so well as the barons wife; he himself having added to his name in common appellation this syllable Sir, which is the title whereby we call our knights in England...

Esquire (which we commonlie call squire) is a French word, and such are all those which beare armes, or testimonies of their race from whence they be descended. They were at the first bearers of the armes of barons, or knights, & thereby being instructed in martiall knowledge, had that name for a dignitie given to distinguish them from common souldiers when they were togither in the field.

Gentlemen be those whome their race and bloud (or at least their vertues) make noble and knowne...whosoever can live without manuell labour, and thereto is able and will beare the charge and countenance of a gentleman, he shall for monie have a cote and armes bestowed upon him by heralds...and be called master, which is the title that men give to esquiers and gentlemen, and reputed for a gentleman...

This neverthelesse is generallie to be reprehended in all estates of gentilitie, and which in short time will turne to the great ruine of our countrie, and that is, the usuall sending of noblemens & meane gentlemens sonnes into Italie, from whence they bring home nothing but mere atheisme, infidelitie, vicious conversation, & ambitious and proud behaviour, whereby it commeth to passe that they returne far worse men than they went out...Such men as this last, are easilie knowen; for they have learned in Italie, to go up and downe in England, with pages at their heeles finelie apparelled, whose face and countenance shall be such as sheweth the master not to be blind in his choice...

Citizens and burgesses have next place to gentlemen, who be those that are free within the cities, and are of some likelie substance to beare office in the same. But these citizens and burgesses are to serve the commonwealth in their cities and boroughs, or in corporate towns where they dwell. And in the common assemblie of the realme wherein our lawes are made, for in the counties they beare but little swaie (which assemblie is called the high court of parlement) the ancient cities appoint foure, and the boroughs two burgesses to have voices in it, and give their consent or dissent unto such things as passe or staie there in the name of the citie or borough, for which they are appointed.

Merchants often change estate with gentlemen, as gentlemen doo with them, by a mutuall conversion of the one into the other...among the Lacedemonians it was found out that great numbers of merchants were nothing to the furtherance of the state of the commonwealth: wherefore it is to be wished that the huge heape of them were somewhat restrained, as also our lawyers so should the rest live more easilie upon their owne, and few honest chapmen be brought to decaie...the high prices of wares are kept up, now they have gotten the onelie sale of things (upon pretence of better furtherance of the commonwealth) into their owne hands: whereas in times past we had sugar for foure pence the pound, that now is halfe a crowne, raisons or currants for a penie that now are holden at six pence, and sometimes at eight pence and ten pence the pound: nutmegs at two pence halfe penie the ounce: ginger at a penie an ounce, prunes at halfe pence farding: great raisons three pound for a penie, cinamon at foure pence the ounce, cloves at two pence, and pepper at twelve, and sixteen pence the pound. Whereby we may see the sequele of things not alwayes to be such as is pretended in the beginning...alas I see not by all their travell that the prices of things are anie whit abated.

Yeoman are those, which by our law are called *Legales homines,* free men borne English, and may dispend of their owne free land in yearlie revenue, to the summe of fortie shillings sterling (or six pounds as monie goeth in our times)...the word (Yeoman) signifieth a settled or staid man, such I meane as being married and of some yeares, betaketh himselfe to staie in the place of his abode for the better maintenance of himselfe and his familie, whereof the single sort have no regard, but are likelie to be still fleeting now hither now thither, which argueth want of stabilitie in determination and resolution of judgement, for the execution of things of anie importance. This sorte of people have a certeine preheminence, and more estimation than labourers & the common sort of artificers, & these commonlie live wealthilie, keepe good houses, and travell to get riches. They are also for the most part farmers to gentlemen...or at the leastwise artificers, & with grazing, frequenting of markets, and keeping of servants (not idle servants as gentlemen doo, but such as get both their owne and part of their masters living) do come to great welth, in somuch that many of them are able and doo buie the lands of unthriftie gentlemen, and often setting their sonnes to the schooles, to the universities, and to the Ins of the court; or otherwise leaving them sufficient lands whereupon they may live without labour, doo make them by those means to become gentlemen: these were they that in times past made all France afraid. And albeit they be called not master as gentlemen are, or sir as to knights apperteineth, but onelie John and Thomas, &c; yet have they beene found to have doone verie good service: and the kings of England in foughten battels, were wont to remaine among these yeomen as the French kings did among their horsemen: the prince thereby shewing where his chiefe strength did consist.

The fourth and last sort of people in England are day labourers, poore husbandmen, and some retailers, copie holders, and all artificers, as tailers, shomakers, carpenters, brickmakers, masons, &c. As for slaves and bondmen we have none...This fourth and last sort of people therefore have neither voice nor authority in the commonwealth, but are to be ruled and not rule other: yet they are not altogither neglected, for in cities and corporate townes, for default of yeomen, they are faine to make up their inquests of such maner of people. And in villages they are commonlie made churchwardens, sidemen, aleconners, constables, and manie times injoye the name of headboroughs. (Unto this sort also may our great swarmes of idle serving men be referred, of whom there runneth a proverb; Young serving men, old beggers: bicause service is none heritage...)...this furthermore among other things I have to say of our husbandmen and artificers, that they were never so excellent in their trades as at this present. But as the workemanship of the later sort was never more fine and curious to the eye, so was it never lesse strong and substantiall for continuance and benefit of the buyers. Neither is there anie thing that hurteth our artificers more than haste, and a barbarous or slavish desire to turne the penie, and by ridding their worke to make speedie utterance of their wares: which inforceth them to bungle up and dispatch manie things they care not how so they be out of their hands, whereby the buyer is often sore defrauded, and findeth to his cost, that haste maketh waste, according to the proverbe.

Oh how manie trades and handicrafts are now in England, whereof the common wealth hath no need? how manie needfull commodities have we which are perfected with great cost, &c: and yet may with farre more ease and lesse cost be provided from other countries if we could use the meanes. I will not speake of iron, glasse, and such like, which spoile much wood, and yet are brought from other countries better cheepe than we can make them here at home; I could exemplifie also in manie other. But to leave these things and proceed with our purpose, and herein generallie to speake of the commonwealth of England, I find that it is governed and mainteined by three sorts of persons.

1 The prince, monarch, and head governour, which is called the king, or the queene; in whose name and by whose authoritie all things are administred.

2 The gentlemen, which be divided into two sorts, as the baronie or estate of lords and also those that be no lords, as knights, esquiers, & simple gentlemen, as I have noted alreadie.

3 The third and last sort is named the yeomanrie, of whom and their sequele, the labourers and artificers, I have said somewhat even now. Whereto I ad that they be called not masters and gentlemen, but goodmen, as goodman Smith, goodman Cornell, goodman Mascall, &c: & in matters of law these and the like are called thus, Edward Mountford yeoman, Iames Cocke yeoman, Herrie Butcher yeoman, &c: by which addition they are exempt from the vulgar and common sorts.

Chapter 12. Of the maner of building and furniture of our houses

The greatest part of our building in the cities and good townes of England, consisteth onelie of timber, for as yet few of the houses of the communaltie (except here and there in the West countrie townes) are made of stone, although they may in diverse places be builded so good cheape of the one as of the other. In old time the houses of the Britons were slightlie set up with a few posts & manie radels, with stable and all offices under one roofe, the like whereof almost is to be seene in the fennie countries and northerne parts unto this daye, where for lacke of wood they are inforced to continue this ancient maner of building. It is not in vaine therefore in speaking of building to make a distinction betweene the plaine and wooddie soiles:

. . .where plentie of wood is, they cover (everie countrie house) with tiles, otherwise with straw, sedge, or reed, except some quarrie of slate be neere hand, from whence they have, for their monie, so much as may suffice them. . .Of chalke also we have our excellent Asbestos or white lime, made in most places, wherewith being quenched, we strike over our claye workes and stone walls, in cities, good townes, rich farmers and gentlemens houses. . .Within their doores also, such as are of abilitie doo oft make their floores and parget of fine alabaster burned, which they call plaster of Paris, whereof in some places we have great plentie, and that verie profitable against the rage of fire.

In plastering likewise of our fairest houses over our heads, we use to laye first a layer or two of white morter tempered with haire, upon laths, which are nailed one by another, and finallie cover all with the aforesaid plaster, which beside the delectable whitenesse of the stuffe it selfe, is layed on so even and smoothlie, as nothing in my judgement can be done with more exactnesse. The walls of our houses on the inner sides in like sort be either hanged with tapisterie, arras worke, or painted cloths, wherin either diverse histories, or hearbes, beasts, knots, and such like are stained, or else they are seeled with oke of our owne, or wainescot brought hither out of the east countries, whereby the roomes are not a little commended, made warme, and much more close than otherwise they would be. . .This also hath been common in England, contrarie to the customes of all other nations, and yet to be seene (for example in most streets of London,) that many of our greatest houses have outwardlie been verie simple and plaine to sight, which inwardlie have beene able to receive a duke with his whole traine, and lodge them at their ease. Hereby moreover it is come to passe, that the fronts of our streets have not beene so uniforme and orderlie builded as those of forreine cities, where the utterside of their mansions have oft more cost bestowed upon them, than all the rest of the house, which are often verie simple and uneasie within, as experience doth confirm. Of old time, our countrie houses, in stead of glasse, did use much lattice, and that made either of wicker, or fine rifts of oke in checkerwise. I read also that some of the better sort, in and before the times of the Saxons did make panels of horne in stead of glasse, & fix them in woodden calmes. But as horne in windows is now quite laid downe in everie place, so our lattices are also growne into lesse use, bicause glasse is come to be so plentifull, and within a verie little so good cheape as the other...onelie the clearest glasse is most esteemed: for we have diverse sorts, some brought out of Burgundie, some out of Normandie, much out of Flanders, beside that which is made in England, which would be so good as the best, if we were diligent and carefull to bestow more cost upon it, and yet each one that may will have it for his building...

The furniture of our houses also exceedeth, and is growne in maner even to passing delicacie: and herein I doo not speake of the nobilitie and gentrie onelie, but likewise of the lowest sort in most places of our south countrie, that have anic thing at all to take to. Certes, in noble mens houses it is not rare to see abundance of Arras, rich hangings of tapisterie, silver vessell, and so much other plate, as may furnish sundrie cupbords, to the summe oftentimes of a thousand or two thousand pounds at the least: whereby the value of this and the rest of their stuffe dooth grow to be almost inestimable. Likewise in the houses of knights, gentlemen, merchantmen, and some other wealthie citizens, it is not geson to behold generallie their great provision of tapisterie, Turkie worke, pewter, brasse, fine linen, and thereto costlie cupbords of plate, worth five or six hundred (or a thousand) pounds, to be deemed by estimation. But as herein all these sorts, doo far exceed their elders and predecessors, (and in neatnesse and curiositie, the merchant all other), so in times past, the costlie furniture stayed there, whereas now it is descended yet lower, even unto the inferiour artificers and manie farmers, who have learned also to garnish their cupbords with plate, their joined beds with tapisterie and silke hangings, and their tables with carpets and fine napery, whereby the wealth of our countrie doth infinitlie appeare...and whilest I behold how that in a time wherein all things are growen to most excessive prices, we doo yet find the means to obtain and achieve such furniture as heretofore hath been impossible. There are old men yet dwelling in the village where I remaine, which have noted three things to be marvellouslie altred in England within their found remembrance; (& other three things too too much increased.) One is, the multitude of chimnies latelie erected, whereas in their young dayes there were not above two or three, if so manie, in most uplandish townes of the realme (the religious houses, & manour places of their lords alwayes excepted, and peradventure some great personages) but ech one made his fire against a reredosse in the hall, where he dined and dressed his meat.

The second is the great amendment of lodging, for (said they) our fathers (yea) and we ourselves (also) have lien full oft upon straw pallets, covered onelie with a sheet, under coverlets made of dagswain or hopharlots (I use their owne termes), and a good round log under their heads in steed of a bolster, or pillow. If it were so that our fathers or the good man of the house, had within seven yeares after his mariage purchased a matteres or

542

flockebed, and thereto a sacke of chaffe to rest his head upon, he thought himself to be as well lodged as the lord of the towne, that peradventure laye seldome in a bed of downe or whole fethers; so well were they contented, and with such base kind of furniture: which also is not verie much amended as yet in some parts of Bedfordshire, and elsewhere further off from our southerne parts. Pillowes (said they) were thought meet onelie for women in childbed. As for servants, if they hade anie sheet above them, it was well, for seldome had they anie under their bodies, to keepe them from the pricking straws that ran oft through the canvas of the pallet, and rased their hardened hides.

The third they tell of, is the exchange of vessell, as of treene platters into pewter, and woodden spoones into silver or tin. For so common were all sortes of treene stuffe in old time, that a man should hardly find foure peeces of pewter (of which one was peradventure a salt) in a good farmers house, and yet for all this frugalitie, they were scarce able to live and paye their rents at their dayes without selling of a cow, or an horsse, or more, although they paid but foure pounds at the utter most by the yeare...in my time, although peradventure foure pounds of old rent be improved to fortie, fiftie, or an hundred pounds, yet will the farmer thinke his gaines verie small toward the end of his terme, if he have not six or seven yeares rent lieng by him, therewith to purchase a new lease, beside a faire garnish of pewter on his cupbord, three or four featherbeds, so manie coverlids and carpets of tapisterie, a silver salt, a bowle for wine (if not an whole nest) and a dozzen of spoones to furnish up the sute...

And as they commend these, so they speake also of three things that are growen to be verie grievous unto them, to wit, the inhansing of rents, latelie mentioned; the dailie oppression of copyholders, whose lords seeke to bring their poore tenants almost into plaine servitude and miserie...The third thing they talk of is usurie, a trade brought in by the Jewes, now perfectlie practised almost by everie christian, and so commonlie, that he is accompted for a foole that dooth lend his monie for nothing.

Chapter 22. Of woods and marishes

It should seeme by ancient records, and the testimonie of sundrie authors, that the whole countries of Lhoegres and Cambria, now England and Wales, have sometimes been verie well replenished with great woods & groves, although at this time the said commoditie be not a little decayed in both, and in such wise that a man shall oft ride ten or twentie miles in ech of them, and find verie little, or rather none at all, except it be neere unto townes, gentlemens houses, & villages, where the inhabitants have planted a few elmes, okes, hasels, or ashes, about their dwellings, for their defense from the rough winds, and keeping of the stormie weather from annoyance of the same. This scarcitie at the first grew either by the industrie of man, for maintenance of tillage, or else thorough the covetousnesse of such, as, in preferring of pasture for their sheepe and greater cattell, doo make small account of firewood and timber: or finallie, by the crueltie of the enimies, whereof we have sundrie examples declared in our histories...Although I must needs confesse that there is good store of great wood or timber here and there, even now in some places of England, yet in our dayes it is far unlike to that plentie, which our ancestors have seen heretofore, when statelie building was lesse in use...in times past, men were contented to dwell in houses, builded of sallow, willow, plumtree, hardebeame, and elme, so that the use of oke was in maner dedicated wholie unto churches, religious houses, princes palaces, noblemens lodgings, & navigation: but now all these are rejected, and nothing but oke anie whit regarded...

...our workmen are growne generallie to such an excellence of devise in the frames now made, that they far passe the finest of the old. And such is their husbandrie in dealing with their timber, that the same stuffe which in time past was rejected as crooked, unprofitable, and to no use but the fire, dooth now come in the fronts and best part of the worke. Whereby the common saying is... 'no oke can grow so crooked but it falleth out to some use'...

We have manie woods, forests, and parks, which cherish trees abundantlie, although in the woodland countries there is almost no hedge that hath not some store of the greatest sort, beside infinit numbers of hedgerowes, groves, and springs, that are mainteined of purpose for the building and provision of such owners as doo possesse the same. Howbeit...there is not anie wood, parke, hedgerow, grove, or forrest, that is not mixed with diverse, as oke, ash, hasell, hawthorne, birch, beech, hardebeame, aspe, poplars, wild cherie, and such like, whereof oke hath alwayes the preheminence, as most meet for building and the navie, whereunto it is reserved. This tree bringeth forth also a profitable kind of mast, whereby such as dwell neere unto the aforesaid places doo cherish and bring up innumerable heards of swine...I might ad in like sort the profit insuing by the barke of this wood, whereof our tanners have great use in dressing of leather, and which they buye yearlie in Maye by the fathome, as I have oft seene...

Of all oke growing in England, the parke oke is the softest, and far more spalt and brittle than the hedge oke. And of all in Essex, that growing in Bardfield parke is the finest for joiners craft: for oftentimes have I seene of their workes made of that oke so fine and faire, as most of the wainescot that is brought hither out of Danske, for our wainescot is not made in England. Yet diverse have assayed to deale withoute okes to that end, but not with so good successe as they have hoped, bicause the ab or juice will not so soone be removed and cleane drawne out, which some attribute to want of time in the salt water. Neverthelesse, in building, so well the hedge as the parke oke go all one waye, and never so much hath beene spent in an hundred years before, as is in ten yeare of our time; for everie man almost is a builder, and he that hath bought anie small parcell of ground, be it never so little, will not be quiet till he hath pulled down the old house (if anie were there standing), and set up a new after his owne devise. But whereunto will all this curiosity come?

Of elme we have great store in everie high waye and elsewhere, yet have I not seene thereof anie togither in woods or forrests, but where they have beene first planted, and then suffered to spread at their owne willes. Yet have I knowen great woods of beech and hasell in manie places, especiallie in Barkeshire, Oxfordshire, and Buckinghamshire, where they are greatlie cherished, & converted to sundrie uses by such as dwell about them. Of all the elms that ever I saw, those in the south side of Dover court, in Essex neere Harwich, are the most notable, for they grow in crooked maner, that they are almost apt for nothing else but navie timber, great ordinance, and beetels; and such thereto is their naturall qualitie, that being used in the said behalfe, they continue longer...than anie the like trees in whatsoever parcell else of this land, without shaking, or cleaving, as I find.

Appendix II

Extracts from *An Academie or Store House of Armory & Blazon,* by Randle Holme of Chester Gent. (1627-99).

As found in Part II, Roxburghe Club 1905, ed. I.H. Jeayes. British Library C.101.h.2.

Randle Holme (called the Third) of Chester was an heraldic painter by profession. Heraldry and blazonry were apparently twin consuming passions for him, and resulted in his compiling ten remarkable volumes of manuscript, the first part of which was published in 1688 and is more commonly known under the shorter title of the *Academy of Armory.* It is stated that the work was prepared in 1648-49, but many additions and amendments must have been made before publication in 1688. He had earlier held the post of Deputy Garter for Cheshire, Shropshire, Lancashire and North Wales; and in 1664 was appointed Sewer of the Chamber Extraordinary to Charles II, a sinecure which enabled him to devote more time to pursue his studies of Heraldry.

The manuscripts were sold in 1707 by the executors of Randle Holme IV, and were purchased by agents of Robert Harley (Earl of Oxford), eventually being absorbed into the Harleian Collection of Manuscripts. The particular volumes containing the *Academy* are now in the British Museum (Harl. Mss. 2026-2035). The second part was not published until 1905, when I.H. Jeayes edited them for the Roxburghe Club, and a small edition was issued by subscription.

In his work, Randle Holme attempted to present links between everyday objects and their heraldic interpretations. Many of the ideas are heavily contrived, and he is rarely at a loss to find an example of existing heraldic badges — e.g., when discussing the primitive three-legged stool (75), he finds that "...Argent, such a stoole sable is borne by *Die Schoner Van Sturbenhart,* a Germane familey..."

For our purposes the most interesting section is a group of pictures and text with objects and descriptions relevant to the mid- and later seventeenth century English home (facing p.18 in the Roxburghe edition). Unfortunately, Randle Holme was not attempting to describe or explain these objects, merely to interpret them for heraldic purposes. As a result his comments are tantalisingly brief and inconsistent, but we can nevertheless learn a good deal about nomenclature and usage and there are lists of necessary furnishings for a dining-room and bedchamber:

65. ...This kind of cabinett is such as Ladyes keepe their rings, necklaces, Braclett, and Jewells In: it stands constantly on the table (called the dressing table) in their Bed chamber.

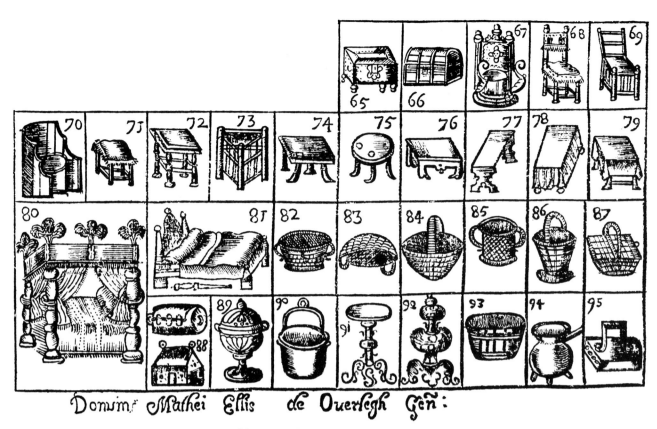

Donum Mathei Ellis de Ouerlegh Gen:

66. ...a Usurers Trunke, or coffer or Trunke or Caskett...bound with plates, or Iron Hoopes. These kind of coffers and trunks were first invented to be thus garded by old usurers, or covetous Misers, to keep safely that treasure committed to it, as unto a castle strongly fortified with Iron grates and Bars: makeing it thereby the token of negligence and niggardlyness by over much keeping of worldly pelse and muck: whereas they signifie of themselves diligence and virtuous studie.

A coffer is called in Latine *scrinium,* being a necessary thing for the safe keeping of pretious, and secrete things; as Jewells, Money, Ornaments; as also bookes, evidences, and records of Judgments.

If it have a streight, and flat cover, it is called a Chest; which in all other things represents the coffer, save the want of a circular lid, or cover.

67. ...a Throne, a chair Royall, or a Cathedre (from it Latine terme).
68. ...a Chaire. This is a chaire made up by an Imbrautherer...being all of one colour...(or)...of contrary colours, as when it is made up of needle, or turky worke then the fringe is diverse coloured; In such cases blazon it thus: a chaire...covered with Turkey work (or the seate and back of Needle work)...ffringed answerable thereunto, Garnished (or set with Nayles). Some will say onely, a Turky worke Chaire. Some blazon this a stoole-chaire, or back stoole. If the chaire be made all of Joyners worke, as back and seate then it is termed a Joynt chaire, or a Buffit chaire. Those which have stayes on each side are called Arme chaires or chaires of ease.
69. ...a Turned chaire with Armes. These kind of chaires are (also) borne without Armes.
70. ...This is the old way of makeing the chaire. Some term it a settle chaire, being so weighty that it cannot be moved from place to place, but still abideth in it owne station, haveing a kind of box or cubbert in the seate of it.

546

There is another kind of these chaires called Twiggen chaires because they are made of Owsiers, and Withen twigs: haveing round covers over the heads of them like to a canapy. Thes are principally used by sick and infirm people, and such women as have bine lately brought to bed; from whence they are generally termed, Growneing chaires, or Child-bed chaires.

71. ...a stoole...or after some thus, a Stool (or stoole frame), covered and Fringed, studed, or garnished.

72. ...a Joynt stoole. It is so called because all made and finished by the Joyner, haveing a wood cover: In most places in Cheshire it is termed a Buffit stool.

73. ...a Turned stoole. This is so termed because it is made by the Turner, or wheele wright all of turned wood, wrought with Knops, and rings all over the feete, these and the chaires, are generally made with three feete, but to distinguish them from the foure feet, you may term them three footed turned stoole or chaire.

74. ...a countrey stoole, or a planke, or Block stoole, being onely a thick peece of wood, with either 3 or 4 peece of wood fastned in it for feet. Note that if these be made long, then they are termed, either a Bench, a Forme, or a Tressell; of some a long seate.

Some of these stooles have but three feete, then they are termed three footed stooles, as in the next example.

75. ...a round three footed stoole, or a countrey stoole made round with three feete.

76. ...a nursing stoole. In some places it is called a crickett, or low stoole, or a childs stoole.

77. ...a Joynt Forme, or Bench.

These are termed Joynt formes, because wholy and workmanlike made, by Artist of the Joyners craft. Some are made with turned feete, 4 or 6, according to its length, haveing railes or Barres both above, for the seate to be fixed upon, and below, to hold the feete firme and stiddy. If the covers be broad then they are blazoned, Tables.

78. ...a Long Table...covered (with a cloth).

79. ...a Table, or square Table, covered with a Carpett. Some are covered with a carpett of Turky work, or needle worke, and such like.

Things necessary for and belonging to a dineing Rome.

The Rome well wanscoted about, either with Moontan and panells or carved as the old fashion was; or els in larg square pannell.

The Rome hung with pictures of all sorts, as History, Landskips, Fancyes, &c.

Larg Table in the midle, either square to draw out in Leaves, or Long, or Round or oval with falling leaves.

Side tables, or court cubberts, for cups and Glasses to drink in, Spoons, Sugar Box, Viall and Cruces for Viniger, Oyle and Mustard pot.

Cistern of Brass, Pewter, or Lead to set flagons of Beer, and Bottles of win in.

A Turky table cover, or carpett of cloth or Leather printed. Chaires and stooles of Turky work, Russia or calves Leather, cloth or stuffe, or of needlework. Or els made all of Joynt work or cane chaires.

Fire grate, fire shovell, Tongs, and Land Irons all adorned with Brass Bobbs and Buttons.

Flower potts, or Allabaster figures to adorn the windows, and glass well painted and a Larg seeing Glass at the higher end of the Rome.

A Faire with-drawing Rome at the other end of the dineing Rome well furnished with a Table, Chaires and stooles &c.

80. ...a Bed Royall, the vallance, curtaines (turned about the posts) and counter pane laced and fringed about: with a foote cloth of Turky worke about it: the Tester adorned with plumbes, according to the colours of the bed. This I have not seen in a coat, but for the badge and cognisance of an house in the citty of London, whose Indweller I suppose, was the Kings, or Queenes Maiesties, Upholsterer.

Things usefull about a Bed, and bed-chamber.

Bed stocks, as Bed posts, sides, ends, Head and Tester.

Mat, or sack-cloth Bottom.

Cord, Bed staves, and stay or the feet.

Curtain Rods and hookes, and rings, either Brass or Horn.

Beds, of chaffe, Wool or flocks, Feathers, and down in Ticks or Bed Tick.

Bolsters, pillows.

Blankets, Ruggs, Quilts, Counterpan, caddows.

Curtaines, Valens, Tester head cloth; all either fringed, Laced or plaine alike.

Inner curtaines and Valens, which are generally White silk or Linen.

Tester Bobbs of Wood gilt, or covered suteable to the curtaines.

Tester top either flatt, or Raised, or canopy like, or half Testered.

Basis, or the lower Valens at the seat of the Bed, which reacheth to the ground, and fringed for state as the uper Valens, either with Inch fring, caul fring, Tufted fring, snailing fring, Gimpe fring with Tufts and Buttons, Vellem fring, &c.

The Chamber

Hangings about the Rome, of all sorts, as Arras, Tapestry, damask, silk, cloth or stuffe: in paines or with Rods, or gilt Leather, or plaine, else Pictures of Friends and Relations to Adorne the Rome.

Table, stands, dressing Box with drawers, a large Myrour, or Looking glass. Couch, chair, stooles, and chaires, a closs-stoole.

Window curtaines, Flower potts.

Fire grate, and a good Fire in the winter, Fire shovel, Tongs, Fork and Bellows.

81. ...a Bed with...blankett or Cadow or Rugg: or covering: the sheets turned down, and boulster...this is a bed prepared for to lodge in, but haveing no Tester. Such are termed Truckle beds, because they trundle under other beds: or being made higher with an head, so that they may be set in a chamber corner, or under a cant roofe, they are called a field Bed or cant Bed. If it be soe, that it may have a canapy over it (that is a halfe tester)

then it is termed a Canapy Bed: to which bed belongs curtaines and Vellance.

In the base of this square ly's a Bed staffe, of some termed a Burthen staffe.

88. ...(lower half) an Arke or safe: a kind of little house made of wood, and covered with haire cloth, and so by two rings hung in the midle of a Rome, thereby to secure all things put therein from the cruelty of devouring Rats, mice, Weesels and such kind of Vermine. Some have the pannells of the Arke made all of Tyn, with small holes for aire, others of woode.

91. ...a Stand: a little round table, set upon one pillar, or post, which in the foote branches it selfe out into three or foure feete, or toes. It is used for to set a Bason on whilest washing, or a candle to read by.

Appendix III

The Life of Humphrey Beckham of Salisbury (1588-1671)

So rarely are we able to identify the work of minor pre-Restoration furniture makers, that it must be worthwhile recording such small biographical details as can be gathered for one of them; the joiner Humphrey Beckham of Salisbury, Wiltshire. Some attributions are surveyed in Chapter Four (Figures 4:61-67), where some excellent carving is thought now to be by his hand, and related pieces are possibly from his workshop or that of his family. Obviously, some hundreds of provincial joiners are eligible for investigation in this way, but in Beckham we have a craftsman who emerges quite clearly as both a personality and a minor artist.

It is tempting to compare his life and achievements with those of the emigrant joiner Thomas Dennis of Ipswich, Massachusetts. Dennis was elevated to the status of a folk hero as a result of the series of articles by Irving Lyon (Antiques Magazine, November 1937 — August 1938); and although the number of items and the quality of work attributed to Dennis has since been severely diminished, his reputation as an accomplished joiner-carver remains largely unquestioned.

Yet, by comparison, Beckham's skill and achievements are considerably superior. His work is modest enough beside that of the major sculptors and the metropolitan joiners of his time; yet he met with a large measure of local success during his working life, and his abilities were acclaimed by his friends and patrons. Since 1771, he has been the subject of occasional biographical notes (see below), and has remained identified as a personality in the folk memory of local people right down to the present day (even if the aspect they remember best is the myth of his boastful nature). Though only a joiner by trade, his work is imbued with a suave sculptural sense which is entirely more respectable than the acknowledged work of Thomas Dennis.

The known facts of Beckham's life are few. Some of these are spelt out in the excerpt from *Antiquitates Sarisburiensis* quoted below, and these are filled out by numerous instances of payments for work in the account books of Salisbury institutions, such as those of the churchwardens of Sarum St. Thomas. The Beckhams had a close association with the parish and church where Humphrey was a sidesman and assistant churchwarden in 1636, where he lies buried, and where his tomb panel still remains (Figure 4:64).

Although he is said to have come from a family of clothiers, there are references to other Beckhams which show that several were joiners. As early as 1573, Reynold Beckham was paid for making "ye frame for the Quenes Armes" which still remains at Sarum St. Thomas. Humphrey and his brother John both served as Chamberlains and later Wardens of the Joyners' Company. In 1634 John Beckham was paid for an important civic commission, "for that he hath artificiallye set up ye waynscott and carved workes in the Counsell House". In his will of January 1671, Beckham left the residue of his estate, which included his house, workshop, tools, timber and "new wares" to a second brother, Benjamin, who was also a joiner. Many years earlier a third brother, William, appeared in the existing Joyners' Company Accounts for 1618-21.

After a search, Beckham's will and probate inventory were recently brought to light (1978) at the Wiltshire Record Office at Trowbridge. The will is long and detailed, but several interesting facts emerge, including the identification of another Beckham joiner, his kinsman Nathaniell. Even at the advanced age of eighty-three, Humphrey is found to have a current apprentice, Thomas Deverall, and the completion of his training is entrusted to Benjamin and Nathaniell. One clause offers a bequest of twenty shillings to the "Society of Carpenters and Joyners" (the Joyners' Company), and instructs that the money be used specifically "to helpe encrease their Stock" (cf. Chapter Two, p.48). The inventory (Appendix IV) provides the usual picture of a rather sparsely furnished home, but once again certain details emerge to clothe Beckham's circumstances. The workshop and yard contain a store of timber and tools, and further evidence of his continuing active life is provided by the "new wares" stored in the workshop and chambers.

Biographical notes on Humphrey Beckham have been published in several places, more notably in *Old and New Sarum, or Salisbury,* by Robert Benson and Henry Hatcher, London 1843; and in *The Ancient Trade Guilds and Companies of Salisbury,* by Charles Haskins, Salisbury 1912; but the main source would seem to have been *Antiquitates Sarisburiensis,* printed and sold in Salisbury by E. Easton in 1771. Coincidentally, this small book was produced one hundred years after Beckham's death, but the sources of the information are not revealed. Perhaps the circumstances of Beckham's life were still common knowledge locally, or else the author had access to manuscript notes. In the extract which follows, more interesting than the sparse biographical detail is the author's strong opinion of Beckham's worth, and his conviction that the earthy and homespun virtues of (what we would now call) folk art should be applauded for their own sakes; a view which echoes William Hogarth's motives when he set up an exhibition of sign-makers' work in London only a few years previously in 1762. It was not until the twentieth century that the works of so-called 'primitive' painters and sculptors were seriously considered again as works of art.

This account of Humphrey Beckham appears, alongside other local worthies, in Chapter 6 of *Antiquitates Sarisburiensis* (The Lives of Eminent Men, Natives of Salisbury).

HUMPHREY BECKAM

It is of little importance where a man of Genius is born; the place can add nothing to, whatever it may receive from, such a birth. Beckam's family originally came from a place of that name in the Hundred of Fordingbridge, but had for some generations resided in Salisbury, where Humphrey was born in 1588.

In early life the mind being free from the fetters of Education and Prepossession, displays its propensity without fear of censure, or the hope of praise; indeed where the inclination is strong, no future institution can supersede or extinguish this natural bent. Beckam exemplified this; his parents would have brought him up to the clothing business, which was what they were engaged in, had it been possible to alter a pre-disposition to another Art. He was constantly shaping rude figures in wood and clay, instead of applying to his intended profession. This determined his father to place him with one Mr. Rosgrave a painter and carver in the city.

These Arts, particularly the last, had arrived at tolerable perfection, because more cultivated than others. The Church had constant occasion for Croziers, Crucifixes, Images of Saints, &c. But what animated Artists was the building of Sepulchres, and the expensive Decorations of Monuments...and in truth, many of those antient works to be seen at this day, shew a richness of invention and a regularity of disposition that is admirable, the execution also is vastly superior to what we can well conceive of in such remote times, and performed by artists with no higher titles, than those of Carvers, Marblers, Glaziers, &c.

The Reformation had not only demolished all the monuments raised to inferior persons, but even those of higher ranks could not preserve theirs, except by removing every superstitious appendage. The tide now ran as strong against images, as ever it had done for them, the Arts dependant thereon were consequently reduced to a low ebb. At this unfavourable era was Beckam born, with talents capable of advancing sculpture, or if you please carving and statuary to their utmost limits. *Rosgrave,* his Master, knew nothing of designing or any thing else except the mechanical part of his profession; books were scarce on these subjects, Beckam's learning reached no further than being able to read the Testament or Psalms, so that want of money added to other circumstances precluded him from all improvement. Humphrey instead of grinding colours, was either daubing the walls, or spoiling the tools about images, or gazing at the Statue of Henry III in a niche over the Arch of the close gate. 'Tis very extraordinary what an impression this statue made on Beckam's mind, he contemplated it from his infancy, and formed his works to that model as nearly as possible.

Some things done by Humphrey were noticed and commended by several Citizens, which encouraged his master to set him to carve statues and other ornaments for some houses then building in the City. Of these many are yet remaining in Mr. Thomas Dennis's parlour, in Brown-street, and in other places. Some are in the dresses of the times, and others seem to be taken from the Cuts in Hollinshed's chronicle, —a book, says a contemporary writer conteyning manie delectable histories and portraictures of our auncient Kynges, —and in much repute at that time.

A modern Critic will look on these figures as only fit for Bart'lmy Fair, or to be admired by old women and children; He will ask, of what materials are these works made; when he is answered of Beech, Ash, and such-like as England produced, how much more valuable, replies he, were they of snow-white Ivory, of Parian or Penthelian marble, of Porphyry, Granite or Basaltes; this however is talking like a stone mason rather than a man of taste; tis not the materials but the workmanship that stamps the merit. Look into any collection of Antiquities, that of the *Comte de Caylus* for instance, what a grand style and wonderful expression does he discover in some half demolished Egyptian, Etruscan or Grecian Statues, Busto or Relievo! 'Tis antique, that is enough. Let us lay aside our prejudices, and applaud a countryman, when he has merit. Beckam's figures are all varied and finely imagined, the countenance is strongly marked, the attitude graceful, the draperies hang light, and the execution is easy and free.

Soon after James I's accession to the throne, he came down to Lord Pembroke at Wilton; the King complimented the City of Salisbury with a visit, and received the congratulations of his new subjects from some eloquent Mayor or Recorder; Beckam mixt with the croud, but little attentive to the speechifying Orator, he was impressing on his imagination the capital traits of the Monarch's face; accordingly from memory, he has most happily expressed them in a statue still extant. His Majesty has a sharp Scotch face, like his profile on a gold coin struck in Scotland, in 1575.

Charles the First had some taste for the fine Arts, and made a large collection of Paintings and statues, but the troubles which continued most part of his reign, prevented the spreading of an improved manner in these through the Kingdom.

Beckam lived to see it thought meritorious to destroy with more than Gothic barbarity, the statues of Saints and eminent men, and every remains of antient ingenuity; no place was a greater sufferer than the Cathedral of Salisbury; numberless statues... and the brazen arms on the Monuments of the deceased, were defaced and carried away under the notion of removing superstition.

Beckam now advanced in years, his Genius was in decline: The troubles of a family prevented him from attending to that walk in which he could excel, he spent the remainder of his life, in obscurity, yet above want. Some time before his decease he carved his monument on the west wall of St. Thomas's church; it represents the Lord appearing to the shepherds. The design, execution and perspective are not inconsiderable for the hand of untutored nature...

The last-mentioned 'monument' is the oak tomb panel (Figure 4:64) which still hangs in the church, though now on the south wall. It is no doubt this panel which gave rise to Beckham's reputation for boastfulness and self-advertisement; but in fact Beckham probably made it many years earlier for his own private domestic use, as a chimney overmantel. It can no doubt be identified as one of the two "chimney peeces" mentioned in his probate inventory (Appendix IV). His brother Benjamin inherited the house, the business and all the furnishings, and no doubt it was family pride that prompted him to set up an example of his brother's own work, to stand as the most suitable of all possible monuments to a joiner-carver.

Appendix IV

Selections from the Probate Inventories of Provincial Woodworkers

As we have seen, before the reign of Charles II furniture makers were drawn from the ranks of the anonymous artisan classes, and none are known to us in the same way as the virtuoso personalities of later generations. Those master-craftsmen who rose to serve as joiners or upholders to the Crown or the aristocracy must have been men of considerable skill and accomplishment, but they were regarded by their patrons as nothing more than tradesmen and suppliers, whose identities were of far less interest than their capabilities and the quality of their work. Inigo Jones was perhaps the first English architect/designer to be granted some prestige during his lifetime, as a result of his work for James I and Charles I, in the same way that some painters had begun to receive status in the eyes of their contemporaries.

In the last quarter of the seventeenth century, some patrons began to see that recognition was due to the better calibre of cabinetmakers, such as Gerrit Jensen, and for the first time patrons were pleased that the supplier of their furniture should be known by name. In the next century, the cult of the designer grew to a pitch which has barely been matched since.

But the provincial joiners, carpenters and turners who made the furniture illustrated in these pages were men of no such distinction. Few of them were known to any but their closest friends and neighbours, and most of their work will always remain irretrievably anonymous. Until recent years, almost none of their work had been identified by name, and one of the tasks which faces the modern furniture historian is that of cataloguing further some of these men and their products, though it is a task fraught with problems and lost information.

Evidence of their low station in life is provided by the poor lists of chattels in their inventories, four examples of which are given here. Of these, only Humphrey Beckham has been rescued from anonymity (see Chapter Four and Appendix III). Edward Bickerton would appear to have been in possession of a thriving business at the time of his death, with £63 8s. 6d.-worth of timber in his yard and elsewhere. This represents a considerable capital investment for a man worth only slightly more than £100, and is by far the largest item in his estate. The other three were doubtlessly old men, and retired from business, or partially so (only John Day no longer owned the necessary tools of his trade). Indeed, we know that Beckham was aged eighty-three yet he had an apprentice, a stock of new wares in his house, and £40-worth of timber in his yard. Both Beckham and Rathbane held bonds to the value of £70 (perhaps on loan as working-capital to other and younger craftsmen or kinsmen), and so the only very poor member of the group was old John Day the carpenter, with his few sticks of sorry and indifferent furniture worth only £8 13s. Rathbane is described as a 'gentleman', yet his household goods are valued at a mere £17 8s.; which, with his turning tools "in the shopp", suggests that his occupation was that of a jobbing turner.

These probate inventories are of interest to us, not only because of the testators' occupations, but for the insight which they provide into the domestic conditions of real people at this time. They are the only glimpse we shall ever have into the homes of ordinary people in the seventeenth century, and they contain as much magic as more literary descriptions. Even Humphrey Beckham, who we know had achieved a fair measure of local success in his working life, furnished his house in a very modest manner.

The Joiner and the Turner

The Joiner, 1.
smootheth hewn Boards, 2.
with a Plain, 3.
upon a Work-board, 4.
he maketh them very smooth
with a Little plain, 5.
he boreth them thorough
with an Augre, 6.
carveth them with a Knife, 7.
fasteneth them together
with Glue and Cramp-irons, 8.

and maketh Tables, 9.
Boards, 10.
Chests, 11. &c.
  The Turner, 12.
sitting over the Treddle, 13.
turneth with a Throw, 15.
upon a Turner's Bench, 14.
Bowls, 16.
Tops, 17.
Puppets, 18.
and such like Turners Work.

(From Joh. Amos Comenius, 'Orbis Pictus or The Visible World', ed. 1777)

It was required by law that an inventory be taken of the movable goods and chattels of the deceased, and that it be produced in evidence as a fair valuation at the granting of probate of a will. Inventories are not entirely reliable as complete descriptions of the furnishings of a house, since they did not include items fixed to the freehold, the property of a spouse, nor many of those little personal belongings which make even the most modest house into a home. Nevertheless, they contain many invaluable references to the common furnishings of their time, showing that furniture was by no means the rare luxury that some modern commentators would have us believe. Many hundreds of inventories and wills have been published, often in local groups, and these are the source for most of the quotations to be found in these pages.

The original manuscripts were usually prepared on long, narrow sheets of paper (or sometimes vellum), and they often follow a predictable course around the house, naming each room in turn. The phonetic spellings are sometimes difficult for the modern reader to follow, but it is worth struggling with them, both for the richness of the expressions used and for the occasional insight they may grant us into the development of names for things. The inventories are signed by two or more appraisers, and are headed by a more or less standard preamble.

Humphrey Beckham of Salisbury in Wiltshire, Joiner, 1671[1]

A True and perfect Inventory of all the Goods of Humphrey Beckham of the City of New Sarum in County Wilts Joyner. Taken and Appraised by those whose names are hereunder subscribed the ffifth Day of ffebruary

Anno Dom 1671

	£	s	d
IN THE CHAMBER OVER THE SHOP			
One ffeather Bead Bolster & Pillows	2	10	0
One fflock Bead & two fflock Bolsters	0	10	0
One Rugg & one Civirlead	1	0	0
One High Beadstead Curtaines and Vallons Rods matt & Coard		12	0
One Couch 2 trunks 4 Chaires & a Chimney Peece			
one Desk & one Coffer	2	00	0
	6	12	0
IN THE CLOSSETT			
Two fflitches of Bacon & 2 Cheeses	1	3	0
In new Ware in the Chambers	5	0	0
	6	3	0
IN YE LITTLE CHAMBER			
One ffeather Bead 2 fflock Bolsters 4 Civirings			
a trundle Beadstead Matt & Coard	1	0	0
ffor ye Timber in ye Backside	30	0	0
ffor the Timber in th Backhouse	10	0	0
	41	0	0
IN THE SHOP			
ffor New Ware	3	0	0
A Grinding Stone & for Tooles & Lumber in ye Shop	2	0	0
	5	0	0
IN THE KITCHEN			
In Brass & Pewter	2	10	0
A Jack a Spitt 2 fire Pannes a pr of Tongs a pr of			
Cotterells Billowes & a pr of Iron Andirons	0	10	0
A Table Board Cubbord & ye Lumber & 5 Pictures	0	15	0
A Leaden Pumpe	0	10	0
In Bookes	0	05	0
A Chimney Peece		05	0
	4	5	0

1. Previously unpublished, held at Wiltshire County Record Office, Trowbridge.

His Wearing Apparrell	5	0 0
Y Cowles Tubs & for Lumber in the Cockloft	0	10 0
ffor the Linnin	1	10 0
Debts Owing on Bond	70	0 0
Other Debts owing	02	0 0
	77	10 0
Sum Tot	142	10 0

Nathaneill Beckham
William Cawly

Edward Bickerton of Evesham in Worcestershire, Joiner, 1668[2]

Imprimis, his wearing apparell.	£5 0s. d.
Item, Timber in his house and abroad.	£63 8s. 6d.
Item, *In the Kitchen,* Brass and Pewter, with one furnace, at	£6 13s. 4d.
One joined cubard, one table, 4 joined stools, four chairs.	£1 10s. 0d.
Item, one Jacke, one Gunne, 2 Spitts, fire shovell and tongs, one lanthorn, 2 dripping panns.	19s. 6d.
Item, *In the Hall,* One joined cupboard, one table and stools, 5 bedposts.	£1 6s. 0d.
Item, *In the Chamber Over the Hall,* one joined Bedstead, one Tester bed with the furniture thereto belonging, one trundell bed with a flock bed and furniture thereto belonging. 2 trunckes, one forme and a warming pan.	£4 13s. 4d.
Item, *In the Chambers Over the Kitchen,* Two bedsteads, one fetherbed with the furniture belonging to them both.	£6 0s. 0d.
Item, one table, one little cubbard.	6s. 8d.
Item, one box of linning, *In the Top Loft.*	£1 13s. 4d.
Item, *In the Brew House,* One Malt Mill, two stools, with other brewing vessells.	£1 13s. 4d.
Item, *In the Cellar,* Two hogsheads of Beare.	£2 0s. 0d.
Item, one hogshead and 7 half hogsheads.	£1 0s. 0d.
Item, all his working tools,	£5 0s. 0d.
	£101 6s. 6d.

Gamaliell Rathbane of Writtle in Essex, Gent (? Turner), 1663[3]

IN THE BEST CHAMBER — One featherbedd, one Flocke bedd, one feather Bolster, one Pillowe, one Bedsted with Matt and Corde, Two Coverletts, Three Blanketts, Three Curtaine Rodds, Three Blanketts, Three old stayned Curtaines, 4*li.*

MORE IN THE BEST CHAMBER — Three Chests, two Trunkes, two little Tables, six Jointstooles, one Joynd chaire, Three Cushions, one Glasse Case, two lookinge Glasses, a Birdinge peece, one paire of Cobirons, a fire shovell and Tonges, a paire of Bellowes, a Saltboxe, a paire of Trammells, fower old Candlesticks, a smoothinge Iron, Two paire of flaxen sheets, three Pillowbeeres, a Dozen of Napkins, Three Towells, two shirts, two Table Cloathes, 4*li.* 8*s.*

IN THE OLD CHAMBER — One Cupboard with Drawers, two Chests, one Trunke, fower boxes, a Napkin Presse with two swords & other Lumber, 2*li.* 10*s.*

2. Published by John West, *Village Records,* Macmillan & Co., London, 1962, p.116.
3. Published by Francis W. Steer, *Farm & Cottage Inventories of Mid-Essex. 1635-1749.* Essex Record Office Publications, No. 8, Chelmsford, 1950, p.98, No.40.

MORE IN THE OLD CHAMBER — A parcell of Bookes, Twenty Pewter Dishes, Twelve Sawcers, sixe Porrengers, one Pewter Bason, one Quart pott, one Pewter Chamber pott, three Brasse Potts, one Chaffer, one Pestle and Morter, Three Skilletts, Two small kettles, one fryinge Panne, one Drippinge Pann, Three Spitts, an Iron Spade, 6*li*. 10*s*.

IN THE SHOPP — Turninge Tooles, 13*s*. 4*d*.

IN WEARINGE APPARELL AND MONEY IN HIS PURSE — 9*li*. 19*s*. 4*d*.

Due to the deceased in debts upon bond & otherwise about — 70*li*.
The whole summe of this Inventary...doth amount unto — 98*li*. 0*s*. 8*d*.

John Day the elder of Highwood in Essex, Carpenter, 1725[4]

IN THE HALL — One long table, 6 joynt stooles, two other small tables, 4 old chairs, one cuberd, fire shovel and tongs, 3 small spits, 6 peuter dishes, 6 pleats, one bras candle stick, som other small implements, one clock, one worming pan, £2 10*s*.

IN THE PARLER — One indeferant bed, & bedsted with all belonging too it, one chest of drauers, one pres cubard, one small table, 2 sorry old chairers, 1 4*s*.

IN THE BUTTRE — Two half hogsheds, one iron porridg pots, 7*s*.

IN THE DARY — One chespres, one stand, 3 woden trays, and a few earthen pans, and other small implements, 7*s*.

IN THE BREWHOUSE — One small copper, four tubs, one bras cettle, other small things, £1 5*s*.

IN THE CHAMBER OVER THE PARLER — One sorry bed with a linciwolcy teeke (linsey-woolsey tick), and bedsted, one small table, three hutchis, 2 truncks, £1 10*s*.

IN THE HALL CHAMBER — Two beds with what belongs to them very mean, one cubbard, 2 huthis, £1 10*s*.

Two cows that are kept upon the Commans, £4.
Waring clothis and mony in his purs, £1 10*s*.
Linlin — 4 pair of sheets, 6 napkins, 3 board cloths, £1 3*s*.
(Total) — £15 6*s*. (Appraisers — Samuel Shettleworth, William Middleton.)

4. Ibid., p.260, No.224.

Appendix V

Distribution of Population in the British Isles, 1662.

Estimates of population sizes and densities are highly unreliable for most English towns and counties in the seventeenth century. Most censuses at this time were concerned only with the taxable aspects of population and property; but at least in the case of the Hearth Tax, we have a set of figures which reflects both the relative sizes of populations and the general wealth of individual towns: both factors which must be directly related to the bulk and quality of furniture production. The map and table in Figure 4:56 are based on figures published by W.G. Hoskins in his *Local History in England,* 1959, using information supplied by C.A.F. Meekings of the Public Record Office. The figures are based mainly on the Hearth Tax Returns for 1662, a year which is central to the range of regional and vernacular furniture types (see Chapter Four). Though subject to small local adjustments, the relative importance suggested by the table is probably highly accurate.

Thus Figure 4:56 gives us a chart of the towns in which we are most likely to find some evidence of furniture production at a high standard, and it is hoped that the map and table may be of some use in pointing the way towards a future scheme of regional studies on an urban basis. The influence of these towns as markets and cultural centres extended over a considerable area of the surrounding countryside, and full account should be taken of the local topography.

But the larger towns still accounted for only a small percentage of the total population at this date (perhaps one-eighth out of about seven millions), and so we should also look at the rural areas to find in which regions the bulk of the population was concentrated. The sketch-map on the next page is intended to provide only the broadest indications of relative population densities in 1662, since accurate figures are not available. The information for this map was based partly on the county densities published in the *Reader's Digest Atlas of the British Isles,* 1965 — one of the very few sources available, and tempered by considerations of the relief structure of the British Isles. The natural regions of Britain, which are largely defined for us by major lowlands and coastal profiles, must be seen as more relevant to regional furniture studies than the more arbitrary county boundaries (even if the counties are more readily understandable).

In 1662 the majority of people lived in the southern and eastern areas of the British Isles, and their distribution was closely related to the productive agricultural lowlands. The greatest densities of population were in the immediate areas of London and the Dublin Pale, though most of the towns in Figure 4:56 were overcrowded to some extent, especially in the poorer districts of the town centres. The most highly populated agricultural counties (with an overall figure of one to two hundred persons per square mile) were the whole of East Anglia, Kent, Surrey, Gloucestershire, Somerset, Devon, Lancashire, Midlothian (Edinburgh), Kinross, Fife and County Meath (Dublin). In addition, the map indicates interesting concentrations in the embryonic industrial areas of South Yorkshire and East Lancashire (textiles — the Clothing Dales), Nottingham and Durham (coal and iron). The most empty areas were those of highland, wasteland or sheeplands (such as the undrained Fen, the Breckland or Salisbury Plain).

In the second half of the seventeenth century, the pattern shifted somewhat with the growth of the towns. Industrial towns in particular grew at a considerable rate, and by 1700 the list of larger towns included Birmingham, Manchester, Liverpool and Sunderland. All the major ports increased their populations, wealth and influence in the seventeenth century as a direct result of overseas trade and expansion; as in the case of Liverpool, which grew as an outlet for Lancashire textiles and as an inlet for colonial and Irish imports.

Relative population densities in the British Isles, 1662. It is important not to gain an exaggerated impression of the total population from this map. Even the more populous counties were fairly sparsely settled by today's standards. Settlements were surrounded by areas of farmland, and these alternated with vast areas of uncleared forest and 'wasteland'. The total population of the British Isles was not much in excess of seven million.

Appendix VI

The Private and Public Collector

An appreciation of the unique virtues of early oak furniture has been expressed by many writers in many different moods. At one time or another it has represented most things to most men (see p.155), but one of the most sympathetic views was that taken by William Cobbett, who noted fervently in his *Cottage Oeconomy* of 1822 that "...In household goods the warm, the strong, the durable, ought always to be kept in view. Oak-tables, bedsteads and stools, chairs of oak or of yew-tree, and never a bit of miserable deal board. Things of this sort ought to last several life-times. A labourer ought to inherit something besides his toil from his grandfather..." Cobbett was at pains to offer sound advice to the struggling poor, and the pleasure he found in the strong and simple homes of country folk shines through his descriptions of farmhouse life. During one of his rural rides (in 1825) he visited a farmhouse which was amply furnished with "...tables, and stools, and benches of everlasting duration...Everything about this farmhouse was formerly the scene of plain manners and plentiful living. Oak clothes-chests, oak bedsteads, oak chests of drawers, and oak tables to eat on, long, strong, and well supplied with joint stools. Some of the things were many hundreds of years old..."

Cobbett's angle was that of a practical man, a pragmatist passionately interested in the welfare of the agricultural labouring classes. He advised them to stick to the old ways because he believed in their integrity and value for money. He urged the farmer with money to spare for luxuries not to throw out the old furniture in favour of "...the mahogany table, and the fine chairs, and the fine glass, and all as bare-faced upstart as any stock-jobber in the country can boast of..."

Literary references to cottage life in the nineteenth century abound with images of snug little nests like Old Sally's cottage, described by Flora Thompson in *Lark Rise to Candleford*, where "...there was a good oak, gate-legged table, a dresser with pewter and willow-pattern plates, and a grandfather's clock...the inner room — 'the house', as it was called — was a perfect snuggery, with walls two feet thick and outside shutters to close at night and a padding of rag rugs, red curtains and feather cushions within..." Cottages and farmhouses of this description were to prove a treasure trove for later generations of collectors and dealers, who were scouring the country for negotiable merchandise long before the end of the century. Farmhouses had long been furnished with good plain joiner-made furniture, but the association of panelled wainscot furniture with the cottages of the poor dates only from the later eighteenth and the nineteenth century. As oak furniture became unfashionable for persons of means, some remarkably fine pieces were passed down to servants, farmhands and

Figure ia. *Joined 'Imprisoning' chair. Oak, c.1775, in the style of c.1530.*

Figure ib. *The 'Imprisoning' chair, shown when sprung. This is the sort of toy which has always delighted collectors, and was probably made for Horace Walpole's collection at Strawberry Hill. The coat-of-arms on the side cases is probably that of Walpole, but identification is uncertain without the tincture. In 1660, Samuel Pepys had noted a similar chair at the home of his friend, Sir W. Batten, where he was made "...very welcome. Among other things he showed me in my Lady's Closet, wherein was a great store of rarities; as also a chair, which he calls King Harry's Chaire, where he that sits is catched with two irons that come round about him, which makes good sport..." Batten's chair must have been very similar to the present example, which is in the style of Henry VIII. The seat is spring-loaded, and the unwary sitter finds that two iron bars spring out from the side cases to trap him by the legs. No doubt Walpole wanted his friends to believe that the chair had some ancient sinister purpose, but in fact such chairs were probably never more than a practical joke in England.*

1. For further details see the account by Simon Jervis in Furniture History, Volume X, 1974.

poorer neighbours, and entered into a new lease of serviceable cottage life. Regrettably, many pieces were cut and altered to fit into smaller rooms, and sets of chairs and stools were broken up between different homes; but at least this process led to the eventual survival of many items which would otherwise have been chopped up and burned.

The collector of early furniture had first entered on the scene in the middle of the eighteenth century, though individual items had found their way into collections of curiosities at a much earlier date. This usually meant that the piece was asssociated with an historic personality, or that it possessed some characteristic which appealed to the contemporary mind (Figure i a and b); and items of furniture were thrown together with stuffed animals, sea shells, Egyptian mummies, semi-precious stones, fossils, Roman bronzes, Medieval armour and Eskimo spears, in a magnificent cornucopia (which only recently died out with the passing of the true old-fashioned junk shop). Such catholicity of taste was still apparent in the collections of Horace Walpole in the second half of the eighteenth century, but by then he had at least started to analyse the characteristics of *style* in old furniture, and had (however imperfectly interpreted) begun to form some cohesive view of historic *periods* of furniture design. His main interest focused on a rather hazy vista of the Middle Ages and the Elizabethan Age, though in the face of much derision from his contemporaries, and the catalogue of his collections at Strawberry Hill includes Gothic carvings and Renaissance furniture (see Figure 4:34).

The Gothic splendours of Strawberry Hill were not dispersed until the sale of 1842 (Walpole died in 1797), before which the house was much-visited and influenced the thinking of many collectors such as William Beckford and Thomas Baylis. Although their expertise was over-shadowed by their fervour, Baylis and his friend Lechmere Whitmore set up a house and collection at the Pryorsbank, Fulham, which contained a vast and picturesque collection of 'venerable' oak furniture, carved panelling, arms and armour and textiles, as well as many other splendid but unrelated items.[1] In the 1840s the house was a meeting place for many of their antiquarian friends, and the atmosphere contributed to the ideals of men like Joseph Nash (author and illustrator of the *Mansions of England*) and C.J. Richardson, whose watercolour drawings of furniture and interiors are invaluable records of long-vanished pieces.

The most important element of the collective taste of the time was a subjective and somewhat self-indulgent view of the 'picturesque' and the 'quaint'. A growing army of collectors and connoisseurs relied more heavily on their intuitive reactions than on objective observation, and this passionate approach set a pattern in taste and scholarship which persisted until long after 1900. The modern collector values early pieces in a pure and unadulterated form, but many nineteenth century collectors were not above 'beautifying' their acquisitions to conform more closely to a preconceived ideal. This usually took the form of 'carving-up' plain pieces, or adding bits of old carving to them. The bedstead in Figure iib is a perfect example of a genuine piece which has been added to in this way. An early exercise in decorating a house in this manner may still be seen at Plas Newydd, near Llangollen in Denbighshire (Clwyd). This house was occupied from 1778 until 1831 by 'The Ladies of Llangollen' (Lady Eleanor Butler and Sarah Ponsonby), where they created a Gothic retreat in the romantic landscape of the Vale of Llangollen. The ladies acquired hundreds of pieces of old carved oak with which to decorate the structure of the house, and to reconstruct fantastic pieces of furniture, a phase which they entered in earnest after c.1810.

Whether the ladies were actually responsible themselves for breaking up genuine furniture, we cannot now be sure, but the supply of period carvings was by then a common trade. Newspapers carried advertisements for quantities of old carvings, and J.C. Loudon noted in his *Encyclopaedia* of 1829: "...The exterior of chests or wardrobes might be rendered curious, and highly interesting, though we do not say in correct or architectural taste, by covering them with the Elizabethan, Dutch, Louis XIV., or Francis I. ornaments, which are now to be purchased in abundance..."[2] Furniture of this sort is still to be found in large numbers, and such things are still accepted as genuine by the unwary and thoughtless collectors. Gullibility was by no means exclusive to the amateur in the nineteenth century, for in 1890 the bed in Figure iib was acquired from Christie's by no less august an institution than the Victoria and Albert Museum, for the sum of £357.

Such a casually indulgent approach can only be followed in a market where the supply of good pieces far outweighs the demand for them. As late as 1902, Fred Roe was able to note that "...linen-panelled chests, early or late, can be obtained without difficulty up to the present day; their importation and manufacture must have at one time literally glutted the market...", adding that "...a perfect mania for destroying old receptacles seems to have existed till lately, even at the present time it is not wholly extinct..."

It was not until after the First World War that the first signs appeared of an approaching shortage of high-quality goods. By that time the first great definitive book on the subject was well established (Percy Macquoid's *History of English Furniture,* especially Volume One — *The Age of Oak*), and prices began to rise steeply with the increasing quality of scholarship and the availability of post-war industrial fortunes. A taste for early oak furniture coincided with the euphoria of the early 1920s, and by 1925 the prices paid for individual pieces had passed the £1,000 mark. Less ambitious pieces were still available very cheaply to those collectors of small means, but there was a wide group of rich collectors whose houses and collections of furniture and accessories are chronicled in such prestigious publications as Country Life (see the series *In English Homes,* edited by Charles Latham and Avray Tipping), *Early English Furniture and Woodwork* by Cescinsky and Gribble, and the *Dictionary of English Furniture* by Macquoid and Edwards. An enormous contribution to the volume of published material was made by such periodicals as the *Connoisseur, Apollo, Old Furniture,* the *Burlington Magazine,* the *Antique Collector,* and the American magazine *Antiques.*

Unfortunately, there is as yet no published account of the attitudes and achievements of early collectors and scholars in this field, and the reader must browse for himself through old sale catalogues and the above-mentioned publications, in order to gain some impression of the way in which such collections were assembled, the scope of their contents, and the manner in which they were used to furnish and decorate some fine old houses. Most of these collections were dispersed on the death of their owners and creators, and the contents are to be found in museums and private collections in Britain and America, and elsewhere. A list of the more interesting collections would include those of Sir George Donaldson, Sir Edward Barry, Arthur Radford, Morgan Williams, Sir Charles Lawes-Wittewronge, Sir Harold Peto, Seymour Lucas, the Rev. Meyrick-Jones, Sir William Burrell, William Randolph Hearst, Geoffrey Hart, J. Thursby-Pelham and many more; besides the more influential dealers on whom

2. Many collectors and interior decorators genuinely believed that they were doing a valuable job in rescuing such items from destruction and converting them to a practical use; as witness Thomas Baylis's slogan printed at the head of his catalogue of c.1840: "...the Preservation of Ancient Works By their application to Modern Purposes..." Most modern observers would count this an admirable intention, but performed in very questionable taste, since early fragments can be displayed in far better ways than by nailing them willy-nilly to fireplaces, bedsteads or wardrobes.

Figure iib. *Joined tester bedstead. English. Oak, dated 1593, with the arms of Courtenay and considerable later additions. This is basically a genuine bed, which has been smothered by an accretion of later bits of carving and other nonsense. The practice of 'beautifying' old specimens by the addition of carved appendages was noted early in the nineteenth century, e.g. at Plas Newydd, but connoisseurs seem to have learned nothing of the practice by 1890, when this bed was acquired by the Victoria and Albert Museum.*

Figure iia. *Mid-nineteenth century engraving of the Courtenay bed of 1593. This is a rather naïve Victorian view of the bed and an equally nonsensical armchair, both of which reflect the contemporary uncritical and uninformed view of old furniture.*

many of these collectors relied (perhaps too heavily), such as Murray Adams-Acton (of Acton-Surgey Ltd.), Sir Charles Allom (of White Allom & Co.) and S.W. Wolsey. The part played by these men in the formation of modern connoisseurship and scholarship would merit careful analysis, and would be of great interest to modern collectors and curators.

Perhaps the greatest of these collections was that of Sir William Burrell, who guaranteed himself a place of importance by leaving his vast assemblage of objects and works of art to his native city of Glasgow in 1944. The collection is significant not only for the quality of its contents, but also for the eclectic range of its coverage, which remains to us intact. There are over five hundred items of early furniture,[3] though this forms only a small section of the collection as a whole. From 1927 Sir William lived at Hutton Castle, outside Berwick-on-Tweed, and two of the rooms are shown here as he lived in them (Figures iii-v). The photographs demonstrate the large measure in which Sir William and Lady Burrell conformed to the current taste of their generation for a balanced mixture of oak furniture, early arms and armour, tapestries and Oriental carpets (though the quality of the tapestries in the Burrell Collection is wholly exceptional). As we contemplate the photographs of this and similar houses, we are left with the distinct feeling that their owners were often more concerned with their furniture as mere decoration, than with scholarly speculation; the legacy of an approach where the aesthetic value of old furniture far outweighed its importance as an historical and social document.

Private collectors are free to indulge their whims and prejudices to an extent which is not available to the public collector — the curators and directors of public museums, whose responsibility to the taxpayer is largely an educational one. A good public collection should be administered and developed in such a way that its contents provide a touchstone by which others may be judged. The pieces on display in a museum do not all have to be of the finest quality, but they should offer a very high level of authenticity. In the areas of research and interpretation, the curator is

3. See Victor Chinnery, *A Scottish Collector Par Excellence — Oak Furniture in the Burrell Collection,* Antique Collecting/Finder, Volume 11, No. 8.

responsible for pushing forward the boundaries of knowledge, yet some of the great public collections of early oak furniture have lain virtually dormant since they were formed earlier in this century. Such stagnation is the result of many factors, not least the desperate shortage of funds; the moral and political intricacies involved in trying to 'weed out' past purchases and donations of the more unfortunate kind; and the fact that, outside of a very limited circle, early oak furniture was decidedly out of fashion in the post-war years after 1945.

During this quiet period (1945-70) in which both real prices and the supply of money dropped dramatically, a new breed of collector evolved. Low prices and lack of competition enabled them to put together some very interesting collections. In contrast with an older generation, they were profoundly sceptical of the 'Gothic' furniture and other extravagant pieces to be found in the early books. When older collections were dispersed in auction, many of these 'important' pieces were weighed in the balance and found sadly lacking. The younger collectors turned their attention to the simpler vernacular furniture of the sixteenth and seventeenth centuries, and insisted on a high degree of purity and authenticity in the items which they chose to buy. As with any reaction against an older regime, the scepticism of the new generation was sometimes overdone, and many perfectly good items were condemned on no better grounds than an unfounded suspicion. Yet, their rigorous example has encouraged the present climate of objectivity, and high standards of approach are evolving.

Many collectors today show a high degree of skill and judgement in the selection of their purchases, though for the individual the acquisition of desirable pieces must remain a matter of conscience between his inclinations and his pocket, whereas the 'official' curator (where he has any purchase-fund at all) must eschew any inclinations towards *taste* and try to retain a detached and objective approach. This is not the place to enter a discussion on the aesthetics and impulses of collecting (different people collect for different motives), but we must assume that both kinds of collector must adhere to some absolute standards if their work is to attain some measure of credibility. Private collectors and professional curators may not share the

Figure iii. *The dining room at Hutton Castle, the home of Sir William Burrell. Taken during the Burrells' occupancy, before the collection was donated to the City of Glasgow.*

Figure iv. *Another view of the dining room at Hutton Castle. When the new museum opens, which is to house the Burrell Collection in Glasgow, this and other rooms are to be shown as reconstructions after the photographs.*

Figure v. *The drawing room at Hutton Castle, when it was the home of Sir William Burrell.*

same motives and opportunities, but they must expect to share the same themes and interests.

The joy of collecting is a very personal and private pleasure, which crystallises for most people at that exciting moment when the eye alights on the quarry, when the price is right, and that 'I-must-have-it' sensation floods into the brain. But for the serious collector, that moment is far more than a mere involuntary and intuitive flash of light. It is the culmination of a long process of learning and experience, in which he must see, feel, live with, read about and talk over all the rich and varied aspects of his chosen subject.

Having run his quarry to earth (and any collector will agree that my analogy with hunting is not inapt), the prospective purchaser must enter a second and quieter phase in which he brings to bear the weight of his experience to decide whether the object really is what he hopes it to be, and in which he balances up its qualities.

So, what are the criteria used by the modern collector of early oak furniture in this exercise of discrimination?

The vexed question of fakes is the one which always rears its ugly head in this imperfect world. As a definition, we may accept that a copy or reproduction does not become a fake until it is sold, displayed or otherwise presented as genuine. Despite modern attempts to identify fakes with the aid of irrefutable scientific methods, very little progress has been made in the case of furniture. It is now possible to date certain timbers by means of dendrochronology, or archaeological tree-ring dating. This method involves measuring the relative thicknesses of the annual growth rings in a given specimen of wood, so that quarter-sawn oak panels present an ideal subject since the rings emerge uniformly at right angles to the surface. By comparing the pattern of growth, the scientist is often able to determine the years in which the sample of wood was growing; and if the layers of sapwood and bark are still present, he can even determine the year in which the tree was felled.

This method has been successfully applied to house timbers in many countries, but dendrochronology must be seen to have a severely limited application to furniture, for the following reasons:

* The method involves laying bare a considerable area of end grain for inspection. Unless the end grain is exposed naturally (as for example in the

Figure vi. *Underneath view of the backstool in Figure 4:139, showing the dry, clean surface under the seat, which contrasts sharply with the rich patination of the turnings and the upper surface of the seat-rail.*

Figure vii. *Under view of court cupboard, detail of Figure 3:248. The fine dry surface of the oak is very apparent under the top, behind the apron piece and spandrels, and at the top of the leg. Note the grading of the patinated surface where the polish ends above the turning; and the lack of finish on the under surfaces.*

case of Figure 2:36), this would be bound to entail some damage to the piece, and that is unacceptable in an area where untouched condition is valued very highly.

* The method is costly in terms of time and research — often more costly than the value of a given piece of furniture.

* It is necessary to know, fairly exactly, the region in which the wood was grown. Despite advances in locating regional styles, it is still impossible to ascertain the specific origins of most furniture.

* Dendrochronology can only provide the dates during which the wood was growing. It cannot provide the actual date of construction of a piece of furniture, and could not conclude on a fake made from wood of the correct period, or on a late piece made from re-used earlier timber. It could not conclude on the date of a genuine piece, other than to confirm the age of the timber. In the final analysis, it could only tell us whether a piece were not genuine: i.e. made from wood of later growth than its appearance would suggest.

In the foreseeable future, it must seem that we shall not be provided with some handy tool which will pronounce for us on the authenticity of items of early furniture, and for many years the most reliable guide must still be (perhaps will always be) the hand and eye of experience.

As he grows in his experience, the collector will begin to recognise intuitively the little signs of construction and surface character which are the hallmarks of the genuine piece. The single factor which matters most to the serious collector of today is paradoxically referred to as 'original surface', that is the colour and texture of the matured patination. This surface is the result of generations of wear and polishing in the case of domestic furniture, and is the result of a subtle blend of circumstances which reflect the history and treatment of the piece concerned. Furniture from churches or public institutions will not normally have a fine glossy surface, owing to the rigours of damp or neglect; but when domestic furniture has been cared for by generations of diligent housewives, this is reflected in the hard bronze-like glow of the patination. The best colour is a rich and varied combination of black, chestnut-red and golden brown. In the crevices and mouldings will lie a deposit of hard grey dust, left behind where the polishing cloth cannot reach. Underneath and behind, where the polish and wear have never touched, the rough-sawn or riven surface of the timber should be a dry greyish biscuit colour (Figures vi-vii).

Figure viii. *Rear view of joined court cup-board in Figure 3:247. The roughly finished surfaces at the rear are typical of early joiners' work. The labels are the old depository tickets which are often found on the back of old furniture.*

567

Figure ixa. *(Left) Joined stool. English; Salisbury. Oak, c.1620. This stool is a pair with Figure 4:62, but was in a seriously dilapidated state.*

Figure ixb. *(Right) The same stool after expert restoration and colouring. Careful inspection would be necessary to determine which parts are replaced, and whether the patination were not entirely genuine.*

Careful consideration should be given to the degree to which a piece of period furniture has been damaged and repaired. If a piece is in entirely original condition, then it has had a fortunate escape from attack by woodworm, damp and careless or neglectful people. But many items have suffered a hard life, and the potential buyer should be very wary of replaced parts, since these can seriously undermine the value of an otherwise worthy piece. Modern restorers are sometimes very clever at repairing and colouring quite highly-damaged objects, witness the joined stool in Figure ix a and b. This was a highly-neglected church stool (one of a pair with the perfectly-preserved stool in Figure 4:62), which was expertly restored a couple of years ago. It is a highly contentious matter whether such pieces should be restored or not, and many collectors would prefer to see a fine piece such as the chair in Figure x left as it was found. As always, individual cases must be decided on their merits.

Genuine wear is a prime indicator of age, and as such is an acceptable (even desirable) feature of a piece of old furniture. In the past, worn stretchers and other parts were often needlessly replaced, and this is to be regretted. The budding collector should study the effects of genuine wear very carefully, since it is difficult to imitate well. In particular he should note the angles of the different sorts of wear to be found on stretchers, seats and the arms of chairs; and the tenuous relationship between wear and colour, for in well-worn areas the colour must be thinner and paler than elsewhere.

For anyone used to the precise engineering and sophisticated finish of Georgian and Victorian cabinetwork, early oak furniture must seem both badly made and coarsely finished. The execution of carving and inlay is often so carefree as to be thought careless, whilst the scribe lines which mark out the joints and areas of carving are normally left for all to see on the polished surface of structural members. Worse still, if you turn over an early cupboard or table, the nether surfaces are 'unfinished' and cobwebbed to a degree which shocks the fastidious. But is is this very directness and honesty of approach that holds the key to the attraction for the oak lover. Most joined furniture is the sound product of honourable toil, and embodies a generous use of materials, a fitness of purpose, and a sufficiency for the demands of a simpler age. The niceties of this

Figure x. *Joined armchair. English. Oak, dated 1612. This chair is of excellent quality and very fine colour, but the 'untouched condition' also means that a number of parts are missing and damaged. It is a serious dilemma for the modern collector as to whether or not such a piece should be restored. As a general rule, it is best to leave well alone, though this is not always possible or desirable.*

craftsmanlike ethic hold a particular delight for the purist, and great account is made of the polished and projecting heads of tenon pegs, or the oval cross-section of a well-seasoned turning.

The problem of attributing accurate dates to early items is one which gives rise to great uncertainty and discussion. In fact, many collectors are over-obsessed by the question of dates, especially in cases where it is impossible to estimate a date within fine tolerances. It would be a remission not to remind ourselves of the great importance of dated furniture in providing a guide for their undated brethren. Similarly, documented or provenanced pieces may be used for purposes of comparison, both stylistic and structural. Yet the whole problem of 'guessing' at dates is hedged about with provisions and restrictions. In most cases it is unwise to look for a range of less than thirty to forty years, even with the help of dated comparables. In extreme cases, as in the conservative traditions of Westmorland, it is difficult to be dogmatic within a range of eighty to a hundred years. The best we can do is to bear in mind the date at which a particular feature first appeared, then decide how long it remained in currency. It must often be a matter of intuition as to whether it be a late or an early example of the type. It is *not* good practice to assume that better examples must be earlier. In the case of the two chairs from Salisbury of 1585 and 1622 (p.449), the quality and execution of the later chair is far better than the earlier. There is no evidence of a decline in the quality of joined and carved work through the seventeenth century, as is so often asserted, and this is supported by the many fine pieces dated after 1700, such as Sarah Ward's chest of 1722 (Figure 3:399).

Despite a history of collecting which now extends over a period of two hundred years or more, the amount of solid knowledge and sound research on the history of oak furniture is still deplorably thin. In very recent years some considerable strides have been taken in exploring new avenues of enquiry, such as the chronology of regional styles, problems of terminology and nomenclature, identification of makers and workshop groups, and the nature of the Anglo-American relationship in the seventeenth century. As further results are published in these areas, the collector will take greater account of this information in the management of his activities; and we may soon see the time in which the work of individual makers is collected for its own sake, as styles are more readily classified by workshop or region. The furniture of the sixteenth and seventeenth centuries must be judged by a different yardstick from that used for the eighteenth century cabinetmaker, and the scope for further enquiry is exceedingly promising.

Bibliography

Sidney Oldall Addy, *Evolution of the English House,* George Allen and Unwin, London 1933.

Malcolm Airs, *The Making of the English Country House, 1500-1640,* The Architectural Press, London 1975.

Joseph Aronson, *Encyclopaedia of Furniture,* Batsford, London 1966.

Albert C. Baugh, *A History of the English Language,* Routledge and Kegan Paul, London 1951.

Robert Benson and Henry Hatcher, *Old & New Sarum, or Salisbury,* London 1843.

S.T. Bindoff, *Tudor England,* Pelican, London 1950.

J.P. Blake and A.E. Reveirs-Hopkins, *Little Books about Old Furniture — Volume One, Tudor to Stuart,* Heinemann, London 1922.

Hugh Braun, *Old English Houses,* Faber, 1962.

Herbert Cescinsky, *English Furniture from Gothic to Sheraton,* Garden City Publishing Co., New York 1937.

Herbert Cescinsky and Ernest Gribble, *Early English Furniture and Woodwork,* Routledge & Sons, London 1922.

Herbert Cescinsky and George Hunter, *English and American Furniture,* Garden City Publishing Co., New York 1929.

Sir George Clark, *The Seventeenth Century,* Oxford University Press, 1929.

Peter Clark and Paul Slack, *English Towns in Transition 1500-1700,* Oxford University Press, 1976.

William Cobbett, *Rural Rides,* 1830; *Cottage Oeconomy,* 1822.

Olive Cook and Edwin Smith, *English Cottages and Farmhouses,* Thames and Hudson, London 1954; *The English House through Seven Centuries,* Nelson, London 1968.

G.W. Digby, *Elizabethan Embroidery,* Faber & Faber, London 1963.

E. Easton, Printer, *Antiquitates Sarisburiensis,* Salisbury 1771.

F.G. Emmison, *Elizabethan Life. Home, Work & Land,* Essex Record Office Publications, no.69, Chelmsford 1976.

E.A. Entwisle, *The Book of Wallpaper,* Kingsmead Reprints, Bath 1970.

John Evelyn, *Sylva, or a Discourse of Forest Trees,* 1664; *Diary and Correspondence,* ed. H.B. Wheatley, 1906.

Dean A. Fales, Jr., *American Painted Furniture 1660-1880,* Dutton, New York 1973.

Furniture History Society, Furniture History (Journal), 1965-78.

E.W. Gregory, *The Furniture Collector,* Herbert Jenkins, London n.d.

J.A. Halliwell, *A Dictionary of Archaic and Provincial Words,* pub. John Russell Smith, 1852.

G.B. Harrison (ed.), *The Elizabethan Journals,* 2 vols., Anchor Books, Garden City Publishing, New York 1965.

Rev. William Harrison, *Description of England,* 1577; *Description of Britain,* 1587, ed by F.J. Furnivall, for the New Shakespeare Society, Trubner, London 1877.

Charles Haskins, *The Ancient Trade Guilds and Companies of Salisbury,* pub. by subscription, Salisbury 1912.

Arnold Hauser, *The Social History of Art,* 2 vols., Routledge and Kegan Paul, 1962.

Arthur Hayden, *Chats on Old Furniture,* Benn, London 1905.

Helena Hayward (ed.), *World Furniture,* Paul Hamlyn, London 1965.

Ambrose Heal, *London Tradesmen's Cards of the XVIII Century,* Batsford, London 1925.

Frank Herrman, *The English as Collectors,* Chatto & Windus, London 1972.

Christopher Hill, *The World Turned Upside Down,* Pelican, London 1975.

HMSO, *Handbook of Hardwoods,* 1972; *Handbook of Softwoods,* 1957; *English Chairs,* Victoria and Albert Museum, Large Picture Book no. 10, 1970.

Randle Holme III, *Academie of Armory,* c.1649, ed. I.H. Jeayes, Roxburghe Club 1905.

W.G. Hoskins, *Local History in Britain,* 1959; *The Making of the English Landscape,* Pelican, London 1970.

G. Melvyn Howe, *Man, Environment and Disease in Britain,* Pelican, London 1976.

Therle Hughes, *English Domestic Needlework,* Lutterworth Press, London 1961.

Samuel Johnson, *Dictionary of the English Language,* Millar, London (8th ed.) 1792.

Margaret Jourdain, *English Interior Decoration 1500-1830,* Batsford, London 1950; *English Decoration and Furniture of the Early Renaissance 1500-1650,* Batsford, London 1924.

Patricia E. Kane, *Furniture of the New Haven Colony — The Seventeenth Century Style,* New Haven Colony Historical Society, New Haven 1973.

Bryan Latham, *Timber. A Historical Survey,* Harrap, London 1957.

Charles Latham, *In English Homes,* various volumes, Country Life, London various dates.

Nathaniel Lloyd, *History of the English House,* 1931, re issued by the Architectural Press, London 1976.

Percy Macquoid, *A History of English Furniture,* 4 vols., Collins, London 1919.

Percy Macquoid and Ralph Edwards, *Dictionary of English Furniture,* 3 vols., Country Life, London 1924-27, revised 1954.

Eric Mercer, *Furniture 700-1700,* Weidenfeld and Nicolson, London 1969.

Joseph Moxon, *Mechanick Exercises,* 1703.

Wallace Nutting, *Furniture of the Pilgrim Century,* 1924, Dover Paperbacks, New York 1965.

Samuel Pepys, *Diary,* 1660-1669.

Edward H. Pinto, *Treen, and other wooden bygones,* Bell, London 1969.

I.M.G. Quimby (ed.), *Arts of the Anglo-American Community in the Seventeenth Century,* Winterthur Conference Report, 1974.

Readers' Digest, *Atlas of the British Isles,* London 1965.

F.S. Robinson, *English Furniture,* Methuen, London 1905.

F. Gordon Roe, *English Cottage Furniture,* Phoenix House, London 1961.

Fred Roe, *A History of Oak Furniture,* Connoisseur, London 1920; *Ancient Coffers and Cupboards,* Methuen, London 1902.

John C. Rogers and Margaret Jourdain, *English Furniture,* Spring Books, London 1959.

A.L. Rowse, *The England of Elizabeth,* Macmillan, London 1950.

Hermann Schmitz, *Encyclopaedia of Furniture,* Benn, London 1926.

Henry Shaw, *Specimens of Ancient Furniture,* 1836.

Ivan Sparkes, *The English Country Chair,* Spurbooks, 1973.

Francis W. Steer, *Farm and Cottage Inventories of Mid-Essex 1635-1749,* Essex Record Office Publications, no.8, Chelmsford 1950.

John Stow, *The Survey of London,* 1598.

R.W. Symonds, *Furniture Making in 17th and 18th Century England,* Connoisseur, London 1955.

R.W. Tawney, *Religion and the Rise of Capitalism,* Pelican, London 1938.

E.P. Thompson, *The Making of the English Working Class,* Pelican, London 1968.

Flora Thompson, *Lark Rise to Candleford,* Penguin Classics, London 1973.

Peter Thornton, *Seventeenth Century Interior Decoration in England, France and Holland,* Paul Mellon/Yale University Press, New Haven/London 1978.

H. Avray Tipping, *Old English Furniture — Its True Value and Function,* Country Life, London 1928.

Robert Trent (ed.), *Pilgrim Century Furniture,* Main Street/Universe, New York 1976.

G.M. Trevelyan, *English Social History,* Longmans, London 1926.

L. Twiston-Davies and H. Lloyd-Johnes, *Welsh Furniture,* University of Wales Press, Cardiff 1950.

John West, *Village Records,* Macmillan, London 1962.

Geoffrey Wills, *English Furniture 1550-1760,* Guinness, London 1971.

Wiltshire Record Society, *Churchwarden's Accounts of S. Edmund and S. Thomas Sarum 1443-1702,* Salisbury 1896.

S.W. Wolsey and R.W.P. Luff, *Furniture in England — the Age of the Joiner,* Barker, London 1968.

Margaret Wood, *The English Medieval House,* Phoenix House, London 1968.

Photographic Credits

The author wishes to thank the many private owners who have given permission for their belongings to be photographed and reproduced, though many have wished to remain anonymous. Thanks are also extended to John White, curator/botanist to the Forestry Commission at Westonbirt Arboretum, Gloucestershire, for his careful preparation of the tree silhouettes used in Chapter Two. The other drawings and the maps are the work of the author. The woodcut illustrations used at various points in the book are all of the late sixteenth or seventeenth centuries, and most are the property of the British Museum.

The following photographs are reproduced by courtesy of their owners as listed:

American Antiquarian Society: **2**:93.

American Museum in Britain, Bath: **2**:94, 102, 103, 151. **3**:41, 141, 148, 186, 192, 193, 198, 199, 243, 472, 484, 496. **4**:211, 230, 246, 253-255. **Plate** Nine.

F.E. Anderson & Co., Welshpool, Mont.: **2**:60, 198, 204. **3**:88, 91, 98, 99, 123, 172, 197, 230, 336, 340, 502. **4**:236, 237, 241, 242, 251, 267, 269.

Associated Book Publishers Ltd.: **4**:88.

Avon Antiques, Bradford-on-Avon, Wilts.: **2**:22. **3**:183, 270, 304, 388, 495. **4**:139, 235, 243. **Appendix VI**, vi.

Barling & Co.: **2**:131. **3**:103, 210, 213, 217, 419, 420. **4**:111.

Mary Bellis: **2**:77, 85, 117, 120a, 188, 203, 206, 207, 209, 219, 223a. **3**:7, 24, 35, 111, 115, 117, 134, 153, 181, 214, 234, 247, 248, 318, 368, 370, 372, 377, 380, 383, 418, 467a, 482. **Plate** Three.

Claude Bornoff: **4**:73.

Boston, Museum of Fine Arts, Mass.: (Bequest of Charles H. Tyler) **2**:237. **3**:389, 408. **4**:199, 207, 209, 214, 222. (Samuel Putnam Avery Fund) **4**:191. (Gift of J. Templeton Coolidge) **4**:196. (Gift of Hollis French) **4**:198, 223. (Gift of Maurice Geeraerts in memory of Mr. and Mrs. William R. Roberson) **4**:216. (Gift of Mrs. Henry F. Wardwell) **4**:219. (Gift of Miss Mary S. Wheeler and Edward A. Wheeler) **4**:229.

Bristol City Museums: **3**:1, 95, 374. **4**:81-85, 90, 92, 93, 250.

Shirley Brown: **2**:58, 68. **3**:84, 142, 224, 273, 333. **4**:8, 51, 120.

Burnley Borough Council: **2**:33.

Burrell Collection: **2**:57, 61, 63, 80, 107, 132, 139, 140, 156, 164, 165, 170, 172, 173, 175, 179, 186, 190, 228, 232. **3**:4, 9, 15, 18, 22, 25, 26, 32, 33, 38, 43a, 54, 59, 70, 72, 81, 133, 138, 155, 156, 161, 165, 187, 203, 206, 207, 212, 249, 422, 473. **4**:4, 7, 9, 15, 18b, 22, 31, 33, 36, 39, 55, 66, 70, 79, 80, 95, 112, 114, 232, 264. **Appendix VI**, i, iii-v. **Plates** Eight (boarded chest), Thirteen, Fourteen (stools).

Joyce Caldwell: **4**:127.

Cedar Antiques, Hartley Wintney, Hampshire: **3**:430. **Plates** Twelve, Fifteen, Sixteen.

A. and J. Chinnery: **2**:125.

Christie's: **2**:51, 128, 152, 153, 182. **3**:21, 159, 202, 205, 236, 256, 268, 277, 311, 357, 439. **4**:94, 167, 173.

Olive Cook and Edwin Smith: **1**:7, 8, 10.

Royal Commission for Historical Monuments (Crown Copyright): **1:**5, 9. **2:**1, 3, 35, 83, 122, 129, 134, 229, 233, 234. **3:**78, 293, 442, 444, 445, 448. **4:**170, 176, 178, 179, 180.

Salisbury Cathedral, Dean and Chapter: **3:**40.

Salisbury Corporation: **4:**58-61. **Plate** One.

Sarum St. Thomas, Salisbury, Churchwardens of: **2:**15, 144. **4:**64, 245.

Shakespeare Birthplace Trust: **2:**97, 181, 189, 205, 225, 226. **3:**39, 101, 112, 122, 145, 146, 238, 239, 263, 312, 321, 329, 376a, 485. **4:**65, 72, 78, 86, 122, 158, 159, 288.

Clive Sherwood: **4:**54.

Shrewsbury,The Master of the Drapers' Company: **2:**5, 6, 7, 8, 9, 10, 11. **3:**404.

A.T. Silvester & Sons: **3:**406.

Paul Smith: **4:**113.

Sotheby Parke Bernet: **2:**123a, 168, 200. **3:**13, 19, 56, 157, 160, 241, 253, 254, 258, 317a, 412, 415, 458, 476. **4:**3, 32, 46, 74, 89, 110, 181.

Spink & Co.: **2:**222, 240. **3:**267, 307, 409, 431, 434, 440, 493. **4:**265.

Stair & Co.: **2:**53. **3:**294, 350, 411, 433. **4:**27a, b, c.

Louis Stanton: **2:**45, 59, 74, 108, 145, 193, 194. **3:**86, 89, 118, 158, 177, 227, 297, 314, 317b, 374a, 426, 460. **4:**69b.

Colin Stock: **4:**34.

William Stokes: **2:**21, 24, 81, 218. **3:**10, 14, 60, 62, 128, 169, 171, 233, 261, 269, 285, 371, 376b. **4:**25, 27, 91, 151.

Temple Newsam House, Leeds: **3:**85, 391, 421. **4:**35, 40a, 130, 154-156, 168, 183, 231.

Trinity Hall, Aberdeen: **3:**20. **4:**6, 96, 98-109.

Victoria and Albert Museum: **2:**20, 84, 137. **3:**3, 29. **Plate** Two.

Victoria and Albert Museum (Crown Copyright): **2:**99, 136, 141, 142, 167, 169, 187, 212, 220, 231, 239. **3:**8, 11, 16, 42, 53, 61, 63-66, 94, 136, 137, 184, 211, 259, 282, 284, 306, 326, 358, 364, 394, 403, 424, 446, 456, 463, 467b, 490, 507. **4:**1, 10, 13, 16, 18a, 23, 42-44, 53, 153, 161, 182. **Appendix VI,** ii. **Plate** Fourteen (floral chimney-board).

Wadsworth Atheneum, Hartford, Conn.: **2:**91, 92, 111, 150. **3:**164, 417. **4:**192, 195, 208, 220, 221, 227. (Bequest of Charles H. Tyler) **2:**112. (Nutting Collection) **3:**385, 386, 397, 398. (Goodwin Collection) **3:**413.

Welsh Folk Museum, St. Fagans (National Museum of Wales): **1:**1, 2. **2:**12, 19, 23, 26-32, 65, 76, 78, 79, 118, 124, 177, 178, 217. **3:**5, 27, 28, 69, 76, 129, 143, 144, 167, 168, 237, 252, 276, 278, 325, 328, 339, 361, 362, 399, 449-453, 464, 468, 483. **4:**136, 184, 187, 233, 234, 244, 285, 286. **Plate** Ten.

Willey Mill Antiques: **4:**193.

Robert Williams: **2:**159, 160.

Winterthur Museum: **2:**236. **4:**190, 215, 217.

Yale University Art Gallery, New Haven: (Mabel Brady Garvan Collection) **2:**98. **3:**289, 390, 392, 400, 407. **4:**57 (lower), 193, 203, 204, 206, 225, 226, 228. (Gift of John E. Bray) **4:**202. (Gift of Charles Wyllys Betts) **4:**213. (Anonymous donor) **4:**210.

574

Index

This index covers references in the text only. For more general information, initial reference should be made to the list of contents, pp.9-10. Individual furniture types are listed under: Furniture types. Certain authors are recorded in footnotes or the bibliography, and may be omitted from the index.